SEVENTH CANADIAN EDITION

FOUNDATIONS OF MARKETING

M. DALE BECKMAN
University of Victoria

JOHN M. RIGBY
University of Saskatchewan

Based on *Foundations of Marketing,* by David L. Kurtz, University of Arkansas, and Louis E. Boone, University of South Alabama.

Harcourt Canada

Toronto Montreal Fort Worth New York Orlando
Philadelphia San Diego London Sydney Tokyo

Canadian Cataloguing in Publication Data

Beckman, M. Dale, 1934–
    Foundations of marketing

7th Canadian ed.
ISBN 0-03-922735-9

1. Marketing. 2. Rigby, John Mark, 1957–   . I. Title.

HF5415.B56 2000   658.8   C99-932807-7

Acquisitions Editor: Ken Nauss
Developmental Editor: Lise Dupont
Production Editor: Linh Vu
Supervising Editor: Liz Radojkovic
Production Coordinator: Cheryl Tiongson

Copy Editor: Claudia Kutchukian
Permissions Editors: Patricia Buckley and Cindy Howard
Photo Researchers: Shefali Mehta and Maria DeCambra
Cover and Interior Design: Sonya V. Thursby, Opus House Incoporated
Typesetting and Assembly: Megan Byrne, Water Street Graphics
Technical Art: Brian Lehen Graphic Design Ltd.
Printing and Binding: RR Donnelley & Sons Company

Harcourt Canada
55 Horner Avenue, Toronto, ON, Canada M8Z 4X6
Customer Service
Toll-Free Tel.: 1-800-387-7278
Toll-Free Fax: 1-800-665-7307

This book was printed in the United States of America.
1 2 3 4 5   04 03 02 01 00

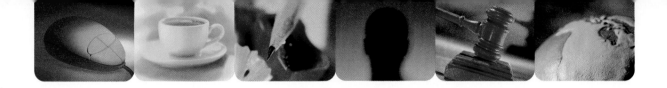

To Bobby and Wendy, with thanks for constant encouragement

Preface

Foundations of Marketing has maintained a leadership role among Canadian marketing textbooks for over twenty years. Faculty and students have returned to this book again and again for several reasons. First, it presents a sound and complete introduction to the subject, and strives to fulfill the "foundations" aspect promised in the book title. Second, the book has been acclaimed for the interesting and lively manner in which the material is presented. Past students have commented that the reading/studying experience is facilitated by the engaging writing style, and readability continues to be a hallmark of this edition. Third, timely publication of new editions ensures that the book includes current marketing topics and reflects contemporary academic thinking and business practices.

Foundations of Marketing, Seventh Canadian Edition, is completely updated but maintains its established focus on the key issues of marketing practice and theory. In addition, a wide variety of interesting photos and advertisements have been added to illustrate the textual material. Design is an important feature in improving readability and involving the audience, so an award-winning design team was commissioned to work on the layout and illustrations of this edition.

To add further interest to the book, six new feature boxes are interspersed throughout the text:

- Internet Impact (pink) showcases the importance and impact of the Internet on marketing.
- The Practising Marketer (yellow) demonstrates practical applications of marketing concepts.
- The Canadian Marketplace (red) contains interesting statistics, marketing trivia, and quotations.
- The Ethical Marketer (green) presents various ethical issues, such as campus monopolies, marketing to children, and telephone advertising.
- The Informed Consumer (orange) provides information to help make readers more knowledgeable consumers and more aware of their legal rights.
- The Roots of Marketing (purple) features anecdotes and quotations that provide a historical perspective on marketing.

Many of these boxes include discussion questions to encourage students to apply the concepts covered in the chapter.

Each chapter begins with a list of Chapter Objectives and concludes with a Summary. In addition, chapters contain Web links, a list of Key Terms, and Interactive Summary and Discussion Questions that are specially designed to ensure understanding and facilitate learning. In this section, portions of chapter material are summarized and the student is asked to answer thought-provoking questions that require more than just reciting textual material—the questions challenge the student to demonstrate mastery of the chapter concepts. An Internet-based discussion question has been included with every chapter. For additional marketing resources and a list of further readings for each chapter, students may refer to the *Foundations of Marketing* Web site at www.marketing-canada.com.

▶ NEW TO THIS EDITION

While much of the popular material of the past edition has been kept, several chapters have been extensively updated and reorganized in *Foundations of Marketing*, Seventh Canadian Edition. The increasing role of technology has been woven in throughout the book, beginning with an overview of the issues in Chapter 2, The Environment for Marketing Decisions. E-commerce — retailing and advertising on the Internet — is discussed extensively, and Internet examples appear in the opening vignettes. Web site addresses (URLs) are provided for many of the companies mentioned in the text. The instructor or the student can then easily follow up on the current situation of these companies. In addition, readers can consult the *Foundations of Marketing* Web site. The Appendix to Chapter 5, which lists and describes marketing research data sources, has also been updated to include both print and Internet sources.

Chapter 6, Marketing Strategy and the Marketing Plan, has been revised to emphasize the role of marketing strategy within overall corporate strategy. Marketing strategy is presented as the foundation that supports the entire marketing program and process. Diagrams and tables highlighting key strategic issues are developed in this chapter and then reiterated throughout the text to reinforce learning. The unique chapter, Total Customer Satisfaction in Marketing (Chapter 7), has been moved from the end of the book to directly follow the chapter on marketing strategy. Thus the importance of striving to create total customer satisfaction is naturally linked to the development of marketing strategy. Chapter 7 has been updated and includes a section on relationship marketing.

Chapter 8, Consumer Behaviour, has been completely reorganized. Business-to-business marketing is now the focus of Chapter 9.

The discussion of services marketing has been updated and expanded in Chapter 12 to deal more extensively with internal marketing and the services marketing triangle.

The chapters on distribution and channels (Chapters 15 to 17) have also been changed significantly to provide a contemporary treatment of this rather complicated topic. To further update this section, material on logistics and supply chain management has been added to Chapter 17.

Chapter 16 reflects the many new and exciting trends that are occurring in retailing, including e-commerce.

The retailing and the marketing communications chapters (Chapters 16, 18, and 19) also deal with the growing trend to using direct response marketing. Thus students will be able to see the opportunities and challenges of this marketing option. The coverage of advertising media is also expanded: Internet advertising is compared and contrasted with other, more traditional media, and a new section introduces students to many other media opportunities (a total of 32, ranging from aerial advertising to video screen advertising).

The importance of global business continues to grow. Consistent with this, international considerations are woven throughout the book as a regular part of the textual discussion. For example, in Part Five, the discussion of pricing is extended from the traditional considerations in the domestic market to the special considerations required when setting prices internationally. Many of the opening vignettes and feature boxes have an international orientation. In addition to this integrated coverage, Chapter 20 is devoted to an up-to-date discussion of the important topic of global marketing.

Foundations of Marketing pays special attention to the topics of marketing strategy, marketing planning, and the marketing mix in a manner that is consistent, clear, and pedagogically appropriate. It uses the terms strategy, marketing planning, and marketing mix in such a way that their meaning is consistent and unclouded. We avoid using these terms until they can be introduced and developed properly. The strategy of a firm, of which marketing strategy is an essential component, is shown to be paramount. A marketing plan is required to implement the marketing strategy, and the marketing mix is part of the marketing plan. By introducing the marketing mix a little later in the course, students are more likely to comprehend the power and usefulness of this concept, rather than viewing the "P's" of the mix as a simple formula that can be understood superficially and treated in a trivial way.

We believe *Foundations of Marketing,* Seventh Canadian Edition, will be a strong pedagogical support for marketing instructors and an interesting introduction to the exciting and varied world of marketing for students. We wish you all the best as you explore this world together.

▶ THE *FOUNDATIONS OF MARKETING* PACKAGE

A full educational package is also available to complete *Foundations of Marketing,* Seventh Canadian Edition:

- **Case Supplement** All new marketing case studies are packaged in a separate supplement to meet the needs of instructors and students by providing cases that are current and fresh. The case studies cover a range of marketing issues and are suitable for class discussion, assignment, and formal presentation.
- **Computerized Test Bank** The updated and revised *Computerized Test Bank* contains more than 2200 multiple-choice, true/false, matching, and fill in the blank questions. Instructors are able to preview and edit test questions as well as add their own. Answers are provided, as well as scoring and grade-recording management.
- **Instructor's Manual** Presented on disk in an easy-to-use format, the *Instructor's Manual* contains chapter summaries, chapter objectives, teaching tips, network activities, answers to end-of-chapter questions, video cases, questions and answers to video cases, and teaching notes to accompany the *Case Supplement.*
- **PowerPoint Presentation Software** This collection of PowerPoint slides covers all the essential topics presented in each chapter of the book and also includes figures, tables, graphs, and other examples to reinforce major concepts and issues. Instructors are able to custom design their own multimedia classroom presentations by adapting or adding slides.

- **Study Guide** This new learning tool is designed to enhance students' understanding of marketing practices by bringing marketing concepts and theories to life. The workbook contains numerous types of exercises that deal with real-life marketing issues and events. Each chapter highlights the content discussed in the corresponding textbook chapter.
- *Foundations of Marketing* **Web Site** Students and instructors who are interested in acquiring additional information on the study of marketing will find links to current marketing information, a variety of marketing-related sites, and other useful learning tools. The site also offers on-line marketing resources, hot new topics, and case resources.
- **Video Cases** This all-new innovative video package adopts a problem-resolution approach to video segments, which are tied to chapter concepts. Nineteen videos were created in partnership with successful, well-known companies, giving students a real-world perspective of how professional marketers meet the challenges and changes of the current marketplace. Overviews and related questions that correspond to the video cases are included in each chapter of the *Instructor's Manual.*
- **Discovering Your Marketing Career CD-ROM** This newly-expanded software package helps students explore career opportunities in marketing based on their personal interests and skills. Through videos, interviews with marketing professionals, and an interactive student study component, this unique CD-ROM program reinforces marketing concepts described in the text and gives students a real-world taste of actual careers and career paths in today's market.
- **Internet Marketing Connection** Students who own a copy of the *Discovering Your Marketing Career CD-ROM* can download this on-line guide to a wide range of marketing titles. Students can link to Web sites that cover current marketing topics, as well as sites where they can identify marketing job opportunities in the career fields covered in the CD-ROM. The *Internet Marketing Connection* is updated regularly to ensure that links are current. The latest version can be reached at http://www.dryden.com/mktng/careercd/.
- **Overhead Transparencies** The approximately 160 full-colour transparencies in this package are described in detail in the notes included with the package.
- **The Marketing Game** This innovative Windows-based computer simulation will help students develop their marketing skills within the framework of an evolving product life cycle in the digital-camera industry.

▶ ACKNOWLEDGEMENTS

Any textbook represents the work and thinking of countless scholars. We recognize and appreciate the stream of knowledge-creating activities of our colleagues from around the world.

This book naturally builds upon the six previous editions, and thus reflects the comments and suggestions of reviewers over the years. It also reflects the work of previous editors, copy editors, and researchers.

Research now flows easily around the world. While writing in Canada and in Australia, we benefited significantly from the day-to-day communication and research efforts of Chris Johnston.

We are also grateful for the time, attention, and suggestions of the following reviewers. We have considered their recommendations carefully and tried to respond to them. This is a better book because of their input.

Simon Curwen, Ryerson Polytechnic University
Brad Davis, Wilfrid Laurier University
Dwight Dyson, Centennial College
Gerard Edwards, Douglas College
Rick Gelsinger, Saskatchewan Institute of Applied Science and Technology
Robert Kansky, Northern Alberta Institute of Technology
Mike LeRoy, University of British Columbia
John Lille, Centennial College
Rajesh Manchanda, University of Manitoba
Jay Rubinstein, Vanier College
Terry Seawright, McMaster University
Carolyn Sterenberg, Mount Royal College
Denis Sullivan, Fanshawe College
Ray Verity, Southern Alberta Institute of Technology

Case writing is a special calling and skill. Those who write cases provide exceptional opportunities for instructors and students to develop understanding through their work in solving case problems together. We acknowledge with thanks their participation in the package of cases that supplements this book.

We also acknowledge the diligent efforts of the Harcourt Canada publishing team. Special thanks go to Lise Dupont for her willing support and patient understanding of sometimes impossible academic schedules. We would also like to thank Ken Nauss, Linh Vu, and Claudia Kutchukian, as well as Sonya Thursby of Opus House.

The sales team deserves specific mention. We recognize that your intelligent and faithful work is a key to the success of this book. We know that you will continue your dependable achievements.

Most importantly, we give thanks to our families. We appreciate their willingness to forgo numerous activities, and even our presence, while we spent the hours necessary to complete this project.

M. Dale Beckman
University of Victoria

John M. Rigby
University of Saskatchewan

A Note from the Publisher

Thank you for selecting *Foundations of Marketing*, Seventh Canadian Edition, by M. Dale Beckman and John M. Rigby. The editor and publisher have devoted considerable time to the careful development of this book. We appreciate your recognition of this effort and accomplishment.

We want to hear what you think about *Foundations of Marketing*. Please take a few minutes to fill in the stamped reader reply card at the end of the book. Your comments and suggestions will be valuable to us as we prepare new editions and other books.

Brief Contents

Contents

▶ PART 5 PRICING

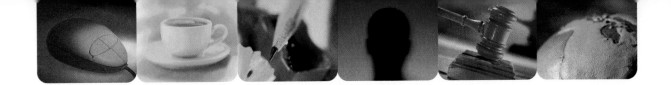

Interest Boxes

▶ **PART 3 CONSUMER BEHAVIOUR**

▶ **PART 4 PRODUCTS**

Part 1
Marketing and Its Environment

The fundamental philosophy of marketing is that an organization should orient itself to serve the customer's needs. Part 1 of *Foundations of Marketing* shows why marketing must identify and respond to these needs. These chapters also provide essential definitions and explain some of the basic concepts on which marketing is based. As well, the relationship of marketing to society at large is explored.

▶ **CHAPTER 1**
The Nature of Marketing

▶ **CHAPTER 2**
The Environment for Marketing Decisions

Chapter 1
The Nature of Marketing

www.coca-cola.com

Coca-Cola® is recognized and found all over the world, even in remote parts of the globe.

What do you get if you take some carbonated water, caramel colouring, flavouring, sugar, and a few other ingredients and mix them all together? If it's you or me doing the mixing, the answer is "not much." On the other hand, if you're The Coca-Cola Company, the answer is a multibillion-dollar enterprise and one of the most widely recognized brand names and products in the world.

The difference between the value of the beverage to you or me, and to The Coca-Cola Company, lies in over 100 years of careful and intelligent marketing. The product itself has been refined and fine-tuned to appeal to a broad spectrum of the population. It has been packaged in several distinctive and convenient forms. It is one of the most widely distributed products in the world—so if you're thirsty, chances are you can find a Coca-Cola nearby. The beverage is priced so that while it always remains affordable, it returns a handsome profit for the company. All of these decisions and plans by The Coca-Cola Company have been supported by a century's worth of advertising and other types of communication that present Coca-Cola as a refreshing, desirable beverage—a message that millions of people accept and act on every day. The result is a thriving company and recognition that The Coca-Cola Company is one of the world's master marketers.

> ▶ **CHAPTER OBJECTIVES**
> After reading and studying this chapter, you should be able to
> 1. Define marketing and describe its primary nature.
> 2. Show how marketing bridges the gap between producer and consumer.
> 3. Outline the functions of marketing.
> 4. Demonstrate the scope of marketing.
> 5. Contrast activities in each of the three orientations of business in the marketing domain.
> 6. Position marketing as one of the basic business functions.

▶ INTRODUCTION

Marketing has changed the face of Western civilization in the past 50 years. Many consumer products are available in the most remote parts of the globe—and products can be found on Canadian shelves that come from the most remote parts of the globe. We are exposed to thousands of marketing messages on any given day. It is hard to imagine what our world would look like if all marketing activity were to suddenly stop.

The practice of marketing has itself changed a great deal and seems destined to continue to evolve rapidly. Today you can apply for a mortgage, buy insurance, order books—or any number of other products or services—over the Internet without ever leaving your home. Marketers are increasingly forming a sort of relationship with their customers based on information gleaned from extensive databases. For example, retailers can and do track your shopping history and custom-design promotional offerings just for you and other people with your shopping habits and tastes. Even a few years ago such possibilities were only dreamed of at futurist conferences.

Even though the practice of marketing is changing at a dizzying speed, the basic, and deceptively simple, underlying principles of marketing are remarkably stable. Against that backdrop of rapid and exciting change, this book is intended to help you learn and understand basic marketing principles and to illustrate and help you learn how the principles can be applied.

Many people think that marketing is really just a synonym for advertising or selling. In fact, marketing is a much broader concept, although advertising and selling can certainly be part of the marketing process. In the most general sense, marketing is all about matching producers' output to customers' activities. As a consumer, you know that sometimes this is done very well and other times not.

▶ THE ROOTS OF MARKETING

www.drucker.com

If we want to know what a business is we have to start with its purpose. And its purpose must lie outside the business itself. In fact, it must lie in society since a business enterprise is an organ of society. *There is one valid definition of business purpose: to create a customer.*[1]

Peter F. Drucker is recognized as one of the most influential management thinkers of the modern era. He has written extensively and is quoted widely. In a salute to his contribution, he has been awarded nineteen honorary doctorates by different universities around the world. He is particularly interested in non-profit organizations and serves as Honorary Chairman of the Peter F. Drucker Foundation for Nonprofit Management, New York, NY.

To learn more about Peter F. Drucker, visit the Peter F. Drucker Canadian Foundation for Nonprofit Innovation Web site.

Generally, this matching process results in a continuous flow of goods and services for consumers, and the economic activity that maintains profitable business and employment.

The idea of matching producers' output to customers' activities sounds less complicated than it really is. There are many product and even company failures, and often people cannot seem to find the product that really satisfies their needs. Poor marketing frequently causes these problems. The cause of poor marketing is usually a lack of focus on customers.

Serving the needs of customers is what business should be all about. A good example is the well-known philosophy of FedEx, which is to strive for 100 percent customer satisfaction and on-time delivery. This philosophy has made FedEx the leader in its field. Marketing is the business function that interprets customer needs to the rest of the organization and brings the resulting offerings of the firm to the consumer.

www.fedex.com/ca/
ca_english

Even with excellent customer focus, meeting customer needs can be difficult. It is as if there is a gap between producers and consumers that marketing must bridge. Many things can contribute to this gap. The most common are consumer perceptions, lack of information, attitudes, time constraints, cost constraints, and space or location. Consider the gap between Cheryl, a university student whose current stereo works, but not very well, and a stereo manufacturer, say Sony, that would like to sell her a new stereo.

www.sony.com

- *Consumer perceptions.* Cheryl may not realize that her stereo is poor quality and may perceive the sound it produces to be acceptable.
- *Lack of information.* Cheryl does not realize that Sony makes mid-priced stereo systems, not only high-end equipment.
- *Attitudes.* Cheryl's friend had problems with his Sony stereo, so Cheryl suspects that the brand is over-rated.
- *Time constraints.* Cheryl is a second-year commerce student and doesn't have a lot of time to shop for and compare stereos.
- *Cost constraints.* Because she's a student, Cheryl does not have much extra cash right now, so even a mid-priced stereo system would stretch her resources.
- *Space or location.* Sony manufactures its stereos in Japan (and other countries), but Cheryl wants hers in Lethbridge.

A careful study of customer needs allows marketing and the rest of the organization to bridge the gap between producer and consumer. This bridge is built through eight **marketing functions**: buying, selling, transporting, storing, grading, financing, risk taking, and information collecting and disseminating.

marketing functions
Buying, selling, transporting, storing, grading, financing, risk taking, and information collecting and disseminating.

One or more of the contributors to the gap between Cheryl and Sony can be addressed by each of the marketing functions. These functions are a part of all marketing transactions, to a greater or lesser degree. They may be shifted to various members of the retail or wholesale trade, or even to the customer, but they cannot be eliminated.

Performing the marketing functions reduces the size of the gap between the organization and the consumer. As we shall see, a reduction in the gap implies an increase in the utility consumers associate with a product or service. The result is that consumers are more likely to enter into an exchange relationship with the marketing organization. Let's first consider the notion of exchange, and then we'll examine how it relates to utility.

Pharmaceutical Manufacturing Plant

St. John's Wort

All drugs come from plants. So why are some taken more seriously than others?

You're probably used to asking a HEALTHWATCH® Pharmacist about medicine from the plant on the left. But what about medicine derived from the plant on the right? The truth is, they can all have an effect on your health and should be treated with respect. That's where our HEALTHWATCH Pharmacists come in. They're trained on an ongoing basis so they can answer questions about all medication, including herbs. If you have questions about herbals, ask your HEALTHWATCH Pharmacist.

HEALTH watch
SHOPPERS DRUG MART

Consumers are faced with increasing numbers of herbal products and the growing perception that they all have health benefits. Shoppers Drug Mart, with its HEALTHWATCH® program, tries to educate consumers and correct misconceptions.

exchange process
The means by which two or more parties give something of value to one another to satisfy felt needs.

▶ THE ESSENCE OF MARKETING

The essence of marketing is the **exchange process**. This is the means by which two or more parties give something of value to one another to satisfy felt needs.[2] In many cases, the item is a tangible good, such as a newspaper, a calculator, or a pair of shoes. In other cases, intangible services, such as a car wash, transportation, or a concert performance, are exchanged for money. In still other instances, funds or time donations may be offered to political candidates, a Red Cross office, or a church or synagogue.

The marketing function is both simple and direct in subsistence-level economies. For example, assume that a primitive society consists solely of Person A and Person B. Assume also that the only elements of their standard of living are food, clothing, and shelter. The two live in adjoining caves on a mountainside. They weave their own clothes and tend their own fields independently. They are able to subsist even though their standard of living is minimal.

Person A is an excellent weaver but a poor farmer, while Person B is an excellent farmer but a poor weaver. In this situation, it would be wise for each to specialize in the line of work that he or she does best. The net result would then be a greater total production of both clothing and food. In other words, specializa-

But I like shopping!

The exchange process satisfies felt needs.

tion and division of labour will lead to a production surplus. But neither A nor B is any better off until they trade the products of their individual labour, thereby creating the exchange process.

Exchange is the origin of marketing activity. In fact, marketing has been described as "the process of creating and resolving exchange relationships."[3] When there is a need to exchange goods, the natural result is marketing effort on the part of the people involved.

The cave-dweller example is simplistic, and our society has a more complicated exchange process. Nonetheless, the basic concept is the same: production is not meaningful until a system of marketing has been established. As Wroe Alderson observes in the Roots of Marketing box, without the possibility of exchange, the world as we know it would not exist.

▶ THE ROOTS OF MARKETING

It seems altogether reasonable to describe the development of exchange as a great invention which helped to start primitive man on the road to civilization.[4]

Professor Wroe Alderson published *Marketing Behavior and Executive Action* in 1957. It has been an extremely influential book, informing and anticipating much of the subsequent theoretical writings in marketing.

Marketing Defined

Ask five people to define marketing, and you will likely get five different definitions. Most of them will be too limited, and wrong. As we mentioned, because of the visibility of personal selling and advertising, many people will say that marketing is selling or that marketing is advertising. But marketing is much more comprehensive than these narrow perspectives.

Marketing can be defined at a micro (or organizational level), or from a macro (or societal) perspective. At a micro level, we can think of marketing as everything that an organization does to stay in tune with its customers or clients in order to ensure that the organization's products or services continue to effectively meet the customer's needs. More formally, the definition of **marketing** is "the process of planning and executing the conception, pricing, promotion, and distribution of ideas, goods, and services to create exchanges that satisfy individual and organization objectives."[5]

marketing
The process of planning and executing the conception, pricing, promotion, and distribution of ideas, goods, and services to create exchanges that satisfy individual and organizational objectives.

This definition implies much more than you may at first think. The rest of this book is required to elaborate it. The definition applies to not-for-profit as well as business organizations. Note also that the definition is specific in pointing out that exchanges created by marketing activities must satisfy individual (consumer) objectives and organizational objectives.

It is important to realize that effective marketing does not happen accidentally—careful planning is part of the definition. Professional marketers have found that success comes about much more easily when planning starts with a thorough analysis of customers and their needs. This is such an important idea, with so many ramifications, that we will spend the next section elaborating it.

The successful organization is geared toward making desired exchanges more likely to occur—that is, closing the gap discussed earlier between the organization and the consumer. Organizations increase the likelihood of desired exchanges taking place through production and marketing. These organizational functions increase **utility**, which can be defined as the want-satisfying power of a product or service. The higher the levels of utility a product possesses, the more attractive it is to a customer. There are four basic kinds of utility: form, time, place, and ownership.

utility
The want-satisfying power of a product or service.

www.tommypr.com

Form utility is created when the firm converts raw materials and components into finished products and services. Ford Motor Company converts glass, steel, fabrics, rubber, and other components into a new Mustang or Taurus. Tommy Hilfiger converts fabric, thread, and buttons into clothes. Symphony Nova Scotia converts sheet music, musical instruments, musicians, a conductor, and the Rebecca Cohn Auditorium into a performance. Although marketing inputs may be important in specifying consumer and audience preferences, actually creating form utility is the responsibility of the production function of the organization.

Marketing directly creates the other utilities: time, place, and ownership. Time utility is created when products and services are available to the consumer when she or he wants to purchase them. Coca-Cola, for example, is available 24 hours a day at 7 Eleven, Mac's, or vending machines. Place utility is created when the product is available at a convenient location, such as a movie theatre in Coca-Cola's case. Ownership utility is created when facilities are available whereby title to the product or service may be transferred at the time of purchase. For low-value goods, such as Coca-Cola, there is an implied contract when the

In this humorous advertisement, Diesel Jeans are touted as having such a high level of form utility that even nuns are buying and wearing them.

customer purchases the product. For high-value products, such as a car, there is a literal contract that transfers ownership from the car dealership to the purchaser.

On the macro level, marketing is defined as the development of systems that direct an economy's flow of goods and services from producers to consumers. This definition shows that, when added up, all marketing activities produce a flow of goods and services that are distributed throughout society. In a sense, at a macro level, marketing is the fuel that drives the engines of the economy.

Three Types of Business Orientation

Most companies have an orientation that fits one of the following three categories: product-oriented, sales-oriented, or market-oriented.[6]

PRODUCT OR PRODUCTION ORIENTATION

In firms with a **product orientation**, the emphasis is on the product itself rather than on the consumer's needs. For the production-oriented firm, the dominant considerations in product design are those of ease or cheapness of production. In either case, market considerations are ignored or de-emphasized. Firms stress production of goods or services,[7] then look for people to purchase them. The prevailing attitude of this type of firm is that a good product will sell itself. Beginning entrepreneurs often take this approach, convinced that their product idea is a sure-fire winner. Such a strategy is very limiting, for it assumes that the producer's tastes and values are the same as those of the market. Often a firm does not consider changing from this narrow approach until it runs into trouble.

product orientation
A focus on the product itself rather than on the consumer's needs.

SALES ORIENTATION

A **sales orientation** is an improvement on a product orientation. The firm is still quite product-oriented, but it recognizes that the world will not beat a path to its door to purchase its products. Therefore, the firm focuses its marketing efforts on developing a strong sales force to convince consumers to buy. "Get the customer to fit the company's offerings" could be a motto of such a sales-oriented strategy. Thus, to be successful, what you really need is an aggressive, high-powered sales organization and advertising program.

sales orientation
A focus on developing a strong sales force to convince consumers to buy whatever the firm produces.

▸ **THE INFORMED CONSUMER**

Bait and Switch

Bait and switch is a high-pressure sales approach that is considered unethical and, in certain circumstances, is illegal. Consumers are often baited with advertisements of a particular item. Once they get to the store, the salesperson will not sell the item because he or she says it is inferior or they have sold out. The salesperson then uses high-pressure sales tactics to sell the consumer a more expensive item.

A 14″ colour TV is advertised for only $200 at McStereo Sales and Service. Pat heads down at opening time to be sure to get one. However, David, the salesperson, tells Pat that several customers have complained about that particular set (that's why it is on sale); it is not guaranteed; and the manufacturer is out of business (so there are no spare parts available). David just *knows* Pat (a person David has never met before) will not be satisfied with the sale set, but there are other sets in the store that are fully guaranteed, are very popular, and only sell for $399. (Pat should head for the nearest exit when this happens.)

Always find a dealer with a good reputation when making major purchases of any kind. Sellers must have reasonable quantities of products they advertise at bargain prices (*The Competition Act*).

Source: Adapted from Sandra Hornung, *Consumer Power: A Guide to the Basics of Consumer Law in Saskatchewan* (Saskatoon: Public Legal Education Association of Saskatchewan, Inc., 1997), p. 30.

As you are watching TV some evening (with your marketing text in your lap), try to identify some ads with a pure sales orientation. For some reason, furniture retailers often use this approach.

Clearly, good, persuasive communication is an important part of a marketing plan. However, selling is only one component of marketing. As marketing expert Theodore Levitt has pointed out, "Marketing is as different from selling as chemistry is from alchemy, astronomy from astrology, chess from checkers."[8]

MARKET ORIENTATION

Many firms have discovered that the product and sales orientations are quite limiting. They have found that it makes a great deal of sense to pay careful attention to understanding customer needs and objectives and then make the business serve the interests of the customer rather than trying to make the customer buy what the business wants to produce. A primary task under a **market orientation**, then, is to develop ways to research and understand various aspects of the market.

A market-oriented strategy can produce any of the benefits of the other two orientations, but it avoids their drawbacks. In addition, it can identify new opportunities and avoid nasty surprises as changes occur in the market.

In a market-oriented firm, the marketing function is not tagged on at the end of the process. It takes a primary role right from the beginning of the planning process. A marketing orientation represents a set of processes that touch on all aspects of the company. It involves much more than just understanding the customer. Three characteristics make a company market-driven:

- *Intelligence generation.* The market-oriented firm generates intelligence in three major areas: customers' current needs, customers' emerging needs, and competitive activity. Understanding the current needs of customers is a rela-

market orientation
A focus on understanding customer needs and objectives, then making the business serve the interests of the customer rather than trying to make the customer buy what the business wants to produce.

tively straightforward matter that involves formal and informal dialogue with target customers. The formal dialogue can take the form of customer surveys and other types of marketing research. The market-oriented firm is not satisfied with simply trying to understand customers' present situation and needs—it also looks to the future to anticipate customers' unfolding needs. Such anticipation usually involves monitoring the environment for legal, technical, or other developments that might influence customers' requirements. Market-oriented computer manufacturers, for example, are monitoring the development and refinement of voice-recognition software, because it represents a potentially superior method of inputting computer data for their customers. The third area of intelligence generation focuses on competitive activity. Companies must have an accurate understanding of what competitors are doing to ensure that their own products or services are not left behind, and to evaluate the attractiveness of different markets.

- *Intelligence dissemination.* Market-oriented firms not only gather intelligence, they make it available throughout the organization. Customer information must reach all areas of the organization, including research and development, engineering, manufacturing, and accounting.
- *Responsiveness.* Up-to-the-minute information that is widely available within the organization serves no purpose unless the organization actually adjusts its products or processes based on that information. A remarkable number of organizations are fully aware that customers are unhappy with some aspect of their product or service delivery—long waits at an automotive service desk, for example—but make no attempt to address the problem. The market-oriented firm does not just understand its customer and its environment, it acts on that understanding.[9]

The Marketing Concept: A Guiding Philosophy for Marketing

The discussion of market orientation is primarily focused on how firms behave: what actions they take to achieve marketing success. Underlying those actions is a particular attitude or philosophy known as the **marketing concept**. The marketing concept is an organization-wide philosophy that holds that the best route to organizational success is to find an unserved or underserved need in society and meet that need better than anyone else, while still meeting long-term organizational objectives.

The marketing concept requires careful analysis and monitoring of competitors' actions. A company that practises the marketing concept holds basic assumptions in relation to its competitors. Management believes that the firm has the capacity to compete, that it is not at the mercy of its competitors and is a force of its own. At the same time, it recognizes that the firm has to be up-to-date on its competitors' actions to make sure that it does not lose its competitive edge. An organization that views itself as dominated by others is incapable of taking new initiatives, even if it identifies major unsatisfied customer needs.[10]

marketing concept
An organization-wide philosophy that holds that the best route to organizational success is to find an unserved or underserved need in society and meet that need better than anyone else, while still meeting long-term organizational objectives.

Ethics and Marketing

The marketing concept is a useful way to think about individual organizations, their missions, and the role they play in meeting the needs of individuals.

▶ THE PRACTISING MARKETER

Consumers Want Benefits not Features

From coffee makers to computer software, home consumer products seem to have been designed by engineers with little thought given to the people who will ultimately use them. In the age of convergence, the electronics industry promises home entertainment mega-devices: televisions combined with computers; digital video discs that hold movies and data; telephones with screens that can access the Internet. Although such appliances will run on digital systems much like computers, manufacturers expect them to also appeal to a mass audience that computers do not reach.

"But first these devices are going to have to work for people," Dr. Kim Vicente warns. The University of Toronto professor of mechanical and industrial engineering adds, "Manufacturers do what's possible, technologically. Whether it's easy to use is secondary. It should be the other way around."

The result is what technology experts call the 80–20 rule. People use 20 percent of the functions in devices such as computers 80 percent of the time, and the other 80 percent just 20 percent of the time.

A product from Toshiba Corp., the Infinia 7220, includes a computer, television, telephone, fax machine, pager, digital video disc player, and surround-sound movie and game centre. The question is how many of these features will all but the most dedicated technology devotees learn and use. Even options included in today's appliances are rarely used, such as picture-within-picture features in TVs and CD players that can be programmed to play selected tracks.

Don Norman, the author of a book called *The Design of Everyday Things,* questions the whole drive to build a convergence appliance that takes in myriad functions. "You can guarantee that it doesn't fit any individual," he says, because people have different needs and abilities.

The electronics industry appears to be listening. Electronics manufacturers attending the 1998 Consumer Electronics Show in Las Vegas, the world's largest showcase for gadgets of the future, acknowledged that their products are too complicated.

Michael Bloomberg, president of Bloomberg Financial Markets, says that people coming home from work want to relax, not "write a term paper on Mesopotamia" or pay bills on-line.

"The real challenge we face is going to be finding out, what does the consumer want, and satisfying that," he says. "If you don't, you are going to get chewed up."

Still, Dr. Vicente hopes that, one day, consumers aware of the issues will reach a critical mass and lead a revolt for simplicity.

"They should ask how easy a product is to use, to put together, and how good is the support once they have it," Dr. Vicente says. "If people demand ease of use, that's going to make companies pay attention, because they won't make money."

What orientation are the manufacturers of consumer electronic products displaying? What changes in orientation would you recommend?

Source: Adapted from Mary Gooderham, "Baffled Consumers Plead for Simplicity," *Dow Jones* in *The Globe and Mail* (December 8, 1998), pp. C1, C10.

Sometimes, though, the success of the organization and the satisfaction of the organization's customers can be at odds with the interests of society as a whole. "Lucky" Luciano, the notorious New York City mobster of the 1920s and 1930s, used many modern management techniques and presumably had at least some satisfied customers.[11] Nonetheless, most people would applaud neither his goals nor his outcomes. Similarly, the tobacco industry as a whole has come under severe attack for using masterful marketing techniques to sell a product everyone but members of the tobacco industry considers addictive and dangerous.

More subtly, perhaps, how is one to judge a legitimate enterprise, such as a steel mill, that makes a necessary, quality product for satisfied customers but in the process contributes inordinately to the deterioration of air quality?

One approach to dealing with these types of concerns is to broaden the marketing concept from its focus on organizations and customers to explicitly include consideration of the long-term benefit of society as a whole. This broader approach is called the **societal marketing concept**. It can be defined as an organization-wide philosophy that holds that the best route to organizational success is to find an unserved or underserved need in society and meet that need better than anyone else, while still meeting long-term organizational objectives and also considering the long-term impact on society.

> **societal marketing concept**
> An organization-wide philosophy that holds that the best route to organizational success is to find an unserved or underserved need in society and meet that need better than anyone else, while still meeting long-term organizational objectives and also considering the long-term impact on society.

The societal marketing concept is a useful perspective, but it does not instantly and easily solve every possible moral dilemma marketers encounter. Companies that operate in more than one country sometimes face particularly thorny issues. Depending on the country, executives can find themselves trying to deal with institutionalized discrimination, systemic corruption (is it ever acceptable to offer a bribe?), or even powerful criminal pressures. The unanswered question of the societal marketing concept that international dealings uncover is "Whose society are we concerned about?" Increasingly, the answer will have to be "The world as a whole."

Even if marketers are committed to operating on the general principles implied by the societal marketing concept, individual decisions can still be bewildering. One of the simplest and most practical approaches to considering moral dilemmas is the TV test. In the TV test, the marketer simply asks, "Would I be able to justify what I'm doing on the 6 o'clock news?" A positive answer suggests that the marketer is at least operating within the ethical norms of society. This approach leaves open the question of whether the norms of society are themselves ethical. An eighteenth-century landowner would have had no difficulty justifying the use of slave labour using the TV test (except, of course, to figure out what a TV was).

▶ THE ETHICAL MARKETER

Marketing to Children

Billboards to Pop Up on Calgary Students' Computers

Elementary school students in Calgary will soon be bombarded by advertisements for Burger King, Pepsi, Kellogg's, and other brands when they turn on their computers. The Calgary public school board has agreed to allow the screen-saver ads in a deal with Screen Ad Billboards Inc. of Brampton, Ont., *Marketing* magazine reports. The pilot program in eight to ten schools could generate about $300 000 for the board if it is expanded to all 11 000 of its computers.

Is this an ethical marketing approach? Does the use that the revenues are put to affect your answer? If you think this example is unethical, do you think it is ever ethical to target marketing activity at children?

www.screenad.com

Source: Excerpted from "Ad Lib, Marketing Shorts," *The Globe and Mail* (October 14, 1998), p. B29. Reprinted with permission from *The Globe and Mail*.

Delving deeply into the philosophical and religious perspectives behind the study of ethics is well beyond the scope of this text. What we will do is periodically highlight ethical issues related to different topic areas in marketing. We will invite you to consider the issues and come to conclusions about the ethical acceptability of different marketing actions. We encourage you to grapple with the examples and use them to examine and perhaps further articulate your own value system. It is much easier to come to conclusions about "the right thing to do" when you are considering textbook examples than when you are facing similar issues for the first time in the workplace.

The Importance of Marketing

Marketing is a core business discipline. It is important to people, companies, and the economy.

- *Importance to people.* Each of us responds to marketing every time we buy a product. Marketing efforts attempt to match goods and services to our needs. An infinite variety of offerings is available, and marketers try to tell us about these offerings. Marketing communications permeate the media and, sometimes, our consciousness. Marketing costs amount to between 40 and 60 percent of everything we buy. From a personal standpoint, studying marketing can make us better-equipped to react to the endless marketing efforts directed toward us.

www.pg.com

  Jobs in marketing are also numerous. Marketing-related occupations account for 25 to 33 percent of the jobs in our country—a good reason to study marketing. Starting salaries rank high, and marketing positions often lead to the most senior company posts. Marketers can be found in virtually every sector of the economy, including government, not-for-profit organizations such as the United Way, financial service providers such as the Bank of Montreal, or large multinationals such as Procter & Gamble.
- *Importance to companies.* As the main revenue-producing function, marketing is essential to a firm. Without sales, the firm dies. As sales increase, fixed costs are spread over more units. This increases profitability and enables firms to compete through lower prices.
- *Importance to the economy.* The benefits brought to people and firms make marketing a vital component of the economy. The more efficient the marketing process, the higher a nation's standard of living.

The study of marketing is therefore truly relevant for students. Furthermore, working in marketing is fascinating because it requires considerable initiative and creativity. Many find great satisfaction in such work. It is little wonder that marketing is now a popular field of academic study.

Marketing in Not-for-Profit Organizations

Most marketing activity is meant to generate a profit for the firm, but nonbusiness public organizations like public art galleries, churches, and charities have also found that they can benefit from applying marketing principles. For instance, the Canadian government is one of Canada's leading advertisers, spending

That pounding
you hear isn't drums.
It's your heart.

🐘 TorontoZoo
The African Savanna Exhibit

Sponsored by: KRAFT ⬛Loblaws ISUZU

Even not-for-profit organizations like The Toronto Zoo must apply marketing principles to survive.

approximately $44 million annually on advertising. World Vision and other charitable groups have developed considerable marketing expertise, some police departments have used marketing-inspired strategies to improve their image with the public, and we are all familiar with the marketing efforts employed in political campaigns. Most arts organizations now employ a director of marketing. Chapter 21 discusses marketing in not-for-profit settings more fully.

▶ WHAT TO EXPECT IN THIS TEXTBOOK

This textbook is organized around two themes: the marketing concept and marketing planning. The marketing concept suggests that our organization's goal must be to serve our customers extremely well while meeting our own long-term objectives. We need marketing planning because "serving customers extremely well" does not happen accidentally but is the conscious outcome of careful thought and consideration.

To consciously serve customers' needs, we must understand what opportunities are available and what difficulties we might encounter. In short, we have to understand the environmental context in which our organization exists. Chapter 2 discusses important concepts within the marketing environment and presents a framework to help you organize and understand information about this environment.

If our goal is to serve a particular group of customers extremely well, it follows that there is simply too much diversity in the marketplace to serve everyone's needs equally well. We must select a subgroup of customers, or market segment, and focus on meeting that subgroup's needs better than anyone else. Chapters 3 and 4 highlight the need for and process of market segmentation.

Another obvious implication of the marketing concept is that if we are planning to meet our chosen customers' needs extremely well, we must know something about those customers and their needs. Chapter 5 introduces the marketing research process.

Once we have basic information about the environment, have chosen our segments, and understand something about them, we have to begin to consciously use that information to form a plan of action. Chapter 6 highlights the process of developing a marketing strategy and marketing plan.

The first six chapters present the basic strategic building blocks of marketing. With this foundation in place, Chapter 7 revisits the issue of serving customer needs and presents in far greater detail what that implies and how it can be accomplished.

In addition to detailed information about our specific customers, a great deal is known about customers in general. As further background for the marketing plan, Chapters 8 and 9 outline consumer behaviour and business-to-business relations in general, highlighting information that is particularly useful as we try to serve our specific customer groups.

The analysis of the environment, organizational goals and objectives, and customers is complete by the end of Chapter 9. The text then examines the tools of marketing, frequently called the marketing mix. Chapters 10 through 19 consider designing and managing a product or service so that it meets customer needs, pricing the product so that it is attractive to the customer, distributing the product so that it is available to customers when needed, and communicating with customers and potential customers the benefits that the organization is offering. The text concludes with the unique issues facing global marketers (Chapter 20) and not-for-profit marketers (Chapter 21).

Throughout the textbook you will find six different types of interest boxes. The Practising Marketer addresses some of the theoretical concepts of marketing. The Ethical Marketer presents possible ethical dilemmas to consider. Internet Impact boxes showcase the importance of the Internet and the impact that it has had—and continues to have—on marketing. The Canadian Marketplace gives interesting facts, figures, and quotations about marketing in Canada. The Informed Consumer highlights issues that you may find useful in your role as a Canadian consumer. The Roots of Marketing points out historical trends or issues in marketing.

▶ SUMMARY

Marketing is a dynamic force in our society. One way to think about marketing is the bridge that closes the gap between customers and producers. That gap can consist of consumer perceptions, lack of information, attitudes, time constraints, cost constraints, and space or location.

The formal definition of marketing indicates that it is really about managing exchange processes between customers and producers. Marketing is defined as "the process of planning and executing the conception, pricing, promotion, and distribution of ideas, goods, and services to create exchanges that satisfy individual and organizational objectives."[12]

Companies can take three common orientations in their business practices. A product or production orientation emphasizes the product itself rather than the customer's needs. A sales orientation emphasizes convincing the customer that the product offered should be purchased. A market orientation tries to understand the customer's needs and organize the company in such a way that those needs are met.

Ethical considerations are becoming an important part of marketing planning. The societal marketing concept is an organization-wide philosophy that holds that the best route to organizational success is to find an unserved or underserved need in society and meet that need better than anyone else, while still meeting long-term organizational objectives and also considering the long-term impact on society.

▶ KEY TERMS

exchange process

market orientation

marketing

marketing concept

marketing functions

product orientation

sales orientation

societal marketing concept

utility

▶ INTERACTIVE SUMMARY AND DISCUSSION QUESTIONS

1. The gap between producer and consumer has the following components: consumer perceptions, lack of information, attitudes, time constraints, cost constraints, and space or location. Choose a product, and explain how marketing could be said to be the force that bridges the gap between producer and consumer.

2. The marketing gap components are satisfied by one or more of the marketing functions. Match functions with gap components in the columns that follow.

buying

selling

transporting

storing

grading

financing

risk taking

information collecting and disseminating

consumer perceptions

lack of information

attitudes

time constraints

cost constraints

space or location

3. The exchange process is the means by which two or more parties give something of value to one another to satisfy felt needs. Explain how this is the core of all marketing activity.

4. Marketing is "the process of planning and executing the conception, pricing, promotion, and distribution of ideas, goods, and services to create exchanges that satisfy individual and organizational objectives." Explain why the definition mentions ideas, goods, and services.

5. In a product-oriented firm, the emphasis is on the product itself rather than on the consumer's needs. Give an example of such a firm, and explain the limitations of this approach.

6. A sales-oriented firm is still quite product-oriented, but it focuses its marketing efforts on developing a strong sales force to convince consumers to buy. Is this what most companies need? Why or why not?

7. A market-oriented firm tries to understand customer needs and then makes the business serve the interests of the customer. How can such an approach be a practical way of making money?

8. Relate the definition of marketing to the concept of the exchange process.

9. Identify the product and the consumer market in the following:
   a. local cable television firm
   b. Vancouver Canucks hockey team
   c. Planned Parenthood
   d. annual boat and sports equipment show in local city auditorium
   e. regional shopping mall

10. Explain the effect of a market orientation on products offered to the market, and on marketing planning.

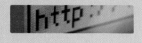

11. Check the Web sites of three major companies. Do they have statements of guiding principles to assist ethical decision making? If so, how do you think the stated principles will actually affect company actions and employee behaviour?

To obtain a list of further readings for Chapter 1, please refer to the *Foundations of Marketing* Web site.

Are these a health hazard?

Chapter 2
The Environment for Marketing Decisions

Taking the stage during a student assembly at Aurora High School in Southern Ontario, Graeme Gilday used two props: a small, $85 bottle of perfume and an equally small, even more expensive electronic device that detects the presence of potentially harmful volatile organic compounds (VOCs) in the air.

The air in a typical science laboratory will contain VOCs in a concentration of about 30 to 50 parts per million, Mr. Gilday, a health and safety officer with the York Region District School Board, told students as he squirted two shots of perfume on his wrist.

A moment later, he held the detector up to his wrist and it began to beep like a smoke alarm.

"Nine thousand four hundred parts per million!" Mr. Gilday exclaimed while the students applauded.

"I have never seen this machine go into alarm mode before," he said.

Mr. Gilday is the first to admit that his presentation—accompanied by an anti-perfume pantomime presented by Aurora High drama students, performed under a banner that declared "No Scents Make Sense"—is more theatre than science.

But he is one of a growing number of activists across North America convinced that perfumes and other scented products present a health hazard and must be suppressed in the same manner as tobacco.

"If you go from the fifties to the nineties and look at smoking, guess what's going to happen with scents?" he said. "It's interesting."

The campaign, which is causing a growing number of public buildings and offices across Canada to declare themselves "scent-free," is also setting off alarms among the companies that produce such products.

"I think a lot of people looked at this and said, 'It can't be serious. How can it be serious?'" industry spokesman Carl Carter said.

> **▶ CHAPTER OBJECTIVES**
> After reading and studying this chapter, you should be able to
> 1. Identify the environmental factors that affect marketing decisions.
> 2. Identify three categories of competition faced by marketers, and outline the issues to consider in developing a competitive strategy.
> 3. Illustrate the association between marketing plans and the technological environment.
> 4. Demonstrate how the sociocultural environment influences marketing decisions.
> 5. Show how the economic environment has a bearing on marketing planning.
> 6. Explain the major legislative framework that regulates marketing activities.

Business's failure to take the situation seriously, Mr. Carter said, allowed the antiscent movement to "build without being challenged. It's only in the last year or two that industry has said, 'Enough's enough.'"

There is a lot at stake. Mr. Carter is a spokesman for the recently established Scented Products Education and Information Association of Canada, which draws support from an array of industry bodies: the Allied Beauty Association; the Canadian Association of Chain Drug Stores; the Canadian Cosmetic, Toiletry and Fragrance Association (these two share office space in Mississauga); the Canadian Fragrance Materials Association; the Canadian Manufacturers of Chemical Specialties Association; the Direct Sellers Association; the Nonprescription Drug Manufacturers Association of Canada; and the Soap and Detergent Association of Canada.

Every year, he said, Canadian sales of "fine fragrance" products alone (excluding such scented goods as detergents and candies) range between $400-million and $500-million. Now Mr. Carter and other industry representatives travel the country attacking the scientific basis of the scent bans proliferating in Canadian schools and workplaces.

But that doesn't mean they're succeeding. In some areas of the country, especially Nova Scotia, "scent-free" is becoming as common as "smoke-free."

"We have scent-free Tim Hortons, scent-free restaurants and scent-free offices everywhere here," said Karen Robinson of Halifax, an activist and parent of two children who attend different schools, both of them officially scent-free.

She estimated that 80 percent of the schools in the Halifax Regional School Board have similar policies, and she is lobbying for a system-wide ban, which the board is scheduled to debate this month.

"Many of the chemicals found in smoke and second-hand smoke are the same chemicals that are found in perfume products," Ms. Robinson said, rhyming off a witches' brew of VOCs—"acetones, benzene, benzopyrene, formaldehyde, phenol, toluene."

Some perfumes contain as many as 600 different petrochemical-derived compounds, she said.

When exposed to perfume, some people go into anaphylactic shock, a massive, potentially fatal allergic reaction, Ms. Robinson said. In her case, she said, exposure leads to headaches and difficulty in concentrating.

One such attack occurred when she gave a presentation during a school-board meeting also attended by a group of opponents who had applied large amounts of perfume as a protest.

As a result of the fumes, Ms. Robinson said, she was unable to complete her presentation and was forced to withdraw to a corner of the room.

"If they had recognized what they were doing, they would probably never do that, but they don't recognize it or understand it," she said. "They think it's just a bunch of foolishness. They don't realize the impact on people's abilities and health.

"The main point we've been making is that it's a health issue, not a matter of likes and dislikes."

That point is controversial, but an increasing number of health-care authorities are willing to grant it.

"Perfume isn't made from flowers any more," noted Audrey Barrett, a registered nurse with the Nova Scotia Environmental Health Centre in Fall River, a clinic devoted to researching and treating environmentally triggered illness.

Source: Excerpted from John Barber, "Is Your Perfume a Health Hazard?" *The Globe and Mail* (May 14, 1999), pp. Al and A9. Reprinted with permission from *The Globe and Mail.*

▶ INTRODUCTION

Organizations operate in an environment that is constantly shifting and changing. Assumptions that held yesterday may no longer be valid today. Opportunities that are pursued enthusiastically today may disappear tomorrow, while threats to the company's existence, unthought of today, may occupy a major portion of the manager's time in the future. That is certainly the situation facing the perfume industry. A few years ago, it didn't occur to anyone that the relatively small proportion of people who find perfume objectionable or who have allergic reactions to it would be able, or even bother to try, to mount a widespread grassroots effort to ban scents in public places. Now, the industry finds itself desperately trying to put together some sort of coherent response, one that does not ignore public concerns but that protects the fragrance industry from extinction.

The perfume industry is experiencing a fairly rapid change, or at least sudden vocalization, of widely held attitudes of the Canadian public. These attitudes make up part of the sociocultural environment of Canada. Industry representatives are very concerned that these changes will in turn lead to changes in the political–legal climate that might restrict or, in the worst case, from the industry's perspective, prohibit the use of scents outright. As serious as these problems are, they represent only two aspects of the environment that face the perfume industry and all other businesses.

▶ ENVIRONMENTAL SCANNING

The marketing environment seems to be in a state of constant flux. If marketing managers are to make informed, intelligent decisions, they must develop methods of monitoring environmental changes. **Environmental scanning** is the process by which the marketing manager gathers and sorts information about the marketing environment.

environmental scanning
The process by which the marketing manager gathers and sorts information about the marketing environment.

Information can come from formal or informal sources. It can be gathered periodically, in the form of major focused market research projects, or it can be gathered continuously, by systematic ongoing market research, by tracking trade publications, commercially available reports, the general media, information made public by competitors, government press releases, internal company records, and even conversations with people both inside and outside the company.[1]

Simply gathering information, of course, is not enough: the information must be analyzed and acted upon in some way. The smaller the company, the more likely action will be taken to try to recognize and adjust to new environmental realities. Environmental changes can also be positive from an individual company's perspective, and they can represent significant opportunities for growth or competitive advantage.

If an issue arises that affects an industry as a whole, sometimes industry players will cooperate to try to shape or manage environmental realities. Air bags in cars were developed jointly by car manufacturers in response to government pressure to make cars safer. Kellogg's and Quaker have cooperated to try to have restrictions on health claims of food products eased (see Chapter 4 for further discussion). Even modest shifts in one or more of the environmental elements can alter the results of marketing decisions. For example, technical changes are now permitting people to download digital music over the Internet. This development could have profound effects on how musical recordings are sold. Not only does it make the traditional retailer potentially redundant, it makes creating and distributing pirated recordings of studio quality a very simple matter.

The environment for marketing decisions may be classified into five components: the competitive environment, the technological environment, the sociocultural environment, the economic environment, and the political–legal environment. This is the structure upon which marketing decisions are made, as well as the starting point for marketing planning. Figure 2.1 illustrates this relationship. The remainder of this chapter looks at the different components of the environment in more detail.

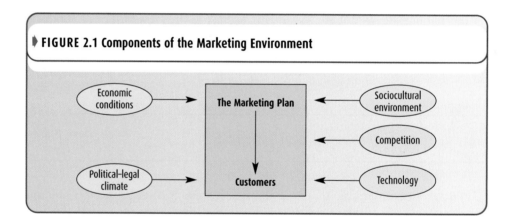

▶ **FIGURE 2.1 Components of the Marketing Environment**

▶ THE COMPETITIVE ENVIRONMENT

competitive environment
The interactive process that occurs in the marketplace in which different organizations seek to satisfy similar markets.

The interactive process that occurs in the marketplace in which different organizations seek to satisfy similar markets is known as the **competitive environment**. Marketing decisions by an individual firm influence consumer responses in the marketplace; they also affect the marketing strategies of competitors. As a consequence, marketers must continually monitor and adjust to the marketing activities of competitors—their products, channels of distribution, prices, and communication efforts.

In a few instances, organizations enjoy a monopoly position in the marketplace. Utilities, such as natural gas, electricity, water, and cable television service, accept considerable regulation from government in such marketing-related activities as rates, service levels, and geographic coverage in exchange for exclusive rights to serve a particular group of consumers. However, such instances are relatively rare. In addition, portions of such traditional monopoly industries as telephone service have been deregulated in recent years, and telephone companies currently face competition in such areas as selling telephone receivers, providing some long-distance services, and installing and maintaining telephone systems in larger commercial and industrial firms.

In many industries, the competition among firms is fierce. For example, consider the retail food industry. For supermarkets, the profit margin on most items is quite low. Therefore, to make an adequate return on investment, a store must generate a high volume of sales. Supermarkets are thus very sensitive to fluctuations in sales caused by the actions of competitors. If one competitor advertises a sale on certain products, another will be inclined to match those sale prices. Or if a new store format (such as Loblaws superstores) is developed, it will be countered (as was done with Safeway's Food for Less outlets).

Types of Competition

Marketers face three types of competition. The most direct form is inter-product or direct competition, which is among marketers of similar products. Xerox photocopiers compete with models offered by Canon, Sharp, and Olivetti. Estée Lauder cosmetics face competition from Lancôme and Revlon. Competitors are as likely to be from abroad as from the local market.

A second type of competition is product-substitute or indirect competition, which is among products that can be substituted for one another. In the construction industry and in manufacturing, steel products by Stelco may compete with similar products made of aluminum by Alcan. Paper bags compete with plastic bags. In circumstances where a change such as a price increase or an improvement in the quality of a product occurs, demand for substitute products is directly affected.

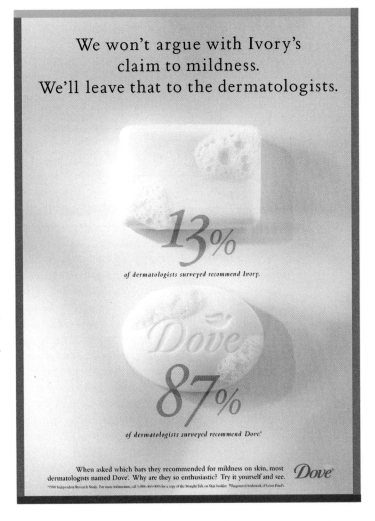

We won't argue with Ivory's claim to mildness. We'll leave that to the dermatologists.

13% *of dermatologists surveyed recommend Ivory.*

87% *of dermatologists surveyed recommend Dove.*

When asked which bars they recommended for mildness on skin, most dermatologists named Dove. Why are they so enthusiastic? Try it yourself and see.

One of the greatest inter-product competitions is among soap brands. Dove, in this advertisement, uses the results of a study among dermatologists to claim superiority over a key rival—Ivory.

The final type of competition is alternative-gratification, sometimes called total-dollar, competition. This involves all organizations that compete for the consumer's purchases. Traditional economic analysis views competition as a battle among companies in the same industry or among substitutable products and services. Marketers, however, accept the argument that *all* firms are competing for a limited amount of discretionary buying power. The Ford Focus competes with a vacation in the Bahamas; the local live theatre centre competes with pay television and the Leafs, Blue Bombers, or Expos for the consumer's entertainment dollars.

Changes in the competitive environment can wipe out a product, or an entire business, in short order. Marketers must therefore continually assess the marketing strategies of competitors, as well as monitor international business developments.

New product offerings with technological advances, price reductions, special promotions, or other competitive actions must be monitored in order to adjust the firm's marketing program in the light of such changes. Among the first purchasers of any new product are the product's competitors. Carefully analyzing the product—its physical components, performance attributes, packaging, retail price, service requirements, and estimated production and marketing costs—allows competitors to forecast its likely competitive impact. If necessary, current marketing procedures may be adjusted as a result of the new market entry. The competitive environment is a fact of life for most marketers. They ignore it at their peril! Competitive analysis is discussed in more detail in Chapter 6.

▶ THE TECHNOLOGICAL ENVIRONMENT

technological environment
The applications of knowledge based on scientific discoveries, inventions, and innovations.

The **technological environment** consists of the applications of knowledge based on scientific discoveries, inventions, and innovations. Technology, especially computer technology and the Internet, is reshaping the face of marketing. Virtually every aspect of the marketing program has been affected.

Existing products have been redesigned. Everything from cars to hearing aids to toasters incorporates computer technology. The performance of many products has improved, while size and cost have often fallen. Some products we see everywhere today, such as palm-sized computers, didn't even exist a few years ago.

Today manufacturers are planning to incorporate night-vision technology from the military in cars, and some models already have satellite-based on-board navigation systems as an option.[2] Some appliance manufacturers are musing about smart appliances that are directly wired to the Internet. Frigidaire has developed a refrigerator that can keep a running inventory of its contents and automatically order fresh groceries as required (if only it would also identify the container full of green fuzzy things on the back shelf).

Service design is also changing. The Internet has simultaneously become a huge communication device and a global shopping mall. Some storefronts exist only in cyberspace. Probably the best known of these "e-tailers" is Amazon.com.

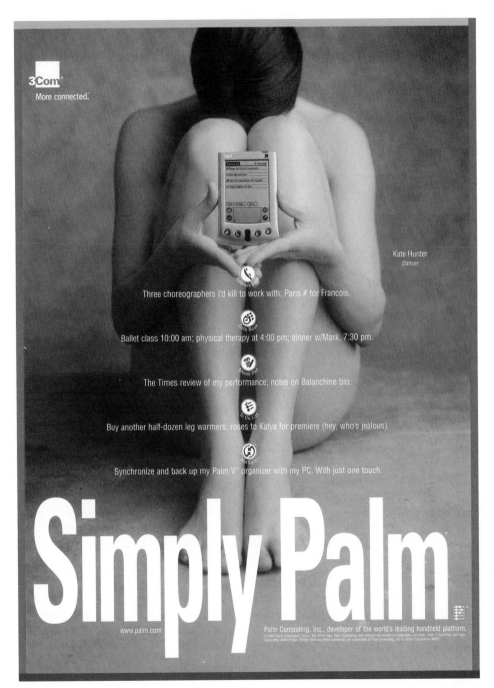

Recent technological advances have given rise to such new products as the Palm V™, a palm-sized electronic organizer that is competing against paper-based day planners and diaries.

(There is, of course, considerable irony in the fact that one of the Internet's earliest and largest retailers sells books!) Internet-based businesses, or e-businesses, are attracting a great deal of interest both from the media and from investors. It's worth noting, though, that virtually none of them has turned a profit—although that may just be a matter of time. The following notice in *Maclean's* magazine captures the dynamics:

www.etoys.com

Shares of Santa Monica, California-based eToys more than quadrupled on their first day of trading in a much-anticipated initial public offering. Demand for the offering, representing eight percent of the toy company, exceeded most expectations and signalled that investors still have an appetite for Internet issues. eToys has yet to make a profit.[3]

▶ INTERNET IMPACT

On-line Book Sales

Amazon.com Inc. is the undisputed heavyweight of Internet book selling—grabbing both the lion's share of the market and investor interest.

But analysts say several up-and-comers jousting for position in the burgeoning business of on-line bookstores have the potential to steal both market share and investing dollars.

Barnes & Noble Inc., Borders Group Inc., Chapters Inc., and German publishing giant Bertelsmann AG, which plans to enter the United States, all have strategies for gaining a toehold in the market that Amazon.com pioneered from its Seattle base.

Analyst Derek Brown of Volpe Brown Whelan in San Francisco estimates the on-line book market could swell to annual sales of between $2.5-billion and $3-billion (U.S.) in 2002.

www.amazon.com

Amazon.com, he estimates, could command 30 to 40 percent of that market. Amazon.com has an advantage over rivals, Mr. Brown believes, because it pioneered the on-line book market, and the company's management has executed more effectively than competitors such as New York–based Barnes & Noble, whose bread-and-butter business is selling books in traditional retail shops.

Amazon.com has also locked up agreements to be the exclusive book merchant on several popular Web sites, including that of America Online Inc. of Dulles, Va.

www.barnesandnoble.com

Barnes & Noble plans to spin off 20 percent of the on-line division, known as barnesandnoble.com, in a public offering later this year.

The division had about $12.5-million in sales in the second quarter, up 470 percent from the same period last year.

New York–based Prudential Securities Inc. analyst Amy Ryan forecasts the on-line business will generate revenue of between $60-million and $65-million in 1998, and $200-million in 1999. She said the public entity could be worth as much as $800-million, about four times next year's predicted revenue, or about half of the multiple now accorded to Amazon.com.

www.chapters.ca

The Canadian entry into the fray is Toronto-based Chapters, which launched its on-line bookstore in the fall of 1998.

Montreal-based analyst Patricia Baker of Merrill Lynch Canada Inc. said Chapters' on-line investment will hurt profitability in the short term but will deliver long-term returns. "Their competitive advantage is their knowledge of the Canadian market."

If you were the owner of an independent bookstore in Edmonton, Alberta, what actions would you take to counter the appearance of Amazon.com and Chapters.ca?

Source: Excerpted from Carolyn Leitch, "Book Giants Target Internet Selling," *The Globe and Mail* (September 28, 1998), pp. B1 and B8. Reprinted with permission from *The Globe and Mail*.

To remain competitive in the book retailing market, which is dominated by the likes of Amazon.com, Chapters has launched its own on-line bookstore.

Less visibly, advances in computing and communications technology have allowed marketers to maintain more detailed records and to access those records in more useful ways. This in turn allows them to identify and track major accounts and regional and customer sales figures in depth and more quickly. The Royal Bank of Canada used improved databases to divide its clients into A-, B-, and C-level clients based on profitability. The bank assigned the A-level customers to account managers who now call these customers several times a year to discuss specific products. In a two-year period, the average profit per A client increased 292 percent.[4]

Advances in technology have also helped in inventory management by reducing the level of inventory necessary while avoiding stock-outs and automating the reorder process. Many of these topics are discussed in more detail in Chapter 16.

Marketers should take note of several points when analyzing technological changes in their environment. The first is not to be left behind by these changes—marketers must keep abreast of developments that might affect their business and be willing to adjust to those developments. The other side of the story, though, is that marketers should not be seduced by technology. Technological change and innovation should be driven by customer needs. Adopting new technology will not be successful if it works only to the benefit of the company while ignoring the customer. The Practising Marketer box describes frustrations that some customers have with banks' use of technology.

▸ THE PRACTISING MARKETER

New Banking Technologies

Kevin Sheridan wrote the following wry article as an introduction to a special issue of *Bank Marketing*:

Welcome to the spandex-and-rocket-belt edition of *Bank Marketing* magazine. Our special section this month features a glimpse into the Jetsonesque future of banking technologies and their impact. Part of the section introduction notes that, on the bleeding edge of tech, the ability to do something too often substitutes as the reason for doing so.

This was forcefully driven home as I recently tried to stay on deadline while visiting the doctor. During the editing of this issue's special section, my semiannual dalliance with dental hygiene occurred, and so I found myself in a waiting room, marking up an article on new and enhanced uses for ATMs.

The dentist's office was packed with the sort of random sampling of people that warms the empiric hearts of focus-group brokers. Professional people were interspersed with stay-at-home parents; older patients sat next to younger ones; and the room was almost perfectly gender-balanced.

Mary Jane, who has been my dentist's receptionist as long as I can remember, looked up from her desk to see me, as usual, editing a manuscript. "What's it about this time, Kevin?" she called across the waiting room.

"It's a story about new uses for ATMs—especially during the transaction itself, if you really want to know," I replied.

The roomful of people looked first at me and then back at Mary Jane. "Kevin, here, works for a banking magazine," the now-obligated receptionist explained to the group of patients.

"You're writing about ATMs?" asked an older woman on my right. "Well, you know what I hate? When you're standing there waiting to get your money—right out there on the street—and they show you a commercial. I really hate that." *(continued)*

▶ THE PRACTISING MARKETER *(continued)*

This opened the floodgates. Everyone in the waiting room began complaining to me, the hapless and unwilling representative of banks everywhere. Basically, they all groused about how much they disliked being held hostage to advertising messages while they waited for their cash to be dispensed. Two things impressed me about my fellow dental patients—how quickly they revved up their annoyance (obviously, it had been festering) and how impassioned they were (imagine the angry villagers in a Frankenstein movie).

One man gave me a squint uncomfortably like that of Clint Eastwood—and eloquently told me this: "I can't stand being sold things at my ATM—but it makes me think, if they have the know-how to do these ads, why can't the machines remember how much money I usually withdraw or give me the ability to change the denominations in my withdrawal? That way, at least, I'd feel in control of my own money." The other patients engaged in much vigorous head-nodding at this.

Dutifully listening to all the griping, I recognized the rather creepy irony of the manuscript in my lap, opened to the great and glorious marketing opportunity awaiting banks that push ads at their ATM customers. And, indeed, from a bank perspective, it does make wonderful sense to do so. But what is not taken into account (or perhaps simply ignored), is how the customers would react to such an arrangement. ("Not well" is the answer, if the waiting room-cum-focus group is any indication.)

Essentially, what that eloquent patient was asking for is bank technology that benefits him, and not merely the bank. The fact that this simple, understandable desire feels like break-through thinking is indicative of how far many financial institutions have to go in terms of savvy implementation of technology and customer service/satisfaction.

As this issue of *Bank Marketing* causes you to reflect on the implications of new technologies, also think about this: The most effective impact of bleeding edge bank tech may be in the ways it makes life easier for customers, not bank staff. Otherwise, we're just tech-ing to ourselves.

How do the author's observations relate to the discussion of the marketing concept in Chapter 1?

Source: Kevin Sheridan, "Are We Tech-ing to Ourselves?" *Bank Marketing* 31:4, p. 5. Reprinted with permission from the Bank Marketing Association.

Any time of significant change represents tremendous opportunity for those companies that anticipate and correctly adjust to and incorporate the change. It can be a time of catastrophe for those who do not. In the next ten years, new forms of business organizations will probably appear. Undoubtedly, some established businesses will disappear. What will be most interesting to watch, and what will require the greatest managerial skill and vision, are established businesses that are able to embrace the environmental change and be transformed into new and exciting marketing organizations.

▶ THE SOCIOCULTURAL ENVIRONMENT

A probation officer and his wife have found a novel way of marrying people who do not belong to an organized religion or who prefer not to get married in a church. Edward and Ruth Simmons have formed a company called Weddings and have opened chapels in Hamilton and Burlington, Ontario. Weddings offers five different ceremonies: four religious and one secular. The rituals are open to change, at clients' request.

Edward Simmons says that he came up with the idea when he saw couples being married in the courts. "They would go in happy and come out with a stunned look on their faces. I don't think they realized the abruptness of the proceedings. That really bothered me," he says. "Religion doesn't always meet the needs of a secular society," he adds. "In many cases, a place of worship won't marry couples who don't belong to it, people who have been divorced, couples that have been living together, and those who have crossed religious barriers."[5]

A few years ago, the success of the Simmons' company would have been doubtful. However, changes in the sociocultural fabric of Canada now make this type of business quite viable. This example illustrates the importance of understanding and assessing the relevant social and cultural components when making marketing decisions. The **sociocultural environment** is the mosaic of societal and cultural components that are relevant to the organization's business decisions. Obviously, many different aspects are significant. One important category is the general readiness of society to accept a marketing idea; this aspect was important in the Simmons' decision.

sociocultural environment
The mosaic of societal and cultural components that are relevant to the organization's business decisions.

Another important category involves the trust and confidence of the public in business as a whole. Such relationships have been on the decline since the mid-1960s. Opinion polls suggest that people have lost confidence in major companies (although they maintain faith in the private-enterprise system). These declines should, however, be viewed in perspective. All institutions have lost

---

▶ THE CANADIAN MARKETPLACE

Feeding a Need to Eat on the Run

Hungry but starved for time? Has your get-up-and-go got up and gone? If so, you're the prime target for a group of products whose recent sales growth has been nothing short of phenomenal—energy bars and drinks.

They come with names like Powerbar, Ensure Plus, and Boost, and Canadians bought $1.72-millon worth of them at food stores and pharmacies in 1996. In 1997, however, we spent $3.46-millon on them, an increase of just over 100 percent. Sales in 1998 look set to post a 70-percent leap over 1997.

"It's a lifestyle thing," said Peter Elgersma, a business manager with the market-research firm A.C. Nielsen. "Life is fast and you often need an energy lift."

Raminder Bindra, brand manager for Mead Johnson Nutritionals, says his company's Boost drinks are intended more as a breakfast food, while the bars are designed for snacks during the day for people on the run who want something more than a candy bar.

The energy bars are dense and chewy but pleasantly flavoured. And they contain a few things you won't find in a Mars bar: phosphorus, magnesium, iron, zinc, copper, manganese, and chromium.

What changes in the sociocultural environment are contributing to the success of energy bars?

Source: Adapted from Philip Jackman, "Feeding a Need to Eat on the Run," *The Globe and Mail* (December 3, 1998), p. A30. Reprinted with permission from *The Globe and Mail*.

THE CANADIAN MARKETPLACE

Small Towns Getting Bigger (and Smaller)

Canada's small towns and rural communities have achieved a remarkable feat: They're growing and shrinking at the same time.

As always, it all depends on how you look at the figures. According to Statistics Canada, rural and small-town populations have increased with each census since 1976, although the rates of growth have varied widely from province to province. Therefore, these communities are growing.

On the other hand, populations in the large cities have been growing at a faster pace. Therefore, the percentage of Canadians living in small towns and rural areas is shrinking. About 34 percent of Canadians lived outside big cities in 1976. Twenty years later it was 22 percent.

Changes in boundaries are another ingredient to add to the mix. Since 1976, many local boundaries have been reclassified, and small towns have been gobbled up by the commuting zones of big cities, which further complicates the issue.

In general, the rural and small-town population grew most in retirement communities and on the edge of the commuting zones of large urban areas. Major growth in retirement destinations took place north of Montreal in the Laurentians, north of Toronto in the Muskoka area, and in the Okanagan Valley of British Columbia. However, since 1976, rural and small-town populations have declined in most rural areas of Saskatchewan, in the Gaspé region of Quebec, and in every region of Newfoundland.

Nevertheless, Newfoundland is still the only province with more than 50 percent of its population living outside cities.

▶ Percentage of Canada's Population Living in Small Towns and Rural Areas

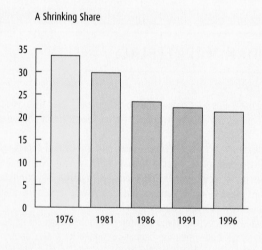

A Shrinking Share

What are some of the social implications of changes in the balance of Canada's urban–rural population? What products might be particularly affected by these changes?

Source: Philip Jackman, "Small Towns Getting Bigger (and Smaller)," *The Globe and Mail* (March 15, 1999), p. A22. Reprinted with permission from *The Globe and Mail*. Graph: Statistics Canada and *The Globe and Mail.*

public confidence to some degree. In fact, some would argue that governments and labour unions are even less popular than business.

The sociocultural environment for marketing decisions has both expanded in scope and increased in importance. Today, no marketer can initiate a strategy without taking the social context into account. Marketers must be aware of the way in which this context affects their decisions. The constant flux of social issues requires that marketing managers place more emphasis on solving these questions as part of the marketing decision process. Some firms have created a new position—manager of public policy research—to study the changing social environment's future impact on the company.

One question facing contemporary marketing is how to measure the accomplishment of socially oriented objectives. A firm that is attuned to its social environment must develop new ways of evaluating its performance. Traditional income statements and balance sheets are no longer adequate. This issue is one of the most important problems facing contemporary marketing.

Many marketers recognize societal differences among countries, but assume that a homogeneous social environment exists at home. Nothing could be further from the truth! Canada is a mixed society composed of varied submarkets that can be classified by age, place of residence, gender, ethnic background, and many other determinants. For example, the Quebec market segment has enough distinctive characteristics that separate marketing programs are sometimes developed for that province.

Gender is another increasingly important social factor. The feminist movement has had a decided effect on marketing, particularly promotion. Television commercials now feature women in less stereotyped roles than in previous years.

Since social variables change constantly, marketers must continually evaluate this dynamic environment. What appears to be out-of-bounds today may be tomorrow's greatest market opportunity. Consider the way that previously taboo subjects, such as condoms, are now commonly advertised.

The social variables must be recognized by modern business executives, since these variables affect the way consumers react to different products and marketing practices. One of the most tragic—and avoidable—of all marketing mistakes is failing to appreciate social differences within our own domestic market.

The rise of consumerism can be partly traced to the growing public concern with making business more responsible to its constituents. Consumerism is an evolving aspect of marketing's social environment. Certainly the advent of this movement has influenced the move toward more direct protection of consumer rights in such areas as product safety and false and misleading advertising. These concerns will undoubtedly be amplified and expanded in the years ahead.

▶ THE ECONOMIC ENVIRONMENT

Marketers must understand economic conditions and their impact on the organization. An economy with growing monetary resources, high employment, and productive power is likely to create strong demand for goods and services.

economic environment
The factors in a region or country that affect the production, distribution, and consumption of its wealth. Key elements are monetary resources, inflation, employment, and productive capacity.

In a deteriorating **economic environment**, on the other hand, many firms experience a decline. However, such conditions may represent good news for other companies. As inflation and unemployment go up and production declines, consumer buying patterns shift. Flour millers note that flour sales go up. Automobile repairs and home improvements also increase. Greeting card firms report that consumers buy fewer gifts but more expensive cards. Hardware stores show higher sales. The economic environment considerably affects the way marketers operate.

Stages of the Business Cycle

Within the economic environment, there are fluctuations that tend to follow a cyclical pattern comprising three or four stages:

1. recession (sometimes involving such factors as inflation and unemployment)
2. depression[6]
3. recovery
4. prosperity

No marketer can ignore the economic climate in which a business functions, because the type, direction, and intensity of a firm's marketing strategy depend on it. In addition, the marketer must be aware of the economy's relative position in the business cycle and how it will affect the position of the particular firm. This requires the marketer to study forecasts of future economic activity.

Of necessity, marketing activity differs with each stage of the business cycle. During prosperous times, consumers are usually more willing to buy than when they feel economically threatened. For example, during a recent recession, personal savings climbed to high levels as consumers (fearing possible layoffs and other workforce reductions) cut back their expenditures for many products they considered nonessential. Marketers must pay close attention to the consumer's relative willingness to buy. The aggressiveness of one's marketing strategy and tactics often depends on current buying intentions. More aggressive marketing may be called for in periods of lessened buying interest, as when automakers use cash rebate schemes to move inventories. Such activities, however, are unlikely to fully counteract cyclical periods of low demand.

While sales figures may experience cyclical variations, the successful firm has a rising sales trend line. Achieving this depends on management's ability to foresee, correctly define, and reach new market opportunities. Effective forecasting and research is only a partial solution. Marketers must also develop an intuitive awareness of potential markets. This requires them to be able to correctly identify opportunities.[7]

Besides recession, two other economic subjects have been of major concern to marketers in recent years: inflation and unemployment.

Inflation

inflation
A rising price level that results in reduced purchasing power for the consumer.

Inflation, which can occur during any stage in the business cycle, critically influences marketing strategy. Inflation is a rising price that results in reduced purchasing power for the consumer. A person's money is devalued in terms of what it can buy. Traditionally, inflation has been more prevalent in countries outside North America. However, in the late 1970s and early 1980s, Canada experienced double-digit inflation, an inflation rate higher than 10 percent a year. Although the rate of inflation has declined considerably since then, experiences of inflation's effects have led to widespread concern over political approaches to controlling interest rates and stabilizing price levels, and over ways in which the individual can adjust to such reductions in the spending power of the dollar.

Stagflation is a word that has been coined to describe a peculiar brand of inflation that Canada experienced in the 1970s, an economy with high unemployment and a rising price level at the same time. Formulating effective strategies is particularly difficult under these circumstances.

stagflation
High unemployment and a rising price level at the same time.

Unemployment

Another significant economic problem that has affected the marketing environment in recent years is unemployment. The ranks of the unemployed—officially defined as people actively looking for work who do not have jobs—fluctuate as a result of the business cycle. Since 1966, the unemployment rate in Canada has ranged from 4.4 percent to 12.4 percent.

In the severe recession of the early 1980s, numerous businesses failed, production slowed, many factories ceased operation entirely, and thousands of workers found themselves out of work. The consequences of reduced income and uncertainty about future income were reflected in the marketplace in many ways. Similar conditions were experienced in Canada during some of the 1990s.

GOVERNMENT TOOLS FOR COMBATTING INFLATION AND UNEMPLOYMENT

The government can attempt to deal with the twin economic problems of inflation and unemployment by using two basic approaches: fiscal policy and monetary policy. **Fiscal policy** concerns the receipts and expenditures of government. To combat inflation, an economy can reduce government expenditures, raise its revenue (primarily through taxes), or both. It could also use direct controls such as wage and price controls. **Monetary policy** refers to the manipulation of the money supply and market rates of interest. In periods of rising prices, the government may take actions to decrease the money supply and raise interest rates, thus restraining purchasing power.

fiscal policy
The receipts and expenditures of government.

monetary policy
The manipulation of the money supply and market rates of interest.

Both fiscal and monetary policy have been used in our battles against inflation and unemployment. Their marketing implications are numerous and varied. Higher taxes mean less consumer purchasing power, which usually results in declining sales for nonessential goods and services. However, some taxes that have been collected may find their way into various job-creation programs. Income earned from these tends to be spent on basic goods and services. Lower federal spending levels make the government a less attractive customer for many industries. A lowered money supply means that less liquidity is available for potential conversion to purchasing power. High interest rates often lead to a significant slump in the construction and housing industries.

Both unemployment and inflation affect marketing by modifying consumer behaviour. Unless employment insurance, personal savings, and union supplementary unemployment benefits are sufficient to offset lost earnings, unemployed individuals have less income to spend in the marketplace. Even if individuals are completely compensated for lost earnings, their buying behaviour is likely to be affected. As consumers become more conscious of inflation, they are likely to become more price-conscious in general. This can lead to three possible outcomes that are important to marketers. Consumers can (1) elect to buy now in the belief that prices will be higher later (car dealers often use this argument in their commercial messages), (2) decide to alter their purchasing patterns, or (3) postpone certain purchases.

Demarketing—Dealing with Shortages

Shortages—temporary or permanent—can be caused by several factors. A brisk demand may exceed manufacturing capacity or outpace the response time required to gear up a production line. Shortages may also be caused by a lack of raw materials, component parts, energy, or labour. Regardless of the cause, shortages require marketers to reorient their thinking.[8]

demarketing
The process of cutting consumer demand for a product, because the demand exceeds the level that can reasonably be supplied by the firm or because doing so will create a more favourable corporate image.

Demarketing, a term that has come into general use in recent years, refers to the process of cutting consumer demand for a product, because the demand exceeds the level that can reasonably be supplied by the firm or because doing so will create a more favourable corporate image. Some oil companies, for example, have publicized tips on how to cut gasoline consumption as a result of the gradual depletion of oil reserves. Utility companies have encouraged homeowners to install more insulation to lower heating bills. And growing environmental concerns have resulted in companies' discouraging demand for plastic packaging for their products.

Shortages sometimes force marketers to be allocators of limited supplies. This is in sharp contrast to marketing's traditional objective of expanding sales volume. Shortages require marketers to decide whether to spread a limited supply over all customers so that none are satisfied, or to back-order some customers so that others may be completely supplied. Shortages certainly present marketers with a unique set of marketing problems.

▶ THE POLITICAL–LEGAL ENVIRONMENT

political–legal environment
The laws and interpretation of laws that require firms to operate under competitive conditions and to protect consumer rights.

It would be absurd to start playing a new game without first understanding the rules, yet some businesspeople exhibit a remarkable lack of knowledge about marketing's **political–legal environment**—the laws and interpretation of laws that require firms to operate under competitive conditions and to protect consumer rights. Ignorance of laws, ordinances, and regulations can result in fines, embarrassing negative publicity, and possible lawsuits.

It requires considerable diligence to develop an understanding of the legal framework of marketing. Numerous laws, often vague and legislated by a multitude of different authorities, characterize the legal environment for marketing decisions. Regulations affecting marketing have been enacted at the federal, provincial, and local levels as well as by independent regulatory agencies.

Our existing legal framework was constructed on a piecemeal basis, often in response to a concern over current issues.

Canada has tended to follow a public policy of promoting a competitive marketing system. To maintain such a system, competitive practices within the system have been regulated. Traditionally, pricing and promotion have received the most legislative attention.

Society's Expectations Create the Framework

We live in and want a "free-enterprise society"—or do we? The concept of free enterprise is not clear and has been gradually changing. At the turn of the century, the prevalent attitude was to let business act quite freely. It was expected that new products and jobs would be created as a result and the economy would develop and prosper. Currently, the former communist countries are trying to make free enterprise develop their chaotic economies.

In North America, an uncontrolled approach provided great freedom for the honest and the dishonest. Although many businesses sought to serve their target markets in an equitable fashion, abuses did occur. Figure 2.2 shows an example of dishonest marketing practices. Such advertisements were not unusual in the late 1800s and early 1900s. Advancing technology led to the creation of many products in many fields. Often the buying public did not have the expertise needed to choose among them.

With the increasing complexity of products, the growth of big, impersonal business, and the unfair or careless treatment of consumers by some firms, soci-

▶ **FIGURE 2.2 An Example of Dishonest Advertising**

I CURE FITS!

When I say cure I do not mean merely to stop them for a time and then have them return again. I mean a radical cure. I have made the disease of FITS, EPILEPSY or FALLING SICKNESS a life-long study. I warrant my remedy to cure the worst cases. Because others have failed is no reason for not now receiving a cure. Send at once for a treatise and a Free Bottle of my infallible remedy. Give Express and Post Office.

H. G. ROOT, M.C., 183 PEARL ST., NEW YORK.

Source: Excerpted from S. Watson Dunn and Arnold M. Barban, *Advertising: Its Role in Modern Marketing,* 5th ed. (Hinsdale, IL: Dryden, 1982), p. 84. Copyright © 1982 by the Dryden Press, reprinted by permission of the publisher.

ety's values changed. "Government should regulate business more closely," we said. Over time, governments at the federal and provincial levels have responded to this shift: many laws have been passed to protect consumers, and to attempt to maintain a competitive environment for business. Large bureaucracies have grown with this increase in market regulation.

A significant development in the legal environment at the federal level was the consolidation in 1967 of consumer and business regulation programs into Consumer and Corporate Affairs Canada (now called the Competition Bureau of Industry Canada), and the appointment of a cabinet minister to represent these interests at the highest level. Previously these functions had been scattered among several different government departments. Following the lead of the federal government, most provinces have established consumer and corporate affairs branches and have generally streamlined the regulation of these sectors.

strategis.ic.gc.ca/
SSG/ct01254e.html

The Competition Act Sets the Standards

The Competition Act (formerly the Combines Investigation Act) has the most significance in the legal environment for marketing decisions. The Act dates back to 1889, when it was enacted to protect the public interest in free competition. Since then, various revisions have occurred in response to changes in social values and business practices.

The Act prohibits rather than regulates. That is, it does not spell out in detail the activities that industry may undertake, but greatly discourages certain activities through the threat of penal consequences.

The provisions of the Act fall into three main classes. Generally, they prohibit the following:

1. combinations that prevent, or lessen unduly, competition in the production, purchase, sale, storage, rental, transportation, or supply of commodities, or in the price of insurance
2. mergers, monopolies, or abuses of dominant market position that may operate to the detriment of the public
3. deceptive trade practices, including

   - price discrimination
   - predatory pricing
   - certain promotional allowances
   - false or misleading representations, by any means, to promote the sale of a product or to promote a business
   - unsubstantiated claims of performance
   - misleading warranties or guarantees
   - misrepresentation of the ordinary price
   - misleading testimonials for a product or service
   - double ticketing
   - pyramid sales
   - referral selling
   - nonavailability of advertised specials
   - sale above advertised price
   - promotional contests

▶THE ROOTS OF MARKETING

Evolution of Major Combines Legislation

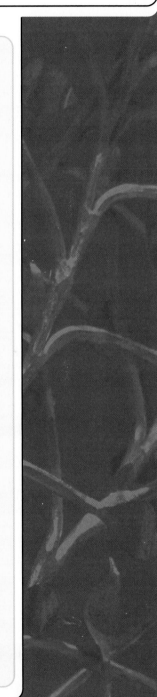

DATE	LEGISLATION	REASON FOR LEGISLATION
1888	Combines Investigation Commission	To protect small businesses that suffered from monopolistic and collusive practices in restraint of trade by large manufacturers.
1889	Act for the Prevention and Suppression of Combinations Formed in Restraint of Trade	To declare illegal monopolies and combinations in restraint of trade.
1892	Above Act incorporated into the Criminal Code as Section 502	To make the above a criminal offence.
1900	Above Act amended	To make the Act effective, because as it stood, an individual would first have to commit an illegal act within the meaning of common law. Now, any undue restriction of competition became a criminal offence.
1910	Additional legislation passed to complement the Criminal Code and assist in the application of the Act	To stop a recent rush of mergers that had involved some 58 firms.
1919	Combines and Fair Prices Act	To prohibit undue stockpiling of the "necessities of life" and prohibit the realization of exaggerated profits through "unreasonable prices."
1923	Combines Investigation Act	To consolidate combines legislation.
1952, 1960	Amendments to the above	
1976	Bill C-2; amendments	To include the service industry within the Act, to prohibit additional deceptive practices, to give persons the right to recover damages, and to protect the rights of small businesses.
1986	Competition Act replaces Combines Investigation Act	To facilitate prosecutions of illegal combinations, mergers, and monopolies.

Despite the long history of the Combines Investigation Act, it proved remarkably powerless for prosecuting those who appeared to contravene either of the first two categories. The passage of the Competition Act to replace the Combines Investigation Act in June 1986 was an important change. Classified as civil law, it corrected many problems in the strictly criminal, proof-beyond-a-reasonable-doubt approach of the old Act. The new Competition Act also created a quasi-judicial body, known as the Competition Tribunal, to deal with matters via the civil route and to make certain rules.

Combines and Restraint of Trade

It is an offence to conspire, combine, agree, or arrange with another person to prevent or lessen competition unduly. The most common types of combination relate to price fixing, bid rigging, market sharing, and group boycotting of competitors, suppliers, or customers.

While the list covers much territory, it should be noted that in the following circumstances agreements between businesspeople are lawful:

- exchanging statistics
- defining product standards
- exchanging credit information
- defining trade terms
- cooperating in research and development
- restricting advertising

Consequently, it is permissible to report statistics centrally for the purpose of analyzing factors relating to industrial operation and marketing, as long as competition is not lessened unduly.

Mergers

Until the passage of the Competition Act in 1986, the law regarding mergers was largely ineffective. Important provisions in the new Act changed the situation. The Competition Tribunal has the power to stop mergers that substantially lessen competition without offering offsetting efficiency gains. Furthermore, the Tribunal must be notified in advance of large mergers (transactions larger than $35 million in sales or assets, and/or companies with combined revenues or assets of more than $400 million). This enables the review and modification of large, complex mergers that are difficult to reverse once consummated. Four of Canada's chartered banks ran afoul of this legislation when they were refused permission to merge into two very large banks in 1999.

Deceptive Trade Practices

This is an extremely important section for marketing decision makers, as it contains a number of directly related provisions. There are real teeth in the legislation, which the marketer should be aware of. Many successful prosecutions have been made under this section.

▶ THE ROOTS OF MARKETING

First Antimonopoly Case after Passage of Competition Act

The first antimonopoly case after the new Competition Act was passed in 1986 was laid in 1989. NutraSweet Co., a subsidiary of U.S. chemical giant Monsanto, was charged with "abuse of dominance" (monopoly) in the Canadian market for aspartame, an artificial sweetener. The Bureau of Competition Policy said in a statement that NutraSweet, the sole supplier of aspartame in the United States, had captured more than 95 percent of the Canadian market. It claimed that NutraSweet demanded contracts with customers that precluded them from buying aspartame from anyone other than NutraSweet. Where exclusive contracts were not made, it claimed, NutraSweet insisted that customers give the company a chance to match the lowest price charged by a competitor. The Bureau also charged NutraSweet with selling aspartame in Canada at a price below its acquisition cost or below its long-run average cost, with the result of substantially lessening competition.

NutraSweet issued a statement disagreeing with the Bureau's charges and believed that the issue would be decided in its favour.[9] However, a few months later, in a precedent-setting decision, the Competition Tribunal ruled that NutraSweet had effectively maintained monopolistic powers over the $25 million domestic aspartame market at the expense of potential competitors.

NutraSweet invented aspartame in the 1960s, but health testing delayed its introduction in many countries, including Canada, until the early 1980s. Soon afterward, NutraSweet's patents on the product began running out. In Canada, that took place in 1987. But in preparation, NutraSweet tied up its customers in exclusive contracts. Under the Tribunal's order, NutraSweet can no longer enforce existing contracts or sign new ones that make it the exclusive aspartame supplier. Nor can NutraSweet sign contracts that give it the right to match, in the future, a competing bid from another aspartame producer. As well, it has been prohibited from giving financial inducements on the sale of aspartame to companies that display NutraSweet's swirl insignia on their products. The director of the Bureau of Competition Policy called the Tribunal's ruling a significant sign that anticompetitive behaviour by companies will not be tolerated.[10]

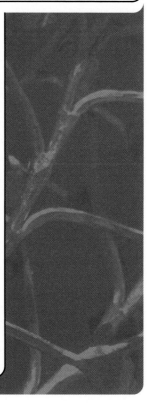

MISLEADING ADVERTISING

False statements of every kind (even in the picture on a package) made to the public about products or services are prohibited. For example, in 1998 The Bay was fined $600 000 for misrepresenting how long sale prices would be in effect (see the Practising Marketer box).

Often carelessness has been seen as responsible for the offence, and over the years, numerous advertisers have been prosecuted under the misleading-advertising provisions of the Combines Investigation Act. The fines meted out have been surprisingly small. The Bay's fine was quite large by comparison.

It is an offence to make unsubstantiated claims. Therefore, claims for a product are expected to be based on an adequate and proper test. Significantly, the onus is on whoever is making the claim to prove its efficacy, rather than on someone else to prove that the product is not as claimed. This reverse onus has been challenged before the courts under the Charter of Rights as being unconstitutional, because it purports to put the onus on the accused to prove innocence, but the section was upheld. One example, and there are many, concerns Professional Technology of Canada, which was convicted in Edmonton on May 27, 1986, for promoting a gas-saving device that claimed to offer 10 to 35 percent better mileage for cars. The company was fined $12 500.[11]

▸ THE PRACTISING MARKETER

www.hbc.com

An Example of False Advertising

Hudson's Bay Co., which led its customers into a misleading "feeling of urgency" when it advertised that there was a time limit on its bicycle sales, was fined $600 000 on May 4, 1998. Crown prosecutor Robert Hubbard, in an agreed statement of facts, added that The Bay had a "prior record of convictions [for false advertising]," most recently in 1991, when a fine of $70 000 was imposed. He said, however, that The Bay has since implemented a compliance program to guard against a further offence.

Madam Justice Anne Molloy of the Ontario Court's General Division accepted the $600 000-fine recommendation made by both The Bay and the Crown.

Charges were laid after investigators from the federal Department of Consumer and Corporate Affairs made about 90 in-store visits in the seven provinces where The Bay does business. They discovered that in 1989, Canada's largest department store stuck to its sale prices for bicycles after the expiry dates in the ads had passed, Mr. Hubbard said.

On May 4, 1998, The Bay pleaded guilty to a charge of false advertising relating to the ads but was acquitted on two similar charges relating to the advertisements of sales on mattresses and pillows. In 1989, flyers, newspaper advertisements, and in-store displays promoted mountain, 12-speed, and family bicycles and stated that sales were in effect for a limited time, Mr. Hubbard said. "They led consumers to believe that they had to purchase bicycles during the stated limited-time period in order to take advantage of the sale price when the sale in fact continued for much longer periods of time." Edward Greenspan, the lawyer for The Bay, told Judge Molloy that the resulting charges were supposed to represent a test case that would clear up the existing legislation on advertising. But a bill before Parliament has now "clarified the law."

Mr. Greenspan said later that a bill before Parliament would amend the Competition Act so such quasi-criminal conduct could be dealt with at an administrative level rather than through the courts.

It took nine years to get the case to court because The Bay brought a motion to quash, which was taken to the Ontario Court's General Division, the Ontario Court of Appeal, and the Supreme Court of Canada before The Bay eventually lost.

The federal government initially laid 17 charges against The Bay and two individuals, but this was boiled down to three charges. Those against the individuals were among the ones dropped.

"It's a big case," Mr. Greenspan said, but when the federal government indicated there would be amending legislation "the importance of this case was fast diminishing." The Bay has more convictions for similar offences but Mr. Greenspan said most were regional in nature. He noted that The Bay has been in business since 1670, so it amounts to "a couple of convictions every century."

Mr. Greenspan said the federal government at first wanted a higher fine, and The Bay wanted a lower one. The $600 000 represented a compromise. It was, he said, "an unhappy result for both sides."

Mr. Greenspan implies that The Bay's convictions for false advertising are of no particular significance or consequence, amounting to "a couple of convictions every century." Do you agree with his assessment? How were consumers harmed by The Bay's actions?

Source: Adapted from Donn Downey, "Hudson's Bay Fined $600 000 for False Ads," *The Globe and Mail* (May 5, 1998), p. B3. Reprinted with permission from *The Globe and Mail*.

Another important fact of the misleading-advertising legislation concerns pricing. Many businesses seem to be unaware that much care needs to be taken when advertising comparative prices. It is, for example, considered misleading for a retailer to advertise a television set as follows:

Manufacturer's suggested list price $680
On sale for $500

if the manufacturer's suggested list price is not normally followed in this retail trading area, and the usual price is around $600. Although the retailer *is* offering a bargain, the magnitude of the saving is not indicated accurately.

Retailers may try to get around this provision by choosing different comparative expressions, such as "regular price," "ordinarily $ ...," "list price," "hundreds sold at," "compare with," "regular value," and the like. But such tactics may nevertheless be problematic. For example, in Moncton, Best for Less (a division of Dominion Stores Ltd.) compared its price with a "why pay up to" price on in-store signs, and depicted the savings. It was established that items were available from competitors at lower prices than the "why pay up to" prices, and the firm was convicted and fined $7650.[12]

The businessperson who genuinely seeks to comply with this provision should ask two questions:

1. Would a reasonable shopper draw the conclusion from the expression used that the figure named by way of comparison is a price at which goods have been, are, or will ordinarily be sold?
2. If the answer is yes, would such a representation be true?

PRICING PRACTICES

It is an offence for a supplier to make a practice of discriminating in price among purchasers who are in competition with one another and who are purchasing like quantities of goods. Selling above the advertised price is also prohibited. Furthermore, the lowest of two or more prices must be used in the case of double-ticketed products. This latter provision has led to the development of easy-tear-off, two-price stickers, so that the sale price can readily be removed after a sale.

If you are a ski manufacturer and wish all ski shops to sell your skis at your suggested list price, can you force them to do so? No; it is an offence under the Act to deny supplies to an outlet that refuses to maintain the resale price. Thus, resale price maintenance is illegal, and a reseller is generally free to set whatever price is considered appropriate.

The Competition Act includes several other prohibitions, including ones against bait-and-switch selling, pyramid selling, and some types of referral selling and promotional contests.

Other Provisions of the Competition Act

PROTECTION AGAINST EXTRATERRITORIAL LAWS AND DIRECTIVES

Foreign companies that do business in Canada have sometimes been constrained by laws or judgements in their home country to the detriment of competition in Canada, or of opportunities for Canadian international trade. For example, Canadian subsidiaries of American companies have felt constrained by American laws against doing business with countries the United States is having disputes with. This is theoretically no longer the case, because the Restrictive Trade Practices Commission (established under the anticombines provisions of the Competition Act) has been given power to rule against such interference in Canadian affairs. In practical terms, companies can still face strong external government pressures. For example, in 1996 the United States demanded that any foreign company that wished to do business with the United States must stop trading with Cuba. Wal-Mart Canada Ltd., which at the time sold Cuban-made pyjamas, found itself having to choose between violating U.S. law by selling the pyjamas or violating Canadian law by pulling them because they were made in Cuba. The company pulled them.[13]

CIVIL DAMAGES

In some situations, people have the right to recover damages incurred as a result of a violation by others. This has profound implications. In some jurisdictions, not only can an individual sue for damages, but if he or she wins, that judgement will apparently serve as evidence for anyone else who has experienced a similar loss. Would this mean that a company could face the possibility of virtually every purchaser of a product claiming damages? Consider the millions of dollars involved for an automobile manufacturer, for example. To our knowledge, there have been no such cases in Canada.

Regulation, Regulation, and ... More Regulation

So far, only some of the provisions from the federal Competition Act have been cited. Provincial governments are also very active in this area. Fortunately, each marketer need not be aware of all provisions, for many are specific to the situation, time, place, and products.

In addition, provincial and municipal governments have other laws and by-laws that must be considered when developing marketing plans. For example, regulations vary from province to province concerning the amount and nature of advertising directed at children. Some other significant laws or regulations relate to bilingual specifications for packaging and labelling; there are special language requirements in Quebec.

From a broad point of view, the legal framework for relations between business and consumers is designed to encourage a competitive marketing system that employs fair business practices. In many respects, various laws have resulted in more effective competition, although many feel that business is overregulated and others think that more regulations are needed. There is little doubt that consumers in Canada are protected as well as or better than consumers in any other country in their dealings with sellers, especially regarding truth in advertising. It is clear that governments will continue to act in response to society's expectations of a fair and honest marketplace.

Marketers in Canada must be aware of how government regulations affect business. For example, they must ensure that packaging and labels are in both English and French, as shown on this Realemon juice label.

▶ SUMMARY

Marketers must understand and monitor the five aspects of their environment. The competitive environment is the interactive process that occurs in the marketplace in which different organizations seek to satisfy similar markets. Competition occurs on three levels: similar products, substitutable products, and all organizations that compete for the consumer's purchases.

The technological environment consists of the applications of knowledge based on scientific discoveries, inventions, and innovations. Computer-based innovations, particularly the Internet, are having a tremendous impact on the practice of marketing.

The sociocultural environment is the mosaic of societal and cultural components that are relevant to the organization's business decisions.

The economic environment—the general national and global economic conditions—sets the framework for developing marketing plans.

The political–legal environment consists of the laws and the interpretation of laws that require firms to operate under competitive conditions and to protect consumer rights.

▶ KEY TERMS

competitive environment
demarketing
economic environment
environmental scanning
fiscal policy
inflation

monetary policy
political–legal environment
sociocultural environment
stagflation
technological environment

▶ INTERACTIVE SUMMARY AND DISCUSSION QUESTIONS

1. The competitive environment is the interactive process that occurs in the marketplace in which competing organizations seek to satisfy markets. Give an example of how the competitive environment might be viewed for the following firms:
   a. McCain Foods
   b. local aerobics exercise centre
   c. Swiss Chalet franchise
   d. Avon products
   e. Sears catalogue department
   f. local television station

2. Marketers face three types of competition: similar products, products that can be substituted for one another, and all organizations that compete for the consumers' purchases. Give an example of each for three different organizations that you are familiar with.

3. The technological environment consists of the applications of knowledge based on scientific discoveries, inventions, and innovations. Discuss the relevance of the technological environment for the firms listed in question 1.

4. Identify some aspects of the sociocultural environment that would likely be of specific relevance to the firms listed in question 1.

5. Where are we now in the business cycle? Give examples of how the economic environment currently could be affecting the marketing practices of the firms listed in question 1.

6. The political–legal environment consists of the laws and the interpretation of laws that require firms to operate under competitive conditions and to protect consumer rights. Give examples of how the political–legal environment might apply to the six firms listed in question 1.

7. Explain how the expectations of society can be said to create the legal framework for business practice.

8. Can the consumerism movement be viewed as a rejection of the competitive marketing system? Defend your answer.

9. The Competition Act has the most significance in the legal environment for marketing decisions. In which areas has the Act had little effect, and for what types of business practices has it been productive?

10. Would a gas station that sold gasoline to a city's police department for one cent a litre less than its price for other customers be in violation of the Competition Act? Why or why not?

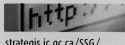

strategis.ic.gc.ca/SSG/
ct01250e.html

11. Visit the home page of the Competition Bureau, and follow the links to the section on deceptive telemarketing (http://strategis.ic.gc.ca/SSG/ct01067e. html). How might the restrictions outlined affect legitimate telemarketers? As a consumer, do you think that a company that follows the Competition Bureau's guidelines would make telemarketing more acceptable to you? Explain your answer.

To obtain a list of further readings for Chapter 2, please refer to the *Foundations of Marketing* Web site.

Part 2
Foundations of the Marketing Plan

The starting point for marketing is recognizing that organizational success comes from identifying and meeting an unmet or poorly met need in society better than anyone else. In Chapter 1 we call this notion the marketing concept. Chapter 2 suggests that the environment affects our ability to meet needs—either positively or negatively. Recognizing that we cannot meet needs accidentally, the focus of the five chapters in Part 2 is planning—*anticipating the future and determining the courses of action designed to achieve organizational objectives.* In order to plan effectively, we must decide whose needs we will try to meet. Chapters 3 and 4 discuss market segmentation, which is the process of making that decision. The premise of Chapter 5 is that if we are going to satisfy unmet needs, we have to know something about those needs. We gather that information through market research. Chapter 6 discusses developing the marketing strategy and plan, and Chapter 7 covers the importance of total customer satisfaction in marketing.

GET TOGETHER with an ADESEPHONE.

See your adesephone dealer.

Chapter 3
Market Segmentation: Finding a Base to Start

Adesemi (formerly the African Communications Group, ACG) Communications International's "small" thinking is leading to big results. By catering to neglected or underdeveloped markets in Africa, Asia, Eastern Europe, and Latin America—those ignored by large companies—this telecommunications company has identified a unique market segment.

No one can accuse Monique Maddy of thinking small just because she runs a telecommunications company out of her basement and concentrates on markets the heavy hitters won't touch.

In her rare idle moments, the supremely confident president and chief executive officer of Adesemi Communications International dreams of becoming the next generation's Rupert Murdoch by carving a media and communications empire out of the world's last remaining frontier territories.

The Liberian-born Ms. Maddy, 35, and her Canadian partner, Come Laguë, 31, are busy installing wireless pay phones and paging services in Tanzania and Ghana. There are also plans to bring their low-cost formula to other neglected or underdeveloped markets in Africa, Asia, Eastern Europe, and Latin America. Adesemi targets regions where there are enough phone-deprived people earning between $200 (U.S.) and $1000 a month each.

"These are our ideal customers," Ms. Maddy says. "And each of these regions have pockets of these types of populations we can serve, whether it's in the main city or a rural area."

But providing basic phone service to the have-littles of the world is only the first step, Ms. Maddy and Mr. Laguë said in an interview at their modest headquarters in a town house near Harvard University. Ms. Maddy lives upstairs and her living room doubles as a waiting area for visitors to the company.

Their eventual goal is to build Adesemi into a full-fledged provider of everything from cable television to electronic publications. The company started as a class project at Harvard Business School and it now boasts millions of dollars in funding from U.S. and European investors.

"The idea would be to move into other forms of media once we've established a footprint in these markets," says Ms. Maddy, whose lilting voice still reflects both her West African roots and her boarding school years in England. By then, Adesemi plans to be a publicly traded company or to be gobbled up by one of the global telecom giants looking for a ready-made platform in smaller markets where they currently pay scant attention. The need for capital will likely be too great to sustain with private funds.

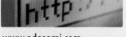

www.adesemi.com

▶ **CHAPTER OBJECTIVES**
After reading and studying this chapter, you should be able to

1. Explain the concept of the marketing plan.
2. Define market segmentation.
3. Discuss and apply five types of market segmentation in consumer markets.
4. Illustrate some aspects of the Canadian market in terms of the five types of consumer market segmentation.
5. Discuss and apply the main types of segmentation in industrial markets.

Ms. Maddy believes Adesemi will one day be attractive to an expansion-minded major such as SBC Communications Inc. of San Antonio, Tex., or Bell Canada International Inc., "when we have quite a big footprint and a number of established systems in different countries."

But for now, the company will settle for getting its toes in the doorways of countries that are just starting to open sectors such as telecommunications to outside players.

Ms. Maddy and Mr. Laguë, the company's Montreal-born chief operating officer, started with initial funds of $200 000. They have since managed to raise about $28-million, and they have a small ownership stake, with the rest held by HarbourVest and a number of other investors.

A key boost for Adesemi came from early supplier SR Telecom Inc. of St. Laurent, Que., which provided a credit of about $800 000 (Canadian) for leased radio transmission equipment. After a three-year grace period, Adesemi has started to pay off the debt.

"They did perhaps the most thorough work I've ever seen in analyzing situations," says Mike Morris, SR's vice-president of corporate affairs. "These people are not hand-wavers. They know what it takes to build a telecommunications network." The core strategy for the business, the entrepreneurs say, is cheaply applying new wireless technology in areas where there is little old telecommunications infrastructure.

Adesemi keeps its services simple and its costs low. It looks for partners in each country who know the ropes and can plot their way through any bureaucratic minefields, and it sets up shop with local hires.

Ms. Maddy and Mr. Laguë have just acquired a controlling stake in a telecommunications company in Ivory Coast. They are also teaming up with a local venture capital fund to acquire a similar business in Sri Lanka, and they are negotiating to install a service from scratch in Zimbabwe. Adesemi's basic operating model—integrating wireless public pay phones with voice mail and paging service—can be installed quickly. The hard part is assessing the political and market risks, finding the right local partners, and winning the licences.

The pagers, which are the most basic available on the market, are sold for no more than $25 (U.S.) each, and callers wanting to leave messages pay the fee, so there are no subscription or collection headaches. The phones operate only with prepaid cards, which reduces vandalism.

Because Adesemi is small and flexible, it can move quickly to take advantage of opportunities.

"That's what you need to succeed in these niche markets. For the big companies, its just not cost-effective," Ms. Maddy says. "They're looking at the Chinas and Indias of the world, the huge markets."

New York–based telecommunications consultant Francis MacInerney agrees. "The big guys aren't interested. They often have trouble justifying putting people in the field where they can't quickly generate sales and profits."

Adesemi is using market segmentation analysis as the basis of its marketing plan. Markets are not usually homogeneous. They consist of many different groups of people from many geographical locations, with a multitude of differing lifestyles, needs, and economic realities. Ms. Maddy has identified a segment of potential customers, which is currently being ignored by larger telecommunications companies, that she believes her company can serve profitably. In order to reach this segment, she and her partner have made decisions specifying an appropriate product and service package, an affordable price, methods of communicating the availability of the service to potential customers, and details on how the product will actually be distributed to the customers. In combination, these decisions are known as the marketing plan. Truly effective marketing plans always flow from consideration of market segments.

Source: Adapted from Brian Milner, "Phone Startup Stakes Out Final Frontiers," *The Globe and Mail* (July 27, 1998), p. B11. Reprinted with permission from *The Globe and Mail.*

▶ INTRODUCTION

Developing the marketing plan is one step of the strategic marketing planning process, a process that involves the consideration of many factors. Two of these factors, customer needs and environmental analysis, have already been introduced in Chapters 1 and 2. Those chapters provide an important base for the rest of this book. We now want to begin building on that base by introducing the strategic marketing planning process, and seeing the role of market segmentation within that process.

If you have a product to market, a decision must be made about the *target market*—that is, to whom will you market the product? In most cases, you will achieve greater success by focusing on part of the entire market. Therefore, an analysis of appropriate target market segments is necessary. Other aspects of strategic marketing planning include taking a careful look at what competitors are doing and at your own firm's situation and resources. Marketing research is also required. A marketing manager and his or her staff take all these elements into consideration in forecasting sales and developing a unique marketing plan that will enable the organization to compete successfully in the marketplace.

Figure 3.1 shows a model of the strategic marketing planning process. It will provide a preliminary perspective on the role each of Part Two's chapter topics plays in the marketing planning process. An expanded discussion of the model is included in Chapter 6. We will start the discussion of marketing planning with the topic of market segmentation.

▶ DEVELOPING A STRATEGIC MARKETING PLAN

Although marketers may face hundreds of decisions in developing an effective plan for achieving organization objectives, these decisions may be summarized as two fundamental tasks:

- Marketers must identify, evaluate, and ultimately select a target market.
- Once the target market has been selected, marketers must develop and implement a marketing program that is designed to satisfy the chosen target group.

These two tasks reflect the philosophy of consumer orientation in action. The choice of a target market is based on recognizing differences among consumers and organizations within a heterogeneous market. The starting point is to understand what is meant by a *market*.

What Is a Market?

A market is *people*. It is also business, not-for-profit organizations, and government—local, provincial, and federal purchasing agents who buy for their "firms."

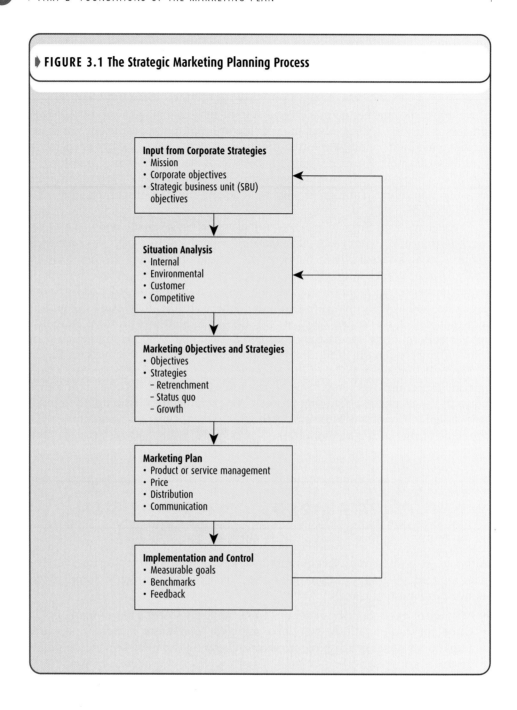

FIGURE 3.1 The Strategic Marketing Planning Process

Input from Corporate Strategies
- Mission
- Corporate objectives
- Strategic business unit (SBU) objectives

Situation Analysis
- Internal
- Environmental
- Customer
- Competitive

Marketing Objectives and Strategies
- Objectives
- Strategies
  - Retrenchment
  - Status quo
  - Growth

Marketing Plan
- Product or service management
- Price
- Distribution
- Communication

Implementation and Control
- Measurable goals
- Benchmarks
- Feedback

But people alone do not make a market. The local dealer for foreign cars is unimpressed by news that 60 percent of the marketing class raise their hands in response to the question "Who wants to buy a new BMW?" The next question is, "How many of them are waving cheques in their outstretched hands?" A **market** consists of people with the willingness, purchasing power, and authority to buy.

One of the first rules that the successful salesperson learns is to determine who in the organization or household has the authority to make particular pur-

market
People with the willingness, purchasing power, and authority to buy.

chasing decisions. Much time can be wasted convincing the wrong person that a product or service should be bought.

Types of Markets

Products may be classified as consumer or industrial goods. **Consumer goods** are those products and services purchased by the ultimate consumer for personal use. **Industrial goods** are those products purchased to be used, either directly or indirectly, in the production of other goods or for resale. Most of the products you buy—books, clothes, milk—are consumer goods. Refined nickel is an industrial good for the mint; rubber is a raw material for Michelin. It is important to make the distinction, because often the motivations and buying process in each case are quite different. The marketing of industrial goods is often called business-to-business marketing.

Sometimes the same product is destined for different uses. The new set of tires purchased by your neighbour are clearly consumer goods, yet when they are bought by Chrysler Corporation to become part of a new Neon, they are classified as industrial goods, since they become part of another good that is destined for resale. The key to the proper classification of goods lies in the purchaser and in *the reasons for buying the good.*

consumer goods
Those products and services purchased by the ultimate consumer for personal use.

industrial goods
Those products purchased to be used, either directly or indirectly, in the production of other goods or for resale.

▶ MARKET SEGMENTATION

A country is too large and filled with too many diverse people and firms for any single marketing plan to satisfy everyone. Unless the product is an item such as an unbranded commodity, trying to satisfy everyone may doom the marketer to failure. Even a seemingly functional product like hand soap is aimed at a specific market segment. Ivory positions itself as a pure, wholesome product; Dove emphasizes moisturizing qualities; while Dial focuses on deodorizing.

The auto manufacturer who decides to produce and market a single car model to satisfy everyone will encounter seemingly endless decisions to be made about such variables as the number of doors, type of transmission, colour, styling, and engine size. In its attempt to satisfy everyone, the firm may be forced to compromise in each of these areas and, as a result, may discover that it does not satisfy anyone very well. Other firms that appeal to particular segments—the youth market, the high-fuel-economy market, the large-family market, and so on—may capture most of the total market by satisfying the specific needs of these smaller, more homogeneous target markets. Although everyone is different, we can group people according to their similarity in one or more dimensions related to a particular product category. This aggregation process is called **market segmentation**.

Once a specific market segment has been identified, the marketer can design an appropriate marketing approach to match its needs, improving the chance of sales to that segment. Market segmentation can be used by both profit-oriented and not-for-profit organizations.[1]

market segmentation
Grouping people according to their similarity in one or more dimensions related to a particular product category.

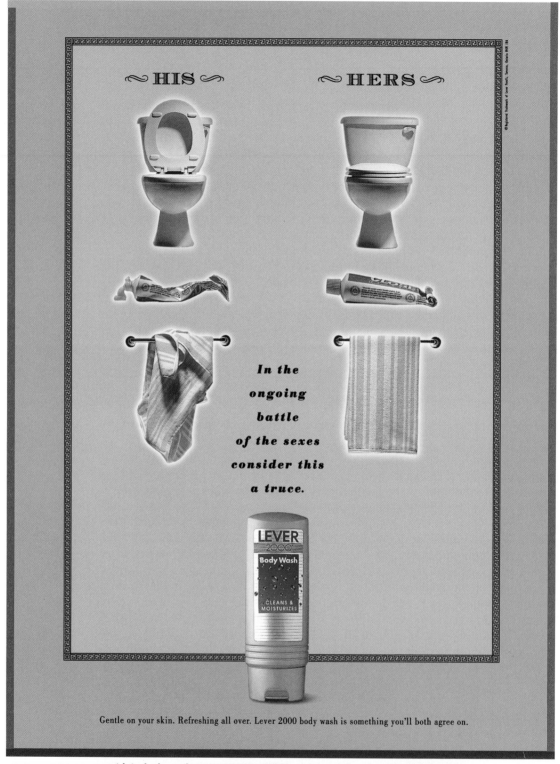

With its body wash, Lever 2000 appeals to couples and to the oldest battle of all times—the battle of the sexes. The advertisement claims that the market segment of couples will, for once, agree on something—its gentle and refreshing cleanser.

▶ SEGMENTING CONSUMER MARKETS

Market segmentation results from determining the factors that distinguish a certain group of consumers from the overall market. These characteristics—such as age, gender, geographic location, income and expenditure patterns, and population size and mobility, among others—are vital factors in the success of the overall marketing strategy. A toy manufacturer such as Mattel studies not only birthrate trends, but also shifts in income and expenditure patterns. Colleges and universities are affected by such factors as the number of high-school graduates, changing attitudes toward the value of college educations, and increasing enrolment of older adults. Figure 3.2 identifies five commonly used bases for segmenting consumer markets. The first two are descriptive, while the next three are behavioural approaches.

▶ FIGURE 3.2 Bases for Market Segmentation

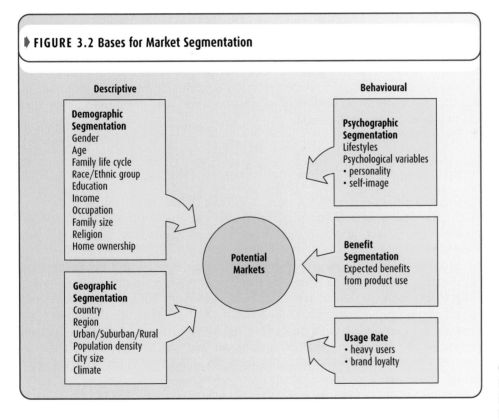

Geographic segmentation, dividing an overall market into homogeneous groups based on population location, has been used for hundreds of years. The second basis for segmenting markets is **demographic segmentation**—dividing an overall market on the basis of characteristics such as age, gender, and income level. Demographic segmentation is the easiest way of subdividing total markets, and is therefore often used.

geographic segmentation
Dividing an overall market into homogeneous groups based on population location.

demographic segmentation
Dividing an overall market on the basis of characteristics such as age, gender, and income level.

psychographic segmentation
Uses behavioural profiles developed from analyses of the activities, opinions, interests, and lifestyles of consumers in identifying market segments.

benefit segmentation
Depends on advanced marketing research techniques that focus on benefits the consumer expects to derive from a product.

usage rate
Divides the market by the amount of product consumed, and/or the degree of brand loyalty.

The third and fourth bases require more sophisticated techniques to implement. **Psychographic segmentation** uses behavioural profiles developed from analyses of the activities, opinions, interests, and lifestyles of consumers in identifying market segments. **Benefit segmentation** depends on advanced marketing research techniques that focus on benefits the consumer expects to derive from a product. Product attributes can then be designed to provide desired benefits. These segmentation bases can be important to marketing strategies provided they are significantly related to differences in buying behaviour. The final segmentation base, **usage rate**, divides the market by the amount of product consumed, and/or the degree of brand loyalty.

▶ GEOGRAPHIC SEGMENTATION

A logical starting point in market segmentation is to find out where buyers are. It is not surprising, therefore, that one of the first bases for segmentation to be considered is geographic. Country and regional variations in consumer tastes often exist. In Japan, for example, consumers are much more particular about the type of rice they use and the way it is cooked than most Canadians. In Canada, per capita consumption of seafood is higher in the Maritimes than in Alberta. Brick and stone construction, a mainstay in many homes in Ontario, is much less common in the West.

Geographic Location of the Canadian Population

Canada's population has grown from 3 million in 1867 to about 30 million in 1999.[2] The Canadian population, like that of the rest of the world, is not distributed evenly. In fact, it is extremely uneven; large portions of this country are uninhabited.[3]

In Canada, about 7 percent of the land surface is occupied farmland.[4] The inhabited space in Canada is depicted in Figure 3.3. This map shows dramatically that a relatively small strip along the American border is the land area most heavily settled and utilized. Business and social activities therefore must operate in an east–west manner, over tremendous distances. It is thus not surprising to see the emergence of various distinct market segments, such as Central Canada (Ontario and/or Quebec), the Maritimes, the Prairies, and British Columbia.

Not only do provinces vary widely in total population (see Figure 3.4 and Table 3.1), but pronounced shifts also occur. People tend to move where work and opportunities exist. Thus, Ontario and British Columbia have been continuously attractive to those on the move. In the late 1970s, Alberta experienced large population influxes because of the oil-induced prosperity there. Many left during the recession of the early 1980s.

Natural factors and immigration also influence population. Growth has occurred as a result of natural increase (births minus deaths) and net migration (immigration minus emigration). Overall, the rate of natural increase has been

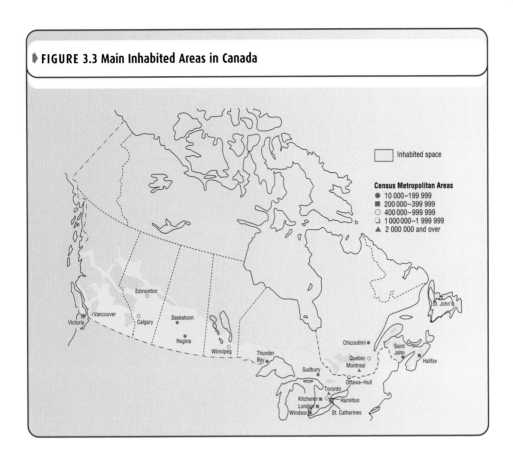

▶ FIGURE 3.3 Main Inhabited Areas in Canada

somewhat higher than that of net migration.[5] In fact, the Atlantic provinces and Saskatchewan depend on natural increase to restore population levels lost by emigration. On the other hand, Ontario, British Columbia, and Alberta have shown significant total population increases because on balance they have received migration flows plus a natural increase. In recent years natural increases have been declining.

Immigration has had a tremendous impact on Canadian society. The injection of a steady stream of British immigrants and short bursts of Central, Eastern, and Southern Europeans and Southeast Asians into the Canadian population have created social pressures in assimilation and citizenship. Some areas have attracted much more immigration. In fact, Ontario contains 54.8 percent of Canada's living foreign-born people.[6] The western provinces contain the greatest percentages of foreign-born "old-timers" (people who immigrated before 1946).

Postwar immigration tended to be from European urban centres to Canadian cities, whereas immigration before World War II was largely from European rural areas to Canadian rural areas.

A remarkable influence has been the immigration–emigration flow in Canada. Despite the fact that 8 million people entered the country through immigration between 1851 and 1961, it is estimated that more than 6 million *left*. From Confederation to 1967, Canada's growth was due largely to natural increase (14.5 million), whereas net migration produced only a 2.4-million increase.[7]

▶ **FIGURE 3.4 Percentage Distribution of the Canadian Population by Province, 1998**

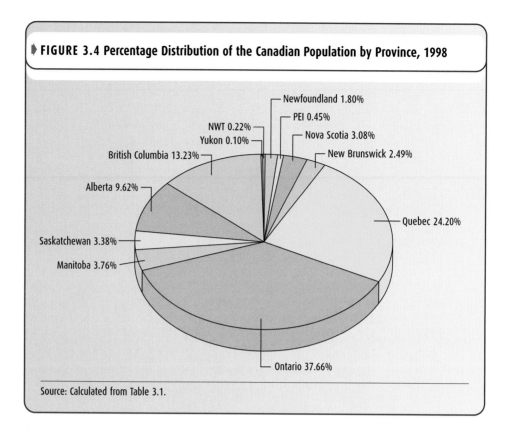

Source: Calculated from Table 3.1.

▶ **TABLE 3.1 Provincial and Territorial Populations, 1985, 1994, 1998**

| | POPULATION (THOUSANDS) | | |
REGION	1985	1994	1998
Newfoundland	580.9	582.4	544.4
Prince Edward Island	128.1	134.5	136.4
Nova Scotia	887.7	936.7	934.6
New Brunswick	726.1	759.3	753.0
Quebec	6690.3	7281.1	7333.3
Ontario	9334.4	10927.8	11411.5
Manitoba	1084.6	1131.1	1138.9
Saskatchewan	1028.8	1016.2	1024.4
Alberta	2311.1	2716.2	2914.9
British Columbia	2990.0	3668.4	4009.9
Yukon	24.6	30.1	31.7
Northwest Territories	55.0	63.1	67.5
Canada	25841.6	29246.9	30300.5

Source: Statistics Canada, *Annual Demographics Statistics, 1998,* Catalogue No. 91-213. Reproduced by permission of the Minister of Supply and Services Canada.

It is estimated that emigration has decreased in recent years. However, the tremendous immigration and emigration in proportion to the size of Canada's population has resulted in a somewhat unstable set of common goals and ends for Canadian society. The character of Canadian society has continually been pulled in various directions through the infusion of different ethnic groups at varying periods of history via immigration.

These factors have traditionally affected the political outlook of Canada's geographic regions. Marketers also recognize that they must take geographic market segments into account.

PEOPLE ARE IN THE CITIES

Canada's population is predominantly urban. People have been migrating to the cities for many years. Figure 3.5 shows that by 1991, the percentage of rural dwellers had dropped to 26 percent, whereas urban dwellers made up 74 percent of the population. In 1996, the percentage of rural dwellers was 22 percent, whereas urban dwellers made up 78 percent of the population.[8] Table 3.2 shows populations and growth rates for Canada's 25 largest metropolitan areas. The three largest—Toronto, Montreal, and Vancouver—already contained approximately 33.1 percent of Canada's total population by 1998, and approximately 61 percent of Canada's population lived in cities of 100 000 and over.[9]

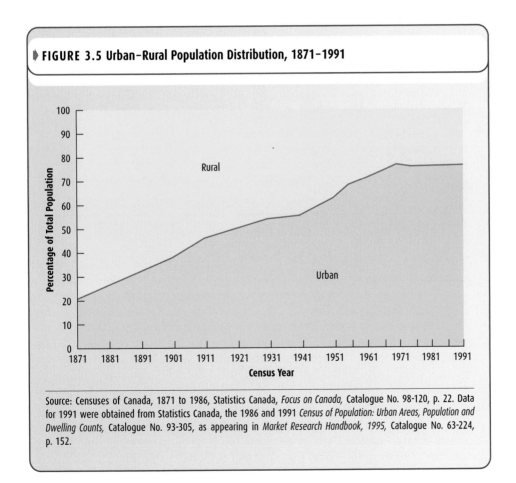

▶ **FIGURE 3.5 Urban-Rural Population Distribution, 1871–1991**

Source: Censuses of Canada, 1871 to 1986, Statistics Canada, *Focus on Canada,* Catalogue No. 98-120, p. 22. Data for 1991 were obtained from Statistics Canada, the 1986 and 1991 *Census of Population: Urban Areas, Population and Dwelling Counts,* Catalogue No. 93-305, as appearing in *Market Research Handbook, 1995,* Catalogue No. 63-224, p. 152.

▶ **TABLE 3.2 The 25 Largest Metropolitan Areas in Canada, 1996**

RANK	AREA	1996 POPULATION (THOUSANDS)	AVERAGE ANNUAL GROWTH RATE, 1988–96 (PERCENT)
1	Toronto	4445	1.9
2	Montreal	3359	1.0
3	Vancouver	1891	2.7
4	Ottawa–Hull	1031	1.9
5	Edmonton	892	1.2
6	Calgary	852	2.3
7	Quebec	698	1.2
8	Winnipeg	677	0.5
9	Hamilton	650	1.1
10	London	416	1.5
11	Kitchener	403	2.1
12	St. Catharines–Niagara	390	1.0
13	Halifax	347	1.3
14	Victoria	313	1.5
15	Windsor	292	1.2
16	Oshawa	281	2.6
17	Saskatoon	222	0.6
18	Regina	199	0.3
19	St. John's	178	0.7
20	Chicoutimi–Jonquière	167	0.4
21	Sudbury	166	0.9
22	Sherbrooke	150	1.1
23	Trois-Rivières	144	0.8
24	Thunder Bay	131	0.34
25	Saint John	129	0.3

Source: *Census of Canada 1996*, Statistics Canada, CANSIM, Matrix 6231 reproduced in Statistics Canada, *Canada Year Book 1999*, Catalogue No. 11-402-XPE, p. 94.

The Canadian population, along with the American and the Australian, is one of the most mobile in the world. The average Canadian moves twelve times in a lifetime, as compared with eight times for the average English citizen and five for the typical Japanese.[10] However, this trend may be waning. The slowdown may be due to a number of factors: poor job prospects elsewhere, the tendency of wage earners in two-income families to refuse transfers, an aging population, and a heightened concern about the quality of life.

Using Geographic Segmentation

There are many instances where markets for goods and services may be segmented on a geographic basis. Country and regional variations in taste often exist. Breakfast in Germany normally includes bread, cheese, and cold meat. In countries with large Chinese populations, this segment will eat rice porridge and other "nonbreakfast" items (by Canadian standards). Quebec has long been known for its interest in fine and varied foods.

Residence location within a geographic area is another important geographic variable. Urban dwellers may eat more meals in restaurants than their suburban and rural counterparts, while suburban dwellers spend proportionally more on lawn and garden care than do people in rural or urban areas. Both rural and suburban dwellers may spend more of their household income on gasoline and automobile needs than do urban households.

Climate is another important factor. Snow blowers, snowmobiles, and sleds are popular products in many parts of Canada. Residents of southwestern British Columbia may spend proportionately less of their total income on heating and heating equipment than other Canadians. Climate also affects patterns of clothing purchases.

Geographic segmentation influences decisions about which sales regions to enter, where sales force offices are located, and where retail outlets are located.

Geographic segmentation is useful only when true differences in preference and purchase patterns for a product emerge along regional lines. Geographic subdivisions of the overall market tend to be rather large and often too heterogeneous for effective segmentation for many products without carefully considering additional factors. In such cases, it may be necessary to use other segmentation variables as well.

▶ DEMOGRAPHIC SEGMENTATION

The most common approach to market segmentation is to group consumers according to demographic variables. These variables—age, gender, income, occupation, education, household size, and others—are typically used to identify market segments and to develop appropriate market mixes. Demographic variables are often used in market segmentation for three reasons:

- They are easy to identify and measure.
- They are associated with the sale of many products and services.
- They are typically referred to in describing the audiences of advertising media, so that media buyers and others can easily pinpoint the desired target market.[11]

Vast quantities of data are available to assist the marketing planner in segmenting potential markets on a demographic basis. Gender is an obvious variable for segmenting many markets, since many products are gender-specific. Electric-razor manufacturers have used gender as a variable in successfully marketing such brands as Lady Remington. Diet soft drinks have often been aimed at female markets. Even deodorants are targeted at males or females.

Age, stage in the family life cycle, household size, and income and expenditure patterns are important factors in determining buying decisions. The often distinct differences in purchase patterns based on such demographic factors justify their frequent use as a basis for segmentation.

Segmenting by Age

The population of Canada is expected to grow by 10 percent between 1999 and 2006, but this growth will be concentrated in persons aged 45 and older. This group represents two potentially profitable target markets.

The older and senior middle-aged adult segment (45–64) includes households where the children have grown up and most have left home. For many, housing costs are lower because mortgages are paid off. In general, this group finds itself with substantial disposable income because it is in a peak earning period, and many basic purchases for everyday living have been completed. This disposable income is often used for luxury goods, new furniture, and travel. While this segment currently represents 20.8 percent of the Canadian population, it will account for 65 percent of the growth in population between 1999 and 2006.

▶ THE CANADIAN MARKETPLACE

A Life and Death Experience

Hardly a day passes without news of some new drug or genetic technique to help us live longer.

How would such improvements in health care work out? There are two broad theories about this. One says that medical science will improve the chances of surviving at any age and extend the lives of all, so that as many as half of us would live into our second centuries.

The other says that the chances of survival will improve dramatically in youth and middle age, but that death will finally come not much later than it does now; aging cannot be stopped, only mitigated.

One way of envisaging these changes is to take a group of 1000 babies, then plot the number of survivors year by year into their old age. As the chart shows, as recently as 1951 the number of survivors began to plunge rapidly in middle age. At 45 there were 900 survivors of a typical group; by age 70 there were only 600; by 90 a mere 60 survivors.

The first theory, life extension, means that a higher proportion would be alive at each age. The chart looks ahead to the year 2071, to allow known and unknown medical miracles to mature. By then, there will still be over 900 survivors at age 60, nearly 800 at 90, 55 even at 120. Being 100 years old in 2071 would be like being 70 in 1951.

The second theory, sometimes described as "squaring the survivor curve" (note the shape on the chart), means something different. There would be over 900 survivors of the original 1000 at age 75, but not a lot more at age 95 than in 1951. The assumption is that efforts to beat aging will be abandoned and scientists will concentrate instead on a healthier life during the normal span.

For many businesses and services, the differences will be large. Consider the impact on insurance companies, obviously, but also for people caring for the elderly, governments planning taxes, and pension plans.

▶ **Actual and Hypothetical Survival Patterns of 1000 Births**

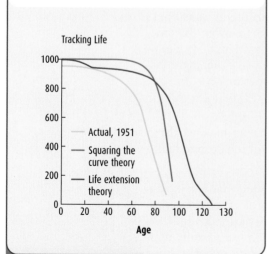

Tracking Life

Actual, 1951
Squaring the curve theory
Life extension theory

Age

Source: John Kettle, "A Life and Death Experience," *The Globe and Mail* (February 25, 1999), p. B11. Reprinted with permission from the author. Graph: Statistics Canada and John Kettle, *The Globe and Mail.*

Not so many years ago, there was no such thing as a senior-citizen market, since few people reached old age. Now, however, some 12.3 percent of the total population is 65 or older.[12] Not only is it comforting for this year's retiree to learn that at age 60 her or his average life expectancy is at least another 22.2 years,[13] but the trend also creates a unique and potentially profitable segment for the marketing manager. The manager of course will not ignore the youth segment, which will decline in proportion to the whole population but remain large. Figure 3.6 shows the changing profile of the Canadian population.

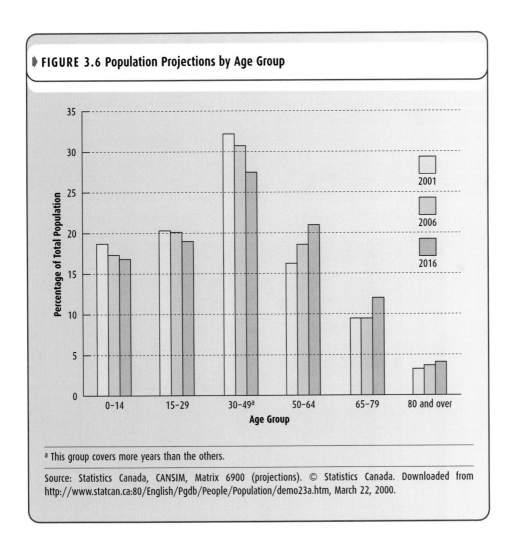

▶ **FIGURE 3.6 Population Projections by Age Group**

^a This group covers more years than the others.

Source: Statistics Canada, CANSIM, Matrix 6900 (projections). © Statistics Canada. Downloaded from http://www.statcan.ca:80/English/Pgdb/People/Population/demo23a.htm, March 22, 2000.

Each of the age groups in Figure 3.6 represents different consumption patterns, and each serves as the target market for particular firms. For instance, Gerber Products Company has been extremely successful in aiming at the parents-of-infants market, and prepackaged tours appeal to older consumers. Table 3.3 lists some of the types of merchandise often purchased by the various age groups.

TABLE 3.3 Buying Patterns for Different Age Groups

AGE	NAME OF AGE GROUP	MERCHANDISE
0–5	Young children	Baby food, toys, nursery furniture, children's wear
6–19	Schoolchildren (including teenagers)	Clothing, sports equipment, records, school supplies, food, cosmetics, used cars
20–34	Young adults	Cars, furniture, houses, clothing, recreational equipment, purchases for younger age groups
35–49	Younger middle-aged adults	Larger homes, better cars, second cars, new furniture, recreational equipment
50–64	Older middle-aged adults	Recreational items, purchases for young marrieds and infants
65+	Senior adults	Medical services, travel, drugs, purchases for younger age groups

Young children, representing the 0–5 age group of the family life cycle, are an important age segment. Toys such as Lego attract both children (the target market), who enjoy this timeless product, and parents (the product buyers), who seek educational toys for their children.

▶ THE CANADIAN MARKETPLACE

Teen Consumers in Canada

A dozen teens sit in a fashionable Toronto office loft taking part in a focus group organized by Youth Culture Inc., a company that tracks trends. YCI's creative director Gary Butler and Sean Saraq, a demographer with Environics Research Group, want to know what exactly prompts kids to spend their money on CDs, movies, video games, and fashion. Their responses? Annie Grainger, 16, says she is wary of commercials and market- ing, yet spends $50 a pop for body-piercing. Eighteen-year-old Mike Landon proudly wears hip-hop clothes with the Phat Farm label and says: "Show me a commercial that says 50-percent off—that's a good commercial to me." Chi Nguyen, 18, says she "would like a world that didn't respond to advertising." So much for gaining insight into the mind-set of the "average" teen. The message: there *is* no such thing as an average teen. "The deeper people dig," says the 34-year-old Saraq, "the more they realize that teens are all over the map."

Why do companies want to pin kids down? Call it a Youthquake. Call it Teen Power. Whatever, for the first time since the baby boom, kid culture is king. Teens have more money in their pockets than ever before, and their influence is everywhere—in music stores with CDs by bands ranging from The Moffatts and Britney Spears to Korn and The Offspring; in clothing stores with labels such as JNCO and Snug. MuchMusic's teen audience has grown 80 percent since 1996. "It's all about pop culture," says Grainger, an eleventh-grader from Toronto. "And pop culture is all about buying."

In fact never before has so much been pitched to so many who are so young. Advertisers are pursuing kids on TV, in print, and even in schools. Their quarry comprise the so-called Echo or Y Generation (born between 1980 and 1995), the largest demographic in Canada next to their baby boomer parents (those born between 1947 and 1966). University of Toronto economics professor David Foot, author of the best- selling *Boom, Bust & Echo 2000,* says the Echo Generation is a nationwide phenomenon with its highest con- centrations in Ontario and the West. Statistics Canada predicts that by July [of 1999], there will be 4.1 mil- lion Canadians between 10 and 19 years of age. By the year 2006, that number will swell to 4.4 million. And don't doubt their clout: in 1998, 9- to 19-year-olds spent an astonishing $13.5 billion in Canada. "That number is going to do nothing but go up," says Lindsay Meredith, a professor of marketing at Simon Fraser University in Burnaby, BC. "This is the gold rush."

Advertisers and marketers divide the demographic into two distinct groups—9- to 14-year-old "tweens" and 15- to 19-year-old teens. In Canada, there are 2.4 million tweens with $1.5 billion to spend, according to a Creative Research International Inc. survey commissioned by the cable channel YTV. Seventeen percent of tweens have ATM bank cards, and each tween spends roughly $137 per year on back-to-school gear. Seventy-six percent have Internet access either at home or at school. Susan Mandryk, vice-president of mar- keting with YTV, says the key to reaching tweens lies in understanding their "age aspirations—we never tell a tween that they are a tween." Tweens want to be teens; they buy products that make them feel sophisticated. Environics Research findings show that on average 12-to-14-year-olds want to be 18, while 15-to-19-year-olds want to be 20.

So while tweens spend to feel like teens, teens buy to cultivate their stature as "young adults." In 1998, there were 2.5 million teens between 12 and 17 years old, according to Statistics Canada. And unlike Generation Y, the 1980s teens who were maligned as "slackers" after running into the reality of inflation and unemployment, the current crop has high expectations. "They are totally optimistic," says Victor Thiessen, a sociology professor at Dalhousie University in Halifax. "Teens have not had an experience where the world kept them back. They take for granted that they are going to work." Meanwhile, they are going to spend: Youth Culture Inc.'s Butler estimates the average teen has a disposable income of $500 a month.

They also consider themselves immune to the tricks of the advertising trade. Bombarded from birth, they know they are being pitched and are suspicious. They recognize their own power. At the Youth Culture focus group, there are nods of agreement when 18-year-old Liane Balaban remarks: "I like the idea of a bunch of advertising executives sitting in a room sweating and pulling their hair out trying to figure out how to sell to us."

If you were the one tearing your hair out trying to sell to teens, what steps might you take?

Source: Adapted from Andrew Clark, "How Teens Got the Power," *Maclean's* (March 22, 1999), pp. 42–43.

Segmenting by Family Life Cycle

family life cycle
The process of family
formation, development,
and dissolution.

The **family life cycle** is the process of family formation, development, and dissolution. Using this concept, the marketing planner combines the family characteristics of age, marital status, presence or absence of children, and ages of children in developing the marketing strategy. Patrick E. Murphy and William A. Staples have proposed a six-stage family life cycle with several subcategories. These stages are shown in Table 3.4.

The behavioural characteristics and buying patterns of people in each life-cycle stage often vary considerably. Young singles have relatively few financial burdens, tend to be early purchasers of new fashion items, are recreation-oriented, and make purchases of basic kitchen equipment, cars, and vacations. By contrast, young marrieds with young children tend to be heavy purchasers of baby products, homes, television sets, toys, and washers and dryers. Their liquid assets tend to be relatively low, and they are more likely to watch television than young singles or young marrieds without children. The empty-nest households in the middle-aged and older categories with no dependent children are more likely to have more disposable income; more time for recreation, self-education, and travel; and more than one member in the labour force than their full-nest counterparts with younger children. Similar differences in behavioural and buying patterns are evident in the other stages of the family life cycle.[14]

▶ **TABLE 3.4 Family Life-Cycle Stages**

1. Young Single

2. Young Married without Children

3. Other Young
   a. Young divorced without children
   b. Young married with children
   c. Young divorced with children

4. Middle-Aged
   a. Middle-aged married without children
   b. Middle-aged divorced without children
   c. Middle-aged married with children
   d. Middle-aged divorced with children
   e. Middle-aged married without dependent children
   f. Middle-aged divorced without dependent children

5. Older
   a. Older married
   b. Older unmarried (divorced, widowed)

6. Other
   All adults and children not accounted for by family life-cycle stages

Source: Adapted from Patrick E. Murphy and William A. Staples, "A Modernized Family Life," *Journal of Consumer Research* (June 1979), p. 16, published by the University of Chicago Press.

Analyzing life-cycle stages often gives better results than relying on single variables, such as age. The buying patterns of a 25-year-old bachelor are very different from those of a father of the same age. The family of five headed by parents in their 40s is a more likely prospect for a Ford Windstar minivan than the childless 40-year-old divorced person.

Marketing planners can use published data such as census reports to divide their markets into more homogeneous segments than would be possible if they were analyzing single variables. Such data are available for each classification of the family life cycle.

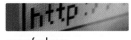

www.ford.com

Segmenting by Household Size

Half the households in Canada are composed of only one or two persons, and the average household size is three persons. This development is in marked contrast to households that averaged more than four persons before World War II. Married couples still form the largest segment of households, but in relative terms their numbers are decreasing.

There are several reasons for the trend toward smaller households. Among them are lower fertility rates, the tendency of young people to postpone marriage, the increasing desire among younger couples to limit the number of children, the ease and frequency of divorce, and the ability and desire of many young single adults and elderly people to live alone.

Over 2.6 million people live alone according to the 1996 Census.[15] The single-person household has emerged as an important market segment with a special title: **SSWD** (single, separated, widowed, or divorced). SSWDs buy approximately 25 percent of all passenger cars, but a much higher proportion of specialty cars. They are also customers for single-serving food products, such as Campbell's Soup-for-One and Green Giant's single-serving casseroles.

SSWDs
Single, separated, widowed, or divorced people.

www.campbellsoup.ca

Segmenting by Income and Expenditure Patterns

Earlier, markets were defined as people and purchasing power. A very common method of segmenting consumer markets is on the basis of income. For example, fashionable specialty shops that stock designer-label clothing obtain most of their sales from high-income shoppers.

www.greengiant.com

Income statistics can be analyzed by family structure. Families can be divided into two groups: husband–wife families and lone-parent families. The latter can be further subdivided by the sex of the parent. Significant changes have occurred in the structure of families over time, as Table 3.5 shows. Between 1985 and 1996, the number of husband–wife families increased by 16.7 percent, while that of male lone-parent families increased by 15.2 percent. However, the number of female lone-parent families increased by 17.8 percent. The three groups fared differently with respect to their incomes over the five-year period. Each group experienced a significant increase in real income. The average income in the husband–wife families increased almost twice that in female lone-parent families. In 1985, the average income in male lone-parent families was 63 percent higher than in female lone-parent families, but lowered to 53 percent in 1996.[16]

▶ TABLE 3.5 Percentage Distribution by 1985 and 1996 Family Income Groups by Family Structure, Canada

FAMILY INCOME GROUP (1993 DOLLARS)[a]	HUSBAND – WIFE FAMILIES		MALE LONE-PARENT FAMILIES		FEMALE LONE-PARENT FAMILIES	
	1985	1996	1985	1996	1985	1996
Under $10 000	5.2	1.7	15.3	2.8	33.6	9.4
$10 000–14 999	7.1	2.2	10.0	7.6	16.4	16.3
15 000–19 999	8.7	3.7	9.9	7.3	11.9	15.5
20 000–24 999	8.5	6.4	9.8	5.4	10.5	10.8
25 000–34 999	19.0	12.4	20.4	19.0	14.0	16.1
35 000–49 999	25.2	18.1	19.8	25.5	9.2	17.7
50 000 and over	26.2	55.4	14.8	32.3	4.4	14.2
Total	99.9	99.9	100.0	99.9	100.0	100.0
Number (in thousands)	5 881	6 863	151	174	702	827
Average income (in dollars)	40 222	60 847	31 252	45 376	19 177	29 694
Median income (in dollars)	35 758	53 558	27 405	38 933	15 005	24 079

[a] The dollar figures have not been adjusted for inflation.

Source: The 1985 data have been obtained from Statistics Canada, *Income Distribution by Size in Canada, 1985*, Catalogue No. 13-207, p. 71. The 1996 data have been obtained from Statistics Canada, *Income Distribution by Size in Canada, 1996*, Catalogue No. 13-207-XPB, p. 96.

A household's expenditures may be divided into two categories: (1) basic purchases of essential household needs, and (2) other purchases that can be made at the discretion of the household members once the necessities have been purchased (disposable income). Total Canadian disposable income is estimated to have tripled in constant dollars since 1961,[17] a substantial increase.

Engel's Laws

How do expenditure patterns vary with increased income? More than 100 years ago a German statistician named Ernst Engel published three general statements — **Engel's Laws** — based on his studies of spending behaviour. According to Engel, as family income increases:

1. A smaller percentage of expenditures goes for food.
2. The percentage spent on housing and household operations and clothing will remain constant.
3. The percentage spent on other items (such as recreation, education, etc.) will increase.

Engel's Laws As family income increases, (1) a smaller percentage goes for food, (2) the percentage spent on housing and household operations and clothing will remain constant, and (3) the percentage spent on other items will increase.

Are Engel's Laws still valid today? Figure 3.7 supplies the answers. A small decline in the percentage of total income spent for food occurs from low to high incomes. Note the emphasis on the word *percentage*. The high-income families will spend a greater absolute amount on food purchases, but their purchases will represent a smaller percentage of their total expenditures than will be true of low-income households.

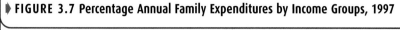

FIGURE 3.7 Percentage Annual Family Expenditures by Income Groups, 1997

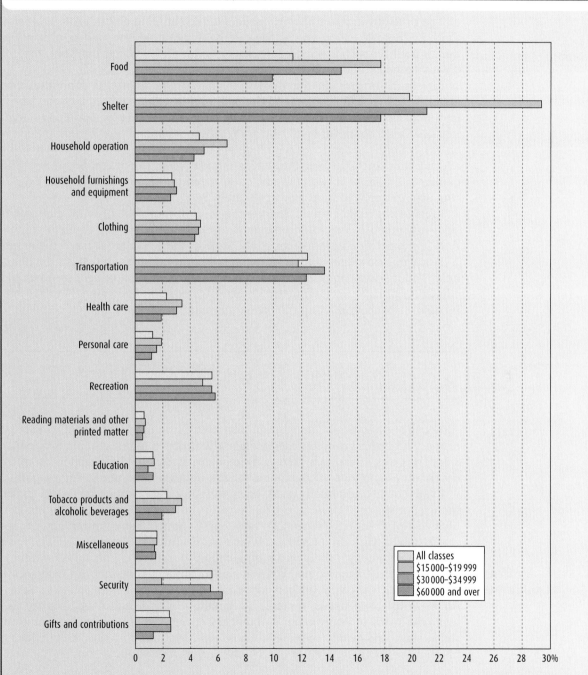

Source: Data from Statistics Canada, *Family Expenditure in Canada, 1997*, Catalogue No. 62-555, as appearing in *Market Research Handbook, 1999*, Catalogue No. 63-224-XPB, pp. 66–67. Reproduced by permission of the Minister of Supply and Services Canada.

With respect to Engel's second law, expenditures for shelter decline rather than remain constant. However, as predicted, there is relatively little change in the percentage of income spent on household operations and in household furnishings and equipment, as well as on clothing.

The third law is also true with respect to recreation and education. However, there are notable exceptions to the original generalization, such as transportation. It has become a much greater part of family expenditures than Engel might have dreamed.

Engel's Laws provide the marketing manager with useful generalizations about types of consumer demand that will evolve with increased income. These laws may also be useful when evaluating a foreign country as a potential target market. Other countries may well have different expenditure patterns, however. For example, in countries with high population densities, such as Hong Kong and parts of England, housing that is equivalent to North American size and quality is available only to the rich. The marketer cannot assume that Engel's conclusions apply without checking carefully.

In general, demographic segmentation is useful for estimating segment size — it's much easier to determine the size of demographic-based segments than it is to get an accurate picture of the size of the behavioural-based segments.

Demographic segmentation influences the choice of local distribution channels. The marketer looks for channels that cater to different age, income, and education groups. Similarly, the choice of media is determined by the age, income, or education group the product is designed to serve.

▶ PSYCHOGRAPHIC SEGMENTATION

Although geographic and demographic segmentation have traditionally been the primary bases for grouping customers and industries into segments to serve as target markets, marketers have long recognized the need for richer, more in-depth representations of consumers for use in developing marketing programs.

Even though traditionally used variables such as age, gender, family life cycle, income, and population size and location are important in segmentation, lifestyles of potential consumers often prove much more important. Demographically, a truck driver and a college professor may be the same age and have the same income, yet their purchasing behaviour will likely be very different.

lifestyle
The mode of living.

Lifestyle refers to the mode of living of consumers. Consumers' lifestyles are regarded as a composite of their individual behaviour patterns and psychological makeup—their needs, motives, perceptions, and attitudes. A lifestyle also bears the mark of many other influences—those of reference groups, culture, social class, and family members. Thus, segmentation by lifestyles provides a much more complete picture of customer needs and wants.

psychographics
The use of psychological attributes, lifestyles, and attitudes in determining the behavioural profiles of different consumers.

Psychographics

A technique that is more comprehensive than lifestyle segmentation is **psychographics**. Psychographics is the use of psychological attributes, lifestyles, and attitudes in determining the behavioural profiles of different consumers. These profiles are usually developed through market research that asks for agreement or disagreement with statements dealing with activities, interests, and opinions. Because of the basis of the statements (activities, interests, and opinions), they are sometimes referred to as **AIO statements**.

Goldfarb Consultants and Environics Research have each produced psychographic groupings of the Canadian market. Their findings are somewhat different, but both provide some interesting insights into the marketplace.

AIO statements
Statements about activities, interests, and opinions that are used in developing psychographic profiles.

THE GOLDFARB SEGMENTS[18]

There are six Goldfarb segments, divided neatly into *more* or *less* traditional, with 56 percent of the population falling into the *more* traditional segment. The Goldfarb segments are as follows:

- *Day-to-Day Watchers* are quite satisfied with what life has to offer. They are early followers rather than leaders, but they keep a close eye on the world around them.
- *Old-Fashioned Puritans* are conservative to the point of being defensive, traditional to the point of inflexibility, and indifferent to the point of apathy. This is not the best group for new-product advertising.
- *Responsible Survivors* are a cautious group; they are very brand-loyal and are heavy TV viewers.
- *Joiner–Activists* are leading-edge thinkers, but tend to be nonconformists.
- *Aggressive Achievers* are confident, success-oriented people. They want to be leaders, love status-signalling goods, and need to have their psyches stroked regularly.
- *Disinterested Self-Indulgents'* TV viewing is similar to the previous group. Their music tastes are a little more conservative, learning to pop rock and oldies. They are also above-average pay TV viewers and VCR users (see Figure 3.8).

You can visit the Goldfarb Consultants Web site and fill out a short twenty-question survey. Based on your answers, you will link to another Web page that explains your particular psychographic profile.

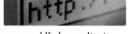

www.goldfarbconsultants.
com

THE ENVIRONICS SEGMENTS[19]

Environics has produced a slightly more complicated scheme than Goldfarb's. First they divide the population into three main age groups: the Elders (age 50 +), the Boomers (ages 30–40), and Generation X (ages 15–29). Each age group is then subdivided into various psychographic segments as follows:

Elders

- *Rational Traditionalists* (15 percent of total population, 54 percent of Elders) are motivated to achieve and preserve financial independence, stability, and security. Key values include religiosity and primacy of reason.
- *Extroverted Traditionalists* (7 percent of total population, 26 percent of Elders) are motivated by traditional community, institutions, and social status. Key values include religiosity and family.
- *Cosmopolitan Modernists* (6 percent of total population, 20 percent of Elders) are motivated by traditional institutions and experience seeking. Their key values include a global world-view, respect for education, and desire for innovation.

> **FIGURE 3.8 Application of Psychographic Analysis**

Old-Fashioned Puritan

- Heavy TV viewers—preference for game shows, soaps, family dramas, miniseries, and children's cartoons
- Light radio listeners—preference for country and "oldies"
- Low pay TV/VCR use

Disinterested Self-Indulgent

- Medium/heavy TV viewing—preference for sitcoms, variety, suspense/crime drama, and sports
- Heavy radio listening—preference for top 40, hard rock, "oldies," and hockey and football broadcasts
- Above-average pay TV use—Nashville Network, TSN, First Choice/Super Channel
- Above-average VCR use
- Never delete commercials

Source: John Chaplin, "Pigeonholes for Consumers," *Marketing Magazine* (October 16, 1989), p. 1.

Boomers

- *Autonomous Rebels* (10 percent of total population, 25 percent of Boomers) are motivated by personal autonomy and self-fulfillment. They have a strong belief in human rights, are skeptical toward traditional institutions, and are suspicious of authority. They also value freedom, individuality, and education.
- *Anxious Communitarians* (9 percent of total population, 20 percent of Boomers) are motivated by traditional community, institutions, and social status. They value family, community, and duty and need respect.

- *Connected Enthusiasts* (6 percent of total population, 14 percent of Boomers) are motivated by both traditional and new communities and are experience seekers. They value family, community, hedonism, and immediate gratification.
- *Disengaged Darwinists* (18 percent of total population, 41 percent of Boomers) seek financial independence, stability, and security. They are nostalgic about the past.

Generation X

- *Aimless Dependents* (8 percent of total population, 27 percent of Gen Xers) are motivated to achieve financial independence, stability, and security. They desire independence.
- *Thrill-Seeking Materialists* (7 percent of total population, 25 percent of Gen Xers) are motivated by traditional communities, social status, and experience seeking. They desire money and material possessions, recognition, respect, and admiration.
- *New Aquarians* (4 percent of total population, 13 percent of Gen Xers) are experience seekers interested in new communities. They value egalitarianism, ecology, and hedonism.
- *Autonomous Postmaterialists* (6 percent of total population, 20 percent of Gen Xers) are motivated to achieve personal autonomy and self-fulfillment. They value freedom and respect for human rights.
- *Social Hedonists* (4 percent of total population, 15 percent of Gen Xers) are experience seekers interested in new communities. They value aesthetics, hedonism, sexual permissiveness, and immediate gratification.

Environics has a Web site where you can see which profile you best match.

erg.environics.net/surveys

What can be done with such segment analyses? Each segment can be related to product preference and use. There are many possibilities. For example, when two of Goldfarb's sets of lifestyle clusters were cross-tabulated against questions about radio or TV listening/watching, Old-Fashioned Puritans were found to be heavy TV viewers and light radio listeners. They have a preference for game shows, soaps, family dramas, miniseries, and children's cartoons. In radio listening, they have a preference for country music and "oldies." They have low ownership of VCRs and low pay TV usage.

Such information is extremely useful to broadcasters and advertisers, because they know what types of messages and products to feature on different shows. The procedure used for broadcasting could be applied to many other goods and services as well. The insights developed by such a process go far beyond demographic segmentation and influence product positioning (see Chapter 4), advertising themes, and media choice.

Psychographic segmentation is often part of an overall segmentation strategy in which markets are also segmented on the basis of demographic/geographic variables. These more traditional bases provide the marketer with accessibility to consumer segments through orthodox communications channels such as newspapers, radio and television advertising, and other promotional outlets. Psychographic studies may then be implemented to develop lifelike, three-dimensional profiles of the lifestyles of the firm's target market. When combined with demographic/geographic characteristics, psychographics emerges as an important tool for understanding the behaviour of present and potential target markets.[20]

▶ BENEFIT SEGMENTATION

Benefit segmentation is based on the attributes of products as seen by the customer. Segments are developed by asking consumers about the benefits they perceive in a good or service. Since many people perceive and use the same product differently, those who perceive benefits that are similar are clustered into groups. Each group then constitutes a market segment.

Many marketers now consider benefit segmentation one of the most useful methods of classifying markets. One analysis of 34 segmentation studies indicated that benefit analysis provided the best predictor of brand use, level of consumption, and product type selected in 51 percent of the cases. In a pioneering benefit segmentation investigation, Daniel Yankelovich revealed that much of the watch industry operated with little understanding of the benefits watch buyers expect in their purchases. At the time of the study, most watch companies were marketing relatively expensive models through jewellery stores and using prestige appeals. However, Yankelovich's research revealed that less than one-third of the market was purchasing a watch as a status symbol. In fact, 23 per-

▶ THE ROOTS OF MARKETING

Benefit Segmentation of the Toothpaste Market, 1968

	SEGMENT NAME			
	THE SENSORY SEGMENT	THE SOCIABLES	THE WORRIERS	THE INDEPENDENT SEGMENT
Principal benefit sought	Flavour, product appearance	Brightness of teeth	Decay prevention	Price
Demographic strengths	Children	Teens, young people	Large families	Men
Special behavioural characteristics	Users of spearmint-flavoured toothpaste	Smokers	Heavy users	Heavy users
Brands disproportionately favoured	Colgate, Stripe	MacLean's, Plus White, Ultra Brite	Crest	Brands on sale
Personality characteristics	High self-involvement	High sociability	High hypochondriasis	High autonomy
Lifestyle characteristics	Hedonistic	Active	Conservative	Value-oriented

Source: Russell I. Haley, "Benefit Segmentation: A Decision-Oriented Research Tool," *Journal of Marketing* (July 1968), p. 33. Reprinted by permission of the American Marketing Association.

cent of his respondents reported they purchased the lowest-price watch, and another 46 percent focused on durability and overall product quality. The Timex Company decided to focus its product benefits on those two categories and market its watches in drugstores, variety stores, and discount houses. The rest is history. Within a few years of adopting the new segmentation approach, it became the largest watch company in the world.[21]

The Roots of Marketing box illustrates how benefit segmentation might be applied to the toothpaste market. The box reveals that some consumers are primarily concerned with price, some with preventing tooth decay, some with

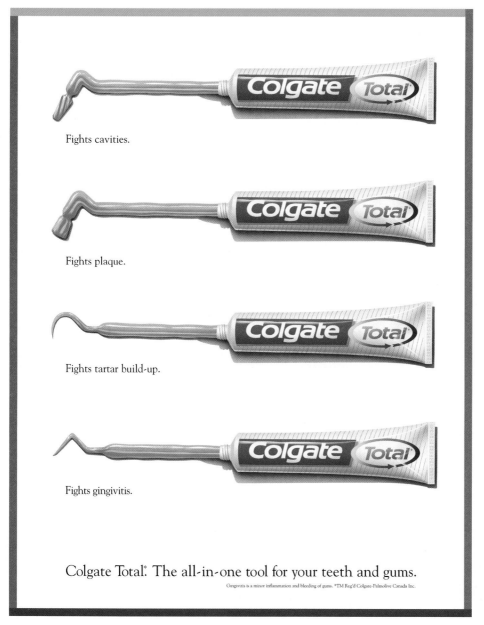

Fights cavities.

Fights plaque.

Fights tartar build-up.

Fights gingivitis.

Colgate Total.* The all-in-one tool for your teeth and gums.

Gingivitis is a minor inflammation and bleeding of gums. *TM Reg'd Colgate-Palmolive Canada Inc.

For the market segment seeking an all-benefits-in-one toothpaste, Colgate Total offers the solution.

taste, and others with brightness "benefits." Also included are the demographic and other characteristics used in focusing on each subgrouping.[22] Although this segmentation scheme was first published in 1968 and some of the information in it seems dated by today's standards, it is still a classic example of how benefit segmentation can be used.

▶ PRODUCT USAGE RATE SEGMENTATION

A final common way of segmenting consumer markets is by product usage rate. Marketers are especially interested in identifying and serving the heavy user of a particular product. Many markets follow a rule of thumb known as the 80/20 rule. That is, about 80 percent of a company's sales will tend to come from 20 percent of its customers. The 80/20 rule is not always a rigid literal relationship; the real point is that a disproportionate amount of sales tend to come from a relatively small group of customers. It only makes sense, then, to try to identify and cultivate that small group.

www.coca-cola.com

www.pepsiworld.com

Brand loyalty is also an important issue. Someone who drinks five or six cans of Coca-Cola—and only Coca-Cola—a day, is a far more valuable customer to The Coca-Cola Company than is the person who only drinks one or two cans of cola a month and doesn't much care if they're drinking Coca-Cola, Pepsi, or President's Choice. Again, identifying and cultivating the brand-loyal heavy user can be extremely profitable for the marketer.

To attract heavy users, companies may create different product size offerings, promotions that reward frequent purchasers, or special financing terms for heavy users.

Table 3.6 summarizes the different methods of segmentation and some of the marketing decisions that are affected by those choices.

▶ THE ETHICAL MARKETER

Problems with Heavy Users

For most products and services there is no particular ethical problem with targeting and attempting to increase the heavy user segment. But what if your product tends to lead to physical addiction, psychological compulsion, negative health outcomes, or all three?

Tobacco marketers and, to a somewhat lesser degree, alcohol marketers have faced this situation for decades. It is also one of the principal arguments made by opponents to legalized gambling. The fear is that a very large proportion of gambling revenues will come from a small number of gamblers—who likely cannot afford the losses.

What do you think? Are there ethical options for the marketers of such products?

▶ **Table 3.6 Consumer Marketing Decisions Affected by Segmentation Choices**

SEGMENTATION BASIS	DECISIONS AFFECTED
Geographic	• Choice of sales region • Sales force location • Retail location
Demographic	• Estimates of segment size • Choice of local distribution channels or channels that cater to different age, income, and education groups • Choice of media that serve different age, income, and education groups
Psychographic	• Product/service positioning • Advertising themes • Choice of media
Benefit	• Product/service design—different models with different features • Advertising themes • Sales training
Product Usage Rate	• Special products (sizes and quality) • Special services • Frequent-user promotions • Special financial terms

Source: Adapted from Peter R. Dickson, *Marketing Management,* 2nd ed. (Fort Worth, TX: Dryden Press, 1997), p. 187. Copyright © 1997 by Harcourt, Inc., adapted by permission of the publisher.

▶ SEGMENTING BUSINESS-TO-BUSINESS MARKETS

While the bulk of market segmentation research has concentrated on consumer markets, the concept can also be applied to business-to-business marketing. The overall process is similar. Four industrial market segmentation approaches have been identified: geographic segmentation, product segmentation, end-use application segmentation, and account size and potential segmentation.

Geographic Segmentation

Geographic segmentation is useful in industries where the bulk of the customers are concentrated in specific geographical locations. This approach can be used in such instances as the automobile industry, concentrated in the central

Ontario area, or the lumber industry, centred in British Columbia and Quebec. It might also be used in cases where the markets are limited to just a few locations. The oil-field equipment market, for example, is largely concentrated in cities like Calgary and Edmonton. Geographic segmentation is especially helpful when organizing a sales force and making sales management decisions.

Product Segmentation

It is possible to segment some business-to-business markets in terms of their need for specialized products. Industrial users tend to have much more precise product specifications than do ultimate consumers, and such products often fit very narrow market segments. For example, special rivets for bridge-building might be a market segment. Therefore, the design of an industrial good or ser-

▶ THE PRACTISING MARKETER

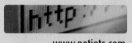

www.netjets.com

www.bombardier.com

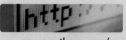

www.raytheon.com/rac

Time Sharing Fuels Jet Sales

The heady growth of "time-sharing" programs that allow companies and wealthy individuals to buy only part of a private jet is helping fuel a boom in business aircraft sales, pitting Bombardier Inc. against U.S. tycoon Warren Buffett.

The $725-million (U.S.) purchase last month of Montvale, N.J.–based Executive Jet Inc. by Mr. Buffett's Berkshire Hathaway Inc. has focused attention on "fractional" aircraft ownership. It is considered by many observers to be the fastest-growing and most hotly contested segment of the business aviation industry.

The New Jersey company pioneered the concept a decade ago and remains the largest industry player with about 130 planes—including 16 superluxurious Gulfstream IV-SPs—divided among 850 owners.

Unlike its main competitors in the fractional ownership game—Montreal-based Bombardier and Raytheon Aircraft Co. of Wichita, Kan.—Executive Jet does not manufacture planes. But with annual revenue of almost $900-million, its Netjets program has become the world's biggest purchaser of business aircraft and currently has about 200 planes on order worth more than $2-billion.

Bombardier, however, has spurned its business. The Canadian aerospace giant, which is the only manufacturer that offers a complete line of lower-end and luxury corporate jets, says it needs to reserve all of its available output for its own three-year-old FlexJet program. FlexJet occupies the No. 2 industry spot behind Executive Jet with 46 aircraft split among more than 200 owners. The program employs more than 400 people, about half of them pilots.

Bombardier's Business Jet Solutions Inc. (BJS), which runs the FlexJet program out of Dallas, expects to have sold 63 planes through its fractional ownership program by the end of 1998. The division also has about 60 planes on order to meet anticipated customer demand. The aircraft on order include the company's newest models, the long-range Learjet 45 and superluxury Global Express.

"The industry is growing by between 50 percent and 70 percent a year," said Michael Riegel, BJS's vice-president of marketing and sales. "Right now we are struggling to get as many aircraft as we can into the program, so we don't have any spare capacity to sell to [Executive Jet]."

Raytheon, which started up its fractional ownership program a year ago, has taken a different tack and gladly peddles its planes to Executive Jet. "We believe the market is big enough to support selling airplanes to a competitor," said Tony Marlow, director of marketing for Raytheon's Travel Air program.

What segmentation approach are Bombardier and Raytheon using?

Source: Konrad Yakabuski, "Time Sharing Fuels Jet Sales," *The Globe and Mail* (August 4, 1998), p. B1. Reprinted with permission from *The Globe and Mail.*

vice and the development of an associated marketing plan to meet specific buyer requirements is a form of market segmentation.

The **North American Industrial Classification System (NAICS)**—formerly the Standard Industrial Classification, or SIC—is a coding system used to categorize different types of businesses and products. The NAICS codes are the business-to-business equivalent of demographic and psychographic consumer information and can be used in much the same way.[23] Chapter 9 discusses NAICS codes in more detail.

North American Industrial Classification System (NAICS)
A coding system used to categorize different types of businesses and products (formerly the Standard Industrial Classification, or SIC).

www.census.gov/epcd/
www/naics.html

End-Use Application Segmentation

A third segmentation base is end-use applications—that is, precisely how the industrial purchaser will use the product. (This is similar to benefit segmentation in consumer markets.) A manufacturer of, say, printing equipment may serve markets ranging from a local utility to a bicycle manufacturer to Agriculture Canada. Each end use may dictate unique specifications of performance, design, and price. The market for desktop computers provides a good example: IBM has several computers for different market sizes. Caterpillar has equipment designed for road construction as well as for other industrial applications. End-use segmentation affects product design, sales force training, and advertising and communications emphasis.

Account Size and Potential Segmentation

A final way to segment business-to-business customers is by account size and growth potential.[24] Using this segmentation base is similar to segmenting on the usage rate in consumer markets. The benefits to the marketer are also similar in that this technique allows the marketer to concentrate resources where they will have the biggest payoff.

▶ **Table 3.7 Business-to-Business Marketing Decisions Affected by Segmentation Choices**

SEGMENTATION BASIS	DECISIONS AFFECTED
Geographic	• Choice of sales region • Sales force organization
Product (including NAICS)	• Product design • Media choices • Trade show choices
End-Use Application	• Product design • Sales force training • Advertising emphasis
Account Size and Growth Potential	• Account and relationship management

Source: Adapted from Peter R. Dickson, *Marketing Management,* 2nd ed. (Fort Worth, TX: Dryden Press, 1997), p. 196. Copyright © 1997 by Harcourt, Inc., adapted by permission of the publisher.

Business-to-business segmentation choices and the marketing decisions affected are summarized in Table 3.7. Regardless of how it is done, market segmentation is as vital to industrial marketing as it is in consumer markets.

This chapter has introduced the concept of market segmentation and has explained the main bases for segmenting both consumer and industrial markets. Some segmentation procedures are quite simple; others require the use of advanced research techniques. The next chapter examines how segmentation concepts may be applied to market segmentation strategies.

▶ SUMMARY

It is impossible to serve all possible customers equally well. Therefore, in developing a marketing plan, managers must select a target market segment and then develop and implement a marketing program for that segment.

A market consists of people with the willingness, purchasing power, and authority to buy. Products are classified as consumer products or industrial products based on their end use. Some products can be classified as both consumer and industrial products. Market segmentation is the grouping of people according to their similarity in one or more dimensions related to a particular product category.

Five commonly used bases for segmenting consumer markets are geographic, demographic, psychographic, benefit, and usage rate. Commonly used bases for segmenting industrial markets are geographic, product, end-use application, and account size and potential.

▶ KEY TERMS

AIO statements
benefit segmentation
consumer goods
demographic segmentation
Engel's Laws
family life cycle
geographic segmentation
industrial goods
lifestyle

market
market segmentation
North American Industrial
   Classification System (NAICS)
psychographic segmentation
psychographics
SSWDs
usage rate

▶ INTERACTIVE SUMMARY AND DISCUSSION QUESTIONS

1. In developing a marketing plan, managers must select a target market, then develop and implement a marketing program for that segment. Explain how these tasks reflect the philosophy of consumer orientation in action.

2. A market consists of people with the willingness, purchasing power, and authority to buy. Illustrate the application of this concept in the case of a salesperson for a photocopier company who is trying to make a sale to the Royal Bank.

3. Illustrate how some products can be classified as both consumer and industrial products. Why is it important to make a distinction between the two?

4. Market segmentation is the grouping of people according to their similarity in one or more dimensions related to a particular product category. Show how segmentation might be advantageous in developing a marketing plan for the following products:
   a. textbooks
   b. women's clothing
   c. chain saws
   d. life insurance

5. Five commonly used bases for segmenting consumer markets are geographic, demographic, psychographic, benefit, and usage rate. Suggest one descriptive segmentation approach and one behavioural segmentation approach for each item in the list in question 4. Give as detailed an example as possible.

6. Suggest two different types of geographic segmentation approaches that could be used in each of the following markets:
   a. Canada
   b. United States
   c. Mexico
   d. Germany
   e. Japan
   f. Italy
   g. Hong Kong

7. Canadian census data reveal that a significant number of Canadians have a mother tongue other than English or French (mother tongue is defined as the language first learned and still understood). Some of the larger language groups are Italian (approximately 484 500 people), German (approximately 450 140 people), Chinese (approximately 715 640 people), and Ukrainian (approximately 162 695 people).[25] How could a marketer use this demographic information? How could a behavioural segmentation approach enhance the demographic segmentation?

8. Industrial market segmentation methods are geographic segmentation, product segmentation, end-use application segmentation, and account size and potential segmentation. Give an example of how Xerox Corporation might use each segmentation method.

9. Explain and describe the use of AIO questions.

10. How might a fast-food marketer such as Harvey's respond to the changing age-group projections shown in Figure 3.6?

11. Visit the Goldfarb Consultants Web site and the Environics Web site, and complete your psychographic profile. Which approach do you think best captures who you are? Which would be most useful to marketers? Explain.

www.goldfarbconsultants. com

erg.environics.net/surveys

To obtain a list of further readings for Chapter 3, please refer to the *Foundations of Marketing* Web site.

Chapter 4
The Market Segmentation Process

Wear a Helmet

WWW.JONESSODA.COM™

Vancouver's Urban Juice and Soda Co. has found a niche with its nostalgia-evoking and trendsetting drinks. With unique, award-winning label designs, the firm's products are finding success among young consumers.

"See honey? That's the soda Mommy drank when she was a little girl." Hamilton Rousseau hears these words a lot from customers—usually followed by the whirring of a cash register, as Mommy buys some bottled nostalgia for herself and another soda for the kid. Mr. Rousseau owns and operates Ifs Ands & Butts, a Dallas-based retailer specializing in cigars and designer sodas. He stocks 125 varieties of small-batch sodas, ranging from Vernor's, first bottled in Detroit in the late 1800s, to Skeleteens Brainwash, a California-brewed concoction with a skull and crossbones label.

"There's a whole world out there beyond Coke and Pepsi," Mr. Rousseau says.

That may be, but it's a small and crowded world, where smaller companies count on sophisticated graphics, breezy Web sites, and quirky marketing strategies to grab attention and shelf space.

Also called micro, premium, or specialty sodas, designer sodas are carbonated, flavoured drinks made by small, often regional producers. They account for a relative drop in a global pop bucket dominated by Atlanta-based Coca-Cola Co. and Pepsi-Cola Co. of Somers, NY.

▶ CHAPTER OBJECTIVES
After reading and studying this chapter, you should be able to

1. Explain the factors underlying market segmentation strategy choices.
2. Outline the stages in the market segmentation process.
3. Explain the concept of positioning within market segments.
4. Show how target market decision analysis can be used in market segmentation.
5. Show how target market decision analysis can be used to assess the assortment of products offered to the market.

One of the most successful in building brand loyalty has been Vancouver-based Urban Juice & Soda Company Ltd., which sells and manufactures Jones Soda, along with Wazu Natural Spring Water.

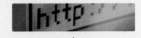

www.jonessoda.com

Launched in 1996, the Jones line combines old-fashioned flavours like cream soda and vanilla cola with funky labels that feature black and-white photographs of Jones drinkers.

Instead of radio, television, and print campaigns, president and founder Peter van Stolk has focused on deals that resonate with a youthful target audience, such as sponsoring top snow-boarders. For distribution, he concentrates on venues such as pool halls and corner stores.

www.coca-cola.com

When taken as a whole, the soft drink market is huge and is dominated by The Coca-Cola Company and Pepsi. It would be just short of impossible to dislodge either of them from their perch atop the market. But that doesn't mean that there are no opportunities in soft drinks. The trick is to find segments that are too small for the major companies to bother with but are large enough to be worth your while to pursue. That is exactly what Mr. Van Stolk is doing with his Jones line of flavoured colas and other soft drinks. Once these segments are identified and an appropriate product is developed, the rest of the marketing plan, including price, commu-nication, and distribution, must be developed. In fact, developing the marketing plan, at least in outline, is a necessary part of deciding whether the segment is viable.

www.pepsiworld.com

Source: Adapted from Wendy Stueck, "Specialty Soda Makers Sell Rebel Image," *The Globe and Mail* (September 30, 1998), p. B29. Reprinted with permission from *The Globe and Mail.*

▶ INTRODUCTION

This chapter continues the discussion of market segmentation. Chapter 3 dis-cussed the role of market segmentation in developing a marketing strategy, and the bases for segmenting the consumer market (geographic, demographic, psy-chographic, usage rates, and benefit segmentation). In this chapter, the empha-sis shifts to the process of market segmentation.

We will consider the rationale for and process of matching product offerings to specific market segments. As we will see, selecting an appropriate strategy depends on a variety of internal and external variables facing the firm.

▶ ALTERNATIVE MARKET MATCHING STRATEGIES

Market segmentation may take many forms ranging from treating the entire market as a single homogeneous entity to subdividing it into several segments and providing a separate marketing plan for each segment.

The very core of the firm's strategies is to match product offerings with the needs of particular market segments. To do so successfully, the firm must take the following factors into consideration:

- *Company resources.* These must be adequate to cover product development and other marketing costs.
- *Differentiability of products.* Some products can be easily differentiated from others. Some can be produced in versions designed specially for individual segments.
- *Stage in the product life cycle.* As a product matures, different marketing emphases are required to fit market needs. (Product life cycles are discussed in detail in Chapter 10.)
- *Competitors' strategies.* Strategies and product offerings must be continually adjusted in order to be competitive.
- *Size of segment.* The potential segment must be large enough to make it worthwhile to develop.

Essentially, the firm makes a number of goods/services offerings to the market in view of these determinants. One firm may decide on a **single-offer strategy**. This is the attempt to satisfy a large or a small market with one product and a single marketing program. Such a strategy may be adopted for different rea-

single-offer strategy
The attempt to satisfy a large or a small market with one product and a single marketing program.

HOT INVESTMENT TIPS. YOU CAN'T MISS IT.

The *National Post,* Canada's newest daily paper, uses a single-offer strategy to attract a mass market, including business readers and general news readers.

sons. A small manufacturer of wheelbarrows might concentrate on marketing one product to retailers in only one city because it does not have the resources to serve a mass market. A large producer of drafting equipment might offer a single product line with a marketing program aimed at draftspersons because it believes that only this limited segment would be interested in the product. A single-offer strategy aimed at one segmentation is often called *concentrated marketing;* when aimed at mass markets it is often call *undifferentiated* or *mass marketing.* For close to 100 years, until the early 1980s, the marketing of Coca-Cola was an example of the latter.

On the other hand, another company with greater resources may recognize that several segments of the market would respond well to specifically designed products and marketing programs. It adopts a **multi-offer strategy**. This is the attempt to satisfy several segments of the market very well with specialized products and unique marketing programs aimed at each segment. A bank designs particular services to fit the unique needs of different consumer and commercial market segments. A multi-offer strategy is also called *differentiated marketing.* Since about 1982 the Coca-Cola Company has gradually moved to a multi-offer strategy by marketing Coke II, Diet Coke, Cherry Coke, Diet Cherry Coke, and Coca-Cola Classic.

multi-offer strategy
The attempt to satisfy several segments of the market very well with specialized products and unique marketing programs aimed at each segment.

PROVOCATIVE COLUMNISTS. YOU CAN'T MISS IT.

When these determinants are combined with markets segmented on the dimensions discussed in Chapter 3, the firm is able to develop a market matching strategy. A successful match of products to segments through developing a marketing program with the appropriate product design, pricing strategy, distribution strategy, and communication strategy is vital to the market success of the firm.

www.can.ibm.com

Many firms, large and small, practise a multi-offer strategy in today's environment. Procter & Gamble markets Tide, Dash, Duz, Cheer, Bold, Gain, Oxydol, and Bonus, among other detergents, to meet the desires of specific groups of detergent buyers. IBM offers huge mainframe computers, mid-range size tailored for medium-sized organizations, and computers designed for the home market.

Generally speaking, the company with a multi-offer marketing strategy should produce more sales by providing higher satisfaction for each of several target markets than would be possible with only a single-offer strategy. However, whether a firm should choose a single- or a multi-offer strategy depends on

▶ THE ROOTS OF MARKETING

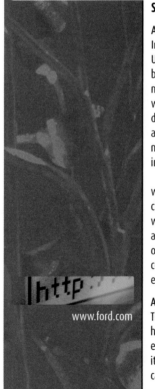

www.ford.com

Single- versus Multi-Offer Strategies

A Single-Offer Strategy—Ford Motor Company in 1908

In 1908, Henry Ford introduce the Model T and revolutionized the automobile business around the world. Until the late 1920s, he sold only the Model T car and Model T truck. Ford's strategy was based on the belief that if he could get the price of a serviceable, utilitarian car low enough, he could develop a large mass market. His competitors were several hundred manufacturers who were producing vehicles that were virtually custom-built, with short production runs and high costs. Ford's strategy generated unprecedented sales. A dealership organization evolved that carried spare parts and service facilities to users across North America and through much of Europe. The marketing program, including an excellent service network, quickly made Henry Ford a multimillionaire and contributed to economic development by improving the transportation system.

Some dangers are inherent in a single-offer strategy, however. A firm that attempts to satisfy a very wide market with a single product of service *fairly well* is vulnerable to competition from those who choose to develop more specialized products that appeal to and serve segments of the larger market very well. Over time, General Motors and Chrysler developed a wider variety of models, price ranges, styles, and colour options. What worked superbly in 1908 faltered in the 1920s, and Ford had to move to a multi-offer strategy. The firm developed the Model A and the Model B, offering them with various options. The company differentiated the product line further in the 1930s by introducing the first mass-produced V-8 engine, which was a company hallmark for years.

An Extensive Multi-Offer Strategy—Ford Motor Company in the Early 2000s

The market matching strategy of the Ford Motor Company today is quite different from that of 1908. It has evolved with the changing environment that faces the automobile industry. Ford's product line is much expanded from the Model T days, but the company still does not produce products for all markets. Instead, it serves those markets where its resources, marketing skills, product strengths, and competitive offerings can best be exploited. Table 4.1 compares the product lines then and now.

Can a firm use a single-offer strategy today? Using one or more of the five segmentation approaches discussed in Chapter 3, write a short description of the segment served by each of the Ford cars listed in Table 4.1.

management's goals, as well as on the economics of the situation — whether the company has the resources, and whether greater profits can be expected from the additional expense of a multi-offer strategy.

▶ **TABLE 4.1 Market Matching Strategies**

| | PRODUCT OFFERINGS | | | |
| | Ford Motor Company | | Audi/Volkswagen/Porsche | |
MARKET SEGMENT	1908 Single-Offer Strategy	Early 2000s Multi-Offer Strategy	1955 Single-Offer Strategy	Early 2000s Multi-Offer Strategy
General-Purpose Cars				
Small	Model T	Focus	Beetle	Golf
Medium	Model T	Taurus		Jetta
				Passat
Large		Crown Victoria		
Sporty Cars				
Low-priced		ZX2 Escort		new Beetle
				GTI
Medium-priced		Cougar		Cabrio
		Mustang		Audi TT
				Porsche Boxster
High-priced		Jaguar XK8		Porsche 911
		Aston Martin DB7		
Luxury Cars				
Medium-priced		Lincoln Continental		Audi A4
		Lincoln Town Car		
High-priced		Jaguar S-Type		Audi A6
				Audi A8
Vans		Windstar		EuroVan
		Econoline		
Trucks				
Small	Model T (truck)	Ford Ranger		
Medium		Ford "F" series		
Sport Utility Vehicles (SUVs)		Explorer		
		Expedition		
		Excursion		
		Lincoln Navigator		

▶ THE ROOTS OF MARKETING

www.vw.com

Segmentation Strategies Reflect Other Competitive Considerations

A Single-Offer Strategy for Different Reasons—Audi/Volkswagen/Porsche in 1955
When Volkswagen decided to enter the North American market, it chose to do so with only the "Beetle" for a variety of reasons. First, the company was strapped for funds and could not expand its production facilities, which were stretched to the limit in trying to supply automobile-short postwar Europe. It also recognized that a dealer-support system and spare-parts inventory had to be developed from scratch if it was to compete successfully in North America. With these constraints in mind, Volkswagen marketers determined that the serviceable Beetle was the answer. The Beetle was relatively low-priced, was supported by an imaginative promotional campaign, and became an immediate success with those who wanted a small, relatively basic car. Volkswagen sold a much wider variety of products in Europe (and continued to introduce new products in that market much earlier than in North America). It deliberately chose to make a single offer to the North American market.

A Strategic Move to a Multi-Offer Strategy—Audi/Volkswagen/Porsche in the Early 2000s
Today, products under the Volkswagen parent company's control compete for a much broader number of market segments than did the Beetle. The changes are indicative of a major change in the segmentation strategies. The company has not only the products but also the resources and the marketing infrastructure to serve more segments.

▶ THE STAGES OF MARKET SEGMENTATION

The marketer has a number of potential bases for determining the most appropriate market matching strategy. Geographic, demographic, psychographic, usage rate, and benefit bases are often used in converting heterogeneous markets into specific segments that serve as target markets for the consumer-oriented marketer. The industrial marketer segments geographically, by product, by end-use application, or by account size and potential. In either case, a systematic five-stage decision process is followed. This framework for market segmentation is shown in Figure 4.1.

No single basis for segmentation is necessarily the best, so the firm should segment the market in a way that most suits the situation. For example, demographic segmentation may be used in planning an advertising campaign that uses print media, because magazines are normally aimed at specific demographic segments. The marketer thus often experiments with segmenting markets in several ways in the process of discovering which of the marketing elements can be changed for greatest effect. (Similarly, marketing opportunities are sometimes discovered by rating how well competitors have served segments differentiated on a particular dimension.) This is part of the interactive process of analysis. The systematic five-stage decision process shown in Figure 4.1 lends form to what are otherwise often complex and unstructured problems.[1]

Stage 1: Identify Market Segmentation Bases

The decision process begins when a firm identifies characteristics of potential buyers as bases that will allow the marketer to classify them into market segments. For example, IBM might segment on the basis of computer usage (accounting firms) or by company size. Segmentation bases should be selected so that each segment contains customers who have similar needs, so that specific marketing programs can be designed to satisfy those needs. For example, before Procter & Gamble decides to market Crest to a segment made up of large families, management should be confident that most large families are interested in preventing tooth decay and thus receptive to the Crest marketing offer. In some cases, this objective is difficult to achieve. Consider the marketer trying to reach the consumer segment that is over 50 years of age. Saturday-evening television commercials can reach this group, but much of the expenditure may be wasted since the other major viewer group at that time consists of teenagers.

www.pg.com

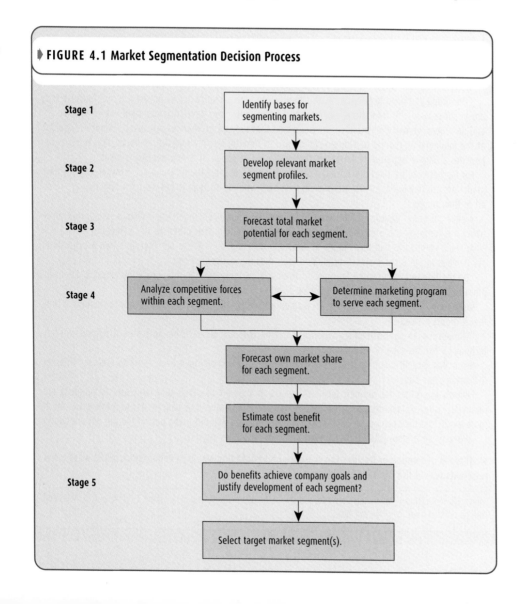

▶ **FIGURE 4.1 Market Segmentation Decision Process**

Stage 1 — Identify bases for segmenting markets.

Stage 2 — Develop relevant market segment profiles.

Stage 3 — Forecast total market potential for each segment.

Stage 4 — Analyze competitive forces within each segment. ↔ Determine marketing program to serve each segment.

Forecast own market share for each segment.

Estimate cost benefit for each segment.

Stage 5 — Do benefits achieve company goals and justify development of each segment?

Select target market segment(s).

▸ INTERNET IMPACT

Segmentation on the Web

The Internet can be a powerful tool for marketers to reach women—as long as they know where to find them, says the woman who heads IBM's electronic commerce business in Canada.

More Canadian women are going on-line every day, says Shahla Aly, vice-president and general manager of E-business for IBM Canada Ltd. Close to half of all Internet users are women, Ms. Aly says, but the way they use the technology generally is much different from men.

"I would say women use [the Internet] in a more focused fashion. They use it to fulfill a need, not necessarily to browse."

For that reason, she says marketers looking for a female audience need to do their homework and figure out where in cyberspace their target market is apt to hang out.

That could be a discussion group or one of a growing number of portals designed specifically for women, such as planetgirl.com, women.com, or girlson.com.

Ms. Aly—who goes far and wide when she surfs the Net herself—says the no-nonsense approach most women adopt on the Internet means that they are more likely to take advantage of a portal site that will link them quickly to Web sites that are geared to their interests.

"It's like being able to do all your shopping in one mall," she says.

That tendency to congregate in certain areas can work to the advantage of marketers who do their homework well, she adds.

"One thing you have to keep in mind is that women are easier to access on the Internet because they are in some ways the most time-impoverished," she says. "You have to understand where women go, and go where women go. You have to understand that they do go there in a focused fashion." Speaking at the inaugural Marketing to Women conference in Toronto, Ms. Aly told the audience that the Internet provides a unique opportunity for companies to pitch a message at a very specific market.

For instance, rather than purchasing banner ads on the home page of a popular browser, Ms. Aly says marketers can pay to have their message appear only when users type in key search words that are related to their product.

A seller of baby furniture might want to have its ad appear when someone does a search on "pregnancy." A company that makes calcium supplements could link their message to "osteoporosis."

As well, companies can buy "point of decision" ads, she says. These ads pop up when a cybershopper decides to put a competitor's product in their electronic shopping cart.

"On the Internet, you can be far more focused in your segmentation than you could possibly be in the physical world," Ms. Aly said in an interview following her presentation.

Ms. Aly notes that research has shown women are ready and willing to use Internet technology if they feel it meets a need.

"Women like to use technology when it is useful, whereas research has indicated that men will buy technology for the sake of technology."

Given that fact, it is not surprising that women business owners have been quick to embrace Internet technology, she says.

"What's important for women business owners is that on the Web two inhibitors to progress are removed." She explains that in cyberspace, women entrepreneurs can gain access to information much more easily and they can get through to key decision-makers without being part of the old boys network.

"Women are finding [the Internet] more and more useful every day."

What types of companies besides those mentioned might find Ms. Aly's comments useful? What other segments would the Internet be able to address?

Source: Elizabeth Church, "Marketers Search for Women on the Web," *The Globe and Mail* (June 3, 1999), p. B10. Reprinted with permission from *The Globe and Mail*.

Stage 2: Develop Relevant Profiles for Each Segment

Once segments have been identified, marketers should develop a profile of the relevant customer needs and behaviours in each segment.

Segmentation bases provide some insight into the nature of customers, but typically not enough for the kinds of decisions that marketing managers must make. Managers need precise descriptions of customers in order to match marketing offers to their needs. In other words, the task at this stage is to develop profiles of the typical customer in each segment with regard to lifestyle patterns, attitudes toward product attributes and brands, brand preferences, product-use habits, geographic location, demographic characteristics, and so on. For example, one regional retail chain surveyed female customers and identified the following profile: ages 25–55, 147–160 cm tall, 38–55 kg, career-oriented, and having a household income of $20 000 or higher. The retailer used this profile to set up separate "petites" sections, one of the fastest-growing segments in the women's fashion industry.[2]

Stage 3: Forecast Market Potentials

In the third stage, market segmentation and market opportunity analysis are used together to produce a forecast of market potential within each segment. Market potential is the upper limit on the demand that can be expected from a segment and, combined with data on the firm's market share, sales potential.

This stage is management's preliminary go or no-go decision point as to whether the sales potential in a segment is sufficient to justify further analysis. Some segments will be screened out because they represent insufficient potential demand; others will be sufficiently attractive for the analysis to continue.

Consider the segments of the CD market. A producer must think carefully about whether it will be profitable to enter the reggae segment given the existing competition.

Stage 4: Forecast Probable Market Share

Even when the segment is large enough, a firm may not be able to compete in it successfully. Therefore, once market potential has been estimated, the share of that market that can be captured by the firm must be determined. This requires analyzing competitors' positions in target segments. At the same time, the specific marketing strategy and tactics should be designed for these segments. These two activities should lead to an analysis of the costs of tapping the potential demand in each segment.

Procter & Gamble once outsold Colgate nearly two to one in dishwashing liquids. Colgate also ran behind in heavy-duty detergents and soaps. A realistic assessment indicated that for most directly competitive products, Colgate had little chance of overtaking P&G. So Colgate diversified its product line. Today, many of the firm's offerings do not face a directly competitive Procter & Gamble product, and those that do compete effectively.

Stage 5: Select Specific Market Segments (Target Markets)

target market
A market segment that a
company chooses to serve.

Finally, the accumulated information, analyses, and forecasts allow management to assess the potential for achieving company goals and justify developing one or more market segments. These are known as **target markets**. Demand forecasts combined with cost projections are used to determine the profit and return on investment that can be expected from each segment. Analyses of marketing strategy and tactics will determine the degree of consistency with corporate image and reputation goals, as well as with unique corporate capabilities that may be achieved by serving a segment. These assessments will, in turn, determine management's selection of specific segments as target markets.

At this point of the analysis, the costs and benefits to be weighed are not just monetary, but also include many difficult-to-measure but critical organizational and environmental factors. For example, the firm may not have enough experienced personnel to launch a successful attack on a segment that has the potential to be an almost certain monetary success. Similarly, a firm with a product that is suitable for export may choose one country over another because management likes that country better. A public utility may decide not to encourage higher electricity consumption because of possible environmental and political repercussions. Assessing both financial and nonfinancial factors is a vital and final stage in the decision process.

There is not, and should not be, any simple answer to the market segmentation decision. The marketing concept's prescription to serve the customer's needs and to earn a profit while doing so implies that the marketer has to evaluate each possible marketing program on how it achieves this goal in the marketplace. By performing the detailed analysis outlined in Figure 4.1, the marketing manager can increase the probability of success in profitably serving consumers' needs.

▶ OVERALL EVALUATION OF MARKET SEGMENTS

In general, attractive market segments share five traits: uniqueness, responsiveness, actionability, stability, and profitability.[3]

Uniqueness implies that there are real differences between the segment and the rest of the population. There is no point, for example, in designing a plastic food wrap specifically for second- and third-generation Ukrainians living in the Prairie provinces if there is no difference in how that group uses plastic food wrap compared with the rest of the population.

Responsiveness means that the identified segment will actually be influenced by marketing activity. For example, there is a segment of homeowners who, one could charitably say, are somewhat disinterested in yard care. The marketer of easy-to-use yard care products may have difficulty targeting this group, because they are so disinterested that they will ignore even easy-to-use products.

An actionable segment is one that the marketing manager can actually direct marketing activity toward. Sometimes behaviourally based segments, in particular, are difficult to address if the marketing manager is unable to match the behaviour with classification (demographic) variables.

A stable segment will exist for a reasonable period. The Practising Marketer box illustrates that teenagers are becoming an attractive market segment after having been somewhat ignored for a while because there were too few of them. On the other hand, during the last part of 1998 and 1999, a segment emerged that might be labelled "millennium worriers." This group was a bit of a windfall for manufacturers of generators and staple foods. Obviously though, these people do not represent a viable long-term segmentation opportunity.

Finally, the chosen segment must be sufficiently profitable to be worth the effort. As the opening vignette of this chapter illustrates, what constitutes "sufficiently profitable" varies from one company to the next.

▶ THE PRACTISING MARKETER

Teens Are a Viable Segment

The resounding power of the Echo Generation seems to be a North American phenomenon. Europe did not have the same baby boom that North America experienced, so there is not the accompanying "boomlet." In the United States, however, the Echo market is staggering; Teenage Research Unlimited, a Northbrook, Ill.—based demographics firm, says there are 26 million teens who last year spent $141 billion (U.S.)—almost twice as much as a decade ago. That has U.S. companies battling for a slice of that pie, and their products spill over into Canada. *Teen People* boasts 10 million readers each issue. Launched in 1998, its circulation has grown from 500 000 to 1.2 million, making it one of the fastest-growing magazines in American publishing history. "It wasn't cool to be a teen in the '70s or '80s," says managing editor Christina Ferrari. "The teenage population hasn't taken centre stage like this since the '50s and '60s."

Where does all their money come from? Studies show that while the popularity of after-school jobs is important it is not the source of the vast majority of kids' cash. A recent report by the Canadian Council on Social Development showed the youth labour market is actually at its lowest point in 25 years— fewer than half of 15- to-19-year-old students worked in 1997, down from two-thirds in 1989. The big money instead comes from family sources. Economics professor David Foot calls teens "six-pocket kids" who get money from mom, dad, grandparents, and often step-parents. Family money gets divided up into bigger chunks by fewer siblings, since Canadians are having smaller families (on average 1.7 children each).

How useful is this information? What differences would you expect between marketing to teens in Canada and marketing to teens in Europe?

Source: Excerpted from Andrew Clark, "How Teens Got the Power," *Maclean's* (March 22, 1999), p. 43.

Teenagers comprise an important market segment for many marketers. From television shows to clothes to magazines, the many products aimed at teens indicate the significance of this group's buying power.

▶ TARGET MARKET DECISION ANALYSIS

Identifying specific target markets is an important aspect of overall marketing strategy. Clearly delineated target markets allow management to effectively employ marketing efforts like product development, distribution, pricing, and advertising to serve these markets.

target market decision analysis
The evaluation of potential market segments.

Target market decision analysis, the evaluation of potential market segments, is a useful tool in the market segmentation process. Targets are chosen by segmenting the total market on the basis of any given characteristics (as described in Chapter 3). The example that follows illustrates how target market decision analysis can be applied.[4]

▶ THE PRACTISING MARKETER

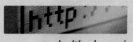

www.kraftfoods.com/
kool-aid/ka_index.html

Selecting a Target Market

Kraft Inc.'s Kool-Aid is launching a new flavour targeted at Hispanic consumers in the United States, marking its first foray into ethnic marketing.

Mandarina-Tangerine is the 19th entry in Kool-Aid's powdered drink lineup, but is the first with bilingual packaging in the U.S. market. The rollout in February will be supported by a national Spanish-language television campaign.

How long before the Kool-Aid Man starts chanting, "Yo quiero Kool-Aid?"

Do you think this product, which is intended for the U.S. market, would be successful in Canada? Are there other specific ethnic groups in Canada that Kool-Aid could target?

Source: Excerpted from John Heinzl, "The Ethnic Kool-Aid Acid Test," *The Globe and Mail* (January 22, 1999), p. B25. Reprinted with permission from *The Globe and Mail*.

A Useful Method of Identifying Target Markets

Sometimes marketers fail to take all potential market segments into consideration. A useful process is the "divide-the-box" procedure. Visualize the entire market for the product category as a single box. Then divide this total market box into realistic boxes or cells, with each cell representing a potential target segment (see Figure 4.2). How the cells are defined is up to you. They can be based on consumer benefits desired; on geographic, demographic, and psychographic characteristics; or on some combination of these. While this concept is simple, it can be extremely complex in practice, and it requires creativity.

Consider the decisions of an airline company's marketing manager who wishes to analyze the market potential for various levels of passenger service. The company wants to delineate all possible target markets and to assess the most profitable multi-offer strategy.

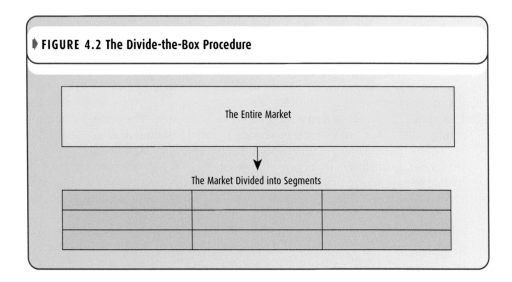

▶ **FIGURE 4.2 The Divide-the-Box Procedure**

As a tool for outlining the scope of the market, the marketing manager devises a grid like the one in Figure 4.3. This enables the company to match the possible types of service offerings with various customer classifications. The process of developing the target market grid forces the decision maker to consider the entire range of possible market matching strategies. New or previously underserved segments may be uncovered. The framework also encourages the marketer to assess the sales potential in each of the possible segments, and aids in properly allocating marketing efforts to areas of greatest potential.

▶ **FIGURE 4.3 Market for Airline Passenger Travel**

Market	First Class	Extra-Service Business Class	Regular Tourist Class	Seat-Sale Class	Age Specials	Charter
Senior executives	X	X	?			X
Employees of large firms		X	X	?		X
Employees of small businesses		X	X	X		
Wealthy individuals	X	X				?
Other individuals			X	X		X
Senior citizens			?	X	X	X
Youth			X	X	X	X

X = Probable demand for service   ? = Uncertain or limited demand

Once the cells of the grid have been identified, the marketer can then evaluate the wants, needs, and motivations of each market segment. For example, it appears that senior executives would be the appropriate targets for the first-class and extra-service categories. Further research could confirm or modify these evaluations and enable the marketer to determine whether the market segment's size makes it worth developing a special offering for. Apparently, airlines have analyzed the needs and motivations for this segment. They provide roomier seating, better food, and check-in service to satisfy the needs thus identified. Market segmentation thus enables appropriate marketing plan design.

The cross-classification in Figure 4.4 shows that the matrix can be further subdivided to gather more specific data about the characteristics of the proposed target market and to accurately develop a suitable marketing mix. The potential bases for segmenting markets are virtually limitless. For example, the segments might have been based on psychographic data or on the benefits sought. In the latter instance, prestige, comfort, and basic transportation might be some benefits that would assist in designing market offerings. Such divisions are sometimes made intuitively in the first place, but the final decisions are usually supported by concrete data.

FIGURE 4.4 Employees of Large Firms, Extra-Service Class

Service Benefit Desired	Heavy-Traffic Regions	Southern Canada	Northern Canada
Schedules	X		
Food			
Attendant service			
Legroom			

Using Target Market Decision Analysis in Assessing a Product Mix

product mix
The assortment of product lines and individual offerings available from a company.

Product mix, a concept we will take a detailed look at in Chapter 11, refers to the assortment of product lines and individual offerings available from a company. Target market decision analysis can be used to assess a firm's product mix and to point out needed modifications. For example, one telephone company has used the concept to evaluate its product offerings.[5] The company segments the total market by psychographic categories as shown in Figure 4.5. Two of these categories are "belongers" and "achievers." Belongers were defined in this instance as those who are motivated by emotional and group influences. Achievers were defined as those whose dominant characteristic is the need to get ahead.

> ▶ **FIGURE 4.5 Using Target Market Decision Analysis to Evaluate a Product Mix**

Product Offering	Psychographic Category		
	Belongers	**Achievers**	**Etc.**
Romantic	Phone M Phone A Phone C		
Character		Phone R Phone Y	
Contemporary			

Source: "Properly Applied Psychographics Add Marketing Luster," *Marketing News* (November 12, 1982), p. 10. Used by permission of the American Marketing Association.

The telephone company's rule is to offer two — and only two — types of telephones in a given market segment in order not to have too complicated a market offering. Belongers were thus offered a regular phone and a romantic-type phone to appeal to their sentiments. Achievers were offered the regular phone plus one designed to suggest efficiency and character. This analysis helped to select a product from the assortment shown in Figure 4.5.

Target market decision analysis can go beyond merely identifying target markets. It can play a crucial role in actually developing marketing strategies such as product mixes.

▶ PRODUCT POSITIONING

After a target market has been selected, the task has just begun. Your firm will naturally find others competing in that segment. The challenge is to develop a marketing plan that will enable your product to compete effectively against them. It is unlikely that success will be achieved with a marketing program that is virtually identical to competitors', for they already have attained a place in the minds of individuals in the target market and have developed brand loyalty. Since people have a variety of needs and tastes, market acceptance is more easily achieved by **positioning** — shaping the product and developing a marketing program in such a way that the product is perceived to be (and actually is) different from competitors' products.

Consider, for example, a simple positioning map of the cola market (see Figure 4.6). By plotting brands on a price-reputation/quality matrix the relative positions of the brands listed can be determined. The perceptual map shows the positions of Pepsi and Coca-Cola being threatened by brands such as Cott and

positioning
Shaping the product and developing a marketing program in such a way that the product is perceived to be (and actually is) different from competitors' products.

▶ **FIGURE 4.6 Positioning Map of Cola Market**

Well-Known Brand/Quality

• Coca-Cola/Pepsi

• Cott Cola
• President's Choice

Lower Price   **Higher Price**

• Z Cola

• Private-label store brands

Unknown Brand/Quality

President's Choice. Many consumers position the quality of the newer brands near Pepsi and Coca-Cola, and are quite aware that they cost less. If you were a potential newcomer to the cola market segment, a positioning analysis such as this would be essential. Where would you position a new brand of cola?

The positioning process requires a careful analysis of the features and strengths of competitive offerings, as well as a good understanding of the needs and wants of the target market. From comparing the two, the marketer tries to find a niche of significant size that is currently poorly served, and to develop an offering to fit that opportunity. Positioning can sometimes be accomplished by using advertising to differentiate a product.

Cadillac positions its cars, including its latest innovation, Night Vision, as unique—cars that cause heads to turn.

9 out of 10 moose prefer Night Vision.

Coming this Fall from Cadillac. That's right, Cadillac

7-Up used promotion as the sole element in positioning. The firm discovered that its product was missing the primary market for soft drinks—children, teenagers, and young adults—because of 7-Up's image as a mixer for older people's drinks. The firm used its now well-known "uncola" campaign to reposition 7-Up by first identifying the product as a soft drink and then positioning it as an alternative to colas in the soft-drink market. Since then the company has continued its focus on advertising that emphasizes youth and action.

Another classic positioning campaign was that used by Avis to position itself against Hertz with the theme "Avis is only number two, why go with us? Because we try harder." In this case, the service was also adjusted to make the claim true.

A total marketing program is often dictated to secure position. An example is the establishment of CFM Inc. In 1987, Colin Adamson and Heinz Rieger were senior managers for a wood-burning fireplace maker. In the fireplace market, they saw an opportunity to develop a product to position against wood-burning and gas fireplaces, so they formed their own company and began to develop a product. They positioned their product away from the more traditional style of gas fireplace—a row of uniform, nonflickering blue flames coming from a steel pipe decorated, perhaps, with a poor imitation of a log. Instead, Adamson and Rieger developed a way to produce dancing yellow flames that simulate a wood fire, and surrounded them with natural-looking logs. The product could then be positioned as a realistic-looking alternative to wood.

CFM has now developed a range of products to enhance its gas fireplace position. Colin Adamson says, "A lot of people make things and then try to sell the market on them, [but] success comes from making what people want."[6] The firm has developed a loyal group of dealers, and therefore has the distribution system necessary to move its products from manufacturer to consumer. In product development, CFM pays much attention to regional tastes in materials, trims, and sizes. CFM's positioning strategy enabled the company to focus on developing product and marketing plans that led to achieving a sales volume of over $13 million by 1994.

Using product positioning to evaluate and develop marketing strategies in the light of competitive offerings in the market is a valuable and basic concept. It should follow naturally from the market segmentation decision.

▶ SUMMARY

Market segmentation ranges from treating the entire market as one segment to subdividing it into a number of segments. No single basis for segmentation is necessarily the best, so the firm should segment the market in a way that most suits the situation.

A single-offer strategy is an attempt to satisfy a large or a small market with one product and a single marketing program. A multi-offer strategy is a bid to satisfy several segments of the market very well with specialized products and unique marketing programs aimed at each segment. Because of resource constraints or management inclination, a firm may choose to adopt a single-offer strategy in a market that has several obvious market segments.

The stages of the market segmentation process are as follows: (1) identify segmentation bases, (2) develop relevant profiles for each segment, (3) forecast market potentials, (4) forecast probable market share, and (5) select specific market segments. Attractive segments will be unique, responsive, actionable, stable, and profitable.

Positioning is shaping the product and developing a marketing program in such a way that the product is perceived to be different from competitors' products. Positioning can sometimes be accomplished through advertising alone, and sometimes requires a total marketing program.

▶ KEY TERMS

multi-offer strategy	single-offer strategy
positioning	target market
product mix	target market decision analysis

▶ INTERACTIVE SUMMARY AND DISCUSSION QUESTIONS

1. Market segmentation ranges from treating the market as one to subdividing it into a number of portions. Give examples of firms that have adopted each of the two alternatives. In your opinion, have these firms made the correct decision?

2. A single-offer strategy is an attempt to satisfy a large or a small market with one product and a single marketing program. Give an example of where this seems to be working well for a company, as well as an example of where this strategy may not be so beneficial to the company.

3. A multi-offer strategy is a bid to satisfy several segments of the market very well with specialized products and unique marketing programs aimed at each segment. Explain how a company that is marketing in Canada and Europe might manage this.

4. A firm may choose to adopt a single-offer strategy in a market that has several obvious market segments. Explain why.

5. Give an example of how a not-for-profit organization might apply a multi-offer segmentation strategy.

6. "No single base for segmentation is necessarily the best, therefore the firm should segment the market in a way that most suits the situation." Explain.

7. The stages of the market segmentation process are (1) identify segmentation bases, (2) develop relevant profiles for each segment, (3) forecast market potentials, (4) forecast probable market share, and (5) select specific target markets. Explain how each of these steps would apply to a marina and to a radio station.

8. Assume you are a manufacturer of computers and related hardware. Using the divide-the-box procedure, identify the various target markets among college students.

9. Positioning is shaping the product and developing a marketing program in such a way that the product is perceived to be different from competitors' products. Draw a positioning matrix for a product category that you are familiar with.

10. Positioning can sometimes be accomplished through advertising alone, and sometimes requires a total marketing program. Give an example of each situation.

11. Reread the opening vignette of this chapter. Visit The Coca-Cola Company's and Pepsi-Cola's Web sites. Compare them with Jones Soda's Web site. How has Jones Soda differentiated itself from Coca-Cola and Pepsi?

www.coca-cola.com

www.pepsiworld.com

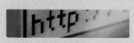
www.jonessoda.com

To obtain a list of further readings for Chapter 4, please refer to the *Foundations of Marketing* Web site.

Chapter 5
Obtaining Data for Marketing Decisions

Introducing Gillette®
MACH3™

THREE REVOLUTIONARY BLADES...
AND SO MUCH MORE.

3 SPECIALLY POSITIONED BLADES.
To shave progressively closer in a single stroke.

PATENTED DLC™ COMFORT EDGES.
With MACH3, you experience less drag and pull for an extraordinary comfortable shave.

INDICATOR™ LUBRICATING STRIP.
Signals when you're no longer experiencing the optimal MACH3 shave.

RESPONSIVE SPRINGS.
To sense and adjust to every contour of your face.

NEW PIVOT DESIGN.
So the blades are always in an optimal shaving position.

SOFT, FLEXIBLE MICROFINS.
To protect your skin while gently setting up your beard.

RUBBERIZED CONTOUR GRIP.
For better handling.

SINGLE POINT DOCKING.
For easy loading.

THE CLOSEST SHAVE
IN FEWER STROKES
WITH LESS IRRITATION

Gillette
The Best a Man Can Get

www.MACH3.com   © 1999 The Gillette Company

The Gillette Company, a world leader in developing and marketing shaving systems and other products, continually conducts market research to better understand its customers and improve its products.

CHAPTER OBJECTIVES
After reading and studying this chapter, you should be able to

1. Describe the development and current status of the marketing research functions.
2. Present the steps of the marketing research process.
3. Discuss the nature and sources of primary and secondary data.
4. Outline the methods of collecting survey data.
5. Discuss the nature of marketing information systems, and relate them to the marketing research function.

The Gillette Company is a world leader in developing and marketing shaving systems and other products. Just when it seems that it is not possible to develop a more complex or sophisticated razor, another new one appears on the market. These new products are available almost simultaneously in many parts of the world.

Founded in 1901, Gillette is the world leader in male grooming, a category that includes blades, razors, and shaving preparations. Gillette also holds the number one position worldwide in selected female grooming products, such as wet shaving products and hair epilation devices. The company is the world's top seller of writing instruments and correction products, toothbrushes, and oral care appliances. In addition, the company is the world leader in alkaline batteries.

www.gillette.com

Gillette sales in 1998 amounted to $10.1 billion. Manufacturing operations are conducted at 60 facilities in 24 countries, and products are distributed in over 200 countries and territories around the world. The company employs 43 100 people, nearly three-quarters of them outside the United States.

Gillette expects that the company's strong profitable growth will be sustained through continued emphasis on the growth drivers of research and development, capital spending and advertising, and geographic expansion.

The Gillette Company's stable of powerful global brands makes it a formidable player in the world's consumer marketplace. Gillette products are found in a vast number of retail outlets. Its channel of distribution structure is one of the most extensive in the world. In addition to this extensive distribution structure, the company has established a Web site (www.theEssentials.com) where customers can purchase some products on-line.

Gillette has a values statement that includes emphasis on employee development and compensation and high standards of achievement. Another value is good citizenship in whatever country the company operates.

The third important category of values is customer focus: "We will offer consumers products of the highest levels of performance for value. We will provide quality service to our customers, both internal and external, by treating them as partners, by listening, understanding their needs, responding fairly and living up to our commitments."

Marketing research is thus a key element of the company's strategy. What kinds of information enables Gillette to analyze customer needs, test products, and advertise successfully to a large global market? Following are the types of marketing research studies conducted by Gillette:

- *Annual National Consumer Studies* The objectives of these annual studies are to determine what brand of razor and blade was used for the respondents' last shave, to collect demographic data, and to examine consumer attitudes toward the various blade and razor manufacturers. These studies rely on personal interviews with national panels of male and female respondents, who are selected by using probability sampling methods.

- *National Brand Tracking Studies* The purpose of these studies is to track the use of razors and blades to monitor brand loyalty and brand switching tendencies over time. These studies are also conducted annually and use panels of male and female shavers. However, the information for them is collected via mail questionnaires.

- *Annual Brand Awareness Studies* These studies are aimed at determining the "share of mind" Gillette products have. This information is collected by annual telephone surveys that employ unaided as well as aided recall of brand names and advertising campaigns.

- *Consumer Use Tests* The key objectives of the use-testing studies are to ensure that "Gillette remains state of the art in the competitive arena, that our products are up to their desired performance standards, and that no claims in our advertising, packaging, or display materials are made without substantiation." At least two consumer use tests are conducted each month by Gillette. In these tests, consumers are asked to use a single variation of a product for an extended period of time, at the end of which their evaluation of the product is obtained.

- *Continuous Retail Audits* The purpose of the retail audits is to provide top management with monthly market share data, along with information regarding distribution, out-of-stock, and inventory levels of the various Gillette products. This information is purchased from the commercial information services providing syndicated retail audit data. The information is supplemented by special retail audits, which Gillette conducts itself, that look at product displays and the extent to which Gillette blades and razors are featured in retailer advertisements.

- *Laboratory Research Studies* These studies are designed to test the performance of existing Gillette products and to help in the design of new products. They include having people shave with Gillette and competitor products and measuring the results, as well as determining the number of whiskers on a man's face, how fast whiskers grow, and how many shaves a man can get from a single blade.

Marketing research–generated information helps to define target markets. It also helps managers understand consumer needs and responses to product offerings in those target markets. The process of generating, analyzing, and transmitting that information is a core part of the marketing research approach.

Sources: Adapted from the Gillette Web site (www.gillette.com/company/ataglance.html and www.gillette.com/company/mission.html). Marketing research study categories excerpted from Gilbert A. Churchill, Jr., *Marketing Research* (Fort Worth, TX: Dryden Press, 1999), p. 63.

▶ INTRODUCTION

The quality of all marketing planning decisions depends on the quality of the information on which they are based. A variety of sources of marketing information are available to the marketing decision maker. Some involve the regular information flow that occurs in a company—for example, sales-force reports, accounting data, and other internal statistics. Sophisticated firms apply the power of computers to analyze such internal data, and to simulate the effects of changes in strategy.

marketing research
The systematic gathering, recording, and analyzing of data about problems relating to the marketing of goods and services.

Another important source of information is **marketing research**. Marketing research is the systematic gathering, recording, and analyzing of data about problems relating to the marketing of goods and services. This is the function that links the consumer to the company through information—information that is used to identify and define marketing opportunities and problems; to generate, refine, and evaluate marketing actions; to monitor marketing performance; and to improve understanding of marketing as a process.

Marketing research specifies the information required to address these issues, designs the method for collecting information, manages and implements the data collection process, analyzes the results, and communicates the findings and their implications.[1]

The critical task of the marketing manager is decision making. Managers earn their salaries by making effective decisions that enable their firms to solve problems as they arise, and by anticipating and preventing the occurrence of future problems. Many times, though, they must make decisions with limited information that is of uncertain accuracy. If the decision maker undertakes some marketing research, much valuable additional information can be gained to help with the decision. Although the marketing research does not *make* the decision, it does make it easier for the manager to do so.

Most of the market segmentation procedures outlined in Chapters 3 and 4 are based on information collected through marketing research. There is a growing

▶ THE ROOTS OF MARKETING

The First Full-Time Researcher

Marketing research in Canada may be said to have existed since there first were buyers and sellers. However, the day on which marketing research became a full-time profession was January 2, 1929. On that day, Henry King became the first full-time marketing researcher in Canada. His employer was an advertising agency, Cockfield Brown.[2]

In 1932, through the encouragement of Cockfield Brown, the first independent research company—Ethel Fulford and Associates—was founded in Toronto. In 1937, the Fulford company became known as Canadian Facts. Marketing research firms are now found in most major centres.

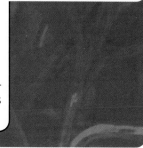

use of marketing research for developing marketing plans. Its regular use is now considered indispensable by most successful companies.

Marketing research studies generate data that may serve many purposes, for example, developing sales forecasts, determining market and sales potential, designing new products and packages, analyzing sales and marketing costs, evaluating the effectiveness of a firm's advertising, and determining consumer motives for buying products.

Many companies do not have their own marketing research departments. The function is often at least partly contracted out to specialists, because the research skill and activity levels are quite variable for different projects. Even large firms typically rely on outside agencies to conduct interviews. Such agencies have a large number of trained interviewers and the appropriate systems in place to conduct the studies.

There are two basic types of marketing research organizations that a firm may use. The first can be categorized as a *full-* or *partial-service research supplier.* Full-service firms handle all aspects of the research and provide a final report to management, whereas those offering partial service specialize in some activity, such as conducting field interviews.

The second type of external research organization is known as a *syndicated service.* A syndicated service provides a standardized set of data on a regular basis to all who wish to buy it. Normally, such research firms specialize in providing information on a small number of industries. For example, the Consumer Panel of Canada regularly gathers information on consumer purchases of food and other household items from 7000 households. These data inform marketers about brand preferences, brand-switching, and the effects of various promotional activities. Since all major products in the category are reported, a purchaser of this information can see how competitors are doing as well.

Research is likely to be contracted to outside groups when

www.npd.com/cpc.htm

- Problem areas can be defined in terms of specific research projects that can easily be delegated.
- There is a need for specialized know-how or equipment.
- Intellectual detachment is important.[3]

▸ THE MARKETING RESEARCH PROCESS

Infotech, a provincially based organization, was intrigued by the possibilities of stimulating in the province a computer software industry that would specialize in producing software for use in schools (known as "courseware"). Such an industry could be on the leading edge in the rapidly growing computer sector and thus could stimulate much economic growth in the province. In order to know whether such a strategy was worthwhile, Infotech commissioned a marketing research study. It wanted to know (a) the size of the courseware market in North America, (b) the trends in courseware for education usage, (c) what channels of distribution exist in the courseware industry and what it costs to use them, and (d) the marketing and financial aspects of courseware development.

Given the need for information, how is marketing research actually conducted? Normally, there are five steps in the marketing research process: (1) formulate the problem, (2) develop the research design, (3) determine the data collection method, (4) collect the data, and (5) interpret and present the information.

Figure 5.1 diagrams the marketing research process from the information need to the research-based decision.

Defining the problem is the first step in the marketing research process.

Formulate the Problem

Problems are barriers that prevent the accomplishment of organizational goals. A clearly defined problem helps the researcher to focus the research process on securing data that are necessary to solve the problem. Someone once remarked that well-defined problems are half solved.

Defining the problem is not always easy. Suppose a tennis player with a sore knee and other symptoms goes to the doctor for treatment. His "problem," he tells the doctor, is a sore knee. However, on further investigation, it is discovered that the knee pain is merely a symptom of the real problem: damage to an Achilles tendon. Sometimes it is easy to pinpoint the business problem that requires research information to solve. However, it is often difficult to determine the specific problem, since what the researcher is confronted with may be only symptoms of the real underlying problem. To focus research properly, the research must look beyond the symptoms. This is done through exploratory research.

"Memo to all employees—according to my research, our company wastes about 1800 hours a year wishing each other good morning ... "

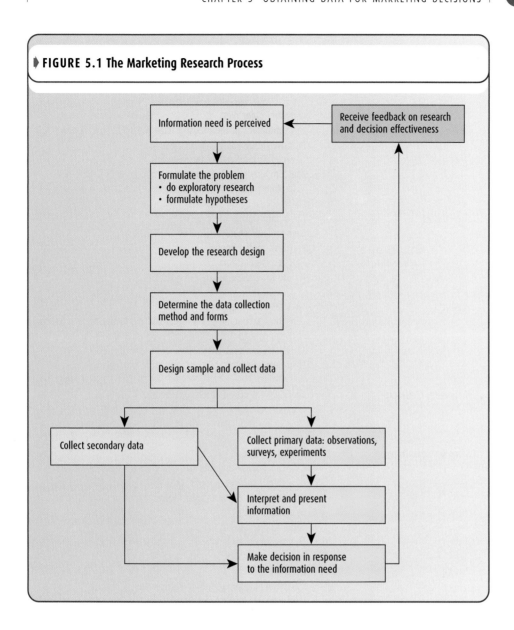

▶ **FIGURE 5.1 The Marketing Research Process**

DO EXPLORATORY RESEARCH

Exploratory research can help to formulate the problem. In searching for the cause of a problem, the researcher will learn about the problem area and begin to focus on specific areas for study. This search, often called **exploratory research**, consists of discussing the problem with informed sources within the firm and with wholesalers, retailers, customers, and others outside the firm, and examining secondary sources of information. Marketing researchers often refer to internal data collection as *situation analysis* and to exploratory interviews with informed persons outside the firm as *informal investigation.* Exploratory research also involves evaluating company records, such as sales and profit analyses of its own and its competitors' products. Table 5.1 provides a checklist of topics that might be considered in an exploratory analysis.

exploratory research
Learning about the problem area and beginning to focus on specific areas of study by discussing the problem with informed sources within the firm (a process often called situation analysis) and with knowledgeable others outside the firm (the informal investigation).

▶ **TABLE 5.1 Topics for the Exploratory Analysis**

The Company and Industry	• Company objectives • The companies in the industry (size, financial power) and industry trends • Geographic locations of the industry • The company's market share as compared with competitors' • Marketing policies of competitors
The Market	• Geographic location • Demographic characteristics of the market • Purchase motivations • Product-use patterns • Nature of demand
Products	• Physical characteristics • Consumer acceptance—strengths and weaknesses • Package as a container and as a promotional device • Manufacturing processes, production capacity • Closeness and availability of substitute products
Marketing Channels	• Channels employed and recent trends • Channel policy • Margins for resellers
Sales Organization	• Market coverage • Sales analysis by number of accounts per salesperson, size of account, type of account, etc. • Expense ratios for various territories, types of product, size of accounts, etc. • Control procedures • Compensation methods
Pricing	• Elasticity • Season or special promotional price cuts • Profit margins of resellers • Legal restrictions • Price lines
Advertising and Sales Promotion	• Media employed • Dollar expenditures as compared with competitors' • Timing of advertising • Sales promotional materials provided for resellers • Results from previous advertising and sales promotional campaigns

In the Infotech case, exploratory research was done through a review of the literature about courseware; then in-person and telephone interviews were undertaken with knowledgeable people in departments of education and the school systems. Before a specific research plan could be designed, the researchers needed to know more about the subject and about the existing trends in the industry. Only then was it possible to begin planning a more complete research program. It was determined that the next steps should be (1) to systemically explore every current article written on the subject, and (2) to develop a plan to obtain information directly from different market groups. In some research projects, the next step might have been formulating hypotheses, but this did not seem appropriate in the Infotech situation.

▶ THE ETHICAL MARKETER

Toyota Faces Battle Over Customer Data

Toyota Canada Inc. dealers have warned that the automaker is heading toward a potential battle over ownership of customer data after it announced an exclusive agreement with information systems supplier Reynolds and Reynolds Canada Ltd.

www.toyota.ca

www.reyrey.com

The key issue, one Toyota dealer said, is "who truly owns those customers"—the sales outlet or the head office. Dealers also fear that Toyota may be setting up an Internet-based sales network that would sell directly to customers, then allocate those sales to various dealerships.

Under the deal, Reynolds and Reynolds will provide information systems to all Toyota dealers in Canada and create "a revolutionary retailing solution enabling Toyota Canada dealers to deliver superior value to Canadian car buyers," Pierre Blais, vice-president of Reynolds Canada Ltd., said.

The battle over customer information and who controls it is one of the key issues in the revolution sweeping the automotive retailing industry in North America, industry observers say. "Factories want to control the information, they want to control the customer data," said one industry insider. "The factory can't tell you who their customers are, so [information] systems, from a factory standpoint, are critical."

If the automakers don't control the information, they must rely on dealers to tell them who their customers are and unless a dealer does so, the car companies can't maintain contact with their customers once they've bought a car, truck, or minivan.

What are the implications and issues for consumers of trading personal information in data banks?

Source: Adapted from Greg Keenan, "Toyota Faces Battle Over Customer Data," *The Globe and Mail* (December 3, 1998), p. B5. Reprinted with permission from *The Globe and Mail*.

FORMULATE HYPOTHESES

After the problem has been defined and an exploratory investigation has been conducted, the marketer should be able to formulate a **hypothesis**, a tentative explanation about the relationship between variables as a starting point for further testing. In effect, the hypothesis is an educated guess.

A marketer of industrial products might formulate the following hypothesis: "Failure to provide 36-hour delivery service will reduce our sales by 20 percent." Such a statement may prove correct or incorrect. Formulating a hypothesis does, however, provide a basis for investigation and an eventual determination of its accuracy. It also allows the researcher to move to the next step: developing the research design.

hypothesis
A tentative explanation about the relationship between variables as a starting point for further testing.

Develop the Research Design

research design
A series of advance decisions that, taken together, make up a master plan or model for conducting the investigation.

The research design should be a comprehensive plan for testing the hypotheses formulated about the problem. **Research design** refers to a series of advance decisions that, taken together, make up a master plan or model for conducting the investigation. Developing such a plan allows the researcher to control each step of the research process. Table 5.2 lists the steps involved in the research design.

The research design for Infotech was quite complicated. No fewer than five individual data collection procedures were planned. These included surveys of (1) departments of education across Canada and in selected American states, (2) principal textbook and software publishers, (3) key hardware and software manufacturers in Canada, and (4) a sampling of the teacher population.

Determine the Data Collection Method

Data can be obtained in many ways. These include finding existing statistics and information, as well as collecting new data through surveys and experiments. These topics are covered in greater detail later in this chapter. There is a great deal of science, as well as art, in choosing the best data collection method. As always, these decisions are affected by the importance of the decision and the budget available.

Collect the Data

After the research design has determined what data are needed, the data must then be collected. Collecting data is a major part of the marketing research project. Two types of data are typically obtained: primary data and secondary data. **Primary data** refer to data being collected for the first time during a study. Primary data are normally the *last* to be collected.

primary data
Data being collected for the first time.

Bell Canada collects customer data through various methods, including direct mail. As a result of such market research efforts, the company understands its customers better and is able to focus its advertising campaigns.

TABLE 5.2 Questions Typically Addressed at Various Stages of the Research Process

STAGE IN THE PROCESS	TYPICAL QUESTIONS
Formulate the problem	• What is the purpose of the study—to solve a problem? identify an opportunity? • Is additional background information necessary? • What information is needed to make the decision at hand? • How will the information be used? • Should research be conducted?
Develop the research design	• How much is already known? • Can a hypothesis be formulated? • What types of questions need to be answered? • What type of study will best address the research questions?
Determine data collection method and forms	• Can existing data be used to advantage? • What is to be measured? How? • What is the source of the data to be collected? • Are there any cultural factors that need to be taken into account in designing the data collection method? If so, what are they? • Are there any legal restrictions on the collection methods? If so, what are they? • Can objective answers be obtained by asking people? • How should people be questioned? • Should the questionnaires be administered in person, over the phone, or through the mail? • Should electronic or mechanical means be used to make the observations? • What specific behaviours should the observers record? • Should structured or unstructured items be used to collect the data? • Should the purpose of the study be made known to the respondents? • Should rating scales be used in the questionnaires?
Design sample and collect data	• Who is the target population? • Is a list of population elements available? • Is a sample necessary? • Is a probability sample desirable? • How large should the sample be? • How should the sample be selected? • Who will gather the data? • How long will the data gathering take? • How much supervision is needed? • What operational procedures will be followed? • What methods will be used to ensure the quality of the data collected?
Analyze and interpret the data	• Who will handle the editing of the data? • How will the data be coded? • Who will supervise the coding? • Will computer or hand tabulation be used? • What tabulations are called for? • What analysis techniques will be used?

(continued)

> **TABLE 5.2 (continued)**

STAGE IN THE PROCESS	TYPICAL QUESTIONS
Prepare the research report	• Who will read the report? • What is their technical level of sophistication? • What is their involvement with the project? • Are managerial recommendations called for? • What will be the format of the written report? • Is an oral report necessary? • How should the oral report be structured?

Source: Adapted from Gilbert A. Churchill, Jr., *Basic Marketing Research,* 7th ed. (Fort Worth, TX: Dryden Press, 1999), p. 68. Reprinted by permission of the publisher.

secondary data
Previously published matter.

Secondary data are previously published matter. They serve as an extremely important source of information for the marketing researcher.

COLLECT SECONDARY DATA

Not only are secondary data important, they are also abundant in many areas that the marketing researcher may need to investigate. In fact, the overwhelming quantity of secondary data available at little or no cost often challenges the researcher, who wants to select only pertinent information.

Secondary data consists of two types: internal and external. *Internal secondary data* include company records of sales, product performances, sales-force activities, and marketing costs. *External data* are obtained from a variety of sources. Governments — local, provincial, and federal — provide a wide variety of secondary data. Private sources also supply secondary data for the marketing decision maker. The appendix at the end of this chapter describes a wide range of secondary data sources.

Government Sources The federal government provides the country's most important sources of marketing data, the most frequently used being census data. Although the government spends millions of dollars in conducting the various censuses of Canada, the information obtained thereby is available at no charge at local libraries and Statistics Canada offices, or it can be purchased at a nominal charge in various electronic forms for instant access. In fact, Statistics Canada produces several different censuses. Table 5.3 briefly describes the main ones. In addition, there are monthly and annual surveys of important economic sectors, such as manufacturing.

The current data are so detailed for large cities that breakdowns of population characteristics are available for areas comprising only a few city blocks (census tracts) or by postal code. Thus local retailers or shopping-centre developers can easily gather detailed information about the immediate neighbourhoods that will constitute their customer bases without spending time or money conducting a comprehensive survey.

So much data are produced by the federal government that the marketing researcher often purchases summaries such as the *Canada Year Book* or *Market Research Handbook* or subscribes to *Statistics Canada Daily.* The latter is the vehicle for first (official) release of statistical data and publications produced by Statistics Canada. It provides highlights of newly released data with source information for more detailed facts, contains weekly and monthly schedules of upcoming major news releases, and announces new nonprint products and new services.

The Official Release Unit also produces *Infomat,* a weekly review of Canadian economic and social trends (also available electronically at order@statcan.ca). Or it can be found, along with many other resources, in the nearest Statistics Canada Regional Reference Centre.

The other main Statistics Canada publications are

- *CANSIM.* The Canadian Socio-Economic Information Management System (CANSIM) is a time series database containing more than 650 000 items. CANSIM can be accessed through the Internet at http://www.statcan.ca/English/CANSIM.
- *Canadian Social Trends.* This on-line quarterly publication that discusses the social, economic, and demographic changes affecting the lives of Canadians contains the latest figures for major social indicators.

A number of other Statistics Canada publications can be found on its Web site at http://www.statcan.ca. Many statistics are also available on CD-ROM.

▶ **TABLE 5.3 Major Statistics Collected by Statistics Canada**

Census of Canada
Conducted once each decade, with certain categories checked every five years. It provides a count of all residents of Canada by province, city or town, country, or other suitable division, and, in large cities, by census tract. Particularly useful to marketers are the data provided by economic rather than political boundaries, such as greater metropolitan areas. Data are also gathered on age, gender, race, citizenship, education level, occupation, employment status, income, and family status of inhabitants. A less detailed census is conducted at the halfway point in the decade.

The Economy—The Latest Indicators
Key monthly and quarterly measures of economic performance for Canada and each province.

The Economy in Detail
Annual data covering most aspects of Canada's economy.

The Land
Statistics on Canada's land area, plant and animal life, and environment.

The People
Statistics on Canada's population traits and trends, plus education, culture, and health.

The State
Statistics on government finances and employment, justice, and elections.

Web sites associated with the above data can readily be accessed on the Internet at http://www.canada.gc.ca.

www.nationalpost.com

www.acnielsen.com

Provincial and city governments are other important sources of information on employment, production, and sales activities.

Private Sources Numerous private organizations provide information for the marketing executive. In *Canadian Markets,* published by the *National Post,* the marketer will find a wide range of valuable data. Other good summary data can be found in the annual survey of buying power published by *Sales and Marketing Management* magazine (which can be accessed at http://www.salesandmarketing.com). For activities in a particular industry, trade associations are excellent resources. Advertising agencies continually collect information on the audiences reached by various media.

Several national firms offer information to business on a subscription basis. The largest of these, A.C. Nielsen Company, collects data that are reported weekly on product sales, retail prices, and promotional activities. The company also reports on consumer purchase behaviour, which is sourced from its 12 000 member Home Scan panel, an electronic consumer-based household panel. The Consumer Panel of Canada also gathers information on consumer purchases.

Advantages and Limitations of Secondary Data Using secondary data offers two important advantages over that of primary data:

- Assembling previously collected data is almost always less expensive than collecting primary data.
- Less time is involved in locating and using secondary data. Table 5.4 shows the estimated time involved in completing a research study that requires primary data. The time involved will naturally vary considerably depending on such factors as the research subject and the scope of the study.

The researcher must be aware of two potential limitations to using secondary data: (1) the data may be obsolete, and (2) the classifications of the secondary data may not fit the information needs of the study. Published information has an unfortunate habit of quickly going out of date. A marketing researcher ana-

---

▶ TABLE 5.4 Time Requirements for a Primary-Data Research Project

STEP	ESTIMATED TIME REQUIRED FOR COMPLETION
Define problem	1–3 days
Develop methodology	1–3 days
Design questionnaire	1–2 weeks
Pretest questionnaire and evaluate pretest results	1–3 weeks
Conduct field interviews	1–6 weeks
Code returned questionnaires	1 week
Transfer data to computer	1 week
Do data processing and statistical analysis	7–10 days
Interpret output, write report, and present findings	1–2 weeks
Total elapsed time	7–18 weeks

lyzing the population of the Calgary metropolitan market in 2002, for example, may well discover that much of the 2001 census data are already obsolete due to an upturn or downturn in the economy or new developments in the oil and gas industry.

Data may also have been collected previously on such bases as county or city boundaries, when the marketing manager requires it to be broken down by city blocks or census tracts. In such cases, the marketing researcher may not be able to rearrange the secondary data in a usable form and must therefore collect primary data. Figure 5.2 provides an outline of how to get started when searching for published sources of secondary data.

Secondary information proved very valuable in the Infotech study. A wide range of information sources was found. For example, relevant articles were found in such magazines as *Maclean's, Popular Computing,* and *Businessweek.* An especially valuable publication was *Electronic Learning,* which had no fewer than eight articles relating to the topic.

www.macleans.ca

▶ FIGURE 5.2 How to Start Searching for Published Sources of Secondary Data

1. Identify what you wish to know and what you already know about your topic.

↓

2. Develop a list of key terms and names.

↓

3. Search several of the general guides, directories, and Web sites for papers and/or reports.

↓

4. Compile the literature you have found. Rework your list of key words and authors if necessary.

↓

5. Consult the reference librarian.

↓

6. Consult the various directory guides.

↓

7. Identify authorities in the area and consult them.

Source: From Figure 6.2 in Gilbert A. Churchill, Jr., *Basic Marketing Research,* 7th ed. (Forth Worth, TX: Dryden Press, 1999), p. 226. Reprinted by permission of the publisher.

In addition to such periodicals, the researchers found eleven different special reports on various aspects of the educational use of computers. Report titles included "School Uses of Computers" (from Johns Hopkins University, in the United States) and "Phase Two: A Periodical Reporting on Education Computing in Scotland."

Studying such secondary sources gave the researchers immense insight into the fundamental issues involved in using courseware in the educational system. But some important information was still needed before a decision could be made about proceeding with the courseware project. Thus, it was time to plan a primary-data collection process.

DESIGN AND EXECUTE SURVEY

Since secondary data are incomplete or do not fully relate to the problem at hand, the necessary information must be obtained through one of several primary research methods. If hypotheses have been stated, facts should be gathered in such a way as to allow direct testing of the hypotheses.

Collecting primary data requires a considerable amount of technical expertise. Companies have found that they get the best information when specially trained individuals handle the design and execution of the research.

COLLECT PRIMARY DATA

The marketing researcher has three alternative methods for collecting primary data: observation, survey, or controlled experiment. No one method is best in all circumstances.

The Observation Method Observational studies are conducted by actually viewing (either directly or through mechanical means such as hidden cameras) the overt actions of the respondent. Examples of this approach include conducting traffic counts at a potential location for a fast-food franchise, checking licence plates at a shopping centre to determine the area from which shoppers are attracted, or using supermarket scanners to record sales of certain products.

The observation method has both advantages and drawbacks. The advantages are that observation is often more accurate than questioning techniques like surveys and interviews, and that it may be the only way to get information about such things as actual shopping behaviour in a supermarket. Observation may also be the easiest way to get specific data. The drawbacks include observer subjectivity and errors in interpretation. For instance, researchers might incorrectly classify people's economic status because of the way they were dressed at the time of observation.

Sometimes firms use the observation method in evaluating advertisements. A specialist research service is hired to study patterns of viewer eye movements when looking at advertisements. This is done under laboratory conditions. The results from one such eye-tracking test led the advertiser to move the headline from the bottom of the ad to the top, since a majority of eye movements flowed to the top. Observation could also be used to determine the route shoppers take once inside a supermarket. From this information, positioning of items might be determined.

The Survey Method The amount and type of information that can be obtained through merely observing overt consumer acts is limited. To obtain information on attitudes, motives, and opinions, the researcher must ask questions. The survey method is the most widely used approach to collecting primary data. There are three kinds of surveys: telephone interviews, self-completed surveys, and personal interviews.

Telephone interviews are inexpensive and fast ways to obtain limited quantities of relatively impersonal information. Many firms have leased WATS[4] services, which considerably reduce the cost of long-distance calls.

Telephone interviews account for the majority of all primary marketing research. They are limited to a small number of simple, clearly worded questions. Such interviews have two drawbacks: it is extremely difficult to obtain information about the personal characteristics of the respondent, and the survey may be prejudiced since two groups will be omitted — those households without telephones and those with unlisted numbers. One survey reported that alphabetical listings in telephone directories excluded one-quarter of large-city dwellers, and that they underrepresented service workers and separated and divorced persons. In addition, the mobility of the population creates problems in choosing names from telephone directories. As a result, a number of telephone interviewers have resorted to using digits selected at random and matched to telephone prefixes in the geographic area to be sampled. This technique is designed to correct the problem of sampling those with new telephone listings and those with unlisted numbers.

Self-completed surveys (often distributed by mail) allow the marketing researcher to conduct national studies at a reasonable cost. While personal interviews with a national sample may be prohibitively expensive, by using the mail the researcher can reach each potential respondent for the price of a postage stamp. Costs may be misleading, however, since *returned* questionnaires for such a study range between 10 and 80 percent, depending on the length of the questionnaire and respondent interest (a 20 percent return is not uncommon). When returns are low, the question arises as to the opinions of the majority (who did not respond). Some surveys use a coin or other incentive to gain the reader's attention, an approach that can increase returns but also increases costs. Unless additional information is obtained from nonrespondents, the results of the study are likely to be biased, since there may be important differences between the characteristics of these people and the characteristics of those who took the time to complete and return the questionnaire. For this reason, a follow-up questionnaire is sometimes mailed to nonrespondents, or telephone interviews may be used to gather additional information. These extra steps naturally add to the survey's cost. In spite of these difficulties, mail surveys are widely used.

Mail questionnaires must be carefully worded and pretested to eliminate any potential misunderstanding by respondents. But misunderstandings can occur with even the most clearly worded questions. When a truck operated by a government agency killed a cow, an official responded with an apology and a form to be filled out. It included a space for "disposition of the dead cow." The farmer responded "kind and gentle."

Personal interviews are typically the best means of obtaining more detailed information, since the interviewer has the opportunity to establish rapport with the respondent. The interviewer can also explain questions that might be confusing or vague to the respondent.

Personal interviews are slow and are the most expensive method of collecting data. However, their flexibility — coupled with the detailed information that can be collected — often offset these limitations. Marketing research firms sometimes rent locations in shopping centres, where they have greater access to potential buyers of the products in which they are interested. Downtown retail districts and airports are other on-site locations for marketing research.

The focus group interview is a special type of personal interview. *Focus group interviews* are widely used to gather preliminary research information. Eight to twelve people are brought together to discuss a subject of interest. Although the moderator typically explains the purpose of the meeting and suggests an opening discussion topic, he or she is interested in stimulating interaction among group members in order to develop the discussion of numerous points about the subject. Focus group sessions, which are often one to two hours long, are usually taped so that the moderator can devote full attention to the discussion. This process gives the researcher an idea of how consumers view a problem. Often it uncovers points of view that the researcher had not thought of. On the basis of these findings a broader study can be developed to verify the preliminary findings.

▶ THE PRACTISING MARKETER

www.campbellsoup.ca

As a result of garbology, a marketing research technique used by the *Saturday Evening Post*, Campbell's found its real customer.

Using Unobtrusive Marketing Research

Sometimes it is better to use unobtrusive methods of marketing research than to ask people direct questions about their attitudes or behaviour. "Garbology"—a technique whereby the researcher monitors consumption behaviour by rummaging through selected garbage—is a good example of such a method.

The *Saturday Evening Post* used this technique during the early 1900s to convince Campbell Soup that working-class, not upper-class, families were the appropriate target market for canned soup. Empty soup cans were widely found in trash in working-class neighbourhoods but not upper-class neighbourhoods. The success of this project resulted in Campbell becoming a regular advertiser in the *Saturday Evening Post*.

Restaurant managers have used garbology for years to monitor customer satisfaction. Patrons throw away what they don't want to eat or don't have room for. Thus, quality or quantity of food can be flagged by this method.

Can you think of other applications for garbology?

The Controlled Experiment Method The final and least-used method of collecting marketing information involves using *controlled experiments*. An experiment is a scientific investigation in which the researcher controls or manipulates a test group and observes this group as well as another group that did not receive the controls or manipulations. Such experiments can be conducted in the field or in a laboratory setting.

Although a number of marketing-related experiments have been conducted in the controlled environment of a laboratory, most have been conducted in the field. To date, the most common use of this method has been in test marketing.

Marketers face great risks in introducing new products. They often attempt to reduce this risk by **test marketing**: selecting areas considered reasonably typical of the total market, and introducing a new product to these areas with a total marketing campaign to determine consumer response before marketing the product nationally. Frequently used cities include Calgary, Lethbridge, and Winnipeg. Consumers in the test-market city view the product as they do any other new product, since it is available in retail outlets and is advertised in the local media. The test-market city becomes a small replica of the total market. The marketing manager can then compare actual sales with expected sales and project them on a nationwide basis. If the test results are favourable, the risks of a large-scale failure are reduced. Many products fail at the test-market stage; thus, consumers who live in these cities may purchase products that no one else will ever be able to buy.

The major problem with controlled experiments is the difficult task of controlling all the variables in a real-life situation. The laboratory scientist can rigidly control temperature and humidity, but how can the marketing manager determine the effect of varying the retail price through refundable coupons when the competition decides to retaliate against or deliberately confuse the experiment by issuing its own coupons?

In the future, experimentation will become more frequent as firms develop more sophisticated simulated competitive models that require computer analysis. Simulating market activities promises to be one of the great new developments in marketing.

In the Infotech market study, primary data were collected through four different research methods: (1) telephone surveys of departments of education across Canada and in selected American states, (2) personal and telephone interviews of principal Canadian textbook suppliers, (3) personal and telephone interviews of key hardware and software manufacturers and distributors, and (4) in-class surveys of teachers taking summer-school courses.

test marketing
Selecting areas considered reasonably typical of the total market, and introducing a new product to these areas with a total marketing campaign to determine consumer response before marketing the product nationally.

THE DATA COLLECTION INSTRUMENT

Most of the data collection methods depend on the use of a good questionnaire. Developing a good questionnaire requires considerable skill and attention. It should be done with reference to specified objectives concerning information that is needed to complete the study. With this list as a foundation, specific questions are written for the questionnaire. The questionnaire must then be pretested; a small sample of persons similar to those who will be surveyed are asked to complete it. Discussions with these sample respondents help uncover points that are unclear. The nature, style, and length of the questionnaire will vary depending on the type of data collection technique chosen. After pretesting and revising until the questionnaire works well, the researcher plans the necessary computer-coding setup on the questionnaire to facilitate later data analysis.

The actual execution of the survey is beyond the scope of this book. Other important issues that need to be dealt with in planning the study are selecting, training, and controlling the field interviewers; editing, coding, tabulating, and interpreting the data; presenting the results; and following up on the survey. It

IMPORTANT! PLEASE FILL OUT AND RETURN WITHIN THE NEXT 10 DAYS.

1. 1. ☐ Mr.   2. ☐ Mrs.   3. ☐ Miss

GNB02-01

First Name / Family Name

Street / Apt. No./Suite No.

City / Province / Postal Code

E-mail Address:

The IKEA

$10,000 Shopping Spree

It's your chance to take home the store.

CONTEST DETAILS: To enter, deposit completed Official Entry Form in a designated box at participating IKEA stores or mail to IKEA SHOPPING SPREE, c/o ConsumerLink, PO Box 2730, Station "A", Toronto, ON M5W 1H3. NO PURCHASE NECESSARY. There will be one (1) Grand Prize awarded consisting of a $10,000 IKEA SHOPPING SPREE awarded in the form of a $10,000 IKEA Gift Certificate. Odds of winning depend on total entries received. To win, selected entrant must correctly answer a skill-testing question and sign a declaration and release. Entries must be received on or before the closest closing date of July 31, 1999. Québec residents may submit litigation regarding this contest to the Régie des loteries et courses du Québec. For Full Rules, mail a self-addressed stamped envelope to: IKEA SHOPPING SPREE RULES, c/o ConsumerLink, PO Box 2730, Station "A", Toronto, ON M5W 1H3.

2. Telephone #: (   )   –

3. Your date of birth: MM / DD / YYYY

About Your Household

4. **Marital status:**   1. ☐ Married   2. ☐ Single

5. **Not including yourself, what is the GENDER and AGE (in years) of children and other adults living in your household?**
   1. ☐ No one else in household   2. ☐ Child under 1 year

Male	Female	Age		Male	Female	Age
1. ☐	2. ☐	___ yrs.		1. ☐	2. ☐	___ yrs.
1. ☐	2. ☐	___ yrs.		1. ☐	2. ☐	___ yrs.

6. **Which group describes your annual family income?**
   1. ☐ Under $20,000   6. ☐ $60,000-$74,999
   2. ☐ $20,000-$29,999   7. ☐ $75,000-$99,999
   3. ☐ $30,000-$39,999   8. ☐ $100,000-$149,999
   4. ☐ $40,000-$49,999   9. ☐ $150,000-$199,999
   5. ☐ $50,000-$59,999   10. ☐ $200,000+

7. **Level of education:** (check highest level completed)
   1. ☐ Completed High School   3. ☐ Completed Graduate School
   2. ☐ Completed College

8. **What is the primary language spoken in your household?** (check only one)
   1. ☐ English   4. ☐ Cantonese
   2. ☐ French   5. ☐ Mandarin
   3. ☐ Spanish   6. ☐ Other

About Your Shopping Activities

9. **Not counting this visit, how many times have you visited IKEA within the last 12 months?** (check only one)
   1. ☐ 1 time   4. ☐ 4 times   6. ☐ 6 times
   2. ☐ 2 times   5. ☐ 5 times   7. ☐ 7+ times
   3. ☐ 3 times

10. **Did you or any member of your household make a purchase at IKEA during this visit?**   1. ☐ Yes   2. ☐ No
    If yes, what was the total dollar amount of your purchase today? $ ___,___.00

11. **Where have you purchased furnishings in the past year?**
    01. ☐ Brault et Martineau   06. ☐ Home Depot   11. ☐ Pier 1
    02. ☐ The Bay   07. ☐ Idomo   12. ☐ Reno Depot
    03. ☐ The Brick   08. ☐ Kmart   13. ☐ Structube
    04. ☐ Eatons   09. ☐ Leons   14. ☐ Wal-Mart
    05. ☐ Ethan Allen   10. ☐ Linen Chest   15. ☐ Zellers

12. **Which credit cards do you use regularly?** (check all that apply)
    1. ☐ IKEA credit card   4. ☐ Mastercard/Visa/Discover
    2. ☐ American Express   5. ☐ Do not use credit cards
    3. ☐ Diners Club

13. **How much did you spend on home furnishings in the last 12 months?** (check only one)
    1. ☐ Under $500   3. ☐ $1,000 - $1,499   5. ☐ $2,500 +
    2. ☐ $500 - $999   4. ☐ $1,500 - $2,499

14. **How many times in the last 12 months have you purchased from:**
    (A) A catalog: ___ times   (B) Online (internet): ___ times

About Your Experience With IKEA

15. **How would you rate IKEA for the following?**

	Poor	Fair	Good	N/A
A. Overall satisfaction	1. ☐	2. ☐	3. ☐	4. ☐
B. Catalog	1. ☐	2. ☐	3. ☐	4. ☐
C. Restaurant/café	1. ☐	2. ☐	3. ☐	4. ☐
D. Furniture styles	1. ☐	2. ☐	3. ☐	4. ☐
E. Home accessories	1. ☐	2. ☐	3. ☐	4. ☐
F. Merchandise selection	1. ☐	2. ☐	3. ☐	4. ☐
G. Prices	1. ☐	2. ☐	3. ☐	4. ☐
H. Items in stock	1. ☐	2. ☐	3. ☐	4. ☐

16. **Have you ever placed a phone order with IKEA?**   1. ☐ Yes   2. ☐ No

17. **If yes, how would you rate our phone order service?**

	Poor	Fair	Good	N/A
A. Knowledge of service representative	1. ☐	2. ☐	3. ☐	4. ☐
B. Courtesy of service representative	1. ☐	2. ☐	3. ☐	4. ☐
C. Timing of merchandise delivery	1. ☐	2. ☐	3. ☐	4. ☐
D. Condition of merchandise upon arrival	1. ☐	2. ☐	3. ☐	4. ☐

Companies often use questionnaires to collect data, which helps them better understand their customers and improve their relationships with customers. To encourage customer participation, this IKEA questionnaire is designed as a contest with a $10 000 shopping spree as its grand prize.

population or **universe**
The total group that the researcher wants to study.

census
A collection of marketing data from all possible sources.

is crucial that marketing researchers and research users cooperate at every stage in the research design. Too many studies go unused because marketing managers view the results as not meaningful to them.

For the Infotech study, a team of four researchers worked almost full-time for approximately three months to collect the secondary data, design and pretest questionnaires, and gather the primary data. The data were analyzed and presented in a 195-page report to the client.

The report highlighted the size and growth of the market. It also showed that despite the favourable market size, the idea as originally conceived would be extremely difficult to implement. As a result of the study, the sponsor was able to make an informed decision about whether or not to go ahead. The marketing research presented information that saved the sponsor a great deal of time and money.

SAMPLING TECHNIQUES

Sampling is one of the most important aspects of marketing research. The total group that the researcher wants to study is called the **population** or **universe**. For a political campaign, the population would be all eligible voters. For a new cosmetic line, it might be all women in a certain age bracket. If this total group is contacted, the results are known as a **census**. Unless the group is small, the cost of such a survey will be overwhelming. Even the federal government attempts a full census only once every ten years.

Information, therefore, is rarely gathered from the total population during a survey. Instead, researchers select a representative group called a *sample*. Samples can be classified either as probability samples or as nonprobability samples. A **probability sample** is a sample in which every member of the population has a known chance of being selected. Because **nonprobability samples** are arbitrary, standard statistical tests cannot be applied to them. Marketing researchers usually base their studies on probability samples, but it is important to be able to identify all types of samples. Some of the best-known ones are outlined below.

A **convenience sample** is a nonprobability sample based on the selection of readily available respondents. Broadcasting's "on-the-street" interviews are a good example. Marketing researchers sometimes use such samples in exploratory research, but not in definitive studies, because of the weakness of this method.

A nonprobability sample of people with a specific attribute is called a **judgement sample**. Election-night predictions are usually based on polls of "swing voters" and are a type of judgement sample.

A **quota sample** is a nonprobability sample that is divided so that different segments or groups are represented in the total sample. An example would be a survey of imported-car owners that includes 33 Honda owners, 31 Toyota owners, 7 BMW owners, and so on.

A **cluster sample** is a probability sample that is generated by randomly choosing one or more areas or population clusters and then surveying all members in the chosen cluster(s). This approach can be helpful in a situation where it is difficult to obtain a complete list of all members of the population, but where there is good information on certain *areas* (such as census tracts).

The basic type of probability sample is the **simple random sample**, a sample in which every item in the relevant universe has an equal opportunity of being selected. Provincial lotteries are an example. Each number that appears on a ticket has an equal opportunity of being selected, and each ticket holder has an equal opportunity of winning. Using a computer to select 200 respondents randomly from a mailing list of 1000 would give every name on the list an equal opportunity of being selected.

A probability sample that takes every nth item on a list, after a random start, is called a **systematic sample**. Sampling from a telephone directory is a common example. This is a frequently used sampling procedure.

Interpret and Present the Information

After going through the many steps to choose the best research method and the often complicated process of collecting data, the researcher faces the daunting task of making sense of the information. The researcher is faced with a mass of numbers that must be compiled, organized, and interpreted. Computer programs are available to help with the task, but the responsibility of drawing conclusions and writing a report remains. Once this process is complete, it is common procedure to present the analysis and conclusions to others in the marketing team. The team will then combine the findings with other information to make strategic decisions and create marketing plans.

probability sample
A sample in which every member of the population has a known chance of being selected.

nonprobability sample
A sample chosen in an arbitrary fashion so that each member of the population does not have a representative chance of being selected.

convenience sample
A nonprobability sample based on the selection of readily available respondents.

judgement sample
A nonprobability sample of people with a specific attribute.

quota sample
A nonprobability sample that is divided so that different segments or groups are represented in the total sample.

cluster sample
A probability sample that is generated by randomly choosing one or more areas or population clusters and then surveying all members in the chosen cluster(s).

simple random sample
A probability sample in which every item in the relevant universe has an equal opportunity of being selected.

systematic sample
A probability sample that takes every nth item on a list, after a random start.

▶ THE PRACTISING MARKETER

www.tigercat.com

Data Collection at Tigercat Industries Inc.

Obtaining and using information is a key component of Tigercat Industries' success.

Tigercat Industries Inc. is a successful manufacturer of logging equipment. The company engineers, assembles, and markets logging equipment for cutting down, transporting, and bundling trees. The machines range in size from 14 to 32 tons and cost between $210000 and $500000. Close to 70 percent of Tigercat's sales are to the southeast United States.

Two important aspects of information collected by the company are sales analysis and personal interviews with users. A year-old company study of customers found that 70 percent of sales were to repeat customers. A more recent look found that the percentage had changed to 50 percent. The company concluded that this change indicated that more customers were on board. Personal interviews are done by company engineers. They take regular trips into the forests with loggers to get a good feel for what they need and the conditions they are dealing with.

The combination of knowing what customers want and being dedicated to producing the highest-quality products has paid off. In a shrinking market for logging machines, Tigercat has been growing in the range of 165 percent annually over the past five years. In 1998 the company was selected one of Canada's 50 Best Managed Companies.

How would you classify the types of data collected by the company? Do you agree or disagree with the assessment that more customers were on board because of the decline in repeat purchases?

Source: Adapted from "Seeing the Forest and the Trees," *Financial Post* (December 28, 1998), p. C17. Reprinted with permission.

▶ MARKETING INFORMATION SYSTEMS

For all companies, some market data flow in on a regular basis from sales and other marketing activities. And companies that undertake marketing research gain other periodic bursts of facts from such studies.

The value of such material can vary significantly. Data and information are not necessarily synonymous terms. *Data* refer to statistics, opinions, facts, or predictions categorized on some basis for storage and retrieval. *Information* is data that is relevant to the marketing manager in making decisions. Often, the right information does not seem to be available when a marketing decision has to be made because the company simply does not have it, or because the information is not readily available in the firm's system.

The solution to the problem of obtaining relevant information appears simple—establish a systematic approach to information management by installing a planned marketing information system (MIS). Establishing an effective information system is, however, much easier said than done, as evidenced by the large number of firms that have attempted to develop an MIS and have succeeded only in increasing the amounts of irrelevant data available to them.

A **marketing information system** is a set of routine procedures to continuously collect, monitor, and present internal and external information on company performance and opportunities in the marketplace. Properly constructed, the MIS can serve as the nerve centre for the company, providing instantaneous information that is suitable for each level of management. It can act like a thermostat, monitoring the marketplace continuously so that management can adjust its actions as conditions change.

The analogy of an automatic heating system illustrates the role of marketing information in a firm's marketing system. Once the objective of a temperature setting (perhaps 20°C) has been established, information about the actual temperature in the house is collected and compared with the objective, and a decision is made based on this comparison. If the temperature drops below an established figure, the decision is made to activate the furnace until the temperature reaches some established level. On the other hand, a high temperature may require a decision to turn off the furnace.

Deviation from the firm's goals of profitability, return on investment, or market share may necessitate changes in price structures, promotional expenditures, package design, or numerous marketing alternatives. The firm's MIS should be capable of revealing such deviations and possibly suggesting tactical changes that will result in attaining the established goals.

Some marketing executives feel that their company does not need a marketing information system, for various reasons. Two arguments are most often given: (1) the size of the company's operations does not warrant such a complete system, and (2) the information provided by an MIS is already being supplied by the marketing research department.

These contentions arise from a misconception regarding the services and functions performed by the marketing research department. Marketing research has already been described as typically focusing on a specific problem or project; the investigations involved have a definite beginning, middle, and end. Marketing information systems, on the other hand, are much wider in scope and involve continually collecting and analyzing marketing information. Figure 5.3 indicates the various information inputs—including marketing research studies—that serve as components of a firm's MIS.

By focusing daily on the marketplace, the MIS provides a continuous, systematic, and comprehensive study of areas that indicate deviations from established goals. The up-to-the-minute data allow problems to be corrected before they adversely affect company operations. Furthermore, such a system can be designed to collect information on the activities and effects of competitors. Competitor analysis is a very important component of a company's strategic planning process.

marketing information system
A set of routine procedures to continuously collect, monitor, and present internal and external information on company performance and opportunities in the marketplace.

Roots of Marketing Information Systems

Robert J. Williams, creator of the first and still one of the most notable marketing information systems in 1961 at the Mead Johnson division of Edward Dalton Company, explains the difference between marketing research and marketing information systems this way:

The difference between marketing research and marketing intelligence is like the difference between a flash bulb and a candle. Let's say you are dancing in the dark. Every 90 seconds you're allowed to set off a flash bulb. You can use those brief intervals of intense light to chart a course, but remember everybody is moving, too. Hopefully, they'll accommodate themselves roughly to your predictions. You may get bumped and you may stumble every so often, but you can go along.

On the other hand, you can light a candle. It doesn't yield as much light, but it's a steady light. You are continually aware of the movements of the other bodies. You can adjust your own course to the courses of the others. The intelligence system is a kind of candle. It's no great flash on the immediate state of things, but it provides continuous light as situations shift and change.[5]

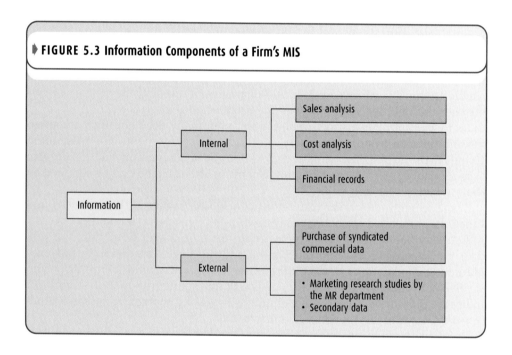

▶ FIGURE 5.3 Information Components of a Firm's MIS

Successful Marketing Information Systems

The Monsanto Company and General Mills Incorporated are examples of firms that have a successful MIS in operation.

Monsanto has designed one of the most advanced marketing information systems in operation. The system provides detailed sales analyses by product, sales, district, type of mill, and end use. Computer analyses are obtained from a continuing panel of households that represent a cross section of the national market. Information is collected on purchase patterns by socioeconomic group and is then analyzed to determine current buying trends.

Monsanto also collects survey data to record the actions of competitors. In addition, the system generates short-, medium-, and long-range forecasts for the company and industry. Short-term forecasts are developed for each of about 400 individual products.

www.monsanto.co.uk

The General Mills computer supplies each zone, regional, and district manager with a daily report on the previous day's orders by brand and a comparison of current projections of monthly sales with the monthly total projected the week before. Each of approximately 1700 individual products is analyzed in terms of current profitability and projected annual profitability as compared with target projections made at the beginning of the year. The "problem" products that require management attention are then printed out on the daily reports. A similar report looks for problem areas in each region and breaks down the nature of the problem according to cause (i.e., profit margins, over- or underspending on advertising and sales promotion).[6]

www.generalmills.com

As marketing research becomes increasingly scientific and is combined by a growing number of organizations into fully functional information systems, decision makers benefit by making informed decisions about problems and opportunities. Sophisticated computer simulations make it possible to consider alternative courses of action by posing a number of "what if?" situations.

This chapter has shown that information is vital for marketing decision making. No firm should operate without detailed information on consumer, competitors, and conditions in its market. Marketing research information enables the company to identify market segments and serves as a basis for developing the marketing plan.

The first five chapters of this book have been designed to serve as building blocks for marketing planning. The next chapter will show how a marketing plan is developed.

> **SUMMARY**

Marketing research is the systematic gathering, recording, and analyzing of data about problems related to the marketing of goods and services. It is the function that links the consumer to the company.

The five steps of the marketing research process are (1) formulate the problem, (2) develop the research design, (3) determine the data collection method, (4) collect the data, and (5) interpret and present the information. The research design is a master plan or model for conducting the research.

Secondary data are previously published matter. They include any useful information published by sources such as Statistics Canada, information from the Web, and others. Secondary data can be very useful in that they provide a ready source of useful information at low or no cost. On the other hand, the value of the data may be limited because they might not directly relate to the problem, and the quality of the information may not be verifiable.

Primary data are data collected for the first time, by observation, survey, or controlled experiment. The three kinds of surveys are telephone interviews, self-completed surveys, and personal interviews.

Full- and partial-service research suppliers are often hired to handle various amounts of specific research needed by a firm. Another type of company, the syndicated service organization, collects and sells regularly collected information.

In drawing a sample of consumers to research, firms can choose between probability and nonprobability samples. Probability samples represent all elements of the desired population because every member of the population has a known chance of being selected. A nonprobability sample is chosen in an arbitrary way that does not give everyone a chance of being selected.

A marketing information system (MIS) is a set of routine procedures to continuously collect, monitor, and present internal and external information on company performance, competitors' actions, and opportunities in the marketplace. Marketing information systems can provide better information for management decisions than periodic marketing research surveys.

▶ KEY TERMS

census	population or universe
cluster sample	primary data
convenience sample	probability sample
exploratory research	quota sample
hypothesis	research design
judgement sample	secondary data
marketing information system	simple random sample
marketing research	systematic sample
nonprobability sample	test marketing

▶ INTERACTIVE SUMMARY AND DISCUSSION QUESTIONS

1. Marketing research is the systematic gathering, recording, and analyzing of data about problems that relate to the marketing of goods and services. Does information collected in such a scientific manner reduce the scope of management decision making? Explain.

2. Full- and partial-service research suppliers handle various amounts of specific research needed by a firm. Syndicated service organizations collect and sell regularly collected information. Give examples of when each of these types of service would be used by a company.

3. The five steps of the marketing research process are (1) formulating the problem, (2) developing the research design, (3) determining the data collection method, (4) collecting the data, and (5) interpreting and presenting the information. A small firm recognizes that it has the ability to develop high-quality air-monitoring equipment. Illustrate how the marketing research process might be applied to help management decide whether or not to enter this market.

4. Explain how problem definition in marketing research can sometimes be confused with symptoms.

5. Research design is a master plan or model for conducting the investigation. Differentiate between research design and the steps of the marketing research process.

6. Secondary data are previously published matter. Give examples of sources of external secondary data.

7. Discuss the advantages and limitations of secondary data.

8. Primary data are data collected for the first time, by observation, survey, or controlled experiment. Give examples of each of these data collection methods.

9. The three kinds of surveys are telephone interviews, self-completed surveys, and personal interviews. Discuss the advantages and disadvantages of each.

10. Test marketing is one of the experimental designs used for collecting information. Why would a firm undertake test marketing? Why don't all firms do so?

11. In drawing a sample to research, firms can choose between probability and nonprobability samples. Why are nonprobability samples generally considered to be unreliable?

12. A marketing information system is a set of routine procedures to continuously collect, monitor, and present internal and external information on company performance and opportunities in the marketplace. Explain how a marketing information system could provide better information for management decisions than periodic marketing research surveys.

13. Assume that you are asked by your employer to research the market potential for a line of new miniature, but high-quality, speakers for computers. You are asked to start with an analysis of the British market. Go to the Web and write a report on the relevant information to be found there.

To obtain a list of further readings for Chapter 5, please refer to the *Foundations of Marketing* Web site.

Appendix
Locating Secondary Data *

As mentioned earlier in the chapter, secondary data can be an extremely important element in making business decisions. This appendix introduces you the key sources of information. They will be helpful in working on your assignments for this course as well as others, and will serve as a valuable reference after graduation.

The publications and Internet sites listed and described in this appendix refer mainly to the Canadian market. Some international marketing sources are covered in the final sections. These are by no means all the sources of secondary data available for Canada or for international markets. However, it is hoped that these sources will serve as a representative list and as a starting point in the search for secondary sources of marketing data.

Several practical comments are appropriate in regard to the Internet sites. Universal resource locators (URLs) can change or become obsolete due to many factors, such as a change of server or lack of maintenance. The most current URLs have been provided, but be prepared for a nonfunctioning address.

Also note that a print publication, such as a directory, may have a so-called Internet equivalent, but in reality the Internet version, while providing a search capability, may not replicate the actual printed pages of the directory. This can reduce the usefulness of an electronic version of a printed publication.

▶ CANADIAN GOVERNMENT PUBLICATIONS

The federal government generates a vast array of publications through its various departments and agencies. Two services are useful in keeping track of these publications. The *Weekly Checklist of Canadian Government Publications* put out by the Depository Services Program, Public Works and Government Services Canada, lists the book and serial titles that have been released during the week by the Parliament of Canada, federal departments, and Statistics Canada. Depository institutions (those that have negotiated a depository status agreement with the federal government to receive the publications free) use the *Checklist* to select publications for their collections. Most major universities and provincial legislative libraries in Canada have full depository status. Check on the status of a library when using its federal government publications.

dsp-psd.pwgsc.gc.ca

The second service is the Canadian Government Publishing's Internet site. The *Weekly Checklist* is also available electronically at this location. In addition, the full *Weekly Catalogue* is available for searching back issues of the *Checklist*. The records in the *Catalogue* go back to 1993. The titles can either be ordered or sought out in the libraries across Canada that collect government publications, particularly those with depository status. Links are also provided to other federal government databases accessible through the Internet. This includes Strategis, Industry Canada's site, described below.

* This appendix was developed by Dennis Felbel, Head, A.D. Cohen Management Library, University of Manitoba. He is also responsible for developing the appendix in the previous edition.

Industry Canada

strategis.ic.gc.ca/engdoc/
main.html

Strategis, Industry Canada's Internet site, is the federal government's major initiative in providing information on business, trade, and investment in Canada as well as on the international business environment. For information on major export opportunities, international intelligence, and key business contacts, one enters the site through the Trade and Investment, International Business Opportunities section. For domestic information, Strategis has a company directory section, a business information by sector section, and a consumer information section, among others. The Strategis site contains over 50 000 reports.

Sector Competitiveness Frameworks Series

Industry Canada has published a series of sector analyses under the series name *Sector Competitiveness Frameworks*. Some 29 industrial sectors are covered, including the automotive industry, forest products, household furniture, and primary steel. Each focuses on the opportunities, both domestic and international, and challenges that face each sector. Each sector analysis covers the highlights and key points of an industry, changing conditions and industry responses, and growth prospects. The series is available in both print and electronic format via Industry Canada's Strategis Web site, described above. Within Strategis, select Business Information by Sector from the main menu.

Statistics Canada

Statistics Canada publishes extensive statistical information that is gathered through various sources. In addition to standard print publications, data are disseminated on computer printouts and microform and in electronic format. Maps and other geographic reference materials are also available for some types of data. With hundreds of titles available, it is not practical to describe all the publications and services. However, detailed information can be obtained in several ways. There are Statistics Canada regional centres in the following cities:

- Halifax
- Montreal
- Ottawa
- Toronto
- Winnipeg
- Regina
- Edmonton
- Calgary
- Vancouver

Each centre has a collection of current Statistics Canada publications and reference materials that can be consulted or purchased. Copying facilities for printed materials and microform are also available, as is access to CANSIM (Statistics Canada's computerized database).

STATISTICS CANADA CATALOGUE

This catalogue is no longer published on a regular annual basis. For example, the 1997 edition was the first full catalogue published since 1994. In addition, the

1997 catalogue contains only print products. Electronic data products and services are not listed in the catalogue, but rather are found in Statistics Canada's electronic catalogue known as Information on Products and Services (IPS) via its Web site. However, the *Statistics Canada Catalogue* still contains useful information in appendices that helps the first-time user of Statistics Canada products to understand the catalogue numbering system as well as to find and order their publications.

As a federal government agency, Statistics Canada publications are available at university and provincial legislative libraries across Canada that have a depository status agreement with the federal government.

www.statcan.ca

STATISTICS CANADA'S WEB SITE

The Statistics Canada Web site is available in both English and French. It is relatively easy to browse through the approximately twelve major sections. Newly released data or new products and services are described in a Daily News section. The Canadian Statistics section presents free tabular data on all aspects of Canada's economy, land, people, and government. This free data is normally extracted from CANSIM, Statistics Canada's on-line statistical database. One can also access CANSIM and retrieve more detailed data at a nominal cost. The CANSIM time series database is also available to colleges and universities who have paid an annual fee via the Data Liberation Initiative. Free census data are available, as well as the option to purchase more detailed data series. All of Statistics Canada's publications and services, print and electronic, are listed in the Information on Products and Services (IPS) Catalogue. Particularly useful is the Links to Other Sites Feature, whereby one can access other statistical Web sites, both provincial and international.

CANADIAN ECONOMIC OBSERVER

Generally, the most readily available Statistics Canada publication is likely to be the *Canadian Economic Observer*. It was titled the *Canadian Statistical Review* up to 1988. It is published monthly and, as of September 1993, has been split into two parts, a journal with feature articles and economic analysis, and a statistical summary. The journal provides authoritative commentary on Canadian and international economic trends, analysis of current economic conditions (including the composite leading indicator), and a monthly feature article. The statistical summary provides a complete range of hard data on critical economic indicators, prices, markets, trade, and demographics. Data on the provinces and the G7 international scene are also compiled. An annual historical statistical supplement that compiles monthly data is also available individually or as part of a subscription to the *Canadian Economic Observer*.

▶ PROVINCIAL GOVERNMENT PUBLICATIONS

The provincial governments publish thousands of documents through their various departments and agencies. These publications cover a variety of topics, reflecting the nature of the departments from which the documents originated.

They range across the entire information spectrum, from agriculture to urban affairs.

As the available documents are too numerous to describe individually, it is the best to begin with the major sources that list and describe the documents published by the provincial governments. As an illustration, here is how one would find publications generated by the province of Manitoba. Documents published by other provincial jurisdictions can be identified and obtained in a similar way.

The Province Of Manitoba

www.gov.mb.ca/
index.en.html

Like a number of provinces, Manitoba makes its publications available through a department or agency of the government. It publishes the *Manitoba Government Publications Monthly Checklist,* which lists the publications received during the month by the Legislative Library of Manitoba. The publications are listed by their issuing department, which means by department, their branches and subdivisions, as well as boards, committees, and other agencies or bodies of the government. The publications can be obtained from their issuing body or from Statutory Publications, a government department, as indicated in the *Checklist.*

Manitoba government publications are also available in eight major libraries in the province that operate under a provincial depository program. These depository libraries automatically receive current Manitoba government publications.

The province of Manitoba also has an agency known as the Manitoba Bureau of Statistics. Its main publication, the *Manitoba Statistical Review,* presents statistical information of a socioeconomic nature for both the government and the private sector. In general, the *Review* publishes statistics in the areas of population, the labour force, economics, and industrial sectoral analysis.

The Manitoba government, like other provincial jurisdictions, also maintains a site on the Internet. The site provides access to the Statutory Publications department and the services offered at cost via the Internet. Links to other government sites are also provided.

▶ CHAMBERS OF COMMERCE

Most major cities and towns have a Chamber of Commerce, which is an association established to further the business interests of its community. The Chambers in most metropolitan cities publish information and maintain Web sites about their cities for promotional reasons. The types of information one can expect to find at most Chambers of Commerce include economic facts, employment figures, government descriptions, demographic data, and quality of life statistics.

www.winnipegchmbr.mb.ca

As an illustration, the Winnipeg Chamber of Commerce maintains a Web site that provides a description of Chamber services, member listings, and resource links.

▶ OTHER BUSINESS AND GOVERNMENT AGENCIES

www.winnipegedw.com

Municipalities, cities, and towns, in their promotional efforts to stimulate business development, often create special agencies to promote economic development. As part of their efforts, such agencies create resource material that can be of great value to the researcher when gathering secondary material at the local level.

An example of such an agency is Economic Development Winnipeg (EDW), a business development initiative of the City of Winnipeg. EDW promotes success stories and business news, tracks Winnipeg events, and markets the city itself. It generates publications about the city that highlight and focus on the strengths of Winnipeg as a place to do business. EDW's major publication is the *Winnipeg Community Profile,* which outlines Winnipeg's economic strengths, manufacturing diversity, transportation network, and workforce, along with other features of the city that make it an attractive location for business. Most of the information provided through EDW is available elsewhere, but having all the information in one place makes the research process easier.

Organizations that are similar to EDW exist in other jurisdictions across the country. The researcher seeking marketing data must be aware of their existence and potential usefulness.

▶ MARKET REPORTS, SURVEYS, DIRECTORIES, SPECIAL ISSUES, MAGAZINES, AND NEWSLETTERS

Many of the publications listed in the remainder of this appendix are available through university, public, and special business libraries. As many of them can be either fairly expensive or difficult to locate, consult with a librarian as to their cost and possible locations where they may be held.

Free on-line searching of Internet sites is often available at university and public libraries, although printing costs may apply. Also remember that what one finds on an Internet site may not match the published print version in content and format.

Once again, the annotated publications that follow are not meant to be comprehensive, but rather are a sampling of some of the more significant publications in each of the fields. The publications are listed under major headings that describe the industry, trade, or sector to which they pertain. Remember that the headings are not clear cut; there may be some overlap, so you may need to consult more than one heading.

Some "special issues" may appear in libraries under the title of the magazine with which they are associated. Furthermore, some of the "annual" publications may not always be published on a regular basis, and new special issues may appear with little or no prepublication announcement.

Advertising

CANADIAN ADVERTISING RATES AND DATA
Published monthly. Known by its acronym *CARD*. Advertises itself as Canada's media information network. Provides addresses, advertising rates, circulation, mechanical requirements, and personnel and branch office information for radio and TV stations, newspapers, magazines, and Web advertising sites for all of Canada. (Maclean Hunter Publishing)

CANADIAN MEDIA DIRECTORS' COUNCIL MEDIA DIGEST
Published annually as a supplement to *Marketing Magazine,* formerly called *Marketing.* Profiles the advertising industry in a statistical format. Provides net advertising revenues by medium as well as analysis of each medium, including the Internet, television, radio, newspapers, business publications, and consumer magazines. Also contains a useful media terminology dictionary. (Maclean Hunter Publishing)

ETHNIC MEDIA AND MARKETS
Published twice yearly by *Canadian Advertising Rates and Data (CARD).* Provides the same information on the ethnic media. Coverage includes print media, radio and TV stations and programs, and ethnic media support services. (Maclean Hunter Publishing)

GUIDE TO MARKET RESEARCH SERVICES
Published annually in a May issue of *Marketing Magazine.* Lists by Canadian city firms that are involved in market research. Provides a description of the services offered along with addresses. (Maclean Hunter Publishing)

NATIONAL LIST OF ADVERTISERS
Published annually in December. Provides the addresses, telephone numbers, brand names, and personnel of over 4300 major advertisers in Canada. In a special section, the companies are arranged by their North American Industrial Classification System codes. Also lists advertising agencies. (Maclean Hunter Publishing)

PUBLICATION PROFILES
An annual supplement to *Canadian Advertising Rates and Data.* Gives the editorial profile of all the major consumer, farm, and business publications published in Canada. An Internet version of the *Publication Profiles* supplement, searchable by keyword, is available. (Maclean Hunter Publishing)

www.cardmedia.com

Canadian Market, General

BANK OF CANADA REVIEW
Published quarterly, with monthly statistical supplements, as opposed to its former monthly schedule. Combines articles and news items on monetary policy with extensive charts and tables on the major financial and economic statistical

www.bank-banque-
canada.ca/english

indicators collected and analyzed by the Bank. In summer 1999 the format changed to two distinct publications, the *Bank of Canada Review* and the *Bank of Canada Banking Financial Statistics.* The Bank of Canada makes available most of the articles from the *Review,* other publications, and selected financial statistics on its Web site. (Bank of Canada)

CANADA YEAR BOOK

Published every two years. Records in narrative and statistical format the developments in Canada's economic, social, and political life. Useful for determining "where Canada is at" on general topics. (Statistics Canada)

CANADIAN ECONOMIC OBSERVER

Published monthly but now in two parts, a journal with feature articles and economic analysis, and a statistical summary. The data in both parts are retrieved from CANSIM, Statistics Canada's computerized data bank. An annual historical statistical supplement that compiles monthly data is also available. All three combine to become the definitive source for Canadian statistical information. For a more complete description of the *Canadian Economic Observer,* see earlier in this appendix under Statistics Canada. (Statistics Canada)

CANADIAN OUTLOOK: ECONOMIC FORECAST

Published quarterly. Features forecasts on the major components of the Canadian economy, including consumer expenditures, housing, government, business, international trade, energy, employment, labour force, costs and prices, and the financial markets. Statistical tables covering the same range of topics follow. An *Executive Summary* of *Canadian Outlook* is also available on a quarterly basis. (Conference Board of Canada)

ECONOSCOPE

Published monthly. Provides economic forecasts for the Canadian economy in both narrative and statistical formats. The forecasts and indicators are provided for both Canada and the United States, which makes comparisons convenient. (Royal Bank)

EDITOR AND PUBLISHER MARKET GUIDE

Published annually. A compilation of marketing data on all Canadian and U.S. markets where daily newspapers are published. The main sections survey each of the cities or communities that support a daily. Other sections provide a nationwide summary of population, income, housing, and retail sales. Market ranking tables are shown for population, disposable income, income per household, and total retail sales. Retail sales are in turn broken down into nine categories. (Editor and Publisher Company)

FP MARKETS, CANADIAN DEMOGRAPHICS

Published annually. One of the most extensive sources for demographics on Canadian urban markets. Provides data and projections for population, households, retails sales, and personal income for markets nationwide. The markets are defined by the census divisions. Buying power indices are developed, allowing for market comparisons. Municipal and provincial profiles are also provided. (National Post)

MARKET RESEARCH HANDBOOK
Published annually. An authoritative source of socioeconomic information on local and national markets in Canada based on the latest census data available as well as estimates of that data. It is very useful for locating target markets. The data are divided into a number of broad categories, including population, employment and earnings, expenditures, industry statistics, and projections. (Statistics Canada)

PROVINCIAL OUTLOOK: ECONOMIC FORECAST
Published quarterly. Similar in format to *Canadian Outlook,* but with individual sections for each of the Canadian provinces. Key economic indicators for each province follow the forecasts. An *Executive Summary* of *Provincial Outlook* is also available on a quarterly basis. (Conference Board of Canada)

SURVEY OF BUYING POWER AND MEDIA MARKETS
Published annually in August as a supplement to *Sales and Marketing Management.* Provides data from U.S. geographic markets and media markets in the form of market rankings, population, effective buying income, retail sales, buying power indices, merchandise line sales, and projections. It is known as the reference guide to American purchasing influence. (Bill Communications)

Clothing

CANADIAN TEXTILE JOURNAL MANUAL
Published annually. A comprehensive source of information that provides access to textiles, chemical specialties, yarn sources (importers and domestic producers), Canadian machinery agents, and textile mills. The largest section is a buyer's guide that lists products and services, with the companies paying a fee for the listing. Other information sources cover business opportunities, associations, and conferences. (Canadian Textile Journal Inc.)

STYLE: BUYERS' GUIDE
Published annually as a special issue of *Style.* A comprehensive guide to companies, services, agencies, designers, suppliers, associations, showrooms, and fashion schools in the Canadian clothing sectors. (Style Communications)

Computers and Information Technology

COMPUTING CANADA
Published weekly in newspaper format. Intended for professionals in information technology management. Provides news on current developments. Normally contains a special report featuring some aspect of the field. Companies are indexed for each issue, and articles providing industry statistics are com-

mon. Special issues published irregularly are devoted to major trends. (Plesman Publications)

FINANCIAL POST MAGAZINE BRANHAM 200

Published annually in March. The Branham 200 ranks Canada's leading software and information technology service companies. The information technology industry is also analyzed, and major companies are profiled. (National Post)

INFORMATION WEEK

Published weekly. Intended for business and technology managers. Two regularly released special issues are of note. The *Outlook* issue published in January forecasts developments for the near term, looking at spending, networking, Web commerce, and other industry developments. In September *Information Week 500* highlights and ranks the top 500 information technology users. (CMP Media Inc.)

PC MAGAZINE'S TOP 100 WEB SITES

www.zdnet.com/pcmag

Published annually and expanded in the 1999 edition to cover twenty categories. Although a number of the recommended sites are more appropriate for personal use, this listing will fill many information needs. Each site is described briefly. The categories covered include finance, news, reference, search engines, and software downloads. A continually updated *Top 100* is available on the *PC Magazine* Internet site. (ZD Inc.)

PC WORLD'S BEST FREE STUFF ONLINE

www.pcworld.com

Published annually. As more and more Web sites begin charging for information content, *PC World* has compiled a guide to useful free sites. These range from financial information sites, to government sites, to Web and browser services. (PC World Communications)

Electronics

ELECTRONIC BLUEBOOK

Published annually. Lists the names, products, and companies of the electrical equipment industry. (Kerrwil Publications)

ELECTRONIC PRODUCTS AND TECHNOLOGY (EP&T): ELECTROSOURCE PRODUCT REFERENCE GUIDE AND TELEPHONE DIRECTORY

www.ept.ca

Intended audience includes buyers, technicians, and engineers in Canada's electronics industry. Lists companies, products and their suppliers, U.S. and foreign manufacturers, and manufacturers' representatives and distributors. An Internet version of the *Electrosource Directory*, searchable by company or product, is also available. (Lakeview Publications)

Financial and Insurance

CANADIAN INSURANCE: ANNUAL REVIEW OF STATISTICS

Published annually in June as a special issue of *Canadian Insurance*. Reviews the Canadian insurance industry in a largely statistical format. The major portion of the publication is taken up by the company exhibits, which provide five years of underwriting experience for insurers in Canada. Five-year data are also provided for the various classes of insurance, such as liability, aircraft, accident and sickness, and marine insurance. Recent developments and trends in the industry are also highlighted in narrative form. (Stone and Cox Ltd. Publishers)

CANADIAN UNDERWRITER: ANNUAL STATISTICAL ISSUE
Published annually in May as a special issue of *Canadian Underwriter*. Provides insurance company financial results for the previous year. The summary tables are arranged by type of insurance and by company. The company tables also contain five-year underwriting results. A five-year record by class of insurance is included. Leading companies are also ranked by type of insurance and by their rank within their provincial jurisdiction. (Southam Magazine Group)

DIRECTORY OF EMPLOYEE BENEFITS CONSULTANTS
Published annually in August as a special section of *Benefits Canada*. Contains the services offered by benefits consultants, listed geographically by province. (Maclean Hunter Publishing)

DIRECTORY OF GROUP INSURANCE
Published annually in May as a special section of *Benefits Canada*. Group insurance companies are arranged alphabetically, with address, contact, telephone number, and branch office information provided. Various rankings are also available in table format. (Maclean Hunter Publishing)

DIRECTORY OF PENSION FUND INVESTMENT SERVICES
Published annually in November as a special section of *Benefits Canada*. The 1998 *Directory* includes a subdirectory of pension money managers, a subdirectory of investment consultants, and a top 40 money managers listing. A snapshot of the pension fund investment management business is provided.

In 1999 *Benefits Canada* began to publish semiannually in May and October the *Canadian Pension Fund Investment Directory*. It contains the three above-mentioned directories and is available in both print and electronic copy. For this new directory, see the *Benefits Canada* Web site. (Maclean Hunter Publishing)

www.benefitscanada.com

Food and Restaurants

DIRECTORY OF RESTAURANT AND FAST FOOD CHAINS IN CANADA
Published annually. Provides coverage for more than 600 companies, listing head and regional office information, personnel, financial and advertising data, and expansion plans. (Maclean Hunter Publishing)

FOOD IN CANADA
Published nine times a year to serve the Canadian food and beverage processing industry. It publishes special reference issues such as *The Top Food and Beverage Processors in Canada and Economic Review*, the *Guide Book of Associations, Resources, and Events*, and a *Buyers' Guide*. (Maclean Hunter Publishing)

www.foodincanada.com

FOOD IN CANADA'S BUYERS GUIDE DIRECTORY ONLINE

The trade publication *Food in Canada* maintains an Internet site that is described as the resource tool for suppliers across Canada. It is searchable by product, manufacturer, and distributor.

Forestry

www.cppa.org/index.htm

CANADIAN PULP AND PAPER ASSOCIATION (CPPA) HOME PAGE

The library at the CPPA site provides access to the publications of this national association. Of particular note are the *Annual Review* and the *Trade Directory*. The former provides key statistics relating to the industry's economic and environmental performance. The latter lists products manufactured by member companies of the association. Links are supplied to member companies, government agencies, and other forestry organizations.

MADISON'S CANADIAN LUMBER DIRECTORY

Published annually. Provides product and service listings, addresses, phone and fax numbers, key contacts, and names for all sectors of the Canadian forest industry. Also provides statistics and five-year price graphs for the industry. (Madison's Canadian Lumber Reporter)

PULP AND PAPER CANADA: ANNUAL AND DIRECTORY

Published annually for professionals in the pulp and paper industry. Lists information on products, personnel, mills and their equipment, suppliers, and other sources required for purchasing. (Southam Magazine Group)

Franchises

CANADIAN BUSINESS FRANCHISE DIRECTORY

Published annually. Contains over 1000 franchise listings in some 35 categories. In addition to a supporting services section, this publication contains articles on the basics of buying and running a franchise. (CGB Publishing)

DIRECTORY OF FRANCHISING ORGANIZATIONS

This *Directory* is in its thirty-eighth edition. It is American in focus and lists 1300 franchise opportunities in 45 categories. (Pilot Books)

ENTREPRENEUR: ANNUAL FRANCHISE 500

Published annually for twenty years. Ranks and rates Canadian and U.S. franchises based on financial strength and stability, growth rate, and size, among other criteria. (Entrepreneur)

ENTREPRENEUR INTERNATIONAL: WORLD'S TOP 200 FRANCHISES

Published as a supplement to *Entrepreneur*. Provides addresses and descriptions of the top 200 franchisers seeking foreign franchisees. Also contains articles on worldwide franchising. (Entrepreneur)

MINING REVIEW: EXPLORATION AND DEVELOPMENT REVIEW

Published annually as a special issue of *Mining Review*. Focuses on exploration and new developments in the Western Canadian mining industry over the past twelve months. (Naylor Communications)

Photography

PROFESSIONAL PHOTOGRAPHERS OF CANADA DIRECTORY

Published annually. Contains member listings broken down by province. Also contains a buyers' guide for photographic supplies and manufacturers. (Craig Kelman and Associates)

Printing, Publishing, and Graphic Arts

CANADIAN PRINTER: BUYERS' GUIDE AND DIRECTORY

Published annually. Provides information on equipment, supplies, and suppliers, as well as statistical information on the printing industry. A searchable, on-line version of the *Buyers' Guide* is available. (Maclean Hunter Publishing)

www.bizlink.com/printer

ESTIMATORS' AND BUYERS' GUIDE

An annual guide for the graphics industry by the publisher of *Graphic Monthly*. Lists companies and graphic arts services of relevance to the graphics industry. (North Island Sound Ltd.)

Product Design and Engineering

DESIGN ENGINEERING: FLUID POWER BUYERS' GUIDE

Published annually as a special issue of *Design Engineering*. Lists information on suppliers, systems, and products in the engineering/fluid power sector. (Maclean Hunter Publishing)

DESIGN ENGINEERING: MECHANICAL POWER TRANSMISSION BUYERS' GUIDE

Published annually as a special issue of *Design Engineering*. Lists information on products, suppliers, and manufacturers in the mechanical power transmission industry. (Maclean Hunter Publishing)

www.design-engineering. com

Both of these *Design Engineering Buyers' Guides* have an on-line equivalent that is searchable by product, manufacturer, and distributor.

Retailing

CANADIAN DIRECTORY OF SHOPPING CENTRES

Published annually. Provides information on 1850 major shopping centres across the country. Lists include tenant and manager/owner contact information. Statistical data includes rental costs, traffic, sales, and market population. (Maclean Hunter Publishing)

CANADIAN GROCER

A trade journal that monitors all the latest trends and news in food retailing. Special directory issues are published regularly, such as the *National Directory of Food Brokers and Brands* and the *Annual Survey of Chains and Groups.* (Maclean Hunter Publishing)

DIRECTORY OF RETAIL CHAINS IN CANADA

Published annually. Provides information on over 2000 chains, including store location and size, head office details, and key contacts. Other details include projected openings and buyers names. (Maclean Hunter Publishing)

MONDAY REPORT ON RETAILERS

Published weekly as a newsletter. Provides articles on the expansion plans of the major chain retailers in North America. Contains no advertising. (Maclean Hunter Publishing)

Transportation

CANADIAN TRANSPORTATION LOGISTICS: BUYERS' GUIDE

Published annually as a special issue of *Canadian Transportation Logistics.* Arranged by transportation carrier: air, sea, motor, and rail. Other transport-related companies are listed under services such as customs brokers, logistic providers, and transportation intermediaries. (Southam Magazine Group)

www.modernpurchasing.com

MODERN PURCHASING: TRANSPORTATION SERVICES DIRECTORY

Published annually. The *Directory* provides information on the major transportation carriers used by the purchasing sector, including air cargo, couriers, freight forwarders, and ports. The *Directory* is also available on-line. (Maclean Hunter Publishing)

Regional and City Business Magazines

A number of regional and city business magazines published in Canada devote themselves to a restricted geographic area. They often provide a wealth of information and analysis on the local scene that is available nowhere else. Some examples follow, with their respective publishers.

BC BUSINESS MAGAZINE

Features an annual Top 100 Companies issue and profiles award-winning local entrepreneurs in a special issue. (Canada Wide Magazines)

MANITOBA BUSINESS
Includes special issues focusing on the Top 100 Manitoba Companies and the 50 Fastest-Growing Manitoba Companies. (Canada Wide Magazines)

NORTHERN ONTARIO BUSINESS
Reports on all aspects of business and industry that relate to Northern Ontario, in newspaper format. (Laurentian Publishing)

City business magazines like *Toronto Business Magazine* (Zanny Ltd.) and *Montreal Business Magazine* (Quebec Inc.) focus on the current business events of their respective cities. Other city magazines exist for urban areas across Canada generally, providing a combination of business and consumer information for those cities.

▶ TRADE DIRECTORIES

CANADIAN NATIONAL SERVICES DIRECTORY
Published annually. Contains listings of Canadian businesses in the service industry only. These businesses have to have twenty or more employees, annual revenue of $1 million or more, and a North American Industrial Classification System code in the service industry sector. Address and company-specific information are provided. Also contains a business by NAICS code and geographic index. (Dun & Bradstreet)

CANADIAN TRADE INDEX
Published annually. A multivolume directory that provides a classified list of some 55 000 Canadian products and an alphabetical list of some 24 000 Canadian companies. Also includes sections on distributors and export businesses and their areas of trade, as well as a trademark section with some 80 000 trade names. (Alliance of Manufacturers and Exporters Canada)

FP SURVEY OF INDUSTRIALS
Published annually. Covers all publicly traded Canadian manufacturing and service companies. Describes the companies' operations and highlights of events over the past year, plus financial data and ratios that are useful for investment purposes. The companies are also listed by North American Industrial Classification System codes. (National Post)

FRASER'S CANADIAN TRADE DIRECTORY
Published annually in four volumes. Provides a comprehensive listing of manufacturers by product classification, as well as an alphabetical listing. Trade names and their manufacturers, and international firms who have agents or distributors in Canada, also have their own specific listings. (Maclean Hunter Publishing)

MOODY'S INTERNATIONAL MANUAL

Published annually, with an updating service. One of eight *Moody's Manuals,* this one provides coverage of major international corporations in over 110 countries, including Canada. Each entry contains a company history, business and product description, subsidiary and personnel listings, and financial statements. (Financial Communications Inc.)

SCOTT'S INDUSTRIAL DIRECTORIES

Published annually. The four major *Scott's Directories* are Atlantic, Quebec, Ontario, and Western. They have identical formats, with three main sections. The first is a list of Canadian manufacturers in alphabetical order. The second is alphabetical by geographic location of the company, with addresses, products, and number of employees. The third lists companies by their product, arranged by North American Industrial Classification System code. (Southam Information Products)

▶ INTERNATIONAL MARKETING PUBLICATIONS

EUROPEAN MARKETING DATA AND STATISTICS

Published annually. This major reference work is a compendium of statistical information on the countries of Western and Eastern Europe, which can be very useful for market planning. Some 24 principal subject areas are broken down into subcategories covering over 470 pages. Representative subject areas are demographic trends/forecasts, economic indicators, labour force indicators, and advertising/media patterns. Within the subject of labour force indicators, for example, there are ten subcategories ranging from employment level to average working week in manufacturing. The data compilation dates back to 1977, which allows for analyzing trends and forecasting. The data are presented in spreadsheet format. The data for Eastern Europe are not quite as extensive and complete as those for Western Europe, for obvious reasons. For example, countries that emerged from former Czechoslovakia, Yugoslavia, and the USSR in the early 1990s are included as far as possible. Prior to that period, the data are provided under the former country name. Brief geographic sketches and maps for each European country are included in a separate section. There is also a special chapter arranged by country that identifies the major information sources one can turn to for further research on the European market. (Euromonitor)

INTERNATIONAL MARKETING DATA AND STATISTICS

Published annually. A publication similar in format to *European Marketing Data and Statistics,* except that the 24 principal subjects deal with the Americas, Asia, Africa, and Oceania. The country coverage includes over 160 countries and is particularly useful for smaller countries for which it is difficult to find statistical information. Also includes a chapter that deals with other major information sources that can be consulted. (Euromonitor)

STATISTICAL YEARBOOK

Published annually. Provides information on some 200 countries and territories that are members of the United Nations. The data are presented mainly in table format. Some of the specific areas covered include education, science and technology, libraries, book publication, cultural information, and radio and television broadcasting. UNESCO maintains a Web site from which many of its documents can be identified, ordered, and downloaded. (UNESCO)

www.unesco.org

WORLD ECONOMIC OUTLOOK

Published biannually. This survey of prospects and policies resulting from the International Monetary Fund (IMF) draws on information provided through member countries. The analysis is both current and detailed. The 1998 releases dealt with the turbulence in the economies of Asia, South America, and Russia. Implications of this turbulence for the world economy as well as mature financial markets in the United States and Europe are addressed. The narrative is supported in a comprehensive fashion by an extensive array of tables, boxes, and figures on all aspects of country, regional, and world statistics. A large number of IMF titles appear in full on its Web site; others have to be ordered. (International Monetary Fund)

www.imf.org

YEARBOOK OF LABOUR STATISTICS

Published annually. Summarizes the principal labour statistics for some 190 countries, usually covering the most recent ten-year period. Data are drawn from national statistical services and are presented in nine chapters on such topics as wages, unemployment, and hours of work. A companion volume to the annual is the *Retrospective Edition on Labour Statistics, 1945–1989*. This volume pulls together data for the period and thus offers an opportunity to analyze participation rates of the population in the labour force over a 25-year period. The majority of free data is in the Library section of the International Labour Organization's Web site. (International Labour Organization)

www.ilo.org

▶ BIBLIOGRAPHIC DATABASES

ABI/INFORM

This database is available in CD-ROM and Internet versions. It contains thorough indexing and abstracting of articles from international business and management journals, including all the major marketing journals. The CD-ROM version known as *ABI Power Pages* carries more than 1000 journal titles, while the Internet version known as *Proquest Direct* carries more than 1500 journal titles. Over 400 of the journals in *ABI Power Pages* allow you to print entire articles. For *Proquest Direct,* articles in over 750 titles can be viewed, printed, or e-mailed to a specific address. *ABI/INFORM* has search capabilities that make it easy to search for articles on a specific industry or company. The CD-ROM version is updated monthly, while the Internet version is updated on a continuous basis.

Coverage for indexing and abstracting dates back to 1981, and for full access to 1987. *ABI/INFORM* is user-friendly, with users requiring only a few minutes of instruction in order to feel comfortable with the system. It is available in many university and business libraries (URL will vary with library). (University Microfilms International)

CANADIAN BUSINESS AND CURRENT AFFAIRS (CBCA)

This database, available on CD-ROM and the Internet, provides indexing and abstracting to over 600 Canadian periodicals, including business, popular, trade, special interest, and academic publications, along with the major Canadian daily newspapers. Coverage goes back to 1982, with the full text of articles available from 1993 on for a select number of titles. Many of the special issues of periodicals described in the previous sections of this appendix are indexed in this database. Company, product, and industry information are readily searchable. CBCA is available in many public, university, and business libraries (URL will vary with library). It is relatively easy to use after a few minutes of instruction. (Micromedia Ltd.)

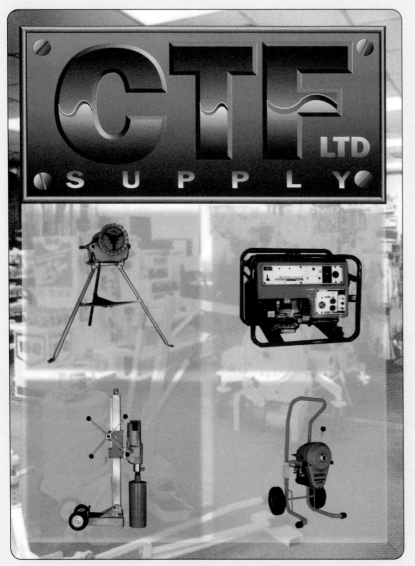

Named one of the *Financial Post*'s 50 Best Managed Private Companies, CTF Supply's sales tripled from $5 million in 1993 to $16 million in 1998. What is the company's secret to success? Strategic market planning.

Chapter 6
Marketing Strategy and the Marketing Plan

▶ **CHAPTER OBJECTIVES**
After reading and studying this chapter, you should be able to

1. Explain the importance of a strategic orientation for marketing.
2. Show the connection between organization strategy and marketing strategy.
3. Show the connection between marketing strategy and the marketing plan.
4. Show that a marketing plan should be based on a good analysis of the character of the external environment.
5. Discuss in detail the steps in the marketing planning process.
6. Explain the connection between the marketing plan and the marketing mix.
7. Describe how the elements of the marketing mix can be combined to produce synergistic effects.

What would a construction company be without the tools and equipment to get the job done? Enter CTF Supply Ltd. of Toronto. CTF, with 60 employees in six Ontario branches and two in British Columbia, rents and sells portable electric power tools, concrete anchors, screw products, and safety equipment to the construction industry—25 000 different items, to be exact.

In 1998, sales topped $16-million, a far cry from 1993, the lowest ebb of the recession. "By that year, we were down to $5-million in sales," says Robert Todd, president.

www.ctfsupply.com/
about.htm

"We'd lost five of our top 10 customers to bankruptcy; one was a suicide. I sat down with our guys and told them we had to get back to work. We had to look at everything we were doing and why we were doing it."

Mr. Todd and his managers created a list of what they wanted to accomplish—a total of 43 items—and then dug in. They created a 700-page catalogue, created a Web site to take customer orders, added nine new product lines, changed 16 suppliers, and began opening new stores. Stock on hand grew to four times its previous size.

"Now every manager submits a business plan," he says. "So does every counter person. To keep on track we have biweekly conference calls. We became much, much better planners."

Staff wasn't overlooked either. Along with greater responsibility came greater benefits. There's profit-sharing for people not on commission, for example, and a condo at the Deerhurst Resort for holidays.

"This company now has a team of highly trained professionals," he says. "We knew the business wasn't going anywhere unless we changed it, so change it we did."

CTF is a story of successful strategic market planning. Faced with near disaster, Mr. Todd and his executives analyzed their environment, identified opportunities, set marketing objectives, developed a marketing plan to achieve those objectives, and then regularly monitored performance to ensure that the plan was in fact unfolding as intended. No doubt the original plan, made in 1993, has been revised and modified many times over the ensuing years. In 1998, CTF was designated one of Canada's 50 Best Managed Private Companies by the *Financial Post*.

Source: Adapted from Deborah Stokes, Terrance Belford, and Robert Gibbens, "Finding Focus," *Financial Post* (December 28, 1998), p. C18. Reprinted with permission.

▶ INTRODUCTION

Long-term organizational success is never accidental. It results from managers being committed to providing benefits that customers need and want—or being market-oriented, as we discussed in Chapter 1. In Chapter 2 we saw that long-term success also implies that managers understand the environment in which the organization operates and are adapting to that environment. Chapters 3 and 4 pointed out that customer needs are too complex for any one product to satisfactorily meet everyone's needs, so the successful organization segments its markets. Chapter 5 highlights the fact that managers of successful organizations need information to aid their decision making.

Market orientation, sensitivity to the operating environment, segmentation, and market information are not in and of themselves sufficient to assure organizational success. These factors must be thoughtfully combined into a marketing strategy and plan that guide the organization.

Two main aspects of strategy formulation will be discussed in this chapter: strategy for the organization as a whole (corporate strategy), and marketing strategy. After marketing strategy has been established, the marketing plan can be developed (see Figure 6.1). You will find that discussing these concepts is relatively simple, but practitioners know that implementing them is extremely difficult.

▶ **FIGURE 6.1 An Overview of the Strategy and Marketing Planning Process**

▶ STRATEGY FOR THE ORGANIZATION AS A WHOLE

Strategy is the overall purpose and direction of the organization that is established in the light of the challenges and opportunities found in the environment, as well as available organizational resources. This is often referred to as **corporate strategy**. The process of developing a corporate strategy starts with analyzing market and environmental opportunities and threats facing the company as a whole. Simultaneously, the company undertakes an analysis of its own strengths and weaknesses. From this external and internal examination, the organization generates a list of *possible* alternative courses of action and objectives that could be followed. The next step involves evaluating and selecting the *most appropriate* alternative options for the organization. Finally, implementation and control programs must be planned for the strategy that has been developed. Figure 6.2 shows all five stages of the corporate strategy process.

Developing the corporate strategy is the responsibility of the head of the organization, and requires input from all the functional areas of the company (for example, finance, production, and marketing). The corporate strategy, in turn, gives direction in the form of objectives and intended resource allocation to the subunits of the corporation. These subgroups are often set up as distinct profit centres within the corporation and are usually referred to as strategic business units, or SBUs.

The strategy chosen is often expressed in a *mission statement*. This formal statement channels all of the organization's activities. From the mission statement, all individuals can determine which activities are appropriate to engage in and which are not. This keeps activities within the scope considered most suitable for the company. An example of a mission statement can be found in Table 6.1.

corporate strategy
The overall purpose and direction of the organization that is established in the light of the challenges and opportunities found in the environment, as well as available organizational resources.

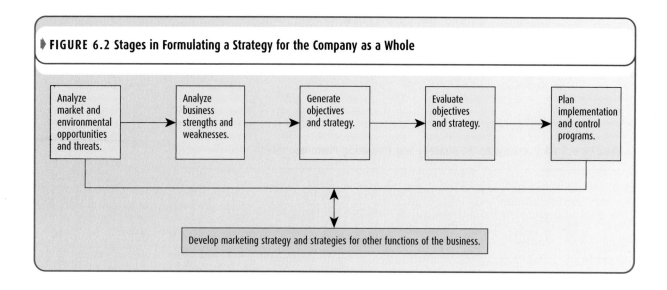

▶ **FIGURE 6.2 Stages in Formulating a Strategy for the Company as a Whole**

▶ **TABLE 6.1 Example of an Organizational Mission Statement**

Mission and Values
The Gillette Company is a globally focused consumer products company that seeks competitive advantage in quality, value-added personal care and personal use products. We compete in four large, worldwide businesses: personal grooming products, consumer portable power products, stationery products and small electrical appliances.

As a Company, we share skills and resources among business units to optimize performance. We are committed to a plan of sustained sales and profit growth that recognizes and balances both short- and long-term objectives.

Mission
Our mission is to achieve or enhance clear leadership, worldwide, in the existing or new core consumer product categories in which we choose to compete.

Source: Gillette Web site, "Mission and Values" page (http://www.gillette.com/company/mission.html), August 9, 1999.

▶ MARKETING STRATEGY

marketing strategy
A strategy that focuses on developing a unique long-run competitive position in the market by assessing consumer needs and the firm's potential for gaining competitive advantage.

Marketing strategy, which is based on the strategy set for the company as a whole, focuses on developing a unique long-run competitive position in the market by assessing consumer needs and the firm's potential for gaining competitive advantage.[1] Day and Wensley add that "[marketing] strategy is about seeking new edges in a market while slowing the erosion of present advantages.[2]

Knowing everything there is to know about the customer is not enough. To succeed, marketers must know the customer in a context that includes the competition, government policy and regulation, and the broader economic, social, and political macroforces that shape the evolution of markets. In other words, a strategic approach is necessary.

Figure 6.3 illustrates a marketing-oriented approach to strategy formulation and evaluation. This model extends the corporate strategy model depicted in Figure 6.2 and shows the important components of marketing strategy.

After receiving input from corporate-level strategies, the strategic marketing planning process unfolds in four main steps. (1) The **situation analysis** con-

situation analysis
Considers the internal circumstances of the organization or product, the external environment, competitive activity, and characteristics of the customer that may be relevant to the marketing plan.

▶ **FIGURE 6.3 The Strategic Marketing Planning Process**

Input from Corporate Strategies
• Mission
• Corporate objectives
• Strategic business unit (SBU) objectives

Situation Analysis
• Internal
• Environmental
• Customer
• Competitive

Marketing Objectives and Strategies
• Objectives
  – Profitability
  – Market share
  – Volume
• Strategies
  – Retrenchment
  – Status quo
  – Growth

Marketing Plan
• Product or service management
• Price
• Distribution
• Communication

Implementation and Control
• Measurable goals
• Benchmarks
• Feedback

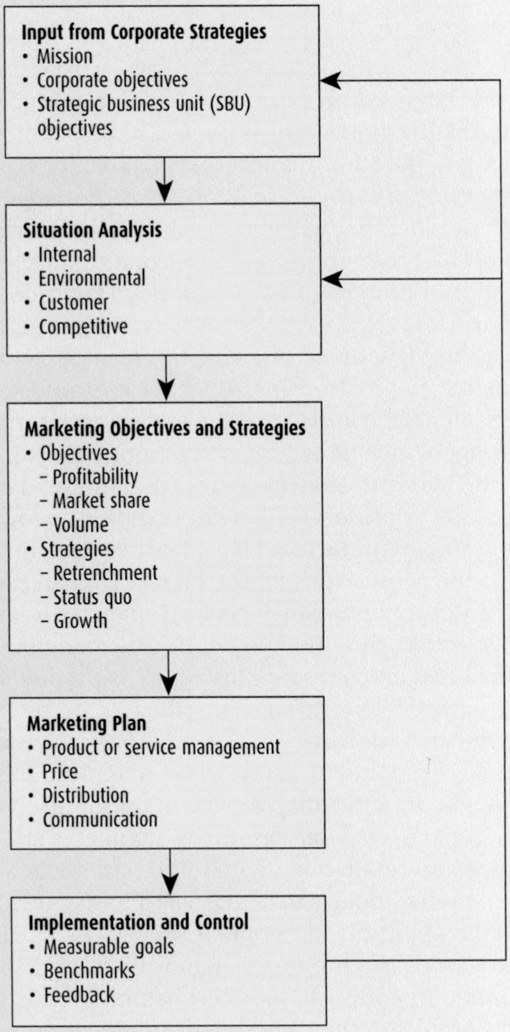

siders the internal circumstances of the organization or product, the external environment, competitive activity, and characteristics of the customer that may be relevant to the marketing plan. (2) The **marketing objectives and strategy** flow from the situation analysis. They are a statement of what the organization intends to accomplish with its marketing program and the general strategic approach it will take. (3) The **marketing plan** is a specific detailed statement of how the marketing mix will be used to realize the marketing strategy. (4) **Implementation and control** consist of putting the marketing plan into action as well as doing ongoing monitoring and gathering feedback on how well the plan is accomplishing the stated marketing objectives.

marketing objectives and strategy
Flow from the situation analysis. They are a statement of what the organization intends to accomplish with its marketing program and the general strategic approach it will take.

marketing plan
A specific detailed statement of how the marketing mix will be used to realize the marketing strategy.

implementation and control
Consist of putting the marketing plan into action as well as doing ongoing monitoring and gathering feedback on how well the plan is accomplishing the stated marketing objectives.

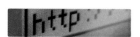

www.mcdonalds.com

www.harleycanada.com

www.pg.com

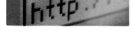

www.gm.com

▶ SITUATION ANALYSIS

Internal Analysis

A situation analysis begins with an internal analysis. Managers consider both the nature of the organization itself as well as the specific product or service being marketed. A key question managers will consider is whether the organization has, or can create, a *sustainable competitive advantage,* or SCA. An SCA is some aspect of the product that will give it value in the marketplace that cannot be easily duplicated by other companies. McDonald's has an SCA of consistency in its restaurants and product offerings. Harley-Davidson, on the other hand, builds on its SCA of legendary mystique. Robert Todd of CTF Supply Ltd., discussed in the opening vignette of this chapter, created an SCA of breadth and availability of construction tool inventory for his customers.

A realistic assessment of company resources is an important part of an internal analysis. Managers decide whether the organization has the financial resources to pursue certain strategies. Production, managerial, and human resources must also be considered. Sheldon Birney, the founder of Reliance, a Winnipeg company that manufactures plastic water jugs, related his mixed feelings when, early in the company's history, he received an extremely large order from a well-known department store chain. Convinced that he could not successfully service the order and unwilling to risk his fledgling company's reputation, he politely declined and set about building his production and sales capacity. Today, many years later, Reliance products can be found all over the world—including in that department store.[3] Many companies without Mr. Birney's managerial insight and discipline have outgrown their resource base by overly rapid expansion only to collapse back in on themselves.

In addition to SCAs and available resources, managers should review the past market performance and reputation of a product. Products that have performed well and have strong reputations can be used as a basis for further market gains. Procter & Gamble has built on the original success of its Head and Shoulders dandruff shampoo to create a full line of dandruff-related shampoos that share the same brand name. In contrast, poor-performing products with poor reputations must be supported in other ways or even discontinued. General Motors stopped producing the Corvair in the 1960s after the car's safety record was attacked.

A final important issue that must be considered when analyzing a company's internal situation is the product portfolio. The **product portfolio** is the complete collection of products or services that a company produces. Portfolio analysis is a very useful tool to apply when reviewing a firm's overall product mix.

A particularly well-known approach to portfolio analysis was developed by the Boston Consulting Group (BCG). The **BCG growth-share matrix**, shown in Figure 6.4, plots market share relative to the market share of the largest competitor, against market growth rate. All of a firm's various businesses or products can be plotted in one of the four quadrants. The resulting quadrants are labelled Cash Cows, Stars, Dogs, and Question Marks, and BCG suggests a unique marketing strategy for each one.

product portfolio
The complete collection of products or services that a company produces.

BCG growth-share matrix
Plots market share relative to the market share of the largest competitor, against market growth rate.

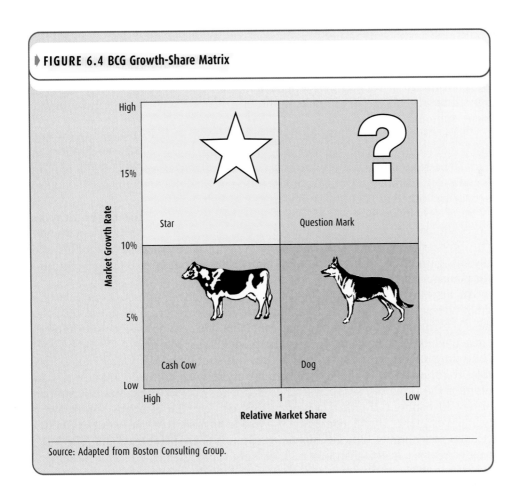

▶ **FIGURE 6.4 BCG Growth-Share Matrix**

Source: Adapted from Boston Consulting Group.

- *Cash Cows* (dominant market share in a market with low growth): Cash Cows are the main source of earnings and cash to support growth areas. Marketing planners want to maintain this situation for as long as possible, since it produces a strong cash flow. The objective is to maximize cash flow while maintaining market share.
- *Stars* (dominant market share in a market with high growth): While this type of business produces profits, it requires heavy cash consumption to maintain

a leading market position. If this share can be maintained until growth of the market slows, Stars may become high dollar earners. In the meantime, Stars may even produce a negative cash flow. Such products require considerable management attention.

- *Dogs* (small market share in a market with low growth): This type of business generally consumes too much management attention. Usually, the company should minimize its position in this market area, pulling investment from it and withdrawing completely if possible.
- *Question Marks* (small market share in a market with high growth): Question Mark enterprises must achieve a dominant position before growth slows, or they will be frozen in a marginal position and become Dogs. Because they demand a heavy commitment from limited financial and management resources, their number in the portfolio should be restricted. These situations require that marketers make a basic go–no go decision. Unless Question Marks can be converted to Stars, the firm should pull out of these markets.

The BCG matrix highlights the importance of creating a mix that works to the best advantage of the firm. It emphasizes the importance of having common agreed-upon goals for all products in the firm's portfolio. Many variations of this basic approach are now in use.

There are some difficulties with the matrix. Many so-called Dogs can be, and are, extremely profitable. Further, whether a product is labelled a Dog or a Cash Cow depends on how the product's market is defined. If we look at the market for cars, for example, a Lamborghini is a Dog; if we define our market as luxury sport cars valued at $200 000 or higher, it's a Cash Cow.

More seriously, critics of the BCG approach argue that the health of Cash Cows can be seriously damaged if resources are constantly being drained without appropriate levels of reinvestment. As with all management models, the insights gained by applying the BCG matrix should not be used as a substitute for managerial ability.

www.ge.com

An alternative to the market growth–market share approach to portfolio analysis was developed by General Electric. Usually referred to as the GE business screen, it is a 3 x 3 matrix that considers business strengths and industry attractiveness. The basic premise of the model is that businesses should be concentrating on opportunities in which they are strong and the industry is attractive. If either or both of those factors are merely average, a company should monitor the situation, accept earnings that it may be enjoying, but be cautious of new investment. If either or both factors are poor, the company should avoid new investment. If the company is already involved in the area, it should attempt to withdraw. The GE business screen is shown in Figure 6.5. The business screen is a useful planning tool, because it provides an effective method of evaluating SBUs at the corporate level and individual product opportunities at the SBU, or marketing, level. In actual practice, applying the screen is an extremely sophisticated matter that involves the careful quantitative analysis and rating of up to twelve different factors for each axis.

When the various aspects of the internal situation have been considered, the internal analysis is usually summarized as a list of strengths and weaknesses. Strengths are any internal factor, such as a well-known and respected brand name, that a company can use to contribute to future success. Weaknesses are any internal shortcomings, such as a poorly trained sales force, that must be overcome before the company can achieve success.

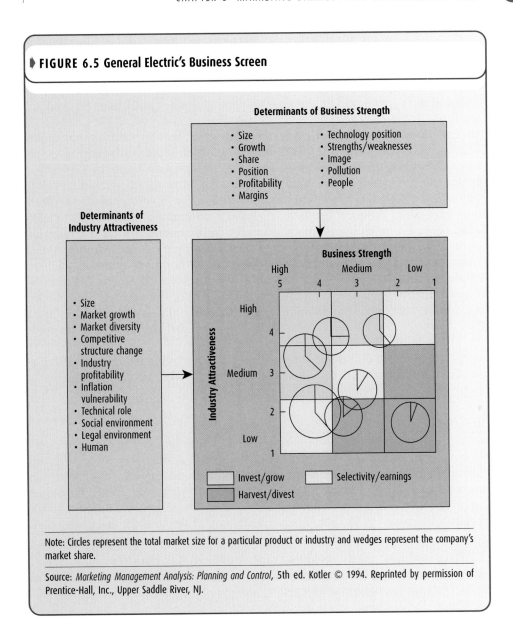

FIGURE 6.5 General Electric's Business Screen

Determinants of Business Strength

- Size
- Growth
- Share
- Position
- Profitability
- Margins
- Technology position
- Strengths/weaknesses
- Image
- Pollution
- People

Determinants of Industry Attractiveness

- Size
- Market growth
- Market diversity
- Competitive structure change
- Industry profitability
- Inflation vulnerability
- Technical role
- Social environment
- Legal environment
- Human

Business Strength

	High	Medium	Low
	5 4	3	2 1

Industry Attractiveness

High — 4
Medium — 3
Low — 2
1

Invest/grow   Selectivity/earnings
Harvest/divest

Note: Circles represent the total market size for a particular product or industry and wedges represent the company's market share.

Source: *Marketing Management Analysis: Planning and Control*, 5th ed. Kotler © 1994. Reprinted by permission of Prentice-Hall, Inc., Upper Saddle River, NJ.

Environmental Analysis

When the internal examination of the company is complete, the situation analysis continues with an environmental analysis. Chapter 2 discussed the importance of the environment in detail. From a marketing planning perspective, the understanding of the environment should be distilled into major issues, events, or trends that could affect, positively or negatively, an organization's success in the marketplace. This distillation of issues is often presented under the headings of opportunities and threats. Opportunities are environmental issues or trends that a company can use to its advantage. Threats are issues or trends that may interfere with an organization's ability to thrive. Sometimes the same factor can be an opportunity for one company but a threat for another. For example, the demographic trend of an aging population is an opportunity for developers of retirement communities, for manufacturers of products traditionally used by an older population such as Metamucil, or even for funeral homes. On the other hand, it could be perceived as a threat by Fisher-Price or Gerber baby food company, both of whom depend on a growing base of young children and babies for success.

SWOT analysis
The combined summary of the internal analysis and the environmental analysis. Stands for *strengths, weaknesses, opportunities,* and *threats.*

The combined summary of the internal analysis and the environmental analysis is widely abbreviated as a **SWOT analysis**, which stands for *strengths, weaknesses, opportunities,* and *threats.* Examining the first two boxes of Figure 6.2 reveals that corporate planners have already gone through a parallel exercise. Although the description of the process is similar for large corporations, these steps imply very different levels of analysis. A corporate planner at The Coca-Cola Company, for example, might consider "thirst quenchers" as the relevant competition, and based on that analysis, give input to the Minute Maid, Powerade, and Diet Coke units of the company. In contrast, a market planner within the Diet Coke unit would probably concentrate on Diet Pepsi as the primary competition while also monitoring the actions of store brands of diet cola. In a similar way, all of the strategic analysis undertaken at the corporate level of large organizations tends to be at a higher level of abstraction than at the product, or marketing, level. At the same time, for smaller organizations, there is often little practical difference between strategic marketing planning and strategic corporate planning, with the one flowing seamlessly into the other.

www.coca-cola.com

Customer Analysis

We have emphasized repeatedly that understanding and being in tune with the customer's needs is the very heart of successful marketing. Customer analysis has an important role to play in developing marketing strategy. In customer analysis, both market segmentation, discussed in Chapters 3 and 4, and market research, discussed in Chapter 5, have a role to play. In general, there are seven questions marketers should ask about their customers:

1. Who are our actual and potential customers?
2. Why do they buy our product?
3. Why do noncustomers *not* buy our product?
4. Where do our customers buy our product?
5. How do they buy it?
6. When do they buy it?
7. What do they do with our product?[4]

With the seven customer usage questions answered, plus additional input from market research, the marketer can then consider the issue of segmentation.

Each segment must first be subjected to an analysis by positioning. This means that the competing companies and brands in each segment are identified, and their positioning in the segment is indicated. For example, in the business microcomputer segment, Compaq, IBM, Apple, and a number of other manufacturers compete. IBM and Compaq position themselves as the firms with leading-edge technology and high quality. Apple is positioned as providing the most user-friendly and versatile quality computer. Several clones also compete in this segment, and will be positioned as providing various combinations of features at a low price (see Figure 6.6). IBM and Compaq are adopting a head-to-

www.compaq.ca/English/
atcompaq/atcompaq.htm

www.can.ibm.com

www.apple.com

head positioning strategy—directly taking each other on in the microcomputer market. On the other hand, Apple with its iMac has chosen to follow a differentiation strategy—distinguishing itself from IBM and Compaq on user-friendliness. In its 1999 advertisements, Apple used its multicoloured computer casings as an indicator, or cue, of that difference.

▶ **FIGURE 6.6 Positioning Map for Business Microcomputer Segment**

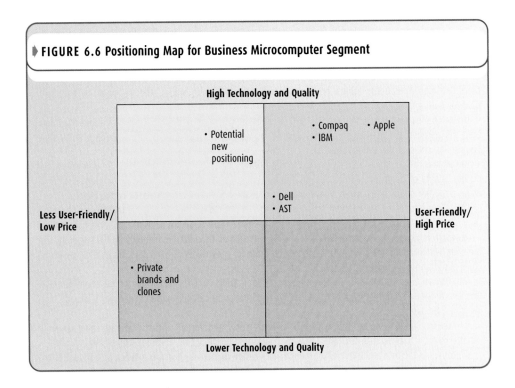

High Technology and Quality

• Potential new positioning

• Compaq • Apple
• IBM

• Dell
• AST

Less User-Friendly/ Low Price

User-Friendly/ High Price

• Private brands and clones

Lower Technology and Quality

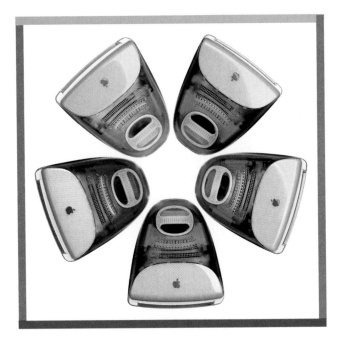

In the business microcomputer segment, Apple positions its computers as the most user-friendly. The company's new "fruit-flavoured" iMac even *looks* friendly—and stands out.

▶ THE PRACTISING MARKETER

www.secondcup.com

Second Cup Is Stirring Up Business

Second Cup Ltd. is now offering its coffee on planes, trains, and grocery aisles and making little money at it. That's the plan.

For example, the Toronto-based specialty coffee retailer says its effort to land partnerships with Air Canada and Via Rail in the past 18 months isn't meant to make a bundle on the more than 22 million cups consumed in transit each year, but to give passengers a taste of what they might be missing.

"I don't make a lot of money on those programs," says Randy Powell, chief executive officer of Second Cup's Canadian operations. "Those programs aren't meant to make money, they're meant to be a self-paid-for trial vehicle."

Under the leadership of chairman and CEO Michael Bregman, Second Cup has already more than doubled the number of Canadian stores this decade, as well as established control of the 316-unit Coffee People Inc. chain in the United States.

In Canada, the company built its market-leading brand the way most restaurateurs do. It concentrated on the quality of its product, store design, and locations, Mr. Powell says. "The only problem with that, or let's say the opportunity when I got here, was that we had very low household penetration.

"Very few people in Canada were actually coming into our stores because for one reason—not because they didn't like us, they loved it when they tried us—they were unaware of us."

Research indicates that only between 5 and 5.5 percent of Canadian households visit a specialty coffee shop within a two-week period, leaving much room for growth, Mr. Powell says. He estimates Second Cup's penetration at about 2.5 percent.

(Mr. Powell used to work for Toronto-based Campbell Soup Co. Ltd., which has a household penetration in a month of about 98 percent. "You try growing the soup category when everybody's already buying you," he says.)

One reason this part of the coffee sector has such a low penetration is that there are many areas in Canada where it's difficult to find any specialty coffee retailer, let alone a Second Cup outlet.

Vancouver is the most mature market for specialty coffee in Canada. And if it is taken as a model, there is room for the industry to more than double the number of cafés or outlets in Canada's top markets alone, Mr. Powell says. If Seattle is taken as the model, then there is potential to almost triple the number of stores, he adds.

To get Second Cup's share of that potential, Mr. Powell has set a two-prong strategy for its Canadian operations.

Second Cup, known for its quality coffees and in-store ambiance, is seeking to grow its customer base.

Caramel Corretto
A tempting blend of espresso with creamy caramel and mellow vanilla, topped with caramel drizzled over frothed milk.

Crème Brûlée RISTRETTO
A delectable espresso creation with the caramelized sugar taste of a classic crème brûlée, crowned with caramel drizzled over whipped cream.

Mocca Mandarino
A velvety medley of espresso, rich chocolate and orange under a cloud of foamed milk sprinkled with tangy orange zest.

First, Second Cup will continue to expand locations in order to get closer to more customers.

Second, the company is striving to raise awareness of its brand through increased marketing and partnerships with transportation firms and grocers that are designed to drive more customers into its cafés.

Andrew Stodart, president of Toronto-based Brand Builders, says the partnerships are a good strategy for Second Cup to attract new customers, but the company must ensure it delivers the same quality that it does in the café.

"If they can't do that, then I think they have a serious problem because what they're setting themselves up for is trial and rejection," Mr. Stodart says.

It's something that has concerned Second Cup in the past. The company argues it's more in the business

(continued)

> ► **THE PRACTISING MARKETER** *(continued)*

of supplying the social experience of a café than simply selling coffee. Could they deliver that experience in a jet 35 000 feet above ground?

"That's the reason we stayed away from it in the past," Mr. Powell says. "We didn't think we could duplicate the experience. You don't have to. All you have to do is drive a little awareness, a little trial, and get them into the cafés where the full experience can be had."

Second Cup is taking the same approach in the grocery sector, where it has established stand-alone displays of ground and whole bean coffee for sale in several supermarkets in Quebec, Ontario, and Alberta since August 1998.

The company will closely study the results of 12 planned test sites, as well as the use of such tie-ins as coupons on the grocery packaging that can be redeemed at the cafés, Mr. Powell says.

Because the program is designed to improve sales in its chain, Second Cup has secured guarantees from the grocers that they won't undercut the prices charged by the cafés for the same coffee, he says.

The company itself expects to make some money from the grocery program, but it won't be much, Mr. Powell says.

"That's not why we're doing it, though. That to me is all gravy," he says. "The reason we're doing it is to get people back in the cafés. And you know and I know I make my money in cafés."

Is Second Cup practising penetration, product development, market development, or diversification?

Source: Excerpted from Casey Mahood, "Second Cup Stirring Up Business," *The Globe and Mail* (August 24, 1998), pp. B1 and B6. Reprinted with permission from *The Globe and Mail*.

The result of this analysis is the identification of certain segments and positions that are deemed worthy of further consideration. Many different reasons could lead to the decision to consider a segment further — for example, size of market, an opportunity to position a product where there is little competition, or evidence that existing competition can be overcome.

Next, as Chapter 4 discusses, a more thorough analysis of the selected segments is undertaken. One method of doing this is by conducting a more focused SWOT analysis. A SWOT analysis helps to develop a picture of the situation faced by a business. For example, within the above-mentioned microcomputer segment, a firm might have a unique product (a strength), but limited additional funds for advertising (a weakness). This strongly affects the type of marketing program that can be developed.

Following this, the positioning analysis shown in Figure 6.6 makes it possible to clearly identify areas of opportunity. In our example, the upper left quadrant has no other direct competitors. If the size of that market is significant, the company might design a product to match that segment.

It is also necessary to have a realistic assessment of the current or potential threats faced within the market segment. For example, companies with two closely positioned products, such as Compaq and IBM, can see that there are threats posed by each other, as well as by other companies that might be trying to move in for a share of their position. Management should carefully select the most desirable bases for segmentation and positioning to encompass all of the firm's current and potential offerings.

Competitive Analysis

A major objective in strategic planning is to create and sustain competitive advantage. Therefore, along with customer analysis, competitor analysis is fundamental. In addition to identifying the relative positions of competitors, an effective strategy for dealing with competitors is essential. For example, if you should develop a new soft drink that is as good as or better than Pepsi, you would be foolish to develop a plan for marketing it without taking into consideration the competitive response of Pepsi if that company thought you might threaten its market share.

Competitive analysis is an important component of situation analysis.

PEANUTS reprinted by permission of United Feature Syndicate, Inc.

Competitor assessment leads some firms to specialize in particular market segments. Others with greater resources compete in a broad range of product markets in several areas of the world. Determining a competitive strategy involves answering five questions:

1. Who are our competitors, and what are their strengths and weaknesses?
2. What is our competitors' strategy, and what will be their likely response to our competitive moves?
3. Should we compete?
4. If so, in what markets should we compete?
5. How should we compete?

The first question, "Who are our competitors?" focuses attention on the various potential challenges to be faced to gain a share of the market. Firms sometimes enter a market with an inadequate understanding of the extent of the competition. Or, if they are already established, firms sometimes respond poorly to the entrance of a new and powerful competitor. In Canadian retailing, the responses of various firms to the entrance of the powerful Wal-Mart chain is a good example. Zellers and Canadian Tire anticipated that they would be some of the most affected retailers. Each studied the Wal-Mart operation carefully and made adjustments to its pricing and advertising to compete. As discussed in Chapter 2, two types of competition must be clearly identified: inter-product, and product-substitute competition.

HOW TO ASSESS COMPETITIVE ADVANTAGE

Peter Chandler suggests two steps for thinking strategically about gaining competitive advantage:

1. Think through your own organization's strategic capabilities, and also how you can link these business processes to serve customer needs in a way that is superior to your competitors.
2. Read everything you can about how other organizations in other industries and countries are gaining competitive advantage. "To be ignorant of how others are succeeding is a bit like fighting set piece trench warfare as occurred in World War I. The smart commander will be looking outside the square to see what new forces or approaches can be brought to bear."[5]

The second question, "What is our competitors' strategy?" points out that a marketing strategy cannot be developed in a vacuum. It must be at least as good as, more effective than, or different from that of competitors. Often a great deal of creativity is required to come up with a winning plan.

The third question, "Should we compete?" should be answered based on the resources and objectives of the firm and the expected profit potential for the firm. In some instances, potentially successful ventures are not considered due to a lack of a match between the venture and the overall organizational objectives. For example, a clothing manufacturer may reject an opportunity to diversify through purchasing a profitable chain of retail clothing stores. Or a producer of industrial chemicals might refrain from entering the consumer market and instead sell chemicals to another firm that is familiar with serving consumers at the retail level.

In other cases, a critical issue is expected profit potential. If the expected profits are insufficient to pay an adequate return on the required investment, then the firm should consider other lines of business. Many organizations have switched from less profitable ventures quite efficiently. This decision should be subject to continual re-evaluation so that the firm avoids being tied to traditional markets with declining profit margins. It is also important to anticipate competitive responses.

"In what markets should we compete?" Whatever decision is made acknowledges that the firm has limited resources (engineering and productive capabilities, sales personnel, advertising budgets, research and development, and the like) and that these resources must be allocated to the areas of greatest opportunity. Too many firms have taken a "shotgun" approach to market selection and thus do an ineffective job in many markets rather than a good one in selected markets.

"How should we compete?" is the fifth question. It requires the firm's marketers to make the decisions involved in setting up a comprehensive marketing strategy.

▶ THE CANADIAN MARKETPLACE

How We Get Pizza at Home

Pizza restaurants that deliver are facing stiff competition not only from each other but from homemade and frozen pizza as well. What should restaurants do to increase their share of the total pizza market?

(continued)

▶ THE CANADIAN MARKETPLACE *(continued)*

▶ **How We Get Pizza at Home, October 1997–March 1998**

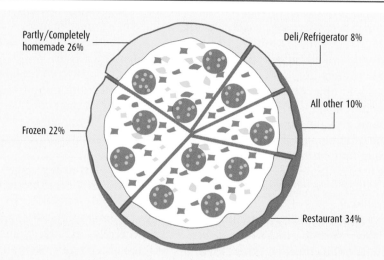

Partly/Completely homemade 26%

Deli/Refrigerator 8%

All other 10%

Frozen 22%

Restaurant 34%

Source: Casey Mahood, National Eating Trends, "Pizza Makers Say It's Tougher to Make Dough," *The Globe and Mail* (January 18, 1999), p. B4.

Who can tell it from take out?

McCain Rising Crust Pizza

DELUXE

Pizza restaurants face stiff competition from frozen pizzas, such as those made by McCain.

▶MARKETING OBJECTIVES AND STRATEGY

Profit-oriented firms usually state objectives in terms of desired market share, or sales or profitability targets. Frequently, more than one issue will be considered simultaneously. For example, a firm might set an objective of a 15 percent return on investment, subject to market share remaining at or above 22 percent. In other words, the firm's objectives imply that executives might be willing to sacrifice profits in the short term in order to protect market share.

Not-for-profit organizations more often express their objectives in terms of level of services provided, number of clients served, and funds raised. Each year, the United Way establishes a national objective and then a city-by-city objective for fundraising. Once objectives are established, strategies must be developed to achieve the objectives.

At the level of the marketplace—what you see as you watch commercials, check out flyers, and walk around retail outlets—there is an endless variety of marketing strategies and accompanying tactics. When reduced to their most basic level, though, there are really three strategies that a firm can pursue: retrenchment, status quo, or growth.

Firms can choose to pull back from the marketplace by following a *retrenchment* strategy. Retrenchment implies that a company has narrowed its product line, reduced its geographic scope by closing some locations, or tried to cut costs in some significant way. More often, retrenchment involves all three activities. Major retrenchment signals a retreat from the marketplace and is usually only pursued in times of crisis. Eaton's went through a retrenchment in the late 1990s by closing more than twenty unprofitable stores and shedding some low-margin, high-cost product lines such as major appliances. By the end of 1999 it was clear that even these actions would not save the venerable retailer, and it was forced into bankruptcy. The history of Eaton's is discussed in more detail in Chapter 16. Kmart, another retailer, was forced to take even more drastic retrenchment measures than Eaton's. A few years after Wal-Mart entered the Canadian retailing scene, Kmart sold its Canadian operations to Zellers and retreated to its U.S. base.

www.walmart.com

Status quo strategies are an attempt to maintain competitive equilibrium in a market. A firm that uses this strategy defends its position in a market but does not aggressively pursue increased market share. Some would argue that the entire Canadian retail sector was pursuing a status quo strategy before the appearance of Wal-Mart and the big-box stores such as Home Depot and Costco. A status quo strategy tends to leave a firm open to attack by aggressive competitors, as happened to Canadian retailers, and as a result it is rarely a marketer's conscious choice. In practice, most firms are pursuing a growth strategy.

www.zellers.ca

The product–market growth matrix, illustrated in Figure 6.7, is a convenient way to think about growth opportunities. The matrix is based on the observation that growth must come from some combination of existing or new products and existing or new markets. Growth strategies can take four forms.

Growth that comes from selling existing products in existing markets is penetration. It implies that current customers are buying more of the product. The dairy industry, with its many milk advertisements, pursues a penetration strategy. Growth through new products in existing markets is called product devel-

> **FIGURE 6.7 Product–Market Growth Matrix**

MARKET \ PRODUCT	Present	New
Present	Penetration	Product development
New	Market development	Diversification

www.generalmills.com

opment. When General Mills produced Honey Nut, Frosted, and Apple Cinnamon Cheerios, it was following a product development strategy. Selling existing products in new markets is called market development. The strategy involves either appealing to buyers in a different geographical area or appealing to a different segment in a served area. Finally, creating new products for new markets is called diversification.

Within each of the three broad strategies and each of the growth strategies that a firm can follow, several more specific strategies can be considered: focus, niche, low-cost, and differentiation.

Microsoft is a very large company, but it became large by pursuing a very focused strategy and market—high-volume microcomputer software. Most other companies of Microsoft's size are widely diversified across many different markets. Focused strategies concentrate on single, but large, markets.

Netscape, in contrast to Microsoft, has been following a niche strategy, concentrating on Web browser software. Niche strategies pursue smaller subsegments of large markets. Adesemi Communications, discussed in the opening vignette of Chapter 3, is pursuing a niche strategy.

Low-cost strategies are difficult to accomplish but extremely powerful if achieved. Wal-Mart is feared by other retailers because it has persistently and aggressively reduced its costs until they are lower than competitors'. That implies that Wal-Mart can set prices in a range that severely squeezes, or eliminates altogether, other retailers' profit margins while still making a profit for itself. (Note the distinction between a low-cost strategy and low prices—it's easy to lower prices but very difficult to lower costs.)

Finally, a differentiation strategy seeks to create a point of distinction between a product or service and that of competitors. Differentiation is the foundation of most successful marketing campaigns. Dr. Pepper has cheerfully pursued a differentiation strategy for years. Differentiation is the strategy behind product positioning and market segmentation discussed in Chapters 3 and 4.

Each of these strategies has different implications for the total marketing program put together by the organization. Those implications must be systematically considered and accommodated in the marketing plan.

▸ THE ETHICAL MARKETER

The Dark Side of Hockey Cards

There's a hidden danger lurking in the harmless activity of collecting hockey cards, a California law firm claims.

Every time a child buys a pack of cards, they're being lured into an illegal and exploitative racket, says the firm Milberg Weiss Bershad Hynes & Lerach. It has begun a class-action lawsuit against the National Hockey League, the NHL Players Association, and six other professional sports organizations, claiming sports cards are a kind of lottery with the odds stacked against collectors.

Kids buy the cards in the hopes of finding valuable "chase cards" randomly inserted into the packages. Buyers stand only a small chance of getting those coveted cards, such as the rare Wayne Gretzky card that contains small patches of a jersey he wore during a game.

As these are worth $500 or more to collectors, consumers are manipulated to keep buying until they find a package with one of the "artificially scarce" cards, the suit claims. This creates a "chase mania" and keeps kids spending until they hit a winner, it says.

The plaintiffs contend that sports card marketing satisfies the criteria for a lottery because consumers pay for a chance by buying the card package, have certain odds of receiving a chase card, and, if they're lucky, receive a prize with a cash value in the form of a chase card.

"Major league sports claim they're anti-gambling, and they're out there encouraging kids to gamble" said lawyer Kevin Roddy, who leads the litigation.

Mr. Roddy has assembled statements from addiction experts who will testify that "chase mania" is a form of gambling.

"What is particularly scary to the experts is that, whatever it is that makes certain adults get addicted to gambling, it's four times stronger in kids," he said. "They are less able to resist."

The NHL disagrees. "We do not believe that this case has any merit, and we intend to defend it vigorously," said Frank Brown, vice-president for media relations. The defendants have moved to dismiss the claim.

www.nhl.com/nhlhq

From the NHL's perspective, the organization is practising market penetration—encouraging its current customers to buy more of its products. Do you feel that the approach the NHL has taken is ethical, or do you agree with Mr. Roddy? If you feel that the NHL is not behaving ethically, is it possible to have an ethical penetration strategy when marketing a product that will be purchased primarily by children? Explain.

Source: Excerpted from Glen McGregor, "Lawyers Talk of Dark Side of Collecting Hockey Cards" *The Ottawa Citizen* in the *National Post* (February 1, 1999), pp. A1 and A2. Reprinted with permission.

▸ THE MARKETING PLAN

The marketing plan is a detailed statement of how the marketing mix will be used to realize the marketing strategy. In marketing planning, the first question to be addressed is "What should be included in the plan?" How can the planner have confidence that the marketing plan developed accomplishes the strategy that has been set out and includes the appropriate planning elements? The criterion for a marketing plan should be that it leads to organization effectiveness.

▶ THE PRACTISING MARKETER

www.globalte.com

Global Thermoelectric Inc. Fires Up New Products

The U.S. Army was looking for a few good vehicle heaters—ones that wouldn't catch fire and explode as previous models had during the Persian Gulf War.

Meanwhile, Global Thermoelectric Inc. of Calgary was eager to diversify its product line beyond a narrow niche of low maintenance, gas-fired generators.

It was a match made in heaven—or hell, considering Uncle Sam's tough specifications. The army wanted a heater that could start up in -48°C weather.

"We're good at applications involving heat and electricity. That's what our generators are, so the idea of heaters was not difficult to come up with," Global president Jim Perry says.

In a testing showdown, Global's prototype vehicle heater beat out entries from two U.S. rivals. It landed the $18-million army contract in 1996 for two-foot-long, tube-shaped heaters.

Production of the vehicle heaters began in 1998, marking a key stage in the diversification of this small, formerly one-product company. Global has been looking for ways to smooth out its annual sales between giant contracts for its trademark generators.

Winner of a Canada Export Award for 1998, Global is now supplying heaters for 2000 of the army's vehicles, including tanks and personnel carriers, with a possibility to provide up to 2000 more.

Global is hardly an overnight success story. Founded in 1975, its mainstay product has been its generator technology, adapted from models developed by the Minnesota Mining & Manufacturing Co. (3M) for moon landings.

While the original 3M generator used radioactive isotopes for fuel on the moon, Global's version relies on natural gas. Because it has no moving parts, the device requires as little as one hour of maintenance a year.

But while Global had a unique product, the company was largely run by scientists until 1993. Without a strong business orientation, it hobbled along for two decades as a mainly scientific venture, kept alive in part by research grants and later through an Alberta government ownership stake.

It was only in 1993, when the government sold its stake to Edmonton venture capital firm Foundation Equity Corp., that Global began to take full commercial advantage of its technology. It went public in 1994 with a preferred share offering on the Alberta Stock Exchange.

The company worked to smooth out its spotty profit record and solidify its position as the leading supplier of thermoelectric generators for remote use—now with more than 95 percent of the world market.

Global's main customers are natural gas pipeline manufacturers that need electricity along the pipe route to power cathodic protection that keeps the metal from rusting.

"Whenever anybody builds a gas pipeline we are one of the only good choices," says Mr. Perry, 51, a former petroleum executive recruited in 1997.

In fact, annual revenue has grown at the compound rate of 37 percent over the past five years, to $16.3-million in fiscal 1998 from $3.4-million in 1993.

But despite this growth, Global realized years ago it had to develop alternative sources of revenue, in addition to its large generator contracts. For example, sales in 1998 exceeded 1997 levels by 68 percent, largely because of two major contracts—a $3.2-million deal with India and a $1.8-million pact with China.

"The market doesn't like lumpy sales and lumpy earnings," says analyst Michael Hill with Acumen Capital Partners in Calgary, who follows Global.

When it came to diversification, Global had built up a rich base of research after 20 years of scientific tinkering, but nothing commercial had emerged beyond the gpenerators.

What the U.S. Army's heater contract offered Global was a chance to take some of its existing technology and adapt it.

Growth was rapid at Global in 1998 as production of the heaters came on line at its manufacturing facility in Bassano, Alta., 100 kilometres east of Calgary.

(continued)

▶ THE PRACTISING MARKETER *(continued)*

The company has boosted its work force by more than 20 percent to 100, including highly skilled welders who have been in great demand in Alberta's hot economy. Global's recruiting task grew easier in 1998 as plunging oil prices cooled down a hot labour market.

Meanwhile, Global is finding other markets for its generators, including telecommunication repeater stations and long-distance monitoring of oil and gas wells.

Next on the diversification drawing board are solid fuel cells for higher-power applications. Global has purchased the technology from a German lab and is working to develop cells fuelled by gas that can power cell towers or cable TV systems in remote locations.

What were Global Thermoelectric's objectives? What strategy was the company following?

Source: Adapted from Steven Chase, "Global Fires Up New Products," *The Globe and Mail* (October 16, 1998), p. B11. Reprinted with permission from *The Globe and Mail*.

How does a manager know whether the plans made will be effective or not? Contingency theory, which originated in the organizational behaviour literature, provides some excellent guidance. This theory argues that managerial decisions are not right or wrong per se. They must be made and assessed in the light of the circumstances surrounding the decisions. For example, if profits are falling because of declining sales, a decision to reduce or increase advertising might depend on whether the drop is caused by lack of awareness of the product or adverse economic conditions (people know about the product but have no money). Therefore, a marketing plan should be based on a careful analysis of the key factors in the business environment. In a generic sense, most firms face the following conditions. Since the importance of each condition varies according to the individual firm's situation, it is impossible to present an exhaustive set.

Increasing Competition

The current environment is characterized by intense and increasing competitiveness. Some authors have argued that marketing strategy should be based on a competitive rather than a marketing orientation.[6] This is an extreme position. However, increased competition can be observed in several ways:

- *Intertype competition.* Firms readily cross industry lines to compete if they think they can apply their technology to another field (for example, agricultural companies may begin producing recreational vehicles, or computer software firms may play a leading role in producing machine tools and industrial robots).
- *International competition.* A fundamental strategy of most countries today is to increase exports. Alert companies are responding. Consequently, domestic firms are finding aggressive new competitors facing them in traditional domestic markets.

- *More demanding economic conditions.* As a result of the economic decline in the early 1980s, virtually all firms had to become more efficient and aggressive in order to survive. Many continued this posture as the economy turned around. Through the business cycles of the 1990s, it was clear that a prolonged period of intense domestic and worldwide competition had turned into the norm for business.

To take account of these conditions, a marketing plan should have a realistic assessment of the competitive domestic and worldwide industry environment. It should also include a statement of current market share, and a recognition of the shares and strategies of leading competitors. The plan should include an analysis of competitive strengths and weaknesses, and a forecast of market demand.

Dynamic Consumer Society

Today's marketplace is characterized by fragmented, rapidly changing, sophisticated consumers. More products have emerged to more precisely meet tastes and higher consumer expectations. International travel and world communication have added to this sophistication. A marketing plan must include a thorough analysis of current customer motivations and trends.

Hi-Tech Environment

Computers have revolutionized products and services. The inherent nature of many products, as well as their design and production, has changed. For example, the microchips now commonly built into such products as telephones and tools enable functions unheard of a few years ago. Many services are similarly affected.

Social Consciousness

An acute sensitivity to ecological issues continues to grow. The marketplace is showing evidence of the desire for a clean environment, as well as environmentally friendly products. In a related development, the requirements for socially responsible business behaviour continue to increase. If changes do not happen voluntarily, governmental regulation and legislation may be expected.

A comprehensive marketing plan should explicitly take such factors into consideration. Failing this, contingency theory suggests that it would be more difficult for the organization to be effective and competitive, and that the firm will sooner or later fall out of phase with its competitors and the environment.

Planning Process Requirements

For every marketing plan statement, a system for expeditiously developing a complete plan is necessary. Possible elements of such a system include identifying problems and opportunities, conducting a postmortem of previous plans, stating alternative strategies considered, identifying risk factors, stating objectives, stating an action plan, and developing contingency plans.

Operational Organizational Requirements

In order to make it operational, each plan should also include a statement of objectives, a budget statement, a section identifying those responsible for executing the plan, and specific timetables and controls for the new plan.

Table 6.2 presents a model of how these important environmental features might be identified. It also shows the corresponding marketing planning activities required to operate effectively in the environment. This model can serve as a comprehensive guide for marketing planning.

When this model is used as a base for developing a marketing plan, decisions about whether to include a component of the plan are contingent on the conditions found in the environment. Following a contingency approach enables a firm to be more relevant in its planning. Because the process begins with a careful analysis of the environment, current conditions that are of direct significance as well as long-term trends can be identified and responded to. This process should also lead to a more comprehensive plan, as outlined in the right-hand column of the table.

What, then, should be included in a marketing plan? The answer can be determined from Table 6.2. The left-hand column shows the environmental conditions that must be addressed. The marketing plan should meet these new conditions. The right-hand column outlines the marketing plan components that are required to meet the conditions in the illustration. Obviously, as conditions change, different marketing plan components will be included, excluded, or emphasized.

Identifying key elements of the environment that must be responded to ensures that the marketing plan is focused on the right things. A further important advantage of this approach is that the marketing plan is not focused solely on current conditions. To properly understand the environment requires taking long-term trends into consideration. Providing that the organization's reward structure is not excessively focused on short-term results, a marketing plan based on current environmental conditions, as well as the forces behind them, will have a longer-term perspective. A more common description of a process for developing a marketing plan is shown in Figure 6.8. (It should in fact look familiar—we saw a less detailed version early in Chapter 3.)

Benetton has become famous for its signature social-awareness advertising campaigns. Its "United Colors" slogan, as seen in this advertisement, alludes to racial harmony.

▶ TABLE 6.2 Marketing Planning Model Based on Environmental Antecedents

ENVIRONMENTAL ANTECEDENTS	MARKETING PLAN REQUIREMENTS
Increasing Competition • Intertype competition • Increasing complexity of economic conditions • International competition	• Statement of market share • Recognition of shares and strengths of leading competitors • Analysis of competitive strengths and weaknesses • Forecast of market demand
Dynamic Consumer/Buyer Society • Rapid changes in tastes and behaviour • High customer expectations • Exposure to varied domestic and international mass media • Highly fragmented customer groups • Increasing customer sophistication	• Consideration of the changing needs of customers • Product life-cycle analysis • Market segmentation analysis • Product portfolio position analysis
Hi-Tech Environment • Effect of technology on – product design – product performance – price • Automation of production	• Technological trends statement
Social Consciousness • Health and safety issues • Clean/pure environment issues • Increasing expectations for responsible business behaviour • Expectations for proactive governmental regulation/ legislation	• Environmental issues statement • Consideration of government regulatory issues
Planning Process Requirements • Existence of a system for expeditiously developing a complete plan	• Identification of problems and opportunities • Postmortem of previous plans • Statement of alternative strategies considered • Identification of risk factors • Statement of objectives • Statement of action plan • Development of contingency plans
Operational Organizational Requirements • Guidance • Control • Financial responsibility • Efficiency	• Statement of objectives • Budget statement of proposed plan • Responsibility for execution pinpointed • Timetables and controls for the new plan specified

▶ **FIGURE 6.8 The Strategic Marketing Planning Process**

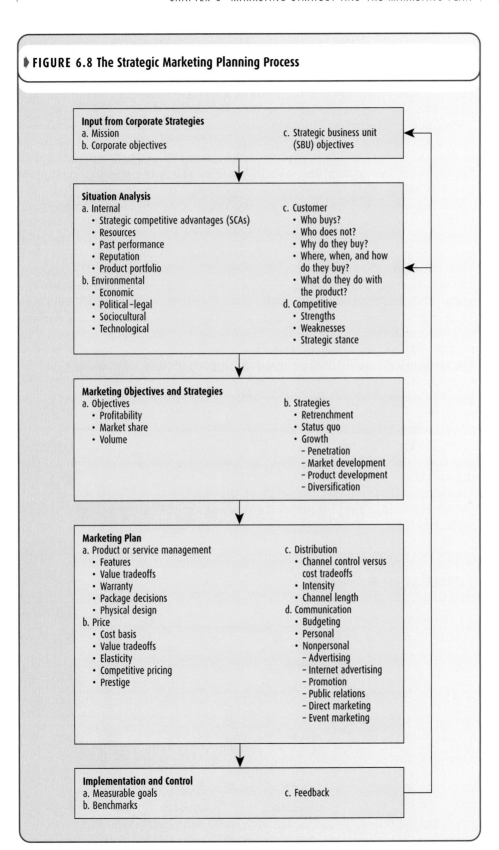

The Marketing Mix

Marketing plans address four main elements: product or service management, pricing, distribution, and communication. Each is an essential part of the marketing mix.

product management
Decisions about what kind of product is needed, its uses, package design, branding, trademarks, warranties, guarantees, product life cycles, and new product development.

Product management includes decisions about what kind of product is needed, its uses, package design, branding, trademarks, warranties, guarantees, product life cycles, and new product development. The marketer's concept of product takes into account the satisfaction of all consumer needs in relation to a good or service.

Pricing involves decisions concerning the methods of setting competitive, profitable, and justified prices. Most prices are freely set in Canada. However, some prices, such as those for public utilities and housing rentals, are regulated to some degree, and are therefore subject to public scrutiny.

pricing
The methods of setting competitive, profitable, and justified prices.

Distribution decisions involve the selection and management of marketing channels and the physical distribution of goods. **Marketing channels** are the steps or handling organizations that a good or service goes through from producer to final consumer. Channel decision making entails selecting and working with the institutional structure that handles the firm's goods or services. This includes wholesalers, retailers, and other intermediaries.

distribution
The selection and management of marketing channels and the physical distribution of goods.

Communication includes personal selling, advertising, sales promotion, and publicity. The marketing manager has many decisions to make concerning when, where, and how to use these elements of communication so that potential buyers will learn about and be persuaded to try the company's products.

marketing channels
The steps or handling organizations that a good or service goes through from producer to final consumer.

The marketing mix is sometimes called the "four P's" for ease of remembering: product, price, place, promotion. The rest of this book will be devoted largely to explaining these four marketing elements. The elements of the marketing mix are shown in Figure 6.9.

Starting with a careful evaluation of the market—using market segmentation—every marketing plan must take into consideration the appropriate prod-

communication
Personal selling, advertising, sales promotion, and publicity.

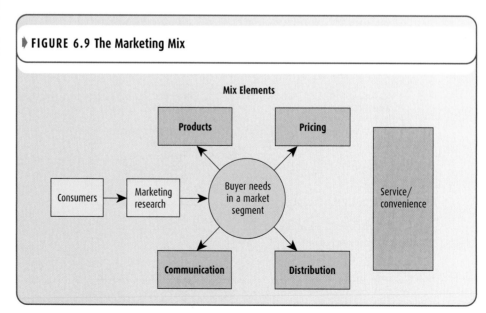

▶ **FIGURE 6.9 The Marketing Mix**

uct for a particular segment, the price that should be charged for it, and the appropriate outlet in which it ought to be sold. All of this information must be effectively communicated to the target market.

A quick examination of various companies' marketing programs shows that, even though they each have all the marketing variables, no two programs use them in exactly the same way. The *emphasis* and *use* of each can vary markedly. For example, the target market for McDonald's might be families with children. The company's products are standardized and reliable, but not considered to match the same calibre as those of Dubrovnik's, a famous Winnipeg restaurant that one might visit on an evening out. Dubrovnik's target market would be couples celebrating a special event or businesspeople entertaining their clients. Prices at McDonald's are low compared with those at the fine restaurant. In terms of distribution, it is important for McDonald's to have outlets at many locations, because consumers are not prepared to drive great distances to visit them. In contrast, people are fully prepared to drive downtown to the one Dubrovnik's location. McDonald's employs a communication program that involves extensive television advertising. Dubrovnik's counts on favourable word-of-mouth publicity, and purchases only a limited number of advertisements in local magazines and theatre guides.

▶ THE ROOTS OF MARKETING

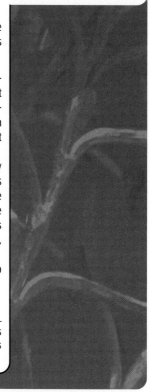

Interaction within the Marketing Mix

Since the notion of the marketing mix was first popularized by Neil H. Borden, many other writers have elaborated on it. In 1985 Benson P. Shapiro pointed out how important it is that the individual elements of the marketing mix fit together. His argument is summarized below.

The marketing mix concept emphasizes the fit of the various pieces and the quality and size of their interaction. There are three degrees of interaction. The least demanding is *consistency*—a logical and useful fit between two or more elements. It would seem generally inconsistent, for example, to sell a high-quality product through a low-quality retailer. It can be done, but the consumer must understand the reason for the inconsistency and respond favourably to it. Even more difficult is maintaining such an apparent inconsistency for a long time.

The second level of positive relationship among elements of the mix is *integration.* While consistency involves only a coherent fit, integration requires an active, harmonious interaction among the elements of the mix. For example, heavy advertising is sometimes harmonious with a high selling price because the added margin from the premium price pays for the advertising, and the heavy advertising creates the brand differentiation that justifies the high price. National brands of consumer packaged goods such as Tide laundry detergent, Campbell soup, and Colgate toothpaste use this approach. This does *not* mean, however, that heavy advertising and high product pricing are always harmonious.

The third—and most sophisticated—form of relationship is *synergy,* whereby each element is used to the best advantage in support of the total mix and results in effects greater than the sum of the parts.

Explain how an intelligent application of these concepts will provide customer satisfaction.

▸ THE ROOTS OF MARKETING

The First Marketing Mix List

▸ Elements of the Marketing Mix of Manufacturers

While we normally talk of the four main categories of the mix, it should be clearly understood that each of the mix elements can, and should, be divided into many subcategories when developing a marketing plan. For example, *communication* includes decisions about advertising, selling, and point-of-purchase promotion, to name a few. Neil Borden, who first coined the term "marketing mix," used to use the following much more extensive list in his teaching and consulting:

1. **Product Planning**
   Policies and procedures relating to
   a. Product lines to be offered—qualities, design, etc.
   b. Markets to sell—whom, where, when, and in what quantity.
   c. New-product policy—R & D program.

2. **Pricing**
   Policies and procedures relating to
   a. Price level to adopt.
   b. Specific prices to adopt—odd-even, etc.
   c. Price policy—one price or varying price, price maintenance, use of list prices, etc.
   d. Margins to adopt—for company, for the trade.

3. **Branding**
   Policies and procedures relating to
   a. Selection of trademarks.
   b. Brand policy—individualized or family brand.
   c. Sale under private label or unbranded.

4. **Channels of Distribution**
   Policies and procedures relating to
   a. Channels to use between plant and consumer.
   b. Degree of selectivity among wholesalers and retailers.
   c. Efforts to gain cooperation of the trade.

5. **Personal Selling**
   Policies and procedures relating to
   a. Burden to be placed on personal selling and the methods to be employed in:
      • Manufacturer's organization.
      • Wholesale segment of the trade.
      • Retail segment of the trade.

6. **Advertising**
   Policies and procedures relating to
   a. Amount to spend—i.e., burden to be placed on advertising.
   b. Copy platform to adopt:
      • Product image desired.
      • Corporate image desired.
   c. Mix of advertising—to the trade, through the trade, to consumers.

7. **Promotions**
   Policies and procedures relating to
   a. Burden to be placed on special selling plans or devices directed at or through the trade.
   b. Form of these devices for consumer promotions, for trade promotions.

8. **Packaging**
   Policies and procedures relating to
   a. Formulation of package and label.

9. **Display**
   Policies and procedures relating to
   a. Burden to be put on display to help effect sale.
   b. Methods to adopt to secure display.

10. **Servicing**
    Policies and procedures relating to
    a. Providing service needed.

11. **Physical Handling**
    Policies and procedures relating to
    a. Warehousing.
    b. Transportation.
    c. Inventories.

12. **Fact-Finding and Analysis**
    Policies and procedures relating to
    a. Securing, analyzing, and using facts in marketing operations.

Source: The twelve elements are from Neil H. Borden, "The Concept of the Marketing Mix," *Journal of Advertising Research* (June 1964), pp. 2–7. Reprinted by permission of the Advertising Research Foundation.

The point is that each firm uses the elements of marketing differently—the marketing elements are harmonized in a unique way to form the main aspects of the marketing plan. This blending of the four elements of marketing to satisfy chosen consumer segments is known as the **marketing mix**. The marketing mix concept is one of the most powerful ever developed for marketers. It is now the main organizing concept for countless marketing plans. It gives executives a way to ensure that all elements of their program are considered in a simple yet disciplined fashion.[7]

The marketing planner must actually make wise decisions about *many* subelements of the marketing mix. This takes much skill and attention.

marketing mix
The blending of the four elements of marketing to satisfy chosen consumer segments.

▶ THE ROLE OF THE MARKETING MANAGER

To conclude our examination of marketing strategy and the marketing plan, Figure 6.10 illustrates some aspects of the role of the marketing manager in the process of developing a marketing plan. The responsibility of developing and implementing the marketing plan falls on the marketing manager. In the light of the opportunities and constraints perceived in the environmental framework, appropriate market segments are selected.

▶ **FIGURE 6.10 The Role of the Marketing Manager**

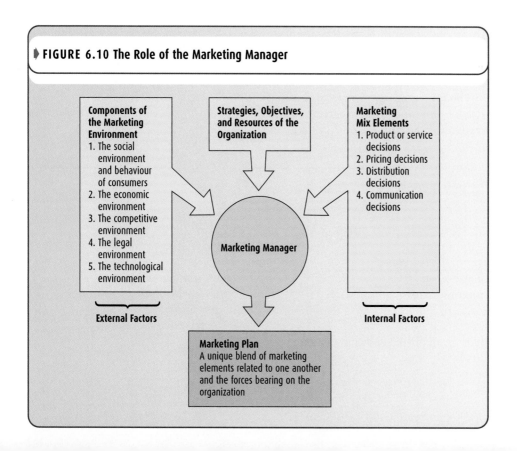

Based on the strategy, objectives, and resources of the firm, the manager and his or her team establishes marketing strategy and then develops a competitive marketing plan. Products or services, pricing, distribution, and communication are blended in a unique way to make up the marketing mix. The result wins customers, sales, and profits for the firm.

This is the essence of the first six chapters of this text. Chapter 7 introduces the important concept of total customer satisfaction. Total customer satisfaction is becoming the overarching objective of all informed marketing activity. Its principles and philosophies have broad implications for the implementation of the marketing plan, including the types of feedback and control systems employed.

The rest of the book will elaborate on the many considerations involved in formulating and implementing marketing strategy and subsequent marketing plans, as well as managing the elements of the marketing mix.

▶ SUMMARY

Corporate strategy is the overall purpose and direction of the organization that is established in the light of the challenges and opportunities found in the environment, as well as available organizational resources.

Corporate strategy gives input to marketing strategy. Setting marketing strategy begins with a situation analysis, which consists of analyzing internal, environmental, customer, and competitive issues. Marketing objectives can include profitability objectives, market share, or volume objectives. Most companies pursue growth strategies, which can include penetration, market development, product development, and diversification.

The four main elements of the marketing plan are product or service, price, distribution, and communication plans. Together, these elements are known as the marketing mix.

▶ KEY TERMS

BCG growth-share matrix
communication
corporate strategy
distribution
implementation and control
marketing channels
marketing mix
marketing objectives and strategy

marketing plan
marketing strategy
pricing
product management
product portfolio
situation analysis
SWOT analysis

▶ INTERACTIVE SUMMARY AND DISCUSSION QUESTIONS

1. Corporate strategy is the overall purpose and direction of the organization that is established in the light of the challenges and opportunities found in the environment, as well as available organizational resources. Using a small firm that you are familiar with as an example, write a hypothetical statement of strategy for the organization using the above definition. Make your statement as comprehensive as possible.

2. Marketing strategy is based on the strategy set for the company as a whole, and focuses on developing a unique long-run competitive position in the market by assessing consumer needs and the firm's potential for gaining competitive advantage. Explain, using an example, the relation between corporate strategy and marketing strategy.

3. The marketing plan is a program of activities that lead to the accomplishment of the marketing strategy. Using the text discussion as a base, explain how the manager can make sure that the plan includes the appropriate elements for the conditions facing the enterprise.

4. A marketing plan must take into consideration six major factors: increasing competition, dynamic consumer society, hi-tech environment, social consciousness, planning process requirements, and operational organizational requirements. Using the following organizations as examples, specify key elements that a marketing plan should include under each of the above headings:
   a. Canadian Tire store
   b. exporter of apples to Japan

5. Marketing plans consist of four main elements: product or service, pricing, distribution, and communication. Describe the marketing mix for the following:
   a. Canadian Tire store
   b. Clearly Canadian mineral water
   c. Royal Bank mortgage service
   d. Tide detergent

6. "The 'mix' concept is very important in marketing." Discuss.

7. In marketing planning, it is helpful to think of a broader list of subelements of the marketing mix. Explain.

8. Illustrate why it is important for the marketing planner to base the plan on a competitive analysis as well as on a consumer analysis.

9. Figure 6.10 illustrates some aspects of the role of the marketing manager in the process of developing a marketing plan. Translate this into an example based on the job of the marketing manager of a city transit system.

10. Visit the Web sites for Tide and Cheer, both Procter & Gamble brands. How are the marketing strategies for the brands similar? How are they different? Who are the brands targeting? What competitive advantage do the products seem to be emphasizing?

www.tide.com

www.cheer.com

To obtain a list of further readings for Chapter 6, please refer to the *Foundations of Marketing* Web site.

Chapter 7
Total Customer Satisfaction in Marketing

Compaq's commitment to quality customer service is reflected in its chain of service centres across Canada.

"We're really chasing customer satisfaction; that's the name of the game," said Rae Strathdee, Vice-President, Customer Services at Compaq Canada Inc., in explaining the company's new and greatly expanded approach to maintaining the most satisfied customer base in Canada.

"In the past we've really focused on break/fix maintenance. But that was before [our merger with Digital]. Now, to reflect our goal of becoming the leading information technology company globally, we've dedicated a lot of time, effort, and money to bring new capabilities to the table."

Mr. Strathdee groups those new capabilities for improved customer service under three main headings: hardware and software support, installation and start-up services, and management services support.

"Perhaps our biggest change is that we've also shifted from a reactive to proactive attitude. Our focus in all areas of customer service is to try and determine issues and problems before they arise. We want to make sure that customers' systems don't go down and that levels of service and maintenance don't degrade over time."

That commitment is reflected in Compaq's chain of service centres. There are five stand-alone centres across Canada, and the company has also launched a new type of service centre, located on college and university campuses.

The first was opened at Algonquin College in Ottawa. The second was set up at Wilfrid Laurier University in Waterloo, Ont. Others are scheduled to open soon.

For customers who want to do maintenance themselves, there is a Compaq team that uses the marvels of direct-dial technology. The team can connect through telephone lines with a customer's system and conduct error checks, then pass the information on to the client and suggest fixes.

The company maintains around-the-clock help desks, plus integration and software support for other companies. "For example," Mr. Strathdee said, "We have a staff of 25 [in Hull] who diagnose problems before a repair technician is dispatched. About 65 percent of the time we can solve a problem on the phone. If not, these support experts deliver an accurate diagnosis so the repair technician always brings along the right parts and equipment to solve the problem."

For routine help desk needs, there is a staff of 160 providing quick responses to Compaq customers, plus another 75 employees dedicated to the needs of commercial clients.

To top off this army of support specialists, there are another 300 Compaq experts continually at work on customer sites across the country.

Furthermore, the company provides management services support with the addition of more than 4000 business partners across Canada. These are the value added resellers (VARs) and distributors, which have traditionally been Compaq's only sales channel. Compaq has created an extensive certification program for business partners and their staffs to ensure the latest up-to-the-minute training is available, and even compulsory.

"They bring customers incredible experience and proven track records in the complete spectrum of IT applications, installation, service, and ongoing support. We also are able to provide instant backup if and when they need help," Mr. Strathdee said.

"The result is a new multilevelled, comprehensive, complete support infrastructure. Customer satisfaction is truly the name of the game."

This example is only one illustration of the growing importance leading firms place on providing total customer satisfaction. Other companies ignore this trend at their peril.

Source: Adapted from Terry Belford "Chasing Customer Satisfaction," *The Globe and Mail Advertising Supplement* (October 14, 1998), p. 7. Reprinted with permission of the author.

www.compaq.ca

▶ INTRODUCTION

This book is about finding and serving customers profitably. In discussing the issue, we have developed an understanding of the many elements involved in the marketing planning process. As shown in the previous chapter, the final aspect of the marketing planning process is *control*—determining whether the objective of achieving consumer satisfaction has been met and marketing plans realized. Achieving these goals leads to accomplishing the objective of obtaining competitive advantage and profits for the firm.

The criterion for assessing success in this area should be more than satisfaction—it must be *total* customer satisfaction. **Total customer satisfaction** means that a good or service fully and without reservation conforms to the customer's requirements. For example, when asked by a waiter, "How was your meal?" how many times have you said, "Fine," even though you were not really satisfied? Our objective must be to create "raving fans" if we are to assume a position of leadership and profitability in the market in which we have chosen to compete. Only by systematically reviewing the outcome of the process can improvements be made in the marketing plan. Note that this approach recognizes that goods

total customer satisfaction
Providing a good or service that fully and without reservation conforms to the customer's requirements.

and services must be designed for specific target markets. It is difficult, if not impossible, to meet everyone's needs.

Consider the following scenario:

"How is your company performing?" William Brand asked. "Sales and profits are up," the president replied. "In fact, our financial people tell me this year we will have one of our best 'bottom lines' ever!"

Mr. Brand was reviewing with the president the recent accomplishment of a manufacturer of computer components as they prepared to set the stage for planning the company's strategy for next year.

"Today's financial results measure the outcomes of strategic initiatives taken in the past. Are you monitoring the critical factors that will create success in the future?" Brand challenged.

"What do you mean? Aren't strong financial controls the proper measuring tools to monitor business performance?" the president said, somewhat taken aback.

Financial measures, used alone, are like driving a car while watching the rear-view mirror. They tell a company where it has been. A manager also needs a forward-looking view toward building success in the areas that lead to a long-run competitive advantage. The key success factors include product quality, after-sale service, corporate flexibility, and employee innovativeness.[1]

In a study of the marketing planning practices of the top 500 Canadian firms, this author found that only 57.8 percent of firms developed a written marketing plan. Furthermore, only 25.4 percent included a postmortem of the past year's results in their current marketing plan. How could such performance lead to total customer satisfaction?

▶ LIFETIME-CUSTOMER VALUE (LCV)

Total customer satisfaction is more than just an intangible concept. There are very sound, quantifiable business reasons that affirm the benefit of providing total customer satisfaction.

Some firms operate their business from the perspective of treating each customer transaction as a single event that has little or no connection with future transactions. They pay limited attention to the long-term relationship a firm has with its customers, or at least they do not explicitly recognize the long-term value of this relationship.

Another way of thinking about customers is to recognize that a relationship developed with a customer can provide long-term value to the firm as well as the customer. With every additional interchange between company and customer, trust in the company and its product grows. Thus, it takes progressively fewer resources to make additional sales. Customers put the company high on their list. The benefit to the firm is called the **lifetime-customer value (LCV)**. Lifetime-customer value is the sum of all future-customer revenue streams minus product and servicing costs, acquisition costs, and remarketing costs. The sum of the value of a firm's customers and prospects (total LCV) is *customer equity*. Customer equity measures the total-asset value of a company's customers.

lifetime-customer value (LCV)
The sum of all future-customer revenue streams minus product and servicing costs, acquisition costs, and remarketing costs.

There are four steps to computing LCV:

1. Determine acquisition and retention response rates .
2. Compute relevant costs.
3. Determine acquisition and retention costs per customer.
4. Use retention and acquisition rates to compute LCV.[2]

It is thus possible to increase profit primarily by retaining existing customers. Researchers Dawkins and Reichheld[3] have shown that a 5 percent increase in the customer retention rate increases the net present value of customers by between 25 and 85 percent in a wide range of industries, from credit card to insurance brokerage and from auto services to office building management. The reasons are that (1) the relative costs of generating cash inflows from existing customers are lower than the costs for new customers, and (2) as these customers stay, sellers save money that they would have spent on replacing them, and the costs of retaining existing customers are less than the costs of generating new ones.[4]

Focusing on LCV can change the marketing strategy of a company. As can be seen in Figure 7.1, the marketing management function is divided into two primary activities: customer management and marketing mix management. Customer management concentrates on determining how to acquire customers, retain them, and sell them additional products and services (add-on selling). Marketing mix management focuses on products, pricing, marketing communications, and distribution.[5] There is a strong link between the two, but it helps to analyze these functions separately. Companies with such an orientation work very hard to provide total customer satisfaction and build relationships to maximize the lifetime value of each customer.

Focusing on LCV concentrates an organization on managing customers as critical assets of the firm. Customers are no longer transactions but relationships. It is important to develop a good database to achieve these results (a later

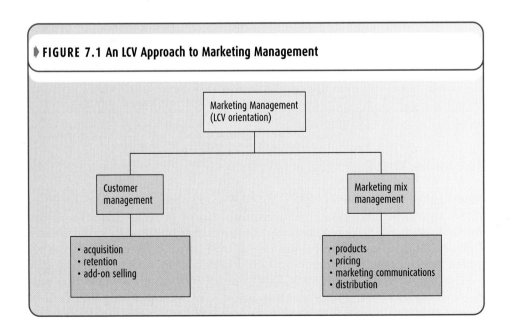

▶ **FIGURE 7.1 An LCV Approach to Marketing Management**

section will discuss this further). Furthermore, financial measures such as quarterly sales and profits should be enhanced by other measures, such as retention levels, add-on selling, cost of customer acquisition versus long-term lifetime value, and changes in total LCV. For example, Sears believes the cost of making the first sale to a new customer is twenty times greater than a sale to a regular customer. Office Depot estimates the lifetime value of a customer at $10 000.

Figure 7.2 provides a perspective of the importance of concentrating on customer satisfaction. Customer satisfaction leads to increasing levels of trust in the organization. The stock of trust that is built in turn enhances the image of the company in the customer's view, and results in company and brand loyalty. This positive image and company loyalty are related to company reputation, and the customer may develop a strong relationship with the company. All of this leads to increased profits and market share.

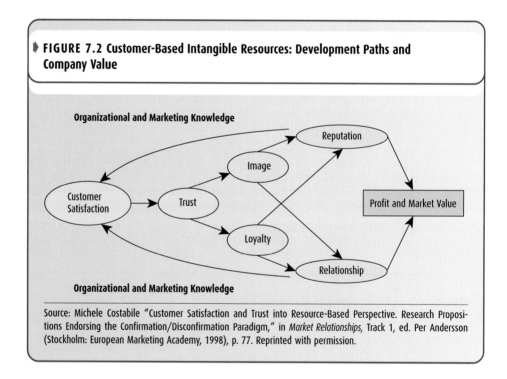

▶ **FIGURE 7.2 Customer-Based Intangible Resources: Development Paths and Company Value**

Source: Michele Costabile "Customer Satisfaction and Trust into Resource-Based Perspective. Research Propositions Endorsing the Confirmation/Disconfirmation Paradigm," in *Market Relationships,* Track 1, ed. Per Andersson (Stockholm: European Marketing Academy, 1998), p. 77. Reprinted with permission.

The Value Vision

Most managers have been taught to manage *activity* rather than *value.* Strategic plans for production, sales, and administration of business units are often focused on short-term gross volume improvements rather than on long-term value-building. These plans reward on the basis of quantity rather than value added, which skews performance toward activity and short-term gain.[6]

The vision of an organization should be to add value for customers and employees. Without a clear understanding of value, all marketing activity is in danger of falling into the activity trap. *Activity is the process by which value is created.* Value should be the heart of organizational purpose.

Quality in customer
service often means
customer satisfaction.

What is value? **Value** is a subjective term, and is defined by the customer. Each customer defines it somewhat differently. It is too simplistic to say that value is synonymous with customer satisfaction. Value is part of customer expectations. These are often complex and sometimes hidden, and they change. Expectations are a combination of cost, time, quantity, quality, and human factors.

Pepsi-Cola is an example of a company that diligently seeks out customer values. It surveyed 10 000 customers to develop sixteen priorities for its total quality effort. For example, it found that customers wanted improved deliveries. Two years later, it followed up with a survey of 2000 customers to see how it was doing.

Johnson & Johnson's McNeil Consumer Products subsidiary, which manufacturers the Tylenol product line, found that it had become too inwardly focused. It set up a special booth in its plant for workers who previously had had no opportunity to interact with customers. In this booth, they can now hear queries and complaints from the outside world that come in on an 800 line.[7]

If a company wants to build value, it has to recognize that value starts with the customer. However, there is a problem with simply asking customers what they want: they often cannot define their wants clearly. There are tow main reasons for this. First, when technology is involved, laypeople are unqualified to judge a product and to specify what they want. Second, customers are focused on their problem, not on the supplier's good or service. The supplier is only a means to helping customers reach their goals.

In spite of this, the marketer must find out which values to offer. Some key questions to ask customers: "What are you trying to achieve?" "What other forces are at work on you?" "What are your problems and opportunities?" "Who is pressuring you?"

value
A subjective term that is defined by the customer; part of customer expectations, which are a combination of cost, time, quantity, quality, and human factors.

www.pepsiworld.com

Customers perceive the well-known Intel Inside® trademark on computers as great value for their money. Intel's processors, a preferred brand, are recognized as compatible and reliable.

Market Challenges

In this context, three significant market challenges[8] highlight the importance of concentrating on providing value: (1) escalating customer expectations, (2) competitive forces, and (3) cost pressures.

ESCALATING CUSTOMER EXPECTATIONS

Customers expect firms to deliver better value, satisfy fragmenting markets, achieve closer relationships with them, and respond faster to their needs.

Better Value The global marketplace provides many options, so providing better value as perceived by the customer is essential. For example, because of competition from Japan and Europe, North American car companies have been forced to produce better engineered and more customer-friendly cars. The competition to provide more customer value is intense.

Satisfy Fragmenting Markets With a growing number of products, customers expect to find products that serve their particular tastes and needs more precisely. Thus businesses need to be more in tune with market needs in order to identify and serve appropriate market segments.

Achieve Closer Relationships with Customers As firms tune in to customer needs more precisely, they can establish closer links with individual customers by using sophisticated databases. This is known as relationship marketing, and will be dealt with in more detail later in this chapter.

Respond Faster Competition and technological developments have also led to rising expectations for rapid responses to consumer needs.

COMPETITIVE FORCES AND COST PRESSURES

Competition leads to pressures to lower prices or to increase value. Much of the easy cost cutting has already been achieved; nevertheless, firms are pushed to continue to seek economies. There is a continuing urgency to do more. This leads to employee layoffs and such activities as requiring customers to provide more input into the transaction, such as self-serve banking and expecting them to endure automated telephone answering systems. Responding to cost pressures while increasing customer satisfaction is a significant challenge.

▶ THE PRACTISING MARKETER

Creating an Environment Customers Want to Return To

Every business believes the one element that sets it apart from the competition is great customer service. But very few companies deliver this level of quality.

The objective is to create an environment where customers want to return and buy again. A consumer will tell at least ten people about a bad service experience, but the same person will only tell three people about a great one.

It takes continuous vigilance to ensure your business provides a positive experience time after time. Here is part of a process you can use to determine whether you have great customer service.

1. Start by surveying your existing customers to determine why they are buying from your company.
2. Set up a continuing process of measuring the perceived service your business provides to customers.
3. Understand the service level expectation in your industry and make sure your company exceeds it.
4. Make sure that customer service permeates the organization.
5. Recognize that employee attitudes are the best indicator of how your business views its customers.
6. Sit down with key customers to discuss their plans over the next few years.
7. Recognize that when you treat a customer badly, it is an opportunity to shine.

Explain the logic behind each of these steps.

Source: Adapted from Larry Ginsberg, "Customer Service Requires Vigilance," *The Globe and Mail* (July 20, 1998), p. B11. This article also appears in *Mind Your Own Business: Ginsberg's Guide to Entrepreneurial Success,* published by CCH.

The Value-Adding Chain

Building value is a function of a five-link chain, as shown in Figure 7.3. This chain links the corporate vision and its human and material assets to the customer's requirements. Any weak link in the value-adding chain breaks the bond between the business and the customer.

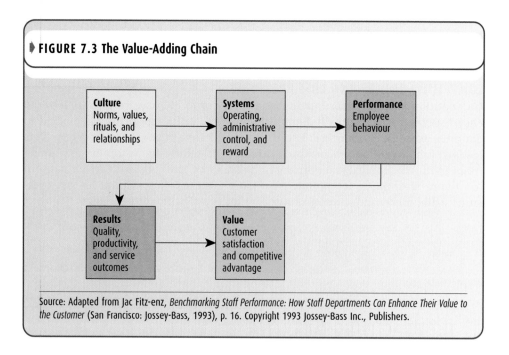

FIGURE 7.3 The Value-Adding Chain

Culture Norms, values, rituals, and relationships → **Systems** Operating, administrative control, and reward → **Performance** Employee behaviour

Results Quality, productivity, and service outcomes → **Value** Customer satisfaction and competitive advantage

Source: Adapted from Jac Fitz-enz, *Benchmarking Staff Performance: How Staff Departments Can Enhance Their Value to the Customer* (San Francisco: Jossey-Bass, 1993), p. 16. Copyright 1993 Jossey-Bass Inc., Publishers.

The *culture* of the organization must be right. Cultural factors spur people to design systems that fit the culture. When a corporation's vision and culture are out of sync, a fatal flaw is exposed and the organization experiences problems. For example, when Jan Carlzon took over the Linjeflyg airline in Sweden (before it was merged into Scandinavian Airlines System in 1993), he started by calling all employees into an empty airplane hangar and asking them for their ideas and help in resurrecting the airline. The result was that Linjeflyg changed from offering high-priced travel that only businesses could afford to offering real travel value to a great number of other customers by dramatically lowering prices. This vision brought about a great change in the culture of the organization. Within two years, the company was profitable.

Systems form the second link in the value-adding chain. They direct employee and management behaviour in the desired direction. Systems are inherently powerful—like a river, they flow along taking everything in their path in one direction. However, like rivers, some systems are lazy, winding, uncertain, and slow. Other rivers are more direct, deep, and strong. When these are flowing in the right direction, they establish a force of tremendously effective power in the marketplace.

The integration of culture and systems affects *performance,* or employee behaviour. This performance produces operating *results,* such as quality, productivity, and service outcomes. The final link, *value,* achieves customer satisfaction and competitive advantage. Every link in the chain should be observed for its impact on customer value.

QUALITY OR VALUE?

Quality is an overworked management term that is used to describe too many things. Quality is just one type of outcome from operations. The other two are productivity and service. Organizations do not survive and prosper because they provide quality. Collectively, quality, productivity, and service should comprise value. Table 7.1 illustrates that customers assess value leaders by considering operational excellence, performance superiority, and customer responsiveness.

▶ **TABLE 7.1 Customer's Views of Value Leaders**

Operational Excellence
"They provide a great deal"
• excellent/attractive price
• minimum acquisition cost and hassle
• lowest overall cost of ownership
"A no-hassles firm"
• convenient
• consistent quality

Performance Superiority
"They're the most innovative"
"Constantly renewing and creative"
"Always at the leading edge"

Customer Responsiveness
"Exactly what I need"
• customized products
• personalized communication
"They're very responsive"
• handling of exceptions
• inducing/building relationships

Source: George Day, adapted from "CSC Index" presentation at ASAC Conference, Lake Louise, May 1993. Reprinted with permission.

▶ BENCHMARKING

The core issue of the marketing plan is how to add value. One way of achieving this is through benchmarking. The computer industry has used the term *benchmarking* for many years to compare the characteristics of computers. A standard software program is run on each computer being tested, and various aspects of their performance are measured. The best performance on each characteristic becomes the standard, or benchmark, against which all others are compared.

The concept of *comparison with the best* is much better than merely setting objectives. It is of little value for one company to set an objective for its computer to increase the number of calculations per second from 500 to 700 when the benchmark rate for another computer is 1100. The only way to be competitive is to meet or beat the benchmark. The Japanese have a word for this concept — *dantotsu* — striving to be "the best of the best."

benchmarking
The comparison of performance with industry best practices.

Benchmarking is the comparison of performance with industry best practices. It is now applied to organizational performance, such as marketing programs. The advantages of using benchmarking are that managers are forced to seek out the best practices in the external environment, and must strive to incorporate these best practices in company marketing planning.

There are four fundamental requirements for using benchmarking as a tool to provide value to customers:[9]

1. *Know your operation.* It is fundamental for a company to develop a good understanding of the strength and weaknesses of its internal operation.
2. *Know the industry leaders and competitors.* Only a comparison with the best practices of leaders and competitors will provide the correct benchmarks to strive for. In addition, knowing their key strengths and weaknesses will lead to good decisions for differentiating products.
3. *Incorporate the best.* As a company finds out the strengths in others, it should not hesitate to learn from them, and copy, modify, or incorporate these strengths into its own operation.
4. *Develop superiority.* As the company's marketing planning and implementation respond by meeting and improving upon the benchmarks set by others, it will be on the right track for providing total customer satisfaction in marketing. Being the best of the best in dimensions that consumers value brings an organization closest to the goal of providing total customer satisfaction.

The Benchmarking Process

Benchmarking comprises five stages: planning, analysis, integration, actions, and maturity. Within these stages there are ten distinct steps.

PLANNING
The process starts with *identifying what is to be benchmarked.* For example, if consumers value competent, friendly service, this should be measured. Other examples might be excellent after-sale service, clear and interesting advertising, or high-quality products.

Identifying leading companies and competitors is the next step. These are the companies that are now doing the best job on these characteristics. Careful attention should be paid to international competitors, as the leaders need to set the standard no matter where they are found. Note that some companies might be better on some benchmark characteristics than others. Therefore, the comparison could be with more than one firm.

Collecting data includes using sound marketing research methodology and the many marketing research techniques. At this stage, it is important to derive quantifiable goals as well as to search out and document the best industry practices.

ANALYSIS

The next step is *determining the current performance gap*. The **performance gap** is the difference between the company's performance and that of the best of the best. This gap can be positive, negative, or nonexistent. Is the benchmarking partner better? Why is it better? By how much? How can its practices be incorporated or adapted for implementation?

Step 5 of the benchmarking process is *projecting future performance levels*. It is also important to project whether current performance, for the benchmark partner as well, is improving or not. Such projections might show that the gap is narrowing or that the gap will be even wider in the competitor's favour in two to five years.

INTEGRATION

Once the findings are established, it is critical to *communicate the benchmark findings and gain acceptance from the rest of the organization*. The organization must have faith in the methodology, and understand and accept the findings, if change is to occur.

Following this, *functional goals must be established*. This is a critical part of the process, as it involves converting benchmark findings into a statement of operational principles. To make the necessary changes, the organization must subscribe to these principles. They will be the criteria upon which the organization will focus in order to provide the value that will lead to customer satisfaction.

ACTION

Implementing these principles involves *developing action plans, implementing specific actions and monitoring progress*, and *recalibrating benchmarks*. Recalibration is necessary over time, as the external environment is constantly changing.

MATURITY

Maturity is reached when the plans have been implemented, and a position of leadership has occurred in each of the benchmarked conditions.

This is the necessary process that will lead to total customer satisfaction. The benchmarking process steps are shown in Table 7.2.

A graphic way of showing how a benchmarking exercise can help a company find where it is positioned is shown in the performance gap chart in Figure 7.4. This shows that the company's historic performance in providing marketing information in comparison with a benchmark competitor is poor, and is likely to get worse if it doesn't adjust.

A similar analysis can be done for each of the salient characteristics that contribute to total value, as perceived by the customer. For example, Pepsi-Cola could undertake such an analysis for each of its sixteen priorities.

performance gap
The difference between the company's performance and that of the best of the best.

▶ WHAT IS CUSTOMER SATISFACTION?

In choosing the value elements to benchmark, marketers need to concentrate on relevant measures that bear on whether or not customer satisfaction has

---

> ▶ **TABLE 7.2 The Benchmarking Process**

Planning
1. Identify what is to be benchmarked.
2. Identify comparative companies.
3. Determine data collection method and collect data.

Analysis
4. Determine current "performance gap."
5. Project future performance levels.

Integration
6. Communicate benchmark findings and gain acceptance.
7. Establish functional goals.

Action
8. Develop action plans.
9. Implement specific actions and monitor progress.
10. Recalibrate benchmarks.

Maturity
- Leadership position attained.
- Practices fully integrated into processes.

Source: Robert C. Camp, *Benchmarking: The Search for Industry Best Practices That Lead to Superior Performance* (Milwaukee, WI: ASQC Quality Press, 1989), p. 17. Reprinted with permission.

---

been achieved. What is customer satisfaction, really? Here are some answers given by managers:[10]

- "You have to start with the definition of customer satisfaction and quality from the customer perspective. Do the diagnostic work. What are they key factors that drive the customer on the good or service?"
- "The customer doesn't care about your system. The customer cares about satisfaction; having problems handled."
- "The customer doesn't care how you track his order. What the customer thinks is, 'I need the answer as to what the status of my shipment is, within the hour.' They don't care about how you execute, only that you do. They care about the *results.*"

There is a common thread in the above responses: customer satisfaction comes down to the ability to better serve your customers. As the managers' comments imply, organizations have to get beyond the lip service paid to satisfaction. One way they are doing this is by going into the marketplace and measuring satisfaction regularly.

www.hp.com

While most companies try to differentiate themselves by providing a succession of new product features, Hewlett-Packard is a company that has chosen not to rely solely on product features to create differentiation. Its European division decided to use customer satisfaction as an additional explicit method of differ-

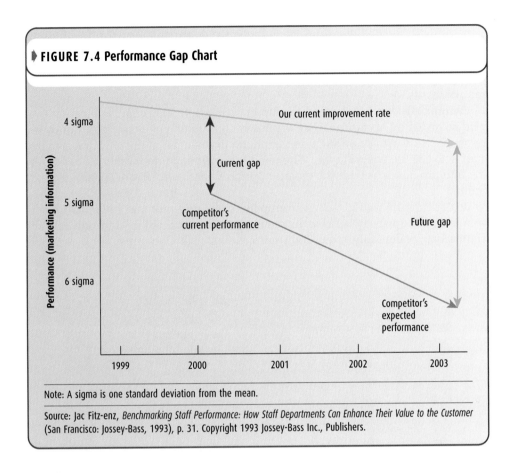

FIGURE 7.4 Performance Gap Chart

Note: A sigma is one standard deviation from the mean.

Source: Jac Fitz-enz, *Benchmarking Staff Performance: How Staff Departments Can Enhance Their Value to the Customer* (San Francisco: Jossey-Bass, 1993), p. 31. Copyright 1993 Jossey-Bass Inc., Publishers.

entiation. Its stated goal is to keep customers forever, and the company has created a new position called "customer satisfaction executive" to help ensure that it achieves this goal.

H-P has also established a customer satisfaction program. The three components of the program are customer feedback input, customer satisfaction surveys, and total quality control. The company carefully monitors and documents customers' complaints as well as compliments. H-P has recognized that it should not always focus on the negative comments but explicitly consider the positive feedback that is received as well. The company administers worldwide "relationship" surveys every eighteen months. These focus on asking how satisfied the customer is with the company as a whole, and how H-P rates against its competition. As well, some product questions are asked. By collecting this information on a regular basis, the company can evaluate whether it is making progress in its goal of providing customer satisfaction from year to year. The third aspect of the customer satisfaction program is a program of total quality control in production and service. With such a comprehensive program, it is not surprising that the worldwide relationship surveys show a steady improvement in customer satisfaction.[11]

Many companies are still behind in the trend toward making customer service number one. They haven't quite realized that customer service is a critically important marketing tool.

Customer satisfaction must be defined from an external, customer-based viewpoint. Marketing executives must lead their organizations to a better understanding of customer satisfaction that is defined in customer terms. Products may be perfectly manufactured, but they will fail if they do not meet market requirements.

For example, when informed consumers see ads proclaiming high-quality service provided by an airline, they are likely to think, "Why waste the money on hype when I can't get through on the phone to make an inquiry?" Furthermore, staff who see the ads will say, "Why put all that money into marketing and nothing into providing us with the means of improving the quality of customer treatment?"

Reassuring the public that the company cares and provides high-quality service is a sound way to build a customer base and profitability, but only if such claims are undeniably true. Total customer satisfaction must be a constant

To meet total customer satisfaction, Canada Post offers direct marketers products and services that match their needs.

byword of managing every facet of the marketing program. Total customer satisfaction means that a good or service totally conforms to the customer's requirements. This, of course, cannot be done without an active program of monitoring customer satisfaction.

Taking Total Customer Satisfaction from Slogan to Substance

It is important to do more than talk about providing total satisfaction for customers. Companies must also develop methods to measure whether those goals are being met. Pillsbury is one company that has made a commitment to measuring how well it is serving customer needs. "For Pillsbury, it's been a revolution. In the past, we only measured performance on cost, but we have found it's no longer adequate. The problem is that if you don't measure it, you can't improve it," said one executive.[12]

www.pillsbury.com

To take total customer satisfaction from slogan to substance, management should follow these guidelines:

1. Identify customer segments and the characteristics that they consider most important for the good or service.
2. Identify specific requirements for each target market.
3. Develop an information system that includes a database of customers, including past purchase behaviour and other relevant data for individual communication and interaction.
4. Translate resolved customer requirements into objectives and specifications for the marketing plan.
5. Identify the steps in the implementation process.
6. Determine the capability of the process to meet the requirements.
7. Select measurements for critical process steps.
8. Implement the program — fulfill customer values relating to the good or service. This must be the overriding goal for every department in the organization. Every service must be measured against the same standard, and every employee should be working toward 100 percent satisfaction of each value attribute.
   - Communicate these goals and standards to all employees, whether or not they communicate with the public. The best salespeople cannot make a company popular and profitable if other aspects of the organization are inefficient or error-prone.
   - Train all employees in a voluntary, cooperative atmosphere. It is woefully inadequate for a vice president or chief executive officer to announce that "all employees should do their best" without universal training in what that means and how to achieve it.
   - Give rewards, financial and otherwise, to those employees whose involvement leads to improvements in customer satisfaction and real cost savings.
9. Evaluate the results of the process, and identify steps for improvement.

The Royal Bank of Canada has an active program of assessing customer satisfaction and loyalty whereby customer feedback is obtained through a telephone interview. In doing so, the company uses a carefully designed nine-page questionnaire. An abbreviated version of the questionnaire, Figure 7.5, illustrates how a company can measure customer satisfaction.

▶ FIGURE 7.5 Royal Bank Quality Service Client Survey

 ROYAL BANK

Integrated Customer Satisfaction and Loyalty ("Client Experience") Survey (1999)
Phase I Short Survey (Revised 6/21/99) *

For the first set of questions, I would like you to think about all your experiences with Royal Bank overall.

OVERALL SATISFACTION AND LOYALTY

2a. Thinking about everything that you have experienced with the Royal Bank in the past three months, how would you rate the Bank overall using a 10-point scale where "1" means "Poor" and "10" means "Superior"?

(Q. 2b should only be asked of 1 in 4 respondents.)

2b. And, thinking of the financial services provided to you by Royal Bank, how would you rate the value for money of those products and services overall?

3. And, if a colleague, friend, or business acquaintance asked you to recommend a financial institution, how likely would you be to recommend Royal Bank using a 10-point scale where "1" means "Not At All Likely" and "10" means "Extremely Likely"?

FINANCIAL INSTITUTION REPUTATION

(This section should only be asked of 1 in 4 respondents.)

5. Thinking about everything you have experienced with Royal Bank in the past three months, including everything you have seen, read or heard about Royal Bank, I would like you to evaluate it in terms of its overall reputation as a financial institution. Compared to other financial institutions, would you say that Royal Bank is the best, better than most, about the same, not as good as most, or one of the worst in terms of its overall reputation?

6. Now I'm going to read you some statements. Thinking of all your experiences with Royal Bank in the past three months, please rate Royal Bank for each statement on a 10-point scale where "1" means "Poor" and "10" means "Superior."

Let's begin.

Randomize:

a. Communicating in a good public image through its advertising
b. Caring about its employees
c. Being visibly involved in support of programs in my community
d. Maintaining my privacy

CUSTOMER SERVICE FROM BRANCH

For the next set of questions, I would like you to think about your experiences with *(branch name)* over the past three months.

7. Thinking of just your last service experience with (branch name), how would you rate the overall customer service you received using a 10-point scale where "1" means "Poor" and "10" means "Superior."

9. Thinking about your <u>last</u> serivce experience with the staff at that branch, please rate the staff for each of the following statements as I read them to you. Please use the same 10-point scale where "1" means "Poor" and "10" means "Superior." Remember, this is about your <u>last</u> experience at that branch.

Randomize:

a. Made me feel like my business was appreciated
b. Was familiar with the products and services I have at Royal Bank
c. Looked for ways to serve me better
d. Gave me straightforward answers to my questions

Still thinking about your last service experience with that branch . . .

e. Completed tasks quickly and efficiently
f. Referred me to the right person if they could not help me themselves
g. Performed services right the first time
h. Had a positive attitude
i. Was professional
j. Was courteous and polite
k. The amount of time I spent waiting to be served
l. Was able to provide service to customers with disabilities
m. Handled my telephone calls quickly and efficiently
n. Returned my telephone calls promptly when I left a message

9.1 And, still thinking about your <u>last</u> service experience at <u>that</u> branch, did the staff . . .

a. Greet you warmly
b. Call you by name
c. Ask you if there was anything else they could help you with
d. Thank you for your business

FINANCIAL PLANNING AND ADVICE

12. Thinking of <u>just</u> the past three months, have you asked for or received financial advice from a representative of any Royal Bank branch?

14. Using a 10-point scale where "1" means "Poor" and "10" means "Superior," how would you rate the last financial advice that you received overall?

15. *(Insert respondent name, i.e., prefix and surname),* again, thinking of the <u>last time</u> you received financial advice, using the same 10-point scale, how would you rate your experience for each of the following?

Randomize:

a. Staff informed me of how new products and services might help me
b. Staff explained financial matters in a way that I could understand
c. Staff explained product and service options without my asking
d. Staff advised me in choosing products and services that are appropriate to me
e. Staff provided financial advice without high pressure selling
f. Staff was knowledgeable about products and services
g. Staff provided unbiased financial advice and recommendations
h. Provided useful and informative newsletters, brochures, and bulletins

PROBLEM RESOLUTION

23. In the past three months, have you experienced any problems or difficulties with your Royal Bank accounts, products or services?

24. And what was the general nature of the one problem that you consider to be the most serious?

---

* *Note that this is an abbreviated version of the original survey. As a result, numbering is not consecutive.*

Source: Royal Bank of Canada, Integrated Customer Satisfaction and Loyalty "Client Experience" Survey, 1999. Reprinted by permission of the Royal Bank of Canada.

▶ RELATIONSHIP MARKETING: SERVING GOOD CUSTOMERS BETTER

Chapter 1 introduced the marketing concept. An ongoing theme of successful marketing is customer orientation—seeking out customer needs and trying to fill them. This chapter takes the concept further by suggesting that the job is not done until the work of the company results in total customer satisfaction.

An important component of this is the determination to develop a long-term relationship with individual customers through generating a base of knowledge about them and tailoring goods, services, and communications to specific needs. This is known as **relationship marketing**. More specifically, relationship marketing involves identifying and establishing, maintaining and enhancing, and, when necessary, terminating relationships with customers and other stakeholders, at a profit, so that the objectives of all parties involved are met, through a mutual exchange and fulfillment of promises. These tasks rely on relational processes such as trust, commitment, and satisfaction.[13]

> **relationship marketing**
> Identifying and establishing, maintaining and enhancing, and, when necessary, also terminating relationships with customers and other stakeholders, at a profit, so that the objectives of all parties involved are met, through a mutual exchange and fulfillment of promises.

In one sense, the local general store manager practised this in Grandma's day. He knew her needs and catered to them. However, as companies grew to serve customers across the country and globally, this became much more difficult. Database technology now makes possible the development of meaningful relationships with customers. It enables customer information to be stored and retrieved, and it allows more efficient communication between the company and its clientele.

The process begins by determining how your customers relate to your product. For example, what do they like and dislike about it, and how do they use it? This information can be used to improve weaknesses, and to maintain and accentuate positive features that can lead to total customer satisfaction.

The next step is to determine what your customer base really looks like. A profile of customers in the database can be very helpful. Especially important is identifying key customers—those who are heavy users. With these profiles you can find other people like them to market to. This information is obtained using database technology and exploiting other communication vehicles, such as advertising, direct marketing, 800 numbers, and the Internet.

One company found that 4 percent of its customers accounted for 45 percent of its sales. It developed a profile of this important customer base, and then developed a marketing program to reach other potential customers with the same profile.

Relationship marketing involves five categories of activities: (1) listening to customers, (2) customizing marketing communication, (3) performing "customer care" activities, (4) customizing products, and (5) rewarding loyal customers.[14]

With respect to *listening* to customers, the focus is on gaining information from individual existing customers. *Customizing marketing communication* implies more individualized communications. *Customer care* activities may also be communication-related. They sometimes involve messages of the "we-care-about-you" type; follow-up messages from car dealers, and Christmas and other greetings are examples. *Customizing products* has often been done in the case of offering services. Flexible manufacturing has also enabled products to be customized. For example, Levi jeans offered made-to-order jeans (since discontinued because it wasn't really what was most important to the customer — see the Canadian Marketplace box).

Having a good relationship with customers is important to many companies. This personalized letter, for example, shows how Canadian Airlines International Ltd. (prior to merging with Air Canada) maintained a relationship with and rewarded its loyal customers.

▶ THE CANADIAN MARKETPLACE

Producing Products That People Can Use

We need to be talking more to customers and finding out what their needs are and servicing those needs.
—Glenn Sato, Levi Strauss's Manager of Retail Operations for Canada, April 1997

www.levistrauss.com

Two years later, Levi Strauss & Co.'s foray into mass customization came to an end in Canada. The San Francisco–based jean maker, which has been reeling from slumping sales, pulled the plug last week on its Personal Pair program that allowed women to order jeans personally sized for them.

The program, which operated out of 30 stores in Canada and about a dozen in the United States, was praised by industry watchers who see mass customization—the ability to produce goods on a large scale, but with personalized features—as a winning formula for today's economy.

Among them was U.S. marketing guru Donald Peppers, who used the Levi Strauss example to illustrate how a large corporation could deploy technology to offer personalized service to its customers and heighten brand loyalty by providing a unique product.

But that's not exactly what happened. Shelley Nandkeolyar, the director of consumer relationships for Levi Strauss & Co. (Canada) Inc., says the company found that the program did not offer women the variety they wanted. "It was targeted at fit and what we realized quickly was that fit was not what the consumer was really looking for. The consumer was looking more and more for style variations."

The Personal Pair system did not technically provide women with made-to-measure jeans. Instead, a pair of "personalized" pants was produced by using a combination of set pattern pieces.

For example, a woman would be measured by staff in a Levi's store and would try on some of the 440 sample pairs each participating store stocked. From that, she would be offered two choices of leg cut, a limited variety of colours, and various size combinations that may not be available off the shelf.

The theory was that a woman with a small waist, long legs, or large hips would finally be able to buy a pair of jeans that fit her unique body type.

But what often happened, Mr. Nandkeolyar says, is that after a customer was measured, the clerk would be able to find a pair of jeans that fit her from Levi's standard inventory. The pair cost $10 less and came without the one-to-three-week wait that a Personal Pair required. "People don't realize the extent of the styles and fits that are available with Levis and the variety that we offer and all the different styles and models."

But that lack of awareness is part of Levi Strauss's problem, as it battles to regain some of the market share it has lost in recent years to designer labels and retailers such as Gap Inc.

The jean maker, which is a private company owned by the descendants of founder Levi Strauss, does not report detailed financial statistics, but disclosed earlier this year that sales were down 13 percent to $6-billion (U.S.) in 1998.

Although Levi Strauss has ended the Personal Pair offering, Mr. Nandkeolyar says that the company still firmly believes in the benefits of mass customization. While there is no replacement program in Canada, in the fall of 1998 the company introduced a new mass customization effort in the United States called Original Spin. Mr. Nandkeolyar says it tries to respond to customers' demand for more style variations and, unlike Personal Pair, is also available to men. That program is now being tested in about 15 U.S. stores, he says, and could be expanded to Canada if it proves successful.

As for Personal Pair, like many corporate ventures that have come and gone, Mr. Nandkeolyar now describes it as an educational experience. "It was one of the green shoots that the company put out to learn from," he says.

Did the company make a marketing mistake in starting the mass customization program?

Source: Adapted from Elizabeth Church, "Personal Pair Didn't Fit into Levi Strauss's Plans," *The Globe and Mail* (May 27, 1999), p. B13. Reprinted with permission from *The Globe and Mail*.

The fifth category of relationship marketing is *rewarding loyal customers*. Hilton Hotels developed a special "Honors Program" for key customers. The company found that the amount of business generated from these top customers accounted for about 33 percent of its revenue.[15] Loyalty programs such as frequent flier or frequent buyer programs are often used to help build databases as well as to generate repeat business. However, it should be noted that rewards are only one aspect of relationship marketing. Some people are confused by this category and tend to think of it as the main part of relationship marketing. A solid relationship marketing program goes beyond these specific activities. Table 7.3 contrasts an earlier transactional view of marketing with a relationship perspective. Note that the objective of the relationship perspective is to satisfy existing customers by delivering superior value.

▶ **TABLE 7.3 A Relationship View of Marketing**

TRANSACTIONAL VIEW	RELATIONSHIP VIEW
• Purpose of marketing is to make a sale	• Purpose of marketing is to create a customer
• Sale is a result and the measure of success	• Sale is beginning of relationship; profit is measure of success
• Business is defined by its products and factories	• Business is defined by its customer relationships
• Price is determined by competitive market forces; price is an input	• Price is determined by negotiation and joint decision making; price is an outcome
• Communications are aimed at aggregates of customers	• Communications are targeted and tailored to individuals
• Marketer is valued for its products and prices	• Marketer is valued for its present and future problem-solving capability
• Objective is to make the next sale and/or find the next customer	• Objective is to satisfy the customer you have by delivering superior value

Source: Presentation by Frederick E. Webster, Jr., at Special Session on "Relationship Marketing," American Marketing Association Educators' Conference (August 1993), Boston, MA. In Michael D. Hutt and Thomas W. Speh, *Business Marketing Management*, 6th ed. (Fort Worth, TX: Dryden Press, 1998), p. 16. Reprinted with permission.

One of the keys to success in relationship marketing is information and how you use it. Before technological developments like the Web and the availability of electronic databases, it was not possible to do sophisticated relationship marketing on a large scale. Now, by using the Web and other direct marketing methods, it is possible to deliver personalized messages. Because of this, there is a trend away from mass market communication to more relationship building and one-to-one communication with customers and prospects. Because of technology we are smarter and can create customized ads and newsletters and have direct dialogue with individual customers. Again, it is important to recognize that using databases is only one tool in relationship marketing. Some people confuse this database activity with the concept of relationship marketing.

The benefits of relationship marketing cannot be realized without securing and maintaining a quality database. It is the database's quality — the information itself and how it is used and acquired — that drives the program, targets customers, and enables the firm to provide the kind of customer satisfaction needed to build long-term relationships.

Flexibility: Facilitating Relationship Marketing and Customer Service

Leading companies have created new possibilities for customers by providing more choices and better response times. They have accomplished this by pushing their operations to perform much more flexibly. Instead of running a production line to produce one specific product for a week, companies are organizing to change production from one product to another within hours. The purpose is to maximize the flexibility of the whole company's response to demand.[16]

For example, product life cycles for low-end computers are measured within months these days, so flexible production lines allow the company to guard against running short of a hot model or overproducing one whose sales have slowed.

Kao Corp., Japan's biggest soap and cosmetics company, has developed incredible flexibility in distribution. The company and its wholly owned whole-

www.kao.co.jp

▸ THE ETHICAL MARKETER

Should You Push Customers?

In Australia, if you are the customer of a certain bank and you still have a passbook, tellers have been advised to check to see if it has a small red sticker attached. That sticker warns tellers to avoid the hard sell with you—they tried it before, and you complained.

Australian banks have transformed themselves from a style of service and personal touches, where customers were often known by name, to a more aggressive sales culture. Every visit by a customer is seen as an opportunity to make another sale: taking out a loan, extending a credit card limit, or transferring money to a "better" account. Tellers and other personnel are pressured to achieve set goals in such efforts, and have been fired for failing to meet them. Rewards are given to those who do.

Also, in the interests of efficiency, the banks have laid off many employees. Customers are not allowed to "bother" the remaining employees with phone calls. Customers cannot phone their local bank branch; instead, all calls are routed to an answering centre. If the staff there cannot answer a question they, not the consumer, call the local branch.

The banks have explained that they are in a very competitive environment and are no different from other businesses that have had to overhaul their thinking and workplace practices since the 1980s. Competition in areas such as home loans and credit cards, coupled with changes in technology such as telephone and computer banking, have forced banks to adapt.

Is there an ethical issue in requiring bank employees to push other products and services than the ones customers went to the bank for? Explain. What would be a total customer satisfaction approach to the problem faced by the banks?

salers can deliver goods within 24 hours to any of 280 000 shops, whose average order is for just seven items. The key is a sophisticated information system. Brand managers see daily sales, stock, and production figures. Within a day, they can learn whether a competitor is running a sale. This network virtually eliminates the lag between an event in the market (e.g., Mrs. Takada buys a bar of soap) and the arrival of the news at the company.

A flexible factory is useless if a company doesn't know what is selling, and it doesn't help to know the market cold if the company can't react to it back at the plant. Building flexibility into an organization enables a firm to add value for customers in several ways. It can provide enhanced product features for specific market segments, lower product prices, rapid change of the product mix, introduction of many new products, and excellent customer response time. Thus, incorporating flexibility into production and marketing can greatly enhance customer satisfaction, and make such organizations extremely competitive in the marketplace.

▶ MARKETING AUDITS: ASSESSING CUSTOMER SATISFACTION

marketing audit
A comprehensive appraisal of the organization's marketing activities. It involves a systematic assessment of marketing plans, objectives, strategies, programs, activities, organizational structure, and personnel.

Marketing audits have been used for years to control and evaluate marketing programs. A **marketing audit** is a comprehensive appraisal of the organization's marketing activities. It involves a systematic assessment of marketing plans, objectives, strategies, programs, activities, organizational structure, and personnel.

A marketing audit can also be used to help determine where an organization stands with respect to providing total quality to its customers. The goal of the audit is to improve the overall marketing efficiency by presenting a corrective action plan to management.

A typical marketing audit includes the following topics:

- environment
- objectives
- strategy
- product decisions
- pricing decisions
- distribution decisions
- marketing communication decisions
- marketing information
- activities and tasks
- personnel

Rothe, Harvey, and Jackson[17] have suggested that five areas also need to be addressed in the marketing audit for the twenty-first century:

1. the degree to which a global focus has been taken
2. support for having a marketing controller position in the organization
3. incorporating and measuring the ecological efforts of the marketing programs in the organization

4. integrating the periodic and continuous marketing control efforts to provide a seamless control mechanism

5. broadening the marketing audit concept to focus on resource management and control

We would suggest a sixth item:

6. broadening the marketing audit concept to focus on and measure total customer satisfaction, which should also include assessing the use of lifetime customer value principles.

In conclusion, the marketing audit, which has traditionally been used to assess marketing effectiveness in the management of the marketing mix, can be broadened to assess how well the firm is doing in managing consumer relationships and providing total customer satisfaction.

▶ SUMMARY

Total customer satisfaction means that a good or service fully and without reservation conforms to the customer's requirements. This approach leads to developing long-term relationships with customers and generating lifetime-customer value (LCV). LCV is the sum of all future customer revenue streams minus product and servicing costs, acquisition costs, and remarketing costs. Focusing on LCV can change the marketing strategy of a company.

Some firms make the mistake of relying solely on traditional financial analysis to determine how they are doing. Financial analysis measures the outcomes of strategic initiatives taken in the past. A manager also needs a forward-looking perspective toward building success in the future as well as calculation of LCV. An emphasis on assessing the amount that total customer satisfaction provides is an important means of accomplishing future success.

Activity is the process by which value is created. Managers have to be careful not to focus on activity rather than value. Value should be the focus of marketing activity, but it is a subjective term and is defined by the customer. Thus a marketing program that tries to provide total customer satisfaction must research the values of target customers.

Building value is the function of a five-link chain composed of culture, systems, performance, and results, which lead to the provision of value. Total quality is a popular management goal, but value is more fundamental.

Benchmarking is the comparison of performance with industry best practices. The concept of "comparison with the best" provides better standards for control of a marketing plan than setting objectives. There are four fundamental requirements to using benchmarking as a tool to provide value to customers: know your operation, know the industry leaders and competitors, incorporate the best practices, and develop superiority.

The performance gap is the difference between a company's performance and that of the best of the best. It is important not only to determine the current performance gap, but to project the future gap as well. This provides a basis on which to develop marketing plans.

Relationship marketing consists of identifying and establishing, maintaining and enhancing, and when necessary, terminating relationships with customers and other stakeholders, at a profit, so that the objectives of all parties involved are met through a mutual exchange and fulfillment of promises. This helps the company to fulfill the mandate of the marketing concept as discussed in Chapter 1. An emphasis on flexibility in production and marketing is a competitive thrust that can provide significant customer value and enable the development of long-term relationships with customers. This is particularly important in a mass marketing situation.

How do you know whether your firm is providing total customer satisfaction? Research is the key. This can be done through regular surveys of customers as well as through a marketing audit that includes a customer satisfaction assessment.

▶ KEY TERMS

benchmarking

lifetime-customer value (LCV)

marketing audit

performance gap

relationship marketing

total customer satisfaction

value

▶ INTERACTIVE SUMMARY AND DISCUSSION QUESTIONS

1. Financial results measure the outcomes of strategic initiatives taken in the past. A manager also needs a forward-looking view toward building success in the future. Explain how an emphasis on total customer satisfaction can assist in directing the company's activities.

2. Activity is the process by which value is created. Why are managers often programmed to manage activity rather than value?

3. Value should be the focus of marketing activity. However, value is a subjective term and is defined by the customer. How, then, can a marketing program that tries to provide total customer satisfaction determine customer values?

4. Building value is a function of a five-link chain composed of culture, systems, performance, and results, which lead to the provision of value. Explain how this chain works.

5. Total quality is a popular management goal, but value is more fundamental. Explain.

6. Benchmarking is the comparison of performance with industry best practices. The concept of "comparison with the best" provides better standards for control of a marketing plan than setting objectives. Give an example to illustrate this concept.

7. There are four fundamental requirements in using benchmarking as a tool to provide value to customers: know your operation, know the industry leaders and competitors, incorporate the best practices, and develop superiority. Using a small business that you are familiar with as an example, explain how these requirements might be explained or applied in terms of that business.

8. The performance gap is the difference between a company's performance and that of the best of the best. Why is it important not only to determine the current performance gap but to project the future gap as well?

9. Review the benchmarking process in Table 7.2. Apply it to two or three marketing features of a local bookstore.

10. Relationship marketing can help to provide total customer satisfaction. Explain how such a program can be implemented for a mass marketer.

11. An emphasis on flexibility is a competitive thrust that can provide significant customer value. Explain how this necessarily involves most aspects of the organization.

12. A marketing audit is based on five variables: customer philosophy, integrated marketing organization, adequate marketing information, strategic orientation, and operational efficiency. Outline the probable steps in a marketing audit for a local dry-cleaning company.

13. In detail, describe how the total customer satisfaction concept could be applied to the marketing management system of a company you are familiar with.

14. Go to the Web site of ten companies of your choice. Determine the degree to which the concept of total customer satisfaction is reflected in the information they provide.

To obtain a list of further readings for Chapter 7, please refer to the *Foundations of Marketing* Web site.

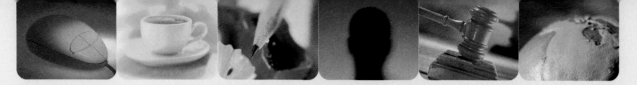

Part 3
Consumer Behaviour

The foundation of the marketing concept involves developing an understanding of the needs and desires of the customer, and then striving to serve those needs. Market segmentation provides a way to identify groupings of customers. After identification, a deeper understanding of the consumer helps establish successful marketing plans. Part 3 discusses some of the many concepts that marketers bring to bear in analyzing consumer behaviour. Both the internal factors and the external influences that affect decision making in consumers and buyers working on behalf of businesses are explored.

Expanding into the Taiwan market taught Purdy's Chocolates, a successful Vancouver-based company, many important lessons about consumer behaviour, including the fact that small chocolates sell and large ones don't.

Purdy's Chocolates is one of the many firms that have discovered that consumers often respond in surprising ways to marketing efforts in other parts of the world. With its 44 shops, the Vancouver-based chocolate producer and retailer is a household name on the West Coast but a relative unknown outside British Columbia and Alberta.

In 1995, the father–daughter team that runs the 90-year-old gourmet chocolate maker decided future growth meant breaking into new markets. They set their sights on Taiwan's capital, Taipei, whose four million residents have a collective sweet tooth. Purdy's owners recognized that sending a perishable food item overseas could be a challenge, and they were up to it.

R.C. Purdy Chocolates Ltd., which makes over 100 different types of chocolates, had been approached many times by would-be partners who wanted to take it into uncharted territory. Company owner Charles Flavelle, 68, and daughter Karen, 39, spurned these offers. "We always said, 'No, no, no, let's stick to our knitting,'" says Ms. Flavelle.

"We're real sticklers for product quality and a big part of that is shelf life. We felt if it goes out of our hands, we lose control of quality, and that made us concerned." But the Flavelle family agreed to consider Taipei after relentless prodding from Taiwan-born businesswoman Lei Mei How, who has lived in Vancouver for 26 years.

Ms. How, a long-time Purdy's aficionado, was convinced the chocolates would be a hit in Asia. In fact, she picked up the tab to fly Purdy's vice-president Neil Hastie to Taipei for five days in spring 1995 to conduct his own market research.

Mr. Hastie was bowled over by the size and energy of the fourth most densely populated city in the world. "It has a huge population with a large disposable income," he says. "Marginal tax rates are very low. Take-home pay is about 80 per-

▶ CHAPTER OBJECTIVES
After reading and studying this chapter, you should be able to

1. Describe how consumer behaviour is affected by two main categories of influence: environmental and individual factors.
2. Explain the role of culture in consumer behaviour.
3. Consider the effect of reference groups on consumer behaviour.
4. Distinguish between needs and motives.
5. Explain perception.
6. Define attitude and its three main components, and explain how attitude influences behaviour.
7. Demonstrate how learning theory can be applied to marketing strategy.
8. Show the steps of the consumer decision process and how environmental and individual factors affect this process.
9. Differentiate among routinized response behaviour, limited problem solving, and extended problem solving.

cent of gross. It's also a marketplace that has a fascination with North American–type goods. There's organized retail—unlike mainland China—in the form of wonderful department stores that showcase North American goods in an upscale environment."

That endorsement was enough for the Flavelles, who formed a partnership with Ms. How, and invested over $200 000 to set up shop in a high-end department store, Mitsukoshi, in Taipei's bustling core.

www.purdys.com

Purdy's had 60 days to get its 34-square-feet of space in order. It opened its doors in October 1995. The company deliberately set its sights low, expecting first-year sales of $200 000 to $250 000. It didn't meet even that target. "We recognized we had a lot to learn, but we didn't think there would be as many roadblocks or that they'd be as big," says Mr. Flavelle.

Some of the hurdles faced were hiring and managing staff from a distance, different tastes in food, packaging preferences (unlike in Canada, small chocolates sell and large ones don't), and hassles in getting products through customs. Another marketing mistake was that they assumed that a product popular with Asian-Canadians—ice cream bars dipped in rolled nuts—would be a winner in Taipei. It wasn't.

The biggest challenge, though, was getting chocolate onto the shelves in an often stifling climate. "We had chocolate melting on the tarmac while we waited to get clearance from Taipei airport."

"What we learned is that the things people of Chinese origin buy in Vancouver are not necessarily a reflection of what will sell in Asia," Mr. Hastie says. "There's a socialization process that they go through when they come here, and depending on how long they've been in this country, their tastes become Canadianized."

In 1996, Purdy's management re-evaluated Taipei. "We said, 'This isn't working,'" Ms. Flavelle says. "So do we abandon it or find a different way of doing it?" Ms. How came up with a solution for the distribution problem. She found a distributor in Konig Foods Ltd. of Taipei, a manufacturer of cakes, cookies, and pastries for high-end stores, and a caterer for weddings and bridal and baby showers.

In February 1997, the three partners teamed up. Now, the Vancouver chocolate maker functions solely as a wholesaler—and Ms. Flavelle is finding that it's working. "Konig arranges to have the product picked up at our factory and it arrives at their door. We wanted to put that responsibility into someone else's hands, and this group has the muscle to do it."

Ms. Flavelle says the company is back on track in its Asian experiment. As a wholesaler, she expects to break even the first year. "It's a give-and-take relationship. They handle the distribution and we bring expertise in imaging and retailing."

Purdy's took some bumps and bruises, but the company didn't bet the store on a risky Taiwanese venture. It deliberately kept its initial investment low to soften the blow if things didn't work out. "To be honest, we wouldn't have gotten anywhere the other way," says Ms. Flavelle of their attempt to sell direct to the public. "Retail needs a lot of supervision and proximity." It also requires a good understanding of the needs and wants of consumers.

She views the first two years as a training ground. "We learned about doing business in an emerging market in a very short time. We aim to take advantage of [the huge market] in China. It's going to come."

Two years later, Purdy's decided to withdraw from the Taiwan market. Sales volume, made even worse by the Asian economic downturn, was not considered high enough to continue. Karen Flavelle believes that "if a company doesn't put ships out, no ships are going to come in." "Every new venture," says Flavelle, "particularly one as different as this, is loaded with difficulties. Being successful in three out of ten tries is considered good—this just happens to be one of the seven out of ten."

The confidence expressed by Ms. Flavelle is based on the lessons learned about consumer behaviour, as well as the behaviour of other business partners. Marketers can win or lose big, depending on how consumers and businesses respond to their offerings. In this case, the venture did not work out. That is why great efforts must be made to try to understand the processes that affect customer decisions.

Source: Adapted from Gayle MacDonald, "Purdy's Tests Asia's Sweet Tooth," *The Globe and Mail* (June 9, 1997), p. B9. Reprinted with permission from *The Globe and Mail*.

▶ INTRODUCTION

This book has made a point of emphasizing the importance of understanding the consumer before developing a marketing plan. Consumer behaviour studies try to apply a microscope to the basic understanding of people and their purchase behaviour. This chapter and the next chapter provide an introduction to the extensive marketing literature concerning consumer behaviour.

Consumer behaviour consists of the activities of individuals in obtaining, using, and disposing of goods and services, including the decision processes that precede and follow these actions.[1] This definition includes both the ultimate consumer and the purchaser of products for business use. However, in the case of business consumers, a major difference is that additional influences from within the organization may be exerted on the purchasing agent. This will be discussed in more detail in the next chapter.

consumer behaviour
The activities of individuals in obtaining, using, and disposing of goods and services, including the decision processes that precede and follow these actions.

"So I told them, 'This Internet thing is just a fad—put your money in gold!'"

Consumer behaviour is sometimes odd and unpredictable.

It is important to develop positive relationships with consumers. Therefore, the basic task of marketing is to understand the customer so sound marketing planning can occur. We can categorize people into various segments, but it is essential to go deeper than that. Marketing planners must consider *what* motivates potential consumers, and *why*. The study of consumer behaviour has become a well-established discipline within the field of marketing.

Much marketing research into consumer behaviour has been undertaken. In addition, the field of consumer behaviour borrows extensively from other areas, like psychology and sociology. The work of Kurt Lewin, for instance, provides an excellent classification of influences on buying behaviour. Lewin's proposition was that

$$B = f(P,E)$$

where behaviour (B) is a function (f) of the interactions of individual factors (P) and the pressures exerted on them by outside forces in the environment (E).[2]

This statement can be rewritten for consumer behaviour as follows:

$$B = f(E,I)$$

where consumer behaviour (B) is a function (f) of the interaction of environmental factors (E) such as culture and social influences, and individual factors and psychological processes (I) such as needs, motives, and attitudes. Understanding consumer behaviour, as Figure 8.1 illustrates, requires careful consideration of the many variables that comprise each of these two major categories.

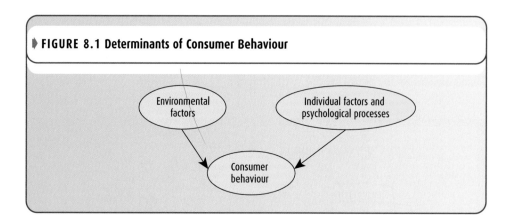

▶ **FIGURE 8.1 Determinants of Consumer Behaviour**

▶ ENVIRONMENTAL FACTORS THAT AFFECT CONSUMER BEHAVIOUR

Countless facets of the environment affect behaviour. Two important groups of factors that can affect consumer behaviour are cultural and social influences. People are social animals. They often buy products and services because of a broad range of perceived influences of others, as well as the culture of which they are a part. The important social influences are group influences, reference groups, social class, and family influences. A general model of the environmental determinants of consumer behaviour is shown in Figure 8.2.

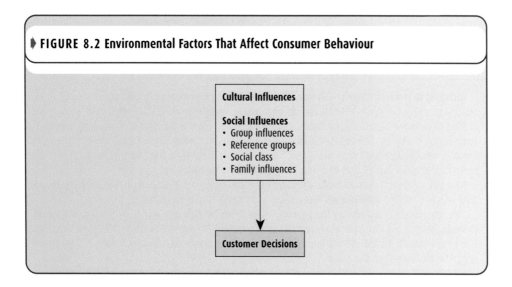

▶ **FIGURE 8.2 Environmental Factors That Affect Consumer Behaviour**

Cultural Influences

Social Influences
- Group influences
- Reference groups
- Social class
- Family influences

Customer Decisions

▶ THE CANADIAN MARKETPLACE

Peasant Chic in the Shower

It's trendy to use a bar of all-in-one shampoo and soap—just like Grandpa in the Old Country.

If washing your hair with a bar of soap conjures images of early pioneers sitting with their knees up in a wooden basin and pouring a pitcher of water over their heads, you're not taking a '90s power shower.

All-in-one shampoo body bars and hair soaps are the new embodiment of the end-of-the-millennium values—convenience, natural ingredients, and bottle-free environmental friendliness.

Available for $8 at select Holt Renfrew stores across Canada, Dr. Hunter's Castile Soap can be used to wash your hair, your kids, your pets, and your laundry. You can also wash fruit and vegetables and brush your teeth with it, even if you didn't say a dirty word.

Aveda, a company known for high-end hair-care products, recently launched its shampoo body bar as part of a new line of men's products. With a suggested retail price of $17, this is one bar of soap you don't want to drop in the shower.

"It was our first launch into a gender-specific market," says spokeswoman Michelle Sahlstrom from Aveda headquarters in Minneapolis, Minn. "Until now, all of our products have been gender neutral!"

The Aveda shampoo body bar is meant for hair, face, and body use. The milky white square contains moisturizers and, according to Aveda, has a built-in conditioner. Sahlstrom says it was created to cater to all hair types and is not for any specific skin type: "It's a shampoo formulation that's been put into the mould of a bar of soap."

The typical consumer is a younger man-on-the-go, but Aveda shops in Toronto and Montreal note that men in their thirties and forties also buy the product. "In many cases your older male population are pretty much set in what they use and what they like," says Sahlstrom.

At Lush, the stores that sell strong-smelling handmade cosmetics, bars of soap for the hair are the second most popular product for both men and women. The shampoo bar, which is not recommended for your body, sells for $4.95 per 100 grams, or $5.95 a puck.

Lush spokeswoman Emma Willis says the shampoo bars are bought mostly by people between the ages of 20 and 30. She says older customers tend to shake their heads at the idea.

(continued)

www.aveda.com

▶ THE CANADIAN MARKETPLACE *(continued)*

According to Professor Mariana Valverde, a sociologist at the University of Toronto and author of *Age of Light, Soap, and Water: Moral Reform in Canada,* poor people and the working class often used a single bar of soap to wash themselves, their clothes, and their children. Then, at the turn of the century, manufacturers began marketing differentiated soaps to a middle-class consumer. "More middle-class people were the ones who bought hand soap like Pears," says Valverde. "The idea was that you wouldn't use the same stuff to clean your clothes and your body, especially your hands and your face."

Now chic companies such as Aveda are going full circle, taking a product and practice formerly associated with poverty and grandparents' tales of the Old Country, and modernizing it.

"We are constantly reinventing the peasant," says Valverde. "It's only when the peasant is a far-off memory that you can start selling peasant things expensively. For people whose parents were peasants, they're not going to be too keen to buy peasant stuff. But for people for whom peasantry is this romanticized far-off thing, then that's fine."

Those who tend to buy all-in-one soaps or shampoo bars are probably thinking less about peasants than they are about convenience, especially when there's no more room along the edges of the bathtub or they are seeking a quick power shower at the gym.

"That's part of the see-saw logic of marketing," says Valverde. "The market creates the problem [by selling multiple products]. Then the same advertisers can sell you the solution to the problem they created in the first place."

Do you agree with this explanation of consumer behaviour? Why or why not?

Source: Mitchel Raphael, "Peasant Chic in the Shower," *National Post* (March 30, 1999), p. B3. Reprinted with permission.

Dr. Hunter and Aveda have reinvented the all-in-one-soap to meet the new millennium values of convenience and environmental friendliness.

Cultural Influences

Culture is the broadest environmental determinant of consumer behaviour. Sometimes it is a very elusive concept for marketers to handle. General Mills knew that few Japanese homes had ovens, so it designed a Betty Crocker cake mix that could be made in the electric rice-cookers widely used in that country. The product failed because of a cultural factor. Japanese homemakers regard the purity of their rice as very important, so they were afraid that a cake flavour might be left in their cookers.[3]

culture
The complex of values, ideas, attitudes, institutions, and other meaningful symbols created by people that shape human behaviour, and the artifacts of that behaviour, transmitted from one generation to the next.

Culture can be defined as the complex of values, ideas, attitudes, institutions, and other meaningful symbols created by people that shape human behaviour, and the artifacts of that behaviour, transmitted from one generation to the next.[4] It is the way of life that is learned and handed down through generations that gives each society its own peculiar characteristics and values.

CORE VALUES IN THE CANADIAN CULTURE

The list in Table 8.1 provides a useful summary of characteristics that are significant to the Canadian culture. There are trends and shifts in cultural values, yet traditionally these changes have been gradual. Nevertheless, marketers must constantly assess cultural norms. One strong cultural thread is an awareness of the distinctiveness of the Canadian "identity," despite the difficulty of being able to easily define it. Thus a number of television programs and commercials created in other countries, including the United States, often do not quite fit in the Canadian context.

▶ **TABLE 8.1 Summary of Significant Canadian Characteristics**

As a Function of Being a Part of the North American Reality
- Modern orientation
- Openness to new ideas
- Egalitarianism
- A rich, developing society with many needs and high materialistic expectations
- Growing, more diffuse middle class

In Relation to the United States
- Conservative tendencies
- Traditional bias
- Greater confidence in bureaucratic institutions
- Collectivity orientation—reliance on institutions such as state, big business, and the church vs. personal risk taking
- Less achievement-oriented
- Lower optimism—less willing to take risks
- Greater acceptance of hierarchical order and stratification
- Tolerance for diversity—acceptance of cultural mosaic
- Family stability
- Selective emulation of the United States—resistance to some American characteristics and dominance, yet willingness to emulate
- Elitist and ascriptive tendencies

CULTURAL INFLUENCES: AN INTERNATIONAL PERSPECTIVE

An awareness of cultural differences is particularly important for international marketers. Different attitudes, mores, and folkways all affect marketing strategy. Examples of cultural influences on marketing strategy are abundant in the international environment. Look at the marketing implications of the following situations:

- In Malaysia and Indonesia, the left hand is considered unclean. Therefore, it is insulting to hand an object to someone using the left hand.

- In Japan, as well as some other Asian countries, it is much easier to get things done, or to get to see a prospective client, if you have been recommended or introduced by a mutual acquaintance.

- In Ethiopia, the time required to make a decision is directly proportional to its importance. This is so much the case that lower-level bureaucrats there attempt to elevate the prestige of their work by taking a long time to make decisions. Unaware North Americans therefore may innocently downgrade their work in the local people's eyes by trying to speed things up.

www.helenecurtis.com

Often a marketing program that has been successful in Canada cannot be applied directly in international markets because of cultural differences. Real differences exist among different countries, and the differences must be known and evaluated by the international firm. Purdy's Chocolates not only discovered that Taiwanese consumers did not like some of their products and packaging, but also that channels of distribution were not what they expected. When Helene Curtis introduced its Every Night shampoo line in Sweden, it renamed the product Every Day, since Swedes usually wash their hair in the morning.

World marketers must become familiar with many aspects of the local population — including their cultural heritage. The local market segments in each country must be thoroughly analyzed prior to developing a marketing plan, just as they are at home. The topic of cultural influences in international marketing is explored more fully in Chapter 19.

SUBCULTURES

microculture
A subgroup with its own distinguishing modes of behaviour.

Within each culture are numerous **microcultures** — subgroups with their own distinguishing modes of behaviour. Any culture as heterogeneous as that existing in Canada is composed of significant microcultures based on such factors as race, nationality, age, rural–urban location, religion, and geographic distribution. The size of such microculture groups can be significant. For example, the Italian population in the Toronto area is about 500 000 — larger than the entire population of most Canadian cities.

Many people on the West Coast display a lifestyle that emphasizes casual dress, outdoor entertaining, and water recreation. Mormons refrain from purchasing tobacco and liquor; orthodox Jews purchase kosher or other traditional foods; Chinese people may exhibit more interest in products and symbols that reflect their Chinese heritage.

The French-Canadian Market Although Canada has many microcultures, the two founding cultures — English and French — are the most influential, through sheer force of numbers. The francophone population is a significant market in Canada. Twenty-two percent of the Canadian population identify French as their mother tongue.[5] While most of this population resides in Quebec, there are significant French-speaking segments in other provinces. Proportionately, the largest is in New Brunswick, where 32.9 percent of the population (or 239 700 people) have French as their mother tongue. Numerically, Ontario has the largest group outside Quebec, with 479 300.

The Quebec market is large enough and different enough to create an entire advertising industry of its own. Quebec's share of Canadian GDP is 21.7 percent.[6] It is the second-largest market in Canada.

While there is no doubt that the Quebec market is substantially different from the rest of Canada, it is difficult to define those differences precisely. Considerable research over the years has suggested many characteristics specific to the area—French-Canadians, for example, are said to be fonder of sweets than other Canadians. However, other data can usually be found to contest any such find, or at least to show that it is no longer true.

Such statements reflect measurement of traits in the Quebec culture at only one particular period. These measurements may be legitimate and necessary for a firm that wishes to market a product in that segment at a particular point in time. However, similar differences can probably be detected between consumers in Nova Scotia and consumers in British Columbia, if you look for them.

▶ THE CANADIAN MARKETPLACE

Is There a Difference? Francophone Quebeckers vs. English Canadians

- Percentage of francophone Quebeckers who prefer people who choose happiness over duty: 51. Of English Canadians: 25.
- Percentage of francophone Quebeckers who think buying something new is one of life's great pleasures: 71. Of English Canadians: 51.
- Percentage of Quebec couples living common-law in 1996: 25. Of couples elsewhere in Canada: 14. Of Quebec couples under 30: 64. Of under-30 couples in the rest of Canada: 42.
- Number of Quebec-made television shows among the ten most highly rated programs in the province during the 1995–96 season: 10. Of Canadian-made shows in the top ten in English Canada: 3.
- Percentage of francophone women who say that dressing elegantly is an important facet of their lives: 45. Of anglophone women: 29.
- Percentage of Quebeckers who conduct their ordinary banking transactions through a credit union or *caisse populaire:* 60. Of English Canadians: 3.
- Percentage of francophone men who said they purchased more than three pairs of shoes in the preceding 12 months: 23. Of anglophone men: 8.
- Percentage of francophone Quebeckers who say they've purchased no-name grocery products: 42. Of English Canadians: 70.
- Percentage of francophone Quebeckers who read the comics section of their newspaper: 17. Of English Canadians: 38.
- Percentage of Quebeckers who acknowledge having had an affair: 16. Of Ontarians: 9.

Do you think there's a difference between francophone Quebeckers and English Canadians? If so, why?

Source: Excerpted from Leger & Leger, Decima Research, Statistics Canada, Nielsen Media Research, and Print Measurement Bureau, in *The Globe and Mail* (July 19, 1997), p. D1.

www.nielsenmedia.com

business.cd-rom-directory. com/cdprod1/cdhrec/003/ 515.shtml

Attention should not be concentrated on *specific* differences between the Quebec market and the rest of Canada, but rather on the fact that there is a basic cultural difference between the two markets. "Culture is a way of being, thinking, and feeling. It is a driving force animating a significant group of individuals united by a common tongue, and sharing the same customs, habits and experiences."[7] Because of this cultural difference, some marketing programs may be distinctly different in Quebec than in the rest of Canada. In the French-Canadian market, it is not the products that are different, but the state of mind. For example, Renault achieved a Quebec market penetration ten times greater than in the rest of Canada. Since the product and price were the same, the difference must have lain in the marketing program attuned to the Quebec market.

As cultures in Canada are affected by similar political and technological influences, the differences in values and consumption patterns also narrow. Nevertheless, it appears that for some francophones some frames of reference and significant cues will continue to be different, requiring the marketer to be astute in dealing with these market segments.

The key to success in this important Canadian market is having marketing specialists who understand people and how to deal in that specific market. Sophisticated marketers now realize this. That is why there are so many Quebec advertising agencies producing unique advertising programs for the francophone market.

Social Influences

The earliest awareness of children confirms that they are members of a very important group—the family—from which they seek total satisfaction of their physiological and social needs. As they grow older, they join other groups—neighbourhood play groups, school groups, Cub Scouts, Brownies, minor league hockey teams—as well as groups of friends. From these groups they acquire both status and role. **Status** refers to relative position in a group. **Role** refers to the rights and duties expected of an individual in a group by other members of the group. Some of these are formal groups (for example, Cub Scouts) and others are informal (friendship groups). But both types supply their members with status and roles and, in doing so, influence the activities, including the consumer behaviour, of each member.

status
Relative position in a group.

role
The rights and duties expected of an individual in a group by other members of the group.

GROUP INFLUENCE AFFECTS CONFORMITY

Although most people view themselves as individuals, groups are often highly influential in purchase decisions. In situations where individuals feel that a particular group or groups are important, they tend to adhere in varying degrees to the general expectations of that group. Consider the pressure faced by young teens to conform to clothing styles.

The surprising impact that groups and group norms can exhibit on individual behaviour has been called the **Asch phenomenon**. The phenomenon was first documented in a classic study by psychologist S.E. Asch:

Asch phenomenon
The impact that groups and group norms can exhibit on individual behaviour.

> Eight subjects are brought into a room and asked to determine which of a set of three unequal lines is closest to the length of a fourth line shown some distance from the other three. The subjects are to announce their judgements publicly. Seven of the subjects are working for the experimenter, and they announce incorrect matches. The order of announcement is arranged such that the naive subject responds last. In a control situation, 37 naive subjects performed the task 18 times each without any information about others' choices. Two of the 37 subjects made a total of 3 mistakes. However, when another group of 50 naive subjects responded *after* hearing the unanimous but *incorrect* judgement of the other group members, 37 made a total of 194 errors, all of which were in agreement with the mistake made by the group.[8]

This widely replicated study illustrates the influence of groups on individual choice making. Marketing applications range from the choice of car models and residential locations to the decision to purchase at least one item at a Tupperware party.

reference group
A group whose value structures and standards influence a person's behaviour.

membership group
A type of reference group to which individuals actually belong.

aspirational group
A type of reference group with which individuals wish to associate.

disassociative group
A type of reference group with which an individual does not want to be identified.

REFERENCE GROUPS

Groups that exert such influence on individuals are categorized as **reference groups**, or groups whose value structures and standards influence a person's behaviour. Consumers usually try to keep their purchase behaviour in line with what they perceive to be the values of their reference group.

The status of the individual within the reference group produces three subcategories: **membership groups**, in which the person actually belongs (as is the case with, say, a country club); **aspirational groups**, a situation where a person wishes to associate with a group; and **disassociative groups**, ones with which an individual does not want to be identified. For example, teenagers are unlikely to enjoy the middle-of-the-road music played on radio stations that cater to their parents' generation.

It is obviously not essential that the individual be a member in order for the group to serve as a point of reference. This partly explains the use of famous athletes and celebrities in advertisements. Even though few possess the skills necessary to pilot a racing car, all racing fans can identify with the Mosport winner by injecting their engines with STP.

The extent of reference-group influence varies widely among purchases. For reference-group influence to be great, two factors must be present:

- The item purchased must be one that can be seen and identified by others.
- The item purchased must also be conspicuous in the sense that it stands out, is unusual, and is a brand or product that not everyone owns.

Figure 8.3 shows the influence of reference groups on both the basic decision to purchase a product and the decision to purchase a particular brand. The figure shows that reference groups had a significant impact on both the decision to purchase a car *and* the type of brand that was actually selected. By contrast, reference groups had little impact on the decision to purchase canned peaches or the brand that was chosen.

SOCIAL CLASSES

Consumer behaviour is affected by **social class**, the relatively permanent divisions in a society into which individuals or families are categorized based on prestige and community status. A six-class system within the social structure has been identified. Families have been grouped into two categories each of

social class
The relatively permanent divisions in a society into which individuals or families are categorized based on prestige and community status.

▶ **FIGURE 8.3 Group Influence as a Function of Product Type and Consumption Situation**

Product or Brand	Publicly Consumed	
	Weak reference group influence (–)	Strong reference group influence (+)
Strong reference group influence (+)	Public necessities Influence: Weak product and strong brand Examples: Wristwatch, automobile, man's suit	Public luxuries Influence: Strong product and brand Examples: Golf clubs, snow skis, sailboat
Weak reference group influence (–)	Private necessities Influence: Weak product and brand Examples: Mattress, floor lamp, refrigerator	Private luxuries Influence: Strong product and weak brand Examples: TV game, trash compactor, icemaker

NECESSITY   LUXURY

Source: William O. Bearden and Michaeli Etzei, "Reference Group Influence on Product and Brand Purchase Decisions," *Journal of Consumer Research* 9 (September 1982), p. 185. Reprinted by permission of the University of Chicago Press.

lower, middle, and upper classes on the basis of occupation, source of income (not amount), education, family background, and dwelling area. Research has shown that activities, interests, opinions, and buying behaviour are significantly affected by social class.

Income is not the main determinant of social-class behaviour, and the view that "a rich person is just a poor person with more money" is incorrect. Pipe-fitters paid at union scale will earn more money than many university professors, but their purchase behaviour may be quite different. For example, a professor may be more interested in expenditures related to the arts and similar entertainment, whereas a pipe-fitter may have quite different tastes and interests in satisfying aesthetic and entertainment needs.

Marketers have found that it is more meaningful to think about such differences in terms of variations in *lifestyle*. Market segmentation by lifestyle is described in the next section.

RELATING SOCIAL-CLASS HIERARCHY AND LIFESTYLES

Analysis of people's lifestyles can be very revealing. It can indicate where they live, how they live, where they travel, what motivates them. More important, it can reveal the kinds of things they purchase, because it is lifestyle, not just income, that determines what a person buys.

Without knowledge of a person's lifestyle it is difficult to intelligently target a product or service. That knowledge provides the means to accurately profile the consumer base. You will know where to market a new product, where to best

---

▶ THE PRACTISING MARKETER

www.clubmed.com

Club Med Adjusts to Changes in Consumer Behaviour

Club Mediterranée, the French company that pioneered sun, sea, and sex holidays, has bowed to the passing of time and acknowledged its customers are now more interested in snoozing.

Club Med was founded in 1950 and became famous for sending well-off hippies to holiday camps in exotic destinations.

However, the company has now recognized that the interests and lifestyles of its customers have changed. The firm therefore launched a huge international advertising campaign that downplays exotic, erotic fun in a tacit admission its holiday-makers have become bald, staid, and a little boring.

"They have fewer beads, less hair, and more children," according to Serge Trigano, son and successor of the firm's founder. The average age of clients is now a decrepit 38. The new message is that Club Med offers customers a chance to recoup and recover from stressful daily routines. The company tells people that they can come to Club Med for a "break from the pace of modern life."

Reborn, Renew, and Reunion are among the slogans in the English-language version of the advertising material.

This recognition of changing consumer behaviour comes none too soon. In 1997, the company ran up losses of $235 million (U.S.). Perhaps closer attention to evolving lifestages would have helped Club Med to avoid the problems they now face.

Source: Adapted from Adam Sage, "Club Med Going for the Older Look," *Financial Post* (October 28, 1998), p. C16. Reprinted with permission.

locate a new store, where to promote with direct mail, where to spend the advertising budget wisely. In fact, lifestyle analysis can provide the answers to most important marketing questions.

To meet marketers' needs for better information, Compusearch has developed a system that groups all the neighbourhoods in Canada into unique clusters. Its PSYTE system identifies 60 different lifestyles (PSYTE cluster profiles) with specific locations across Canada.

Table 8.2 summarizes the PSYTE cluster profiles. Fourteen different major groups are classified as urban, suburban, town, and rural. As an example, the urban subgroup Urban Young Singles (U4) is highlighted. This subgroup is further subdivided into six smaller clusters, including University Enclaves. A brief description of this cluster is shown; Compusearch actually provides a more extensive description. Compusearch calls PSYTE a geodemographic neighbourhood classification system.

According to Compusearch's Web site, the basic tenet of geodemographic neighbourhood classification systems is that people with similar cultural backgrounds, means, and perspectives naturally gravitate toward one another, or form relatively homogeneous communities. Once settled in, people emulate their neighbours; adopt similar social values, tastes, and expectations; and, most important of all, share similar patterns of consumer behaviour toward products, services, media, and promotions. This behaviour is the basis for developing classification systems such as LIFESTYLES, PRIZM, CLUSTER PLUS, and Compusearch's PSYTE system.

Such cluster systems have already proven themselves where it counts — in the marketplace. At a conservative estimate, more than 15 000 companies in Canada and the United States alone used clusters as part of their marketing information mix in 1998.[9]

The major contributions of PSYTE's geodemographic clustering to modern marketing are as follows:

- *Discriminating power.* It is superior to most single-factor demographic measures such as age, gender, income, and so on.
- *Medium of integration.* You can build a consumer target market by profiling your own customer files, or you can use a profile of your particular product or service, and then compare or correlate that profile with more than 50 databases that have been coded with PSYTE. This can help you decide which cluster targets you want. You can then rank TV programs, select names from a mailing list, rank telephone exchanges and postal walks, and target retail distribution, all using the same target definition.
- *Accountability.* The results of cluster targeting can be easily measured. To see if cluster targeting works, companies simply have to track their sales, shipments, subscriptions, or whatever indicator by postal code, summarize them up to each of the 60 clusters, and see if sales have, in fact, increased in the targeted clusters.
- *Longitudinal time series.* PSYTE delivers the ability to track market share for groups of products or individual products on a cluster-by-cluster basis, both at the national and the individual market level, month over month, year over year.
- *Addressable, mapable targets.* Using a desktop mapping system, companies can illustrate targets at any level, right down to individual postal walks, proprietary distribution/sales zones, grocery store trade areas, or whatever.[10]

▶ **TABLE 8.2 PSYTE Cluster Profile, Estimated 1999 Canadian Households**

PSYTE MAJOR GROUPS	NO. OF CLUSTERS	PERCENTAGE OF ALL HOUSEHOLDS
Urban		
Urban Elite (U1)	3	2.66
Urban Ethnic (U2)	3	4.17
Urban Older Singles and Couples (U3)	2	4.76
Urban Young Singles (U4)	**6**	**10.23**
Urban Quebec Grey Collar (U5)	5	8.04
Urban Downscale (U6)	4	5.67
Suburban		
Suburban Affluent (S1)	4	6.78
Suburban Upscale Families (S2)	4	6.70
Suburban Older Singles and Couples (S3)	3	4.21
Suburban Younger Families (S4)	2	6.07
Suburban Quebec (S5)	4	9.80
Town		
Town Upscale (T1)	3	7.66
Town Grey Collar (T2)	5	8.59
Rural		
Rural Comfortable Families (R1)	6	6.41
Rural Downscale (R2)	6	8.23
Total	**60**	**100.00**

URBAN YOUNG SINGLES (U4)	CANADA HOUSEHOLDS	
	(#)	(%)
20 Young Urban Professionals	203 821	1.80
29 Young Urban Mix	223 706	1.97
36 Young Urban Intelligentsia	179 680	1.58
40 University Enclaves	**208 778**	**1.84**
51 Young City Singles	218 135	1.92
56 Urban Bohemia	127 880	1.13
Total Urban Young Singles	**1 162 000**	**10.23**

Cluster 40 (Group U4): University Enclaves (1.84% of Canadian households). Neighbourhood concentrations of urban university students, artists, musicians, etc. Most residents rent high-rise or low-rise apartments or older, subdivided houses. Education levels are very high. Occupations are white and grey collar. There are some immigrants, including recent immigrants, in these areas.

Source: Compusearch Micromarketing Data and Systems. Copyright © 1999 by Compusearch Micromarketing Data and Systems. PSYTE is a trademark of Compusearch.

More detail on the PSYTE system can be found on Compusearch's very interesting Web site at http://www.polk.ca.

OPINION LEADERS

Each group usually contains a few members who can be considered **opinion leaders** or trendsetters. These individuals are more likely to purchase new products early and to serve as information sources for others in a given group. Their opinions are respected, and they are often sought out for advice.

Generalized opinion leaders are rare. Individuals tend to be opinion leaders in specific areas. Their considerable knowledge about and interest in a particular product or service motivates them to seek out further information from mass media, manufacturers, and other sources, and, in turn, they transmit this information to their associates through interpersonal communication. Opinion leaders are found within all segments of the population.

Opinion leaders play a crucial role in interpersonal communication. The fact that they distribute information and advice to others indicates their potential importance to marketing strategy. Opinion leaders can be particularly useful in launching new products.

General Motors once provided a popular small car to college marketing classes as a basis for a course project. Rock stations have painted teenagers' cars for them; of course, the paint job included the stations' call letters and slogans. Politicians sometimes hold issues forums for community leaders. All these efforts are directed at the opinion leaders in a particular marketplace. These people play an important role in how successfully a new or established product, idea, or political candidacy is communicated to consumers.

opinion leaders
Trendsetters—individuals who are more likely to purchase new products early and to serve as information sources for others in a given group.

Family Influences

The family is an important interpersonal determinant of consumer behaviour. The close, continuing interactions among family members are the strongest group influences for the individual consumer.

Most people in our society are members of two families during their lifetime: the family into which they are born, and the family they eventually form as they marry and have children. With divorce an increasingly common phenomenon, many people become involved with three or more families.

The establishment of a new household upon marriage produces marketing opportunities. A new household means a new home and accompanying furniture. The need for refrigerators, vacuum cleaners, and an original oil painting for the living room depends not on the number of people in each household but on the number of *households* themselves.

As children are added to the household, sizes of some products purchased naturally increase. Two litres of milk will be purchased instead of one. Some larger families will purchase larger vehicles. Many other child-related purchases will be made over the period of time the youngsters remain in the home. Marketers find many opportunities in this market segment. For example, Chrysler achieved great success with its minivan, the Magic Wagon, a vehicle with ample capacity for families that nevertheless handled as easily as a car.

Another market evolves as parents are left alone when the children move away from home. These parents find themselves with a four-bedroom "empty nest" and a sizable lawn to maintain each week. Lacking assistance from their children and no longer needing the extra space, they become customers for townhouses, condominiums, and high-rise luxury apartments in the larger cities. This market segment also eventually purchases bifocals, and is a good target for organized tour packages.

IDENTIFYING TARGET MARKETS BY LIFESTAGE

A related approach to understanding consumer behaviour is to identify lifestages—stages in the life of consumers rather than stages within the family. Using this method, one could, for example, categorize young singles who are quite independent but live with their parents without trying to fit them into a category within a family.

The lifestages are *At Home Singles, Starting Out Singles, Young Couples, Young Parents, Single Parents, Mature Singles, Empty Nesters,* and *Left Alone Singles.*

The marketer can determine the type of products each group is buying and how much they are spending on them. It is easy to see that a Starting Out Single's purchases will be quite different from those of a Mature Single. Following this line of analysis, marketers can identify the logical customer for their product and develop a marketing program to appeal to the needs of that customer group.[11]

MARITAL ROLES IN PURCHASE DECISIONS

Although an infinite variety of roles are played in household decision making, four role categories are often used: (1) *autonomic*—situations in which an equal number of decisions is made by each partner, but each decision is made individually by one partner or the other; (2) *husband-dominant;* (3) *wife-dominant;* and (4) *joint*—situations in which decisions are made jointly by male and female.[12] Figure 8.4 shows the roles commonly played by household members in purchasing a number of products.

CHANGING FAMILY ROLES

Two forces have changed the female's role as sole purchasing agent for most household items. First, a shorter workweek provides each wage-earning household member with more time for shopping. Second, a large number of women are now in the workforce. In 1950, only about a quarter of married women were also employed outside the home; by 1981, that figure had doubled. Currently, over half of all married women with school-age children hold jobs outside the home. Women's share of employment is now 48 percent. Between 1989 and 1996, women filled two-thirds of the new managerial and professional jobs. Studies of family decision making have shown that wives who work outside the home tend to exert more influence than wives who work in the home only. Households with two wage earners also exhibit a large number of joint decisions and an increase in night and weekend shopping.

These changing roles of household members have led many marketers to adjust their marketing programs. Men's clothing stores, such as Strollery's in Toronto, now offer suits and accessories for the career woman. Although demand for men's suits has been sluggish in recent years, sales of women's suits increased 70 percent. Meanwhile, a survey of 1000 married men revealed that 77 percent participate in grocery shopping and 70 percent cook. A Del Monte promotional campaign recognized these changes and de-emphasized women as the sole meal preparers. Its theme, "Good things happen when you bring Del Monte home," applies to both male and female food shoppers.

▶ **FIGURE 8.4 Relative Influence of Husbands and Wives in Decision Making**

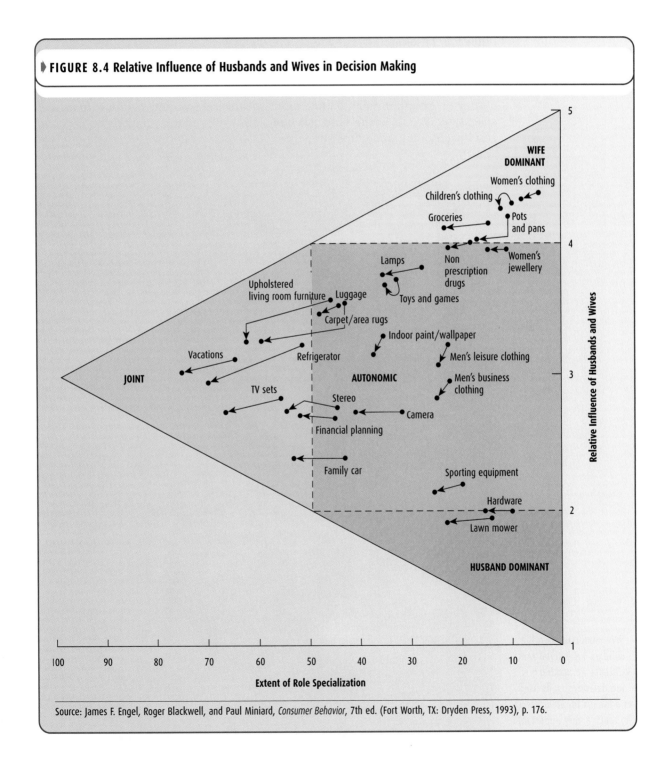

Source: James F. Engel, Roger Blackwell, and Paul Miniard, *Consumer Behavior*, 7th ed. (Fort Worth, TX: Dryden Press, 1993), p. 176.

CHILDREN'S ROLES IN HOUSEHOLD PURCHASING

The role of the children evolves as they grow older. Their early influence is generally centred on toys to be recommended to Santa Claus and the choice of brands of cereals. Younger children are important to marketers of fast-food restaurants. Even though the parents may decide when to eat out, the children often select the restaurant. As they gain maturity, they increasingly influence other purchases.

Young teenage boys spend most of their money on food, snacks, movies, and entertainment. Girls in this same age group buy clothing, food, snacks, movies, entertainment, cosmetics, and fragrances. Older boys spend most of their money on entertainment, dating, movies, cars and gasoline, clothing, food, and snacks, while girls of the same age buy clothing, cosmetics, fragrances, cars and gasoline, movies, and entertainment.

YTV, understanding that children have significant influence on making buying decisions, sells itself as a means for advertisers to reach a very important market segment.

▶ INDIVIDUAL FACTORS AND PSYCHOLOGICAL PROCESSES

In addition to environmental influences on behaviour, many individual factors are involved. These include needs and motives, perceptions, attitudes, and learning. Furthermore, the psychological processes that occur in the development of these factors have a significant bearing on buyer behaviour. After discussing these elements, a model of the consumer decision process will be presented. A general model of the factors that influence consumer behaviour is shown in Figure 8.5.

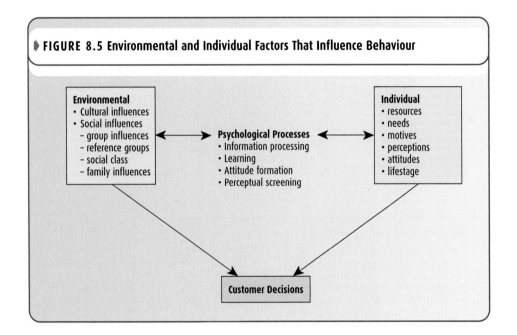

▶ FIGURE 8.5 Environmental and Individual Factors That Influence Behaviour

Needs and Motives

The starting point in the purchase decision process is the recognition of a felt need. A **need** is the perceived difference between the current state and a desired state. The consumer is typically confronted with numerous unsatisfied needs. Note that a need must be sufficiently aroused before it may serve as a motive.

Motives are inner states that direct us toward the goal of satisfying a felt need. The individual is *moved* (the root word of motive) to take action to reduce a state of tension and to return to a state of equilibrium.

HIERARCHY OF NEEDS

Although psychologists disagree on specific classifications of needs, a useful theory that may apply to consumers in general was developed by A.H. Maslow.[13]

need
The perceived difference between the current state and a desired state.

motive
An inner state that directs us toward the goal of satisfying a felt need.

He proposed a classification of needs (sometimes referred to as a hierarchy), as shown in Figure 8.6. It is important to recognize that Maslow's hierarchy *may not apply to every individual,* but seems to be true of groups in general. His theory is based on two important assumptions:

1. People are wanting animals whose needs depend on what they already possess. A satisfied need is not a motivator; only those needs that have not been satisfied can influence behaviour.
2. Once one need has been largely satisfied, another emerges and demands satisfaction.

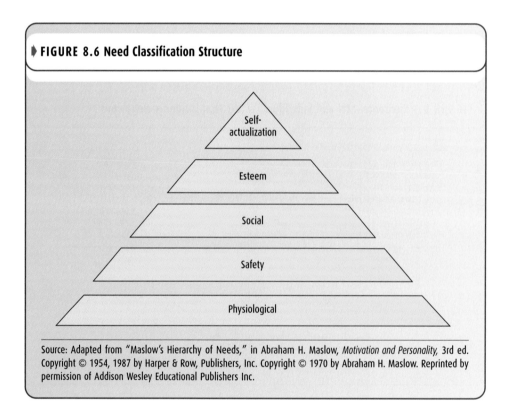

▶ **FIGURE 8.6 Need Classification Structure**

Source: Adapted from "Maslow's Hierarchy of Needs," in Abraham H. Maslow, *Motivation and Personality,* 3rd ed. Copyright © 1954, 1987 by Harper & Row, Publishers, Inc. Copyright © 1970 by Abraham H. Maslow. Reprinted by permission of Addison Wesley Educational Publishers Inc.

Physiological Needs The primary needs for food, shelter, and clothing normally must be satisfied before the higher-order needs are considered. A hungry person is possessed by the need to obtain food, while other needs are ignored. Once the physiological needs are at least partly satisfied, other needs come into the picture.

Safety Needs Safety needs include protection from physical harm, the need for security, and avoidance of the unexpected. Fulfillment of these needs may take the form of a decision to stop smoking, life insurance, the purchase of radial tires, or membership in the local health club. Antismoking advertisements target this need.

Social Needs Satisfaction of physiological and safety needs may be followed by the desire to be accepted by members of the family and other individuals and groups — that is, the social needs. Individuals may be motivated to join various groups and to conform to their standards of dress, purchases, and behaviour, and may become interested in obtaining status as a means of fulfilling these social needs. Social needs seem to be becoming a more important cultural value. Many "lifestyle" advertisements, such as those often used by Coca-Cola and Pepsi, appeal to social needs.

Esteem Needs These higher-order needs are prevalent in all societies. In developed countries with high per capita income, most families have been able to satisfy the basic needs. Therefore, Maslow predicts that such consumers will concentrate more on the desire for status, esteem, and self-actualization. These needs are more difficult to satisfy. At the esteem level is the need to feel a sense of accomplishment, achievement, and respect from others. The competitive need to excel—to better the performance of others and "stand out" from the crowd—is an almost universal human trait.

Esteem needs are closely related to social needs. At this level, however, the individual desires not just acceptance but also recognition and respect in some way. Membership in prestigious organizations or purchase of a specialty car are ways of fulfilling such needs.

Self-Actualization Needs Self-actualization needs are the desire for fulfillment, for realizing one's own potential, for using one's talents and capabilities totally. Maslow defines self-actualization this way: "The healthy man [sic] is primarily motivated by his needs to develop and actualize his fullest potentialities and capacities. What man can be, he must be."[14] The author Robert Louis Stevenson was describing self-actualization when he wrote, "To be what we are, and to become what we are capable of becoming, is the only end in life."

As already noted, Maslow argues that a satisfied need is no longer a motivator. Once the physiological needs are satiated, the individual moves on to the higher-order needs. Consumers are periodically motivated by the need to relieve thirst or hunger, but their interests are most often directed toward the satisfaction of safety, social, and other needs.

Caution must be used in applying Maslow's theory. Empirical research shows little support for a universal hierarchical ordering of needs in *specific individuals*.[15] It would therefore be unsafe to use the theory to explain a particular purchase. The needs hierarchy and motive strength concept may be useful in considering the behaviour of consumers *in general,* however. It has been verified that in consumer buying, previously ignored desires often surface only after a purchase has satisfied a predominant (and *perhaps* lower-order) motive.[16]

Perceptions

In some Asian countries, a prized product is ginseng root. This is used as a key ingredient in certain drinks and medications. The product is not cheap, but demand is huge, because many Asians perceive that ginseng has positive medicinal benefits for a number of conditions. In the West, however, the vast majority see no value in ginseng and are not at all interested in buying or using it.

Individual behaviour resulting from motivation is affected by how we perceive stimuli. **Perception** is the meaning that each person attributes to incoming stimuli received through the five senses.

perception
The meaning that each person attributes to incoming stimuli received through the five senses.

Psychologists once assumed that perception was an objective phenomenon—that is, that the individual perceived what was there to be perceived. It is now recognized that what we perceive is as much a result of what we *want* to perceive as of what is actually there. This does not mean that people view dogs as pigeons. We can distinguish shopping centres from churches, and a retail store stocked with well-known brand names and staffed with helpful, knowledgeable sales personnel is perceived differently from a largely self-serve discount store. Zellers and Birks are both important retailers, but they carry quite different images.

Our perception of an object or event is the result of the interaction of two types of factors:

- Stimulus factors, which are characteristics of the physical object, such as size, colour, weight, or shape. For example, a beautifully decorated and appointed lawyer's office results in a different perception of the lawyer than a plain, "storefront" operation.
- Individual factors, which are characteristics of the perceiver. These factors include not only sensory processes but also past experiences with similar items and basic motivations and expectations. The fancy law office will be reassuring to some and threatening to others.

PERCEPTUAL SCREENS

We are continually bombarded with myriad stimuli, but ignore most of them. In order to have time to function, each of us must respond selectively to stimuli. What stimuli we respond to, then, is the problem of all marketers. How can they gain the attention of individuals so that they will read the advertisement, listen to the sales representative, react to a point-of-purchase display?

perceptual screen
The filter through which messages must pass.

Even though studies have shown that the average consumer is exposed to more than 1000 ads daily, most of them never break through our **perceptual screen**, the filter through which messages must pass. Sometimes breakthroughs may be accomplished in the print media through larger ads, since doubling the size of an ad increases its attention value by approximately 50 percent. Black-and-white TV ads that selectively use one colour, in contrast with the usual colour ads, are another device to break the reader's perceptual screen. Another method of using contrast in print advertising is to include a large amount of white space to draw attention to the ad, or to use white type on a black background. In general, the marketer seeks to make the message stand out, to make it sufficiently different from other messages that it gains the attention of the prospective customer. Piercing the perceptual screen is a difficult task.

With such selectivity at work, it is easy to see the importance of the marketer's efforts to develop brand loyalty to a product. Satisfied customers are less likely to seek or pay attention to information about competing products. They simply tune out information that is not in accord with their existing beliefs and expectations.

CAN SUBLIMINAL MESSAGES SNEAK THROUGH THE PERCEPTUAL SCREEN?

subliminal perception
A subconscious level of awareness.

Is it possible to communicate with people without their being aware of the communication? In other words, does **subliminal perception**—a subconscious level of awareness—really exist? In 1957, the phrases "Eat popcorn" and "Drink Coca-Cola" were flashed on the screen of a New Jersey movie theatre every 5 seconds for 1/300th of a second. Researchers then reported that these messages, although too short to be recognizable at the conscious level, resulted in a 58 percent increase in popcorn sales and an 18 percent increase in Coca-Cola sales. After the publication of these findings, advertising agencies and consumer protection groups became intensely interested in subliminal perception.[17] Subsequent attempts to duplicate the test findings have, however, invariably been unsuccessful.

If used, subliminal advertising would be aimed at the subconscious level of awareness to avoid the perceptual screens of viewers. The goal of the original research was to induce consumers to purchase products without being aware of the source of the motivation. Although subliminal advertising has been universally condemned (and declared illegal in Canada and California), experts believe that it is in fact unlikely that such advertising can induce purchases anyway. There are several reasons for this: (1) strong stimulus factors are typically required even to gain attention, as discussed earlier; (2) only a very short message can be transmitted subliminally; (3) individuals vary greatly in their thresholds of consciousness[18] (a message transmitted at the threshold of consciousness for one person will not be perceived at all by some people and will be all too apparent to others; when exposed subliminally, the message "Drink Coca-Cola" might go unseen by some viewers, while others read it as "Drink Pepsi-Cola," "Drink Cocoa," or even "Drive Slowly");[19] and (4) perceptual defences also work at the subconscious level.

Contrary to earlier fears, research has shown that subliminal messages cannot force the receiver to purchase goods that she or he would not consciously want.[20]

▶ THE PRACTISING MARKETER

What It Takes to Break Through the Perceptual Screen

Many businesses fail to understand what it takes to get attention. They often fail to consider how great a change in stimulus is necessary to make a difference to customers. The relationship between the actual stimulus (such as price, size, loudness, or texture) and the corresponding sensation produced in the individual must be evaluated. This can be expressed as a mathematical equation:

$$\frac{\Delta I}{I} = k$$

where ΔI = the smallest increase in stimulus that will be noticeably different from the previous intensity

I = the intensity of the stimulus at the point where the increase takes place

k = a constant (that varies from one sense to the next)

In other words, the higher the initial intensity of a stimulus, the greater the amount of the change in intensity that is necessary in order for a difference to be noticed.

This relationship, known as **Weber's Law**, has some obvious implications in marketing. A price increase of $300 for a Chrysler Neon is readily apparent for prospective buyers; the same $300 increase on a $70 000 Lexus seems insignificant. A large package requires a much greater increase in size to be noticeable than a smaller-sized package requires. People perceive by *exception*, and the change in a stimulus must be sufficiently great to gain the individual's attention.[21]

How can this finding be applied to advertising?

Weber's Law
The higher the initial intensity of a stimulus, the greater the amount of the change in intensity that is necessary in order for a difference to be noticed.

Attitudes

Perception of incoming stimuli is greatly affected by attitudes regarding these stimuli. In fact, decisions to purchase products are based on currently held attitudes about the product, the store, or the salesperson.

Attitudes may be defined as a person's enduring favourable or unfavourable evaluations of some object or idea. Attitudes are formed over a period of time through individual experiences and group contacts, and are highly resistant to change.

attitudes
A person's enduring favourable or unfavourable evaluations of some object or idea.

COMPONENTS OF AN ATTITUDE

Attitudes consist of three related components: cognitive, affective, and conative. The **cognitive component** is the knowledge and beliefs one has about an object or concept. The **affective component** is one's feelings or emotional reactions. The **conative component** is the way one tends to act or behave. In considering the decision to shop at a warehouse-type food store, a person obtains information from advertising, trial visits, and input from family, friends, and associates (cognitive). A consumer also receives inputs from others about their acceptance of shopping at this new type of store, as well as impressions about the type of people who shop there (affective). The shopper may ultimately decide to make some purchases of canned goods, cereal, and bakery products there, but continue to rely on a regular supermarket for major food purchases (conative).

cognitive component
The knowledge and beliefs one has about an object or concept.

affective component
One's feelings or emotional reactions.

conative component
The way one tends to act or behave.

As Figure 8.7 illustrates, the three components exist in a relatively stable and balanced relationship to one another and combine to form an overall attitude about an object or idea.

PRODUCING ATTITUDE CHANGE

Given that a favourable consumer attitude is a prerequisite to market success, how can a firm lead prospective buyers to adopt a more favourable attitude toward its products? The marketer has two choices: either attempt to change attitudes to bring them into accord with the product, or determine consumer

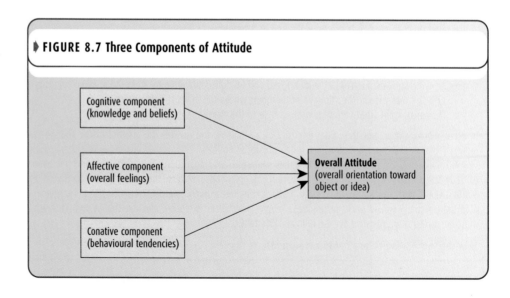

▶ **FIGURE 8.7 Three Components of Attitude**

Cognitive component
(knowledge and beliefs)

Affective component
(overall feelings)

Conative component
(behavioural tendencies)

Overall Attitude
(overall orientation toward object or idea)

attitudes and then change the product to match them. The latter is the easiest choice.

If consumers view the product unfavourably, the firm may choose to redesign the product to better conform with their desires. To accommodate the consumer, the firm may make styling changes, variations in ingredients, changes in package size, and changes in retail stores handling the product. The other course of action — changing consumer attitudes toward the product without changing the product — is much more difficult.

AFFECTING ATTITUDE BY MODIFYING ONE ATTITUDINAL COMPONENT

Attitude change may occur when inconsistencies are introduced among the three attitudinal components. If one component can be influenced, the other two may be brought into congruence with the changed component, and the attitude will be modified.

Cognitive Component One way to create an inconsistency in the cognitive component involves providing new information. In the early 1990s, General Motors mounted a huge advertising program showing that its cars were more fuel-efficient and reliable than Japanese-produced cars. This information was expected to counteract "common knowledge" that Japanese-produced cars were superior on these characteristics. In another instance, beef producers first modified their product, then undertook comparative advertising to show the low amount of fat now contained in beef.

Affective Component The affective component of attitude may be altered by relating the use of the product to desirable consequences for the user. This is a common appeal for health and beauty-aid products. Advertisements for a new perfume or cologne may imply that it will make one more attractive to the opposite sex.

Conative Component The third alternative in attempting to change attitudes is to focus on the conative component by inducing someone to engage in behaviour that is contradictory to the person's currently held attitudes. Attitude-discrepant behaviour of this type may occur if the consumer is given a free sample of a product. Such trials may lead to attitude change.

Learning

Consumers *learn* about the values and uses of products. Since marketing is as concerned with the process by which consumer decisions change over time as with describing those decisions at one point in time, the study of how learning takes place is important. A useful definition of **learning** is changes in knowledge, attitudes, and behaviour, as a result of experience.[22]

The learning process includes several components. The first component, **drive**, refers to any strong stimulus that impels action. Examples of drives include fear, pride, the desire for money, thirst, pain avoidance, and rivalry.

Cues, the second component of the learning process, are any objects existing in the environment that determine the nature of the response to a drive. Cues might include a newspaper advertisement for a new French restaurant, an in-store display, or a Petro-Canada sign on a major highway. For the hungry person, the shopper seeking a particular item, or the motorist needing gasoline, these cues may result in a specific response to satisfy a drive.

learning
Changes in knowledge, attitudes, and behaviour, as a result of experience.

drive
Any strong stimulus that impels action.

cue
Any object existing in the environment that determines the nature of the response to a drive.

▸ THE ETHICAL MARKETER

www.nike.com

www.us.levi.com

www.fila.com

www.tommypr.com

www.adidas.com

Why Teenage Consumers Are Leaving Nike and Levi

Nike Inc. dropped "Just Do It" in favour of "I Can." Levi Strauss & Co. dropped its advertising agency of 68 years.

The key reason in both cases? The companies' images and products weren't cutting it with trendsetting teens who determine what's hot and what's not.

The two mega brands, which are both still leaders in their respective product categories, are losing market share to rivals old and new.

Both are frantically trying to reinvent themselves to be mainstream and cutting-edge hip at the same time—a task that may prove impossible even with their monstrous marketing budgets.

"Nike ha[s] fallen off as the choice for the young influencers, the people who decide what's new and what's hot have sort of fallen out of love with the brand," said Michael Clancy, executive creative director of Brandworks Ltd. of Toronto. "All of a sudden a brand like Fila becomes the brand that black American kids love."

Other brands that are giving the fashion kings trouble are those like Tommy Hilfiger and Adidas, which are brands of choice for urban kids who start and stop trends.

Teenage Research has found that it's only about 10 percent of teens (dubbed the "influencer group") that determines what becomes must-have fashion. Generally, the most popular kids in high school, with good grades and active in sports, are also disproportionately black and Hispanic, more than any other demographic group, Teenage Research says. "The majority of teenagers actually influencing many of the broader teen-embraced trends are nonwhite," says Michael Wood, Teenage Research's director of syndicated research.

Levi is betting it can turn things around with the 14- to 24-year-old set with its "Truth" campaign. The billboard and poster effort revolves around a series of one-line "truths" superimposed on the red tab background such as "Best Friends' Moms Are Usually Sexy" and "Conformity Breeds Mediocrity." TV spots depict youngsters in New York locations "talking about their own raw unedited truths," Levi says. The TV ads are slated to air on shows such as *Dawson's Creek, Buffy the Vampire Slayer,* and *South Park.*

"We want to surround our young consumers with great products and marketing they'll care about," said Robert Holloway, vice-president, youth category for Levi.

Have the research into and marketing efforts to affect teen consumer behaviour gone too far? Explain.

Source: Adapted from Paul Brent, "For Teens, Hip Means Sales," *Financial Post* (November 23, 1998), p. C4. Reprinted with permission.

---

response
The individual's reaction to the cues and drives.

A **response** is the individual's reaction to the cues and drives, such as purchasing a bottle of Pert Plus shampoo, dining at Earl's, or deciding to enrol at a particular university or community college.

reinforcement
The reduction in drive that results from a proper response.

Reinforcement is the reduction in drive that results from a proper response. The more rewarding the response, the stronger the bond between the drive and the purchase of that particular item becomes. Should Pert Plus result in shiny, manageable hair through repeated use, the likelihood of its being purchased in the future increases.

APPLYING LEARNING THEORY TO MARKETING DECISIONS

Learning theory has some important implications for marketing strategists.[23] A desired outcome such as repeat purchase behaviour may have to be developed gradually. **Shaping** is the process of applying a series of rewards and reinforcement so that more complex behaviour (such as the development of a brand preference) can evolve over time. Both promotional strategy and the product itself play a role in the shaping process.

Figure 8.8 shows the application of learning theory and shaping procedures to a typical marketing scenario, in which marketers attempt to motivate consumers to become regular buyers of a certain product. An initial product trial is induced by a free sample package that includes a coupon offering a substantial discount on a subsequent purchase. This illustrates the use of a cue as a shaping procedure. The purchase response is reinforced by satisfactory product performance and a coupon for the next purchase.

The second stage is to entice the consumer to buy the product with little financial risk. The large discount coupon enclosed with the free sample prompts such an action. The package that is purchased has a smaller discount enclosed. Again, the reinforcement is satisfactory product performance and the second coupon.

shaping
The process of applying a series of rewards and reinforcement so that more complex behaviour can evolve over time.

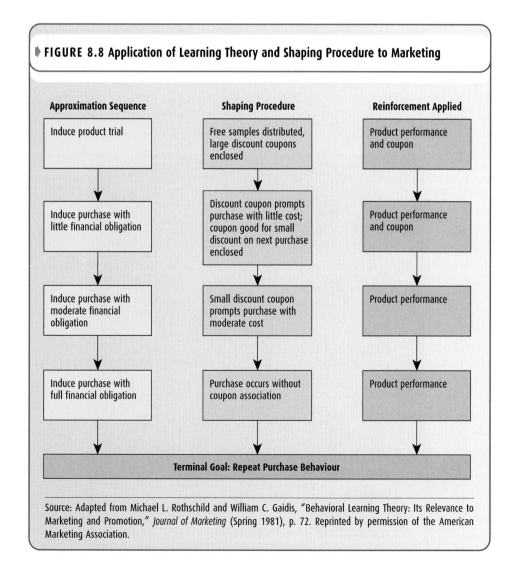

FIGURE 8.8 Application of Learning Theory and Shaping Procedure to Marketing

Approximation Sequence	Shaping Procedure	Reinforcement Applied
Induce product trial	Free samples distributed, large discount coupons enclosed	Product performance and coupon
Induce purchase with little financial obligation	Discount coupon prompts purchase with little cost; coupon good for small discount on next purchase enclosed	Product performance and coupon
Induce purchase with moderate financial obligation	Small discount coupon prompts purchase with moderate cost	Product performance
Induce purchase with full financial obligation	Purchase occurs without coupon association	Product performance

Terminal Goal: Repeat Purchase Behaviour

Source: Adapted from Michael L. Rothschild and William C. Gaidis, "Behavioral Learning Theory: Its Relevance to Marketing and Promotion," *Journal of Marketing* (Spring 1981), p. 72. Reprinted by permission of the American Marketing Association.

The third step would be to motivate the person to buy the item again at a moderate cost. The discount coupon accomplishes this objective, but this time there is no additional coupon in the package. The only reinforcement is satisfactory product performance.

The final test comes when the consumer is asked to buy the product at its true price, without a discount coupon. Satisfaction with product performance is the only continuing reinforcement. Thus, repeat purchase behaviour has literally been shaped.

Kellogg has used learning theory and shaping when introducing some of its cereals. Coupons worth 40 cents off have been distributed to elicit trial purchases by consumers. Inside boxes of the new cereal were additional cents-off coupons of lesser value. Kellogg has clearly tried to shape future purchase behaviour by effectively applying a learning theory within a marketing strategy context.

▶ THE CONSUMER DECISION PROCESS

This chapter has shown that consumer behaviour is the result of two main categories of influences: environmental and individual. The purchase of all goods and services will be affected by some or all of the many variables discussed.

Social status is an environmental factor that influences buying decisions. For example, Lexus is perceived as a car of distinction. Such a consideration may motivate a status-conscious consumer to buy the car.

Move over. Your inner child would like to take the wheel.
The 290-horsepower 1999 LS 400.

THE RELENTLESS PURSUIT OF PERFECTION. ⊘LEXUS

In the light of all this information, researchers have spent considerable effort trying to identify the process that a consumer goes through in making a purchase decision. One commonly accepted hypothesis suggests that the consumer decision process consists of six stages: (1) problem recognition, (2) information search, (3) alternative evaluation, (4) purchase decision, (5) purchase act, and (6) postpurchase evaluation. Figure 8.9 is a model of this process. Each step of the model is covered in the discussion that follows.

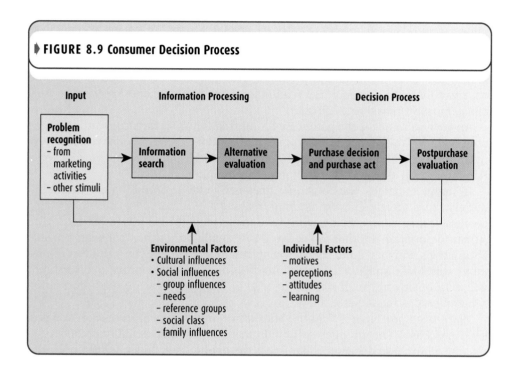

▶ **FIGURE 8.9 Consumer Decision Process**

Problem Recognition

This first stage in the decision process occurs when the consumer becomes aware of a discrepancy of sufficient magnitude between the existing state of affairs and a desired state of affairs. Once the problem has been recognized, it must be defined so that the consumer may seek out methods to solve it. Having recognized the problem, the individual is motivated to achieve the desired state.

What sort of problems might a person recognize? Perhaps the most common is a routine depletion of the stock of products. A large number of consumer purchases involve replenishing items ranging from gasoline to groceries. In other instances, the consumer may possess an inadequate assortment of products. The individual whose hobby is gardening may make regular purchases of different kinds of fertilizers, seeds, or gardening tools as the size of the garden grows.

A consumer may also be dissatisfied with a present brand or product type. This situation is common in the purchase of a new car, new furniture, or a new fall wardrobe. In many instances, boredom with current products and a desire for novelty may be the underlying rationale for the decision process that leads to new-product purchases.

Another important factor is changed financial status. Added financial resources from such sources as a salary increase, a second job, or an inheritance may permit the consumer to recognize desires and make purchases that previously had been postponed due to their cost.[24]

Information Search

Information search, the second stage in the decision process, involves gathering information related to attaining a desired state of affairs. This stage also involves identifying alternative means of solving the problem.

An *internal search* is a mental review of the information that a person already knows that is relevant to the problem. This includes actual experiences and observations, plus remembered reading or conversations, and exposure to various persuasive marketing efforts.

An *external search* is the gathering of information from outside sources. These may include family members, friends and associates, store displays, sales representatives, brochures, and such product-testing publications as *Consumer Reports,* as well as contacts with competing suppliers.

In many instances, the consumer does not go beyond an internal search but merely relies on stored information in making a purchase decision. Achieving a favourable experience flying with Air Canada may sufficiently motivate a consumer to purchase another ticket from Air Canada rather than consider possible alternatives. Furthermore, the Aeroplan frequent flyer program reinforces past purchases. Since an external search involves both time and effort, the consumer will rely on it only in instances in which, for some reason, the information remembered is inadequate.

The search process will identify alternative brands for consideration and possible purchase. The number of brands that a consumer actually considers in making a purchase decision is known as the **evoked set**. In some instances, the consumer will already be aware of the brands worthy of further consideration; in others, the external search process will permit the consumer to identify those brands. Not all brands will be included in the evoked set. The consumer may remain unaware of certain brands, and others will be rejected as too costly or as having been tried previously and considered unsatisfactory. In other instances, unfavourable word-of-mouth communication or negative reactions to advertising or other marketing efforts will lead to the elimination of some brands from the evoked set. While the number of brands in the evoked set will vary by product categories, research indicates that the number is likely to be as few as four or five brands.[25]

evoked set
The number of brands that a consumer actually considers in making a purchase decision.

Alternative Evaluation

The third step in the consumer decision process involves evaluating the alternatives identified during the search process. Actually, it is difficult to completely separate the second and third steps, since some evaluation takes place simultaneously with the search process as consumers accept, discount, distort, or reject some incoming information as they receive it.

Since the outcome of the evaluation stage is the choice of a brand or product in the evoked set (or, possibly, the search for additional alternatives, should all those identified during the search process prove unsatisfactory), the consumer must develop a set of **evaluative criteria**, features the consumer considers in making a choice among alternatives. These criteria can be either *objective* (comparison of gas mileage figures for cars, or comparison of retail prices) or *subjective* (favourable image of Tommy Hilfiger sportswear). Commonly used evaluative criteria include image, price, reputation of the brand, perceived quality, packaging, size, performance, durability, and colour. Most research studies indicate that consumers seldom use more than six criteria in the evaluation process. Evaluative criteria for detergents include suds level and smell as indicators of cleaning power. Style and brand name are key criteria for many people who buy Gap, Eddie Bauer, and Nike products.

evaluative criteria
Features the consumer considers in making a choice among alternatives.

Purchase Decision and Purchase Act

When the consumer has evaluated each of the alternatives in the evoked set using his or her personal set of evaluative criteria, and narrowed the alternatives to one, the result is the purchase decision and the act of making the purchase.

The consumer must decide not only to purchase a product but also where to buy it. Consumers tend to choose the purchase location by considering such factors as ease of access, prices, assortment, store personnel, store image, physical design, and services provided. The product category will also influence the store selected. Some consumers will choose the convenience of in-home shopping by telephone, mail order, or through the Internet rather than complete the transaction in a retail store.[26]

Postpurchase Evaluation

You may have narrowed the choice down to a jacket by Tommy Hilfiger or Eddie Bauer—a discrepancy in your beliefs about which would be best. But after some debate you choose Eddie Bauer. The purchase act results in the removal of the discrepancy between the existing state ("My jacket needs replacing") and the desired state ("I want a stylish jacket so I will look good"). Logically, it should result in satisfaction to the buyer. However, even in many purchase decisions where the buyer is ultimately satisfied, it is common for that person to experience some initial postpurchase anxieties. She or he often wonders if the right decision has been made ("Maybe that Hilfiger jacket would have been better"). This postpurchase doubt is known as cognitive dissonance.

Cognitive dissonance is the postpurchase anxiety that occurs when there is a discrepancy between a person's knowledge and beliefs (cognitions) about certain attributes of the final products under consideration. This occurs because several of the final product-choice candidates have desirable characteristics, making the final decision difficult. Consumers may, for example, experience dissonance after choosing a particular car over several alternative models, when one or more of the rejected models have some desired features that the purchased car lacks.

cognitive dissonance
The postpurchase anxiety that occurs when there is a discrepancy between a person's knowledge and beliefs (cognitions).

Dissonance is likely to increase (1) as the dollar value of the purchase increases, (2) when the rejected alternatives have desirable features that are not present in the chosen alternative, and (3) when the decision is a major one. The consumer may attempt to reduce dissonance in a variety of ways. He or she may seek out advertisements and other information supporting the chosen alternative, or seek reassurance from acquaintances who are satisfied purchasers of the product. At the same time, the individual will avoid information that favours unchosen alternatives. The Toyota purchaser is more likely to read Toyota ads and to avoid Honda and Ford ads. The cigarette smoker may ignore magazine articles that report links between smoking and cancer.

Marketers should try to reduce cognitive dissonance by providing informational support for the chosen alternative. Car dealers recognize "buyer's remorse" and often follow up purchases with a warm letter from the president of the dealership, offering personal handling of any customer problems and including a description of the quality of the product and the availability of convenient, top-quality service.

The consumer may ultimately deal with cognitive dissonance by concentrating on positive aspects of the purchase, changing opinions or deciding that one of the rejected alternatives would have been the best choice, and forming the intention of purchasing it in the future.

Should the purchase prove unsatisfactory, the consumer will revise her or his purchase strategy to obtain need satisfaction. Feedback from the results of the decision process, whether satisfactory or not, will be called upon in the search and evaluation stages of similar buying situations.

Classifying Consumer Problem-Solving Processes

The consumer decision process depends on the type of problem-solving effort required. Problem-solving behaviour has been divided into three categories: routinized response, limited problem solving, and extended problem solving.[27]

ROUTINIZED RESPONSE
Many purchases are made as a routine response to a need. The selection is a preferred brand or is made from a limited group of acceptable brands. The consumer has set the evaluative criteria and identified the available options. Routine purchases of a particular newspaper or regular brands of soft drinks or hand soap are examples.

LIMITED PROBLEM SOLVING (LPS)
Consider the situation in which the consumer has set evaluative criteria but encounters a new, unknown brand. The introduction of a new fragrance line might create a situation that calls for limited problem solving. The consumer knows the evaluative criteria but has not assessed the new brand on the basis of these criteria. A certain amount of time and external search will be required. Limited problem solving is affected by the multitude of evaluative criteria and brands, the extent of external search, and the process by which preferences are determined. Some products — those with little significance, either materially or emotionally — a consumer may purchase first and evaluate later (while using them). These are known as **low-involvement products**.

low-involvement products Products with little significance, either materially or emotionally, that a consumer may purchase first and evaluate later (while using them).

EXTENDED PROBLEM SOLVING (EPS)

Extended problem solving occurs with important purchase decisions when evaluative criteria have not been established for a product category or when the individual wishes to review such criteria. Today, many individuals are in the process of purchasing a scanner for their personal computer. Since many have never owned one before, they generally engage in an extensive search process. The main aspect of this process is determining appropriate evaluative criteria that are relevant to the needs of the decision maker. How much precision is required? Is the scanner to be used for images or optical character recognition (OCR)? What will be the machine's main uses? What special features are required? As the criteria are being set, an evoked set of brands is also established. Most extended problem-solving efforts are lengthy and involve considerable external search. A considerable amount of this research can be done on the Internet. Products for which the purchaser is highly involved in making the purchase decision are known as **high-involvement products**.

high-involvement products
Products for which the purchaser is highly involved in making the purchase decision.

▶ SUMMARY

Consumer behaviour consists of the activities of individuals in obtaining, using, and disposing of goods and services, including the decision processes that precede and follow these actions. Buyer behaviour is a function of the interactions of environmental, individual, and psychological processes, and can be summarized by the formula $B = f(E, I)$.

Environmental factors can be subdivided into cultural influences and social influences. Key social influences are group influence, reference groups, social class, and family influences.

The impact that groups and group norms can exhibit on individual behaviour has been called the Asch phenomenon. Its effect can be seen in the influence of membership, aspirational, and disassociative reference groups. Opinion leaders are individuals who are more likely to purchase new products early and to serve as information sources for others in the group. Therefore, they are important for the marketer when introducing new products.

Marital roles vary in purchase decisions. These roles have been categorized as autonomic, husband-dominant, wife-dominant, and joint.

Individual factors also significantly affect consumer behaviour. These include needs, motives, perceptions, attitudes, and learning. A need is the perceived difference between the current state and a desired state. Abraham Maslow established a need classification system with the following categories: physiological needs, safety needs, social needs, esteem needs, and self-actualization needs.

Motives are inner states that direct us toward the goal of satisfying a felt need.

Perception is the meaning that each person attributes to incoming stimuli received through the five senses. There are so many stimuli that individuals establish a perceptual screen to filter out undesired stimuli.

Attitudes are comprised of three related components: cognitive, affective, and conative. Marketers sometimes try to affect one or more of these components in order to change attitudes and therefore consumer behaviour.

The consumer decision process can be divided into the following steps: problem recognition, information search, alternative evaluation, purchase decision, and postpurchase evaluation. The outcome of this process is affected by environmental influences and individual factors.

Cognitive dissonance is the postpurchase anxiety that occurs after a purchase when there is a discrepancy between a person's knowledge and beliefs (cognitions) about certain attributes of the final products under consideration.

The consumer problem-solving process depends on the type of problem-solving effort that is required: routinized response, limited problem solving, or extensive problem solving. The products that are considered in the purchasing process can be grouped into low-involvement and high-involvement categories.

▶ KEY TERMS

affective component

Asch phenomenon

aspirational group

attitudes

cognitive component

cognitive dissonance

conative component

consumer behaviour

cue

culture

disassociative group

drive

evaluative criteria

evoked set

high-involvement products

learning

low-involvement products

membership group

microculture

motive

need

opinion leaders

perception

perceptual screen

reference group

reinforcement

response

role

shaping

social class

status

subliminal perception

Weber's Law

▶ INTERACTIVE SUMMARY AND DISCUSSION QUESTIONS

1. The work of Kurt Lewin provides a proposition of influences on buying behaviour: $B = f(P,E)$. Explain this equation, and apply it to the purchase of a service.

2. A major category of determinants of consumer behaviour is interpersonal determinants: cultural influences, social influences, and family influences. Based on Figure 8.3, for which of the following products is a reference-group influence likely to be strong?

   a. Rolex watch

   b. skis

    c. shaving foam

    d. mountain bike

    e. deodorant

    f. portable radio

    g. personal computer

    h. contact lenses

3. Compare and contrast influences on product use that you are aware of between two cultural groups. Outline the implications for marketing the product(s) specified.

4. The impact that groups and group norms can exhibit on individual behaviour has been called the Asch phenomenon. Its effect can be seen in the influence of membership, aspirational, and disassociative reference groups. Give an example of each type of group, and how such influence might influence product usage.

5. Opinion leaders are individuals who are more likely to purchase new products early and to serve as information sources for others in the group. Give an example of how a salesperson might make use of the phenomenon of opinion leadership in promoting her or his product.

6. Marital roles vary in purchase decisions. They have been categorized as autonomic, husband-dominant, wife-dominant, and joint. List a number of products whose purchase would be influenced more by a female. Explain how this knowledge could be used in developing an advertising program for a product in this category.

7. Another major factor that affects consumer behaviour is personal determinants, which include needs, motives, perceptions, attitudes, and learning. A need is the perceived difference between the current state and a desired state. Maslow established a need classification system with the following categories: physiological needs, safety needs, social needs, esteem needs, and self-actualization needs. Which needs are being referred to in the following slogans?

    a. No caffeine. Never had it. Never will. (7-Up)

    b. Swedish engineering. Depend on it. (SAAB)

    c. Conformity breeds mediocrity. (Levi Strauss)

    d. Best bed a body can buy. (Simmons)

    e. Don't leave home without it. (American Express)

8. Motives are inner states that direct us toward the goal of satisfying a felt need. Explain this statement using one of Maslow's need categories.

9. Perception is the meaning that each person attributes to incoming stimuli received through the five senses. There are so many stimuli that individuals establish a perceptual screen to filter out undesired stimuli. Name some methods that a marketer might use to break through such a screen. Consider selective perception and Weber's Law in your answer.

10. Attitudes consist of three related components: cognitive, affective, and conative.

    a. Explain each component.

    b. How do attitudes influence consumer behaviour?

    c. How can negative attitudes be changed?

11. The consumer decision process is outlined in Figure 8.9. Relate a recent purchase you made to this consumer decision process model.

12. Cognitive dissonance is the postpurchase anxiety that occurs after a purchase when there is a discrepancy between a person's knowledge and beliefs (cognitions) about certain attributes of the final products under consideration. Describe a purchase situation in which you or someone you know experienced cognitive dissonance. Explain how the company that produced the good or service helped or could have helped to reduce that dissonance.

13. Low-involvement products are those with little significance that a consumer might purchase first and evaluate later. High-involvement products are those for which the consumer is highly involved in making the purchase decision. Explain the type of distribution and advertising messages that would be appropriate for each category.

14. Discuss how access to the Internet might affect the consumer decision process, as outlined in Figure 8.9. Explain both the positive and possible negative aspects.

To obtain a list of further readings for Chapter 8, please refer to the *Foundations of Marketing* Web site.

Chapter 9
Business-to-Business Marketing

Forming an alliance with steelmakers helped International Utility Structures Inc. (IUSI) convince power companies to buy steel utility poles instead of the traditional wooden poles. But it was a tough sell, and as Robert Jack, IUSI's CEO put it, "We were trying to change a 100-year culture...."

Robert Jack found it hard to convince North American power companies to buy his steel utility poles instead of the traditional wooden variety. After all, he had to battle a century of history just to get his foot in the door. "We were trying to change a 100-year culture that was slow to change. That's the best way to describe it," Mr. Jack says. "The message wasn't getting through."

That was before Mr. Jack, chief executive officer of International Utility Structures Inc. (IUSI), came up with a high-powered sales pitch. He started bringing steel-makers—his suppliers are among the biggest buyers of electricity—to sales meetings to help convince power companies they should buy steel poles.

That marketing partnership is starting to pay off for Calgary-based IUSI, says Mr. Jack, adding he sees a dramatic shift in the buying patterns of power utilities. Mr. Jack's argument is that his company's steel poles are stronger and lighter than wooden poles, with at least twice the lifespan. Unlike preserved wood, the steel structures are free of chemicals potentially harmful to human health and the environment.

After factoring in installation, IUSI's steel utility poles cost the same or less than wooden alternatives, insists Mr. Jack.

Steelmakers are happy to work with IUSI. They see this marketing alliance as an opportunity to wring benefits out of the power companies from which they buy so much electricity. The coalition between steel companies and IUSI is forcing power utilities to reconsider their buying patterns. "They say, 'We're buying a whole lot more power than the wood-preserving industry. And we think we deserve to get some of our money back.'"

This new market for steel is music to the industry's ears, because it faces constant competition from other materials, such as plastic and aluminium. The steel companies are collaborating with IUSI and other pole makers to try to gain a 10 percent share of the replacement market for distribution poles in the near future.

www.iusi.ca

> **CHAPTER OBJECTIVES**
> After reading and studying this chapter, you should be able to
>
> 1. Provide an overview of the buying process between business buyers and sellers.
> 2. Differentiate among the three types of business markets.
> 3. Identify the three distinctive features of business markets.
> 4. Explain the characteristics of business market demand.
> 5. Identify the basic categories of business products.
> 6. Describe the nature and importance of government markets.

Not all of IUSI's selling points have proven successful. Mr. Jack discovered it doesn't help to emphasize to utilities the fact steel poles are free of the potentially toxic chemicals used to preserve wooden poles. "We stopped using the environmental argument as a strong push with utilities because they were afraid of it.... They get defensive automatically."

He found many utilities seem afraid to recognize environmental concerns as an argument for switching to steel, because it would mean acknowledging they had been using potentially toxic wooden poles for decades.

In January 1998, IUSI increased its international emphasis. It acquired Petitjean, a European leader in the lamp post and utility pole industry. The company is now geared up to pursue markets overseas. It plans to use Petitjean's vast global distribution network to sell steel utility poles and lamp posts to foreign clients, including developing countries eager for an alternative to less-durable concrete poles. IUSI has found a profitable niche selling to other businesses.

Source: Adapted from Steven Chase, "Steel Pole Firm Makes Powerful Pitch," *The Globe and Mail* (October 2, 1998), p. B24. Reprinted with permission from *The Globe and Mail*.

▶ INTRODUCTION

IUSI does not operate in the consumer market. It is one of a vast number of firms whose market is other businesses. Steel companies not only sell to power pole makers, but also to car and appliance manufacturers and countless other firms. In turn, many of these same companies produce and sell products to steel companies. The huge variety of products and services needed by companies to produce countless products constitutes the business market.

Business-to-business marketing is quite different from the marketing practised by consumer-product companies such as Chanel or Procter & Gamble. Many companies that have consumers that might cross over into the business market, and vice versa, have found that marketing practices that are successful in one market will not necessarily be successful in another.

www.chanel.com

Intuit Inc. offers small businesses easy financial management with QuickBooks accounting software. This tool is marketed as a friendly and efficient timesaver that makes accounting hassle-free, allowing owners to focus on their businesses.

The consumer market consists of individuals who purchase goods and services for *personal* use. The **business-to-business market** consists of firms that produce or acquire goods and services to be used, directly or indirectly, in the production of other goods and services or to be resold. The business-to-business market is also sometimes called the *industrial market.*

Important differences from the consumer market exist in the motivations and buying process followed by business buyers. As a result, marketing planning and the resulting marketing mix for the business-to-business market often are considerably different from those of consumer marketing.

business-to-business market
Firms that produce or acquire goods and services to be used, directly or indirectly, in the production of other goods and services or to be resold.

▶ TYPES OF BUSINESS MARKETS

In assessing the buyer behaviour of businesses, it is helpful to think about it in terms of the types of business markets. The business-to-business market can be divided into three categories: producers, trade industries (wholesalers and retailers), and governments.

Producers are those who transform goods and services through production into other goods and services. Producers include manufacturing firms, farms and other resource industries, construction contractors, and providers of services (such as transportation companies, public utilities, and banks). In the production process, some products aid in producing another product or service (for example, an airplane provides transportation), others are physically used up in the production of a product (wheat becomes part of cereal), and still others are routinely used in the day-to-day operations of a firm (light bulbs and cleaning materials are maintenance items).

producers
Those who transform goods and services through production into other goods and services.

Trade industries are organizations, such as retailers and wholesalers, that purchase for resale to others. In most instances, resale products (for example, clothing, appliances, sports equipment, and car parts) are finished goods that are marketed to customers. In other instances, some processing or repackaging may take place. Retail meat markets may make bulk purchases of sides of beef and convert them into individual cuts for their customers. Lumber dealers and carpet retailers may purchase in bulk, then provide quantities and sizes to meet customers' specifications. In addition to resale products, trade industries also buy cash registers, computers, display equipment, and other products required to operate their business. These products (as well as maintenance items and the purchase of such specialized services as marketing research studies, accounting services, and consulting) all represent industrial purchases. Retailing and wholesaling activities are discussed in separate chapters later in the text.

trade industries
Organizations, such as retailers and wholesalers, that purchase for resale to others.

Governments at the federal, provincial, and local level represent the final category of business purchasers. This important component of the business market purchases a wide variety of products, ranging from highways to education to fighter aircraft. The primary motivation of government purchasing is to provide some form of public benefits, such as transportation infrastructure, education, or health services. Buying behaviour in government markets is discussed separately in this chapter because of its immense size and importance.

▶ THE PRACTISING MARKETER

www.ngl.ca

COMPOSITE WOOD PRODUCTS

NGM
NGM International
DESIGN AND CONSULTING ENGINEERS

Serving Business Customers Very Well

Sitting in Bob Neill's basement in Fredericton, N.B., three engineers came up with a plan. Mr. Neill, formerly with the provincial electric company, Rod Nolan, fresh out of the University of London in Britain, and Harold Gunter knew they wanted to be in business for themselves.

But they were also determined that their firm be different from the dozens of other small engineering firms servicing the local market. "Our vision was much broader," recalls Mr. Nolan.

More than 30 years later, its mission has been accomplished. Neill and Gunter Ltd. is one of the largest design and consulting engineering firms in the country, specializing in factory design. The firm employs over 300 people in Fredericton, Dartmouth, N.S., Scarborough, ME, and Jacksonville, FL, and has clients around the world. The company is also a member of the Mission Air Network; their plane is used by medical patients who need air transport.

President Kenneth Reeder says, "We are focused on growth and on developing new business. We want to broaden our geographic areas as well." Mr. Nolan agrees, but believes it is the quality of their services, and not sheer size or even experience, that sets the firm apart.

"We enjoy a [great] reputation," he says. The secret to this is treating clients—as well as employees—as partners, he adds. "Even if we are only doing one part of a project, we assume responsibility for all of it. We don't want our partners to look at us as an expense, but rather as an investment."

This approach seems to work: staff turnover is low, and 70 percent of the firm's business comes from repeat business. The company's devotion to quality and service was key to their being selected by the *Financial Post* as one of Canada's 50 Best Managed Private Companies.

Suggest some ways that Neill and Gunter might go about finding additional business customers.

Source: Adapted from "Engineering a Reputation with Partners," *Financial Post* (December 28, 1998), p. C16. Reprinted with permission.

Neill and Gunter's winning approach to business has made them a leader in the development and design of industrial facilities.

▶ SCOPE OF THE BUSINESS MARKET

The business market is enormous. As Table 9.1 shows, in the manufacturing sector alone there are over 36 000 establishments, and they employ more than 1.7 million people. The significance of this market is dramatized in the amount of materials and supplies used in their operations—almost $233 billion worth! In total, the industrial market accounts for some 50 percent of purchases of manufactured goods in Canada.

value added
The increase in value of input material when transformed into semifinished or finished goods.

One measure of industrial output is the **value added** by manufacturing: the increase in value of input material when transformed into semifinished or finshed goods. For example, value is added to a tonne of iron ore when it is made into steel plate, and more value is added when the plate is stamped into refrigerator bodies. As shown in Table 9.1, the value added by manufacturing in Canada totalled approximately $164.9 billion in 1996.

▶ TABLE 9.1 Summary of Manufacturers by Province, 1996

PROVINCE	NUMBER OF ESTABLISHMENTS	TOTAL EMPLOYEES	MATERIALS AND SUPPLIES USED ($ MILLIONS)	TOTAL VALUE ADDED ($ MILLIONS)
All Canada[a]	36239	1703734	232872.8	164940.1
Newfoundland	323	10335	734.5	793.0
Prince Edward Island	143	4177	419.7	254.6
Nova Scotia	748	34402	3788.4	2293.5
New Brunswick	705	32069	5235.2	2780.4
Quebec	10603	484068	52261.2	42541.8
Ontario	14471	813504	124541.2	84495.5
Manitoba	1143	53114	4784.7	3949.9
Saskatchewan	800	22298	3155.6	1958.3
Alberta	2884	100746	18154.6	12334.4
British Columbia	4378	148528	19773.0	13517.4
NWT and Yukon	41	493	24.8	21.4

[a] There may be a discrepancy between figures for Canada and the total of all provinces due to varying sources of information.

Source: Statistics Canada, "Principal Statistics on Manufacturing Industries, Canada, Provinces and Territories, 1992–1996," *Market Research Handbook, 1999,* Catalogue No. 63-224-XPB, p. 180. Reproduced by permission of the Minister of Supply and Services Canada.

▶ DISTINCTIVE FEATURES OF THE BUSINESS MARKET

The business market has three distinctive features: geographic market concentration, a relatively small number of buyers, and a complex purchase decision process.

Geographic Market Concentration

The market for business goods in Canada is much more concentrated geographically than that for consumer goods. The largest markets are in Ontario and Quebec. However, business markets for specific items often do not follow the general pattern. As an example, the market for marine engines and fishing gear is concentrated on the Atlantic and Pacific coasts, while that for oil-drilling equipment centres on Alberta, British Columbia, and, to a lesser extent, Saskatchewan. The latter market has now expanded into Newfoundland.

Small Number of Buyers

The business market is concentrated not only on a geographical basis, but also by a limited number of buyers. Although there are approximately 36 000 manufacturing firms in Canada, a small proportion of firms — those with 500 or more employees — typically responsible for approximately half the total value added by manufacturing.

The concentration of the business market greatly influences the strategy used in serving this market. The business marketer can usually make more profitable use of a sales force to provide regular personal contacts with a small, geographically concentrated market than consumer goods companies can provide with ultimate consumers. Wholesalers are less frequently used, and the marketing channel for business goods is typically much shorter than that for consumer goods. Advertising plays a much smaller role in this market, as funds may be more effectively spent on the sales force and other means of promotion than with consumer goods.

Complex Purchase Decision Process

Another distinctive feature of the business-to-business market is the purchase decision process. Compared with the consumer decision process, the business decision process is generally more complex. The magnitude of the decision is greater, more people are involved, and organizations set up more formal procedures that have to be met. This topic will be discussed later in the chapter in more detail.

▶ MARKET DEMAND

Demand for goods and services is affected by many factors. Beyond the strength or weakness of the general economic environment, four primary characteristics distinguish business requirements: derived demand, joint demand, inventory adjustments, and demand variability.

Derived Demand

derived demand
Demand for a product used by business derived from (or linked to) demand for a consumer good.

The demand for products used by business is typically **derived demand** — demand derived from (or linked to) demand for a consumer good. The demand for cash registers (an industrial good) is partly derived from demand at the retail level (consumer products). Lower retail sales may ultimately result in lower demand for cash registers.

The "downsizing" of automobile engines by auto manufacturers in an attempt to develop smaller, fuel-efficient cars adversely affects spark-plug manufacturers like Champion. Since four-cylinder engines use half as many plugs as V-8s, Champion's total sales may decline drastically unless total car sales increase dramatically, or unless Champion can increase its share of the total market. On the other hand, booming personal computer sales, along with advances in computing power, have boosted shipments of CD-ROM disk drives.

Joint Demand

The demand for some industrial products is related to the demand for other industrial goods. There is a **joint demand** for paper and printing ink in the manufacture of newspapers, for example. If the paper supply is reduced, there will be an accompanying reduction in the demand for printing ink.

joint demand
Demand for an industrial product that is related to the demand for other industrial goods.

Inventory Adjustments

Changes in the amounts of materials a manufacturer keeps on hand can have an impact on demand. Suppose a two-month supply of raw materials is considered the optimal inventory in some manufacturing industries. But suppose economic conditions or other factors dictate that this level be increased to a 90-day supply. The raw materials supplier would then be bombarded with a tremendous increase in new orders. Thus, **inventory adjustments** can be a major determinant of demand for products used by business.

inventory adjustments
Changes in the amounts of materials a manufacturer keeps on hand.

Demand Variability

Derived demand in the business market is related to and often creates immense variability in the amount of products required. Assume the demand for industrial product A is derived from the demand for consumer product B—an item whose sales volume has been growing at an annual rate of 10 percent. Now suppose that the demand for product B slowed to a 5 percent annual increase. Management might decide to delay further purchases of product A, using existing inventory until the market conditions were clarified. Therefore, product A's **demand variability** becomes significantly affected by even modest shifts in the demand for product B. The disproportionate impact that changes in consumer demand have on business market demand is called the **accelerator principle**.

An example of shifting demand is in the market for coal. Several countries, including Canada, the United States, South Africa, and Australia, have the potential to produce and sell great quantities of coal, but the market is extremely volatile. Demand has been declining for some time, which has led to significant price falls. One of the reasons for the decline in demand has been technological change. Demand for steel has levelled off, and electric-arc furnaces are being used to make steel from scrap. Also, pulverized coal injection, which allows steelmakers to replace half their coking coal with cheaper steam coal, is eroding the value of sales in the market that remains. Another effect on demand is the availability of substitutes such as gas and oil. As gas supplies have increased, its clean-burning properties have made it the fuel of choice in some applications.

demand variability
In the business market, the impact of derived demand on the demand for interrelated products used in producing consumer goods.

accelerator principle
The disproportionate impact that changes in consumer demand have on business market demand.

Is there any hope for coal? Over the next few years, new materials and technologies for generating electricity from coal are expected to become available. This will increase the percentage of energy in coal that can be converted into electricity. In addition, rapidly developing nations such as China are expected to buy more coal. Demand will fluctuate, but the prospects are not all bad.

▶ BASIC CATEGORIES OF BUSINESS PRODUCTS

capital items
Long-lived business assets that must be depreciated over time.

depreciation
The accounting concept of charging a portion of the cost of a capital item as a deduction against the company's annual revenue for purposes of determining its net income.

There are two general categories of business products: capital items and expense items. **Capital items** are long-lived business assets that must be depreciated over time. **Depreciation** is the accounting concept of charging a portion of the cost of a capital item as a deduction against the company's annual revenue for purposes of determining its net income. Examples of capital items include major installations like new plants and office buildings as well as equipment.

WITHOUT THE RIGHT EQUIPMENT
A BIG JOB CAN SEEM EVEN BIGGER.

WHETHER IT'S HIGH-VOLUME BLACK AND WHITE OR FULL-COLOR SOLUTIONS, CANON HAS THE RIGHT TOOLS FOR THE JOB.
When faced with an overwhelming workload, it's good to have office equipment that's up to the task. Like Canon's high-volume systems. Digital or analog, our high-volume machines are designed so you can handle your biggest jobs with very ANYWARE™ little effort. And all have finishing capabilities that can improve your productivity right from the start. Not to mention the image quality and reliability that have become the standard in the industry. So choose the right equipment — high-volume black and white and full-color solutions from Canon. Suddenly, those big jobs aren't so big anymore.

Canon
1-800-OK CANON

Businesses invest in capital items, such as photocopiers. Canon is known for photocopiers that are designed specifically for commercial use.

Expense items, by contrast, are products and services that are used within a short period of time. For the most part, they are charged against income in the year of purchase. Examples of expense items include the supplies that are used in operating the business, ranging from raw materials and fabricated parts to paper clips and machine lubricants.

expense items
Products and services that are used within a short period of time.

Chapter 10 presents a comprehensive classification of business products. This initial breakdown into capital and expense items is useful, because buying behaviour varies significantly depending on how a purchase is treated from an accounting viewpoint. Expense items may be bought routinely and with minimal delay, while capital items involve major fund commitments and are thus subject to considerable review by the purchaser's personnel.

▶THE NATURE OF BUSINESS PURCHASES

Business purchasing behaviour tends to be more complex than the consumer decision process described in Chapter 8. There are several reasons for this increased complexity:

1. Many people may exert influence in business purchases, and considerable time may be spent obtaining the input and approval of various organizational members.
2. Organizational purchasing may be handled by committees with greater time requirements for majority or unanimous approval.
3. Many organizations attempt to use several sources of supply as a type of insurance against shortages.

Most firms have attempted to systematize their purchases by employing a professional buyer, or purchasing manager, who is responsible for handling most of the organization's purchases and for securing needed products at the best possible price. Unlike the ultimate consumer (who makes periodic purchase decisions), a firm's purchasing department devotes all of its time and effort to determining needs, locating and evaluating alternative sources of supply, and making purchase decisions.

The Complexity of Business Purchases

Where major purchases are involved, negotiations may take several weeks or months, and the buying decisions may rest with a number of people in the organization. The choice of a supplier for industrial drill presses, for example, may be made jointly by the purchasing manager and the company's production, engineering, and maintenance departments. Each of these principals has a different point of view, and these must all be reconciled in making a purchase decision. As a result, representatives of the selling firm must be well versed in all aspects of the product or service and be capable of interacting with the managers of the various departments involved. In the industrial instruments industry, for instance, it takes an average of 4.6 face-to-face presentations to make a sale.[1] The average cost of closing the sale — including salesperson compensation and travel and entertainment expenses — is $1197.80.[2] Table 9.2 shows the sales force total cost as a percentage of sales, the average number of sales calls required to complete a sale in several industries, and the average number of calls made per day.

Many industrial goods are purchased over long periods of time on a contractual basis. A manufacturing operation requires a continual supply of materials, and a one- or two-year contract with a supplier ensures a steady supply of raw materials as they are needed. Other products, such as conveyors, typewriters, and forklifts, generally last several years before they need to be replaced.

Purchase decisions are frequently made on the basis of service, certainty of supply, and efficiency of the products. These factors may be even more important than the prices quoted for the products. Car manufacturers purchase steel,

▶ TABLE 9.2 Sales Call Statistics

INDUSTRY GROUP	AVERAGE SALES FORCE TOTAL COST AS A PERCENTAGE OF SALES	AVERAGE NUMBER OF CALLS TO CLOSE SALE	AVERAGE NUMBER OF CALLS PER DAY
Banking	0.9	3.5	2.5
Business services	10.5	4.2	2.2
Chemicals	3.4	5.4	3.2
Communications	9.9	4.0	3.1
Construction	7.1	6.2	2.2
Educational services	12.7	5.0	1.8
Electronics	12.6	5.0	2.5
Electronic components	4.9	5.0	2.6
Fabricated metals	7.2	3.7	2.5
Food products	2.7	2.3	2.3
Health services	13.4	4.0	3.5
Hotels and other lodging places	1.9	3.8	2.8
Instruments	14.8	4.6	2.8
Machinery	11.3	2.8	3.1
Manufacturing	6.6	4.0	2.6
Office equipment	2.4	3.5	2.9
Paper and allied products	8.2	3.8	2.7
Pharmaceuticals	5.6	0.0	4.0
Printing and publishing	22.2	4.2	4.0
Real estate	2.8	4.9	2.5
Retail	15.3	3.8	2.7
Rubber/plastics	3.6	3.5	4.2
Transportation equipment	6.2	3.8	3.5
Wholesale (consumer goods)	11.2	2.6	3.9
Average	10.0	3.8	3.0

Source: Dartnell Corporation, "Dartnell's 30th Sales Force Compensation Survey" (Palm Beach Gardens, FL: The Dartnell Corporation, 1999), Figures 70 and 104. © 1999, Dartnell Corporation.

glass windows, spark plugs, and batteries as ingredients for their output. Since demand for these parts is derived entirely from the demand for cars, price changes do not substantially affect their sale. Price increases for paint will have little effect on car sales at General Motors, since paint represents a minute portion of the total costs of the car.

Purchasing a Capital Item

A utility company that was considering buying a reinforced Fiberglas utility pole faced a complicated decision process. The sales representative dealt with the members of several departments of the utility company and went through months of negotiations before a purchase was made. The new pole had several advantages over the traditional wood post: it was lightweight, had noncorrosive properties, never needed painting, and met all strength requirements. Its major disadvantage, other than its unfamiliarity to the purchaser, was its high initial purchase price compared with the alternatives. The decision process began when the manager of the utility consulted the engineering head, who in turn brought in the purchasing manager. Purchasing then prepared a list of alternative suppliers and materials, which was approved by engineering. The purchasing manager then discussed the organization's needs in detail with the sales representatives of three suppliers. The salespeople met with the managers of the stores department, the marketing department, and the engineering department. After a series of meetings with the salespeople and numerous discussions among the utility's department heads, the utility company decided to submit the new Fiberglas pole to a test conducted by the engineering department. The results of the test were reported to the various department heads, and bids were then requested from suppliers A, B, and C. These bids were reviewed by the department heads, who ultimately decided to select the Fiberglas pole offered by supplier B. This complex decision process is diagrammed in Figure 9.1.[3]

▶ CLASSIFYING BUSINESS PURCHASING SITUATIONS

Business buying behaviour is affected by the degree of effort and involvement by different levels within the organization. There are three generally recognized industrial purchasing situations: straight rebuy, modified rebuy, and new task buying.

Straight Rebuy

A **straight rebuy** is a recurring purchase decision involving an item that has performed satisfactorily and is therefore purchased again by a customer. This industrial buying situation occurs when a purchaser is pleased with the good or service and the terms of sale are acceptable. Seeing little reason to assess other options, the purchaser follows some routine buying format.

straight rebuy
A recurring purchase decision involving an item that has performed satisfactorily and is therefore purchased again by a customer.

▶ **FIGURE 9.1 The Decision to Purchase a New Type of Utility Pole**

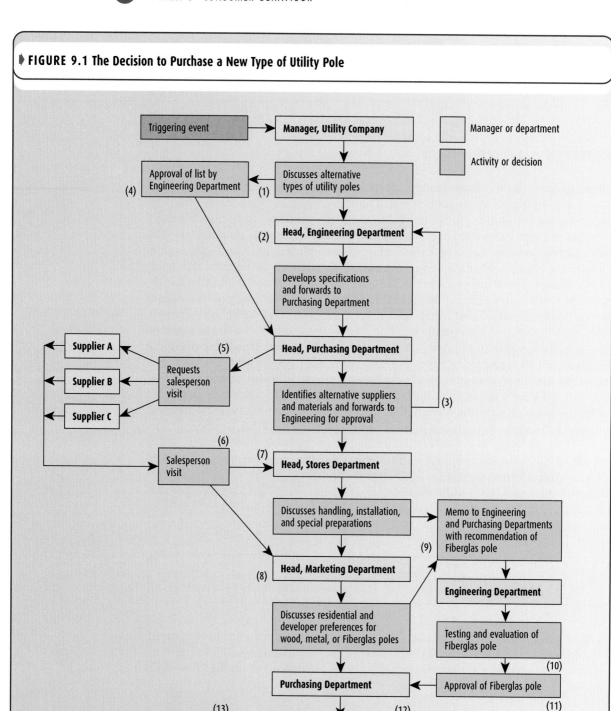

Source: Adapted from Arch G. Woodside, "Marketing Anatomy of Buying Process Can Help Improve Industrial Strategy," *Marketing News* (May 1, 1981), Section 2, p. 11. Used by permission of the American Marketing Association.

Low-cost items like paper clips and pencils are typically rebought. If the purchaser is pleased with the products, their prices, and their terms, future purchases will probably be treated as a straight rebuy from the current vendor. Even expensive items specially designed for a customer's needs can be treated as a straight rebuy in some cases. For example, a manufacturer might be virtually committed to buying additional lathes from a certain company because it purchased them before and wants to keep a standardized production process.

Marketers facing straight rebuy situations should concentrate on maintaining good relations with the buyer through prompt attention and adequate service. Competitors are faced with the difficult task of presenting a unique sales proposal that will break this chain of repurchases.

Modified Rebuy

A **modified rebuy** is a situation in which purchasers are willing to reevaluate their available options. The decision makers feel that it is to their advantage to look at alternative product offerings using established purchasing guidelines. A modified rebuy situation may occur if a marketer allows a straight rebuy situation to deteriorate because of poor service or delivery or if quality, cost, and service differences are perceived by the customer.

Business-to-business marketers want to move purchasers into a straight rebuy position by responding to all their product and service needs. Competitors, on the other hand, try to move buyers into a modified rebuy situation by correctly assessing the factors that would make buyers reconsider their decisions.

modified rebuy
A situation in which purchasers are willing to reevaluate their available options.

New Task Buying

New task buying refers to first-time or unique purchase situations that require considerable effort on the part of the decision makers. Once a need has been identified, evaluative criteria can be established and an extensive search for a product launched. Alternative product and service offerings and vendors are considered. A new task buying situation may arise when a firm enters a new field and has to seek out suppliers of component parts that have not previously been purchased.

Business-to-business marketers should work closely with the purchaser in the case of new task buying situations. This will allow them to study the factors the purchaser considers important and to design their marketing proposal to match the needs of the purchaser.

new task buying
First-time or unique purchase situations that require considerable effort on the part of the decision makers.

▶ THE BUYING CENTRE

buying centre
The key individuals who participate in a buying decision.

The **buying centre** concept is an important key to understanding industrial purchase behaviour. It denotes the fact that important purchases are normally decided with the input of several different individuals, each person often play-

▶ THE PRACTISING MARKETER

www.stssystems.com

STS Systems Inc. equips retail stores, such as Club Monaco, with the hardware and software necessary to run day-to-day operations.

Business-to-Business Marketing in a Global Setting

If you've ever shopped at a Club Monaco or Suzy Shier store in Canada, or a Tommy Hilfiger, Warner Brothers, or Armani store in the United States, you've seen STS Systems Inc. of Pointe-Claire, Que., in action.

You probably didn't notice it, though. STS is the company that provided the information technology that runs those chain stores—the point-of-sale terminals, software, and back-end computers. Doing it and doing it well will see the company posting revenue of $110-million this year, up from $95-million last year—90 percent of it in the United States. With 650 staff and offices in Montreal, New Jersey, Indiana, New York, and Georgia, it's also expanding into Europe through a new office in Britain. "Long term, we want to be a global player," says Howard Stotland, president. "Our new U.K. office is a step in that direction."

While, in the past, STS focused on providing total solutions—its own software plus hardware from business partners General Data and IBM—the company is now also marketing its own packaged best-of-breed products. One such product is AuditWorks—software, Mr. Stotland says, that can manage a retailer's entire audit process. "We're finding best-of-breed packages to be excellent door-openers for our other services," he explains. "Chances are, if they buy one of our solutions, they'll also come to us for other projects."

Behind the company's success is a team of highly motivated, creative people. "We focus on our staff," Mr. Stotland says. "That's what has and will drive this company in the long run.... [We have] a team ... that's always under budget and exceeds expectations."

This is another of the *Financial Post*'s 50 best managed private companies in Canada.

How are the marketing efforts of the company enhanced by having offices in the various world locations?

CLUB MONACO everyday.

Source: Adapted from Deborah Stokes, "Going Global, after a Fashion," *Financial Post* (December 28, 1998), p. C17. Reprinted with permission.

ing a unique role. The buying centre simply refers to the key individuals who participate in a buying decision. For example, a buying centre may include the architect who designs a new research laboratory, the scientist who will use the facility, the purchasing manager who screens contractor proposals, the chief executive officer who makes the final decision, and the vice president of research who signs the formal contracts for the project.

Buying centres are not normally part of a firm's formal organizational structure. They are informal groups whose composition will vary from one purchase situation to another and from one firm to the next. Buying centres typically include anywhere from four to twenty participants, and tend to evolve as the purchasing process moves through its various stages.

Buying centre participants play the roles of users, gatekeepers, influencers, deciders, and buyers in the purchasing decision process. Each of these roles is described in Table 9.3.

A critical task for the business-to-business marketer is to determine the specific role and the relative buying influence of each buying centre participant. Sales presentations and information can then be tailored to the role that the individual plays at each step in the purchase process. Marketers have also found that while their initial, and in many cases most extensive, contacts are with the purchasing department, the buying centre participants with the greatest influence are often elsewhere in the company.

▶ TABLE 9.3 Roles of Buying Group Members

ROLE	EXPLANATION
Users	Individuals who will actually be using the product. They normally have an important role in influencing the purchase decision.
Gatekeepers	Those who control the information about the product. For example, the purchasing agent will likely have catalogues, brochures, and advertisements that may or may not be passed on to the buying group. This individual may control which salespeople get to meet the buying group members.
Influencers	Those who affect the purchasing decision by setting buying specifications, or by providing information (e.g., engineers) or influence (e.g., senior or knowledgeable users).
Deciders	Those who make the purchase decision. The range of possible deciders is wide. They could be users, engineers, purchasing managers, or senior managers. It is important for the marketer to try to determine who the deciders are.
Buyers	Those who have formal authority for making the actual purchase after the decision has been made. Often this is the purchasing manager.

▶ THE PROCESS OF BUYING BUSINESS GOODS AND SERVICES

The exact procedures that are used in buying business goods and services vary according to the buying situation confronted—straight rebuy, modified rebuy, or new task buying. Most business purchases follow the same general process. A model of the business buying process is presented in Figure 9.2.

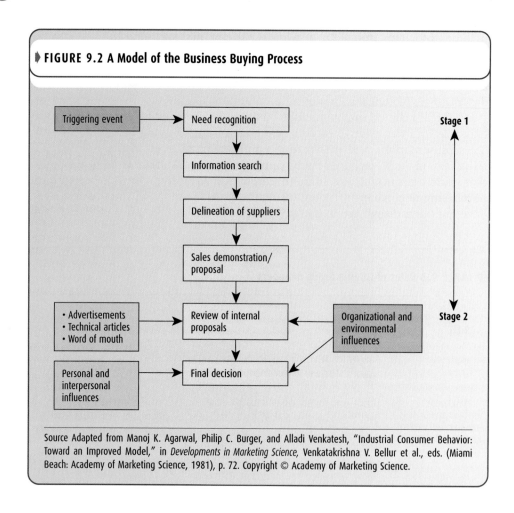

▶ **FIGURE 9.2 A Model of the Business Buying Process**

Source Adapted from Manoj K. Agarwal, Philip C. Burger, and Alladi Venkatesh, "Industrial Consumer Behavior: Toward an Improved Model," in *Developments in Marketing Science*, Venkatakrishna V. Bellur et al., eds. (Miami Beach: Academy of Marketing Science, 1981), p. 72. Copyright © Academy of Marketing Science.

A Model of the Business Buying Process

The specific steps shown in Figure 9.2 are outlined below.

NEED RECOGNITION
A triggering event, such as an equipment failure, stimulates recognition of a perceived need for a business purchase.

INFORMATION SEARCH
Buying centre members begin to collect information on potential suppliers from sales personnel, advertisements, word of mouth, pamphlets, and other sources. The net result is to delineate the technical nature of the purchase and the available alternatives.

DELINEATION OF SUPPLIERS
Given the specifications established in the previous step, potential suppliers are determined. Budget considerations may also be a factor in this step.

SALES DEMONSTRATION/PROPOSAL

Vendor sales representatives are invited to provide demonstrations and sales proposals. These proposals typically include technical and economic options as well as prices.

ADVERTISEMENTS

Advertisements have the effect of informing and persuading. Often, industrial advertising will invite a reader response requesting further information to be supplied.

TECHNICAL ARTICLES

The buying group examines technical articles for an in-depth analysis of the product, its features, and its performance.

WORD OF MOUTH

Buying centre members may then contact current users of the product for their evaluation of its performance. Reliability, costs, and operational abilities are explored. Some vendors are eliminated because of negative information.

PERSONAL AND INTERPERSONAL INFLUENCES

Despite the fact that the business buying process is generally more deliberate and involves more people in the decision, personal and interpersonal influences (as discussed in the previous chapter) also play a significant role in the final decision. For example, some salespeople are *liked* more than others. In other cases, a product will be purchased because it is popular, trendy, or gives a degree of prestige to the buyer or buying organization. The purchase decision may favour a known brand, despite the better promise of an unknown product, as a risk-reducing measure.

ORGANIZATIONAL AND ENVIRONMENTAL INFLUENCES

Often a number of organizational influences affect the purchase decision. For example, in the purchase of a metal milling machine, the marketing and product design group may want the product to be capable of certain performance characteristics. The engineering and manufacturing group has certain specifications that they feel the machine should meet. The production workers also have preferences as to the ease of operation of the machine, and the financial officer wants to see that the purchase price is within budgeted limits.

Environmental considerations are becoming increasingly important. The company must consider whether the product being purchased fits within set standards for pollution and waste. Furthermore, such considerations apply not only to the external but also to the internal environment of the organization. For example, with some photocopiers, proper ventilation has become important for worker safety.

REVIEW OF INTERNAL PROPOSALS

In some business purchase decisions, more than one group within the organization may have an interest in the purchase. For example, accounting, production scheduling, and research and forecasting departments would be interested in the purchase of a new computer system. After all of the information on various systems has been gathered, such interest groups should each be asked to recommend a system. These proposals would be taken into consideration in the process of coming to a final decision.

FINAL DECISION

Eventually a purchase decision is made. In many cases, this extensive process leads to a consensus decision, but some buying centre members have more influence than others in this final decision stage.

Reciprocity

reciprocity
Extending purchasing preference to suppliers who are also customers.

A somewhat controversial practice in a number of business purchasing situations is **reciprocity**, extending purchasing preference to suppliers who are also customers. For example, an office equipment manufacturer may favour a particular supplier of component parts if the supplier has recently made a major purchase of the manufacturer's office equipment. Reciprocal arrangements have traditionally been used in industries with homogeneous products with similar prices, such as the chemical, paint, petroleum, rubber, and steel industries. In the story at the beginning of the chapter, IUSI used reciprocity very effectively.

Two other forms of reciprocity are sometimes used. *Reverse reciprocity* is the practice of supplying parts and raw materials that are in short supply to firms that can provide other needed supplies in return. In times of shortages, reverse reciprocity occasionally emerges as firms attempt to obtain raw materials and parts to continue operations. A more recent reciprocity spinoff is the *voluntary price roll-back,* in which purchasers request vendors to agree to temporary price cuts or freezes. While no threats are made, it is difficult for a supplier to refuse a request from a major purchaser. This sometimes forces the vendor to ask for concessions from its own workforce and suppliers. The various forms of reciprocity are evidence of the close links that exist among the different elements of the industrial marketplace.

▶ NORTH AMERICAN INDUSTRIAL CLASSIFICATIONS

North American Industrial Classification System (NAICS)
A coding system used to categorize different types of businesses and products (formerly the Standard Industrial Classification, or SIC).

The marketer who focuses on the business market is aided by a wealth of information collected by the federal government, including data on the number of firms, their sales volumes, and the number of employees by category for firms in each industry. The data are broken down using a system known as the **North American Industrial Classification System (NAICS)** (formerly SIC) codes. The NAICS codes begin with 20 divisions; under each division is a list of major groups into which all types of businesses are divided. Table 9.4 lists the main divisions and groups.

These broad groups are further divided into classes. For example, Division 31–33 (Manufacturing) and Division 52 (Finance and Insurance) are divided as shown in Table 9.5. Statistics Canada collects statistics for each of the classes. The NAICS code system can thus help greatly in analyzing the business market.

Beyond the NAICS data, trade associations and business publications provide additional information on the industrial market. Many such publications are listed in the Appendix which follows Chapter 5. Such secondary sources often serve as useful starting points for analyzing industrial markets.

Differences in business purchasing behaviour are discussed in the sections that follow.

▶ **TABLE 9.4 North American Industrial Classifications**

DIVISION	INDUSTRY	GROUPS	NUMBER OF GROUPS
11	Agriculture, forestry, fishing and hunting	111–115	5
21	Mining and oil and gas extraction	211–213	3
22	Utilities	221	1
23	Construction	231–232	2
31–33	Manufacturing	311–339	20
41	Wholesale trade	411–419	8
44–45	Retail trade	441–454	12
48–49	Transportation and warehousing	481–493	11
51	Information and cultural industries	511–514	4
52	Finance and insurance	521–526	5
53	Real estate and rental and leasing	531–533	3
54	Professional, scientific, and technical services	541	1
55	Management of companies and enterprises	551	1
56	Administrative and support, waste management, and remediation services	561–562	2
61	Educational services	611	1
62	Health care and social assistance	621–624	4
71	Arts, entertainment, and recreation	711–713	3
72	Accommodation and food services	721–722	2
81	Other services (except public administration)	811–814	4
91	Public administration	911–919	5

Source: Adapted from Statistics Canada, *North American Industry Classification System,* 1997, Catalogue No. 12-501-XME, pp. 17–69. Reproduced by permission of the Minister of Supply and Services Canada.

▶ GOVERNMENT MARKETS

The various levels of government make up a sizable segment of the market for industrial products. There are many similarities between the government market and business markets, for they seek to purchase many similar goods and services. However, the numerous regulations that affect government purchases create differences in the way items are procured.

▶ **TABLE 9.5 NAICS Examples**

DIVISION 31–33—MANUFACTURING

Group	311 Food manufacturing
Class	3111 Animal food manufacturing
	31111 Animal food manufacturing
	311111 Dog and cat food manufacturing
	311119 Other animal food manufacturing
Class	3112 Grain and oilseed milling
	31121 Flour milling and malt manufacturing
	311211 Flour milling
	311214 Rice milling and malt manufacturing

DIVISION 52—FINANCE AND INSURANCE

Group	521 Monetary authorities—Central Bank
Class	5211 Monetary authorities—Central Bank
	52111 Monetary authorities—Central Bank
Group	522 Credit intermediation and related activities
Class	5221 Depository credit information
	52211 Banking
	522111 Personal and commercial banking industry
	522112 Corporate and institutional banking

Source: Adapted from Statistics Canada, *North American Industry Classification System*, 1997, Catalogue No. 12-501-XME. Reproduced by permission of the Minister of Supply and Services Canada.

Government expenditures represent nearly 52 percent of Canada's gross domestic product.[4] More than 60 000 firms supply 20 000 items and services to the various levels of government, whose total spending in 1994–1995 amounted to over $357 billion.[5] Table 9.6 indicates the major categories of government expenditures.

How Governments Buy

bids
Price quotations from
potential suppliers.

Since most government purchases must, by law, be made on the basis of **bids** (price quotations from potential suppliers), the government buyer must develop specifications—specific descriptions of needed items or jobs for prospective bidders (this is often done in the business market also). For the federal government, most of the branded items, such as general-purpose supplies, are purchased by the Department of Supply and Services. Each province generally has a comparable office for such items.

> **TABLE 9.6 Gross General Expenditures, All Levels of Government, 1994–1995**

FUNCTION	$ (MILLIONS)
General services	18237
Protection of persons and property	24477
Transportation and communications	15689
Health	47100
Social services	85783
Education	43920
Resource conservation and industrial development	14119
Environment	8040
Recreation and culture	7215
Foreign affairs and international assistance	4934
Regional planning and development	1615
Debt charges	71325
Other expenditures	791
Total gross general expenditure	357568

Source: Statistics Canada, "Consolidated Federal, Provincial, Territorial and Local Government Expenditure, Fiscal Years 1990/1991 to 1994/1995," from *Public Sector Finance, 1995-1996*, Catalogue No. 68-212, p. 168. Reproduced by permission of the Minister of Supply and Services Canada.

Bidding on Government Contracts

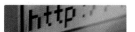

canada.gc.ca

All Canadian business and industrial operations are eligible to bid on federal government contracts. The only requirement is that a firm must indicate interest and be prepared to provide evidence that it can supply needed goods or services in accordance with the specified time, cost, quality, performance, and other terms and conditions.

There are three ways of obtaining bids:

1. An *invitation to tender* is normally used for all purchases of more than $5000. Two or more bids are requested, and the contract award is based on the lowest responsive bid. To ensure fairness, unclassified tenders are opened publicly.

2. *Requests for quotations* may be used for all purchases of less than $5000. They are not opened publicly.

3. *Requests for proposals* are used for all noncompetitive purchases valued at more than $5000, and for competitive purchases where the selection of the supplier cannot be made solely on the basis of the lowest-priced responsive bid. The evaluation of proposals is based on schedule, price, and relevant technical, scientific, financial, managerial, and socioeconomic factors identified in the solicitation. Requests for proposals are not opened publicly.

In addition to the Department of Supply and Services' head office, regional or district suboffices throughout the country purchase for the federal government. Although the details are not exactly the same, similar types of procedures are used by provincial and municipal governments.

Source Lists

The Department of Supply and Services keeps extensive records of thousands of commodity groupings purchased. Matched against these are the names of companies that have indicated they want to be considered as suppliers, and that the department considers capable of carrying out a contract. These records are referred to when requirements arise. A firm that wishes to be listed should write to the Executive Secretary for Supply Administration in Hull, or to the regional or district office in its area. Separate lists are maintained at head office and in each regional or district office.

Selling to Government Markets

Sometimes it is difficult for government to obtain bidders, even for relatively large contracts. Despite its immense size, the government market is often viewed as too complex and unprofitable by many suppliers. Excessive paperwork, bureaucracy, emphasis on low bid prices, decision-making delays, frequent shifts in procurement personnel, and excessive policy changes discourage some suppliers from attempting to service government supply needs.

On the other hand, marketers generally credit the government with being a relatively stable market. Once an item is purchased from a firm by the government, the probability of more sales is good. Other marketers cite such advantages as the instant credibility established by sales to the federal or a provincial government, timely payment, acceptance of new ideas, and reduced competition.

Only a few firms maintain a separate government sales manager or sales force. But many have experienced success with specialized government marketing efforts. It is expected that a growing number of large companies will organize to deal with government purchasers. This is especially true since the North American Free Trade Agreement opened the possibility of selling to U.S. and Mexican governments.

▶ E-BUSINESS OR OUT OF BUSINESS?

In order to implement the various facets of business-to-business marketing in an optimal manner, organizations must utilize the power of Internet interconnectivity. Software producer, Oracle puts it powerfully: "Your competition is on-line. Companies you've never heard of are stealing your customers. 'Business-as-usual' is not an option. Ignoring the Internet means 'no business at all.'"[6]

Some may claim this is overstatement; however, large companies such as Ford are proving that there are benefits to connecting all its suppliers and customers into one electronic exchange network.

An **electronic exchange** is an organized group of buyers and sellers from a specific industry linked together electronically. Electronic exchanges benefit buyers and sellers through the close linkage that they achieve. For example, a

electronic exchange
An organized group of buyers and sellers from a specific industry linked together electronically.

business purchaser might post a request for quotations for 10 000 automotive CD players. An attachment would include drawings and precise specifications. The posting would be placed through an Internet exchange network operated by the company (if the business is large enough) or by other providers. On the closing date, the purchaser would review the quotations that had been received from around the world, and would then issue the purchase order electronically. All other parts of the transaction, except physical delivery and handling, would be handled electronically, including the relaying of information to relevant units of the organization. The CD players would arrive on the production line in the right quantities and at the specified delivery times.

An example of an electronic exchange network is VerticalNet, Inc., a leading creator and operator of numerous vertical trade communities on the Internet, including advanced technologies, communications, food and packaging, healthcare, and other service industries. A **vertical Web community** acts as a comprehensive source of information and dialogue for a particular vertical market.

www.verticalnet.com

vertical Web community
A site that acts as a comprehensive source of information and dialogue for a particular vertical market.

Companies can take advantage of the interactive features and global reach of the Internet to facilitate business-to-business trading. Buyers and sellers from around the world with similar professional interests are brought together in ways that were never possible before the Internet. The VerticalNet Web site features highly focused target markets that draw business Web users to visit the site to obtain information, or to search for products and services to buy and sell. Another site that facilitates business-to-business trade is PurchasePro.com.

corp.purchasepro.com

E-commerce works. Nygard International's Winnipeg production site formerly took five weeks to turn orders around. Today, with electronic ordering that time is cut to a maximum of 72 hours. When a retail customer places an order electronically, a process is triggered that first places automatic orders with fabric and component suppliers linked to the system enabling manufacturing to be scheduled and started quickly. Another firm found that by utilizing a similar system, a purchasing assignment that once took six or seven hours to complete now takes about 45 minutes to an hour.[7]

▶ SUMMARY

The business-to-business market consists of firms that produce or acquire goods and services to be used, directly or indirectly, in the production of other goods and services or to be resold. Important differences from the consumer market exist with business buyers.

Categorizing business buyers is important for assessing buyer behaviour. The three categories are producers, trade industries, and governments. The business market also has three distinctive features: geographic market concentration, a relatively small number of buyers, and a complex purchase decision process.

Business market demand is distinguished by four characteristics: derived demand, joint demand, inventory adjustments, and demand variability.

The business purchase is generally more complex than a typical consumer purchase. The purchase often involves a group of individuals (the buying group) with different interests and skills in assessing the value of the purchase. There are three generally recognized purchasing situations: straight rebuy, modified rebuy, and new task buying. The straight rebuy is the simplest business buying situation.

The business buying process generally involves the following phases: (1) need recognition, (2) information search, (3) delineation of suppliers, (4) sales demonstration/proposal, (5) review of internal proposals, and (6) final decision.

Governments are often very large buyers. Their purchases are normally made on the basis of bids, which are based on specifications.

▶ KEY TERMS

accelerator principle	modified rebuy
bids	new task buying
business-to-business market	North American Industrial
buying centre	Classification System (NAICS)
capital items	producers
demand variability	reciprocity
depreciation	specifications
derived demand	straight rebuy
electronic exchange	trade industries
expense items	value added
inventory adjustments	vertical Web community
joint demand	

▶ INTERACTIVE SUMMARY AND DISCUSSION QUESTIONS

1. Categorizing business buyers is important for assessing buying behaviour. The three categories are producers, trade industries, and government. Why is this categorization useful?

2. The business market accounts for approximately 50 percent of purchases of manufactured goods. What significance does this have for jobs for business graduates?

3. The business market has three distinctive features: geographic market concentration, a relatively small number of buyers, and a complex purchase decision process. Give an example and discuss some of the implications for a marketing program targeted at that market.

4. Business market demand is distinguished by four characteristics: derived demand, joint demand, inventory adjustments, and demand variability. Explain and give examples of each.

5. The two general categories of industrial products are capital items and expense items. Distinguish between the two.

6. Illustrate how a marketing planner can use the North American Industrial Classification System (NAICS).

7. A business purchase is generally characterized by being systematic and complex. Explain and illustrate with an example.

8. There are three generally recognized business purchasing situations: straight rebuy, modified rebuy, and new task buying. Describe each type, and discuss the marketing task in each.

9. Figure 9.2 shows a model of the business buying process. Compare and contrast salesperson influence, advertising influence, and word-of-mouth influence. In which type of buying situations might each be more influential?

10. Prepare a report on a recent purchase by a local organizational buyer. What can be learned from this exercise?

11. The Canadian International Development Agency (CIDA) is a government agency that supports development in less developed countries. Go to the CIDA Web site and prepare a brief report on the business opportunities that exist through its work.

www.acdi-cida.gc.ca

To obtain a list of further readings for Chapter 9, please refer to the *Foundations of Marketing* Web site.

Part 4
Products

The concept of a product is more complex than it may seem at first. The chapters in this section point out the many important attributes that comprise a product. The development and management of products over time is also discussed. The last chapter is devoted to considering one important category of products known as services. A large and growing portion of economic activity is accounted for by services.

Quaker Oats Canada, among others, is lobbying for a change in the Food and Drugs Act that would see many food products repositioned and promoted as having health attributes. Here, Julie Davis of Quaker Oats displays a U.S. package that promotes oatmeal as a food that "can help lower cholesterol."

Chapter 10
Product Strategy

Kellogg and Quaker Oats are enemies at the breakfast table. But they are allies in a larger battle that could revolutionize food marketing in Canada and change the way consumers shop for their weekly groceries.

The cereal makers are part of a powerful food industry lobby that is pushing for the right to link health claims to their products, which is currently prohibited under the federal Food and Drugs Act.

If they succeed—and indications are they will—it would change everything from the types of products sold to the way foods are packaged and advertised.

For the food industry, the stakes are high. It wants to capitalize on the boom in healthy victuals, called nutraceuticals or functional foods, which generate sales of $500-billion or more worldwide, by one estimate.

Quaker Oats Co. of Canada Ltd., based in Peterborough, Ont., says it is developing two ultrahealthy offerings it would launch if the regulations are loosened. For its existing cereals, the company would refocus its advertising to trumpet the benefits of oat bran, which studies have indicated can lower cholesterol levels and reduce the risk of heart disease.

"We would certainly be able to take a much more proactive approach in communicating this information to consumers," says Julie Davis, whose title is manager of Quaker equity. "Right now, the regulations don't allow us to do that."

Kellogg Canada Inc. of Toronto would also shift its marketing if rules are eased, says Christine Lowry, vice-president of nutrition and corporate affairs. "How we present the product to the public in our advertising, that will definitely change ... we'll be able to communicate more effectively."

U.S. rules governing health claims on packaging and in advertising have been liberalized in recent years, permitting companies to link their products with benefits

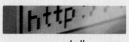

www.kelloggs.com

www.quakeroats.com

such as lowering the risk of heart disease or cancer. In Canada, however, a product that makes a health claim must be classified as a drug, which gives rise to prohibitive costs and marketing restrictions.

But Canada appears to be moving toward the U.S. model. A Health Canada policy paper released this month recommends allowing "structure/function" and "risk-reduction" claims.

The former would encompass a statement, for example, that links calcium in a product to healthy bone development, while the latter would include a claim, for instance, that a diet low in saturated fat may reduce the risk of heart disease. The policy paper recommends against allowing stronger claims that a food can prevent or cure an illness.

It's unclear when, or if, the policy will be implemented, given the huge task of developing new regulations to ensure consumers are protected and food makers are held to rigorous scientific standards in making their claims.

But Laurie Curry, vice-president of public policy and scientific affairs at the Food and Consumer Product Manufacturers of Canada, says she hopes to see health claims on foods by next year.

"It would be a major growth opportunity for the food industry here in Canada, and with respect to innovation and research and development, it would be a tremendous opportunity."

A look at the explosion of functional foods in the United States offers a clue to what Canadians can expect. With baby boomers hungry for products that promise to help them live longer and healthier lives, companies are rolling out mood-lifting soups, calcium-enriched juices, and new-age drinks laced with herbs such as ginseng and echinacea.

There's even a snack called Personality Puffs, presumably for those who have difficulty at cocktail parties, and a product called Brain Gum that purports to improve memory.

Some of these products are spilling across the border. At a Toronto health food store, a reporter purchased Kava Kava Corn Chips, which claim to promote relaxation, and Ginkgo Biloba Rings, labelled as a "memory snack."

www.pg.com

Sensing an enormous marketing opportunity, big U.S. food and consumer products companies are jumping into the functional foods business. This month, Procter & Gamble Co. announced plans to market its laxative Metamucil as a psyllium-rich dietary supplement that promotes a healthy heart. It is the first move into nutraceuticals for P&G, which will revamp its Metamucil package.

Also this month, Kellogg Co. unveiled its first functional foods line. Called Ensemble, it consists of 21 products including frozen entrées, cereal, pasta, and cookies that are rich in psyllium, a soluble fibre that lowers blood cholesterol level. The Ensemble line goes on sale in the U.S. Midwest in March, but Kellogg has no current plans to bring it to Canada. It might reevaluate its plans, however, if it wins the right to tell Canadians about psyllium's benefits.

"We want to supply consumer demand, but we're held back," Ms. Lowry says. "Why [sell] a product you can't promote?"

Strategically, Kellogg and Quaker Oats are trying to accomplish several things. They are trying to influence their legal environment, as discussed in Chapter 2. Beyond that, they are attempting to renew and prolong the life cycle of some of their established products by emphasizing new attributes. They are also planning to expand the depth and width of their product lines by developing and offering new products to their markets. Despite the tremendous success of Kellogg and Quaker Oats over the years, they know that marketers can never rest on their laurels. Managing existing products is essential, as is developing a continuous stream of new ones.

Marketing managers not only face many decisions about designing and positioning new products, but also about managing existing ones. Over the life of each product, they have to determine whether prices should be lowered or raised, whether money should be spent on redeveloping older products, and how such products should be promoted and distributed. Finding and introducing new products and managing older ones are major aspects of marketing management.

Source: John Heinzl, "Food Sector Craves Health Pitch," *The Globe and Mail* (November 18, 1998), p. B29. Reprinted with permission from *The Globe and Mail*.

▶ INTRODUCTION

This is the first of three chapters dealing with the "product" component of the marketing mix. Here the basic concepts and definitions of this marketing element are laid out.

Marketing planning efforts begin with the choice of products to offer the target market. Pricing, marketing channels, and marketing communication (the other variables of the marketing mix) are all based on the nature of the product.

Everyone knows what a product is — or do they? We must first make sure we understand what a product really is.

Product: A Definition

A narrow definition of the word *product* might focus on the physical or functional characteristics of a good that is offered to consumers. For example, a Sony videocassette recorder is a rectangular container of metal and plastic wires connecting it to a television set, accompanied by a series of special tapes for recording and viewing. This is the core product. But purchasers have a much broader view of the VCR. They have bought the convenience of viewing television programs at their leisure; the warranty and service that Sony, the manufacturer, provides; the prestige of owning this fine product; and the ability to rent or purchase recently released movies for home viewing. Thus, the brand image, warranty, and service are also all parts of the product as seen by the consumer.

Marketing decision makers must have this broader concept in mind and realize that people purchase more than just the physical features of products. *They are buying want satisfaction.* Most drivers know very little about the gasoline they regularly purchase. If they bother to analyze it, they discover that it is almost colourless and emits a peculiar odour. However, most drivers do not think of gasoline as a product at all — to them, gasoline is a tax. It is a payment that they must make periodically for the privilege of driving their cars on the streets and highways, and the friendly service-station attendant is a tax collector. Petroleum retailers should be aware of this image in the minds of many customers before spending huge sums to promote dozens of secret ingredients designed to please the motorist.

The shopper's conception of a product may be altered by such features as packaging, labelling, or the retail outlets in which the product may be purchased. An image of high quality has been created for Maytag appliances, whose television commercials describe the Maytag repairer as "the loneliest person in town." More than 30 years ago, the firm's president set a standard of "10 years of trouble-free operation" for washing machines. The company's success in achieving a reputation for high quality is evident in Maytag's continued sales growth record, even though the washer's retail price is higher than the nearest competitor's.

Some products have no physical ingredients. A haircut and blow-dry at the local hairstylist produces only well-groomed hair. A tax counsellor produces only advice. Thus, a broader view of product must also include services.

▶ THE INFORMED CONSUMER

Understanding Warranties

Laws governing warranties are a provincial matter, so there are some differences from province to province. Nonetheless, the provincial legislation is broadly similar. Many consumers are not aware that regardless of written warranties, or the lack of written warranties, they have certain rights assured by legislation.

A new product must be free from encumbrances; that is, the seller must have clear title, or be able to bestow clear title, and must have the right to sell the product in the first place. Descriptions of the product on the package must be accurate. The product must be of acceptable quality unless defects are specifically drawn to the consumer's attention or an inspection of the goods might reasonably be expected to reveal imperfections (e.g., cosmetic imperfections in a paint job). The product must be fit for its purpose. If the purchase is made based on a sample, the purchased goods must match the sample and be of acceptable quality. The product must be of reasonable durability—reasonable will, of course, vary from one product to another. Finally, spare parts and repair facilities must be available, although not necessarily in the immediate vicinity.

On the other hand, many written warranties provide less protection than one might think. Many have an abuse clause by which the warranty will be void if, in the seller's opinion, the problems with the product are caused by abuse. Most manufacturers have that clause to protect themselves from flagrant consumer abuse. A few, however, define abuse as anything that might damage the product, in which case a consumer can literally hear, for example, a golf club manufacturer say, "You must have abused the club, because our clubs don't break in normal play."

Many written warranties have explicit service schedules. Failure to follow the schedule will void the warranty.

Another interesting phrase used in some warranties is "Guaranteed for life." The warranty should specify whether that means the life of the consumer or the life of the product. Obviously, a warranty for the life of the product is not terribly meaningful.

For more information about warranties and consumer rights, visit Industry Canada's Web page on consumer information. The site also has links to provincial pages.

Can you think of an example of a questionable warranty for a product you've recently bought? How could the warranty have been improved to make it more meaningful?

strategis.ic.gc.ca/sc_consu/
engdoc/homepage.html

Source: Based on information from Sandra Hornung, *Consumer Power: A Guide to the Basics of Consumer Law in Saskatchewan* (Saskatoon: Public Legal Education Association of Saskatchewan, 1997), pp. 13–22.

---

product
A total bundle of physical, service, and symbolic characteristics designed to produce consumer want satisfaction.

warranty
A guarantee to the buyer that the supplier will replace a defective product (or part of a product) or refund its purchase price during a specified period of time.

A **product**, then, may be defined as a total bundle of physical, service, and symbolic characteristics designed to produce consumer want satisfaction. Figure 10.1 reflects this broader definition—known as the total product concept—by identifying the various components of the total product.

An important feature of many products is a product **warranty**. The warranty is a guarantee to the buyer that the supplier will replace a defective product (or part of a product) or refund its purchase price during a specified period of time. Such warranties serve to increase consumer purchase confidence and can prove to be an important means of stimulating demand. Sangoma, an electronics components manufacturer, warranties its products for up to 36 months. Many retailers have a broad, unwritten, but frequently honoured warranty of satisfaction or your money back.

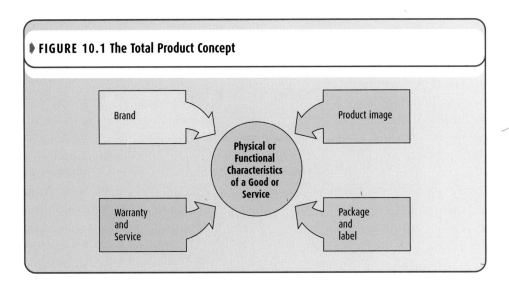

FIGURE 10.1 The Total Product Concept

Brand

Product image

Physical or Functional Characteristics of a Good or Service

Warranty and Service

Package and label

THE PRODUCT LIFE CYCLE

Product *types,* like individuals, pass through a series of stages. The life cycle for humans is quite specific: infancy to childhood to adulthood to retirement to death. Product types also progress through stages, although a product's progress through the stages is sometimes not very clear-cut. This progression of introduction, growth, maturity, and decline is known as the **product life cycle**. An idealized model of the cycle is depicted in Figure 10.2, with examples of products currently at each stage of development.[1] The length of time in each stage varies widely, as represented by the broken line on the bottom axis. The model is representative of many, but not all, situations. For example, there is little evidence that refrigerators enter a decline or death stage.

At each stage of the life cycle, the emphasis and focus of the marketing program should change to fit the requirements at that phase. For example, at the introductory stage, communication efforts should emphasize information. At the growth stage, with competitors entering the market, communication should emphasize comparative features and advantages. Taking into consideration this need to change the marketing mix emphasis, particularly in the introduction and growth stages, can be useful in guiding marketing planning.

product life cycle
A product's progress through introduction, growth, maturity, and decline stages.

Stages of the Cycle

INTRODUCTORY STAGE
The firm's objective in the early stages of the product life cycle is to stimulate demand for the new market entry. Since the product is not known to the public, promotional campaigns stress information about its features. Promotion may also be directed toward channels of distribution to induce them to carry the

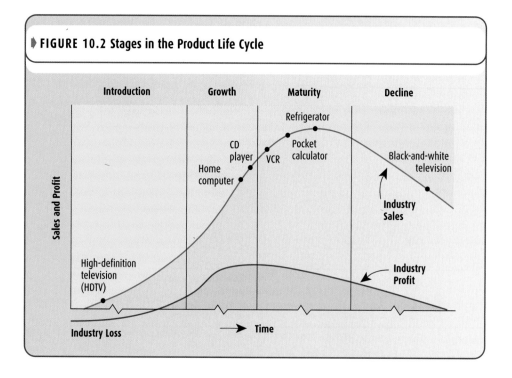

▶ **FIGURE 10.2 Stages in the Product Life Cycle**

product. In this initial phase, the public is being acquainted with the merits of the new product, and acceptance is being gained.

As Figure 10.2 indicates, losses are common during the introductory stage due to heavy promotion as well as extensive research and development expenditures. But the groundwork is being laid for future profits. Firms expect to recover their costs and to begin earning profits when the product moves into the second phase of the cycle—the growth stage.

The costs of development and promotion at this stage are very high. New small business innovators often badly underestimate the costs of even a simple product launch. Big electronics companies such as Philips have spent more than $200 million in this stage of the product life cycle.

www.philips.com

GROWTH STAGE
Sales volume rises rapidly during the growth stage as new adopters make initial purchases and as repurchases are made by the early users of the product. Word of mouth and mass advertising induce hesitant buyers to make trial purchases. Home computers are now in this phase of the cycle.

As the firm begins to realize substantial profits from its investment during the growth stage, it attracts competitors. Success breeds imitation, and firms rush into the market with competitive products in search of profit during the growth stage. As soon as the dramatic market acceptance of mountain bikes was realized, for instance, many manufacturers jumped into the market with their versions of the product.

MATURITY STAGE
Industry sales continue to grow during the early portion of the maturity stage, but eventually reach a plateau as the backlog of potential customers is exhausted.

▶ THE CANADIAN MARKETPLACE

The Growing Popularity of Wireless Phones

They have gone from non-existent to ubiquitous in just over 10 years. Cellular phones have become one of the fastest-growing consumer products in Canadian history.

Actually, we should call them wireless phones, because they come in two types— cellular and PCS (personal communication service). PCS, the newer of the two, offers extras such as fax and e-mail services.

"Canada has some of the lowest prices in the world for cellular and PCS phones," says Marc Choma, director of communications at the Canadian Wireless Telecommunications Association, putting forward one reason for their meteoric rise in popularity.

And he sees no tailing off in demand. Around 15 percent of Canadians now have wireless phones and the CWTA estimates that by 2008 it will be 40 percent. Current users tend to be well-educated, higher income, young to middle-aged males. However, that's changing as more elderly people and women adopt the new technology.

Globally, the growth has also been phenomenal.

It's estimated by the CWTA that by 2005, half the telephone calls in the world will be made on wireless phones.

Telecommunications companies, such as Cantel AT&T, use attractive rates to compete for customers in the booming cellular phone market.

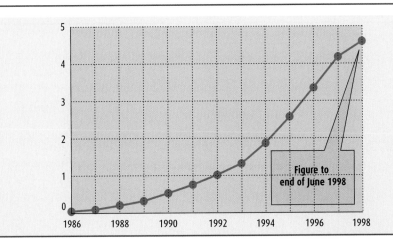

▶ **Millions of Wireless Phone Subscribers in Canada**

Figure to end of June 1998

What stage of the product life cycle are wireless phones in? What does that imply for marketing strategy?

Source: Philip Jackman, ed., "Big Numbers for Wireless Phones," *The Globe and Mail* (September 29, 1998), p. A28. Reprinted with permission from *The Globe and Mail*. Graph: Canadian Wireless Telecommunications Association.

By this time a large number of competitors have entered the market, and profits decline as competition intensifies.

In the maturity stage, differences among competing products have diminished as competitors have discovered the product and promotional characteristics most desired by the market. Heavy promotional outlays emphasize subtle differences among competing products, and brand competition intensifies.

Available products now exceed demand. Companies attempting to increase sales and market share must do so at the expense of competitors. As competition intensifies, the tendency grows among competitors to cut prices in a bid to attract new buyers. Even though a price reduction may be the easiest method of inducing additional purchases, it is also one of the simplest moves for competitors to duplicate. Reduced prices will result in decreased revenues for all firms in the industry unless the price cuts produce enough increased purchases to offset the loss in revenue on each product sold.

DECLINE STAGE

In the final stage of the product's life, new innovations or shifting consumer preferences bring about an absolute decline in total industry sales. The safety razor and electric shavers replace the straight razor, a new Playstation game replaces an earlier version as the latest fad, and the slower personal computer is replaced by a faster, more powerful model. As Figure 10.3 indicates, the decline stage of the old product is often also the growth stage for the new market entry.

Industry profits decline and in some cases actually become negative as sales fall, and firms cut prices in a bid for the dwindling market. Manufacturers gradually begin to leave the industry in search of more profitable products.

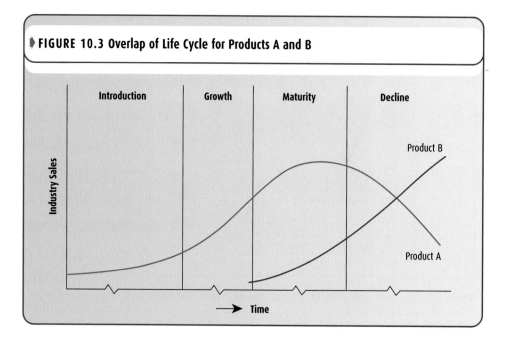

▶ FIGURE 10.3 Overlap of Life Cycle for Products A and B

▶ DEPARTURES FROM THE TRADITIONAL PRODUCT LIFE-CYCLE MODEL

The preceding discussion has examined what is considered the traditional product life cycle, with its four clearly delineated stages. Some marketing theorists divide the life cycle into additional stages, but these four, identified in Figure 10.2, are generally accepted within the marketing discipline.

Yet despite the vast body of material written on the subject, considerable controversy surrounds the format and usefulness of product life-cycle theory. On the one hand, the concept has an enduring appeal because of the intuitive logic of the birth-to-decline biological analogy.[2] As such, it has considerable descriptive value when used as a systematic framework for explaining market dynamics.

However, the simplicity of the concept has led to simplistic uses and expectations for the model, and this has called the concept itself into question. Part of the problem lies in failing to distinguish between the life cycle of a *product type* and that of an *individual brand* within that generic product category. Life-cycle theory is most applicable to product types. A truly new brand is obviously also the generic category for a while, but as competing brands are introduced, it becomes one of several brands within that category. The greatest misuse of product life-cycle theory is to consider it a *predictive* model for anticipating when changes will occur and to presume that one stage will always succeed another. Managers can make grave errors if they naively interpret a particular rise or fall in sales as a sign that a product has moved from one stage to another. Such an interpretation could lead to serious errors in strategy, such as concluding that a product is in decline and removing it from the market.

A second criticism involves the use of the life cycle as a *normative* model, which *prescribes* the alternative strategies that should be considered at each stage. As will be shown later, there are strategies that are generally appropriate at various stages of the life cycle of a product *category*. In the case of an individual brand *within* a product category, however, as Enis, LaGrace, and Prell argue, "[T]he product life cycle [of a brand] is a *dependent* variable.... That is, the brand's stage in the product life cycle depends primarily upon the marketing strategy implemented for that product at a particular time."[3]

A more realistic view is that life-cycle analysis serves several different roles in the formulation of strategy. In the case of both generic product type and individual brand, the life cycle serves as an *enabling condition* in the sense that the underlying forces that inhibit or facilitate growth create opportunities and threats with strategic implications. The stage of the life cycle also acts as a *moderating variable* through its influence on the value of market-share position and the profitability consequences of strategic decisions. In the case of an individual brand, a stage in the life cycle is partly a *consequence* of managerial decisions. Its position is not necessarily a *fait accompli,* which can only be reacted to, but instead is only one of several scenarios that are conditional on the life cycle of the product category, on competitive actions, and on managerial decisions.

Other Life-Cycle Issues

Three other issues that modify the original life-cycle concept are (1) the length of each product life-cycle stage, (2) the existence of product life-cycle variants, and (3) the current role of product and service fashions and fads.

LENGTH OF CYCLE STAGES

Professor John O. King has argued that product life-cycle models should reflect the reality that goods and services move through the cycle at varying speeds. He suggests that the model should be drawn to show a broken horizontal axis to reflect the fact that the stages may be of varying lengths, as we did in Figures 10.2 and 10.3. Research now suggests that product life cycles may be getting shorter, especially in the introductory and growth stages.[4] While definitive conclusions are not yet available, most marketers do accept the fact that product life cycles and their stages show considerable variation in length.

▶ THE PRACTISING MARKETER

www.panasonic.ca

The Video Camcorder Makes a Comeback

Waning after having waxed doesn't mean the tape's run out on a consumer product. After years of buildup and then declining sales, video camcorders are coming back.

In the early days of the product—namely 1987—about 100000 of the devices were sold in Canada, according to the Consumer Electronics Marketers of Canada. That tentative beginning led to a peak of 317000 camcorders sold in 1991.

"When an industry is in its early phases, the purchasers are what we refer to as early adopters, typically hobbyists," explains Barry Murray, a CEMC committee chairman and video market manager for Panasonic Canada Inc. in Toronto. "Later on, the purchaser profile changes."

Today, Mr. Murray estimates that only 35 to 40 percent of camcorder purchasers are hobbyists while the bulk of consumers take the plunge when they are "event-motivated"—about to become parents or grandparents or take an exotic trip.

The recession that ate into the equipment's popularity in the early nineties triggered an industry response of lowered prices and more features. Add the resultant recovering sales to interest in the newly appearing digital camcorders and it again means that no baby's first steps—or police officer's untoward action—will be lost to posterity.

▶ **Camcorder Sales since 1987**

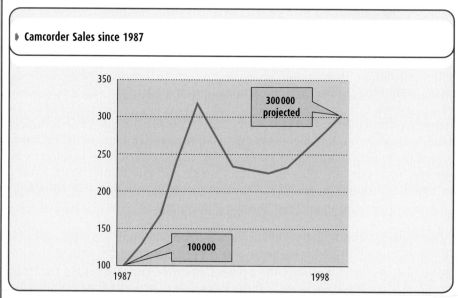

What factors contributed to the downturn in camcorder sales? What has led to the subsequent recovery of sales? In 1992, when sales dropped significantly, how might manufacturers have concluded that camcorders, in fact, had *not* entered the decline stage of their product life cycle?

Source: Salem Alaton, "The Video Recorder Makes a Comeback," *The Globe and Mail* (February 26, 1999), p. A22. Reprinted with permission from *The Globe and Mail*. Graph: Consumer Electronics Marketers of Canada and *The Globe and Mail*.

ALTERNATIVE PRODUCT LIFE CYCLES

Thus far, an idealized product life-cycle model has been presented. Because of the realities of the marketplace, the actual resulting life cycle can take on several other shapes. Some common variants of the traditional model are shown in Figure 10.4.

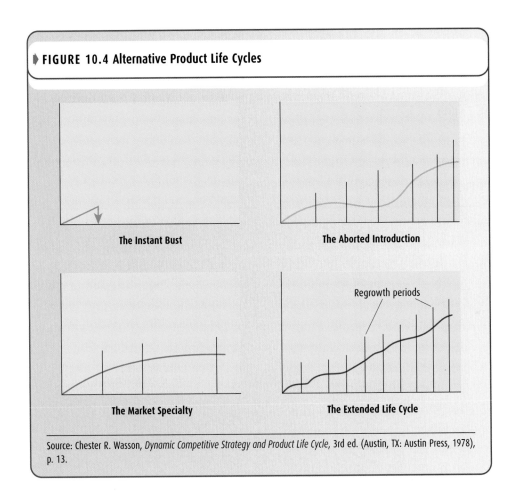

▶ **FIGURE 10.4 Alternative Product Life Cycles**

The Instant Bust

The Aborted Introduction

The Market Specialty

Regrowth periods

The Extended Life Cycle

Source: Chester R. Wasson, *Dynamic Competitive Strategy and Product Life Cycle*, 3rd ed. (Austin, TX: Austin Press, 1978), p. 13.

As shown in Figure 10.4, some products simply do not make it. These can be labelled the "instant busts"—failures that simply do not go through the four steps of the traditional model. Still other products are introduced, but information derived from test-market situations indicates that changes will be necessary if the product launch is to be successful (test markets are described in Chapter 11). The products then have to be modified in some way—such as in design, packaging, or promotional strategy—before they are reintroduced. This type of start-up, start-again launch is labelled the "aborted introduction" in Figure 10.4.

Still other products become market specialty items (discussed later in this chapter) and provide long and stable maturity stages. A common variant is the "pyramid cycle," where the product is adapted through new technology or a revised marketing strategy. The pyramid cycle (also discussed later in this chapter under "Extending the Product Life Cycle") is characterized by a series of regrowth periods.

FASHIONS AND FADS

fashions
Currently popular products that tend to follow recurring life cycles.

fads
Fashions with abbreviated life cycles.

Fashions and fads are also important to marketers. **Fashions** are currently popular products that tend to follow recurring life cycles.[5] The miniskirt was reintroduced in 1982 after being out of fashion for over a decade. In 1990 it appeared again. Wide-leg pants reappeared in the late 1990s after having been the dominant style in the 1970s.

In contrast, **fads** are fashions with abbreviated life cycles. Consider the case of popular music for teenagers. Disco gave way to punk and new wave, which was replaced by the "new music," a take-off on rock and roll. Rap music is another example of the many music fads that come and go. Most fads experience short-lived popularity and then fade quickly. However, some maintain a residual market among certain market segments. Both of these fad cycles are shown in Figure 10.5.

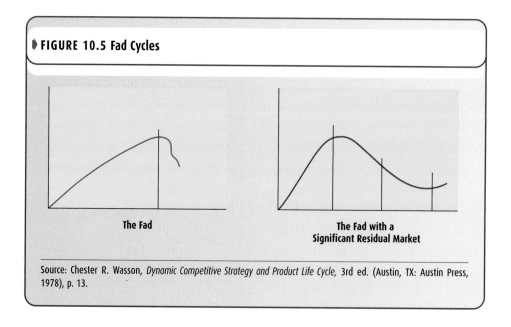

▶ **FIGURE 10.5 Fad Cycles**

The Fad

The Fad with a
Significant Residual Market

Source: Chester R. Wasson, *Dynamic Competitive Strategy and Product Life Cycle*, 3rd ed. (Austin, TX: Austin Press, 1978), p. 13.

▶ PRODUCT LIFE-CYCLE CONSIDERATIONS IN MARKETING STRATEGY

Marketing strategy related to the product life cycle is most useful when it is carried out on an individual *brand* basis rather than a generic product category basis.[6] There are too many uncontrollable variables at the generic level.

The product life cycle—with all its variants—is a useful tool in marketing strategy decision making. The knowledge that profits assume a predictable pattern through the stages and that promotional emphasis must shift from product information in the early stages to brand promotion in the later ones allows the marketing decision maker to take advantage of conditions that often exist in each stage of the product life cycle through appropriate marketing efforts.

A firm's marketing efforts should emphasize stimulating demand at the introductory stage. The emphasis shifts to cultivating selective demand in the growth period. Market segmentation should be used extensively in the maturity period. During the decline, the emphasis again shifts to increasing primary demand. Table 10.1 suggests possibilities for appropriate pricing, distribution, product development, and service and warranty strategies for each life-cycle stage. The reader is again cautioned that the life cycle does not determine the strategy.

Extending the Product Life Cycle

The life cycle of a *brand* can often be affected by managerial strategy. One example is the practice of extending the cycle as long as possible. Marketing managers can accomplish this objective if they take action early in the maturity stage. Product life cycles can sometimes be extended indefinitely by actions designed to accomplish one or more of the following:

1. Increase the frequency of use by present customers.
2. Add new users.
3. Find new uses for the product.
4. Change product quality or packaging.

Examples of such actions follow.

INCREASE THE FREQUENCY OF USE
Noxzema was originally intended as an occasional-use skin medicine, but it was repositioned as a routine-use beauty-care item. This substantially increased the rate of use — and the amount purchased.

ADD NEW USERS
Cadillac introduced its Cimarron, a more sporty model, to attract non-Cadillac buyers who usually purchased cars like BMWs. In 1994, the company announced its intention to move downscale with what was called the LSE, a sedan made in Europe by GM's Opel division. Crest and Colgate have introduced a number of variations ranging from sweeter-tasting gels to appeal to younger consumers to antibacterial formulations aimed at freshening breath and producing healthier gums. Each formulation further extends the life cycles of these well-known brands. Finding new users is often difficult, however. Gerber, for example, failed in attempts to sell its products to the 15-to-22 age group as desserts and snacks. Many still regarded Gerber products as baby food.[7]

A recent market trend has seen the growing use of Eastern herbal medicines, such as ginseng, and the adoption of Eastern exercises, such as Tae Bo. Given the ever-changing marketplace, it is difficult to predict whether products and services that arise from this trend will sustain a long life cycle.

▶ **TABLE 10.1 Organizational Conditions, Environmental Conditions, and Marketing Efforts at Each Stage of the Product Life Cycle**

| INTRODUCTION | GROWTH | MATURITY | | DECLINE |
		Early Maturity	Late Maturity	
Organizational Conditions				
High costs	Smoothing production	Efficient scale of operation	Low profits	
Inefficient production levels	Lowering costs	Product modification work	Standardized production	
Cash demands	Operation efficiencies Product improvement work	Decreasing profits		
Environmental Conditions				
Few or no competitors	Expanding markets	Slowing growth Strong competition	Faltering demand Fierce competition	Permanently declining demand
Limited product awareness and knowledge	Expanded distribution	Expanded market	Shrinking number of competitors	Reduction of competitors
Limited demand	Competition strengthens Prices soften a bit	Heightened competition	Established distribution patterns	Limited product offerings Price stabilization
Marketing Efforts				
Stimulate demand	Cultivate selective demand	Emphasize market segmentation	Ultimate in market segmentation	Increase primary demand
Establish high price	Product improvement	Improve service and warranty	Competitive pricing	Profit opportunity pricing
Offer limited product variety	Strengthen distribution	Reduce prices	Retain distribution	Prune and strengthen distribution
Increase distribution	Price flexibility			

Source: Adapted from Burton H. Marcus and Edward M. Tauber, *Marketing Analysis and Decision Making* (Boston: Little, Brown, 1979), pp. 115–16. Copyright © 1979 by Burton H. Marcus and Edward M. Tauber.

FIND NEW USES

Q-tips cotton swabs were originally sold as a baby-care item, but Cheseborough-Pond's Inc.'s marketers found a new use for them as makeup applicators. Baking soda was used primarily in cooking until its product life cycle was extended by finding new uses for it as a denture cleaner, swimming-pool pH adjuster, cleaning agent, flame extinguisher, first-aid remedy, and refrigerator freshener.

CHANGE THE PRODUCT QUALITY OR PACKAGING

One of the best examples of a product that has been managed well and has avoided the decline stage is Tide. This synthetic detergent, introduced in 1947,

▶ THE CANADIAN MARKETPLACE

Canadians Love Their Kraft Dinner

Canadians eat about 246 000 boxes of Kraft Dinner every day. That's roughly three times, per capita, what Americans eat. Moreover, nine of ten households here have purchased it at one time or another. Canadians even invented the name Kraft Dinner, which was originally a nickname. (Outside Canada, it's called Kraft Macaroni and Cheese.)

West Gidluck, a farmer in Saskatchewan, is the champion of Kraft Dinner consumption. He goes through about 800 boxes a year, and recently won a Kraft Canada contest aimed at finding the most ardent Kraft Dinner fans in Canada.

With a household penetration rate of 90 percent, what steps can Kraft take to continue expanding sales of Kraft Dinner? Have you noticed Kraft making any changes in its marketing approaches in the last year or two?

Source: Adapted from John Heinzl, "Kraft Dinner Serves Up a New Look," *The Globe and Mail* (January 13, 1999), p. B29. Reprinted with permission from *The Globe and Mail*.

kraftfoods.com/index.cgi

dominates the laundry detergent market. But more than 50 modifications of packaging, cleaning performance, sudsing characteristics, aesthetics, and physical properties have been made during its lifetime.

▶ CONSUMER ADOPTION PROCESS

Once a new product is launched, consumers begin a process of evaluating it. This evaluation is known as the **adoption process** — the process whereby potential consumers go through a series of stages from learning of the new product to trying it and deciding to purchase it regularly or to reject it. The process has some similarities to the consumer decision process discussed in Chapter 8. The stages in the consumer adoption process can be classified as follows:

1. *Awareness.* Individuals first learn of the new product but lack information about it.
2. *Interest.* They begin to seek out information about it.
3. *Evaluation.* They consider whether the product is beneficial.
4. *Trial.* They make a trial purchase, test it, or mentally visualize its use to determine its usefulness.
5. *Adoption/Rejection.* If the trial purchase is satisfactory, they decide to make regular use of the product.[8] Of course, rejection may take place at any stage of the process.

Marketing managers need to understand the adoption process so that they can move potential consumers to the adoption stage. Once the manager is aware of

adoption process
A series of stages consumers go through, from learning of a new product to trying it and deciding to purchase it regularly or to reject it.

a large number of consumers at the interest stage, steps can be taken to stimulate sales. For example, when consumer interest in buying a combined shampoo/conditioner began to grow, Procter & Gamble introduced Pert Plus with samples sent to homes in addition to its regular advertising campaign. Sampling, if it is successful, is a technique that reduces the risk of evaluation and trial, moving the consumer quickly to the adoption stage.

Adopter Categories

consumer innovators
The first purchasers—those who buy a product at the beginning of its life cycle.

Some people will purchase a new product almost as soon as it is placed on the market. Others wait for additional information and rely on the experiences of the first purchasers before making trial purchases. **Consumer innovators** are the first purchasers at the beginning of a product's life cycle. They are found to be the first in the community to buy high-definition television (HDTV), for example.

A number of investigations analyzing the adoption of new products have resulted in the identification of five categories of purchasers based on relative time of adoption: innovators, early adopters, early majority, later majority, and laggards. These categories are shown in Figure 10.6, as well as the proportion of the population in each category.

diffusion process
The filtering and acceptance of new products and services by the members of a community or social system.

The **diffusion process** refers to the filtering and acceptance of new products and services by the members of a community or social system. Figure 10.6 shows this process as following a normal distribution. A few people adopt at first, and then the number of adopters increases rapidly as the value of the innovation becomes apparent. The rate finally diminishes as fewer potential consumers remain in the nonadopter category.

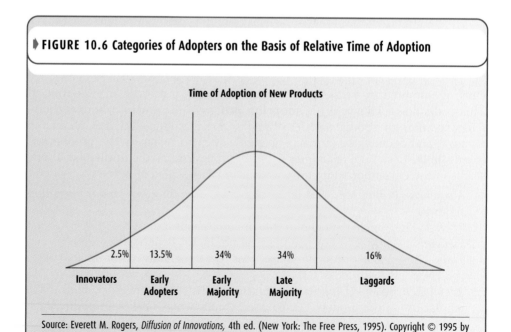

▶ FIGURE 10.6 Categories of Adopters on the Basis of Relative Time of Adoption

Time of Adoption of New Products

| 2.5% | 13.5% | 34% | 34% | 16% |
| Innovators | Early Adopters | Early Majority | Late Majority | Laggards |

Source: Everett M. Rogers, *Diffusion of Innovations*, 4th ed. (New York: The Free Press, 1995). Copyright © 1995 by Everett M. Rogers. Copyright © 1962, 1971, 1983 by The Free Press. Reprinted with the permission of The Free Press, a Division of Simon & Schuster.

Since the categories are based on the normal distribution, standard deviations are used to partition each category. Innovators are defined as the first 2.5 percent of those individuals who adopt the new product; laggards are the final 16 percent to adopt. Excluded from the figure are the nonadopters — people who never adopt the new product.

Identifying the First Adopters

Locating first buyers of new products represents a challenge for the marketing manager. If the right people can be reached early in the product's development or introduction, they may serve as a test market, evaluating the product and possibly making suggestions for modifications. Since early purchasers are frequently opinion leaders from whom others seek advice, their attitudes toward new products are communicated in their neighbourhoods, clubs, and organizations. Acceptance or rejection of the innovation by these purchasers may serve as a kind of signal for the marketing manager that indicates the probable success or failure of the new product.[9]

Unfortunately, people who are first adopters of one new product may not necessarily be first adopters for other products or services. A large number of studies have, however, established some general characteristics possessed by most first adopters.

In general, first adopters tend to be younger, have a high social status, be better educated, and enjoy a higher income. They are more mobile than later adopters, and change both their jobs and their home addresses more often. They are more likely to rely on impersonal information sources than are later adopters, who depend more on promotional information from the company and word-of-mouth communication.[10]

What Determines the Rate of Adoption?

The electronic calculator replaced the slide rule as the engineering student's friend as soon as prices came within range of the student budget. On the other hand, it took thirteen years to convince most corn farmers to use hybrid seed corn — an innovation capable to doubling corn yields — even though some progressive farmers adopted it at once. The adoption rate is influenced by five characteristics of the innovation.[11]

- *Relative advantage.* The degree to which the innovation appears superior to previous ideas. The greater the relative advantage — whether manifested in lower price, physical improvements, or ease of use — the faster the adoption rate.
- *Compatibility.* The degree to which the innovation is compatible with existing facilities or consistent with the values and experiences of potential adopters. The business student who purchases a personal computer will likely buy one that is compatible with those at the school he or she attends or with those of his or her friends.
- *Complexity.* The more difficult it is to understand or use the new product, the longer it will take to be generally accepted in most cases.
- *Divisibility.* The degree to which the innovation may be used on a limited basis. First adopters face two types of risk — financial losses and the risk of

ridicule by others—if the new product proves unsatisfactory. The option of sampling the innovation on a limited basis allows these risks to be reduced and, in general, should accelerate the rate of adoption.

- *Communicability.* The degree to which the results of the product may be observable by or communicated to others. If the superiority of the innovation can be displayed in a tangible form, this will increase the adoption rate.

These five characteristics can be used, to some extent, by the marketing manager in accelerating the rate of adoption. First, will consumers perceive the product as complex, or will its use necessitate a significant change in typical behavioural patterns? Product complexity must be overcome with promotional messages of an informational nature. Products should be designed to emphasize their relative advantages and, whenever possible, be divisible for sample purchases. If divisibility is physically impossible, in-home demonstrations or trial placements in the home may be used. Positive attempts must also be made to ensure compatibility of the innovation with the adopters' value systems.

These actions are based on extensive research studies of innovators in agriculture, medicine, and consumer goods. They should pay off in increased sales by accelerating the rate of adoption in each of the adopter categories.

▶ CONSUMER AND BUSINESS-TO-BUSINESS PRODUCTS

How a firm markets its products depends largely on the product itself. For example, a perfume manufacturer stresses subtle promotions in prestige media such as *Chatelaine* and *Vogue* magazines, and markets the firm's products through exclusive department stores and specialty shops. Cadbury Schweppes Powell Ltd. markets its candy products through candy wholesalers to thousands of supermarkets, variety stores, discount houses, and vending machines. Its marketing objective is to saturate the market and make buying its candy as convenient as possible for potential buyers. A firm that manufactures and markets forklifts may use sales representatives to call on purchasing managers, and ship its product either direction from the factory or from regional warehouses.

Marketing strategy differs for consumer products and business-to-business products. As defined earlier, consumer products are those destined for use by the ultimate consumer, and business-to-business products are those used directly or indirectly in producing other goods for resale. These two major categories can be broken down further.

Characteristics of Consumer Products

The consumer assesses satisfaction by calculating benefits expected minus costs incurred. Costs involve *effort* and *risk*.[12] Effort is the amount of money, time, and energy the buyer is willing to expend to acquire a given product. In addition, there are risks that the product will not deliver the benefits sought. There are five types of such possible risk: financial, psychological, physical, functional, and social.

▶ THE PRACTISING MARKETER

Classifying Consumer and Business-to-Business Products

A product is classified as a consumer or business-to-business product based on its end user rather than on intrinsic attributes. Sometimes the same product is sold both to consumers as a consumer product and to other producers as a business-to-business product.

The Ocean Spray ad is directed towards business customers. What are some examples of Ocean Spray's consumer products? Can you think of other products that have both consumer and business-to-business applications?

Ocean Spray's new product, Sweetened Dried Cranberry, is sold as both a consumer and a business good.

IT COULD BE THE BIGGEST
NEW PRODUCT IDEA
YOUR COMPANY HAS THIS YEAR

There are four categories of products: convenience, preference, shopping, and specialty. Each category can be defined according to the buyer's evaluation of the effort and risk required to obtain the product. Figure 10.7 illustrates the classification system. Two points shown in the figure should be especially noted. First, increasing risk and effort permits the marketer to broaden the scope of marketing strategy (shown by the widening arrow). That is, a wider variety of marketing mix combinations can be used to gain a differential advantage for shopping and specialty products than can be used for convenience and preference products. Second, the concept of high and low product involvement is incorporated into this classification. The yellow area represents low involvement.

CONVENIENCE PRODUCTS

As shown in Figure 10.7, **convenience products** are defined as lowest in terms of both effort and risk. That is, consumers will not spend much money or time in purchasing these products, nor do they perceive significant levels of risk in making a selection. These are the products consumers want to purchase frequently, immediately, and with a minimum of effort; common illustrations are commodities, "unsought" (emergency) items, and impulse products.

Examples of consumer goods that fall into the convenience category include fresh produce and grocery staples, umbrellas, gum, and batteries. Convenience services includes taxis and mass transit.

convenience products
Products that are lowest in terms of both effort and risk.

PREFERENCE PRODUCTS

The second category shown in Figure 10.7 is termed **preference products**. Such products are slightly higher on the effort dimension and much higher on risk

preference products
Products that are slightly higher on the effort dimension and much higher on risk than convenience products.

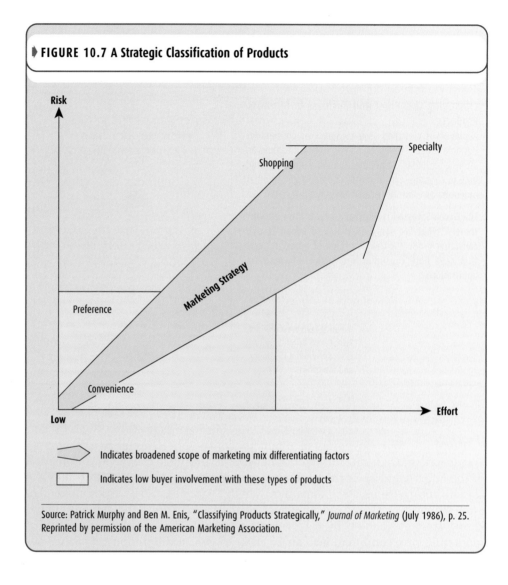

▶ **FIGURE 10.7 A Strategic Classification of Products**

Source: Patrick Murphy and Ben M. Enis, "Classifying Products Strategically," *Journal of Marketing* (July 1986), p. 25. Reprinted by permission of the American Marketing Association.

than convenience products. In fact, the distinction between convenience and preference products is primarily one of buyer-perceived risk. Often the consumer perceives a higher level of risk chiefly due to the marketer's efforts, particularly in branding and advertising. Some companies, for example, have successfully convinced consumers that their brand of a low-priced product conveys greater benefits than competing ones—as, for example, with Bayer aspirin.

The most prominent examples of preference products are in the consumer packaged goods industry (for example, toothpaste and soft drinks). Consumers may "prefer" the taste and image of Diet Coke, based on advertising appeals or brand preference. However, they are likely to substitute Diet Pepsi or perhaps a low-calorie brand of iced tea if the monetary or time effort involved in acquiring the preferred product is too large.

Since the consumer is unwilling to expend much effort in purchasing convenience or preference goods, the manufacturer must strive to make obtaining

www.coca-cola.com

www.pepsiworld.com

them as convenient as possible. Newspapers, soft drinks, and candy are sold in almost every supermarket, variety store, service station, and restaurant. Where retail outlets are physically separated from a large number of consumers, the manufacturers may use vending machines for their customers' convenience. They must protect fragile brand loyalty by ensuring that their product is easily available.

Retailers usually carry several competing brands of preference products and are unlikely to promote any particular brand. The promotional burden therefore falls on the manufacturer. Firms must advertise extensively to develop consumer acceptance of their products.

SHOPPING PRODUCTS

In contrast with convenience goods, **shopping products** are usually purchased only after the consumer has compared competing products on such bases as price, quality, style, and colour in competing stores. Consumers are willing to forgo consumption for a period in order to evaluate product offerings because they anticipate gaining monetary savings or greater satisfaction of needs by evaluating alternatives.

shopping products
Products that are usually purchased only after the consumer has compared competing products.

The purchaser of shopping products lacks complete information prior to the actual purchase and gathers additional information during the shopping trip. A woman who is intent on adding a new dress to her wardrobe may visit many stores, try on perhaps 30 dresses, and spend days making the final decision. She may follow a regular route from store to store in surveying competing offerings and will ultimately select the dress that most appeals to her. New stores that carry assortments of shopping products must ensure that they are located near other shopping-product stores so that they will be included in shopping expeditions.

Shopping products are typically more expensive than convenience or preference products and are most often purchased by women. In addition to women's apparel, shopping products include such items as jewellery, furniture, appliances, shoes, and used cars.

Some shopping products, such as children's shoes, may be classified as *homogeneous*—that is, the consumer views them as essentially the same—while others, such as furniture and clothing, are *heterogeneous*—essentially different. Price is a more important factor in the purchase of homogeneous shopping products, while quality and styling are more important in the purchase of heterogeneous products.

Brands are often less important for shopping than for convenience products. Although some furniture brands may come to mind, they are typically less important than the physical attributes of the product, its price, styling, and even the retail store that handles the brand. And although apparel companies have spent large amounts of money in promoting their brands, the dress buyer knows that the brand is (usually) inside the dress, and is generally more impressed with how the dress looks on her and with its fit than with the hidden label.

Manufacturers of shopping products use fewer retail stores than is common for convenience or preference products, since purchasers can be expected to expend some effort in finding what they want to buy and retailers will expend more effort in selling an exclusively distributed product. Thinness of the market may also affect the number of outlets. Retailers often purchase directly from the manufacturer or its representative rather than going through the wholesalers.

Quality and style are more important than price to the consumer who is purchasing a heterogeneous shopping product. Chintz & Company's rich and stylish offerings appeal to this type of shopper.

Fashion merchandise buyers for department stores and specialty shops make regular visits to Toronto, Montreal, New York, and Winnipeg on buying trips. Manufacturers often visit regional centres such as Vancouver, Edmonton, or Moncton to meet retailers there. Buyers for furniture retailers often go directly to the factories of furniture manufacturers or visit major furniture trade shows.

SPECIALTY PRODUCTS

As the arrowhead in Figure 10.7 shows, marketing managers may attempt to move their shopping products into the specialty category. This means that consumers will no longer "shop" for alternatives but will accept only one brand. The major distinction between shopping products and specialty products revolves around effort rather than risk. The specialty-products purchaser is well aware of what he or she wants and is willing to make a special effort to obtain it. The nearest Leica camera dealer may be 20 km away, but the camera enthusiast will go to that store to obtain what he or she may consider to be the ultimate in cameras. The Campbell River, B.C., collector who longs for a $2500 *objet d'art* of Steuben glassware is willing to journey to Vancouver to find the nearest Steuben dealer.

Specialty products are the highest in both effort and risk, due to some unique characteristics that cause the buyer to prize that particular brand. The buyer possesses relatively complete information about the product prior to the shopping trip and is unwilling to accept substitutes.

Specialty products are typically high-priced and are frequently branded. Since consumers are willing to exert a considerable effort in obtaining such goods, fewer retail outlets are needed. Mercury outboard motors and Porsche sports cars may be handled by only one or two retailers for each 100 000 population.

specialty products
Products that are highest in both effort and risk, due to some unique characteristics that cause the buyer to prize that particular brand.

UNSOUGHT PRODUCTS

Some products are not sought by consumers. They are products that people know about but normally do not think of buying. Products that are usually though of in this category are funerals and life insurance.

Applying the Consumer Goods Classification System

The four-way classification system described above gives the marketing manager additional information to use in developing a marketing strategy. For example, if a new food product sells well in a test market as a preference good, this provides insights about marketing needs in branding, promotion, pricing, and distribution methods. The impact of the product classifications on their associated consumer factors and to marketing mix variables is shown in Table 10.2.

But the classification system also poses problems of which the marketing manager must be aware. One pitfall is that it suggests a neat, four-way series of demarcations into which all products can easily be fitted. Some products do fit neatly into one of the classifications, but others fall into grey areas between categories.

How, for instance, should a new car be classified? It is expensive, is branded, and is handled by a few exclusive dealers in each city. But before it is classified as a specialty good, other characteristics must be considered. Most new-car buyers shops extensively among competing models and dealers before deciding on the best deal. A more effective method of using the classification system, therefore, is to consider it a continuum representing degrees of effort expended by the consumer. The new-car purchase can then be located between the categories of shopping and specialty products, but nearer the specialty-products end of the continuum.

A second problem with the classification system is that consumers differ in their buying patterns. One person will make an unplanned purchase of a new Toyota Corolla, while others will shop extensively before purchasing a car. One buyer's impulse purchase does not make the Corolla a convenience product. Products are classified by the purchase patterns of the *majority* of buyers.

www.toyota.ca

▶ **TABLE 10.2 Managerial Implications of Classifying Products Strategically**

	PRODUCT CATEGORY			
MANAGERIAL FOCUS	**Convenience**	**Preference**	**Shopping**	**Specialty**
Buyer's perception of price	Low effort, low risk	Low effort, medium risk	High effort, medium risk	High effort, high risk
Buyer behaviour	Impulse or habit (auto reorder)	Routine (straight rebuy)	Limited (modified rebuy)	Extensive (new task)
Marketer's objective	Move to preference or shopping category, or dominate via low cost	Brand loyalty	Source or store loyalty	Absolute (source *and* brand) loyalty
Marketer's basic strategy	High volume, cost minimized, or move product	High volume, brand identity, differentiation	High volume or high margin, segmentation	High margin, limited volume, market "niche"
Product strategy	Standard grades and quantities, quality control, innovations copied quickly	Standard grades and quantities, quality control, some R & D	Standard base, many options, much R & D, warranties	Custom design, much R & D, warranties, personalized service
Price strategy	Market	Market	Bundled or negotiated	Negotiated
Monetary, nonmonetary	Minimize time and risk	Minimize time, warrant risk	Accommodate time, warrant risk	Pamper for time and risk
Place strategy	Saturation distribution	Intensive distribution	Selective distribution	Exclusive distribution
Promotion	Point-of-purchase, some sales promotion	Mass advertising, sales promotion, some personal selling	Personal selling, some advertising	Publicity, personal selling, testimony

Source: Patrick Murphy and Ben M. Enis, "Classifying Products Strategically," *Journal of Marketing* (July 1986), p. 35. Reprinted by permission of the American Marketing Association.

Classifying Business-to-Business Products

The foregoing classification system can also be used for business-to-business products. But a more common system categorizes business-to-business products into five categories: installations, accessory equipment, component parts and materials, raw materials, and business-to-business supplies. Business-to-business buyers are professional customers; their job is to make effective purchase decisions. Although details may vary, the purchase decision process involved in buying supplies of flour for General Mills, for example, is much the same as that used in buying the same commodity for Robin Hood. Thus this classification system for business-to-business goods is based on product uses rather than on consumer buying patterns.

INSTALLATIONS

Installations are major capital assets (like factories and heavy machinery) that are used to produce products and services. Installations are the specialty products of the business-to-business market. New aircraft for Air Canada, locomotives for Canadian National, or a new pulp mill for MacMillan Bloedel are examples of installations.

Since installations are relatively long-lived and involve large sums of money, their purchase represents a major decision for an organization. Sales negotiations often extend over a period of several months and involve the participation of numerous decision makers. In many cases, the selling company must provide technical expertise. When custom-made equipment is involved, representatives of the selling firm work closely with the buyer's engineers and production personnel to design the most feasible product.

Price is almost never the deciding factor in the purchase of installations. The purchasing firm is interested in the product's efficiency and performance over its useful life. The firm also wants a minimum of breakdowns. "Downtime" is expensive because employees are nonproductive (but must still be paid) while the machinery is being repaired.

Since most of the factories of firms that purchase installations are geographically concentrated, the selling firm places its promotional emphasis on well-trained salespeople, who often have a technical background. Most installations are marketed directly on a manufacturer-to-user basis. Even though a sale may be a one-time transaction, contracts often call for regular product servicing. In the case of extremely expensive installations, such as computers and electronic equipment, some firms lease the installations rather than sell them outright and assign personnel directly to the lessee to operate or to maintain the equipment.

ACCESSORY EQUIPMENT

Fewer decision makers are usually involved in purchasing **accessory equipment**—second-level capital items that are used in the production of products and services but are usually less expensive and shorter-lived than installations. Although quality and service remain important criteria in purchasing accessory equipment, the firm is likely to be much more price-conscious. Accessory equipment includes such products as desktop calculators, hand tools, portable drills, small lathes, and typewriters. Although these goods are considered capital items and are depreciated over several years, their useful life is generally much shorter than that of an installation.

Because of the need for continuous representation and the more widespread geographic dispersion of accessory equipment purchasers, a wholesaler, often called an **industrial distributor**, may be used to contact potential customers in each geographic area. Technical assistance is usually not necessary, and the manufacturer of accessory equipment can often use such wholesalers quite effectively in marketing the firm's products. Advertising is more important for accessory manufacturers than it is for installation procedures.

installations
Major capital assets that are used to produce products and services.

www.aircanada.ca

www.cn.ca

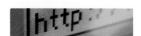
www.mbltd.com

accessory equipment
Second-level capital items that are used in the production of products and services but are usually less expensive and shorter-lived than installations.

industrial distributor
A wholesaler that operates in the business-to-business goods market and typically handles small accessory equipment and operating supplies.

COMPONENT PARTS AND MATERIALS

While installations and accessory equipment are used in producing the final product, **component parts and materials** are the finished business-to-business goods that actually become part of the final product. Champion spark plugs make a new Chevrolet complete, nuts and bolts are part of a Rocky Mountain bike, tires are included with a Dodge pickup truck. Some materials, such as flour, undergo further processing before producing a finished product.

Purchasers of component parts and materials need a regular, continuous supply of uniform-quality goods. These goods are generally purchased on contract for a period of one year or more. Direct sale is common, and satisfied customers often become permanent buyers. Wholesalers are sometimes used for fill-in purchases and in handling sales to smaller purchasers.

RAW MATERIALS

Farm products (such as cattle, wool, eggs, milk, pigs, and canola) and natural products (such as coal, copper, iron ore, and lumber) constitute **raw materials**. They are similar to component parts and materials in that they become part of the final products.

Since most raw materials are graded, the purchaser is assured of standardized products with uniform quality. As with component parts and materials, direct sale of raw materials is common, and sales are typically made on a contractual basis. Wholesalers are increasingly involved in purchasing raw materials from foreign suppliers.

Price is seldom a controllable factor in purchasing raw materials, since it is often quoted at a central market and is virtually identical among competing sellers. Purchasing buy raw materials from the firms they consider most able to deliver in the quantity and the quality required.

SUPPLIES

If installations represent the specialty products of the business-to-business market, then operating supplies are the convenience products. **Supplies** are regular expense items necessary in the daily operation of a firm, but not part of its final product.

Supplies are sometimes called **MRO items**, because they can be divided into three categories: (1) maintenance items, such as brooms, floor-cleaning compounds, and light bulbs; (2) repair items, such as nuts and bolts used in repairing equipment; and (3) operating supplies, such as heating fuel, lubricating oil, and office stationery.

The regular purchase of operating supplies is a routine aspect of the purchasing manager's job. Wholesalers are very often used in selling supplies due to the items' low unit prices, small sales, and large number of potential buyers. Since supplies are relatively standardized, price competition is frequently heavy. However, purchasing managers spend little time in making purchase decisions about such products. They frequently place telephone orders or mail orders, or make regular purchases from the sales representative of the local office-supply wholesaler.

This brings to an end the discussion of products, their classification, and broad management principles that apply in the product life cycle. Product classification analysis has also shown many different strategic needs and opportunities. The next chapter continues with a more detailed look at the numerous considerations required in managing products.

component parts and materials
Finished business-to-business goods that actually become part of the final product.

www.gmcanada.com

www.bikes.com/main.html

www.daimlerchrysler.ca

raw materials
Farm products (such as cattle, wool, eggs, milk, pigs, and canola) and natural products (such as coal, copper, iron ore, and lumber).

supplies
Regular expense items necessary in the daily operation of a firm, but not part of its final product.

MRO items
Business-to-business supplies, so called because they can be categorized as maintenance items, repair items, and operating supplies.

▶ SUMMARY

A product is a total bundle of physical, service, and symbolic characteristics designed to produce consumer want satisfaction. The total product concept includes the brand, image, warranty, and packaging.

Over time, products are characterized by a product life cycle. The stages of this life cycle are introduction, growth, maturity, and decline. The most appropriate marketing strategy changes for different stages of the life cycle. Fads have short life cycles, while other products can have very long life cycles. Marketing activity can extend the product life cycle by increasing the frequency of use of a product, or by changing product quality or packaging. The product life cycle concept applies best to product groups rather than to individual brands.

Consumers go through a process from learning about a product to deciding whether to purchase it or not. This adoption process proceeds in stages consisting of awareness, interest, evaluation, trial, and adoption/rejection. Different people will adopt a particular innovation at different times. Adopters are classified as innovators, early adopters, early majority, late majority, and laggards. Rate of adoption is influenced by the five characteristics of innovation: relative advantage, compatibility, complexity, divisibility, and communicability.

Consumer products can be categorized as convenience products, preference products, shopping products, and specialty products. Business-to-business products are categorized as installations, accessory equipment, component parts and materials, raw materials, and supplies.

▶ KEY TERMS

accessory equipment
adoption process
component parts and materials
consumer innovators
convenience products
diffusion process
fads
fashions
industrial distributor
installations

MRO items
preference products
product
product life cycle
raw materials
shopping products
specialty products
supplies
warranty

▶ INTERACTIVE SUMMARY AND DISCUSSION QUESTIONS

1. A product is a total bundle of physical, service, and symbolic characteristics designed to produce consumer want satisfaction. Explain how this definition applies to
   a. a lawyer's service in drafting a will
   b. a pail of chemical fertilizer used by a farmer
   c. Alfred Sung perfume

2. The product life-cycle stages are introduction, growth, maturity, and decline. Draw the typical life-cycle model, and then the way the model would appear for a fad, a fashion item, and an aborted (re)introduction.

3. At different stages in the product life cycle, the emphasis differs for the elements of the marketing mix. Discuss, and give examples.

4. Fashions are currently popular products that tend to follow recurring life cycles. For some marketers, it would be desirable to speed up the cycle so there would be a revived demand for the new fashion. Is this possible? Why or why not?

5. The life-cycle concept is most applicable to a product category, not to individual brands. Discuss, using examples.

6. The product life cycle may be extended by increasing the frequency of use by present customers, adding new users, finding new uses for the product, or changing product quality or packaging. Discuss the pros and cons of such efforts in comparison with introducing a completely new product.

7. Consumers go through a process from first learning about a product to deciding whether to purchase it or not. This adoption process has the following stages: awareness, interest, evaluation, trial, and adoption/rejection. Discuss how a marketer can use this information.

8. The rate of adoption is influenced by the five characteristics of the innovation: relative advantage, compatibility, complexity, divisibility, and communicability. Using these characteristics, give an example of a product that would be adopted relatively quickly, and one that would be adopted more slowly.

9. Consumer products can be categorized as convenience products, preference products, shopping products, and specialty products. Describe how the marketing mix varies for products in each category.

10. Business-to-business products are categorized as installations, accessory equipment, component parts and materials, raw materials, and supplies. Explain how the marketing mix varies for products in each category.

www.cadbury.co.uk

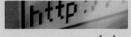

www.ford.ca

11. Compare the Cadbury Web site to the Ford Canada Web site. What types of products are these? How has product type affected the way the products are promoted? How are the Web sites different? Can you attribute any of these differences to differences in product type?

To obtain a list of further readings for Chapter 10, please refer to the *Foundations of Marketing* Web site.

Chapter 11
Product Management

The century-old Indian Motorcycle brand continues to make an impression on consumers, old and young, with its distinctive style.

Amotorcycle legend is about to appear on a street or highway near you. The last large-scale production line Indian Motorcycle model was produced in 1953, but if Rey Sotelo, president of Indian Motorcycle Co., has his way, the fabled bike will again be mass-produced and widely distributed. In 1999, the company produced the Limited Edition Indian Chief. They are planning on producing 15 000 motorcycles a year in the near future. While the motorcycle will have modern mechanics, it will sport the distinctive styling that made Indian so recognizable throughout the twentieth century.

But the motorcycle is only part of the story. The Indian Motorcycle family of companies now owns the right to the nearly 100-year-old brand. In addition to the Limited Edition Indian Chief, the company produces clothing and has opened what they call a "brand shrine" (i.e., a café and lounge, motorcycle dealership, and clothing store) in Toronto. The merchandising rights alone are estimated to be worth millions of dollars.

Whether the attempt to build on the Indian name is successful or not remains to be seen, but the fact that anyone would even consider it is a graphic illustration of the staying power—and value—of a well-established brand.

Recognizing, managing, and protecting the value of a brand, or *brand equity*, are only some of the many facets involved in product management. Having appropriate products and brand names that are attractive and memorable are fundamental tasks of the business.

Source: Susan Bourette, "Firm Vies for Indian Motorcycle Brand," *The Globe and Mail* (November 12, 1998), p. B4; Anonymous, "Leader of the Pack," *The Globe and Mail* (January 22, 1999), p. A14; Ted Latumus, "Legendary Name Returns to the Street," *The Star Phoenix* (March 5, 1999), p. C6.

▶ CHAPTER OBJECTIVES
After reading and studying this chapter, you should be able to

1. Explain the concept of the product mix, and indicate various mix decisions that can be made.
2. Describe the importance of developing a line of related products.
3. Outline new-product strategies and the determinants of their success.
4. Describe various organizational arrangements for new-product development.
5. Examine the stages in the product development process.
6. Discuss the role of brands, brand names, and trademarks.
7. Explain the importance, role, and functions of packaging.

▶ INTRODUCTION

Product management requires continual diligence in assessing the changing needs of the market. Normally it is important to have products that provide a range of opportunities for the company. This range of products is described as a product mix. A **product mix** is the assortment of product lines and individual offerings available from a company. Its two components are the **product line**, a series of related products, and the **individual offerings**, or single products within those lines.

Product mixes are typically measured by width and depth of assortment. Width of assortment refers to the number of different product lines that the firm offers, while depth of assortment refers to the extension or variety within a particular product line. Maple Leaf Foods International offers an assortment of consumer product lines — meats, and several unrelated grocery items such as peanut butter (see Table 11.1). These product lines would be considered the width of the Maple Leaf product mix. The depth is determined by the number of individual offerings within each product line. For example, the company's meat line consists of fresh meats, smoked meats, and processed meats, while the grocery line is represented by peanut butter and several types of canned vegetables. The company also sells a nonedible line of by-products.

product mix
The assortment of product lines and individual offerings available from a company.

product line
A series of related products.

individual offering
Single product within a product line.

www.mlfi.com/specialt.html

▶ TABLE 11.1 The Maple Leaf Foods International Mix

	WIDTH OF ASSORTMENT		
	Meats	Groceries	Nonedible
DEPTH OF ASSORTMENT	Fresh and frozen meats Bacon Sausages Wieners Luncheon meats Canned meat Poultry	Peanut butter Canned vegetables and fruit Vegetable oils Lard Shortening French fries Maple syrup Jams	Byproducts Hides

---

▶ THE EXISTING PRODUCT MIX

The starting point in any product-planning effort is to assess the firm's current product mix. What product line does it now offer? How deep are the offerings within each of the product lines? The marketer normally looks for gaps in the assortment that can be filled by new products or by modified versions of existing products. Expansion or redevelopment of existing product lines is usually the easiest approach for a firm to take, since the market requirements for these lines are generally well known.

Cannibalization

The firm wants to avoid a costly new-product introduction that will adversely affect sales of one of its existing products. A product that takes sales from another offering in a product line is said to be **cannibalizing** the line. Marketing research should ensure that cannibalization effects are minimized or at least anticipated. When Clearly Canadian, the beverage company, introduced new flavours, its marketers were resigned to the fact that sales of their existing brand would be negatively affected.

cannibalizing
Situation involving one product taking sales from another offering in a product line.

Line Extension

An important rationale for assessing the current product mix is to determine whether line extension is feasible. A **line extension** refers to the development of individual offerings that appeal to different market segments but are closely related to the existing product line. If cannibalization can be minimized, line extension provides a relatively cheap way of increasing sales revenues at minimal risk. Oh Henry chocolate bars can be purchased in an ice-cream bar format, in addition to their traditional form. This illustrates the line extension of an existing product.

Once the existing product mix has been assessed and the appropriate line extensions considered, marketing decision makers must turn their attention to product-line planning and new-product development.

line extension
The development of individual offerings that appeal to different market segments but are closely related to the existing product line.

Kellogg has extended its existing product line with its new Honey Crunch Corn Flakes. Which market segment is the firm trying to appeal to?

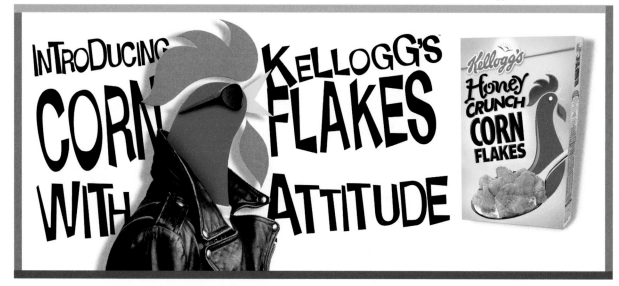

▶ THE IMPORTANCE OF PRODUCT LINES

www.bombardier.com

Firms that market only one product are rare today. Most offer their customers a product line — a series of related products. Bombardier, for example, was formed in 1942 and specialized in manufacturing enclosed multipassenger snowmobiles for military use. In 1959 it introduced the Ski-Doo snowmobile. Ski-Doo was Bombardier's primary product until the early 1970s. In 1974 the company won a contract to build rolling stock for the Montreal subway. Since that time it has diversified well beyond its original product base. In addition to the Ski-Doo and a personal watercraft branded as Sea-Doo, Bombardier manufactures subway and railway stock, corporate and regional commercial jets, short-range surface-to-air defence systems, and the electric Neighborhood Vehicle, or NV, designed to carry people around a golf course, neighbourhood, or other short route. The company also offers various industrial and financial services.[1]

Bombardier's addition of products and product lines has been extremely successful, but the strategy is hardly unique. Several factors account for the inclination of firms to develop complete product lines rather than relying on just one product.

Desire to Grow

A company places definite limitations on its growth potential when it concentrates on a single product. Lever Brothers once introduced 21 new products in a single twelve-month period in its search for market growth and increased profits. A study by a group of management consultants revealed that firms expect newly developed products to account for 37 percent of their sales and 51 percent of their profits over the five years following the products' introduction.[2]

Firms often introduce new products to offset seasonal variations in the sales of their current products. Since the majority of soup purchases are made during the winter months, Campbell Soup Company has attempted to tap the warm-weather soup market. A line of fruit soups to be served chilled was test-marketed, but results showed that consumers were not yet ready for fruit soups. The firm continued to search for warm-weather soups, however, and in some markets it has added gazpacho (and other varieties meant to be served chilled) to its product line.

Making Optimal Use of Company Resources

By spreading the costs of operations over a series of products, a company may find it possible to reduce the average costs of all products. Texize Chemical Company started with a single household cleaner and learned painful lessons about marketing costs when a firm has only one major product. Management rapidly added the products K2r and Fantastik to the line. The company's sales representatives can now call on intermediaries with a series of products at little more than the cost of marketing a single product. In addition, Texize's advertising produces benefits for all products in the line. Similarly, production facilities can be used economically in producing related products. For example, car companies regularly produce a range of products, from convertibles to vans to sports cars, from a basic car design. Finally, the expertise of all the firm's personnel can be applied more widely to a line of products than to a single one.

Increasing Company Importance in the Market

Consumers and marketing intermediaries often expect a firm that manufactures and markets small appliances to also offer related products under its brand name. The Maytag Company offers not only washing machines but also dryers, since consumers often demand matching appliances. Gillette markets not only razors and blades but also a full range of grooming aids, including Foamy shaving cream, Right Guard deodorant, Gillette Dry Look hair spray, and Super Max hair dryers.

www.maytag.com

www.gillette.com

The company with a line of products is often more important to both the consumer and the retailer than is the company with only one product. Shoppers who purchase a tent often buy related items, such as tent heaters, sleeping bags, air mattresses, camp stoves, and special cookware. Recognizing this tendency, the Coleman Company now includes in its product line dozens of items associated with camping. The firm would be little known if its only product was lanterns. Similarly, new cameras from Eastman Kodak help the firm sell more film—a product that carries a significant profit margin.

Exploiting the Product Life Cycle

As its output enters the maturity and decline stages of the life cycle of a product category, the firm must add new products if it is to prosper. The regular addition of new products to the firm's line helps ensure that it will not become a victim of product obsolescence. The car industry continually adds new products, deletes those that are not doing well, and upgrades popular models.

▶ NEW-PRODUCT PLANNING

The product development effort requires considerable advance planning. New products are the lifeblood of many business firms, and a steady flow of new entries must be available if such firms are to survive. Some new products represent major technological breakthroughs. For instance, biotechnology, which permits the transfer of genes from any living organism to another, has the potential to spur the invention of many new pharmaceutical products. Other new products are simple product-line extensions—that is, the "new" product is new only to the company or to the customer. One survey found that for products introduced in one five-year period, about 85 percent were line extensions, and only 15 percent were truly new products.[3]

The Product Decay Curve

New-product development is risky and expensive. In 1989, despite the continuing potential of biotechnology, only 1 of 400 North American start-ups, Geneutech, had made a sustained profit.[4] A Conference Board study of 148 medium and large North American manufacturing companies revealed that one out of three new industrial and consumer products introduced within the previous five years had failed. The leading cause of new-product failure was insufficient or poor marketing research.[5]

Dozens of new-product ideas are required to produce even one successful product. Figure 11.1 depicts the product decay curve from a 1968 survey of 51 companies. Of every 58 ideas produced in these firms, only 12 passed the preliminary screening test designed to determine whether they were compatible with company resources and objectives. Of these 12, only 7 showed sufficient profit potential in the business analysis phase. Three survived the development phase, two made it through the test-marketing stage, and only one, on the average, was commercially successful. Thus, less than 2 percent of new ideas resulted in a successful product.

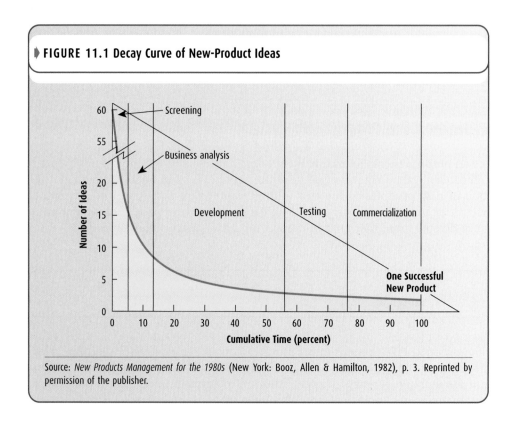

▶ **FIGURE 11.1 Decay Curve of New-Product Ideas**

Source: *New Products Management for the 1980s* (New York: Booz, Allen & Hamilton, 1982), p. 3. Reprinted by permission of the publisher.

A 1981 follow-up study reported that while the success rate had not improved, new-product development was becoming more cost-effective. According to the new data, some 54 percent of total new-product expenditures were made on products that became successes, compared with 30 percent in 1968. Capital investment in new products had fallen from 46 percent to 26 percent of total new-product spending.[6] These figures suggest that new-product development has become more efficient.

Determinants of Success for New Products

What determines the success or failure of a new product? A research effort known as Project New Product suggests the following nine categories as determinants of new-product outcomes:

1. product superiority/quality
2. economic advantage to the user
3. overall company/project fit
4. technological compatibility
5. familiarity to the company
6. market need, growth, and size
7. competitive situation
8. defined opportunity (whether the product has a well-understood category and market, as opposed to truly revolutionary innovations that must define new categories and markets)
9. project definition[7]

These hypothetical variables allowed Robert Cooper of McMaster University to classify types of new products. Cooper contends that the most important key to new-product success lies in the product strategy itself. In his research, he found that in the cases he studied, the best 20 percent of the products had an astounding success rate of 82 percent. In contrast, 20 percent at the other end of the scale (the "me-too" products) suffered a *failure* rate of 78 percent.[8]

▶ CHARACTERISTICS OF THE SUPERIOR PRODUCT

What, then, *is* a superior product? Cooper found that a number of characteristics constituted the superior-product dimension. In descending order of importance, these critical characteristics are as follows:

1. a product that meets customers' needs better than competing products
2. a product that offers features or attributes to the customer that competing products do not
3. a product of higher quality than competitive products (one that has tighter specifications, is stronger, lasts longer, or is more reliable)
4. a product that does a special task or job for the customer — something that cannot be done with existing products
5. a product that is highly innovative, totally new to the market
6. a product that permits the customer to reduce costs[9]

Products with these characteristics, supported by creative marketing strategies, will greatly contribute to a profitable product line.

Product Development Strategies

The firm's strategy for new-product development should vary according to the existing product mix and the determinants cited above. Marketing decision makers also need to look at the firm's current market position. In Chapter 6, we saw that growth opportunities can be summarized using a product/market matrix. Product improvement possibilities can be discussed in a very similar way.

Figure 11.2 provides a means of looking at overall product development strategy. Four forms of product development are suggested: product improvement, market development, product development, and product diversification.

▶ **FIGURE 11.2 Forms of Product Development**

	Old Product	New Product
Old Market	Product improvement	Product development
New Market	Market development	Product diversification

Source: Charles E. Meisch, "Marketers, Engineers Should Work Together in 'New Product' Development Departments," *Marketing News* (November 13, 1981), p. 10. Used by permission of the American Marketing Association. Earlier discussion of these strategies is credited to H. Igor Ansoff, "Strategies for Diversification," *Harvard Business Review* (September–October 1957), pp. 113–24; see also Philip Kotler, *Principles of Marketing*, 2nd ed. (Englewood Cliffs, NJ: Prentice Hall, 1983), pp. 34, 52.

product improvement strategy
A modification in existing products.

A **product improvement strategy** refers to a modification in existing products. Tide is an example of a product that has undergone constant product improvement over the years. Because of such improvements, it continues to be a leading product. Another example is the "Quality Is Job One" program established by Ford. And this was more than just a slogan: Ford's products are now more competitive with Japanese cars.

market development strategy
Finding new markets for existing products.

A **market development strategy** concentrates on finding new markets for existing products. Market segmentation (discussed in Chapters 3 and 4) is a useful tool in such an effort. Penetrating the home market with the fax machine—a product already established in the office—illustrates such a strategy. Cellular phone companies have consistently practised market development. Originally attractive primarily to businesspeople who were frequently away from conventional phones, cell phones are now purchased by consumers for convenience or occasional emergency use.

product development strategy
Introducing new products into identifiable or established markets.

A **product development strategy** refers to introducing new products into identifiable or established markets. Chrysler's Magic Wagon, for example, was a tremendous success because it provided consumers with a spacious vehicle that was as easy to drive, and as comfortable, as a car. This is a major strategy of the

computer industry. A continuous flow of products makes the computer you just bought somewhat obsolete within a few months of purchase.

Sometimes the new product is the firm's first entry in a particular market. In other cases, firms choose to introduce new products into markets in which they have already established positions, in an attempt to increase overall market share.

A **product diversification strategy** refers to the development of new products for new markets. The introduction of the CD-ROM is an example. In some cases, the new target markets complement existing markets; in others, they do not. For example, a computer company might develop a range of products for the home security market.

Each of these strategies has advantages and disadvantages and must carefully be considered in the light of consumer needs and behaviour, competitors' strengths, and the strengths and abilities of the company. New products should be consistent with the firm's overall strategic orientation. Bombardier's recent introduction of a four-wheel all-terrain vehicle (ATV) nicely complements its Ski-Doo and Sea-Doo in its Recreational Products division. It would have made far less sense for Bombardier to have introduced a touring class two-wheel motorcycle. In general, a new product should fit well with the orientation, skills, and resources of the firm.

Many companies adopt a product improvement strategy to attract new and satisfy current customers. Saturn, for example, has modified its regular coupe by adding a third door to provide more convenience.

product diversification strategy
The development of new products for new markets.

▶ THE ORGANIZATIONAL STRUCTURE FOR NEW-PRODUCT DEVELOPMENT

As the above section indicates, new-product planning is a complex area. The critical nature of product-planning decisions requires an effective organizational structure to make them. A prerequisite for efficient product innovation is an organizational structure designed to stimulate and coordinate new-product development. New-product development is a specialized task that requires the expertise of many departments. A company that delegates new-product development responsibility to the engineering department often discovers that engineers sometimes design products that are good from a structural standpoint but poor in terms of consumer needs. Many successful medium and large companies assign new-product development to one or more of the following: (1) new-product committees, (2) new-product departments, (3) product managers, or (4) venture teams.

New-Product Committees

The most common organizational arrangement for new-product development is the *new-product committee.* Such a committee typically comprises representatives of top management in such areas as marketing, finance, manufacturing, engineering, research, and accounting. Committee members are less concerned with conceiving and developing new-product ideas than with reviewing and approving new-product plans.

Since key executives in the functional areas are committee members, their support for a new-product plan is likely to result in its approval for further development. However, new-product committees tend to be slow, are generally conservative, and sometimes compromise in order to expedite decisions so that members can get back to their regular company responsibilities.

New-Product Departments

To overcome the limitations of the new-product committee, a number of firms have established a separate, formally organized department responsible for all phases of a product's development within the firm, including making screening decisions, developing product specifications, and coordinating product testing. The head of the department is given substantial authority and usually reports to the president or to the top marketing officer.

product managers (brand managers)
Individuals assigned one product or product line and given responsibility for determining its objectives and marketing strategies.

Product Managers

Product managers (also called **brand managers**) are individuals assigned one product or product line and given responsibility for determining its objectives and marketing strategies. Procter & Gamble assigned the first product manager back in 1927 when it made one person responsible for Camay soap.[10] The role of product manager is now widely accepted by marketers. Johnson & Johnson, Maple Leaf Foods, and General Mills are examples of firms that employ product managers.

Product managers are deeply involved in setting prices, developing advertising and sales promotion programs, and working to provide assistance to sales representatives in the field. Although product managers have no line authority over the field sales force, they share the objective of increasing sales for the brand, and they try to help salespeople accomplish this task. In multiproduct companies, product managers are key people in the marketing department. They provide individual attention to each product, while the firm as a whole has a single sales force, a marketing research department, and an advertising department that all product managers can use.

In addition to performing product analysis and planning, the product manager must use interpersonal skills and sales skills to gain the cooperation of people over whom he or she has no authority. This occurs with levels above the manager, as well as with those in sales and advertising.

Besides having primary responsibility for marketing a particular product or product line, the product manager often is also responsible for new-product development, creating new-product ideas, and making recommendations for improving existing products. These suggestions become the basis for proposals submitted to top management.

The product manager system is open to one of the same criticisms as the new-product committee: new-product development may get secondary treatment because of the manager's time commitments for existing products. Although a number of extremely successful new products have resulted from ideas submitted by product managers, it cannot be assumed that the skills required for marketing an existing product line are the same as those required for successfully developing new products.[11]

Venture Teams

Many companies have found that new venture teams have provided a good method of bringing new products to the market.

The **venture-team concept** develops new products through combining the management resources of marketing, technology, capital, and management expertise in a team. Like new-product committees, venture teams are composed of specialists from different functions in the organization: engineering representatives for expertise in product design and the development of prototypes; marketing staff members for development of product-concept tests, test marketing, sales forecasts, pricing, and promotion; and financial accounting representatives for detailed cost analyses and decisions concerning the concept's probable return on investment.

Unlike new-product committees, venture teams do not disband after every product developed. Members are assigned to the project as a major responsibility, and the team possesses the necessary authority to both plan and carry out a course of action.

As a means of stimulating product innovation, the team is typically separated from the permanent organization and is also linked directly with top man-

venture-team concept
An organizational strategy for developing new products through combining the management resources of marketing, technology, capital, and management expertise in a team.

agement. One company moved its three-member venture team from its divisional headquarters to the corporate head office. Since the venture-team manager reports to the division head or to the chief administrative officer, communications problems are minimized and high-level support is assured.

The venture team usually begins as a loosely organized group of members with a common interest in a new-product idea. Team members are frequently given released time during the workday to devote to the venture. If viable product proposals are developed, the venture team is formally organized as a task force within a venture department or as a task force reporting to a vice president or to the chief executive officer. When the commercial potential of new products has been demonstrated, the products may be assigned to an existing division, may become a division within the company, or may serve as the nucleus of a new company. The flexibility and authority of the venture team allows the large firm to operate with the manoeuvrability of smaller companies.

▶STAGES IN THE NEW-PRODUCT DEVELOPMENT PROCESS

New-product development strategy should be built on the existing business strategy of the company. Companies that have successfully launched new products are more likely to have had a formal new-product process in place for some time. They are also more likely to have a strategic plan and to be committed to growth through internally developed new products.[12]

Once the firm is organized for new-product development, it can establish procedures for evaluating new-product ideas. The product development process may be thought of as involving seven stages: (1) development of overall new-product strategy, (2) new-product idea generation, (3) screening, (4) business analysis, (5) final product development, (6) test marketing, and (7) commercialization. At each stage, management faces the decision to abandon the project, continue to the next stage, or seek additional information before proceeding further. The process is illustrated in Figure 11.3.

New-Product Strategy

New-product strategy links corporate objectives to the new-product effort, provides direction for the new-product process, and identifies the strategic roles in the product line that the new products should play. It also helps set the formal financial criteria to be used in measuring new-product performance and in screening and evaluating new-product ideas.[13]

Idea Generation

New-product development begins with an idea. Ideas emanate from many sources: the sales force, marketing employees, research and development (R & D) specialists, competitive products, retailers, inventors outside the company, and

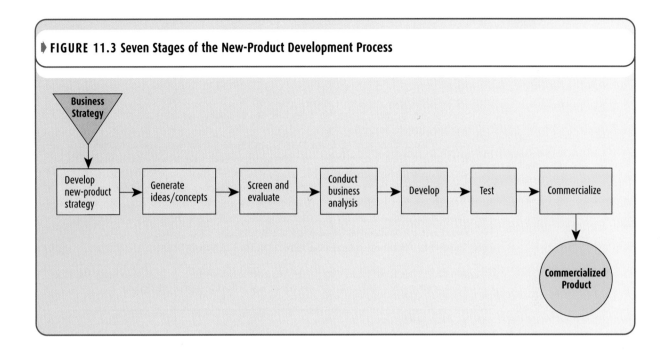

▶ **FIGURE 11.3 Seven Stages of the New-Product Development Process**

customers who write letters asking, "Why don't you …?" It is extremely important for the firm to develop a system of stimulating new ideas and rewarding people who develop them.

Screening

This crucial stage involves separating ideas with potential from those incapable of meeting company objectives. Some organizations use checklists to determine whether product ideas should be eliminated or subjected to further consideration. These checklists typically include such factors as product uniqueness, availability of raw materials, and compatibility of the proposed product with current product offerings, existing facilities, and capabilities. In other instances, the screening stage consists of open discussions of new-product ideas among representatives of different functional areas in the organization. This is an important point in the product development process, since any product ideas that go beyond this point will cost the firm considerable time and money. Table 11.2 lists some issues that should be considered in the screening process.

Business Analysis

Product ideas that survive the initial screening are then subjected to a thorough business analysis. This involves assessing the potential market, its growth rate, and the likely competitive strength of the new product. Decisions must be made about the compatibility of the proposed product with such company resources as financial support for necessary promotion, production capabilities, and distribution facilities.

> ▶ **TABLE 11.2 Basic Criteria for New-Product Screening**

1. *Company's resources and abilities.* Financial resources, R & D skills, engineering skills, marketing research, management, production, sales force and distribution resources and skills, advertising and promotion resources and skills.
2. *Nature of the product.* Newness to the market, newness to the company, how completely the product has actually been planned and technical issues dealt with, fit with current product line, superiority in meeting customer needs, quality relative to current competitive products.
3. *Potential customers for the product.* Similarity to current customers, level of felt need for the product.
4. *Nature of competition.* Similarity to current competition, intensity of competition, presence of price bases competition, number and size of competitors.
5. *Nature of the market.* Size or potential, growth rate, rate of change of needs of customers.

Source: Adapted from Robert Cooper, "The New Prod System: The Industry Experience," *Journal of Product Innovation Management* (June 1992), pp. 125–26. Copyright (1992), with permission from Elsevier Science.

concept testing
A marketing research project that attempts to measure consumer attitudes and perceptions relevant to a new-product idea.

Concept testing, or the consideration of the product idea prior to its actual development, is an important aspect of the business analysis stage. **Concept testing** is a marketing research project that attempts to measure consumer attitudes and perceptions relevant to a new-product idea. Focus groups (see Chapter 5) and in-store polling can be effective methods of assessing a new-product concept.

Product Development

Those product ideas with profit potential are then converted into a physical product. The conversion process becomes the joint responsibility of development engineering, which is responsible for developing the original concept into a product, and the marketing department, which provides feedback on consumer reactions to alternative product designs, packages, features, colours, and other physical appeals. Numerous changes may be necessary before the original mockup is converted into the final product.

Even after basic production processes have been solved, there is often a considerable amount of testing with potential consumers. Such testing is done in many ways. Sometimes employees are given the product and asked to report on performance on a regular, structured basis. As a textbook such as this one is written, it is subject to review by faculty members across the country. In other cases, limited market tests are undertaken under carefully monitored conditions, as discussed in Chapter 5. The series of revisions, tests, and refinements should result in the ultimate introduction of a product with a greater likelihood of success.

Despite such careful testing, further problems are often uncovered in daily use. For example, the first release of computer software often has some "bugs" that have to be corrected. And the first printing of this book might have some typographical or other errors that will be corrected with the next printing a few months later. Cars are sometimes recalled to dealers to replace a part that does not work as expected.

Test Marketing

To determine consumer reactions to their products *and* to the proposed marketing plan under normal shopping conditions, a number of firms test-market their new offerings. Up to this point, consumer information has been obtained by giving free products to consumers, who then gave their reactions. Other information may have been gathered by asking shoppers to evaluate competitive products, but test marketing is the first point at which the product must perform in a "real-life" environment.

Test marketing involves selecting usually one to three cities or television-coverage areas considered reasonably typical of the total market, and introducing a new product to these areas with a total marketing campaign. A carefully designed and controlled test allows management to develop estimates of the effectiveness of marketing mix decisions and projections of sales following full-scale introduction.

test marketing
Selecting areas considered reasonably typical of the total market, and introducing a new product to these areas with a total marketing campaign to determine consumer response before marketing the product nationally.

Some firms omit the test-marketing stage and move directly from product development to full-scale production. They cite three problems with test marketing:

1. Test marketing is expensive. As one marketing executive pointed out,

   > It's very difficult to run a little [test market] for six months or a year in three or four markets across the [country] and then project what your sales volume is going to be two or three years in the future, mainly because you're testing in such small localities, generally to keep your costs down.
   >
   > You simply can't afford to test your products in markets like [Toronto or Montreal]. So you run your test in [smaller cities]. And your test costs are over $1 million even in places like that.[14]

2. Competitors who learn about the test market may disrupt the findings by reducing the price of their products in the test area, distributing cents-off coupons, installing attractive in-store displays, or giving additional discounts to retailers to induce them to display more of their products.

   Test-marketing a new product also communicates company plans to competitors before the product's introduction. The Kellogg Company discovered a new product with suspected sales potential by learning of the test marketing of a new fruit-filled tart designed to be heated in the toaster and served hot for breakfast. Kellogg rushed a similar product into full-scale production and became the first national marketer of the product they named Pop Tarts.

3. Long-lived durable goods (such as dishwashers, hair dryers, and VCRs) are seldom test-marketed due to the major financial investment required for the development, the need to develop a network of dealers to distribute the products, and the parts and servicing required. A company such as Whirlpool invests from $1 million to $33 million in the development of a new refrigerator. To develop each silicon chip in an Apple microcomputer costs approximately $1 million and takes from one to fifteen months. Producing a prototype for a test market is simply too expensive, so the "go/no-go" decision for the new durable product is typically made without the benefit of test-market results.[15]

www.kelloggs.com

www.poptarts.com

A decision to skip the test-marketing stage should be based on there being a very high likelihood of the product's success. The cost of developing a new detergent from idea generation to national marketing has been estimated at $10 million. Even though a firm will experience losses on any product that passes the initial screening process but is not introduced, it will still be much better off if it stops as soon as it discovers that the product cannot succeed. Otherwise, it may be faced with a failure like Corfam, an artificial leather that Du Pont introduced; the company suffered losses of more than $100 million over the lengthy period it tried to make Corfam a success.

Commercialization

The few product ideas that have survived all the steps in the development process are now ready for full-scale marketing. Marketing programs must be established, outlays for production facilities may be necessary, and the sales force, intermediaries, and potential customers must become acquainted with the new product.

▶ THE PRACTISING MARKETER

The Future of Fork Lift Trucks

"Why not for once take an unconventional approach to technology, and get away from the well travelled paths?" asked a German engineering company recently, and so opened a window into the future of fork lift trucks. "Project study RXX" was to look at and, to some extent, test this idea. Important trends have to be recognized and picked up early. What is regarded as futuristic today is likely to be a familiar picture by tomorrow.

The vehicle's outer shape might not be quite as artistic as originally planned, but as far as technology and function are concerned, the same ideas and concepts could soon be finding their way into fork lift truck technology as the standard.

The "intelligent" counterweight is hydraulically adjustable, and makes driving in narrow working aisles much simpler. With the counterweight retracted the wheelbase is smaller, the truck more manoeuvrable. With the counterweight extended the capacity of the truck increases and the tipping stability is greater when working with a raised load. The driver's cab can be raised, thus improving the view over the load. Having to drive backwards because the driver cannot see the front over the raised load will be largely a thing of the past. When stacking, safety is improved because the driver's viewing angle is better.

The hydraulic cylinder, with its star-shaped profile, makes it impossible for the piston to twist, thus a "load bearing" cylinder can act as a lifting device. The result: hardly any restriction of view when driving with or without the load raised. If the driver lowers the cab when stacking, he has a good view below the load. An electronically activated film (LCD screen) is incorporated into the bonded glass of the front windscreen. If the truck is driving backwards, the view to the back taken by the rear view camera is automatically superimposed. At the same time the controller reverses its function—reversing to the right would mean that the steering wheel is turned to the right. The driver remains in the seat facing front but steers backwards in the correct direction—exactly as he does when driving forwards. The reality behind the truck is, so to speak, transposed to the front.

Where is this company in the new-product development process? What does it still have to do? Do you think the company will be able to successfully introduce this innovation?

Source: Adapted from Anonymous, "The Future of Fork Lift Trucks," *International Food Marketing and Technology* 12:4 (August 1998), p. 52. Reprinted with permission.

New-product development should follow the step-by-step approach outlined in Figure 11.3. Systematic planning and control of all phases of development and introduction can be accomplished through the use of such scheduling methods as the Program Evaluation and Review Technique (PERT) and the Critical Path Method (CPM). These techniques map out the sequence in which each step must be taken and show the time allotments for each activity. Detailed PERT and CPM flow charts not only assist in coordinating all activities in the development and introduction of new products, but can also highlight the sequence of events that will be the most critical in scheduling.

▶ PRODUCT DELETION DECISIONS

While many firms devote a great deal of time and resources to developing new products, the thought of eliminating old products from the firm's line is painful for many executives. Often sentimental attachments to marginal products prevent objective decisions to drop products with declining sales. Management finds it difficult to buy an old friend.

If waste is to be avoided, product lines must be pruned, and old unprofitable products must eventually be eliminated from the firm's line. This decision is typically faced in the late-maturity and early-decline stages of the product life cycle. Periodic reviews of all products should be conducted in order to prune weak products or to justify their retention.

In some instances, a firm will continue to carry an unprofitable product so as to provide a complete line of goods for its customers. Even though most supermarkets may not make much money on low-unit-value items such as salt, they continue to carry these items to meet shopper demands.

Other cases arise in which profitable products are dropped because of failure to fit into the firm's existing product line. IBM found that its marketing system, including the training of representatives, was so focused on computers that it was difficult to do an adequate job in marketing printers. Therefore, it removed printers from the main product line and turned them over to a subsidiary company, Lexmark.

▶ PRODUCT IDENTIFICATION

Manufacturers identify their products through the use of brand names, symbols, and distinctive packaging. So do large retailers such as Canadian Tire, with its line of Mastercraft products, and The Bay, with its Beaumark brand. Almost every product that is distinguishable from another contains a means of identification for the buyer. Even a 5-year-old can distinguish a Chiquita banana from other ones. And the California Fruit Growers Exchange literally brands its oranges with the name Sunkist. The purchasing manager for a construction firm can turn over an ordinary sheet of roofing and find the name and symbol for Domtar. Choosing the means of identification for the firm's output often represents a major decision area for the marketing manager.

Brands, Brand Names, and Trademarks

brand
A name, term, sign, symbol, or design (or some combination of these) used to identify the products of one firm and to differentiate them from competitive offerings.

A **brand** is a name, term, sign, symbol, or design (or some combination of these) used to identify the products of one firm and to differentiate them from competitive offerings. A **brand name** is that part of the brand consisting of words, letters, or symbols that make up a name used to identify and distinguish the firm's offerings from those of its competitors.[16] The brand name is, therefore, that part of the brand that can be spoken. A **trademark** is a brand that has been given legal protection and has been granted solely to its owner. Thus, the term "trademark" includes not only pictorial design but also the brand name. Many thousands of trademarks are currently registered in Canada. Today, virtually all trademarks are developed with careful consideration of the visual and emotional impact of the name. Some other common trademarks have emerged through various iterations over the years. The Procter & Gamble "moon and stars" trademark is one example.

brand name
Words, letters, or symbols that make up a name used to identify and distinguish the firm's offerings from those of its competitors.

For the consumer, brands facilitate repeat purchases of products that have been found satisfactory. The brand assures a uniform quality and identifies the firm producing the product. The purchaser associates the satisfaction derived from a carbonated soft drink with the brand name Pepsi-Cola.

trademark
A brand that has been given legal protection and has been granted solely to its owner.

For the marketing manager, the brand serves as the cornerstone around which the product's image is developed. Once consumers have been made aware of a particular brand, its appearance becomes further advertising for the firm. The Shell Oil Company symbol is instant advertising to motorists who view it while driving. Well-known brands also allow the firm to escape some of the rigours of price competition. Although any chemist will confirm that all ASA tablets contain the same amount of the chemical acetylsalicylic acid, Bayer has developed so strong a reputation that it can successfully market its Aspirin at a higher price than competitive products. Similarly, McDonald's "golden arches" attract customers to its outlets.

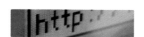

www.pg.com/rumor/
index.html

brand equity
Represents the value customers (and the stock markets) place on the sum of the history the customer has had with a brand.

The "attractiveness" of Bayer, McDonald's, and hundreds of other respected brands is called **brand equity**. Brand equity really represents the value customers (and the stock markets) place on the sum of the history the customer has had with a brand. If a brand has consistently been associated with high quality and resulted in high customer satisfaction, the equity of that brand will be high. Sony is a valuable brand, with high brand equity, because the company has delivered high-quality electronic products for decades. On the other hand, the Russian car manufacturer Lada has struggled for years to overcome an initial public perception of poor quality. Lada is not considered a particularly valuable brand in North America.

We shall see that many brand-related decisions—from initially choosing a name, to protecting the name in court if necessary, to brand extension strategies—are driven by a company's desire to create, preserve, and exploit brand equity.

What Constitutes a Good Brand Name?

Good brand names are easy to pronounce, recognize, and remember. Short names like Vim, Gleem, Dash, and Kodak meet these requirements. Multinational marketing firms face a particularly acute problem in selecting brand names: a brand name that works terrifically well in one country may prove disastrous in another due to language problems.

For 21 years, Nissan Motor Corporation marketers struggled with an easily mispronounced brand name—"Datsun"—for its cars and trucks. Nissan found that in English-speaking nations some people pronounced the *a* like the *a* in *hat,* while others pronounced it like the *o* in *got,* and the difference hindered brand recognition. Finally, Nissan marketers decided to change the name of all its automobile products to "Nissan" beginning with its Stanza model in 1982. Total cost of the change—effected in more than 135 countries—is estimated to have been as high as $150 million.[17]

Every language has "O" and "K" sounds, and "okay" has become an international word. Every language also has a short "a," so that Coca-Cola and Texaco are good in any tongue. An American advertising campaign for E-Z washing machines failed in the United Kingdom because the British pronounce "Z" as "zed," as we do in Canada.

▶ THE ROOTS OF MARKETING

Establishing the Coca-Cola Brand

Coca-Cola and Coke are two one of the world's most widely recognized brands. This high recognition has not been accidental, but rather reflects years of effort and advertising investment by The Coca-Cola Company.

Here is an early advertisement that very explicitly distinguishes Coca-Cola from other colas and also reserves the abbreviation "Coke" as exclusively referring to Coca-Cola.

The company continues to protect its trademarks with great persistence and consistency.

An early advertisement shows the well-recognized brand.

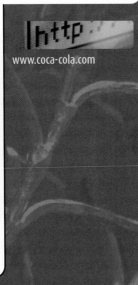

www.coca-cola.com

The brand name should give the buyer the right connotation. Mercury Marine presents favourable images of boating pleasures. The Craftsman name used on the Sears line of quality tools also produces the correct image. Accutron suggests the quality of the high-priced and accurate timepiece made by the Bulova Watch Company. But what can the marketing manager do if the brand name is based on a strange-sounding company name? Sometimes the decision may be to poke fun at this improbable name, as in a promotional campaign built around the theme "With a name like Koogle, it has to be good!"

The Brand Name Should Be Legally Protectable

S.C. Johnson and Son, makers of OFF, lost a court case against Bug Off since it was held that OFF was an improper trademark because it was not unusual enough to distinguish it from other, similar products.

When all offerings in a class of products become generally known by the brand name of the first or leading brand in that product class, the brand name may be ruled a descriptive or **generic name**, after which the original owner loses all right to the exclusive use of it. Generic names like nylon, zipper, kerosene, linoleum, escalator, and shredded wheat were once brand names.

generic name
A brand name over which the original owner has lost exclusive claim because all offerings in the associated class of products have become generally known by the brand name (usually that of first or leading brand in that product class).

Bayer's Aspirin is the only ASA tablet permitted to carry that protected trademark in Canada. All other acetylsalicylic acid tablets are called ASA. In the United States, because Bayer did not protect its trade name, the generic name "aspirin" is given to all acetylsalicylic acid tablets. Most drug purchasers there would not know what an ASA tablet is.

There is a difference between brand names that are legally generic and those that could be perceived to be generic in the eyes of many consumers. Jell-O is a brand name owned exclusively by General Foods. But to most grocery purchasers the name Jell-O is the descriptive generic name for gelatin dessert. Legal brand names—such as Formica, Xerox, Frigidaire, Kodak, Frisbee, Styrofoam, Coke, Kleenex, Scotch Tape, Fiberglas, Band-Aid, and Jeep—are often used by consumers in a descriptive manner. Xerox is such a well-known brand name that it is frequently used as a verb. British and Australian consumers often use the brand name Hoover as a verb for vacuuming.

To prevent their brand names from being ruled descriptive and available for general use, companies must take deliberate steps to inform the public of their exclusive ownership of brand names. They may resort to legal action in cases of infringement. The Eastman Kodak Company developed a series of advertisements around the theme "If it isn't an Eastman, it isn't a Kodak." The Coca-Cola Company and many other companies use the ® symbol for registration immediately after their brand names. Coca-Cola sends letters to newspapers and novelists and other writers who use the name Coke® with a lowercase first letter, informing them that the trademark is owned by Coca-Cola. Walt Disney Co. actively protects its brand names and is prepared to sue if necessary. West Edmonton Mall learned this the hard way when it lost a ten-year court battle with Disney over its indoor amusement park named Fantasyland. It lost an estimated $5 million in replacing all the Fantasyland signs and paraphernalia associated with the name. Thus, companies may face the ironic dilemma of attempting to retain the exclusive rights to a brand name that, chiefly due to the success of their own marketing efforts, could become generic to a large market segment if they do not take appropriate steps to protect their trademarks.

Since any dictionary word may eventually be ruled to be a generic name, some companies create new words to use for brand names. Such brand names as Keds, Rinso, and Kodak have obviously been created by their owners.

Brand Loyalty Categories

Brands vary widely in consumer familiarity and acceptance. While a shopper may insist on Robin Hood flour for use in the family breadmaker, that same shopper may not be able to recall the name of even one brand of powdered milk to be used in the same breadmaker.

Brand loyalty may be measured in three stages: brand recognition, brand preference, and brand insistence.

Brand recognition is a company's first objective for newly introduced products—to make them familiar to consumers. Often the company achieves this goal through advertising. Sometimes it uses free samples or coupons offering discounts for purchases. Several new brands of toothpaste have been introduced on college campuses through free samples contained in Campus Pacs. Once the consumer has used the product, it moves from the "unknown" to the "known" category, and provided the consumer was satisfied with the trial sample, he or she is more likely to repurchase it.

Brand preference is the second stage of brand loyalty. Because of previous experience with the product, consumers will choose it rather than one of its competitors—if it is available. Even if university students prefer Coca-Cola as a means of quenching their thirst, almost all of them will quickly switch to Pepsi-Cola or 7-Up when they discover that the vending machine has no Coca-Cola and the nearest supply is two buildings away. Companies with products at the brand preference stage are in a favourable position with respect to competing in their industries.

The ultimate stage in brand loyalty is **brand insistence**, which occurs when consumers will accept no alternatives and will search extensively for the product. Such a product has achieved a monopoly position with this group of consumers. Even though brand insistence may be the goal of many firms, it is seldom achieved. Only the most exclusive specialty goods attain this position with a large segment of the total market.

THE IMPORTANCE OF BRAND LOYALTY

A study of twelve patented drugs (including well-known drugs like Librium and Darvon) illustrates the importance of brand loyalty. The research indicated that patent expiration had a minimal effect on the drugs' market shares or price levels, a resiliency credited to the brand loyalty for the pioneer product in the field.[18] Another measure of the importance of brand loyalty is found in the Brand Utility Yardstick used by the J. Walter Thompson advertising agency. These rating measure the percentage of buyers who remain brand-loyal even if a 50 percent cost savings is available from generic products. Beer consumers were very loyal, with 48 percent refusing to switch. Sinus-remedy buyers were also brand-loyal, with a 44 percent rating. By contrast, only 13 percent of the aluminum-foil buyers would not switch to the generic product.[19]

Choosing a Brand Strategy

Some brands are so popular that they are carried over to unrelated products because of their marketing advantages. The decision to use a popular brand name for a new product entry in an unrelated product category is known as **brand extension**. This should not be confused with line extension (discussed earlier in this chapter), which refers to adding new sizes, styles, or related products. Brand extension, by contrast, refers only to carrying over the brand name.

---

brand recognition
The first stage of brand loyalty, when a firm has developed enough publicity for a brand that its name is familiar to consumers.

brand preference
The second stage of brand loyalty, when, based on previous experience, consumers will choose a product rather than one of its competitors—if it is available.

brand insistence
The ultimate stage of brand loyalty, when consumers will accept no alternatives and will search extensively for the product.

brand extension
The decision to use a popular brand name for a new product entry in an unrelated product category.

Examples of brand extension are abundant in contemporary marketing. Pears soap has been extended to the Pears shampoo line. Bic applied the brand name developed for its pens to disposable razors. Similarly, General Foods is extending its Jell-O brand: in some markets the company now has Jell-O Pudding Pops, Jell-O Slice Creme, and Jell-O Gelatin Pops.

In other situations a company will choose a new brand name for related products. One reason for this approach is to protect the image of the established brand in case the new introduction fails. In other instances the company may wish to protect the established brand from attack (usually price-based) by competitors. Brands that are intended to protect an established brand from attack are called flanker brands. Loblaws' No Name brand is a flanker brand for its President's Choice brand. No Name offers a low-price alternative to President's Choice but assures that the consumer is still buying a Loblaws brand.

family brand
Brand name used for several related products.

Brands may be classified as family brands or individual brands. A **family brand** is one brand name used for several related products. E.D. Smith markets dozens of food products under the E.D. Smith brand. Black & Decker has a complete line of power tools under the Black & Decker name. Johnson & Johnson offers parents a line of baby powder, lotions, plastic pants, and baby shampoo under one name.

individual brand
Brand that is known by its own brand name rather than by the name of the company producing it or an umbrella name covering similar items.

On the other hand, such manufacturers as Procter & Gamble market hundreds of products with **individual brands** (for example, Tide, Cheer, Crest, Gleem, Oxydol, and Dash). Each such item is known by its own brand name rather than by the name of the company producing it or an umbrella name covering similar items. Individual brands are more expensive to market, since a new promotional program must be developed to introduce each new product to its target market.

▶ THE PRACTISING MARKETER

www.readersdigest.com

Product Management at Reader's Digest

Reader's Digest Association Inc. plans to put its name on credit cards and insurance policies as part of a push to expand further beyond its flagship magazine.

Chief executive officer Thomas Ryder told analysts yesterday the company wants to launch a range of non-publishing products—focusing first on financial services and health—as it continues efforts to revive its profits.

The latest plan seeks to entice readers over 50 to buy other products with the Reader's Digest brands. "Your best customer is your current customer," said spokesman Stephen Morello. "The strength we have right now that we really haven't tapped is in an older audience."

The company said it will explore partnerships with financial services firms to introduce credit cards, insurance, and other financial products. Reader's Digest also is considering taking advantage of its experience in direct marketing to sell pharmaceuticals and vitamins.

Mr. Ryder has been overhauling the company since taking over in April 1998, slashing costs and seeking ways to attract younger customers as the mostly older circulation of its flagship magazine has been declining.

What product and branding strategy is Reader's Digest following? Do you think the company's strategy is likely to succeed? Why or why not?

Source: Adapted from The Associated Press, "Digest Eyes New Range of Products," *The Globe and Mail* (February 26, 1999), p. B7. Reprinted with permission.

Using family brands allows promotional outlays to benefit all products in the line. The effect of the promotion is spread over each of the products. A new addition to the products marketed by the H.J. Heinz Company gains immediate recognition due to the well-known family brand. Family brands also facilitate the task of introducing the product — for both the customer and the retailer. Since supermarkets carry an average of nearly 10 000 items in stock, they are reluctant to add new products unless they are convinced of potential demand. A marketer of a new brand of turtle soup would have to promise the supermarket-chain buyer huge advertising outlays for promotion and evidence of consumer buying intent before getting the product into the stores. The Campbell Soup Company, with approximately 85 percent of the market, would merely add the new flavour to its existing line and could secure store placements much more easily than could a company using individual brand names.

Family brands should be used only when the associated products are of similar quality, or the firm risks the danger of harming its product image. Using the Mercedes brand name on a new, less expensive car model might severely tarnish the image of the other models in the Mercedes product line. Even the most affordable Mercedes starts at a retail price of almost $40 000. With the merger of Chrysler and Daimler-Benz, it is very unlikely that a Mercedes priced below the C-class will appear. Less expensive models will wear a Chrysler brand.

Individual brand names should be used for dissimilar products. Campbell Soup once marketed a line of dry soups under the brand name Red Kettle. Large marketers of grocery products (such as Procter & Gamble, General Foods, and Lever Brothers) employ individual brands to appeal to unique market segments. Unique brands also allow the firm to stimulate competition within the organization and to increase total company sales. Product managers are also more free to try different merchandising techniques with individual brands. Consumers who do not prefer Tide may choose Dash or Oxydol rather than purchase a competitor's brand.

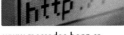
www.mercedes-benz.ca

National Brands or Private Brands?

Most of the brands mentioned in this chapter have been **national brands**, also commonly called **manufacturer's brands**. But, to an increasing extent, large wholesalers and retailers operating over a regional or national market are placing their own brands on the products that they market. These brands offered by wholesalers and retailers are usually called **private brands**. Loblaws' popular President's Choice line is one example. Canadian Tire carries its own brands, such as Mastercraft, MotoMaster, Supercycle, and Playmaker. Safeway store shelves are filled with such company brands as Edwards, Town House, Empress, and Taste Tells. Safeway brands represent a large percentage of all products in an average Safeway supermarket.

For a large retailer such as Loblaws, Canadian Tire, or Safeway, private brands allow the firm to establish an image and to attain greater control over the products that it handles. Quality levels, prices, and availability of the products become the responsibility of the retailer or wholesaler who develops a line of private brands.

Even though the manufacturers' brands are largely presold through national promotional efforts, the wholesaler and retailer may easily lose customers, since the same products may be available in competing stores. But only Canadian Tire

national brand (manufacturer's brand)
A brand promoted and distributed by a manufacturer.

private brand
A brand promoted and distributed by a wholesaler or retailer.

www.canadiantire.ca

▶ THE INFORMED CONSUMER

How to Complain Effectively

Products or services that we purchase are not always satisfactory. The Public Legal Education Association of Saskatchewan, Inc., suggests the following to ensure that your complaints produce some results:

- Complain at once.
- Do complain.
- Get your facts together.
- Talk to the appropriate person.
- Be polite.

- Be specific.
- Keep a record.
- Have a plan of action.
- Organize your action.
- Don't give up.

How Businesses May Say "No"

Be aware of the ways in which the business may try to discourage you. Some methods are

- *The runaround.* The seller and manufacturer may blame each other.
- *Silence.* There is no response to your complaint.
- *The use of the legal system.* One-sided interpretation of the law, use of lawyers, use of court decisions that complicate problems, and the use of legal terms that no one can understand.
- *Blaming the victim.* They say, "It's all your fault."
- *Offering partial refunds or expressing concern.* Despite these, failing to take action.
- *Use of "Sorry, but it's the company's policy."* You have rights regardless of the company's policy.
- *Inefficient management.* These people may be incompetent, as opposed to having bad intentions.

Source: Adapted from Sandra Hornung, *Consumer Power: A Guide to the Basics of Consumer Law in Saskatchewan* (Saskatoon: Public Legal Education Association of Saskatchewan, 1997), pp. 46–49. Reprinted with permission.

handles the Mastercraft line of power tools. By eliminating the promotional costs of the manufacturers' brands, the dealer may be able to offer a private brand at a lower price than the competing national brands — or make higher margins. Both consumers and the company benefit. As private brands achieve increasing brand loyalty they may even enable a retailer to avoid some price competition, since the brand can be sold only by the brand owner.

BATTLE OF THE BRANDS

Competition among manufacturers' brands and the private brands offered by wholesalers and large retailers has been called the "battle of the brands." Although the battle appears to be intensifying, the marketing impact varies widely among industries. One survey showed that private brands represented 36 percent of the market in replacement tires but only 7 percent in portable appliances. A full 52 percent of shoe sales involve private brands. For example, Sears and Bata stores distribute their own private brands. Department stores capture about 53 percent of heavy-appliance sales, most of which are private brands.[20]

Retailers with their own brands become customers of the manufacturer, who place the chains' private brands on the products that the firm produces. Such leading corporations as Westinghouse, Armstrong Rubber, and Heinz obtain an increasingly larger percentage of total sales through private labels.

Manufacturers often debate whether they should serve the private brand market. On the one hand, potential orders are large, so marketing efforts can be reduced. On the other hand, the manufacturer can become dependent on one or two retailers rather than remaining independent by serving a broad range of customers.

▸ THE CANADIAN MARKETPLACE

Branding Boats

Canadians own 2 million recreational boats, including 637 350 canoes, 148 500 sailboats, 349 650 rowboats, 823 200 outboards, and 120 000 other boats of all sorts. For 1998, the estimated expenditures on recreational boating in Canada, including storage, fuel, marina and club rental and membership fees, as well as boats and accessories, total Canadian $2 billion, or 5.2 percent of total estimated world expenditures of U.S. $36 billion. The same year, the United States accounts for 50 percent of the world market, with the equivalent of U.S. $19.2 billion in expenditures at the retail level.

Despite the relatively large size of the recreational boat market, the industry is characterized by many small manufacturers located in virtually all parts of the country. Why is there no dominant brand in this market? What would a boat manufacturer have to do in order to achieve widespread brand recognition?

Source: Industry Canada Web site (http://strategis.ic.gc.ca/SSG/rb01144e.html), downloaded May 20, 1999. Reproduced with the permission of the Minister of Public Works and Government Services Canada.

Generic Products

Food and household staples characterized by plain labels, little or no advertising, and no brand names are called **generic products**. Generic products were first sold in Europe, where their prices were as much as 30 percent below brand-name products. By 1979, they had captured 40 percent of total volume in European supermarkets.

This new version of private brands has received significant acceptance in Canada. Surveys indicate that both professional, college-educated consumers and lower-income, blue-collar consumers are heavy purchasers of generics. Most shoppers have experimented with generic products and formed opinions about those that are acceptable to them.

In the retail food industry there are thus three types of brands. Manufacturers promote their own national brands. Retailers promote, to a limited degree, private brands (for example, Canadian Tire and President's Choice), and generic brands are available at the low end for those who are prepared to accept a wider variation in quality and little information about the product. (Loblaws has muddied the waters somewhat with its No Name brand mentioned earlier. No Name is not a true generic product, but is rather Loblaws' price-fighting brand that it has named, a little perversely, No Name.)

generic products
Food and household staples characterized by plain labels, little or no advertising, and no brand names.

▶ PACKAGING

In a very real sense, the package is a vital part of the total product. Indeed, in an overcrowded supermarket, packaging very often *is* the significant difference between one product and another. In the spring of 2000, for example, Procter & Gamble revamped its Cover Girl line of cosmetics. Carefully redesigned packaging was an important complement to Cover Girl's modified product line and more convenient in-store displays.

Packaging represents a vital component of the total concept. Its importance can be inferred from the size of the packaging industry. Approximately $9.1 billion is spent annually on packaging in Canada.[21] Packaging costs in the food industry as a percentage of net processed food sales range from 4 to 59 percent, averaging about 22 percent. In cases where packaging costs seem to be disproportionately high, costs of ingredients (e.g., salt) have been found to be very low.

The package has several objectives, which can be grouped into three general categories: (1) protection against damage, spoilage, and pilferage; (2) assistance in marketing the product; and (3) cost-effectiveness.

Protection against Damage, Spoilage, and Pilferage

The original purpose of packaging was to offer physical protection. The typical product is handled several times between manufacture and consumer purchase, and its package must protect the contents against damage. Perishable products must also be protected against spoilage in transit, in storage, or while awaiting selection by the consumer.

Another important role of many packages is preventing pilferage, which at the retail level is very costly (even "sampling" from bulk food displays has become a major cost concern for retailers). Many products are packaged with oversized cardboard backings too large to fit into a shoplifter's pocket or purse. Large plastic boxes are used for a similar reason on such products as cassette tapes.

Assistance in Marketing the Product

Package designers frequently use marketing research in testing alternative designs. Increasingly, scientific approaches are used in designing a package that is attractive, safe, and aesthetically appealing. Kellogg, for instance, has been known to test the package for a new product as well as the product itself.[22]

In a grocery store that contains as many as 15 000 different items, a product must capture the shopper's attention. Walter Margulies, chairman of Lippincott & Margulies advertising agency, summarizes the importance of first impressions in the retail store: "Consumers are more intelligent [these days], but they don't read as much. They relate to pictures." Margulies also cites another factor: one of every six shoppers who needs eyeglasses does not wear them while shopping. Consequently, many marketers offering product lines are adopting similar package designs throughout the line in order to create more visual impact in the store. The adoption of common package designs by such product lines as Weight

Watchers foods and Planter's nuts represents attempts to dominate larger sections of retail stores the way Campbell does.[23]

Packages can also offer the consumer convenience. Pump-type dispensers facilitate the use of products ranging from mustard to insect repellent. Pop-top cans provide added convenience for soft drinks and for other food products. The six-pack carton, first introduced by Coca-Cola in the 1930s, can be carried with minimal effort by the food shopper.

A growing number of firms provide increasing consumer utility with packages that are designed for reuse. Peanut butter jars and jelly jars have long been used as drinking glasses. Bubble bath can be purchased in plastic bottles shaped like animals that are suitable for bathtub play. Packaging is a major component in Avon's overall marketing strategy. The firm's decorative reusable bottles have even become collectibles.

Cost-Effectiveness

Although packaging must perform a number of functions for the producer, marketer, and consumer, it must accomplish them at a reasonable cost. Packaging currently represents the single largest item in the cost of producing numerous products. For example, it accounts for 70 percent of the total cost of the single-serving packets of sugar found in restaurants. However, restaurants continue to use the packets because of the saving in wastage and in washing and refilling sugar containers.

Environmentally safer packaging has become a concern in recent years, as evidenced by this example:

> Procter & Gamble has introduced a new, less expensive, more environmentally compatible package for eight of its liquid products. The company estimates that 15 to 25 percent of consumers who use those products will choose to buy them in the new format. That would mean five million fewer plastic bottles — about 700 fewer dump trucks — going to Canadian dumps annually.[24]

An excellent illustration of how packaging can be cost-effective is provided by the large Swedish firm Tetra-Pak, which pioneered aseptic packaging for products like milk and juice. Aseptic packaging wraps a laminated paper around a sterilized product and seals it off. The big advantage of this packaging technology is that products so treated can be kept unrefrigerated for months. Aseptically packaged sterilized milk, for instance, will keep its nutritional qualities and flavour for six months. With 60 percent of a supermarket's energy bill going for refrigeration, aseptic packaging is certainly cost-effective. The paper packaging is also cheaper and lighter than the cans and bottles used for unrefrigerated fruit juices. Handling costs can also be reduced in many cases.[25] These containers have recently been criticized because of ecological concerns over recycling. Tetra-Pak has responded aggressively, showing that its containers can be recycled into such items as picnic furniture.

Labelling

Sometimes the label is a separate item applied to the package, but most of today's plastic packages contain the label as an integral part of the package.

{ pop culture }

The power of pop culture. Take a look around and there's no denying that pop – a.k.a. the pop can, a.k.a. the aluminum can – is a part of our everyday lives. It's environmentally friendly. Totally recyclable. Socially conscious. And here to stay.

Keeps its cool. Aluminum makes an ideal beverage container. It keeps the flavour and carbonation of your favourite soft drink or beer in. And oxygen, light and moisture out. That's not all. It's safe. Shatterproof, lightweight and strong.

 Good for business. In the last ten years, the aluminum industry has invested over $12 billion in the Canadian economy. And aluminum cans are worth between six and twenty times more than other recyclable packaging.

 Environmentally-friendly. When it comes to respecting the environment, the aluminum can has no rivals. You see, when recycled, aluminum is never part of the waste stream. It can be recycled again and again. And get this — aluminum cans can be collected, recycled and will reappear on store shelves as new cans within 60 days.

pop quiz

With all the economic, environmental and social benefits of aluminum cans, why are some governments trying to limit their use through discriminatory regulations?

Find out more.
Call: 1 (416) 598-0016

ALUMINUM IS THE ANSWER

Aluminum is used in containers for such products as soft drinks. Here, the Aluminum Marketing Council is promoting aluminum not just as packaging but as an environmentally friendly— totally recyclable — material that makes good social and business sense.

Labels perform both a promotional and an informational function. A **label** in most instances contains (1) the brand name or symbol, (2) the name and address of the manufacturer or distributor, (3) information about product composition and size, and (4) information about recommended uses of the product.

Government-set and voluntary packaging and label standards have been developed in most industries. The law requires a listing of food ingredients, in descending order of the amounts used, and the labels of such companies as the Del Monte Corporation now show specific food values and include a calorie count and a list of vitamins and minerals. In other industries (such as drugs, fur, and clothing), federal legislation requires various information to be provided and prevents false branding. The marketing manager in such industries must be fully acquainted with these laws and must design the package and label in compliance with these requirements.

The informational aspect of a label is particularly noteworthy. People who condemn all types of elaborate or fancy packaging fail to realize that the information on the label and the nature of the container enhance the product itself. In some cases, the dispenser is almost as important as the contents and is really an integral part of the total "product." Furthermore, with the advent of self-service nearly everywhere, the information on the label takes the place of a salesperson. Self-service improves marketing efficiency and lowers costs.

label
The part of a package that contains (1) the brand name or symbol, (2) the name and address of the manufacturer or distributor, (3) information about product composition and size, and (4) information about recommended uses of the product.

Universal Product Code (UPC)

The Universal Product Code (UPC) designation is another very important part of a label or package. Most grocery items display the bar code UPC on the label or package. The **Universal Product Code**, which was introduced to cut expenses in the supermarket industry, is a code readable by optical scanners that can print the name of the item and the price on the cash register receipt.

The advantages of optical scanning include

- labour savings (because products are no longer individually priced)
- faster customer check-out
- better inventory control, since the scanner can be tied to inventory records
- easier marketing research for the industries involved with it
- fewer errors in entering purchases at the check-out counter

Universal Product Code
A code readable by optical scanners that can print the name of the item and the price on the cash register receipt.

▶ PRODUCT SAFETY

If the product is to fulfill its mission of satisfying consumer needs, it must above all be safe. Manufacturers must design their products in such a way as to protect not only children but all consumers who use them. Packaging can play an important role in product safety. The law requires that bottle tops on dangerous products such as pharmaceuticals be child-proof (some are virtually parent-proof). This safety feature has reduced by two-thirds the number of children under 5 years of age who swallow dangerous doses of ASA. Prominent safety warnings on the labels of such potentially hazardous products as cleaning fluids and drain cleaners inform users about the dangers of these products and urge purchasers to store them out of the reach of children. Changes in product design have reduced the dangers involved in the use of such products as lawn mowers, hedge trimmers, and toys.

The need for fire-retardant fabrics for children's sleepwear was recognized long before federal regulations were established. While fire-retardant fabrics were available, the problems lay in how to produce them to meet consumer requirements for softness, colour, texture, durability, and reasonable cost. Today, government flame-retardancy standards are strictly enforced.

Hazardous Products Act
A major piece of legislation that consolidated previous legislation and set significant new standards for product safety; defines a hazardous product as any product that is included in a list (called a schedule) compiled by Consumer and Corporate Affairs Canada or Health and Welfare Canada.

Federal and provincial legislation has long played a major role in promoting product safety. The **Hazardous Products Act**, passed in 1969, was a major piece of legislation that consolidated previous legislation and set significant new standards for product safety. The Act defines a hazardous product as any product that is included in a list (called a schedule) compiled by Consumer and Corporate Affairs Canada or Health and Welfare Canada. Any consumer product considered to be a hazard to public health or safety may be listed in the schedule. Table 11.3 lists some of the main items and outlines the regulations that affect them.

▶ **TABLE 11.3 Some Hazardous Products Act Regulations**

- Bedding may not be highly flammable.
- Children's sleepwear, dressing gowns, and robes must meet flammability standards.
- Children's toys or equipment may not contain toxic substances (such as lead pigments) beyond a prescribed limit.
- Certain household chemical products must be labelled with appropriate symbols to alert consumers to their hazards.
- Hockey helmets must meet safety standards to protect young hockey players.
- Pencils and artists' brushes are regulated to limit lead in their decorative coating.
- Matches must meet safety standards for strength and packaging.
- Safety glass is mandatory in domestic doors and shower enclosures.
- Liquid drain cleaners and furniture polishes containing petroleum-based solvents must be sold in child-proof packaging.
- Toys and children's playthings must comply with safety standards.
- Crib regulations provide for increased child safety.

The Act itself comprises just fifteen clauses. Those relating to criminal penalties and seizure put sharp teeth in the law. Inspectors designated under the Act have powers of search and seizure. Hazardous products inspectors may enter, at any reasonable time, any place where they reasonably believe a hazardous product is manufactured, prepared, packaged, sold, or stored for sale. They may examine the product, take samples, and examine any records believed to contain information relevant to enforcing the Act. Products that an inspector has reasonable grounds to believe are in contravention of the Act may be seized.

These regulatory activities have prompted companies to voluntarily improve safety standards for their products. For many companies, safety has become a very important ingredient in the broader definition of product.

In conclusion, the management of products is a many-faceted affair. It can involve the way that the organization is structured, both in developing new products and in managing them. Product management also includes an analysis of the product mix, as well as the appropriate branding and packaging of each product. And, as always, such decisions must be made in the light of the marketing strategy, and in harmony with the rest of the elements of the marketing mix.

▶ SUMMARY

A product mix is the assortment of product lines and individual offerings available from a company. Product mixes are typically measured by width and depth of assortment.

A line extension is the development of individual offerings that appeal to different market segments but are closely related to the existing product line.

In product development, many initial ideas fall by the wayside. This is known as the product decay curve.

Contributors to the success of new products include overall superiority, advantages to the user, fit and compatibility of the product with the company, market need, competitive situation, and how well the opportunity and project have been defined.

There are four product development strategies: product improvement, market development, product development, and product diversification.

Organizational structures used to make product-planning decisions are new-product committees, new-product departments, product managers, and venture teams. Product managers are individuals assigned one product or product line who are responsible for determining its objectives and marketing strategies.

The stages of the new-product development process are (1) develop new-product strategy, (2) generate ideas and concepts, (3) screen and evaluate, (4) conduct business analysis, (5) develop the product, (6) test the product, and (7) commercialize it.

In parallel with product introduction decisions, there will normally be product deletion decisions.

A brand is a name, term, sign, symbol, or design (or some combination of these) used to identify and differentiate the products of a firm. Three brand-loyalty categories are brand recognition, brand preference, and brand insistence. Companies choose different types of branding strategy: family brands, individual brands, national brands, and private brands.

Packaging has the following main objectives: protection against damage, spoilage, and pilferage; assistance in marketing the product; and cost-effectiveness.

▶ KEY TERMS

brand	label
brand equity	line extension
brand extension	market development strategy
brand insistence	national brand (manufacturer's brand)
brand name	private brand
brand preference	product development strategy
brand recognition	product diversification strategy
cannibalizing	product improvement strategy
concept testing	product line
family brand	product managers (brand managers)
generic name	product mix
generic products	test marketing
Hazardous Products Act	trademark
individual brand	Universal Product Code
individual offering	venture-team concept

▶ INTERACTIVE SUMMARY AND DISCUSSION QUESTIONS

1. A product mix is the assortment of product lines and individual offerings available from a company. Product mixes are typically measured by width and depth of assortment.
   a. Describe the product mix by depth and width for a company that has ten or more products.
   b. Indicate where each product type is in the life cycle for that product category.

2. A line extension is the development of individual offerings that appeal to different market segments but are closely related to the existing product line. Explain this using the photocopier market as an example.

3. In product development, many initial ideas fall by the wayside. This is known as the product decay curve. Draw a typical decay curve of new-product ideas, indicating the related phases: screening, business analysis, development, testing, and commercialization.

4. Assume you work for the product manager of a company in the consumer electronics business. You have been asked to write your manager a memo on determinants of success for new products. Base your memo on the chapter material.

5. There are four product development strategies: product improvement, market development, product development, and product diversification. In what instances would each strategy be appropriate?

6. Organizational structures used to make product-planning decisions are new-product committees, new-product departments, product managers, and venture teams. Explain and discuss the advantages of each.

7. Product managers are individuals assigned one product or product line and given responsibility for determining its objectives and marketing strategies. Do you think they would do as good a job at suggesting and initiating new products as they do at managing existing products? Why or why not?

8. The stages of the new-product development process are outlined in Figure 11.3. With two or three classmates, develop a product strategy for a product category of your choice. Then brainstorm an extensive list of product ideas. Following this, look more closely at the list and pick out those that seem to have the most potential. Finally, suggest some ways of performing a business analysis for the most promising candidates.

9. In parallel with product introduction decisions, there will normally be product deletion decisions. Give some examples of products that have been (or should be) deleted.

10. A brand is a name, term, sign, symbol, or design (or some combination of these) used to identify and differentiate the products of a firm. What constitutes a good brand name?

11. Three brand-loyalty categories are brand recognition, brand preference, and brand insistence. Explain and discuss the importance of these categories to the marketer.

12. Companies choose different types of branding strategy: family brands, individual brands, national brands, and private brands. Explain and discuss each.

13. Packaging has the following main objectives: protection against damage, spoilage, and pilferage; assistance in marketing the product; and cost-effectiveness. Find examples of products that fulfill all of these objectives.

www.allproducts.com

14. Allproducts.com is a directory of over 60 000 products. Go to their home page and click on the New Products category. Choose two products that look interesting to you. Evaluate them using the criteria listed on page 305. Do you think the products will be successful? Explain.

To obtain a list of further readings for Chapter 11, please refer to the *Foundations of Marketing* Web site.

Chapter 12
Services

INSTALLED HOME IMPROVEMENTS...CALL 1-800-4-MY-HOME™ (1-800-469-4663)

"or where Sears is closed on Sundays, sale prices end Saturday, May 8, 1999, unless otherwise stated, while quantities last

SALE PRICES START MONDAY, APRIL 26 AND END SUNDAY, MAY 9, 1999**

SEARS

1-800-4-MY-HOME™
(1-800-469-4663)

Now for the first time ever!
All installed home improvements on sale!

Plus, use your Sears Card and get double Sears Club points on
selected installed home improvements and pay no interest 'til 2001

Pay in 20 equal monthly payments, interest free, until January 2001. For both offers: On approved credit. Details on page 8
*Excludes duct and carpet cleaning

COME SEE THE MANY SIDES OF SEARS™

▶ CHAPTER OBJECTIVES

After reading and studying this chapter, you should be able to

1. Elaborate on the discussion of products by exploring the "service product."

2. Discuss the similarities and differences between goods and services.

3. Explain the four main characteristics of services.

4. Outline the major issues that must be addressed by marketers for each of the characteristics.

5. Describe the main methods marketers use to address these issues.

Sears is retreating to the home, selling services to "do-it-for-me" and time-crunched homeowners while building on the strength of its in-house brands.

Paul Walters wants to scrub your toilet. He also wants to kill your earwigs, fix your plumbing, and wallpaper the baby's bedroom.

One day in the not too distant future, the president of Sears Canada Inc. wants to be the service overlord of your home, as well as your clothier and the captain of catalogue sales.

"Sears isn't just about wrenches any more," Mr. Walters explains, outlining plans for the evolution of the service side of Sears' business. "The future of the company isn't in bricks and mortar."

If he gets his way, Mr. Walters plans to enlist every Sears customer in a full, home service contract. Within the next few years, the company hopes to expand its panoply of services well beyond its current offerings, such as appliance repairs and carpet installation. It also wants to supply cleaning ladies, interior decorators, and a guy to cut the lawn and shovel the driveway, much of it through subcontractors.

The strategy is to stamp the stalwart Sears brand name on services that have traditionally been performed by mom and pop operations, while building on the strength of its in-house brands.

The big push into home services is the next stage of the $550-million makeover of the Toronto-based company that began in late 1996.

Among other ventures, Sears has launched a 24-hour, 1-800 number service in which people can book a drapery fitting or a bathroom installation. In doing so, the company is hoping to cash in on the newest boomer trend—the "do-it-for-me" home maintenance and repair market—worth an estimated $15-billion in Canada.

"If you look at the whole notion of home services, anything is in the realm of possibility," says Larry Moore, Sears vice-president of service sales. "We see the 'do-it-for-me' customer as the growth market going forward."

Sears is also benefiting from a broader trend—"fortressing"—or a retreat to the home. Boomers are also in their peak spending years when it comes to home merchandise, company research shows.

"The service economy is the money spinner of the future," said John Williams, a retail consultant at J.C. Williams Group in Toronto. "There may not be a lot of money in building the pool. But there will be lots of money in maintaining it." Time-crunched Canadians are willing to pay more for convenience and service, according to a recent survey conducted by Mr. Williams' company.

The strength of the Sears brand—with the added assurance that the company stands by the work of local tradespeople—bodes well for the future of its expansion into more services, adds John Winter, a Toronto retailing consultant.

"What they're really selling is trust. It's one-stop shopping at the end of a 1-800 number."

Source: Adapted from Susan Bourette, "Sears Aims to Clean Up in Home Services," *The Globe and Mail* (October 3, 1998), p. B3. Reprinted with permission from *The Globe and Mail*.

www.sears.ca

▶ INTRODUCTION

As Chapter 1 states, a service is a type of product. For the most part, discussions about the marketing of goods apply to services as well. But services have a number of important special characteristics that differentiate them from goods. One of the most important differences, as Mr. Winter observed in the opening vignette, is that service marketers are really selling *trust*. People have to trust the service enough to buy it *before* they try it.

Figure 12.1 clarifies the relationships among these concepts. General marketing notions, approaches, and theories apply to both goods and services. However, some techniques and ideas are relatively exclusive to services marketing; others, to goods marketing. And within either type of marketing, distinctions may also be made among various industries or various marketing situations.

The service sector today is so large that a good understanding of it is necessary. In Canada, services account for 54 percent of consumer expenditures (compared with 13.5 percent for durable goods, 9.1 percent for semidurable goods, and 23.5 percent for nondurable goods).[1] The World Trade Organization (WTO) estimates that in 1998 total international trade in services was $1.32 trillion (U.S.).[2]

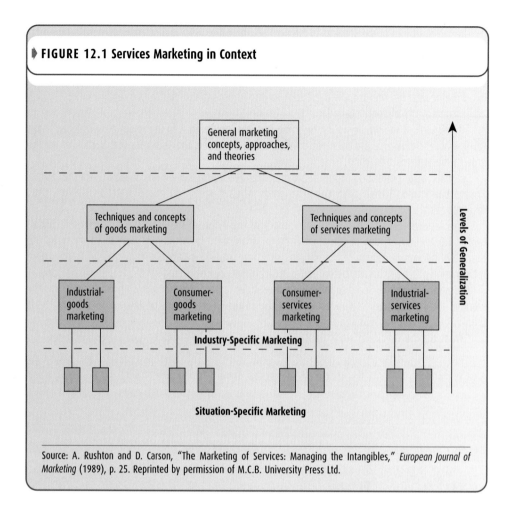

FIGURE 12.1 Services Marketing in Context

General marketing concepts, approaches, and theories

Techniques and concepts of goods marketing

Techniques and concepts of services marketing

Industrial-goods marketing

Consumer-goods marketing

Consumer-services marketing

Industrial-services marketing

Industry-Specific Marketing

Situation-Specific Marketing

Levels of Generalization

Source: A. Rushton and D. Carson, "The Marketing of Services: Managing the Intangibles," *European Journal of Marketing* (1989), p. 25. Reprinted by permission of M.C.B. University Press Ltd.

service
A product without physical characteristics—a bundle of performance and symbolic attributes designed to produce consumer want satisfaction.

tangible attributes
Those attributes that can be experienced by the physical senses, such as sight, touch, and smell.

intangible attributes
Those attributes that cannot be experienced by the physical senses.

SERVICES VERSUS GOODS

A **service** is a product without physical characteristics—a bundle of performance and symbolic attributes designed to produce consumer want satisfaction. Leonard Berry states that "the pivotal difference between goods businesses and services businesses is that goods businesses sell *things* and service businesses sell *performances*."[3] In other words, goods are produced, whereas services are performed.

Despite the relatively clear-cut definition of a service, many products have *both* **tangible and intangible attributes**. For example, a pail of fertilizer sold by a farm-supply dealer to a farmer seems like a pure good. However, if that dealer also provides expertise—for example, counselling about fertilizer application—a service is added. Consequently, it is more accurate to consider products as falling on a spectrum between "tangible elements dominant" and "intangible elements dominant" (see Figure 12.2).

▶ **FIGURE 12.2 The Tangibility Spectrum**

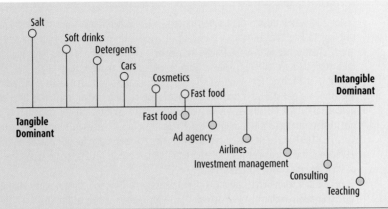

Source: G. Lynn Shostack, "Breaking Free from Product Marketing," *Journal of Marketing* 41 (April 1977), p. 77. Reprinted with permission.

▶ THE ETHICAL MARKETER

What Is an Appropriate Service to Market?

The O.J. Simpson trial and Monica Lewinsky's blue dress have made America more than familiar with the use of DNA evidence. But more than that, the technology is firmly entrenched on Main Street. Above one of Chicago's busiest motorways, a loud neon-pink billboard asks drivers, "Who's the father?" The answer is a telephone call away: 1-800-DNA-TYPE.

The company offering the answer to this potentially explosive question is Identigene, which was founded in Houston in 1993. For $475, it will take cheek swabs from a mother, her child, and the alleged father and, by analyzing them, decide if he really was the dad. The process, it claims, is more than 99.9 percent accurate. It is almost impossible for anyone who is not the child's father to have DNA that matches the specimen so closely.

Identigene also offers other services. Have you, too, found a blue dress in the cupboard with a suspicious stain? For $250, you can learn if that stain is semen; for $900, you can find out whose it is. Don't have quite enough cash on hand for the test? Put down a $100 deposit; Identigene will do the lab work and put the results on the shelf. When you make your final payment, you'll get your answer.

Paternity testing is a growth business, and Identigene is not alone. The American Association of Blood Banks (AABB) has given accreditation to roughly 50 DNA labs around the country. Many others go about their business without bothering to get accredited. The AABB reckons that the number of paternity tests conducted nationwide has grown from 76000 in 1988 to 241000 in 1997. The rise is partly the result of a 1988 change in federal law that requires the states to do a better job of establishing paternity in cases where a mother claims welfare to support a child.

But Identigene is unique in its brazen marketing. The company advertises itself, mainly by those billboards, in about 30 cities, and is adding a new city every month. It boasts that its DNA-testing process is

(continued)

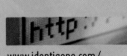

www.identigene.com/
start.html

faster and less intrusive than other procedures, which often require blood samples. As a result, says Caroline Caskey, the company's president, it appeals to many well-to-do couples who want "peace of mind." That peace may prove fragile: researchers doing lineage studies have found that 5–10 percent of their subjects have different fathers from the ones they thought they had.

Is it a good thing for a cutting-edge genetic technology to move so quickly from laboratory to billboard? Some genetic tests may go commercial before the testing system is fully accurate, or before the people taking the tests have any way of coping with the results. There are issues of privacy, and also worries that commercialization might tempt scientists to tilt, or even conceal, their research. A study published in 1997 in the *Journal of the American Medical Association* found that 20 percent of researchers surveyed in the life sciences had delayed publication of their results, or not published them at all, because of their relations with business firms.

For all that, commercialization of genetic research is a good thing, argues Mark Siegler, a professor of medicine and director of the MacLean Centre for Medical Ethics at the University of Chicago. Money and commerce, he argues, are the engines that power scientific development; and perhaps particularly in genetics, where capital has been nimbly jumping from one project to another. Besides, one man's scientific project prematurely rushed to market may be another's life-saver.

Meanwhile, Identigene presses on. Its latest service to parents is to test the DNA of a mother and her newborn baby as soon as they come out of hospital. The proud parents can then be sure they are taking the right baby home. And the company will keep the child's DNA "fingerprints" on file, just in case they should ever be needed.

Is it ethically appropriate to offer DNA testing to the general public? Are there specific applications of this technology that you think would be inappropriate in the marketplace? Do you think a service like this would have the same success in Canada that it seems to be having in the United States?

Source: "A Delicate Question," *The Economist* (April 24, 1999), p. 26. Reprinted with permission.

search qualities
Physical qualities that enable products to be examined and compared. This eases the task of choosing among them.

experience qualities
Characteristics of products that can be assessed mainly through using them.

credence qualities
Qualities for which, even after purchasing, the buyer must simply trust that the supplier has performed the correct service.

Buying Promises

As mentioned earlier, potential customers often have difficulties conceptualizing the service product, because it has no physical properties. Basically, they are buying promises. No product trial or return is possible. Three types of product properties are attached to every good or service: **search qualities**, **experience qualities**, and **credence qualities**.[4] Products that can be physically examined and compared are high in search qualities. Household furniture is high in search qualities. Others are primarily assessed on the basis of the experience of using them. They include a large proportion of both tangible and intangible attributes. A meal at a fine restaurant or a musical performance are both high in experience qualities. Products with credence qualities are those for which, even after purchasing, the buyer must simply trust that the supplier has performed the correct service. Car repairs, medical procedures, and most professional services are high in credence qualities. Figure 12.3 shows this range of product properties. In intangibles, credence (buying a promise) and experience qualities dominate, while search qualities are central for tangible products.

INSURE YOUR WORLDS WITH CHUBB

Your business world and your personal world can both be covered with Chubb Insurance. We can even cover some worlds you haven't yet thought of. Here or almost anywhere else. For more information, contact your insurance broker or Chubb Insurance Company of Canada at (800) 268-4120.

CHUBB INSURANCE COMPANY OF CANADA
www.chubbinsurance.com

INSURE YOUR WORLD WITH CHUBB

Services are often intangible, and marketers have to find ways that will make them tangible to buyers. Chubb Insurance Company, for example, adds tangibility to its service by associating it with people's business and personal world.

▶ FIGURE 12.3 Intangibility and Customer Evaluation

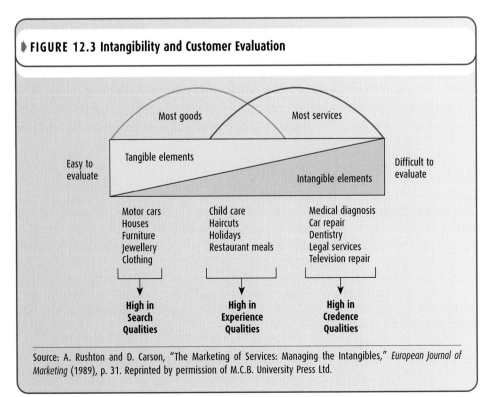

Source: A. Rushton and D. Carson, "The Marketing of Services: Managing the Intangibles," *European Journal of Marketing* (1989), p. 31. Reprinted by permission of M.C.B. University Press Ltd.

▶ CHARACTERISTICS OF SERVICES

Four unique characteristics of services distinguish them from goods: intangibility, inseparability of production and consumption, heterogenetiy, and perishability.

Intangibility

Unlike goods, which can be displayed before the sale, services cannot be seen, smelled, or touched. The student who goes to a counsellor for assistance in deciding what kind of a career to choose cannot foretell the result of that counselling service. J. Bateson believes that besides being physically intangible, services can also be mentally intangible, because it is sometimes hard for the human mind to grasp them.[5]

The intangibility of services creates a number of marketing problems:

- *Services cannot be stored.* An Air Canada plane provides a transportation service for 90 people to fly from Montreal to Vancouver. Revenue from empty seats is lost forever.
- *Services cannot be protected through patents.* Patents apply to physical objects. Thus, because they are intangible, services are ineligible for patents. This can create a real problem for a services marketer, since the service can easily be copied.
- *It is hard to readily display or communicate services.* It is easy to show a good, allowing potential customers to hold, handle, or try it out before purchase. That way, they can get a good idea of whether or not the good will satisfy their needs. In the case of a service, a purchaser must purchase in order to experience it.
- *Prices are difficult to set.* At the best of times, pricing is complex. In the case of a good, each of its components can be costed out, which helps in determining what it is worth. Costing out, say, an accountant's services proves to be much more complex.

www.aircanada.ca

A second complicating factor is that a very high proportion of the cost of some services is fixed. The cost of performing one additional service can be virtually zero. The seat on the Air Canada flight mentioned earlier is a good example. If there is an empty seat on the flight just before takeoff, it costs the airline practically nothing to accept an additional passenger. That's one reason standby tickets—when the passenger flies only if there is an available seat—can be so much cheaper than the regular fare.

The difficulty facing the marketer is to find a price that is low enough to encourage near-maximum usage but high enough to cover all costs over time. Airlines use differential pricing—charging different types of customers different amounts—to try to accomplish this end.

MARKETING STRATEGIES TO SOLVE THE PROBLEMS OF INTANGIBILITY

Some of the problems facing service providers cannot be avoided. But certain marketing strategies can help resolve others, particularly the problem of mar-

"I can tell you this much...it won't be cheap!"

Prices for services are difficult to set.

keting communication. Because services are so intangible, many marketers *stress tangible cues* in advertising and selling. For example, advertisements for long-distance phone calling dramatize the pleasure on the face of a loved one receiving a call. Marketing messages should also *use personal sources more than nonpersonal sources.* Thus a recommendation for life insurance would likely be more persuasive if it came from John Hanchuck, rather than the more impersonal Life Insurance Council. The personal source adds tangibility to the service.

Service marketers also have found that it is helpful to *stimulate word-of-mouth communications.* If a purchaser can be induced — through the superior service received or by other incentives — to speak to friends and acquaintances positively about a service, that service will tend to be purchased by those people. *Engaging in postpurchase communications* is a related useful strategy. For example, a provider of financial counselling services might write a letter to a new client assuring the client of the wise choices she or he made.

Services marketers also try to *create a strong image* of their organization. This is a very important approach affecting the choice of a service. Since potential purchasers cannot physically evaluate the product that is offered, they may be reassured that they are purchasing a service from a well-known organization.

Finally, with respect to the difficulty of setting prices, it has been found useful to *develop a strong cost accounting system.* Such a system enables an accurate and realistic analysis of various costs involved in the operation. This information provides a strong foundation for setting the ultimate price of the service.

SAS AIR CANADA ✦

STAR ALLIANCE ✰

Speak Danish in 8 hours.

Toronto–Copenhagen Nonstøp. Starts May 1.

Services are difficult to market. This Air Canada/ SAS advertisement uses an active, tangible cue— "Speak Danish in 8 hours" —to market its service.

Inseparability of Production and Consumption

Goods are first produced, then sold, and then consumed, but services are first sold, then produced and consumed simultaneously.[6] The customer therefore has an active role during production of the service. For instance, professional legal counselling is consumed at the same time as the service of providing legal advice is performed. The client raises questions, seeks opinions, and responds with the details required by the lawyer.

inseparability
A characteristic of services in which the product is produced and consumed simultaneously.

The **inseparability** of production and consumption also results in marketing problems: (1) consumers are involved in production, so performance depends on the quality of input from the customer, as well as on the relationship between the customer and the provider; (2) other consumers are involved in production; and (3) centralized mass production of services is difficult.

- *Other consumers are involved in production.* Many services are offered in a setting with other people present. For example, the service provided by a restaurant server is performed not just for one customer, but for many simultaneously. This fact can have a number of positive and negative influences on the service actually experienced by an individual buyer. For instance, the presence of others can distract a server, or create so much pressure that service is negatively affected.
- *Centralized mass production of services is difficult.* Services are normally provided where the people are. Whereas Honda might have one or two factories to serve the entire country, Royal Bank must have many "little factories" (branches) in each city. Cost efficiencies and standardization are therefore difficult to achieve because there are so many producers (people) involved.

MARKETING STRATEGIES TO SOLVE THE PROBLEMS OF INSEPARABILITY

With services, since production and consumption occur simultaneously and in the same place, production personnel have a tremendous impact on consumers' perceptions of product acceptability. It is therefore essential to *emphasize the selection and training of public-contact personnel.* Personnel not only have to perform the service well, but must be able to interact positively with the customer. The famous Avis "We Try Harder" program was based on this principle.

Multisite locations may help offset the fact that services cannot be "sent" from a warehouse to a retail outlet. Banking, travel counselling, and other such services must be produced and consumed where consumers shop. Developing, managing, and maintaining so many locations is a major task for the marketer. This is one of the reasons why employment in the service sector is so high.

Managing customer flows also helps to make the "inseparability" condition positive for both buyer and seller. Customer flows can be facilitated by guiding, directing, and expediting their movements and interactions in the service situation. For example, banks channel the flow of customers to tellers through spe-

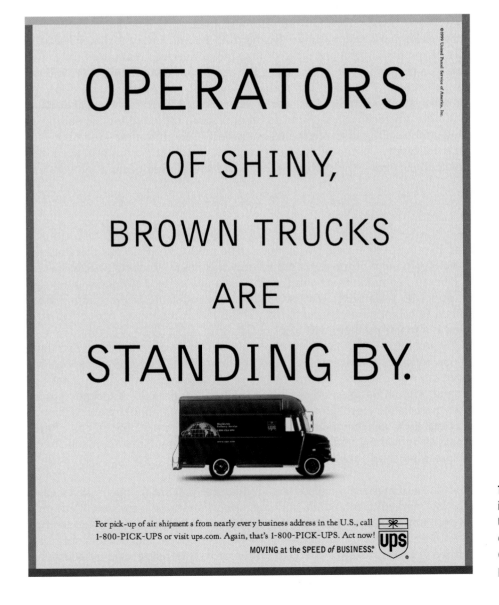

To solve the problems of inseparability of services, UPS emphasizes its pick-up operators, who are the company's public-contact personnel.

cially laid-out queues. Restaurants provide chairs for customers, or seat them in lounges, while they wait for a table to become available.

Increasingly, the Internet is being used to bring service providers and customers together. For example, the Bank of Montreal has created Mbanx, a bank that exists only on-line.

www.mbanx.com

Heterogeneity

Services are highly variable. Because they are performed by a provider who is a fallible human being, they are difficult to standardize. Service providers can vary in skill and training, and individual performance can vary from day to day. Furthermore, performance varies from individual to individual. A customer may pay the same price for a haircut at the same shop on subsequent dates from two different people, with far different outcomes.

The main marketing problem arising from heterogeneity is that standardization and quality control are difficult to achieve. Services marketers try to overcome this problem by industrializing the service or customizing it. To industrialize a service, Theodore Levitt has suggested substituting organized, preplanned systems for individual service operations. For example, a travel agency could offer prepackaged vacation tours to remove the need for the selling, tailoring, and haggling involved in customization.[7] Customization — the opposite of industrialization — is another possible solution. If each service is produced for an individual customer, the problem of standardization disappears.

Perishability

A service cannot be stored. No service can be produced before required and then stocked up to meet future demand. Whatever is not used when available is wasted. Unoccupied motel rooms and airline seats and unused telephone line capacity cannot be reclaimed. Because of this, service businesses frequently find it difficult to balance supply and demand. The fact that services cannot be inventoried is a major problem with services.

The problem of perishability can be solved to some degree by using strategies to cope with fluctuating demand. Restaurants, airlines, and other service businesses often give special discounts to those who use the service in periods of low demand. This shifts some demand from high to low periods. A second approach to the perishability problem is to make simultaneous adjustments in demand and capacity to achieve a closer match between the two. Capacity can often be increased by adding staff or equipment at peak times. This approach may be used simultaneously with the previous solution.

Table 12.1 summarizes the discussion of features that are unique to services, the resulting marketing problems, and suggested marketing solutions. Ziethaml et al. (from whose important study Table 12.1 is adapted) found that service firms did not view most of the problems as especially serious. The authors speculated that this viewpoint may be founded on the providers' being used to facing these problems, or the problems may not in fact be as significant as they first seem.

> **TABLE 12.1 Unique Service Features and Resulting Marketing Problems and Solutions**

UNIQUE SERVICE FEATURES	RESULTING MARKETING PROBLEMS	MARKETING STRATEGIES TO SOLVE PROBLEMS
Intangibility	• Service cannot be stored. • Cannot protect services through patents. • Cannot readily display or communicate services. • Prices are difficult to set.	• Stress tangible cues. • Use personal sources more than nonpersonal sources. • Simulate or stimulate word-of-mouth communications. • Create strong organizational image. • Use cost accounting to help set prices. • Engage in postpurchase communications.
Inseparability	• Consumer involved in production. • Other consumers involved in production. • Centralized mass production of services difficult.	• Emphasize selection and training of public-contact personnel. • Manage consumers. • Use multisite locations.
Heterogeneity	• Standardization and quality control difficult to achieve.	• Industrialize service. • Customize service.
Perishability	• Services cannot be inventoried.	• Use strategies to cope with fluctuating demand. • Make simultaneous adjustments in demand and capacity to achieve a closer match between the two.

Source: Adapted from Valarie A. Zeithaml, A. Parasuraman, and Leonard L. Berry, "Problems and Strategies in Services Marketing," *Journal of Marketing* (Spring 1985), p. 35. Reprinted by permission of the American Marketing Association.

▶ OTHER STRATEGIES IN SERVICES MARKETING

Internal Marketing

Traditionally, the marketing mix is thought to be oriented toward the external market. While services do face a competitive external environment, they must also contend with an internal market — those who provide the service. Since service producers interact so directly with consumers, the way they feel about their task within the marketing strategy is extremely important. In fact, their feelings directly influence the quality of the service they perform. Leonard Berry has suggested that "internal marketing means applying the philosophy and practices of marketing to the people that serve the external customers so that (1) the best possible people can be employed and retained, and (2) they will do the best possible work."[8]

The objective of the **internal marketing** function is to develop motivated, customer-conscious, market-oriented, and sales-minded employees. The successful service company must first sell the job to its employees before it can sell its services to customers.[9]

The interaction between the employee, or service provider, and the customer is critical to the success of the service and the satisfaction of the customer. **Interactive marketing** describes this interrelationship between the employee and the customer.

In total, then, there are actually three aspects of marketing that must take place in order for a service firm to be successful: external marketing, which takes place between the firm and the customer; internal marketing, which takes place between the firm and its employees; and interactive marketing, which takes place between the employees and the customer. External marketing is really making a commitment to customers that certain things will happen in their service encounter. Internal marketing allows that commitment to be carried out. Finally, interactive marketing actually delivers the promise. Figure 12.4, the services marketing triangle, shows that these three tasks are mutually supporting.

internal marketing
A marketing effort aimed at those who provide the service so that they will feel better about their task and therefore produce a better product.

interactive marketing
Term used to describe the interrelationship between the employee and the customer.

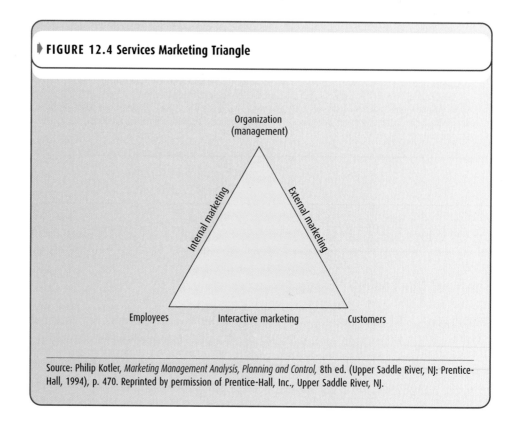

▶ **FIGURE 12.4 Services Marketing Triangle**

Source: Philip Kotler, *Marketing Management Analysis, Planning and Control,* 8th ed. (Upper Saddle River, NJ: Prentice-Hall, 1994), p. 470. Reprinted by permission of Prentice-Hall, Inc., Upper Saddle River, NJ.

Managing Evidence

As discussed earlier, prospective customers like to associate tangibles with a service for cues as to its quality. Marketers, therefore, must try to manage tangibles to convince customers about the service.

Goods marketing tends to give prime emphasis to creating abstract associations with the product. Services marketers, on the other hand, should focus on enhancing and differentiating the "realities" by manipulating tangible cues. Managing evidence comes first for service marketers.[10] There are several ways that the evidence can be managed.

THE ENVIRONMENT

Services are totally integrated with their environment. The physical setting—where the service is performed—has a great influence on the customer's perception. The physical milieu should be intentionally created so as to provide the appropriate situation-specific atmosphere to impress the customer. For example, even though two lawyers may provide identical services, customers still differentiate between the two by the environmental differences. If one lawyer decorates her office with leather and subdued carpeting and the other has a plain painted office with steel-and-formica furniture, customers will judge them accordingly.

▶ THE PRACTISING MARKETER

Restaurants Guilty of Bad Design

Restaurants can be very different in their food, finance, and finesse, but design problems "are overwhelmingly similar," say Susan Davidson and David Schultz, owners of DAS Architects Inc. in Philadelphia.

The two identify ten common eatery pitfalls: inconsistent ambiance, too many designers, a poorly defined target market, improper spacing of tables, greedy use of space, inefficient traffic patterns, unrealistic budgets, offensive colours, a lack of provision for growth, and the number one offender, bad lighting.

As for colour, orange enhances appetites; red, brown, pink, and other "warm" colours make diners look their best.

Source: "Restaurants Guilty of Bad Design," *The Wall Street Journal* in *The Globe and Mail* (September 17, 1998), p. B13. Reprinted with permission of *The Wall Street Journal*.

APPEARANCE OF SERVICE PROVIDERS

The appearance of service providers also affects customers' perception of the product. Salespeople in an optical shop who wear white lab coats look more "professional" than those with ordinary attire.

SERVICE PRICING

Research confirms that there is a high tendency for customers to perceive a direct relationship between price and quality of service.[11] Price is seen as an index of quality. Professional practitioners may charge an unusually high price for their services in order to assure clients. Setting the right price can be critical in differentiating one service from the crowd.

Quality in Services Marketing

Quality in services marketing is generally defined as the degree that customers' experiences match or exceed their expectations. If there is a match the service is of high quality. If there is a gap between customers' expectations and their experiences, the service is of low quality.[12] One of the primary reasons for the success of McDonald's over the years has been its ability to clearly set, and then meet, customer expectations. If you go to a McDonald's you expect a clean facility, quick service, consistent food served at the appropriate temperature, and a relatively low price. The majority of the time, that's exactly what you get.

An experience-based definition implies that quality is somewhat specific to an institution, or at least a type of institution. For example, from a marketing point of view, the McDonald's that meets your expectations is of higher quality than the upscale restaurant that fails to meet your expectations.

Figure 12.5 illustrates that the initial expectations of the customer are a result of word-of-mouth communications, personal needs, and past experience. The gap between customer expectations and perceived service (Gap 5) actually results from four other gaps. Gap 1 is the difference between what customers want from a service and what management *thinks* they want. Reducing Gap 1 involves increasing formal and informal market research.

Gap 2 is the difference between management's understanding of customer expectations and how the service is actually designed. Management may be aware of customer expectations or desires but be unable or unwilling to meet those desires. Many passengers who fly economy class would like, and first-time flyers may innocently expect, more spacious seating. To meet that expectation, though, would reduce the capacity of the airplane and consequently be prohibitively expensive.

Gap 3 is the difference between how management designed the service and how it is actually delivered. Service delivery personnel may not agree with management specifications, may not understand them, or may be unable to fully implement them. The Practising Marketer box on page 348 describes a problem Safeway has had in implementing guidelines for friendlier service.

Gap 4 is the difference between the service and what management has communicated about the service through advertising and other promotions. Overpromising is a particular problem for service industries. A video store that promises to have current titles always in stock and then doesn't creates greater dissatisfaction than if the promise had not been made at all.

The final gap, Gap 5, is the net effect of the other four gaps. If they are small, customers' perceptions should be close to their expectations. If the other gaps are large, customers' perceptions will not match their expectations and they will judge the service provider to have low quality. Figure 12.6 summarizes the five gaps.

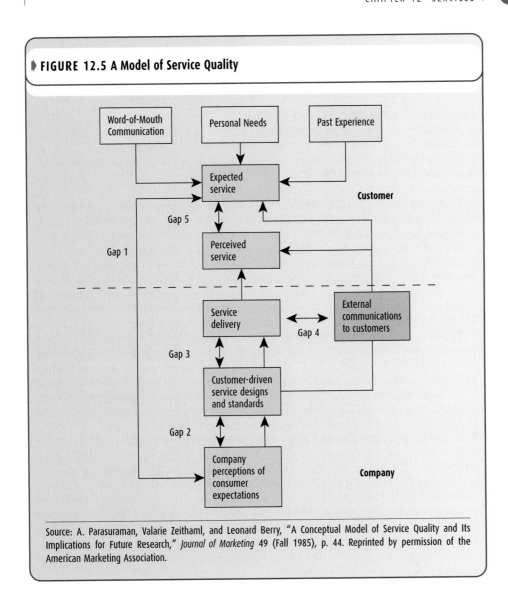

▶ FIGURE 12.5 A Model of Service Quality

Source: A. Parasuraman, Valarie Zeithaml, and Leonard Berry, "A Conceptual Model of Service Quality and Its Implications for Future Research," *Journal of Marketing* 49 (Fall 1985), p. 44. Reprinted by permission of the American Marketing Association.

Organizational Responsibility for Marketing

In many service firms, the organizational responsibility for marketing may be considerably different than in manufacturing companies. In any company there may be confusion about what marketing is. It is frequently considered to be what the marketing department does. Marketing is, however, often carried out by others in the company to some degree. This confusion may be much more acute for service firms than for manufacturing firms, and may in fact constitute an organizational dilemma. In many professional service organizations, the marketing department's role may be limited to handling advertising, sales pro-

▸ THE PRACTISING MARKETER

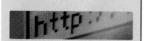

www.safeway.com

Customer Service Programs Can Cause Problems

A Canada Safeway employee in British Columbia had experienced a sudden death in her family. As she tried to pick up the pieces of her life, she came back to work three days a week.

But one day, she was "mystery shopped," union official Tom Fawkes says. That's the customer service practice in which company-hired "plants" pose as shoppers to sniff out the staff's attitudes and responsiveness to customers.

The grieving employee failed the mystery shopper test, says Mr. Fawkes, director of communications of the United Food and Commercial Workers in Vancouver. The union represents 8000 B.C. Safeway employees. The woman was dispatched to what he calls "charm school"—a training program to learn "how to smile and be nice to people." That training is a part of the "superior service" program initiated by Canada Safeway's parent, Safeway Stores Inc. of Pleasanton, Calif. The program demands that employees smile at customers, engage in eye contact with them, and generally respond cheerfully to their wants. Safeway's program is one of a plethora of customer service programs spawned in this era of intense retail competition, including the cheery greeters who welcome customers into stores owned by Gap Inc., Wal-Mart Stores Inc., and Viacom Inc.'s Blockbuster Entertainment Group.

But critics say such practices can infringe on the privacy and personal rights of employees, and expose them to personal danger. Safeway's program has become the target of union protests in Canada and the United States. The UFCW has gone to the B.C. Labour Relations Board protesting against the superior service policy, and is awaiting a hearing date. The supermarket chain defends the policy as simple common sense.

"We're not evaluating employees on the type of smile they're delivering. Our customer service is really common sense—be friendly, courteous, and helpful to the customer," says Toby Oswald, vice-president of public affairs at Canada Safeway. "And the vast majority of employees deliver."

Ms. Oswald says mystery shopping is a time-worn retailing technique for evaluating stores from a customer's point of view. She also says no employee has ever been disciplined or fired as a result of this program. She said things must be put in proper perspective: "In Canada, there has been one grievance [outside of B.C.] out of 30 000 [Canadian employees]." But Safeway, North America's second-largest supermarket chain, has also been under attack on its home front in the United States. One of the company's most contentious rules is requiring employees to smile and make eye contact with shoppers. Some workers complain that some shoppers misinterpret this forced friendliness as flirting, and take it as a signal to hit on or even harass workers.

Apart from that serious side effect, Mr. Fawkes thinks it's just plain stressful—and artificial. "Could you smile at people for four to eight hours every day?"

Safeway also requires staff to:

- Accompany shoppers right to items they can't locate, even if it cuts into employees' job time in, for example, stocking shelves. Verbal instructions that "the canned peas are in aisle seven" aren't enough anymore.
- Thank customers by name if they pay by credit card or cheque.
- Help them out to the car with their groceries.

Mr. Fawkes in Vancouver complains the program is punitive rather than positive because it threatens disciplinary action "up to and including termination," according to an internal Safeway memo from a Vancouver store.

But Mr. Fawkes says he doesn't have a problem with Safeway's program in principle. It's more how it's implemented. "We don't dispute it's working. But the application worries us: You can't threaten staff to be nice to people."

What is Safeway trying to accomplish with its customer service program? Why is Mr. Fawkes objecting? What could Safeway do differently?

Source: Excerpted from Ann Gibbon, "Safeway Staffers Frown on Smile Rule," *The Globe and Mail* (September 17, 1998), p. B3. Reprinted with permission from *The Globe and Mail*.

> **FIGURE 12.6 Summary of the Five Gaps**

Gap	Cause
1	Not knowing what the customer expects
2	Not developing the right service design
3	Not delivering to service standards
4	Not matching performance to promises
5	Not matching experience with expectations

motion, and some public relations. The "sales force" comprises those people who are in direct contact with customers (for example, the branch managers and tellers in a bank). Except for the people in the marketing department, however, staff members are not hired for their marketing know-how but for their ability to produce services. *Yet the person who produces a service must also be able to market that service.* In most cases, what is needed is not professional salespeople but service workers who sell—in effect, producer-sellers.

The dilemma arises when service firms are insufficiently aware of the need to have personnel who can adequately perform both marketing and service-production functions. Furthermore, when the workload is high, too little time may be spent on marketing—an imbalance that will likely have very serious long-term consequences for the organization.

This overview of services concludes our discussion of products. The reader should remember that the term "product" includes services as well as goods. Life-cycle analysis, as well as product classification systems and other product management processes, can be applied to all products. The next two chapters consider issues concerning price, another element of the marketing mix.

▶ SUMMARY

A service is a product without physical characteristics—a bundle of performance and symbolic attributes designed to produce consumer want satisfaction. Buyers of services are often buying promises.

Most products have both tangible and intangible attributes. Tangible goods tend to be high in search qualities, mixed goods high in experience qualities, and intangible goods in credence qualities. Marketers of services must try to manage tangibles to convince customers, as these attributes serve as cues to customers about service quality.

Four characteristics of services distinguish them from goods: intangibility, inseparability of production and consumption, heterogeneity, and perishability.

In addition to marketing to target market customers, services often have to be marketed internally to employees. The employees in turn engage in interactive marketing with customers. External marketing, internal marketing, and interactive marketing make up the services marketing triangle.

▶ KEY TERMS

credence qualities
experience qualities
inseparability
intangible attributes
interactive marketing

internal marketing
search qualities
service
tangible attributes

▶ INTERACTIVE SUMMARY AND DISCUSSION QUESTIONS

1. A service is a product without physical characteristics—a bundle of performance and symbolic attributes designed to produce consumer want satisfaction. Use banking services to explain this definition.

2. Many products have both tangible and intangible attributes. Select three products not discussed in this chapter, and identify for each both types of attributes.

3. Buyers of services are often buying promises. Explain this statement.

4. Four characteristics of services distinguish them from goods: intangibility, inseparability of production and consumption, heterogeneity, and perishability. Explain each of these characteristics.

5. Suggest some marketing strategies to take account of each of the characteristics listed in question 4.

6. In addition to marketing to target market customers, services often have to be marketed internally. Why?

7. Marketers of services must try to manage tangibles to convince customers about the services. Give some examples.

8. Organizational responsibility for marketing services goes beyond those people who are charged with marketing planning. The person who produces a service must also be able to market that service. Why? How can this requirement be implemented?

9. Describe the last transportation service you purchased. What was your impression of the way it was marketed? How could the firm's marketing effort have been improved?

10. Identify three or four service firms, and propose methods they could use to overcome problems with the perishability of their respective services.

11. Visit Merrill Lynch and Apple Canada on the Web. What differences do you see between the two sites? How do these differences relate to some of the unique qualities of their services?

To obtain a list of further readings for Chapter 12, please refer to the *Foundations of Marketing* Web site.

www.ml.com

www.apple.ca

Part 5
Pricing

Pricing is a variable of the marketing mix that assumes widely different roles. It requires a considerable amount of science, as well as art, to manage. Part 5 consists of two chapters on this critical element in the marketing mix. Chapter 13 examines the role of pricing in the marketing mix, as well as price determination in both theory and practice. Chapter 14 examines various pricing decisions that have to be made, as well as the overall management of this function.

As a result of fierce competition in recent years, some companies in the auto industry are lowering or freezing vehicle prices and offering additional financial incentives.

Chapter 13
Price Determination

▶ CHAPTER OBJECTIVES

After reading and studying this chapter, you should be able to

1. Discuss the concept of pricing objectives and their use.
2. Explain basic economic pricing principles and the concept of price elasticity.
3. Identify the practical problems involved in applying economics price theory concepts to actual pricing decisions.
4. Outline the major approaches to price setting.
5. Apply break-even analysis and discuss its use in pricing decisions.
6. Understand the benefits of the marketing approach to pricing.
7. Present a useful model for setting a price.

www.acura.com

www.ford.ca

www.honda.ca

www.toyota.ca

www.gmcanada.com

www.mazda.ca

The sticker price on the 1998 Acura 3.2TL was $42 000. The 1999 version went for $35 000. The 1999 model year kicked off officially at your friendly neighbourhood car dealer with a notable absentee: the annual price increase. For the first time in the 1990s, automakers trimmed prices across the board, freezing them or raising them by tiny percentages at most.

The Acura 3.2TL is perhaps the most extreme example of price cuts—and Acura dealers in Canada were subsidizing the 1998 model with rebates, sweet lease deals, and financing incentives, so the cut wasn't as generous as it appeared on the surface. But it's part of a trend among automakers that started with individual models and now extends to entire fleets.

"There's not much room in Canada for increasing vehicle prices," said Dennis DesRosiers, an industry analyst who heads DesRosiers Automotive Consultants Inc. in Richmond Hill, Ont.

That's clear from 1999 prices announced by several companies:

- Ford Motor Co. of Canada Ltd., car prices down 1 percent, truck prices up 1 percent;
- Honda Canada Inc., prices essentially frozen;
- Toyota Canada Inc., car prices up 0.7 per cent, truck prices up 0.2 percent;
- General Motors of Canada Ltd., prices down 0.8 percent;
- Mazda Canada Inc., prices frozen on most models, but the Millenia luxury sedan was about 6 percent cheaper.

These are manufacturers' suggested retail prices that don't take into account incentives automakers offer consumers to get them to drive those new cars, trucks, and minivans off dealers' lots.

Ford, for example, was offering 4.9-percent financing rates on Escort, Contour, and Mystique compacts, Taurus and Sable mid-sized sedans, and Ranger subcompact pickups and some F-series full-sized pickups.

The key reason for the new pricing era is fierce competition, economists say. The competition is heightened by the decline in value of the Japanese yen against the Canadian dollar in recent years, which gives Honda, Toyota, and other Japan-based companies room to cut prices and offer consumer incentives.

The rush by automakers around the world to add capacity also increases competition as they search for markets to sell their vehicles.

"With all these new plants going up worldwide, there is the risk that some of these vehicles may make their way into North America," said Carlos Gomes, an economist who follows the industry for Bank of Nova Scotia.

"The excess capacity will lead to lower prices," said Kendrick Jordan, senior economist at Bank of Montreal. "Even light trucks, which have experienced strong demand, have begun to witness downward price pressure as a result of the proliferation of products in this category," Mr. Jordan said in a recent industry outlook.

Mr. DesRosiers pointed out that the lower yen is a key factor that helps the Japan-based companies and forces the Canadian units of the Big Three U.S. companies to lower or freeze prices to remain competitive.

"It is likely these lower prices are keeping this market as healthy as it is. It's an undeniable economic fact that when you lower prices, people buy more."

Mr. Gomes of Scotiabank said in a recent report that flat new car prices and the first increase in inflation-adjusted household income in nearly a decade generated the first improvement in new car affordability since 1991.

Pricing decisions are an extremely important part of the marketing mix. Price has the most immediate and direct impact on overall profitability. It is also the only component of the marketing mix that can be changed quickly. As North American car manufacturers realize, many things can affect the appropriateness of a particular price. Along with knowing what the cus-

tomer is willing to pay, competitive activity, industry capacity, international currency strength, and general economic health, to name but a few factors, can all affect the pricing decision.

A price that is well set strengthens a firm's position in the marketplace. Pricing mistakes, on the other hand, can be disastrous.

Source: Adapted from Greg Keenan, "Surprise! The '99 Fleet Is in and Cars Are Cheaper" *The Globe and Mail* (October 3, 1998), pp. Bl and B4. Reprinted with permission from *The Globe and Mail.*

▶ INTRODUCTION

Part 4 examined the first critical element of a firm's marketing mix: the design and management of the goods and services to offer the target market. Part 5 focuses on price, the second element of the marketing mix. Determining profitable and justified prices is the result of pricing objectives and various approaches to setting prices, the topics of this chapter. The following chapter focuses on managing the pricing function and discusses pricing strategies, price–quality relationships, and both industrial pricing and the pricing of public services. The starting place for examining pricing strategy is to understand the meaning of the term *price.*

Price is the value that a buyer exchanges for a good or service. This implies that the value is ultimately determined by customers. In earlier times, the price of an acre of land might have been twenty bushels of wheat, three cattle, or a boat. Price is a measure of what one must exchange in order to obtain a desired good or service. When the barter process was abandoned in favour of a monetary system, price became the amount of money required to purchase an item. As David Schwartz has pointed out, contemporary society uses a number of terms to refer to price:

> Price is all around us. You pay *rent* for your apartment, *tuition* for your education, and a *fee* to your physician or dentist.
>
> The airline, railway, taxi, and bus companies charge you a *fare;* the local utilities call their price a *rate;* and the local bank charges you *interest* for the money you borrow.
>
> The price for taking your car on the ferry to Prince Edward Island or Vancouver Island is a *toll,* and the company that insures your car charges you a *premium.*
>
> Clubs or societies to which you belong may make a special *assessment* to pay unusual expenses. Your regular lawyer may ask for a *retainer* to cover her services.
>
> The "price" of an executive is a *salary;* the price of a salesperson may be a *commission;* and the price of a worker is a *wage.*
>
> Finally, although economists would disagree, many of us feel that *income taxes* are the price we pay for the privilege of making money.[1]

All products have some degree of **utility**, or want-satisfying power. While one individual might be willing to exchange the utility derived from a colour television for a vacation, another may not be willing to make that exchange. Prices are

price
The value that a buyer exchanges for a good or service.

utility
The want-satisfying power of a product or service.

a mechanism that allows the consumer to make a decision. In contemporary society, of course, prices are translated into monetary terms. Consumers evaluate the utility derived from a range of possible purchases and then allocate their exchange power (in monetary terms) so as to maximize satisfaction. Pricing may be the most complicated aspect of the marketing manager's job. It is somewhat difficult to determine the price needed to realize a profit. But an even greater problem is that of determining a price that consumers will respond to positively and that can be maintained in a competitive environment.

Price is fundamental to many aspects of the economic system. Price often serves as a means of regulating economic activity. The employment of any or all of the four factors of production (land, labour, capital, and entrepreneurship) depends on the price received by each.

For an individual firm, prices (along with the corresponding quantity that will be sold) determine the revenue to be received. Prices, therefore, influence a company's profit as well as its use of the factors of production. Early written accounts refer to attempts to develop a fair, or just, price. The "fair price" differs dramatically depending on one's perspective. If you are buying gasoline in Thunder Bay, you will have one set of criteria to judge whether the price is fair. If you are driving late at night on a deserted highway north of Lake Superior and the tank is nearly empty, you will have a different price perception.

▶ PRICE AND THE MARKETING MIX

Just as price is highly important in affecting economic activity, it is a central consideration in developing a marketing mix. A key question when setting a price is "What is the role of price in this marketing mix?" One marketing strategy will assign a major role to price as a means of attracting customers and sales. The discount food chain Save-On Foods is an example. Toward the other end of the spectrum, the marketing strategy of Lexus uses high price as a signal of the value of that fine car. In another marketing mix, price will play a much less important role. It is clear that there are different possible *objectives* for price.

Pricing Objectives

Pricing objectives are a crucial part of a means–end chain from overall company objectives to specific pricing policies and procedures (see Figure 13.1). The goals of the firm and the marketing organization provide the basis for developing pricing objectives, which must be clearly established before pricing policies and procedures are implemented.

A firm may have as its primary objective the goal of becoming the dominant supplier in the domestic market. Its marketing objective might then be to achieve maximum sales penetration in all sales regions. The related pricing goal would be sales maximization (through low prices). This means–end chain might lead to the adopting of a low-price policy implemented by providing the highest cash and trade discounts in the industry.

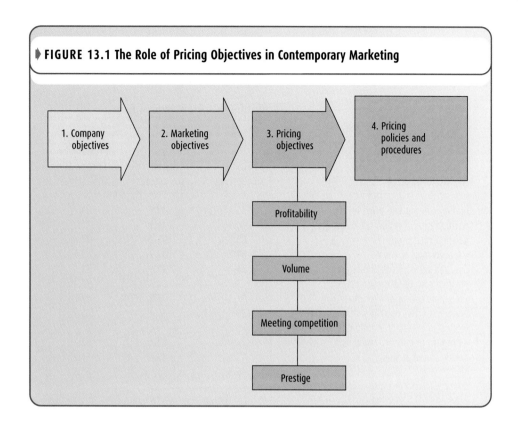

▶ **FIGURE 13.1 The Role of Pricing Objectives in Contemporary Marketing**

Pricing objectives vary from firm to firm. In an interesting U.S. study, marketers identified the primary and secondary pricing objectives of their companies. Meeting competitive prices was most often mentioned, but many marketers ranked two profitability-oriented objectives higher: a specified rate of return on investment and specified total profit levels. These two objectives ranked first and second as *primary* pricing objectives. The findings are shown in Table 13.1.

Pricing objectives can be classified into four major groups: (1) profitability objectives, (2) volume objectives, (3) competition-meeting objectives, and (4) prestige objectives. Profitability objectives include profit maximization and target return goals.

PROFITABILITY OBJECTIVES

Businesses need to make profits in order to survive. How much profits? In classical economic theory, the traditional pricing objective has been to *maximize profits.* In terms of actual business practice, this means that profit maximization would be the basic objective of individual firms.

Profits, in turn, are a function of revenue and expenses:

$$\text{Profits} = \text{Total Revenues} - \text{Total Costs}$$

Revenue is determined by the selling price and the quantity sold:

$$\text{Total Revenue} = \text{Price} \times \text{Quantity Sold}$$

Price, therefore, should be increased up to the point where it causes a disproportionate decrease in the number of units sold. A 10 percent price increase that

---

▶ TABLE 13.1 Primary and Secondary Pricing Objectives of Firms

PRICING OBJECTIVE	PERCENTAGE OF RESPONDENTS RANKING THE ITEMS		
	As Primary Objectives	As Secondary Objectives	As Either Primary or Secondary Objectives
Meeting competitive price level	38.3	43.0	81.3
Specified rate of return on investment	60.9	17.2	78.1
Specified total profit level	60.2	17.2	77.4
Increased market share	31.3	42.2	73.5
Increased total profits above previous levels	34.4	37.5	71.9
Specified rate of return on sales	47.7	23.4	71.1
Retaining existing market share	31.3	35.9	67.2
Serving selected market segments	26.6	39.1	65.7
Creation of a readily identifiable image for the firm and/or its products	21.9	41.4	63.3
Specified market share	15.6	40.6	56.2
Other	5.5	—	5.5

Source: Louis E. Boone and David L. Kurtz, *Pricing Objectives and Practices in American Industry: A Research Paper.* All rights reserved.

---

results in only an 8 percent cut in volume adds to the firm's revenue. However, a 10 percent hike that causes an 11 percent sales decline reduces total revenue.

In terms of the quantity of product that the firm should produce and offer for sale, the point of **profit maximization** is where the addition to total revenue is just balanced by an increase in total cost. This approach is referred to as *marginal analysis.* This is a valuable concept that the reader should understand. Making it work, however, is not so easy. The basic problem centres on the difficulty of achieving this delicate balance between marginal revenue and marginal cost. As a result, relatively few firms actually achieve the objective of profit maximization. A significantly larger number prefer to direct their efforts toward goals that are more easily implemented and measured.

Consequently, target return objectives have become quite common in industry, particularly among the larger firms where public pressure may limit consideration of the profit maximization objective. Telephone and other utility companies are an example of this phenomenon. **Target return objectives** may be either short-run or long-run goals, usually are stated as a percentage of sales or investment. A company, for instance, may seek a 15 percent annual rate of return on investment or an 8 percent rate of return on sales. A specified return on investment was the most commonly reported pricing objective in Table 13.1.

Target return objectives offer several benefits to the marketer. (1) They are likely to result in a more stable and planned profit pattern for the company. This

profit maximization
The point where the addition to total revenue is just balanced by an increase in total cost.

target return objectives
Either short-run or long-run goals, usually stated as a percentage of sales or investment.

contrasts with a profit maximization approach, which can be very unstable. (2) They serve as a means for evaluating performance. (3) They also are designed to generate a "fair" profit, as judged by management, shareholders, and the general public as well. When using such target objectives, management should avoid a short-term perspective. For example, if a product has contributed according to target for a time and now faces price competition, it still could be making a good contribution to overhead and should not be arbitrarily dropped.

VOLUME OBJECTIVES

Some writers argue that a better explanation of actual pricing behaviour is William J. Baumol's belief that firms attempt to **maximize sales** within a given profit constraint.[2] In other words, they set a minimum floor at what they consider to be the lowest acceptable profit level and then seek to maximize sales (subject to this profit constraint) in the belief that increased sales are more important to the long-run competitive picture. The company will continue to expand sales as long as its total profits do not drop below the minimum return acceptable to management.

sales maximization
The pricing philosophy analyzed by economist William J. Baumol. Baumol believes that many firms attempt to maximize sales within a profit constraint.

Another volume-related pricing objective is the **market share objective** — that is, the goal is set to control a specific portion of the market for the firm's product. The company's specific goal can be to maintain or increase its share of a particular market. For example, a firm may want to increase its 10 percent share of a particular market to 20 percent.[3] As Table 13.1 indicates, about two-thirds of all responding firms list retaining existing market share as either a primary or a secondary pricing objective.

market share objective
To control a specific portion of the market for the firm's product.

Market share objectives can be critical to achieving other objectives. High sales, for example, may mean more profit. The extensive *Profit Impact of Market Strategies (PIMS)* project conducted by the Marketing Science Institute analyzed more than 2000 firms and revealed that two of the most important factors influencing profitability were product quality and a large market share.

COMPETITION-MEETING OBJECTIVES

Status quo objectives — objectives based on maintaining stable prices — are the basis of the pricing philosophy for many enterprises. This philosophy usually stems from a desire to minimize competitive pricing action. Maintaining stable prices allows the firm to concentrate its efforts on nonprice elements of the marketing mix, such as product improvement or promotion. Maple Leaf Foods International de-emphasized price competition and developed an advertising campaign emphasizing product features that differentiated its product, Tenderflake lard, from the competition. As a result, market share and profits increased significantly. The company was even able to raise prices gradually. Status quo objectives remain a significant factor in pricing.

status quo objectives
Objectives based on maintaining stable prices.

www.mlfi.com/specialt.html

PRESTIGE OBJECTIVES

Another category of pricing objectives unrelated to either profitability or sales volume is that of prestige objectives. **Prestige objectives** involve establishing relatively high prices in order to develop and maintain an image of quality and exclusiveness. Such objectives reflect marketers' recognition of the role of price

prestige objectives
Establishing relatively high prices in order to develop and maintain an image of quality and exclusiveness.

www.birks.com

www.holtrenfrew.com

http

www.rolls-royce.com

in creating an overall image for the firm and its products and services. It appears that Birks and Holt Renfrew follow this strategy. Many luxury perfume manufacturers also use prestige pricing to suggest quality. And Rolls-Royce has opted for a higher-price image with its Cabriolet convertible model, priced at approximately $150 000.

▶ PRICE DETERMINATION

There are three general approaches to determining price. One is price derivation, which is based on theoretical economic analysis. A second is the cost-plus approach, where the costs of producing the product are determined, and a margin of profit is added on. The third method is the marketing approach. The marketing approach is built on aspects of the economic-analysis and cost-plus methods, and adds an important marketing dimension to come up with a realistic price.

▶ PRICE DETERMINATION IN ECONOMIC THEORY

Demand and consumer type often result in varying prices for a single product or service.

Few businesses follow economic theory strictly in setting prices. Because of this, some students ask why we should bother with reviewing the economic approach to pricing. The reason is that *the concepts of economic price theory are essential to other pricing approaches, and they apply to almost any pricing situation.* These concepts are important building blocks that help us understand what is going on in a particular pricing situation.

The microeconomic approach, or price theory, assumes a profit maximization objective and leads to deriving correct equilibrium prices in the marketplace. Price theory considers both demand and supply factors and thus is a more complete analysis than what is typically found in practice.

Demand refers to a schedule of the amounts of a firm's product or service that consumers will purchase at different prices during a specific period. *Supply* refers to a schedule of the amounts of a product or service that will be offered for sale at different prices during a specified time period. These schedules may vary for different types of market structures.

Would it bother you to hear how little I paid for this flight?

Market Structures

There are four types of market structure: pure competition, monopolistic competition, ologopoly, and monopoly. Very briefly, **pure competition** is a market structure in which there is such a large number of buyers and sellers that no one of them has a significant influence on price. Other characteristics of pure competition include a homogeneous product and ease of entry for sellers, and complete and instantaneous information. This marketing structure is largely theoretical in contemporary society; however, some uncontrolled sectors of the agricultural commodity sector exhibit many of the characteristics of such a market, and provide the closest example of it.

Monopolistic competition is also a market structure with a large number of buyers and sellers. However, in this market there is some degree of heterogeneity in good and/or service and usually geographical differentiation. Customers can distinguish between the companies and will form preferences for one company's product or service over another's product or service. The existence of differentiation allows the marketer some degree of control over price. Most retail stores fall into this category, which partially explains why small retailers can exist with prices 5 to 10 percent higher than their larger competitors.

An **oligopoly** is a market structure in which there are relatively few sellers. Each seller may affect the market, but no one seller controls it. Examples are the car, steel, tobacco, and petroleum-refining industries. Because of high start-up costs, new competitors encounter significant entry barriers. **Oligopsony** is the other side of the coin: a market in which there are only a few buyers.

A **monopoly** is a market structure with only one seller of a product with no close substitutes. Anticombines legislation has tended to eliminate all but *temporary* monopolies, such as those provided by patent protection, and *regulated* monopolies, such as the public utilities (electricity, gas). Regulated monopolies are granted by government in markets where competition would lead to an uneconomic duplication of services. In return for this monopoly, government regulates the monopoly rate of return through regulatory bodies such as the Canadian Transport Commission, the Canadian Radio-television and Telecommunications Commission, the National Farm Products Marketing Council, and provincial public utility regulatory commissions.

pure competition
A market structure in which there is such a large number of buyers and sellers that no one of them has a significant influence on price.

monopolistic competition
A market structure with a large number of buyers and sellers where heterogeneity in good and/or service and usually geographical differentiation allow the marketer some control over price.

oligopoly
A market structure in which there are relatively few sellers.

oligopsony
A market in which there are only a few buyers.

monopoly
A market structure with only one seller of a product with no close substitutes.

Revenue, Cost, and Supply Curves

Within each of these market structures the elements of demand, costs, and supply must be considered. The demand side of price theory is concerned with *revenue curves. Average revenue* (AR) is obtained by dividing *total revenue* (TR) by the *quantity* (Q) associated with these revenues:

$$AR = \frac{TR}{Q}$$

The plotted average revenue line is actually the demand curve facing the firm. *Marginal revenue* (MR) is the change in total revenue (ΔTR) that results from selling an additional unit of output (ΔQ). This can be shown as

$$MR = \frac{\Delta TR}{\Delta Q}$$

To complete the analysis, the supply curves must be determined for each of these market situations. A firm's cost structure determines its supply curves. Let us examine each of the cost curves that apply to price determination.

average cost
Obtained by dividing total cost by the quantity associated with this cost.

Average cost (AC) is obtained by dividing total cost by the quantity (Q) associated with the total cost. *Total cost* (TC) is composed of both fixed and variable components. *Fixed costs* are those costs that do not vary with differences in output, while *variable costs* are those that change when the level of production is altered. Examples of fixed costs include executive compensation, depreciation, and insurance. Variable costs include raw materials and the wages paid to production workers.

average variable cost
The total variable cost divided by the related quantity.

Average variable cost (AVC) is simply the total variable cost (TVC) divided by the related quantity. Similarly, *average fixed cost* (AFC) is determined by dividing total fixed costs (TFC) by the related quantity. **Marginal cost** (MC) is the change in total cost (ΔTC) that results from producing an additional unit of output (ΔQ). Thus, it is similar to *marginal revenue,* which is the change in total revenue resulting from the production of an incremental unit. The point of profit maximization is where marginal costs are equal to marginal revenues.

marginal cost
The change in total cost that results from producing an additional unit of output.

These cost derivations are shown in the following formulas:

$$AC = \frac{TC}{Q} \qquad\qquad AFC = \frac{TFC}{Q}$$

$$AVC = \frac{TVC}{Q} \qquad\qquad MC = \frac{\Delta TC}{\Delta Q}$$

The resulting *cost curves* are shown in Figure 13.2. The marginal cost curve (MC) intersects the average variable cost curve (AVC) and average cost curve (AC) at their minimum points.

In the short run, a firm will continue to operate even if the price falls below AC, provided it remains above AVC. Why is this rational market behaviour? If the firm were to cease operations after the price fell below AC, it would still have some fixed costs, but *no revenue.* Any amount received above AVC can be used

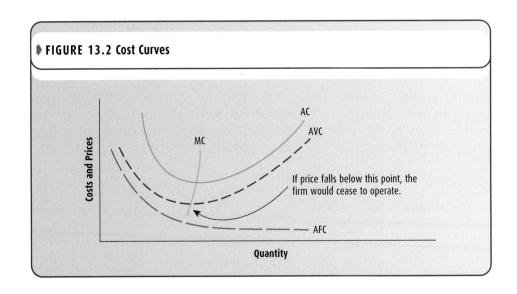

▶ **FIGURE 13.2 Cost Curves**

to cover fixed costs. The firm is acting rationally by continuing to produce as long as price exceeds AVC, since this minimizes losses. If price falls below AVC, the firm would cease operations, because continued operation would result in real losses from out-of-pocket costs per unit, with no control of fixed costs. The **supply curve**, therefore, is the marginal cost curve above its intersection with AVC, since this is the area of rational pricing behaviour for the firm.

How, then, are prices set in each of the product market situations? Figure 13.3 shows how prices are determined in each of the four product markets. The point of profit maximization (MC = MR) sets the equilibrium output (Point A), which is extended to the AR line to set the equilibrium price (Point B). In the case of pure competition, AR = MR, so price is a predetermined variable in this product market.

supply curve
The marginal cost curve above its intersection with average variable cost.

⬧ **FIGURE 13.3 Price Determination in the Four Product Markets**

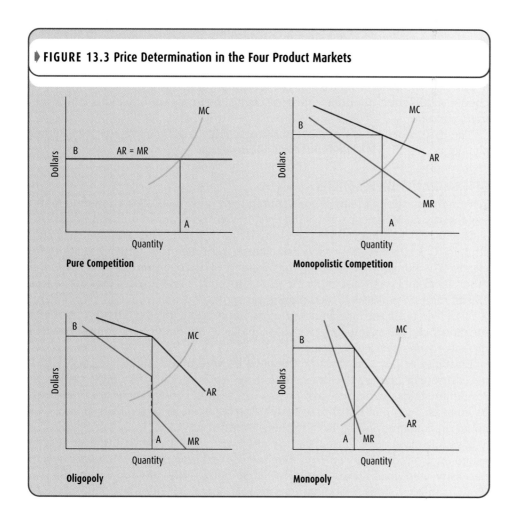

Pure Competition

Monopolistic Competition

Oligopoly

Monopoly

The Concept of Elasticity in Pricing Strategy

Although the intersection of demand and supply curves determines the equilibrium price for each of the market structures, the specific curves vary. To understand why, it is necessary to understand the concept of elasticity.[4]

elasticity
A measure of the responsiveness of purchasers and suppliers to changes in price.

Elasticity is a measure of the responsiveness of purchasers and suppliers to changes in price. The *price elasticity of demand* is the percentage change in the quantity of a product or service demanded divided by the percentage change in its price. A 10 percent increase in the price of eggs that results in a 5 percent decrease in the quantity of eggs demanded yields a price elasticity of demand for eggs of 0.5.

ELASTICITY TERMINOLOGY

Consider a case in which a 1 percent change in price causes more than a 1 percent change in the quantity supplied or demanded. Numerically, that means an elasticity greater than 1.0. When the elasticity of demand or supply is greater than 1.0, it is termed *elastic.*

If a 1 percent change in price results in less than a 1 percent change in quantity, a good's elasticity of supply or demand will be numerically less than 1.0 and is called *inelastic.* The demand for eggs in the example above is inelastic. Gasoline prices can fluctuate quite widely; however, the resulting change in total sales is minimal.

An extreme case occurs when the quantity supplied or demanded does not change at all when the price changes. Then the supply or demand is called *perfectly inelastic.*

The case in which a 1 percent change in price results in exactly a 1 percent change in quantity is called *unit* (or *unitary*) *elastic.*

DETERMINANTS OF ELASTICITY

Why is the elasticity of supply or demand high for some goods and services and low for others? What constitutes the specific determinants of demand elasticity?[5]

One factor that determines the elasticity of demand is the availability of substitutes. If a product or service has close substitutes, the demand tends to be elastic. The demand for olive oil, for instance, is more elastic than it would be if other salad oils were not available as substitutes. The demand for cars is less elastic than it would be if good public transportation was available everywhere. A related factor is the availability of more important complements. The demand for motor oil, for example, tends to be inelastic because it is a complement to the more important good, gasoline.

Elasticity of demand is also influenced by whether a product or service is a necessity or a luxury. For example, dining out is a luxury for most people. If restaurant prices increase, most people can respond by eating at home instead. By contrast, eggs and milk are considered necessities, so price changes have less effect on consumption, at least in the short run.

Elasticity is further influenced by the portion of a person's budget that is spent on a product or service. Matches, for example, are no longer really a necessity, and good substitutes exist. Nonetheless, the demand for matches is thought to be very inelastic because people spend so little on them that they hardly notice a price change. However, the demand for housing and transportation is not perfectly inelastic even though they are necessities. Both occupy a large part of people's budgets, so a change in price cannot be ignored.

Elasticity of demand is also affected by the time perspective under consideration. Demand is often less elastic in the short run than in the long run. Consider the demand for home heating fuel. In the short run, when the price goes up, people find it difficult to cut back on the quantity they use. They are accustomed to living at a certain temperature, dressing a certain way, and so forth. Given time, though, they may find ways to economize. They can better insulate their homes, form new habits of dressing more warmly, or even move to a warmer climate.

All the factors mentioned here are only tendencies, yet often the tendencies reinforce one another. The classic case of inelastic demand is salt, which has no good substitute, is a nutritional necessity, and uses a very small part of one's budget. Sometimes, though, the rules just do not seem to fit. Alcohol and tobacco, which are not necessities and do occupy a large share of some personal budgets, also are subject to notoriously inelastic demand.

It is important to understand that there are actually three kinds of elasticity. **Industry or market elasticity**, which we have been discussing, refers to changes in total demand resulting from general changes in price across the industry. Related concepts, which are also important to the marketer, are company, or brand, elasticity and segment elasticity.

industry or market elasticity
Refers to changes in total demand resulting from general changes in price across the industry.

Company elasticity refers to the sensitivity to changes in price that a particular company or brand faces. Even though the demand for gasoline is very price inelastic, any single retailer's demand is very price elastic. That is, raising a single service station's price even a fraction of a cent above the competition's price will result in significant loss of business. On the other hand, due to their strong reputation, IBM products in general benefit from slightly lower levels of price elasticity than many of the company's competitors. The result is that IBM can sell its products at a premium. In contrast, one would expect that President's Choice Cola is more price elastic than Coca-Cola.

company elasticity
Refers to the sensitivity to changes in price that a particular company or brand faces.

Segment elasticity refers to the sensitivity to changes in price that a particular segment exhibits. Die-hard audiophiles, for example, tend to be very inelastic in their demand patterns, focusing instead on obtaining the best sound reproduction possible. They represent a particularly attractive segment for stereo manufacturers to target—particularly early in the product life cycle.

segment elasticity
Refers to the sensitivity to changes in price that a particular segment exhibits.

ELASTICITY AND REVENUE

There is an important relationship between the elasticity of demand and the way that total revenue changes as the price of a good or service changes. Suppose Montreal wants to find a way to raise more money for its public transportation system. One possible fundraising method is to change the transit fare, but should it be raised or lowered? The correct answer depends on the elasticity of demand for subway rides. A 10 percent decrease in fares is sure to attract more riders, but unless there is more than a 10 percent increase in riders, total revenue will fall. A 10 percent increase in fares will bring in more money per rider, but if more than 10 percent of the riders are lost, revenue will fall. A price cut will increase revenue only if demand is *elastic,* and a price increase will raise revenue only if demand is *inelastic.*

Practical Problems in Applying Price Theory

From the viewpoint of the marketer, price theory concepts are sometimes difficult to apply in practice. What are their practical limitations?

1. Many firms do not attempt to maximize profits. Economic analysis is subject to the same limitations as the assumptions on which it is based, and the assumption of profit maximization often does not hold true.

2. It is difficult to estimate demand curves. Modern accounting procedures provide managers with a clear understanding of their cost structure. The manager, therefore, can readily comprehend the supply side of the price equation. But it is difficult to estimate demand at various price levels. Demand curves must be based on market research estimates that are often not as exact as cost figures. Although the demand element can be identified, it is often difficult to measure in the real-world setting.

3. Inadequate training and communications hinder price theory in the real world. Many businesspeople lack the formal training in economics to be able to apply its concepts to their own pricing decisions. On the other hand, many economists remain essentially theorists who devote little interest or effect to real-world pricing situations. This dual problem significantly hinders the use of economic theory in actual pricing practice.[6]

In spite of these problems, it is very useful for pricing decision makers to consider whether demand for their product is elastic or inelastic, what kind of market structure they are operating in, and other related theoretical matters as a starting point for other pricing approaches.

▶ COST-ORIENTED PRICE SETTING

For many firms, price determination tends to be based on some form of the cost-plus approach.

cost-plus pricing
Pricing technique using base cost figure per unit to which is added a markup to cover unassigned costs and to provide a profit.

Cost-plus pricing uses some base cost figure per unit to which is added a markup to cover unassigned costs and to provide a profit. The only real difference in the multitude of cost-plus techniques is the relative sophistication of the costing procedures employed. For example, the local clothing store may set prices by adding a 40 percent markup to the invoice price charged by the supplier. This markup is expected to cover all other expenses, as well as permit the owner to earn a reasonable return on the sale of the garments.

In contrast to this rather simple pricing mechanism, a large manufacturer may employ a pricing formula that requires a computer to handle the necessary calculations for a sophisticated costing procedure. But in the end, the formula still requires someone to make a decision about the markup. The clothing store and the large manufacturer may be vastly different with respect to the *cost* aspect, but they are remarkably similar when it comes to the *markup* side of the equation.

A major problem associated with cost-oriented pricing is that *costs should not determine prices, since the proper function of cost in pricing is to determine the profit consequences of pricing alternatives.* That is, costs in the long run only determine the floor for the price. Furthermore, it is possible that costs may be too high and not supportable by the marketplace. Unfortunately, this is not always understood by some companies.

Full-Cost Pricing

The two most common cost-oriented pricing procedures are the full-cost method and the incremental-cost method. *Full-cost pricing* uses all relevant variable costs in setting a product's price. In addition, it considers an allocation of the fixed costs that cannot be directly attributed to the production of the specific item being priced. Under the full-cost method, if job order 515 in a printing plant amounts to 0.000127 percent of the plant's total output, then 0.000127 percent of the firm's overhead expenses are allocated to this job. This approach therefore allows the pricer to recover all costs plus the amount added as a profit margin.

The full-cost approach has two basic deficiencies. First, it does not consider the demand for the item or its competition. Perhaps no one wants to pay the price that the firm has calculated. Second, any method of allocating overhead, or fixed expenses, is arbitrary and may be unrealistic. In manufacturing, overhead allocations are often tied to direct labour hours. In retailing, the mechanism is sometimes floor area in each profit centre. Regardless of the technique, it is difficult to show a cause-and-effect relationship between the allocated cost and most products.

Incremental-Cost Pricing

One way to overcome the arbitrary allocation of fixed expenses is by *incremental-cost pricing*, which attempts to use only those costs directly attributable to a specific output in setting prices. For example, consider a small manufacturer with the following income statement:

Sales (10000 units at $10)		$100000
Expenses		
Variable	$50000	
Fixed	$40000	$ 90000
Net Profit		$ 10000

Suppose that the firm is offered a contract for an additional 5000 units. Since the peak season is over, these items can be produced at the same average variable cost. Assume that the labour force would be idle otherwise. To get the contract, how low could the firm price its product?

Under the full-cost approach, the lowest price would be $9 each. This is obtained by dividing the $90000 in expenses by an output of 10000 units. The full-cost pricer would consider this a profitless situation. When pricing in this manner, there is a real problem with using full cost. This is set as a floor below which the price will not be allowed to fall. Instead, the type of costs should be understood. Then they can be viewed as somewhat flexible, and serve as a reference point to which flexible markups are added.

The incremental-cost approach, on the other hand, would permit a price of anywhere from $5.01 upward depending on the competition. If competition were strong, a price of $5.10 would be competitive. This price would be composed of the $5 variable cost related to each unit of production, plus a 10 cents per unit contribution to fixed expenses and overhead. With these conditions of sale, note the revised income statement:

Sales (10 000 at $10 plus 5 000 at $5.10)		$125 500
Expenses		
Variable (15 000 × $5)	$75 000	
Fixed	$40 000	$115 000
Net Profit		$ 10 500

Profits were increased under the incremental approach. Admittedly, the illustration is based on two assumptions: (1) the ability to isolate markets so that selling at the lower price would not affect the price received in other markets, and (2) the absence of certain legal restrictions on the firm. The example, however, does show that profits can sometimes be enhanced by using the incremental approach.

Limitations of Cost-Oriented Pricing

While the incremental method eliminates one of the problems associated with full-cost pricing, it fails to deal effectively with the basic malady: *cost-oriented pricing does not adequately account for product demand.*

The problem of estimating demand is as critical to these approaches as it is to classical price theory. To the marketer, the challenge is to find some way of introducing demand analysis into cost-plus pricing. A well-reasoned approach to pricing should compare the impact of a pricing decision on total sales receipts, or revenue, and on total costs. It involves the increase or decrease in revenue and costs, not just of the product under consideration, but of the business enterprise as a whole.

▶ MARKETING APPROACHES TO PRICING

Marketing is an eclectic discipline. It draws good ideas from many sources. A *marketing approach to pricing* is no exception. A marketing approach recognizes the numerous valuable concepts developed by economic theory. Especially valuable are the concepts of demand estimation and price elasticity. Cost accounting is also considered essential in pricing. Without a thorough understanding of costs, a firm's pricing policies an soon go awry.

A marketing approach to pricing adds the dimension of *consumer analysis* to the economic and cost analysis. For example, this approach might accept that a profit margin of, say, 35 percent would be desirable for the firm. It also considers potential demand for the product, as well as price elasticity. It goes beyond these considerations, however. The marketing approach asks the question of *how potential consumers would respond* to such a price. Would this price cross some possible psychological threshold and be viewed as much higher than it really is? Or would the proposed price seem so low that it would negatively affect the product's image and sales? The astute marketer asks a host of other questions based on the unique perspective of consumer orientation.

In addition to considering the responses of various consumer segments, the marketing approach to pricing considers competitors individually, in addition to as a whole. In some cases, prior experience will have shown that a key competitor will likely respond in a certain way to any pricing moves. For example, car rental firms have quite a good understanding of their competitors' likely response to any pricing change that they might make. Psychological thresholds of key competitors are also important. A particular competitor might not react to a 3 percent price change, for example, but would react to a 5 percent drop.

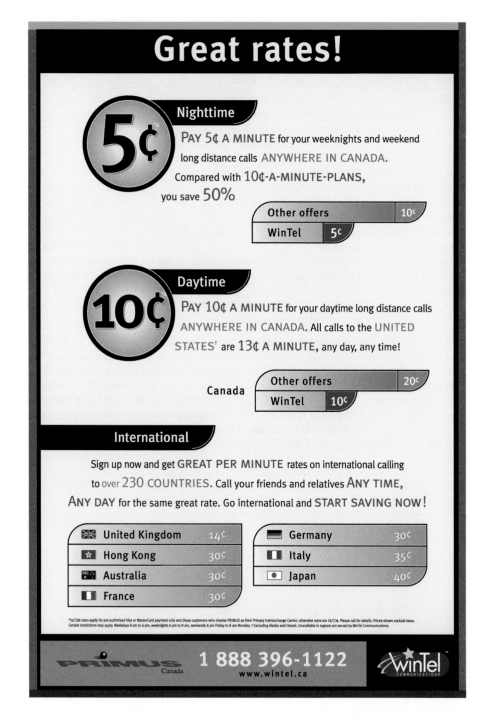

Telephone companies and long-distance carriers use price as the main selling tool in the competition for market share. Here, WinTel Communications offers very attractive rates to long-distance users.

▶ THE PRACTISING MARKETER

Price Wars

Sometimes, particularly with undifferentiated products, it seems to the marketer that the only way to increase market share is to drop the price. The problem is, competitors are usually in a similar situation. To defend their share, they will also drop prices. If the first company tries again, the situation can very quickly degenerate into a scenario that makes no economic sense. The following news story from March 1999 describes a price war in Britain.

Battle to Boost Sales Means Loaves Cost Less than Sheep Feed

LONDON: ASDA Group PLC, yesterday, fired the latest shot in a British supermarket price war that has already made sliced bread so cheap some farmers are feeding it to their sheep.

ASDA, the third biggest British food retailer, announced a new "rollback" promotion, cutting more than 1000 prices at its stores. ASDA's move followed rival Tesco PLC's campaign last month, which cut prices on hundreds of lines. Competition between Britain's Big Four supermarkets—Tesco, J. Sainsbury PLC, ASDA, and Safeway PLC—has slashed the price of some everyday foods dramatically.

Tesco's Value Medium Sliced White bread now costs only seven pence a loaf (17¢ Cdn), making it cheaper than conventional wheat feed given to sheep. Farmers, who themselves have been suffering a slump in sheep prices, have been buying up hundreds of loaves from local stores to feed their flocks.

Britain's food retailers are battling to boost sales and profits in a low-growth and low-inflation environment where price competition seems to have heated up since the start of the year.

They are also facing a probe by the Office of Fair Trading, Britain's competition watchdog, which is expected to publish its findings in March 1999. The OFT investigation into the supermarkets' profitability, launched in July 1998, was responding to concerns raised about their buying power from the farming sector and elsewhere.

The analysts said the key question was whether the price cutting was going to get worse. "Either there will be an uneasy peace or it will get more intense," said one.

There are really only two situations in which a company can win a price war. The first is if it has a real cost advantage over the competition. That is, it can produce its product or service at a lower cost than can the competition. The other situation, which is not nearly as attractive, is when one company has significantly greater resources than the competition. In that case the larger company, if it chooses, can simply accept losses on a particular product and wait out the competition, knowing that it can survive longer. This second case can easily attract the attention of market regulators, depending on the precise details of the situation, as it can amount to an abuse of market power and be perceived as an attempt to reduce competition (by driving competition out of business or out of a particular market).

Source: Adapted from Jane Merriman, "British Supermarkets Slash Prices, Shepherds Flock to Bread Aisle," *Financial Post* (March 9, 1999), p. C14. Copyright Reuters Limited 1999.

From a marketing perspective, a product that is new to the world, as opposed to being merely new to the company, passes through distinctive stages in its life cycle. The appropriate pricing policy is likely to be different at each stage. Perhaps the most difficult task is establishing an initial price for the product. In later stages of the product life cycle, pricing is complicated enough, but at that point, strategic decisions hinge largely on decisions to meet or beat the competition in various ways.

A Pricing Decision Flow Chart

A marketing approach to pricing begins and ends with the company's marketing strategy. The strategy sets the general parameters for pricing decisions (the beginning) and becomes the reference point against which pricing effectiveness is measured (the end) (see Figure 13.4).

▶ **FIGURE 13.4 A Pricing Decision Flow Chart**

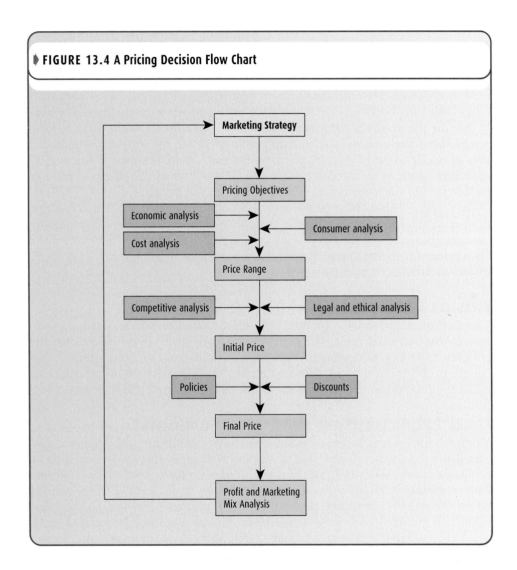

ESTABLISH PRICING OBJECTIVES

Pricing objectives flow from the marketing strategy. As discussed above, objectives can relate to profits, volume, competition, or prestige. Once pricing objectives have been established, economic, cost, and consumer analyses take place. The economic analysis would include a look at the price elasticity of the product.

ESTABLISH A PRICE RANGE

It is helpful to understand the maximum, or ceiling, price and minimum, or floor, price for which a product can be sold. The *ceiling price* comes from the consumer analysis. It is the greatest amount that some segment of the market would be willing and able to pay for this product. The *floor price,* in contrast, is a function of cost. In the short term, the firm cannot price below its variable cost of production without losing money on each sale. In the longer term, there also has to be some contribution to overhead.

ESTABLISH AN INITIAL PRICE

Competitive analysis and legal and ethical analysis will almost always result in a price that is somewhere between the floor and the ceiling. All three factors tend to constrain price decisions down from the price ceiling. If we assume a fairly large range between the firm's floor price and what customers will actually pay for the product, competitive action will usually force the firm to drop prices below the ceiling. That is, competitors will see the large difference and choose to offer a lower price to the same market. In the absence of some other advantage, such as recognized quality or a unique patent, the original firm will be forced to lower its prices to retain its share of the market.

Even with distinct advantages over competition, legal or ethical considerations tend to result in an initial price that is below the ceiling price. Interestingly enough, these considerations can also result in prices that are higher than the floor price, if it can be demonstrated that the purpose of pricing near cost is primarily to damage competition.

ESTABLISH A FINAL PRICE

The final price for which a product is actually sold often will be somewhat different than the initial price. The final price will be affected by the firm's pricing policies regarding skimming, penetration, flexibility, and other issues. Discounts to the trade, freight allowances, and other price promotions will also affect the final price. All of these issues are discussed in Chapter 14.

EVALUATE PROFITABILITY AND MARKETING MIX CONSISTENCY

When the final price has been established, there must be an evaluation process. The first test is to see if the pricing strategy will meet financial goals such as return on investment (ROI), target rate of return on sales, or a payback period. Failure to meet financial goals sends the pricing strategist back to the beginning of the process. In actual practice, the firm will probably have tested the price against its financial goals at several steps along the way. In fact, for new products in particular, it is desirable to make profit plans as early as the concept stage during new-product development. These plans can be updated as the product passes through the development stages.

The second test is to evaluate the selected price in terms of the product, channel, advertising, and personal-selling strategies that will be used in the market segment in question. The role of price in the marketing mix should be specifically identified, and all elements of the mix must blend together. Any inconsistencies must be reconciled by altering the price or one of the other elements of the mix.

A low price is appropriate when the product category is at the mature stage in its cycle. A low price may also be appropriate when there is little promotion, the product is mass-produced, market coverage is intense, production is capital-intensive, technological change is slow, the product is needed to complete the product line, few services are offered, the product is disposable, or the life cycle is short.

▸ INTERNET IMPACT

On-Line Auctions

Another solution to the pricing problem is to put goods up for auction. At an auction, potential buyers state what they are willing to pay for a good by way of a bidding process. Bids can be open or closed. In open bidding, potential buyers know one another's bids and can adjust their bid, and submit follow-up bids, accordingly. In closed bidding, each buyer submits only one bid and does not know what others are bidding.

ebay.com

Auctions tend to be used in three situations: (1) when a seller needs to dispose of goods quickly and either does not have the time or does not have the means to sell them at a preset price (for example, an estate sale); (2) when a seller has been unable to sell a product at a preset price (for example, a used car with high mileage); or when the object is unique and the seller doesn't know what buyers might be willing to pay for it (for example, fine art).

Several auction houses have sprung up on the Internet, in effect making the entire world part of the bidding audience. Of course, a few bugs must be worked out. Recently, a bed believed to have belonged to Sir John A. Macdonald, Canada's first prime minister, was put up for auction by eBay, an Internet auction house. The owners were no doubt thrilled when the winning bid came in at $400 000 U.S. Thrilled, that is, until it was discovered that the bidder had also purchased a Van Gogh sketch, a 1971 Corvette, a medical centre, and various other things that added up to a bill of about $3.2 million U.S. The problem was, the bidder was only 13 years old—and his allowance wouldn't quite cover his commitments.

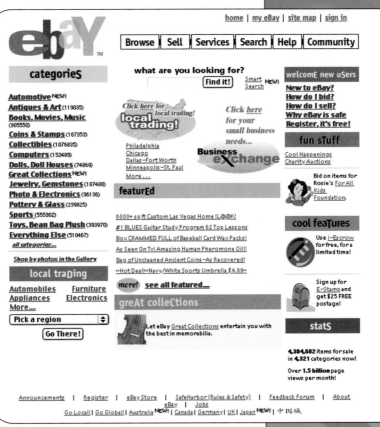

Internet auction houses such as eBay are becoming popular, but work is still needed to prevent hoax bids.

What do you see as some of the advantages and disadvantages of selling goods at auction? Over the Internet?

For details of this story, see Charlie Gillis, "High-Roller on Internet Auction Site Only 13," *National Post* (April 27, 1999), p. 1.

Break-even Analysis: A Useful Tool in Pricing

break-even analysis
A means of determining the number of goods or services that must be sold at a given price in order to generate sufficient revenue to cover total costs.

Break-even analysis is a means of determining the number of goods or services that must be sold at a given price in order to generate sufficient revenue to cover total costs. Figure 13.5 shows the calculation of the break-even point graphically. The total cost curve includes both fixed and variable segments, and total fixed costs are represented by a horizontal shaded bar. Average variable cost is assumed to be constant per unit as it was in the example used for incremental pricing.

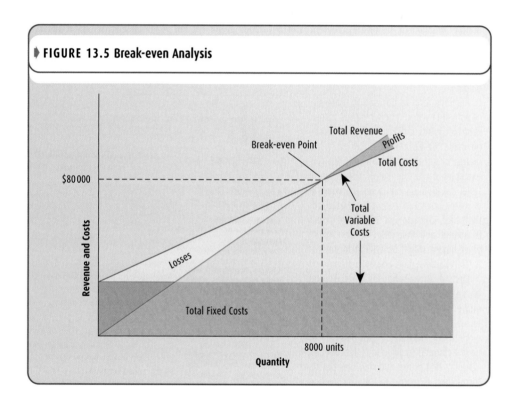

▶ FIGURE 13.5 Break-even Analysis

The break-even point is the point at which total revenue (TR) just equals total cost (TC). It can be found by using the following formulas:

$$\text{Break-even Point (in units)} = \frac{\text{Total Fixed Costs}}{\text{Per-Unit Selling Price} - \text{Average Variable Cost}}$$

$$= \frac{\text{Total Fixed Costs}}{\text{Per-Unit Contribution to Fixed Cost}}$$

$$\text{Break-even Point (in dollars)} = \frac{\text{Total Fixed Costs}}{1 - \dfrac{\text{Variable Cost per Unit}}{\text{Selling Price}}}$$

In our earlier example, a selling price of $10 and an average variable cost of $5 resulted in a per-unit contribution to fixed costs of $5. This figure can be divided into total fixed costs of $40000 to obtain a break-even point of 8000 units, or $80000 in total sales revenue:

$$\text{Break-even Point (in units)} = \frac{\$40000}{\$10-\$5} = \frac{\$40000}{\$5} = 8000 \text{ units}$$

$$\text{Break-even Point (in dollars)} = \frac{\$40000}{1-\dfrac{\$5}{\$10}} = \frac{\$40000}{0.5} = \$80000$$

Break-even analysis is an effective tool for marketers in assessing the sales required to cover costs and achieve specified profit levels. It is easily understood by both marketing and nonmarketing executives and may assist in deciding whether required sales levels for a certain price are in fact realistic goals. Extending this analysis a bit further, a simple profit breakdown is also shown. If a 10 percent profit on sales was desired, sales of $96000 would be required. More data would be needed if a return on investment or some other measure was used as a profitability target.

$$\text{Break-even Profit Point (in dollars)} = \frac{\$40000 + 10\% \text{ of Sales (\$8000)}}{1-\dfrac{\$5}{\$10}} = \frac{\$48000}{0.5} = \$96000$$

Break-even analysis is not without shortcomings. First, the model assumes that costs can be divided into fixed and variable categories. Some costs, such as salaries and advertising outlays, may be either fixed or variable depending on the particular situation. In addition, the model assumes that per-unit variable costs do not change at different levels of operation. However, these may vary as a result of quantity discounts, more efficient use of the workforce, or other economies resulting from increased levels of production and sales. Finally, the basic break-even model does not consider demand. It is a cost-based model and does not directly address the crucial question of whether consumers will actually purchase the product at the specified price and in the required quantities to break even or to generate profits. The challenge of the marketer is to modify break-even analysis and the other cost-oriented approaches to pricing in order to introduce demand analysis. Pricing must be examined from the buyer's perspective. Such decisions cannot be made in a management vacuum in which only cost factors are considered.

The Dynamic Break-even Concept

In Figure 13.5, the break-even analysis was based on the assumption of a constant $10 retail price regardless of quantity. What happens when different retail prices are considered? **Dynamic break-even analysis** combines the traditional break-even analysis model with an evaluation of consumer demand.

Table 13.2 summarizes both the cost and the revenue aspects of a number of alternative retail prices. The cost data are based on the costs used earlier in the basic break-even model. The expected unit sales for each specified retail price are obtained from consumer research. The data in the first two columns of Table 13.2 represent a demand schedule by indicating the number of units consumers

dynamic break-even analysis
Combines the traditional break-even analysis model with an evaluation of consumer demand.

are expected to purchase at each of a series of retail prices. This data can be superimposed on a break-even chart in order to identify the range of feasible prices for consideration by the marketing decision maker. This is shown in Figure 13.6.

▶ **TABLE 13.2 Revenue and Cost Data for Dynamic Break-even Analysis**

	REVENUES			COSTS			
Price ($)	Quantity Demanded	Total Revenue	Total Fixed Costs ($)	Total Variable Costs ($)	Total Cost ($)	TOTAL PROFIT (OR LOSS) ($)
14	3000	42000	40000	15000	55000	(13000)
12	6000	72000	40000	30000	70000	2000
10	10000	100000	40000	50000	90000	10000
8	14000	112000	40000	70000	110000	2000
6	26000	156000	40000	130000	170000	(14000)

As Figure 13.6 indicates, the range of profitable prices exists from a low of approximately $8 ($TR_4$) to a high of $12 ($TR_2$), with a price of $10 ($TR_3$) generating the greatest projected profits. Changing the retail price produces a new break-even point. At a relatively high $14 retail price, the break-even point is 4445 units; at a $10 retail price, the break-even point is 8000 units; and at a $6 price, the break-even point is 30000 units.

The contribution of dynamic break-even analysis is that it forces the pricing decision maker to consider whether consumers are likely to purchase the required number of units of a good or service that will achieve the break-even point at a given price. The analysis demonstrates that a larger number of units sold does not necessarily produce added profits, since—other things being equal—lower prices are necessary to stimulate added sales. Consequently, careful consideration of both costs and consumer demand is necessary in determining the most appropriate price.

Working with Prices: Markups, Markdowns, and Turnover

In working with prices, marketers often must consider three basic concepts: markups, markdowns, and turnover. An ability to handle these is essential for many day-to-day marketing decisions.

markup
The amount a producer or channel members adds to cost in order to determine the selling price.

MARKUPS

A **markup** is the amount a producer or channel member adds to cost in order to determine the selling price. It is typically stated as a percentage of either the

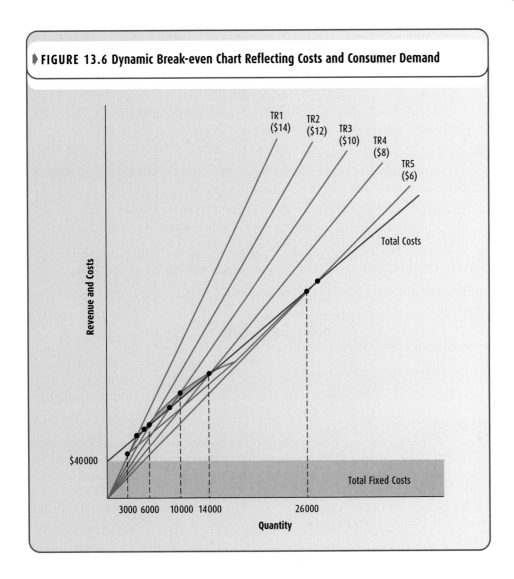

▶**FIGURE 13.6 Dynamic Break-even Chart Reflecting Costs and Consumer Demand**

selling price or the cost. The formulas used in calculating markup percentages are as follows:

$$\text{Markup Percentage on Selling Price} = \frac{\text{Amount Added to Cost (the Markup)}}{\text{Price}}$$

$$\text{Markup Percentage on Cost} = \frac{\text{Amount Added to Cost (the Markup)}}{\text{Cost}}$$

Consider an example from retailing. Suppose an item that sells for $1.00 has an invoice cost of $0.60. The total markup is $0.40. The markup percentages would be calculated as follows:

$$\text{Markup Percentage on Selling Price} = \frac{\$0.40}{\$1.00} = 40\%$$

$$\text{Markup Percentage on Cost} = \frac{\$0.40}{\$0.60} = 67\%$$

To determine the selling price when only cost and markup percentage on the selling price are known, the following formula is used:

$$\text{Price} = \frac{\text{Cost in Dollars}}{100\% - \text{Markup Percentage on Selling Price}}$$

In the example cited above, price could be determined as $1.00:

$$\text{Price} = \frac{\$0.60}{100\% - 40\%} = \frac{0.60}{60\%} = \$1.00$$

Similarly, the markup percentage can be converted from one basis (selling price or cost) to the other by using the following formula:

$$\frac{\text{Markup Percentage}}{\text{on Selling Price}} = \frac{\text{Markup Percentage on Cost}}{100\% + \text{Markup Percentage on Cost}}$$

$$\frac{\text{Markup Percentage}}{\text{on Cost}} = \frac{\text{Markup Percentage on Selling Price}}{100\% - \text{Markup Percentage on Selling Price}}$$

Again, using the data from the example above, the following conversions can be made:

$$\frac{\text{Markup Percentage}}{\text{on Selling Price}} = \frac{67\%}{100\% + 67\%} = \frac{67\%}{167\%} = 40\%$$

$$\frac{\text{Markup Percentage}}{\text{on Cost}} = \frac{40\%}{100\% - 40\%} = \frac{40\%}{60\%} = 67\%$$

MARKDOWNS

A related pricing issue that is particularly important to retailers is markdowns. Markups are based partially on executive judgements about the prices consumers are likely to pay for a given good or service. If buyers refuse to pay the price, however, the marketer must take a **markdown**, a reduction in the price of the item. For purposes of internal control and analysis, the markdown percentage is computed as follows:

markdown
A reduction in the price of an item.

$$\text{Markdown Percentage} = \frac{\text{Markdown}}{\text{``Sale'' (New) Price}}$$

Suppose no one is willing to pay $1.00 for an item and the marketer decided to reduce the price to $0.75. The markdown percentage would be

$$\text{Markdown Percentage} = \frac{\$0.25}{\$0.75} = 33\tfrac{1}{3}\%$$

From a customer's viewpoint, this is only a 25 percent reduction, which is known as the "off-retail percentage." This is the percentage that should be quoted in advertisements. Markdowns are also used for evaluative purposes. For instance, department managers or buyers in a large department store could be evaluated partially on the basis of the average markdown percentage on the product lines for which they are responsible.

TURNOVER

All to often, traditional markup and markdown percentages lead to competitive inertia within an industry. Standard percentages are too frequently applied to all items in a given category regardless of factors such as demand.

A method for avoiding competitive inertia is to use flexible markups that vary with **stock turnover** — the number of times the average inventory is sold annually. The figure can be calculated by one of the following formulas. When inventory is recorded at retail:

stock turnover
The number of times the average inventory is sold annually.

$$\text{Stock Turnover} = \frac{\text{Sales}}{\text{Average Inventory}}$$

When inventory is recorded at cost:

$$\text{Stock Turnover} = \frac{\text{Cost of Goods Sold}}{\text{Average Inventory}}$$

Store A, with $100 000 in sales and an average inventory of $20 000 (at retail), would have a stock turnover of 5. Store B, with $200 000 in sales, a 40 percent markup rate, and an average inventory of $30 000 (at cost), would have a stock turnover of 4.

Store A	Store B
$\text{Stock Turnover} = \dfrac{\$100\,000}{\$20\,000} = 5$	$\begin{aligned} &\$200\,000 \quad \text{Sales} \\ &-\ 80\,000 \quad \text{Markup (40 percent)} \\ &\$120\,000 \quad \text{Cost of Goods Sold} \end{aligned}$
	$\text{Stock Turnover} = \dfrac{\$120\,000}{\$30\,000} = 4$

While most marketers recognize the importance of turnover, they often use it more as a measure of sales effectiveness than as a pricing tool. However, it can be particularly useful in setting markup percentages if some consideration is given to consumer demand.

Table 13.3 indicates the relationship between stock turnover and markup. Above-average turnover, such as for grocery products, is generally associated with relatively low markup percentages. On the other hand, higher markup percentages typically exist in such product lines as jewellery and furniture, where relatively lower annual stock turnover is common and inventory and overhead costs must be covered through higher margins.

This chapter has described the basic considerations for determining price. The next chapter continues the discussion and delves into issues concerning the managing of pricing.

▶ **TABLE 13.3 Relationship between Markup Percentage and Stock Turnover**

STOCK TURNOVER RATE IN RELATION TO THE INDUSTRY AVERAGE	MARKUP PERCENTAGE IN RELATION TO THE INDUSTRY AVERAGE	PRODUCT EXAMPLE
High	Low	Soft Drinks
Average	Average	Motor Oil
Low	High	Sports Cars

▶ SUMMARY

Pricing objectives must be set before a pricing decision can be made. The four pricing objectives are profitability, volume, meeting the competition, and prestige. When focusing on profitability, firms may attempt to maximize profits, or they may aim for a target return. When concentrating on volume, firms can attempt to maximize sales within a given profit constraint, or they can attempt to maximize market share.

Economic approaches to pricing consider supply and demand, marginal revenue, marginal costs, and average revenues and costs. The profit maximizing price is that point where marginal revenue equals marginal costs.

Elasticity of demand is a measure of the responsiveness of buyers to changes in price. Goods can be elastic, or very responsive to price, or inelastic, or not very responsive to price.

Cost-plus pricing uses some base cost figure per unit to which is added a markup to cover unassigned costs and to provide a profit. However, costs should not determine prices. The proper function of cost in pricing is to determine the profit consequences of pricing alternatives. Incremental-cost pricing is superior to full-cost pricing in that it gives a more accurate picture of a particular product's contribution to overall profits.

The marketing approach to pricing takes the price theory and cost-accounting approaches to price into consideration, and adds a pragmatic use of consumer analysis as well as a strategic evaluation of likely competitor response.

Break-even analysis is a means of determining the number of goods or services that must be sold at a given price in order to generate sufficient revenue to cover total costs.

▶ KEY TERMS

average cost	oligopoly
average variable cost	oligopsony
break-even analysis	prestige objectives
company elasticity	price
cost-plus pricing	profit maximization
dynamic break-even analysis	pure competition
elasticity	sales maximization
industry or market elasticity	segment elasticity
marginal cost	status quo objectives
markdown	stock turnover
market share objective	supply curve
markup	target return objectives
monopolistic competition	utility
monopoly	

▶ INTERACTIVE SUMMARY AND DISCUSSION QUESTIONS

1. Pricing objectives must be set before a pricing decision. The four main pricing objectives are profitability, volume, meeting the competition, and pres-

tige. Give one or two product examples for which each objective seems to apply.

2. The two main profitability objectives are profit maximization and target return objectives. Explain the advantages and disadvantages of each.

3. In the case of volume objectives, some firms attempt to maximize sales within a given profit constraint. Others use a market share objective. Explain the advantages and disadvantages of each.

4. Besides trying to make as much money as possible, what are the other advantages of prestige pricing? What are the disadvantages?

5. One approach to determining price is based on theoretical economic analysis, which uses the concepts of supply and demand. Using these concepts, show how price can be determined theoretically.

6. In the short run, a firm will continue to operate even if a price falls below average cost, provided it remains above average variable cost. Why is this rational market behaviour?

7. Elasticity of demand is a measure of the responsiveness of purchasers and suppliers to changes in price. Explain why it is extremely important to take elasticity of demand into consideration in setting prices.

8. Price theory is very useful in understanding many of the forces in the marketplace that should be considered in setting prices, but are quite difficult to apply in practice. Explain.

9. Cost-plus pricing uses some base cost figure per unit to which is added a markup to cover unassigned costs and to provide a profit. However, costs should not determine prices, since the proper function of cost in pricing is to determine the profit consequences of pricing alternatives. Explain.

10. Explain why incremental-cost pricing is a better procedure than full-cost pricing.

11. The marketing approach to pricing takes the price theory and cost-accounting approaches to prices into consideration, and adds a pragmatic use of consumer analysis as well as a strategic evaluation of likely competitor response. Your new boss asks you to write a short memo outlining an approach to pricing a new mountain bike. How might the marketing approach to pricing be applied? What are the broad necessary steps that you would recommend?

12. Break-even analysis is a means of determining the number of goods or services that must be sold at a given price in order to generate sufficient revenue to cover total costs. Calculate the break-even point in dollars and units for a product with a selling price of $25, related fixed costs of $126 000, and per-unit variable costs of $16.

13. Select five different products that are available through the Web as well as through traditional channels. Are the prices quoted on the Web different from those found in traditional channels?

To obtain a list of further readings for Chapter 13, please refer to the *Foundations of Marketing* Web site.

Chapter 14
Managing the Pricing Function

Tom Mihalik, owner of Tom's Place, has more than just a shrewd pricing strategy to boast for his success.

Here's a really bad business idea. Open a store in the stinkiest part of the city, not far from a shop that offers "live carp." Make sure your aisles are good and cramped, and whatever you do, don't put prices on the goods.

To ruin any hope of success, cram the store with upscale items, specifically designer suits and ties. People who buy expensive clothes would never want to put up with all this nonsense, would they?

You bet they would. Tom Mihalik, proprietor of Tom's Place, a discount men's and women's designer clothing store in the heart of Toronto's odorous Kensington Market, is living proof that a retailer can break almost every rule in the book and still become a roaring success.

His store sells about $8-million worth of designer suits, shirts, jackets, blouses, and ties annually. Sales per square foot, a key measure in retail, top $1000—more than twice the industry average. That's impressive, considering the whole store was pulling in less than $100 000 a year when it opened in the early eighties.

His secrets: offer friendly service, good prices, and a little razzle-dazzle. If you've got those, customers will forgive all sorts of sins.

A visitor quickly learns that there are two prices at Tom's Place—a virtual price, which the salespeople initially quote to customers, and Tom's price.

Does he always offer a discount? "Always, always, always. I never sold anything at the asking price, never," he says.

Source: Excerpted from John Heinzl, "Tom's Tactics: Low Prices and Larger than Life," *The Globe and Mail* (July 10, 1998), p. B23. Reprinted with permission from *The Globe and Mail.*

www.toronto.com/E/V/
TORON/0035/32/89/1.html

▶ INTRODUCTION

The previous chapter introduced the concept of price and outlined the three main approaches to determining a price. Beyond this, however, the opening vignette about Tom's Place colourfully illustrates that there are many other pricing issues that the manager must understand. These include the setting of pricing policies, strategic decisions as to the level at which price should be set, and numerous day-to-day issues in pricing management. These will be the subjects of this chapter.

▶ PRICING POLICIES

Pricing policies are important for properly managing pricing. They provide the overall framework and consistency needed in pricing decisions. A **pricing policy** is a general guideline based on pricing objectives that is intended for use in specific pricing decisions. Pricing policies affect the **price structure**, which is an outline of the selling price and the various discounts offered to intermediaries. Price structure decisions take the selected price policy as a given, and specify the discount structure details. Pricing policies have great strategic

pricing policy
A general guideline based on pricing objectives that is intended for use in specific pricing decisions.

price structure
An outline of the selling price and the various discounts offered to intermediaries.

importance, particularly in relation to competitive considerations. They are the bases on which pricing decisions are made. Future Shop, for example, has a policy that it will never be undersold and that if a customer buys from the company and then finds a lower price, a portion of the price difference will be refunded.

Many businesses would be well advised to spend more managerial effort in establishing and periodically reviewing their pricing policies. Companies normally give a great deal of thought and planning to engineering, manufacturing, advertising, and sales promotion policies. It is essential that the same kind of careful study and planning be directed toward the formulation of price policies that will best serve the long-run objectives of the business.

International competition is another reason for establishing clearly formulated price policies. For example, in the retailing sector, the incursion of large U.S. low-price competitors has forced Canadian retailers to quickly rethink their pricing practices. Perhaps if Canadian retailers had been more conscious of the potential international competition, they might have established pricing policies and prices that would have made the Canadian market seem less attractive to foreign competitors.

Pricing policies provide a focus in dealing with varied competitive situations. The type of policy depends on the environment within which the pricing decision must be made. The types of policies to be considered are skimming versus penetration pricing, price flexibility, relative price levels, price lining, and promotional prices. They should all be arrived at through an analysis of the role of pricing in the marketing mix as well as the use of a pricing procedure similar to those described in Chapter 13.

Customers do not always understand pricing policies.

Skimming versus Penetration Pricing Policies

In pricing new products, the initial price that is quoted for an item may determine whether or not the product will eventually be accepted in the marketplace. The initial price also may affect the amount of competition that will emerge. Consider the options available to a company that is pricing a new product. It may price at the level of comparable products, very high, or very low. Figure 14.1 illustrates that the market is made up of different layers of potential customers with varying degrees of willingness and ability to pay depending on whether prices are higher or lower. This is another way of expressing the downward-sloping demand curve that applies to most products.

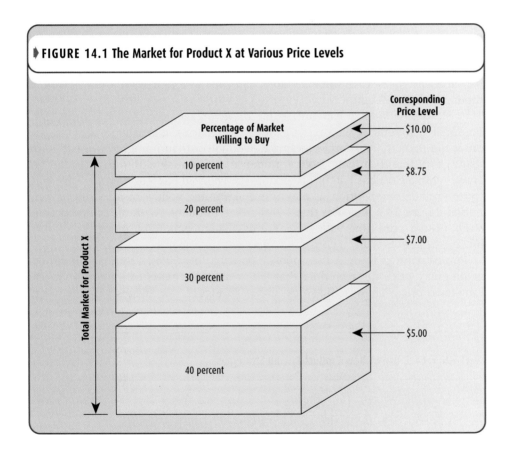

▶ **FIGURE 14.1 The Market for Product X at Various Price Levels**

A **skimming pricing** policy chooses a high entry price. The name is derived from the expression "skimming the cream." The plan is to sell first to consumers who are willing to pay the highest price, and then reduce the price (perhaps introduce a less fancy model) and market to the next level, and so on. One purpose of this strategy is to allow the firm to recover its development costs quickly. The assumption is that competition will eventually drive the price to a lower level, as was the case, for example, with compact discs.

A skimming policy, therefore, attempts to maximize the revenue received from the sale of a new product before the entry of competition. Ballpoint pens

skimming pricing
Choosing a high entry price; to sell first to consumers who are willing to pay the highest price, and then reduce the price.

were introduced shortly after World War II at a price of about $20. Today, the best-selling ballpoint pens are priced at less than $1. Other examples of products that have been introduced using a skimming policy include television sets, Polaroid cameras, videocassette recorders, home computers, and pocket calculators. Subsequent price reductions allowed the marketers of these products to appeal to additional market segments that are more price-sensitive.

A skimming strategy permits the marketer to control demand in the introductory stages of the product's life cycle and to adjust its productive capacity to match demand. A danger of low initial price for a new product is that demand may outstrip the firm's production capacity, resulting in consumer and intermediary complaints and possibly permanent damage to the product's image. Excess demand occasionally results in poor-quality products as the firm strives to satisfy consumer desires with inadequate production facilities.

During the late growth and early maturity stages of the product life cycle, the price is reduced for two reasons: (1) the pressure of competition and (2) the desire to expand the product's market. Figure 14.1 shows that 10 percent of the market for Product X would buy the item at $10, while another 20 percent would buy at $8.75. Successive price declines will expand the firm's market as well as meet new competition.

A skimming policy has one chief disadvantage: it attracts competition. Potential competitors who see the innovating firms make large returns also enter the market. This forces the price even lower than it might have had to be using a different pricing policy under a sequential skimming procedure. However, if a firm has patent protection—as Polaroid had—or a proprietary ability to exclude competition, it may use a skimming policy for a relatively long period. Figure 14.2 indicates that 14.4 percent of the respondents in one pricing study used a skimming policy. Skimming also appears to be more common in business markets than in consumer markets.

penetration pricing
An entry price for a product that is lower than what is estimated to be the long-term price.

Penetration pricing is the opposite policy in new-product pricing. It results in an entry price for a product that is lower than what is estimated to be the long-term price. The pricing study shown in Figure 14.2 suggests that penetra-

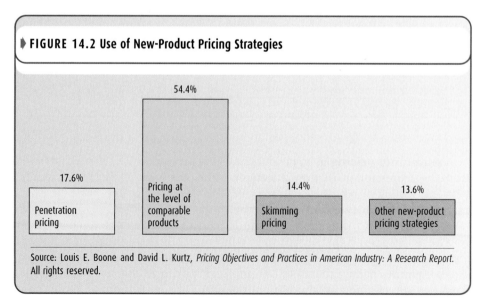

▶ **FIGURE 14.2 Use of New-Product Pricing Strategies**

54.4%

17.6%

14.4%

13.6%

Penetration pricing

Pricing at the level of comparable products

Skimming pricing

Other new-product pricing strategies

Source: Louis E. Boone and David L. Kurtz, *Pricing Objectives and Practices in American Industry: A Research Report.* All rights reserved.

tion pricing is used more often in consumer markets. Soaps and toothpastes are often good examples of this kind of pricing. For instance, a new combined shampoo and conditioner could be introduced with a cents-off label to induce consumers to try it.

The premise is that an initially lower price will help secure market acceptance. Since the firm later intends to increase the price, brand popularity is crucial to the success of a penetration policy. One advantage of such a policy is that is discourages competition from entering, since the prevailing low price does not suggest the attractive returns associated with a skimming policy.

Penetration pricing is likely to be used in instances where demand for the new product or service is highly elastic and large numbers of consumers are highly price-sensitive. It is also likely to be used in instances where large-scale operations and long production runs result in substantial reductions in production and marketing costs. Finally, penetration pricing may be appropriate in instances where the new product is likely to attract strong competitors when it is introduced. Such a strategy may allow it to reach the mass market quickly and capture a large share of the market before the entry of competitors. With penetration pricing, the marketers will likely forgo some profits, at least in the short run.

The key decision, of course, is when to move the price to its intended level. Consumers tend to resist price increases, so correct timing is essential. The solution depends on the degree of brand loyalty that has been achieved. Brand loyalty must be at the point where a price increase would not cause a disproportionate decrease in customers. A series of modest price changes, rather than a single large hike, also can retain customers. Often, firms will use cents-off deals to enter at a lower price. These can then be phased out more easily.

A firm may, of course, decide to use neither a skimming nor a penetration price. It may try to price a new product at the point where it is intended to sell in the long run. All three new-product pricing strategies are common, but it can be seen from Figure 14.2 that this last strategy was chosen in 54.4 percent of new-product pricing situations.

▸ THE PRACTISING MARKETER

New-Product Pricing

Suppose you are the marketing manager of a large candy manufacturer. Your product development team has just come up with a new type of chocolate bar that tastes very similar to fudge. Consumer taste tests have shown that most consumers have a very pronounced preference for the new bar and would be willing to pay a slightly higher price for it than they pay for regular chocolate bars. The best news is, it's actually cheaper to produce the new bar than regular bars. You are unable to patent the bar but are quite confident that it will take at least a year for your competitors to come up with a similar product. You have ample production capacity to manufacture the new bar. Scale and experience economies are not significant.

If your regular bars are priced at 90 cents each, what should be the price of the new bar? Explain your answer.

Price Flexibility

flexible pricing
A variable price policy.

Marketing executives must also determine company policy with respect to **flexible pricing**. Is the firm going to have just one price or pursue a variable price policy in the market? In general, *one-price policies* characterize situations where mass selling is employed, and *variable pricing* is more common where individual bargaining typifies market transactions, for example, the purchase of a car.

A one-price policy is common in Canadian retailing, since it facilitates mass merchandising. For the most part, once the price is set, managers can direct their attention to other aspects of the marketing mix. Flexible prices, by contrast, are found more in wholesaling and business markets. This does not mean that price flexibility exists only in manufacturing industries. A study of the retail home appliance market concluded that people who had purchased identical products from the same dealer had often paid different prices for them. The primary reasons for the differences were customer knowledge and bargaining strength.[1]

While variable pricing has the advantage of flexibility in selling situations, it may result in conflict with the Competition Act provisions. It may also lead to retaliatory pricing on the part of competitors, and it is not well received by those who have paid the higher prices.

Relative Price Levels

Another important pricing policy decision concerns the relative price level. Are the firm's prices to be set above, below, or at the prevailing market price? In economic theory, this question would be answered by supply and demand analysis. However, from a practical viewpoint, marketing managers *administer* prices. In other words, they subjectively set the markup percentages to achieve the price level desired. The decision maker must still develop a basic policy in regard to relative price levels. A fine clothing store, such as Harry Rosen, would probably have a policy of pricing at a level that is higher than most other clothing retailers. Wal-Mart, on the other hand, emphasizes its everyday low prices.

www.walmart.com

Following the competition is one method of negating the price variable in marketing strategy, since it forces competition to concentrate on other factors. Some firms choose to price below or above competition. These decisions are usually based on a firm's cost structure, overall marketing strategy, and pricing objectives.

The price level decision is distinct from the issue of penetration or skimming pricing in that it relates to the long-term price position of the firm. Penetration and skimming relate more narrowly to a new product being introduced to the marketplace.

Price Lining

price lining
The practice of marketing merchandise at a limited number of prices.

Most companies sell a varied line of products. An effective pricing strategy should consider the relationship among the firm's products rather than view each in isolation. Specifically, **price lining** is the practice of marketing merchandise at a limited number of prices. For example, a clothier might have a

www.us.buy.com

▶ INTERNET IMPACT

The Internet's Impact on Pricing

It's possible to buy just about anything on the Internet—used or new. The continued growth of Internet retailing—increasingly dubbed e-tailing—can potentially put price pressure on traditional retail outlets. There are two reasons for this possible pressure.

The first source of price pressure is simply that it is so easy to compare prices on the Internet. Rather than trudging from one store to the next, checking flyers, or spending many happy hours on the telephone, if you start out knowing fairly exactly what you are looking for, you can check out several Internet sites in a matter of minutes.

The second price pressure stems from the fact that several Internet retailers are very aggressively competing on price. Of these, Buy.com currently has the highest profile. They advertise the "lowest prices on Earth" and are prepared to sell products at a loss in order to make good on that claim. Buy.com is discussed in more detail in Chapter 17.

Whether the company has a viable long-term strategy remains to be seen. In the short term, though, its high visibility and aggressive price stance is almost sure to trim the margins of many retailers to some degree.

Do conventional retailers have any way of responding to Internet retailers like Buy.com other than simply trying to match prices? If so, how?

For a more complete discussion of buy.com, see Ross Laver, "Nutty Ideas Worth Billions," *Maclean's* (May 3, 1999), p. 42.

$195 line of men's suits and a $325 line. Price lining is used extensively in retail selling. It can be an advantage to both retailer and customer. Customers can choose the price range they wish to pay, and then concentrate on all the other variables, such as colour, style, and material. The retailer can purchase and offer specific lines rather than a more generalized assortment.

Price lining requires that one identify the market segment or segments to which the firm is appealing. For example, a suitcase manufacturer may see its market not as all luggage, but as the "medium-price, hard-side" portion of the luggage trade. The firm must decide how to *line* its product prices. A dress manufacturer might have lines priced $89.95, $159.95, and $199.95. Price lining not only simplifies the administration of the pricing structure, but also alleviates the confusion of a situation in which all products are priced separately. Price lining is really a combined product/price strategy.

One problem with a price-line decision is that once it is made, retailers and manufacturers have difficulty adjusting it. Rising costs, therefore, put the seller in the position of either changing the price lines, with the resulting confusion, or reducing costs by adjusting production, which opens the firm to the complaint that "XYZ Company's merchandise certainly isn't what it used to be!"

Promotional Prices

A **promotional price** is a lower-than-normal price used as an ingredient in a firm's selling strategy. In some cases promotional prices are recurrent, such as

promotional price
A lower-than-normal price used as an ingredient in a firm's selling strategy.

▸THE INFORMED CONSUMER

www.consumerreports.org

To Buy or Lease?

As consumers buy any big-ticket items, but especially cars, they are increasingly facing a choice of whether to buy the product outright or to lease it. The advantages of leasing include lower up-front costs and lower monthly payments. On the other hand, if you plan to buy the vehicle when the lease expires, it is almost always cheaper overall to just buy it outright. According to *Consumer Reports,* leasing makes sense if

• You do not exceed the annual mileage allowance (in Canada, typically 18 000 to 22 000 km per year). Going over results in additional costs charged per kilometre.

• You do not terminate the lease early—you may risk thousands of dollars in penalties if you do.

• You keep your vehicle in very good shape. "Excess wear and tear" charges at lease-end can be very expensive.

• You prefer to trade in your vehicle every two or three years. If you usually keep a vehicle for more than three years, you're better off buying it from the start.

What are the advantages to automobile manufacturers of leasing arrangements?

Source: Based on "To Lease or Not to Lease?" *Consumer Reports* (April 1999), p. 11. © 1999 by Consumers Union of U.S., Inc., Yonkers, NY 10703-1057, a nonprofit organization. Used by permission.

---

the annual shoe store sale: "Buy one pair of shoes, get the second for one cent." Or a new pizza restaurant may have an opening special to attract customers. In other situations, a firm may introduce a promotional model or brand to allow it to compete in another market.

loss leader
Goods priced below cost to attract customers.

Promotional pricing is often seen at the retail level. One type is **loss leaders**, goods priced below cost to attract customers who, the retailer hopes, will then buy other, regularly priced merchandise. The use of loss leaders can be effective, and is a commonly used means of generating business.

> Probably one of the best innovators of this pricing method was Cal Mayne. He was one of the first men to systematically price specials and to evaluate their effect on gross margins and sales. Mayne increased sales substantially by featuring coffee, butter, and margarine at 10 percent below cost. Ten other demand items were priced competitively and at a loss when necessary to undersell competition. Still another group of so-called secondary demand items were priced in line with competition. Mayne based his pricing policy on the theory that the customer can only remember about 30 prices. Keep prices down on these items and the customer will stay with you.[2]

Some studies have indeed reported considerable price confusion on the part of consumers. One study of consumer price recall reported that average shoppers misquoted the price they last paid for coffee by over 12 percent, toothpaste by over 20 percent, and green beans by 24 percent. While some people hit the prices exactly, others missed by several hundred percent.[3] The use of loss leaders is common in several branches of retailing today.

Three potential pitfalls should be considered when one faces a promotional pricing decision:

▶ THE ETHICAL MARKETER

Johnson & Johnson's Pricing Practice

Pricing decisions can raise some complicated ethical issues. Johnson & Johnson managed to touch on at least two problems with one decision when the company priced the drug levamisole, which it sells under the brand name Ergamisol. Levamisole was discovered to be very effective against colon cancer, the second leading cause of cancer-related deaths. Johnson & Johnson priced the product so that a year's supply ended up costing between $1250 and $1500 (U.S.).

No one argued that $1500 was an unreasonable price for a life-saving drug—until one patient noticed that the active ingredients in her cancer drugs were essentially the same as the ingredients in the deworming medicine she used for her sheep. The deworming medicine sold for more like $14. You might say that the sheep hit the fan for Johnson & Johnson about that point, with accusations of price gouging pouring in from all sides.

Johnson & Johnson, which actually has a stellar reputation for ethical conduct, argues (along with every other major pharmaceutical company) that wide margins are necessary on successful drugs because research costs are so high and it takes so long to develop and bring drugs to market. Furthermore, many research streams are dead ends that never return a profit.

The two issues underlying Johnson & Johnson's dilemma come down to (1) when, if ever, is it ethical to charge different segments different prices for essentially the same product? and (2) is it ethical to take large (or any) margins on products that are necessary to sustain a person's life? What do you think?

The facts presented in this box are drawn from Robert F. Hartley, *Business Ethics: Violations of the Public Trust* (New York: John Wiley & Sons, 1993), pp. 305–307.

www.johnsonandjohnson.com/home.html

- The Competition Act may prohibit some types of promotional pricing practices (see Chapter 2).
- Some consumers are little influenced by price appeals, so promotional pricing will have little effect on them.[4]
- Continuous use of an artificially low rate may result in its being accepted as customary for the product. Bic pens were introduced as a low-price product (with corresponding manufacturing costs). It would be extremely difficult to raise their prices significantly now.

▶ PRICING PRACTICES

Psychological Pricing

Psychological pricing is the use of prices to suggest values of a product or attributes of a product/price offering. Prestige pricing, mentioned in Chapter 13, is one of many forms of psychological pricing.

psychological pricing
The use of prices to suggest values of a product or attributes of a product/price offering.

The psychology of pricing can be complicated. Professor Lee Kreul has found through research that in restaurant newspaper advertisements for a meal costing less than $7, the price usually ends in 9 (e.g., $4.99). This implies a discount. For meals costing above $7, prices usually end in 5. Professor Kreul believes that as prices go up, the ending number changes because it takes more than one cent to create the discount illusion. Furthermore, people interested in paying more than $7 might think that a price ending in 9 suggests discounts, low quality, or hurried service.[5]

odd pricing
Prices are set ending in some amount just below the next rounded number.

Odd pricing is a good example of the application of psychological pricing. Prices are set ending in some amount just below the next rounded number. A price of $16.99 is assumed to be more appealing than $17 (supposedly because it is a lower figure).

Originally, odd pricing was used to force clerks to make change, thus serving as a cash control device within the firm.[6] Now it has become a customary feature of contemporary prices. For instance, one discounter uses prices ending in 3 and 7 rather than 5, 8, or 9 because of a belief that customers regard price tags of $5.95, $6.98, and $7.99 as *regular* retail prices, while $5.97 and $6.93 are considered *discount* prices. Obviously, intuition and experience play a part in establishing an odd pricing policy.

The Price-Quality Concept

One of the most researched aspects of pricing is the relationship between price and the consumer's perception of the product's quality.[7] In the absence of other cues, price is an important factor in the consumer's perception of the product's quality.[8] The higher the price, the better the buyer believes the quality of the product to be. One study asked 400 people what terms they associated with the word *expensive*. Two-thirds of the replies were related to high quality, such as *best*

IKEA furniture and products are priced affordably for most consumers, sometimes creating a perception that low prices mean low quality. To combat this notion, IKEA's catalogue cover showcases its furniture's superior quality and workmanship.

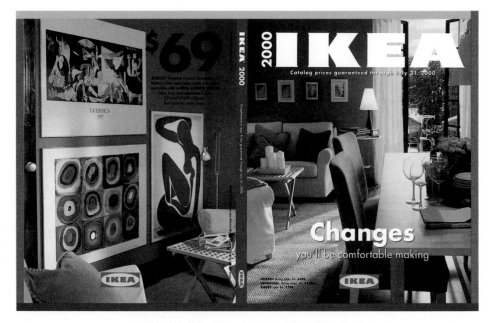

and *superior.*[9] The relationship between price and perceived quality is a well-documented fact in contemporary marketing.

Probably the most useful concept in explaining price–quality relationships is the idea of **price limits**.[10] It is argued that consumers have limits within which product quality perception varies directly with price. A price below the lower limit is regarded as too cheap, while one above the higher limit means it is too expensive. Most consumers do tend to set an acceptable price range when purchasing goods and services. The range, of course, varies depending on consumers' socioeconomic characteristics and buying dispositions. Consumers, nonetheless, should be aware that price is not necessarily an indicator of quality. Alberta Consumer and Corporate Affairs summarized seven price–quality research studies, six covering *Consumer Reports* analyses of 932 products between 1940 and 1977, and one for 43 products tested by *Canadian Consumer* between 1973 and 1977. It found that while there was a positive relationship between price and quality, the correlation was low (Spearman rank correlation = .25). In addition, about 25 percent of products tested had a negative price–quality relation. That is, products ranked lower in performance had higher prices than products deemed superior by the Canadian and U.S. consumer testing organizations.[11]

price limits
Limits within which product quality perception varies directly with price.

Unit Pricing

Consumer advocates have often pointed out the difficulty of comparing consumer products that are available in different-size packages or containers. Is an 800 g can selling for 75 cents a better buy than two 450 g cans priced at 81 cents or another brand that sells at three 450 g cans for 89 cents? The critics argue that there should be a common way to price consumer products.

Unit pricing is a response to this problem. Under unit pricing, all prices are stated in terms of some recognized unit of measurement (such as grams or litres) or a standard numerical count. There has been considerable discussion about legislating mandatory unit pricing. The Consumers' Association of Canada has endorsed unit pricing, and many of the major food chains have adopted it.

unit pricing
Stating prices in terms of some recognized unit of measurement (such as grams or litres) or a standard numerical count.

The real question, of course, is whether unit pricing improves consumer decisions. One study found that the availability of unit prices resulted in consumer savings, and that retailers also benefited when unit pricing led to greater purchases of store brands. The study concluded that unit pricing was valuable to both buyer and seller and that it merited full-scale use.[12] Others have questioned the amount of use of unit pricing by consumers.

www.consumer.ca

▶ PRICE QUOTATIONS

How prices are quoted depends on many factors, such as cost structures, traditional practice in the particular industry, and the policies of individual firms. In this section, we shall examine the reasoning and methodology behind price quotations.

The basis on which most price structures are built is the **list price**, the rate normally quoted to potential buyers. List price is usually determined by one or

list price
The rate normally quoted to potential buyers.

a combination of the methods discussed in Chapter 13. The sticker prices on new cars are good examples: they show the list price for the basic model, and then add the list price for the options that have been included.

Discounts, Allowances, and Rebates

market price
The amount that a consumer pays.

The amount that a consumer pays — the **market price** — may or may not be the same as the list price. In some cases, discounts or allowances reduce the list price. List price is often used as the starting point from which discounts that set the market price are derived. Discounts can be classified as cash, trade, or quantity.

cash discount
Reduction in price that is given for prompt payment of a bill.

Cash discounts are those reductions in price that are given for prompt payment of a bill. They are probably the most commonly used variety. Cash discounts usually specify an exact time period, such as "2/10, net 30." This means that the bill is due within 30 days, but if it is paid in 10 days, the customer may subtract 2 percent from the amount due. Cash discounts have become a traditional pricing practice in many industries. They are legal provided that they are granted to all customers on the same terms. Such discounts were originally instituted to improve the liquidity position of sellers by reducing accounts receivable, lower bad-debt losses, and reduce the expenses associated with collecting bills. Whether these advantages outweigh the relatively high cost of capital involved in cash discounts depends on the seller's need for liquidity as well as alternative sources (and costs) of funds.

trade discount
Payment to channel members or buyers for performing some marketing function normally required of the manufacturer.

Trade discounts, which are also called functional discounts, are payments to channel members or buyers for performing some marketing function normally required of the manufacturer. These are legitimate as long as all buyers in the same category, such as wholesalers and retailers, receive the same discount privilege. Trade discounts were initially based on the operating expenses of each trade category, but have now become more of a matter of custom in some industries. An example of a trade discount would be "40 percent, 10 percent off list price" for wholesalers. In other words, the wholesaler passes the 40 percent on to his or her customers (retailers) and keeps the 10 percent discount as payment for activities such as storing and transporting. The price to the wholesaler on a $100 000 order would be $54 000 ($100 000 less 40% = $60 000, less 10%). Note the sequence in which the discount calculations are made.

quantity discount
Price reduction granted for large purchases.

Quantity discounts are price reductions granted for large purchases. These discounts are justified on the grounds that large-volume purchases reduce selling expenses and may shift a part of the storing, transporting, and financing functions to the buyer. Quantity discounts are lawful provided they are offered on the same basis to all customers.

Quantity discounts may be either noncumulative or cumulative. Noncumulative quantity discounts are one-time reductions in list price. For instance, a firm might offer the discount schedule in Table 14.1. Cumulative quantity discounts are reductions determined by purchases over a stated time period. Annual purchases of $25 000 might entitle the buyer to an 8 percent rebate, while purchases exceeding $50 000 would mean a 15 percent rebate. These reductions are really patronage discounts, since they tend to bind the customer to one source of supply.

Allowances are similar to discounts in that they are deductions from the price the purchaser must pay. The major categories of allowances are trade-ins and

> **TABLE 14.1 A Noncumulative Quantity Discount Schedule**

UNITS PURCHASED	PRICE
1	List price
2–5	List price less 10 percent
6–10	List price less 20 percent
Over 10	List price less 25 percent

promotional allowances. **Trade-ins** are often used in the sale of durable goods such as cars. They permit a reduction without altering the basic list price by deducting from the item's price an amount for the customer's old item that is being replaced.

Promotional allowances are extra discounts offered to retailers so that they will advertise the manufacturer along with the retailer. They are attempts to integrate promotional strategy in the channel. For example, manufacturers often provide advertising and sales-support allowances for other channel members. Many manufacturers offer such allowances to retail dealers.

Rebates are refunds by the seller of a portion of the purchase price. They have been used most prominently by car manufacturers eager to move models during periods of slow sales. Manufacturers' rebates are sometimes used to stimulate sales of small appliances such as coffeemakers or hair dryers. Manufacturers' rebate coupons are placed in the retail outlets near the product being promoted.

trade-in
Deduction from an item's price of an amount for the customer's old item that is being replaced.

promotional allowance
Extra discount offered to retailers so that they will advertise the manufacturer along with the retailer.

rebate
Refund by the seller of a portion of the purchase price.

Geographic Considerations

Geographic considerations are important in pricing when the shipment of heavy, bulky, low unit-cost materials is involved. Prices may be quoted with either the buyer or the seller paying all transportation charges or with some type of expense sharing.

A firm's competitiveness often depends on how it handles the costs of transportation. In the extreme case, where the cost of transportation is high compared with the value of the product (e.g., cement), the competitive limits of a firm's territory can easily be defined. In cases where product margins are high or transportation costs are low, market coverage can be extensive. Furthermore, the more differentiated the product, the easier it is for a company to pass along the costs of distribution in the price.

The seller has several alternatives in handling transportation costs. These are FOB plant, uniform delivered price, and zone pricing.

FOB plant or *FOB origin* pricing provides a price that does not include any shipping charges. The buyer must pay all the freight charges. The seller pays only the cost of loading the merchandising aboard the carrier selected by the

FOB plant
The buyer must pay all the freight charges.

Usually promotional prices are set to attract new customers. This *Canadian Business* magazine promotion offers new subscribers such things as two free issues and $5 off the basic subscription rate.

buyer. The abbreviation FOB[13] means *free on board.* Legal title and responsibility pass to the buyer once the purchase is loaded and a receipt is obtained from the representative of the common carrier.

Prices may also be shown as FOB origin—freight allowed. The seller permits the buyer to subtract transportation expenses from the bill. The amount the seller receives varies with the freight charges charged against the invoice. This alternative, called **freight absorption**, is commonly used by firms with high fixed costs (who need to maintain high volume) because it permits a considerable expansion of their market, since a competitive price is quoted regardless of shipping expenses.

freight absorption
The seller permits the buyer to subtract transportation expenses from the bill.

The same price (including transportation expenses) is quoted to all buyers when a **uniform delivered price** is the firm's policy. Such pricing is the exact opposite of FOB prices. This system is often compared with pricing a first-class letter, which is the same across the country. Hence, it is sometimes called *postage-stamp pricing*. The price that is quoted includes an *average* transportation charge per customer, which means that distant customers are actually paying a lesser share of selling costs, while customers near the supply source pay what is known as *phantom freight* (the average transportation charge exceeds the actual cost of shipping).

uniform delivered price
The same price (including transportation expenses) is quoted to all buyers.

In **zone pricing**, which is simply a modification of a uniform delivered pricing system, the market is divided into different zones and a price is established within each. Canadian parcel post rates depend on zone pricing. The primary advantage of this pricing policy is that it is easy to administer and enables the seller to be more competitive in distant markets. Figure 14.3 shows how a marketer in Winnipeg must divide its market into geographic segments. All customers in zone 1 are charged $10 per unit of freight, while more distant customers pay freight costs based on the zone in which they are located.

zone pricing
The market is divided into different zones and a price is established within each.

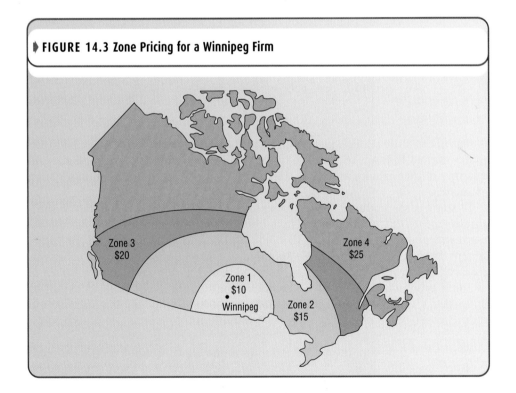

▶ **FIGURE 14.3 Zone Pricing for a Winnipeg Firm**

Zone 3
$20

Zone 4
$25

Zone 1
$10
•
Winnipeg

Zone 2
$15

▶NEGOTIATED PRICES AND COMPETITIVE BIDDING

Many situations that involve government and business procurement are not characterized by set prices, particularly for nonrecurring purchases such as a defence system for the armed forces. Markets such as these are growing at a fast pace. Governmental units now spend nearly half of Canada's GDP!

competitive bidding
A process by which buyers request potential suppliers to make price quotations on a proposed purchase or contract.

Competitive bidding is a process by which buyers request potential suppliers to make price quotations on a proposed purchase or contract. **Specifications** give a specific description of the needed item or job that the government or industrial firm wishes to acquire. One of the most important tasks in modern purchasing management is to describe adequately what the organization seeks to buy. This generally requires the assistance of the firm's technical personnel, such as engineers, designers, and chemists.

specifications
A specific description of a needed item or job that the buyer wishes to acquire.

Competitive bidding strategy should employ the concept of *expected net profit,* which can be stated as

$$\text{Expected Net Profit} = \text{P (Bid} - \text{Costs)}$$

where P = the probability of the buyer accepting the bid.

Consider the following example. A firm is contemplating submitting a bid for a job that is estimated to cost $23 000. One executive has proposed a bid of $60 000, another, $50 000. It is estimated that there is a 40 percent chance of the buyer accepting bid 1 ($60 000) and a 60 percent chance of the buyer accepting bid 2 ($50 000). The expected net profit formula indicates that bid 2 would be best, since its expected net profit is the higher of the two.

Bid 1   ENP = 0.40 ($60 000 – $23 000)
              = 0.40 ($37 000)
              = $14 800

Bid 2   ENP = 0.60 ($50 000 – $23 000)
              = 0.60 ($27 000)
              = $16 200

The most difficult task in applying this concept is estimating the likelihood that a certain bid will be accepted. But this is not a valid reason for failing to quantify one's estimate. Prior experience often provides the foundation for such estimates.

negotiated contract
The terms of the contract are set through talks between the buyer and the seller.

In some cases, industrial and governmental purchasers use **negotiated contracts** instead of inviting competitive bidding for a project. In these situations, the terms of the contract are set through talks between the buyer and the seller. Where there is only one available supplier, or where contracts require extensive research and development work, negotiated contracts are likely to be employed.

Some provincial and local governments permit their agencies to negotiate purchases under a certain limit, say $500 or $1000. This policy is an attempt to reduce costs, since obtaining bids for relatively minor purchases is expensive and there is little prospect of large savings to the agency involved.

escalator clause
Allows the seller to adjust the final price based on changes in the costs of the product's ingredients between the placement of the order and the completion of construction or delivery of the product.

In times of inflation, the fear that inflation may have unknown effects on the economic viability of prices has become a major deterrent to companies bidding for or negotiating contracts that take some time to implement. One response has been to include an **escalator clause**[14] that allows the seller to adjust the final price based on changes in the costs of the product's ingredients between the placement of the order and the completion of construction or delivery of the product. Such clauses typically base the adjustment calculation on commodity indices, the cost-of-living index, or a similar indicator. While an estimated one-third of all business-to-business marketers use escalator clauses in some of their bids, these clauses are most commonly used with major projects that involve long time periods and complex operations.

International pricing takes all of the foregoing into consideration, as appropriate, but requires additional considerations: exchange risk, price escalation through multiplication of channels, and transportation.

Suppose, after looking at costs and exchange rates, you agree to sell your product for 30 000 rubles to a company in Russia and to deliver it in six months. You could lose a great deal of money if the value of the ruble should fall — say, by 25 percent. In this case, the buyer would pay the amount of rubles agreed to, but you would receive only 75 percent of the value you expected. This is known as **exchange risk**. One way of avoiding this risk is to negotiate the price to be paid in Canadian dollars or some other stable currency. There are several other ways of compensating for this risk, which are beyond the scope of this book.

Selling internationally often requires additional channel members to handle the product in another country, resulting **price escalation**. If customary margins are given to all channel members, the market price can escalate beyond what is acceptable to final customers. Thus the international marketer must rethink its expected markup and negotiate lower margins with channel members.

Shipping products overseas may be a significant additional cost for many products. As with price escalation, the international marketer cannot just simply add on the increased transportation costs. Innovative solutions to reducing transportation costs and a willingness to absorb some of these costs may be necessary in order to come up with a price that is acceptable in an international setting.

international pricing
Setting prices to be charged to buyers in other countries taking into consideration exchange risk, price escalation through multiplication of channels, and transportation.

exchange risk
The risk of negotiating a price in another nation's currency and finding upon delivery of the product that the currency's value has dropped in relation to your country's currency.

price escalation
The increase in final price in a foreign market over a domestic price because of having to pay for the services of additional channel members to get the product to that market.

▶THE TRANSFER PRICING PROBLEM

One pricing problem that is peculiar to large-scale enterprises is that of determining an internal **transfer price** — the price for sending goods from one company profit centre to another. As a company expands, it usually needs to decentralize management. **Profit centres** are then set up as a control device in the new decentralized operation. Profit centres are any part of the organization to which revenue and controllable costs can be assigned, such as a department.

In large companies, the centres can secure many of their resource requirements from within the corporate structure. The pricing problem becomes what rate Profit Centre A (maintenance department) should charge Profit Centre B (sales department) for the cleaning compound used on B's floors. Should the price be the same as it would be if A did the work for an outside party? Should B receive a discount? The answer to these questions depends on the philosophy of the firm involved.

The transfer pricing dilemma is an example of the variations that a firm's pricing policy must deal with. Consider the case of UDC-Europe, a Universal Data Corporation subsidiary that itself has ten subsidiaries. Each of the ten is organized on a geographic basis, and each is treated as a separate profit centre. Intercompany transfer prices are set at the annual budget meeting. Special situations, like unexpected volume, are handled through negotiations by the subsidiary managers. If complex tax problems arise, UDC-Europe's top management may set the transfer price.

transfer price
The price for sending goods from one company profit centre to another.

profit centre
Any part of the organization to which revenue and controllable costs can be assigned, such as a department.

▶ PRICING IN THE PUBLIC SECTOR

Pricing public services has also become an interesting, and sometimes controversial, aspect of contemporary marketing. A good example is the price of tuition for college and university courses. Students have watched with alarm as tuition has risen significantly across Canada in the past several years. They fear that a postsecondary education will become unaffordable. At the same time, though, some commentators argue that tuition has in fact been too low.

Traditionally, government services either were very low-cost or were priced using the full-cost approach: users paid all the costs associated with the service. In some cases there have been attempts to set prices using incremental or marginal pricing, which considers only those expenses specifically associated with a particular activity. However, it is often difficult to determine the costs that should be assigned to a particular activity or service. Governmental accounting problems are often more complex than those of private enterprise.

Another problem in pricing public services is that taxes act as an *indirect* price of a public service. Someone must decide the relative relationship between the direct and indirect prices of such a service. A shift toward indirect tax charges (where an income or earnings tax exists) is generally a movement toward charging on the *ability to pay* rather than on the *use* principle.

The pricing of any public service involves a basic policy decision as to whether the price is an instrument to recover costs or a technique for accomplishing some other social or civic objective. For example, public health services may be priced near zero so as to encourage their use. On the other hand, parking fines in some cities are high so as to discourage the use of private cars in the central business district. Pricing decisions in the public sector are difficult because political and social considerations often outweigh the economic aspects. As governments have cut services or transferred them to the private sector, the pricing problem has been simplified somewhat as tax and public policy considerations have been largely eliminated.

▶ SUMMARY

A pricing policy is a general guideline based on pricing objectives that is intended for use in specific pricing decisions. Pricing policies affect the price structure and provide focus in dealing with varied competitive situations.

A skimming policy chooses a high entry price for a new product. A penetration policy chooses a low entry price. Penetration pricing is likely to be used in instances where demand for a new product or service is highly elastic and large numbers of consumers are price-sensitive.

A company's long-term price can be set at, above, or below competition, depending on the rest of the company's marketing mix.

Price lining is the practice of marketing merchandise at a limited number of prices. Psychological pricing is the use of prices to suggest values of a product or attributes of a product/price offering.

Arriving at a final price involves considering a number of other prices and price practices, including market price, cash discounts, trade discounts, and quantity discounts. Price escalation can be an important consideration in long-term contracts. Another set of terms, related to geographical considerations, are FOB plant, freight absorption, uniform delivered price, and zone pricing.

In international marketing, some important additional considerations that affect pricing are exchange risk, price escalation, and transportation.

Pricing in the public sector is complex, because different constituencies with conflicting wishes and needs are often involved.

▶ KEY TERMS

cash discount	price structure
competitive bidding	pricing policy
escalator clause	profit centre
exchange risk	promotional allowance
flexible pricing	promotional price
FOB plant	psychological pricing
freight absorption	quantity discount
international pricing	rebate
list price	skimming pricing
loss leader	specifications
market price	trade discount
negotiated contract	trade-in
odd pricing	transfer price
penetration pricing	uniform delivered price
price escalation	unit pricing
price limits	zone pricing
price lining	

▶ INTERACTIVE SUMMARY AND DISCUSSION QUESTIONS

1. A pricing policy is a general guideline based on pricing objectives that is intended for use in specific pricing decisions. Pricing policies affect the price structure. Give an example of the price structure of a product you are familiar with. What is the likely pricing policy for that product?

2. Pricing policies provide focus in dealing with varied competitive situations. Explain why it is very important to have a pricing policy in such situations.

3. A skimming policy chooses a high entry price. Explain the reasons why a business might choose such a policy. What are the potential disadvantages?

4. Penetration pricing is the opposite policy to a skimming policy in new-product pricing. Explain the reasons why a business might choose penetration pricing. What are the potential disadvantages?

5. Penetration pricing is likely to be used in instances where demand for a new product or service is highly elastic and large numbers of consumers are highly price-sensitive. Explain.

6. A business might set prices relatively higher than those of most competitors. Give an example of such a business, and explain why this might be a good strategy.

7. Price lining is the practice of marketing merchandise at a limited number of prices. In what circumstances is such a practice desirable? Why?

8. Psychological pricing is the use of prices to suggest values of a product or attributes of a product/price offering. Make a list of as many different examples of psychological pricing as you can think of.

9. Behind a list price quotation is a number of other prices and price practices, such as market price, cash discounts, trade discounts, and quantity discounts. Explain each in relation to the list price.

10. Another set of terms related to geographic considerations are FOB plant, freight absorption, uniform delivered price, and zone pricing. Explain each term.

11. In international marketing, some important additional considerations that affect pricing are exchange risk, price escalation, and transportation. Explain how each of these can affect the final realized price.

12. Pricing in the public sector is complex, because different objectives and motives are often involved. Describe how this applies in pricing postsecondary tuition.

13. From time to time, marketers of gasoline are criticized for raising the price of gas almost simultaneously (suggesting collusion) and raising prices seemingly independent of the cost of oil.

    a. Based on your readings, including this chapter, are these accusations justified?

    b. Using the Web, research the literature and government investigations of gasoline pricing practices. What conclusions have been drawn with respect to these issues?

To obtain a list of further readings for Chapter 14, please refer to the *Foundations of Marketing* Web site.

Part 6
Distribution

Part 6 deals with the third element of the marketing mix, the activities and institutions involved in moving products and services to the firm's chosen target market. Topics such as retailing may at first seem very familiar to you, but retailing takes on many different forms and can be quite complex. Much knowledge and strategic planning are required to move products through the various channels efficiently and competitively.

Chapter 15 introduces the basic concepts related to channels of distribution and outlines the functions of wholesaling, which is often the first channel intermediary. Chapter 16 discusses the many aspects of retailing, commonly considered to be the next channel intermediary. Chapter 17 introduces the concepts of logistics and supply chain management. This process of managing and implementing the physical movement of products from source to place of use is the essential linking function of the distribution system.

▶ **Chapter 15**
Channel and Distribution Strategy

▶ **Chapter 16**
Retailing

▶ **Chapter 17**
Logistics and Supply Chain Management

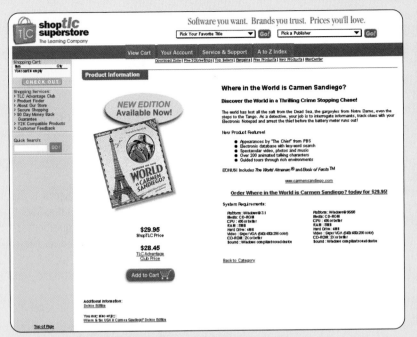

Lessons in distribution from Learning Co.: take advantage of the Internet, and be willing to continually evaluate and modify your distribution methods.

Chapter 15
Channel and Distribution Strategy

Distribution is crucial in the software business, so Learning Co. is making sure it has all the bases covered. The Cambridge, Mass., company headed by Canadians is focusing its efforts squarely on the Internet as the next way to sell its educational and entertainment software. This strategy is aimed at complementing its position as one of the top software vendors in the competitive retail market. "Five years from now, parents and children will be able to turn on some kind of device that connects to the Internet to access what we have today—the best collection of education brands in the world," says Michael Perik, Learning Co.'s 40-year-old chief executive officer. With Montreal-born Kevin O'Leary, who is president of the company, Mr. Perik has helped Learning Co.'s sales jump to $392.4-million (U.S.) in 1997 from about $22-million in 1994 when it was known as SoftKey International Inc. of Toronto.

While Learning Co. wants to be at the forefront of electronic commerce, the market is still in its infancy. A major stumbling block is that many consumers remain reluctant to purchase products on-line out of fear of transmitting their credit card numbers. Nevertheless, Mr. Perik says the company is confident the Internet will boost the software market by offering consumers another buying vehicle.

Learning Co.'s proposed Internet strategy has two distinct components. The first step is to use the Internet as a tool to unlock software stored on a CD-ROM. A consumer who buys a Learning Co. software title at a store could receive additional programs by going to the company's Web site and purchasing the required code to unlock more applications on the CD-ROM.

"We sell millions of CD-ROMs," says Mr. O'Leary, 44. "The beauty of this strategy is rather than making money in five years, we are talking about doing it in the first quarter of next year."

> ▶ **CHAPTER OBJECTIVES**
> After reading and studying this chapter, you should be able to
>
> 1. Discuss channel strategy as one of the elements of the marketing mix.
> 2. Relate channel strategy to the concept of total customer satisfaction.
> 3. Explain the role of distribution channels in marketing strategy.
> 4. Describe the various types of channels of distribution.
> 5. Outline the major strategy alternatives in using marketing channels.
> 6. Identify the conditions under which a manufacturer is likely to assume wholesaling functions rather than use independents.
> 7. Distinguish among merchant wholesalers, agents, and brokers.
> 8. Identify the major types of merchant wholesalers and instances in which each type might be used.
> 9. Provide an overview of the many types of wholesaling intermediaries and their functions.
> 10. Describe conflict and cooperation in the distribution channel.
> 11. Explain the issues involved in changing from the use of one channel intermediary type to a different type.

www.learningco.com

Steven Dube, an analyst with Wasserstein Perella Securities, says Learning Co.'s Internet strategy has potential but the company's bread and butter is still the retail sector, where it has a high profile and strong relationships with the biggest U.S. and Canadian merchants. Learning Co. scored a major coup when it signed an agreement to directly supply Wal-Mart Stores Inc. with its software titles. The deal is expected to reduce Learning Co.'s distribution costs and increase its sales to the world's largest retailer.

"I think Learning Co. and a lot of other people are spending money just exploring and experimenting on the Internet," Mr. Dube says. "They have a very good Web page but I think it's a little premature." A far more important issue for Learning Co., he says, is cementing and enhancing its exposure with mega-retailers such as Wal-Mart and Dallas-based CompUSA Inc., which are knocking smaller rivals out of the market.

One of Learning Co.'s biggest weapons to attack either the Internet or the retail sector is the depth of its product portfolio. Its software—including the popular ReaderRabbit, Sesame Street, and National Geographic titles—has mostly been built through a series of major acquisitions. In one year SoftKey, the Toronto-based company that bought Learning Co. and adopted its name, spent more than $1-billion on acquisitions. "Content is so important in the Internet model," Mr. Perik says. "We made a big bet on that three years ago. Regardless of what the technology or model, owning the content is always a major part of the equation."

Mr. O'Leary started SoftKey as a software distributor in 1983. Analysts expected it to penetrate the $1-billion revenue barrier in the year 2000.

Learning Co.'s willingness to continually evaluate and modify its distribution methods is a very good example for marketers. The company started as a distributor, then acquired products that it distributed through traditional retail channels. It saw the potential of distribution through the Internet, but at the same time continued to make major breakthroughs into giant retailers such as Wal-Mart. It has thus developed an array of options that should continue to provide excellent exposure for and availability of its products.

Experienced marketers know that achieving good distribution for goods and services is one of the most challenging aspects of implementing marketing strategy. There are many options, and the system is quite complex.

Source: Adapted from Mark Evans, "Learning Co. Takes an Internet Course," *The Globe and Mail* (July 22, 1998), p. B25. Reprinted with permission from *The Globe and Mail.*

▶ INTRODUCTION

In Australia, Garry Jones formed a company to produce and market a line of high-class cosmetics for women and men. Where should they be sold? It was not hard to decide that they should be distributed through high-class department stores and cosmetic stores. Jones then bought a company that produced a standard-quality line of cosmetics. The natural distribution outlets for this line were mass marketers such as supermarkets.

How do you get these retailers to carry such products, and how do you distribute these products? Jones could have tried to send salespeople to each outlet and then established a fleet of trucks to deliver the products. However, he knew that a much more efficient system was already available. This was the system of intermediaries (middlemen), such as agents and wholesalers, that would perform the functions of selling, storing, financing, and delivering for him. Such marketing functions always have to be performed, but there is often a choice as to who performs them.

Remarkably, adding more intermediaries to the distribution channel can make distribution more efficient than selling direct. As Figure 15.1 indicates, the number of transactions between manufacturers and their customers is markedly reduced by introducing a wholesaler or retailer.

▶ **FIGURE 15.1 Achieving Transaction Economy with Wholesaling Intermediaries**

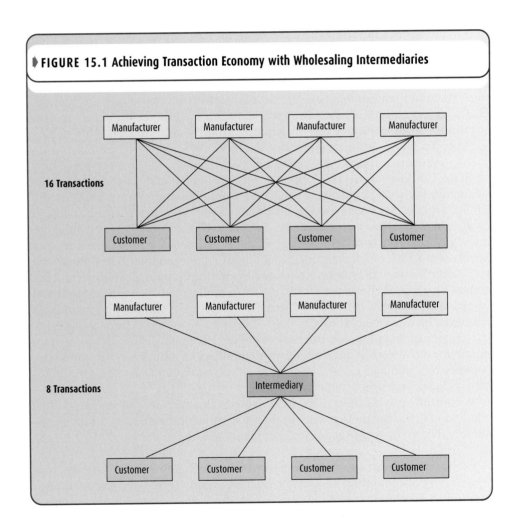

You can have a great product and a great price, but you will fail unless you have worked out a good channel of distribution strategy that is suited to the nature and value of your product.

In Chapter 1 we saw that marketing creates several types of utility. Marketing channels create time, place, and ownership utility in a direct way. Let's take the example of swimwear. Products for the coming spring and summer have already been produced in the months of December and January, and are en route to retail stores throughout the continent. Information from the marketing department has allowed swimwear manufacturers to identify preferences for new colours, styles, and fabrics and to produce products of the highest quality for each market. However, swimwear of even the highest quality will fail to generate adequate sales unless it is delivered to the right place (place utility), at the right time (time utility), and with appropriate legal requirements (ownership utility). Swimwear that meets consumers' quality expectations, is available in the appropriate outlet the first warm day in April, and is accompanied by a sales receipt indicating ownership will be able to provide buyers with form, time, place, and ownership utility — and a little later they'll slip it on, tiptoe across a sunny beach, and dip a pale toe into the chilly water.

A manufacturer of swimwear must therefore work out a clear channel strategy in order for the entire distribution process to work. Let us now consider basic channel strategy as the starting point for a discussion of the distribution function and its role in the marketing mix. An underlying consideration is providing total customer satisfaction. More North American organizations are learning that such an emphasis has a tremendous influence on performance, as measured by cost or customer responsiveness. Products are produced that possess superior technical features and meet the needs and wants of customers, and reach customers through distribution channels.

Carson luggage is made in Ottawa, Staedtler pens and erasers come from Germany, plywood is produced in British Columbia and other provinces, and Timex watches are assembled in Toronto. All are sold throughout Canada. In each case, some method must be devised to bridge the gap between producer and consumer that was discussed in Chapter 1. Distribution channels provide purchasers with a convenient means of obtaining the products that they wish to buy. **Distribution channels** (also called marketing channels) are the paths that goods—and title to these goods — follow from producer to consumer.[1] Specifically, the term *channels* refers to the various marketing institutions and the interrelationships responsible for the flow of goods and services from producer to consumer or industrial user. Intermediaries are the marketing institutions in the distribution channel. A **marketing intermediary** is a business firm operating between the producer and the consumer or business purchaser. The term therefore includes both wholesalers and retailers.

Wholesaling is the activities of intermediaries who sell to retailers, other wholesalers, and business users but not in significant amounts to ultimate consumers. The terms *jobber* and *distributor* are considered synonymous with wholesaler in this book.

Confusion can result from the practices of some firms that operate both wholesaling and retailing operations. Sporting goods stores, for example, often maintain a wholesaling operation in marketing a line of goods to high schools and colleges as well as operating retail stores. For the purpose of this book, we will treat such operations as two separate institutions.

A second source of confusion is the misleading practice of some retailers who claim to be wholesalers. Such stores may actually sell at wholesale prices and can validly claim to do so. However, stores that sell products purchased by individuals for their own use and not for resale are by definition **retailers**, not wholesalers.

distribution channels
The paths that goods—and title to these goods—follow from producer to consumer.

marketing intermediary
A business firm operating between the producer and the consumer or business purchaser.

wholesaling
The activities of intermediaries who sell to retailers, other wholesalers, and business users but not in significant amounts to ultimate consumers.

retailer
A store that sells products purchased by individuals for their own use and not for resale.

▶ THE ROLE OF DISTRIBUTION CHANNELS IN MARKETING STRATEGY

Distribution channels play a key role in marketing strategy, since they provide the means by which goods and services are conveyed from their producers to consumers and users. The importance of distribution channels can be explained in terms of the utility that is created and the functions that are performed.

Distribution Channels Perform Important Functions

The distribution channel performs several functions in the overall marketing system.[2] These include facilitating the exchange process, sorting to alleviate discrepancies in assortment, standardizing transactions, holding inventories, assisting in the search process, and transporting materials and finished products.[3]

FACILITATING THE EXCHANGE PROCESS

The evolution of distribution channels began with the exchange process described in Chapter 1. As market economies grew, the exchange process itself became complicated. With more producers and more potential buyers, intermediaries came into existence to facilitate transactions by cutting down the number of marketplace contacts. For example, if ten orchards in the Okanagan valley each sell to six supermarket chains, there are a total of 60 transactions. If the producers set up and market their apples through a cooperative, the number of contacts declines to 16 (see Figure 15.1).

SORTING TO ALLEVIATE IMBALANCES BETWEEN OUTPUTS AND CONSUMER NEEDS

For economic reasons, a producer tends to maximize the quantity of a limited line of products (limited assortment). For example, one manufacturer may produce 10000 each of a limited line of golf balls. On the other hand, the buyer needs a minimum quantity of a wide selection of alternatives (an assortment of twelve golf balls, one pair of shoes, and one golf jacket). Thus, there is a discrepancy between what one producer has to offer and what the consumers want. **Sorting** is the process that alleviates discrepancies in assortment by reallocating the outputs of various producers into assortments desired by individual purchasers. This is handled by an intermediary such as a wholesaler or retailer that buys large quantities of different goods from several suppliers, and then makes available a customized assortment to fit the needs of its customers.

> **sorting**
> The process that alleviates discrepancies in assortment by reallocating the outputs of various producers into assortments desired by individual purchasers.

Figure 15.2 shows an example of the sorting process. First, an individual producer's output is divided into separate homogeneous categories such as the various types and grades of apples. These apples are then combined with the similar crops of other orchards, a process known as *accumulation*. These accumulations are broken down into smaller units or divisions, such as crates of apples. This is often called *breaking bulk* in marketing literature. Finally, an assortment is built for the next level in the distribution channel. For example, the Okanagan cooperative might prepare an assortment of five crates of Golden Delicious and six crates of Red Jonathan apples for Superstore supermarket in Saskatoon.

▶FIGURE 15.2 The Sorting Process

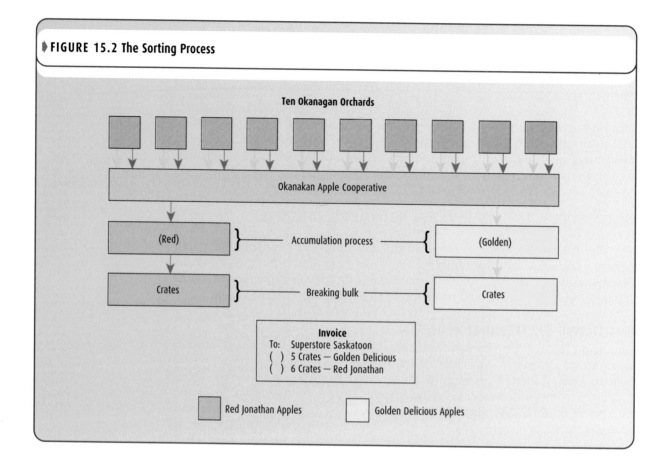

STANDARDIZING TRANSACTIONS

If each transaction in a complex market economy were subject to negotiation, the exchange process would be chaotic. Distribution channels standardize exchange transactions in terms of the product, such as grading of apples into types and grades, and the transfer process itself. Order points, prices, payment terms, delivery schedules, and purchase lots tend to be standardized by distribution channel members. For example, supermarket buyers probably have on-line communications links with the cooperative cited in Figure 15.2. Once a certain stock position is reached, more apples would automatically be ordered from either the cooperative's current output or its cold storage.

HOLDING INVENTORIES

Distribution channel members hold a minimum of inventories to take advantage of economies of scale in transporting and to provide a buffer for small changes in demand. This also makes products available to meet changing consumer demand.

ASSISTING THE SEARCH PROCESS

Distribution channels also accommodate the search behaviour of both buyers and sellers. (Search behaviour was discussed earlier in Chapter 8.) Buyers are searching for specific products and services to fill their needs, while sellers are attempting to find what consumers want. A college student looking for some Golden Delicious apples might go to the fruit section of the Superstore in Saskatoon. Similarly, the manager of that department would be able to provide the Okanagan cooperative with information about sales trends in his or her marketplace.

TRANSPORTING MATERIALS AND PRODUCTS

Storing products in convenient locations for shipment to wholesale and retail establishments allows firms to embody time utility in the product. Place utility is created primarily by transporting the product. Customer satisfaction depends heavily on the reliable movement of products to ensure their availability. Eastman Kodak Company committed a major blunder in the late 1970s when it launched a multimillion-dollar advertising campaign for its new instant camera before adequate quantities had been delivered to retail outlets. Many would-be purchasers visited the stores and, when they discovered that the new camera was not available, bought a Polaroid instead. By providing consumers with time and place utility, physical distribution contributes to implementing the marketing concept.

▶ TYPES OF DISTRIBUTION

There are four main types of distribution channel: direct, one-step, two-step, and multistep. However, no one marketing channel is superior to all others. The "best" channel for Electrolux vacuum cleaners may be direct from manufacturer to consumer through a sales force of 1000 men and women. The "best" channel for frozen french fries may be from food processor to agent intermediary to merchant wholesaler (a wholesaler who takes title) to supermarket to consumer. The marketing manager must therefore analyze alternative channels in the light of consumer needs and competitive restraints to determine the best channel or channels for the firm's products.

Even when the proper channels have been chosen and established, the marketing manager's channel decisions are not over. Channels, like so many of the other marketing variables, change, and today's ideal channel may prove less effective in a few years.

For example, the typical channel for books has been from publisher/producer to local bookstore and department store. Now the smaller stores are being supplanted by superstores such as Chapters, McNally Robinson, Indigo, and others that carry an extensive range of books plus videos, CDs, and a coffee bar. In addition, books are now widely available through the Internet from such suppliers as Amazon.com and the Internet arm of the likes of Indigo.

Figure 15.3 depicts the major channels available for marketers of consumer and business goods. In general, business goods channels tend to be shorter than consumer goods channels because of geographic concentrations of business buyers, a relatively limited number of purchasers, and the absence of retailers from the chain. The term *retailer* refers to the supplier of consumer goods. Service channels also tend to be short because of the intangibility of services and the need to maintain personal relationships in the channel.

www.chapters.ca

www.mcnallyrobinson.com

www.indigo.ca

▶ **FIGURE 15.3 Alternative Distribution Channels**

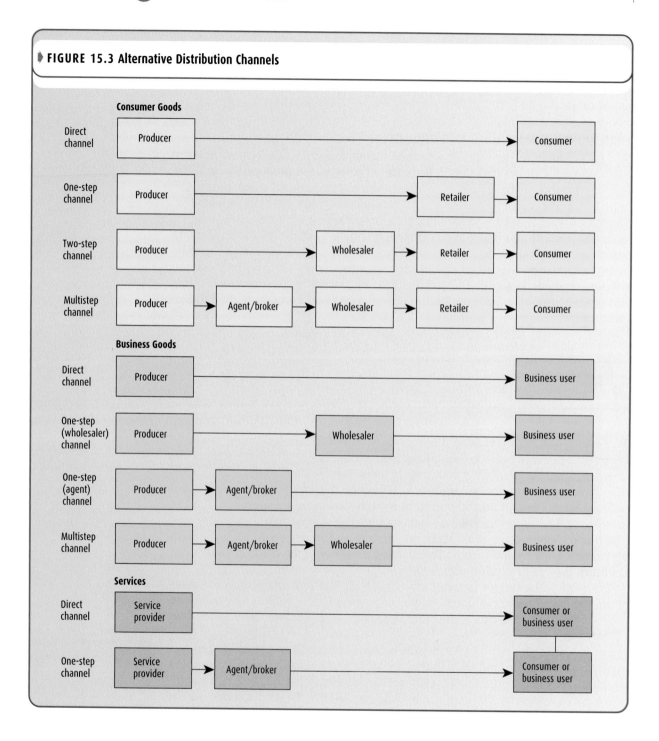

Direct Channel

The simplest, most direct marketing channel is not necessarily the best, as is indicated by the relatively small percentage of the dollar volume of sales that moves directly *from the producer to the consumer.* Less than 5 percent of all consumer goods are candidates for the producer-to-consumer channel. Dairies, Tupperware, Avon cosmetics, and newspapers are examples of firms whose product moves directly from manufacturer to ultimate consumer. Some products, such as milk, are distributed through retail channels as well. The use of multiple channels is quite common for many products. As the use of the Internet increases, the direct channel will likely become a powerful additional channel. For example, since Dell has been so successful in selling computers directly to consumers both through media advertising and through the Internet, Compaq and others have decided that they too will sell directly to customers. Another company offers a bonus of free software for orders placed through the Internet.

Direct channels are much more important in the business goods market, where most major installations and accessory equipment—and many of the fabricated parts and raw materials—are marketed through direct contacts between producer and user.

www.tupperware.com

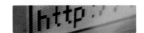

avon.avon.com

The Toronto Star has the largest readership of any newspaper in Canada. It reaches its audience directly via subscription and through one-step channels like convenience stores.

One-Step Channel (Consumer Goods)

www.costco.com/home.asp

This channel is being used more and more, and in many instances it has taken the place of the traditional channel. When large retailers are involved, they are willing to take on many functions performed by the wholesaler—consequently, goods move *from producer to retailer to consumer*. Costco is a good example. It buys in bulk from the producer and sells to individual customers and business customers. No wholesaler has to be involved. A unique aspect of Costco is that is also acts as a wholesaler. It sells to small retailers who in turn sell to final customers. The system works because these small retailers offer the products at a more convenient time and location.

Two-Step Channel (Consumer)

The traditional marketing channel for consumer goods is *from producer to wholesaler to retailer to user*. It is the method used by literally thousands of small manufacturers or companies producing limited lines of products and by as many or more small retailers. Small companies with limited financial resources use wholesalers as immediate sources of funds through their bulk purchases, and as a marketing arm to reach the hundreds of retailers who will stock their products. Smaller retailers rely on wholesalers as *buying specialists* to ensure a balanced inventory of goods produced in various regions of the world.

The wholesaler's sales force is responsible for reaching the market with the producer's output. Many manufacturers also supplement these efforts with their own sales representatives to call on the retailers to assist in merchandising the line. These representatives serve the manufacturer as sources of influence and market information, but will generally not make the sales transaction. If they initiate a sale, they give it to a wholesaler to complete. They are known as *missionary sales representatives*.

Multistep Channel (Consumer)

agent
A wholesaling intermediary that differs from the typical wholesaler in that the agent does not take title to the goods.

The longest channel is *from producer to agent to wholesaler to retailer to consumer*. Where products are produced by a large number of small companies, a unique intermediary—the agent, or broker—appears to perform the basic function of bringing buyer and seller together. **Agents** are, in fact, wholesaling intermediaries, but they differ from the typical wholesaler in that they *do not take title to the goods*.

Agents, merely represent the producer or the regular wholesaler (who does take title to the goods) in seeking a market for the producer's output or in locating a source of supply for the buyer. Say a canner of vegetables in Ontario has 6000 cases of string beans to sell. The firm informs the food brokers (agents) regularly used in various provinces of this fact. A broker in the Maritimes ascertains that the Maritime supermarket chain Sobey's will buy 800 cases. The broker takes the order, informs the canner, and, if the price is acceptable, the canner ships the order to Sobey's. The canner bills Sobey's and sends a commission

▸ THE PRACTISING MARKETER

In a Global Setting

Dell Computer Corp.'s innovative direct sales strategy has taken root in China, paving the way for the company to win a piece of the country's booming personal computer market.

Mr. Michael Dell, company founder, said, "We're implementing the business model that we have used all around the world here in China." Since its founding in 1984, Dell has outstripped established computer rivals IBM Corp. and Compaq Corp. in total U.S. sales by selling custom-built machines direct to the consumer. Now the company hopes to sink its teeth into China, where personal computer sales are expected to exceed 10-million by 2000.

Grounding the effort is a modern production plant in the southeastern port city of Xiamen. "We have since August been delivering machines with a five-day or seven-day lead time, in a custom-configured fashion," he said. With a manufacturing and sales force of 300 people in nine Chinese cities, Dell has replicated its strategy of targeting multinational corporations and government enterprises as prime customers.

"When you get out to the year 2000 or so, 1 percent market share in the China PC industry is about $250-million worth of business," said John Legere, Dell's Asia-Pacific president. Mr. Legere noted that current China sales, which he estimated at $100-million (U.S.) in 1998, were only a fraction of the company's global earnings. "[Nevertheless] we're confident that over the next five years we will see growth rates compound in excess of 100 percent," he said.

A significant portion of Dell's international sales are made over the telephone or Internet, but Mr. Legere said China's market was not yet ripe for such methods. "China has a relatively immature Internet structure, so the great success that Dell has around the world, which is about $6-million a day in Internet sales, will take time," Mr. Legere said. As part of its market push, Dell is also setting its sights on Legend Corp., among China's best recognized computer brand names.

Company officials said Dell would beat local competition by offering top-notch technical support and moving its custom-built machines off the assembly lines in days, rather than weeks.

Explain how a direct channel strategy might be particularly useful in a developing market.

Source: Adapted from "Dell Computer Takes Its Direct Sales Tactics to Growing Chinese Market," *Financial Post* (November 3, 1998), p. C17. Copyright Reuters Limited 1999.

www.dell.com

---

cheque (approximately 3 percent of the sale price) to the food broker for the service of bringing buyer and seller together.

Multistep Channel (Business Goods)

This channel consists of *producer to agent to wholesaler to industrial user.* Similar conditions often exist in the business market, where small producers often use a channel to market their offerings. The agent wholesaling intermediary, often called a manufacturer's representative or manufacturer's agent, is a company that provides an independent sales force for contacting large, scattered wholesalers and some key business buyers. For example, a manufacturer of specialty industrial tapes might use agents to sell to industrial wholesalers and to encourage the wholesaler's sales force to push the product to business users.

One-Step (Agent) Channel (Business)

merchant wholesaler
A wholesaler who takes title to the products carried.

Where the unit sale is small, a **merchant wholesaler** must be used to cover the market economically. By maintaining regional inventories, merchant wholesalers can achieve transportation economies by stockpiling goods and making the final small shipment over a small distance. But where the unit sale is large and transportation costs account for a small percentage of the total product costs, the *producer to agent to business user* channel may be employed. The agent wholesaling intermediaries become, in effect, the company's sales force. For example, a producer of special castings might engage agents who are already calling on potential customers with other lines.

One-Step (Wholesaler) Channel (Business)

industrial distributor
A wholesaler that operates in the business goods market and typically handles small accessory equipment and operating supplies.

Similar characteristics in the business market often lead to the use of wholesalers between the manufacturer and industrial purchaser. The term **industrial distributor** is commonly used in this market to refer to those wholesalers that take title to the goods they handle. These wholesalers are involved in marketing small accessory equipment and operating supplies, such as building supplies, office supplies, small hand tools, and office equipment.

Direct Channel (Services)

Distributing services to both consumers and business users is usually simpler and more direct than for consumer and business goods. In part, this is due to the intangibility of services; the marketer of services does not often have to worry about storage, transportation, and inventory control. Shorter channels, often direct from service provider to consumer or business user, are typically used.

Many services can be performed only on a direct basis, and personal relationships between performers and users are very important. Consumers tend to remain clients of the same bank, car repair shop, or hairstylist as long as they are reasonably satisfied. Likewise, accounting firms and attorneys are retained on a relatively permanent basis by business buyers.

One-Step Channel (Services)

When service providers use marketing intermediaries to reach consumers or business users, these are usually *agents or brokers.* Common examples include insurance agents, securities brokers, travel agents, and entertainment agents.

For instance, travel and hotel packages are sometimes created by intermediaries and then marketed at the retail level by travel agents to both vacationers and firms that want to offer employee incentive awards.

A Special Note on Channel Strategy for Consumer Services

A dominant reason for patronizing many consumer services, such as banks, motels, and car rental agencies, is convenient location. It is absolutely essential to carefully select the retail site. For example, banks locate branches in suburban shopping centres and malls. Automated electronic tellers that enable customers to withdraw funds and make deposits when a bank is closed are a further example of attempting to provide convenience as well as more efficient operations.

Multiple Channels

As mentioned earlier, a common phenomenon is using more than one marketing channel for similar products. These *multiple channels* (or dual distribution) are used when the same product is marketed through several channels as well as both to the ultimate consumer and to business users. Dial soap is distributed through the traditional grocery wholesaler to food stores to the consumer, but a second channel also exists, from the manufacturer to large retail chains and motels that buy direct from the manufacturer. Competition among retailers and other intermediaries that are striving to expand lines, profitability, and customer service has created these multiple channels.

In other cases, the same product is marketed through a variety of types of retail outlets. A basic product such as a paintbrush is carried in inventory by the traditional hardware store; it is also handled by such nontraditional retail outlets as auto accessory stores, building supply outlets, department stores, discount houses, mail-order houses, supermarkets, and variety stores. Each retail store may use a different marketing channel.

Firestone tires are marketed

1. directly to General Motors, where they serve as a fabricated part for new Chevrolets
2. through Firestone stores, company-owned retail outlets
3. through franchised Firestone outlets
4. from the factory to tire jobbers to retail gas stations

Each channel enables the manufacturer to serve a different market.

Reverse Channels

While the traditional concept of marketing channels involves moving products and services from producer to consumer or business user, there is increasing interest in reverse channels. **Reverse channels** are the paths goods follow from consumer to manufacturer or to marketing intermediaries. These channels are normally seen in recycling. For example, metal, paper, and glass are sent back from user to manufacturer for reuse.

reverse channels
The paths goods follow from consumer to manufacturer or to marketing intermediaries.

Reverse channels increase in importance as raw materials become more expensive, and as additional laws are passed to control litter and the disposal of packaging materials such as soft-drink bottles. For recycling to succeed, four basic conditions must be satisfied:

1. A technology must be available that can efficiently process the material being recycled.
2. A market must be available for the end product — the reclaimed material.
3. A substantial and continuing quantity of secondary product (recycled aluminum, reclaimed steel from cars, recycled paper) must be available.

4. A marketing system must be developed that can bridge the gap between suppliers of secondary products and end users on a profitable basis.[4]

In some instances, the reverse channel consists of traditional marketing intermediaries. In the soft-drink industry, retailers and local bottlers perform these functions. In other cases, manufacturers take the initiative by establishing redemption centres. A concentrated attempt by the Reynolds Metals Company in one area permitted the company to recycle an amount of aluminum equivalent to 60 percent of the total containers marketed in the area. Other reverse-channel participants may include community groups, which organize "cleanup" days and develop systems for rechannelling paper products for recycling, and specialized organizations developed for waste disposal and recycling.

REVERSE CHANNELS FOR PRODUCT RECALLS AND REPAIRS

Reverse channels are also used for product recalls and repairs. Ownership of some products (for example, tires) is registered so that proper notification can be sent if there is a product recall. In the case of automobile recalls, owners are advised to have the problem corrected at their dealership. Similarly, reverse channels have been used for repairs to some products. The warranty for a small appliance may specify that if repairs are needed in the first 90 days, the item should be returned to the dealer. After that period, the product should be returned to the factory. Such reverse channels are a vital element of product recalls and repair procedures.

Facilitating Agencies in the Distribution Channel

facilitating agency
An agency that provides specialized assistance for regular channel members (such as producers, wholesalers, and retailers) in moving products from producer to consumer.

A **facilitating agency** provides specialized assistance for regular channel members (such as producers, wholesalers, and retailers) in moving products from producer to consumer. Included in the definition of facilitating agencies are transportation companies, warehousing firms, financial institutions, insurance companies, and marketing research companies.

THE USE OF THE INTERNET IN DISTRIBUTION

The use of the Internet in distribution is growing rapidly. Some products are distributed directly *from manufacturer to consumer,* such as software, music, and computers. But other channel configurations seem to be able make more use of the Internet. This is probably because most producers are not set up to ship directly to the buyer.

The use of the Internet by channel intermediaries is also growing rapidly. This is especially true at the retail level, where everything from books to airline tickets to stocks to bank loans can be obtained through the Internet. This topic will be discussed more extensively in the next chapter.

In business-to-business marketing, suppliers and customers have well-established means of conducting electronic commerce. This can be through the Internet, but it is more likely that they have established other means of direct communication. For example, as components are used by a manufacturer, the supplier is informed electronically, and at a predetermined inventory level the supplier automatically sends components to replenish the manufacturer's inventory.

▶ WHOLESALING

Everyone knows that retailing is an important part of the Canadian economy, but most do not realize that wholesaling is equally important. The total operating revenue of wholesaling is larger than retailing, and wholesale trade as a percentage of GDP is approximately the same (6 percent). Table 15.1 presents a profile of wholesaling and retailing in Canada for selected years. This table also shows the significance of wholesaling in exporting, and also that there are many employment opportunities in wholesaling.

▶ TABLE 15.1 Wholesale and Retail Trade in Canada

YEAR	WHOLESALE TOTAL OPERATING REVENUE (MILLIONS OF CURRENT $)	CANADIAN EXPORTS BY WHOLESALERS (MILLIONS OF CURRENT $)	PERCENTAGE OF WHOLESALE SALES EXPORTED	WHOLESALE TRADE CONTRIBUTION TO GDP (MILLIONS OF CONSTANT $)	WHOLESALE TRADE AS PERCENTAGE OF GDP	EMPLOYMENT IN WHOLESALE TRADE
1985	183560	119474	11.6	21766	5.0	532938
1990	255081	148979	10.8	29819	4.9	631916
1996	351829	275789	10.3	36234	5.4	682582

YEAR	RETAIL TOTAL OPERATING REVENUE (MILLIONS OF CURRENT $)	CONSUMER EXPENDITURES AT RETAIL (MILLIONS OF CURRENT $)	RETAIL TRADE AS PECENTAGE OF CONSUMER EXPENDITURES	RETAIL TRADE CONTRIBUTION TO GDP (MILLIONS OF CONSTANT $)	RETAIL TRADE AS PECENTAGE OF GDP	EMPLOYMENT IN RETAIL TRADE
1985	141346	274100	51.6	27375	6.2	1285004
1990	188160	378933	49.7	31613	6.3	1509944
1996	225537	480956	46.9	38608	5.8	1425194

Source: Statistics Canada, *Wholesaling and Retailing in Canada,* Catalogue No. 63-2361XB, downloaded from http://www.statcan.ca, December 13, 1999. Reproduced by permission of the Minister of Supply and Services Canada.

Wholesalers are more prominent in some distribution channels than others. They are involved in selling to retailers such goods as food, beverages, apparel, and household furnishings. On the other hand, for goods such as metals, machinery and equipment, grain, and petroleum, wholesalers mainly supply industrial and commercial users, farmers, and foreign markets directly. In fact, 65 percent of total wholesale trade activity in Canada does not include retailers.

Wholesaling is the initial marketing institution in many channels of distribution from manufacturers to consumer or business user. Furthermore, there are several different types of wholesaling intermediaries. They are a critical element of the marketing mix of many products. Many intermediaries are also separate business entities with their own marketing mixes. It is essential that a marketer understand this somewhat complex system and the motivations of channel members. With such an understanding, effective competitive channel strategies can be developed. A good starting point is to look at the terminology used in wholesaling.

wholesalers
Wholesaling intermediaries who take title to the products they handle.

Wholesaling involves the activities of people or firms who sell to retailers and other wholesalers or to business users, but not in significant amounts to ultimate consumers. The term **wholesaler** (or merchant wholesaler) is applied only to those wholesaling intermediaries who take title to the products they handle. **Wholesaling intermediaries** (or wholesaling middlemen) is a broader term that describes not only intermediaries who assume title, but also agents and brokers who perform important wholesaling activities without taking title to the products. Under this definition, then, a wholesaler is a *merchant intermediary.*

wholesaling intermediaries
Intermediaries who assume title, as well as agents and brokers who perform important wholesaling activities without taking title to the products.

The route that goods follow on the way to the consumer or business user is actually a chain of marketing institutions—wholesalers and retailers. Only 3 percent of the dollar value of all goods sold to the ultimate consumer are purchased directly from the manufacturer. The bulk of all products sold passes through these marketing institutions.

A common consumer complaint is that prices are too high. The finger of guilt is often pointed at wholesalers and retailers, the intermediaries who allegedly drive prices up by taking "high profits." Discount outlets such as Costco often claim that their prices are lower since they buy direct and eliminate the intermediaries and their profits. Chain stores often assume wholesaling functions and bypass the independent wholesalers.

Are these complaints and claims valid? Are wholesaling intermediaries anachronisms doomed to a swift demise? Answers to these questions can be formulated by considering the functions and costs of these marketing intermediaries.

Wholesaling Functions

A marketing institution will continue to exist only as long as it fulfills a need by performing a required service. Its death may be slow, but it is inevitable if other channel members discover that they can survive without it. Figure 15.4 shows that there are seven possible functions provided by wholesaling intermediaries: buying, selling, storing, transporting, risk taking, financing, and providing market information. It is important to note that numerous types of wholesaling intermediaries exist and that not all of them provide every one of these functions. Producers–suppliers and their customers, who rely on wholesaling intermediaries for distribution, select those intermediaries that provide the desired combination of services.

BUYING AND SELLING

Buying and selling are two key functions of wholesaling. A product does not move from a producer unless a wholesaler is willing to take the risk of buying a quantity for sale to its customers. Because wholesalers are professional purchasers, they have to be convinced that the product will be accepted by ultimate

▶ FIGURE 15.4 Possible Wholesaling Functions for Customers and Producers–Suppliers

Buying
Acts as purchasing agent for customers, anticipates customer demands, possesses knowledge of alternative supply sources.

Selling
Maintains a sales force to call on customers, thus providing a low-cost method of serving smaller retailers and business buyers.

Transporting
Customers receive prompt delivery in response to their demands, reducing their inventory investments. By "breaking bulk" (purchasing in carload or truckload lots, then reselling in smaller quantities), wholesalers reduce overall transportation costs.

Risk Taking
Aids producers by evaluating credit risks of numerous distant retail customers and smaller business users. Extending credit to these customers is another form of risk taking. Risk of possible spoilage, theft, or obsolescence is assumed when the wholesaler is responsible for transporting and stocking goods in inventory.

Storing
Performs a warehousing function, reduces risk and cost of maintaining inventory for producers, and provides customers with prompt delivery service.

Providing Marketing Information
Serves as key marketing research input for producers through regular contact with retail and business buyers. Provides customers with information about new products, technical information about product lines, information on competitive activities and industry trends, and advisory information concerning changes in such areas as pricing and legal rulings.

Financing
Aids customers by granting credit that might not be available if they purchased directly from distant manufacturers. Provides financing assistance to producers by purchasing goods in advance of sale and through promptly paying bills.

users. Thus the task of the supplier is to prove the advantages of the product, and how the supplier will support the wholesaler and other resellers with advertising and other marketing functions.

Once wholesalers agree to carry the product, they implicitly accept the task of selling it to other resellers or users. Wholesalers thus have sales personnel to handle these functions. Because of the large number of products normally carried by a wholesaler, it is difficult for these salespeople to give individual products intensive attention. That is why manufacturers often have their own missionary sales representatives to add to the efforts of the wholesaler's sales force.

TRANSPORTING AND STORING PRODUCT

Wholesalers transport and store products at locations that are convenient to customers. Manufacturers ship products from their warehouses to numerous whole-

Kulin, a wholesaler of imported giftware, provides customers with a full-colour catalogue for viewing and buying its products.

salers, who then ship smaller quantities to retail outlets that are convenient to the purchaser. A large number of wholesalers and most retailers assume the inventory function (and cost) for the manufacturer. The retailer benefits from the convenience afforded by local inventories, and the manufacturer's cash needs are reduced since the firm's products are sold directly to the wholesaler or retailer.

At the wholesale level, costs are reduced by making large purchases from the manufacturer. The wholesaler receives quantity discounts from the manufacturer—along with reduced transportation rates, since economical carload or truckload shipments are made to the wholesaler's warehouses. At the warehouse, the wholesaler breaks bulk into smaller quantities and ships to the retailer over a shorter distance than would be the case if the manufacturer filled the retailer's order directly from a central warehouse.

Costs are often lowered when intermediaries are used, since the sales force of the retailer or wholesaler can represent many manufacturers to a single customer. As Figure 15.1 indicates, the number of transactions between manufacturers and their customers is reduced by introducing an intermediary (a wholesaler or retailer). Reduced market contacts can lead to lowered marketing costs. When a wholesaling intermediary is added, the number of transactions in this illustration is reduced from sixteen to eight, thereby creating economies of scale by providing an assortment of goods with greater utility and at lower cost than would be the case without such an intermediary.

PROVIDING MARKETING INFORMATION

Because of their central position between the manufacturer and retailers or business buyers, wholesalers serve as important information links. Wholesalers provide their customers with useful information about new products. They also supply manufacturers with information concerning market reception of their product offerings.

RISK TAKING

Wholesalers must evaluate the credit risks of retail customers and business users. Risk is assumed by extending credit to its customers. Wholesalers are also faced with a barrage of new products that they must evaluate to determine the likelihood for market acceptance. In addition, the wholesaler is responsible for transporting goods and stocking them in inventory, as well as assuming the risk of possible spoilage, theft, or obsolescence.

FINANCING

Wholesalers provide a financing function as well. Wholesalers often provide retailers with goods on credit. By purchasing goods on credit, retailers can minimize their cash investments in inventory and pay for most of their purchases as the goods are being sold. This allows them to benefit from the principle of *leverage:* a minimum investment inflates their return on investment. For example, a retailer with an investment of $1 million and profits of $100000 will realize a return on investment (ROI) of 10 percent. But if the necessary invested capital can be reduced to $800000 through credit from the wholesalers, and if the $100000 profits can be maintained, the retailer's ROI increases to 12.5 percent.

Wholesalers of goods for the business market provide similar services. In the steel industry, intermediaries called metal service centres currently market approximately one-fifth of the steel shipped by Canadian mills. Such a centre may stock as many as 6500 items for sale to many of the thousands of major metal users who buy their heavy-usage items in large quantities directly from the steel mills, but who turn to service centres for quick delivery of special orders and other items in small quantities. While an order from the mills may take 90 days to be delivered, a service centre can usually deliver within 24 to 48 hours. Such service reduces the investment needed in stock.

Distribution Channel Functions Can Be Assumed by Other Channel Members

While wholesaling intermediaries often perform all seven of the above functions for their producer, retailer, and other wholesale clients, these functions could be performed by other channel members. Manufacturers may choose to bypass independent wholesaling intermediaries by establishing networks of regional warehouses, maintaining large sales forces to provide market coverage, serving as sources of information for their retail customers, and assuming the financing function. In some instances, they may decide to push the responsibility for some of these functions through the channel on to the retailer or the ultimate purchaser. Large retailers who choose to perform their own wholesaling operations face the same choices.

www.walmart.com

A fundamental marketing principle is that *marketing functions must be performed by some member of the channel; they may be shifted, but they cannot be eliminated.* Either the large retailers such as Wal-Mart who bypass the wholesaler and deal directly with the manufacturer will assume the functions previously performed by wholesaling intermediaries, or these functions will be performed by the manufacturer. Similarly, a manufacturer who deals directly with the ultimate consumer or with industrial buyers will assume the functions of storage, delivery, and market information previously performed by other marketing intermediaries. Intermediaries themselves can be eliminated from the channel, but the channel functions must be performed by someone.

The potential gain for the manufacturer or retailer who might be considering bypassing wholesaling intermediaries can be estimated from the profit structure of the wholesaling industry. After-tax profitability runs about 1.7 percent on income, and 11.4 percent on equity.[5] These amounts could theoretically be saved *if* channel members performed the wholesale functions as efficiently as independent wholesaling intermediaries. Such savings could be used to reduce retail prices, to increase the profits of the manufacturer or retailers, or both. In general, profit levels are low. High turnover is therefore a necessity to provide adequate returns on investment.

Types of Wholesaling Intermediaries

As mentioned previously, various types of wholesaling intermediaries are present in different marketing channels. Some provide a wide range of services or handle a broad line of products, while others specialize in a single service, product, or industry. Table 15.2 classifies wholesaling intermediaries based on two characteristics: *ownership* (whether the wholesaling intermediary is independent, manufacturer-owned, or retailer-owned) and *title flows* (whether title passes from the manufacturer to the wholesaling intermediary or not). There are, in turn, three basic types of ownership: (1) independent wholesaling, which can involve either merchant wholesalers (who do take title to goods) or agents and brokers (who do not);[6] (2) manufacturer-owned sales branches and offices; and (3) retailer-owned cooperatives and buying offices.

MANUFACTURER-OWNED FACILITIES

Increasing volumes of products are being marketed directly by manufacturers through company-owned facilities. There are several reasons for this trend:

▶ INTERNET IMPACT

How the Internet Affects the Music Industry's Distribution Channels

Recently, the music industry has come face to face with the Internet — and it's scared. New formats for storing music, especially the one called MP3, make it a snap to share over the Net recordings that can be played, in full stereo, on PCs with speakers, in regular CD players, and on Walkman-like devices designed for MP3. Last year listeners downloaded literally billions of songs from Web sites and paid for next to none of them.

Welcome to yet another chapter of The Internet Changes Everything. This particular one is a profile of two men on opposite ends of the music business spectrum: Val Azzoli, co-chairman and co-CEO of $700-million-plus-a-year Atlantic Group, which sells the work of artists like Hootie & the Blowfish, Jewel, and Sugar Ray; and Michael Robertson, CEO of a privately held Web site called MP3.com, which gives away digitized songs by artists you've mostly never heard of and yet is perhaps the key company in this digital revolution. The men have never met; they are two of the many people, at companies ranging from Real Networks in Seattle and Microsoft in Redmond, Wash., to IBM in Armonk, NY, and Bertelsmann in Germany, who are either defending against or promoting this new technology.

The problem the $38-billion-a-year recording industry faces is that the ability to ship music directly may shift the balance of economic power. If artists can deliver to fans via the Net, who needs labels and distributors? The threat is nascent—North Americans spent almost nothing on downloaded music last year and just $134 million on CDs ordered via the Web vs. nearly $14 billion on tunes bought in stores. But there is evidence of change: The Recording Industry Association of America says MP3 piracy may have helped drive a slight decline in music sold to the 15–24 age group in the past two years. "The barbarians are at the gate," says Robert Goodale, CEO of Ultrastar, a New York firm that helps artists connect with fans and promote music on their own Web sites. "They're in the moats, and they're climbing up the sides of the castle."

The Attila the Hun of this latest digital revolution is a blond, baby-faced 31-year-old named Michael Robertson, CEO of MP3.com. "We're working for a higher purpose," he says, earnest as a preacher. "We're providing artists with an option besides the traditional industry route—an avenue in which they have control of their destiny and keep ownership of their work."

Robertson's business consists of a site, www.mp3.com, where you can click on any of several thousand recordings and download it onto your computer's hard drive. At that point the song is, for all intents and purposes, yours to listen to on your computer's speakers or your stereo system, to transfer to an MP3 player like the Diamond Rio (a machine the RIAA would like to ban, but that's sold in places like CompUSA for $200), or to post to a pirate Web site where thousands of your best friends can share them. The songs on MP3.com are *not* pirated, unlike many of the music files available on the Net—artists place their music here as a way of introducing listeners to their work.

Is this approach to distribution "piracy"? What do you think will be its impact on other channels of distribution?

Source: Excerpted from Jodi Mardesich, "How the Internet Hits Big Music," *Fortune* (May 10, 1999), pp. 96–98. Reprinted with permission.

some products are perishable, some require complex installation or servicing, others need more aggressive promotion, and still others are high-unit-value goods that the manufacturer wishes to control through the channel directly to the purchaser. Among the industries that have largely shifted from using independent wholesaling intermediaries to using company-owned channels are paper, paint, lumber, construction materials, piece goods, and apparel manufacturers.[7] More than 50 percent of all business goods are sold directly to users by the manufac-

> **TABLE 15.2 Categorizing Wholesaling Intermediaries**

Classification Based on Ownership of the Intermediary
• Independent wholesaling intermediaries
• Manufacturer-owned sales branches and offices
• Retailer-owned cooperatives and buying offices

Classification Based on Title Flows
• Merchant wholesalers (take title)
• Agents and brokers (do not take title)

turer, and slightly more than one-third of *all* products are marketed through manufacturer-owned channels.

This does not mean that independent wholesalers are being squeezed out. Their numbers remain in the thousands, and their volume of trade in the billions of dollars.

sales branch
Manufacturer-owned facility that carries inventory and processes orders to customers from available stock.

Sales Branches and Offices The basic distinction between sales branches and sales offices is that the **sales branch** of a company carries inventory and processes orders to customers from available stock. The branch duplicates the storage function of the independent wholesaler and serves as an office for sales representatives in the territory. Sales branches are prevalent in marketing commercial machinery and equipment, petroleum products, motor vehicles, and chemicals.

sales office
Manufacturer-owned facility that does not carry stock but serves as a regional office for the firm's sales personnel.

A **sales office**, by contrast, does not carry stock but serves as a regional office for the firm's sales personnel. Maintaining sales offices in close proximity to the firm's customers helps reduce selling costs and improve customer service. The firm's listing in the local telephone directory and *Yellow Pages* may result in sales for the local representative. Many buyers prefer to deal with a local representative rather than take the time to contact distant suppliers.

public warehouse
Independently owned storage facility.

Since warehouses represent a substantial investment in real estate, small manufacturers and even larger firms developing new sales territories may choose to use **public warehouses**. These are independently owned storage facilities. For a rental fee, the manufacturer may arrange to store its inventory in one of the nation's many public warehouses for shipment by the warehouse to customers in the area. The warehouse owner will break bulk (divide up a carload or truckload), package inventory into smaller quantities to fill orders, and even bill the purchaser for the manufacturer. The public warehouse can provide a financial service for the manufacturer, too, by issuing a warehouse receipt for the inventory. The receipt can then be used as collateral for a bank loan.

trade fairs
Periodic shows at which manufacturers in a particular industry display their wares for visiting retail and wholesale buyers.

Other Outlets for the Manufacturer's Products In addition to using a sales force and regionally distributed sales branches, manufacturers also market their products through trade fairs and exhibitions and merchandise marts. **Trade fairs** or trade exhibitions are periodic shows at which manufacturers in a particular industry display their wares for visiting retail and wholesale buyers. Suppliers show their latest products to retail and wholesale buyers, for example. In addition, members of the media attend and provide a great deal of publicity through articles written about the show. The Montreal toy show and the Toronto, Montreal, and Calgary furniture shows are annual events for both manufacturers and purchasers of toys and furniture.

Trade fairs are very important in international marketing. Many companies get their first foothold in a foreign market by attending a trade show in the country of interest. By displaying its products at international shows, the potential international marketer can often get a very good idea about the potential interest in its products from businesses that attend. Furthermore, such events often result in finding suitable distributors for the products in the new market.

A **merchandise mart** provides space for permanent exhibitions at which manufacturers may rent showcases for their product offerings. One of the largest is Place Bonaventure in Montreal, which is approximately a block square and several storeys high. Thousands of items are on display there. A retail buyer can compare the offerings of dozens of competing manufacturers and make many purchase decisions in a single visit to a trade fair or merchandise mart.

merchandise mart
Permanent exhibition at which manufacturers rent showcases for their product offerings.

The Montreal Gift Show gives gift manufacturers a forum in which to display and sell their new products.

Merchandise marts also provide a means for international buyers to quickly learn about the products of a region or country. In Taiwan, a gleaming, multi-storied World Trade Centre has space for trade fairs on the main floor. As well, it has several floors comprising hundreds of small glass-fronted rooms. Each one displays the products of a producer. The interested buyer can enter and find more information about the products, their prices, and their availability. Thus, instead of a Canadian buyer flying to Taipei and trying to wade through the Taiwanese *Yellow Pages* to find appropriate suppliers, he or she can just go to the World Trade Centre.

INDEPENDENT WHOLESALING INTERMEDIARIES

As has been mentioned earlier, there are many independent wholesaling intermediaries. They perform vital functions in the marketing of goods and services, and their role and categorization should be understood clearly. These intermediaries may be divided into two categories: merchant wholesalers, which take title to the products, and agents and brokers, which may take possession of the products, but do not take title to them. Merchant wholesalers account for approximately 85 percent of all sales handled by independent wholesalers. As Figure 15.5 indicates, they can be further classified as full- or limited-function wholesalers.

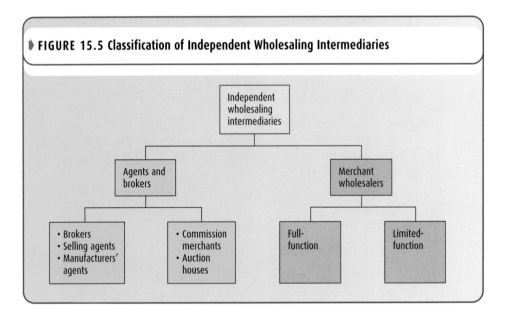

▶ **FIGURE 15.5 Classification of Independent Wholesaling Intermediaries**

Merchant Wholesalers *Full-function merchant wholesalers* provide a complete assortment of services for retailers or business purchasers (Figure 15.4). They are found in convenient locations, thus allowing their customers to make purchases on short notice. To minimize their customers' inventory requirements, they usually maintain a sales force that regularly calls on retailers, makes deliveries (sometimes), and extends credit to qualified buyers. In the business goods market, the full-function merchant wholesaler (often called an *industrial distributor*) usually markets machinery, less expensive accessory equipment, and supplies.

Full-function merchant wholesalers prevail in industries where retailers are small and carry large numbers of relatively inexpensive items, none of which is stocked in depth. The hardware, drug, and grocery industries have traditionally been serviced by these intermediaries.

A unique type of service wholesaler emerged after World War II as supermarkets began to stock high-margin nonfood items. Since the supermarket manager possessed little knowledge of such products as toys, housewares, paperback books, records, and health and beauty items, the **rack jobber** provided the necessary expertise. This wholesaler provides the racks, stocks the merchandise, prices the goods, and makes regular visits to refill the shelves. In essence, the rack jobber rents space from the retailer on a commission basis. Rack jobbers have expanded into drug, hardware, variety, and discount stores.

rack jobber
Wholesaler that provides the racks, stocks the merchandise, prices the goods, and makes regular visits to refill the shelves.

Since full-function merchant wholesalers perform a large number of services, their costs are sometimes as high as 20 percent of sales. Attempts to reduce the costs associated with dealing with the full-function wholesaler have led to the development of a number of *limited-function* intermediaries. Four types of limited-function merchant wholesalers are cash-and-carry wholesalers, truck wholesalers, drop shippers, and direct-response wholesalers.

Cash-and-carry wholesalers perform most wholesaling functions except financing and delivery. They first appeared on the marketing stage in the grocery industry during the Depression era of the 1930s. In an attempt to reduce costs, retailers drove to the wholesaler's warehouse, paid cash for their purchases, and made their own deliveries. By eliminating the delivery and financing functions, cash-and-carry wholesalers were able to reduce operating costs to approximately 9 percent of sales. Costco acts as a cash-and-carry wholesaler for many small retailers and restaurants.

cash-and-carry wholesaler
Limited-function merchant wholesaler that performs most wholesaling functions except financing and delivery.

Although feasible in servicing small stores, such wholesalers have generally proven unworkable for the large-scale operation. The chain store manager is unwilling to perform the delivery function, and the cash-and-carry operation typically operates today as one department of a regular full-service wholesaler.

Truck wholesalers, or truck jobbers, market products that require frequent replenishment. One category is food items such as bread, potato chips, candy, and dairy products. They make regular deliveries to retail stores and simultaneously perform the sales, delivery, and collection functions. Another category is supply items for service stations and garages. The relatively high cost of operating a delivery truck and the low dollar volume per sale account for their relatively high operating costs of 15 percent. The truck wholesaler does, however, provide aggressive promotion for these product lines.

truck wholesaler
Limited-function merchant wholesaler that markets products that require frequent replenishment.

The **drop shipper** takes orders from customers and places them with producers, which then ship directly to the customers. Although drop shippers take title to the products, they never physically handle—or even see—the goods. Since they perform no storage or handling function, their operating costs are a relatively low 4 to 5 percent of sales.

drop shipper
Limited-function merchant wholesaler that takes orders from customers and places them with producers, which then ship directly to the customers.

Drop shippers operate in fields where the product is bulky and customers make purchases in carload lots. Since transportation and handling costs represent a substantial percentage of the total cost of such products as coal and lumber, drop shippers do not maintain an inventory and thereby eliminate the expenses of loading and unloading carload shipments. Their major service is in developing a complete assortment for customers. For example, drop shippers constitute a highly skilled groups of sellers of lumber products from British Columbia. While the major forest-product firms, such as MacMillan-Bloedel and

British Columbia Forest Products, have their in-house lumber traders, independent drop shippers compete head to head with them in selling the output of independent sawmills to eastern Canada and the United States.

direct-response wholesaler
Limited-function merchant wholesaler that relies on catalogues rather than on a sales force to contact retail, industrial, and institutional customers.

The **direct-response wholesaler** is a limited-function merchant wholesaler that relies on catalogues rather than on a sales force to contact retail, industrial, and institutional customers. Purchases are made by mail or telephone by relatively small customers in outlying areas. Mail-order operations are found in the hardware, cosmetics, jewellery, sporting goods, and specialty-food lines, as well as in general merchandise.

Table 15.3 compares the various types of merchant wholesalers in terms of the services they provide. Full-function merchant wholesalers and truck wholesalers are relatively high-cost intermediaries because of the number of services they perform, while cash-and-carry wholesalers, drop shippers, and direct-response wholesalers provide fewer services and thus have relatively low operating costs.

▶ **TABLE 15.3 Services Provided by Merchant Wholesalers**

| | | LIMITED-FUNCTION WHOLESALERS | | | |
SERVICES	FULL-FUNCTION WHOLESALERS	Cash-and-Carry Wholesalers	Truck Wholesalers	Drop Shippers	Direct-Response Wholesalers
Anticipates customer needs	Yes	Yes	Yes	No	Yes
Carries inventory	Yes	Yes	Yes	No	Yes
Delivers	Yes	No	Yes	No	Yes (by mail)
Provides market information	Yes	Rarely	Yes	Yes	No
Provides credit	Yes	No	No	Yes	Sometimes
Assumes ownership risk by taking title	Yes	Yes	Yes	Yes	Yes

Agents and Brokers A second group of independent wholesaling intermediaries — agents and brokers — may or may not take possession of the products they handle, but they never take title to them. They normally perform fewer services than the merchant wholesalers and are typically involved in bringing together buyers and sellers. Agent wholesaling intermediaries may be classified into five categories — commission merchants, auction houses, brokers, selling agents, and manufacturers' agents.

Commission merchants predominate in the marketing of agricultural products. The **commission merchant** takes possession when the producer ships goods to a central market for sale. The commission merchant acts as the producer's agent and receives an agreed-upon fee when a sale is made. Since customers will inspect the products and prices may fluctuate, the commission merchant is given considerable latitude in making decisions. The owner of the goods may specify a minimum price, but the commission merchant will sell them on a "best price" basis. The commission merchant deducts the appropriate fee from the price, and the balance is remitted to the original seller.

A valuable service in such markets as used cars, livestock, antiques, works of art, fur, flowers, and fruit is performed by agent wholesaling intermediaries known as **auction houses**. They bring buyers and sellers together in one location and allow potential buyers to inspect the merchandise before purchasing through a public bidding process. A commission, often based on the sale price, is charged by the auction company for its services. Auction houses tend to specialize in merchandise categories such as agricultural products and art. Sotheby's is a world-famous auction house specializing in art and related products.

The task of **brokers** is to bring buyers and sellers together. They operate in industries characterized by a large number of small suppliers and purchasers — real estate, frozen foods, and used machinery, for example. They may represent either buyer or seller in a given transaction, but not both. The broker receives a fee from the client when the transaction is completed. The service performed is finding buyers or sellers and negotiating for exchange of title. The operating expense ratio for the broker, which may be as low as 2 percent, rises depending on the services performed.

Because brokers operate on a one-time basis for buyers or sellers, they cannot serve as an effective marketing channel for manufacturers seeking regular, continuing services. A manufacturer that seeks to develop a more permanent channel using agent wholesaling intermediaries must evaluate the services of either the selling agent or the manufacturers' agent.

For small, poorly financed, production-oriented manufacturers, **selling agents** may prove an ideal marketing channel. These wholesaling intermediaries have even been referred to as independent marketing departments, since they are responsible for the total marketing program for a firm's product line. They typically have full authority over pricing decisions and promotional outlays, and they often provide financial assistance for the manufacturer. The manufacturer can concentrate on production and rely on the expertise of the selling agent for all marketing activities. Selling agents are common in the textile, coal, sulphur, and lumber industries. Their operating expenses average about 3 percent of sales.

Instead of a single selling agent, a manufacturer may use a number of manufacturers' agents. A **manufacturers' agent** is essentially an independent salesperson (or a company with a sales force) who works for a number of manufacturers of related by noncompeting products and receives a commission based on a specified percentage of sales. Manufacturers' agents can be thought of as an independent sales force. Although some commissions may be as high as 20 percent of sales, they usually average between 6 and 7 percent. Unlike the selling agent, who may be given exclusive world rights to *market* a manufacturer's product, the manufacturers' agent *sells* in a specified territory.[8]

commission merchant
An agent wholesaling intermediary that takes possession when the producer ships goods to a central market for sale.

auction house
An agent wholesaling intermediary that brings buyers and sellers together in one location and allows potential buyers to inspect the merchandise before purchasing through a public bidding process.

www.sothebys.com

broker
An agent wholesaling intermediary that brings buyers and sellers together; operates in industries with a large number of small suppliers and purchasers.

selling agent
An agent wholesaling intermediary that is responsible for the total marketing program for a firm's product line.

manufacturers' agent
An independent salesperson who works for a number of manufacturers of related but noncompeting products.

Manufacturers' agents reduce their selling costs by spreading the cost per sales call over a number of different products. An agent in the plumbing supplies industry may represent a dozen different manufacturers.

Producers may use manufacturers' agents for several reasons. First, when they are developing new sales territories, the costs of adding new salespeople to "pioneer" new territories may be prohibitive. The agents, who are paid on a commission basis, can perform the sales function in the new territories at a much lower cost to the manufacturer.

Second, firms with unrelated lines may need to employ more than one channel. One line of products may be marketed through the company's sales force. A second, unrelated line might be marketed through independent manufacturers' agents. This is particularly common where the unrelated product line is a recent addition and the regular sales force has no experience with the products.

Finally, small firms with no existing sales force may turn to manufacturers' agents to gain access to the market. A newly organized firm producing computer disks may use office equipment and supplies manufacturers' agents to reach retail outlets and industrial purchasers.

The importance of selling agents is somewhat limited, because many manufacturers desire better control of their marketing programs. However, the role played by manufacturers' agents is essential for the success of many newer ventures.

The various types of agents and brokers are compared in Table 15.4.

▶ **TABLE 15.4 Services Provided by Agents and Brokers**

SERVICES	COMMISSION MERCHANTS	AUCTION HOUSES	BROKERS	SELLING AGENTS	MANUFACTURERS' AGENTS
Anticipates customer needs	Yes	Some	Some	Yes	Yes
Carries inventory	Yes	Yes	No	No	No
Delivers	Yes	No	No	No	Infrequently
Provides market information	Yes	Yes	Yes	Yes	Yes
Provides credit	Some	No	No	Some	No
Assumes ownership risk by taking title	No	No	No	No	No

RETAILER-OWNED FACILITIES

Retailers have also assumed numerous wholesaling functions in attempting to reduce costs or to provide special services. Independent retailers have often banded together to form buying groups to achieve cost savings through quantity purchases. Other groups of retailers have established retailer-owned wholesale facilities by forming a cooperative chain. IGA (Independent Grocer's Alliance) is an example. Large chain retailers often establish centralized buying offices to negotiate large-scale purchases directly with manufacturers for the members of the chain.

This rather long discussion of channel intermediaries could have been expanded even further, for this is an important and complex topic. It is important for you to learn the names and functions of these intermediaries in order to take advantage of the many possibilities that exist in developing an appropriate channel strategy. For example, the set of channel distribution options for a newly developed lightweight hair dryer would likely be quite different depending on whether Black and Decker or a new start-up venture had developed it. Reputation and resources would make it much easier for Black and Decker to get the product into the traditional channels. The new company would probably have to use a different route. The next section considers the major issues in selecting an appropriate channel strategy.

www.blackanddecker.com

▶ CHANNEL STRATEGY DECISIONS

Marketers face several channel strategy decisions. The selection of a specific distribution channel is the most basic of these, but the level of distribution intensity and the issue of vertical marketing systems must also be addressed (see Figure 15.6).

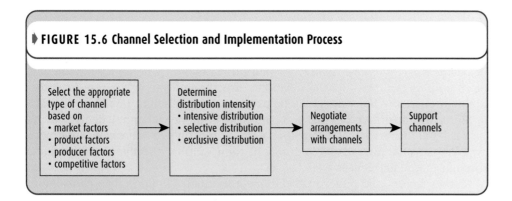

▶ FIGURE 15.6 Channel Selection and Implementation Process

Select the appropriate type of channel based on
• market factors
• product factors
• producer factors
• competitive factors

→

Determine distribution intensity
• intensive distribution
• selective distribution
• exclusive distribution

→

Negotiate arrangements with channels

→

Support channels

Select the Appropriate Distribution Channel

What is an appropriate marketing channel if you want to sell bottled water to Japan? What makes a direct channel (manufacturer to consumer) best for the Fuller Brush Company? Why do operating supplies often go through both agents and merchant wholesalers before being purchased by an industrial firm? Why do some firms employ multiple channels for the same product? The firm must answer many such questions when it determines its choice of marketing channels. The choice is based on an analysis of the market, the product, the producer, and various competitive factors. Each is often of critical importance, and all are often interrelated.

MARKET FACTORS

A major determinant of channel structure is whether the product is intended for the consumer or the business market. Business purchasers usually prefer to deal directly with the manufacturer (except for supplies of small accessory items), but most consumers make their purchases from retail stores. Products sold to both business users and the consumer market usually require more than one channel.

The geographic location and the needs of the firm's potential market also affect channel choice. Direct sales are possible when the firm's potential market is concentrated in a few regions. For example, industrial production tends to be concentrated in a relatively small geographic region, making direct contact possible. The small number of potential buyers also increases the feasibility of direct channels.

On the other hand, consumer goods are purchased by every household everywhere. Since consumers are numerous and geographically dispersed, and purchase a small volume at a given time, intermediaries must be employed to market products to them efficiently.

In Canada, population distribution is an extremely influential factor in channel decisions. For example, the markets for fishing nets are on the two coasts, with smaller markets on the Great Lakes, Lake Winnipeg, and a few other large lakes. The Rockies and the Canadian Shield effectively divide markets and strongly affect channels of distribution. Our relatively smaller and widely dispersed centres of population tend to result in less specialized wholesaling and retailing institutions than in the United States and other developed, heavily populated countries. This may limit the range of channel opportunities available to the marketing manager.

Order size will also affect the marketing channel decision. Manufacturers are likely to employ shorter, more direct channels in cases where retail customers or business buyers place relatively small numbers of large orders. Retail chains often employ buying offices to negotiate directly with manufacturers for large-scale purchases. Wholesalers may be used to contact smaller retailers.

www.toysrus.com

Shifts in consumer buying patterns also influence channel decisions. As newer retail forms such as Superstore, Costco, and Toys R Us have become more popular, manufacturers have had to shift their emphasis to distribute products through these channels as well.

Market factors and buyer expectations are equally important to consider in developing international distribution and channel structures. For example, in Japan many more channel intermediaries are typically used. In the distribution of soap, for instance, the product goes from manufacturer to large wholesaler to smaller wholesaler to very small wholesaler, and finally to the retailer.

PRODUCT FACTORS

Product characteristics also play a role in determining optimum marketing channels. *Perishable products,* such as fresh produce and fruit, and fashion products with short life cycles, *typically move through relatively short channels* direct to the retailer or to the ultimate consumer. Old Dutch Potato Chips are distributed by company salespeople–truck drivers direct to retail shelves. Each year, Hines & Smart Corporation ships over 2 million kg of live lobsters by air, in specially designed insulating containers, directly to restaurants and hotels throughout North America.

Complex products, such as custom-made installations or computer equipment, are typically sold direct from the manufacturer to the buyer. As a general rule, *the more standardized a product, the longer the channel will be.* Such items will usually be marketed by wholesalers. Also, products that require regular service or specialized repair services usually avoid channels that employ independent wholesalers. Cars are marketed through a franchised network of regular dealers whose employees receive regular training on how to service their cars properly.

Another generalization concerning marketing channels is that *the lower the unit value of the product, the longer the channel.* Convenience goods and business supplies with typically low unit prices are frequently marketed through relatively long channels. Installations and more expensive business and consumer goods go through shorter, more direct channels.

PRODUCER FACTORS

Companies with adequate resources — financial, marketing, and managerial — will be less compelled to use intermediaries in marketing their products. A financially strong manufacturer can hire its own sales force, warehouse its products, and grant credit to the retailer or consumer. A weaker firm relies on intermediaries for these services (although some large retail chains may purchase all of the manufacturer's output, making it possible to bypass the independent wholesaler). Production-oriented firms may be forced to use the marketing expertise of intermediaries to replace the lack of finances and management in their organization. In the international marketplace, producers often rely on intermediaries because they know the market better, and it is usually cheaper than setting up a new distribution system.

A firm with a broad product line is better able to market its products directly to retailers or business users, since its sales force can offer a variety of products to customers. Larger total sales allow the selling costs to be spread over a number of products and make direct sales more feasible. The single-product firm often discovers that direct selling is an unaffordable luxury.

The manufacturer's need for control over the product will also influence channel selection. If aggressive promotion for the firm's products at the retail level is desired, the manufacturer will choose the shortest available channel. For new products, the manufacturer may be forced to implement an introductory advertising campaign before independent wholesalers will handle the item.

COMPETITIVE FACTORS

Some firms are forced to develop unique marketing channels because of inadequate promotion of their products by independent intermediaries. Avon concentrated on house-to-house selling rather than being directly involved in the intense competition among similar lines of cosmetics in traditional channels. This radical departure from the traditional channel resulted in tremendous sales by the firm's thousands of neighbourhood salespeople. Similarly, Honeywell discovered that its home security system was being inadequately marketed by the traditional, wholesaler-to-retailer channel and switched to a direct-to-home sales force.

Table 15.5 summarizes the factors that affect the choice of optimal marketing channels and shows the effect of each characteristic on the overall length of the channel.

▶ TABLE 15.5 Factors Affecting Choice of Distribution Channels

FACTOR	CHANNELS TEND TO BE SHORTER WHEN
Market Factors	
Consumer market or business market	Users are in business market
Geographic location of target market	Customers are geographically concentrated
Customer service needs	Specialized knowledge, technical know-how, and regular service needs are present
Order size	Customer places relatively small number of large orders
Product Factors	
Perishability	Products are perishable, either because of fashion changes or physical perishability
Technical complexity of product	Products are highly technical
Unit value	Products have high unit value
Producer Factors	
Producer resources—financial, managerial, and marketing	Manufacturer possesses adequate resources to perform channel functions
Product line	Manufacturer has broad product line to spread distribution costs
Need for control over the channel	Manufacturer wants to control the channel
Competitive Factors	
Need for promotion to channel members	Manufacturer feels that independent intermediaries are inadequately promoting products

Determine Distribution Intensity

Adequate market coverage for some products such as fine furniture could mean one dealer for each 50 000 people. On the other hand, Procter & Gamble defines adequate coverage for Crest toothpaste as almost every supermarket, discount store, drugstore, and variety store, plus many vending machines.

intensive distribution
A form of distribution that attempts to provide saturation coverage of the potential market.

INTENSIVE DISTRIBUTION
Producers of convenience goods that attempt to provide saturation coverage of their potential markets are the prime users of **intensive distribution**. Soft drinks, bread, candy, and chewing gum are available in convenient locations to enable purchasers to buy with a minimum of effort.

Bic pens can be purchased in thousands of retail outlets in Canada. TMX Watches of Canada LTD. uses an intensive distribution strategy for its Timex watches. Consumers may buy a Timex in many jewellery stores, the traditional retail outlet for watches. In addition, they may find Timex in discount stores, variety stores, department stores, hardware stores, and drugstores.

www.timex.com

Mass coverage and low unit prices make the use of wholesalers almost mandatory for such distribution. An important exception to this generalization is products sold and delivered on a direct-to-customer basis. For example, Avon operates direct to the consumer through a nationwide network of neighbourhood salespeople who purchase directly from the manufacturer, at 60 percent of the retail price, and service a limited area with cosmetics, toiletries, jewellery, and toys. Other examples are Tupperware, Mary Kay, and other multilevel marketing companies.

It must be remembers that while a firm may want intensive distribution, the retailer or industrial distributor will carry only products that sell in enough volume to make a profit. If demand is low, the producer may have to settle for less than complete market coverage.

SELECTIVE DISTRIBUTION

As the name implies, **selective distribution** involves the selection of a small number of retailers to handle the firm's product line. This can work *if* consumers are willing to shop around for the product category. By limiting its retailers, the firm may reduce its total marketing costs, such as those for sales force and shipping, while establishing better working relationships within the channel. This practice may also be necessary to give the retailers an incentive (through having a product available to a limited number of sellers) to carry the product and promote it properly against many competing brands. Cooperative advertising (where the manufacturer pays a percentage of the retailer's advertising expenditures and the retailer prominently displays the firm's products) can be used to mutual benefit. Marginal retailers can be avoided. Where product service is important, dealer training and assistance is usually forthcoming from the manufacturer. Finally, price cutting is less likely, since fewer dealers are handling the firm's line.

selective distribution
The selection of a small number of retailers to handle the firm's product line.

EXCLUSIVE DISTRIBUTION

When manufacturers grant exclusive rights to a wholesaler or retailer to sell in a geographic region, they are practising **exclusive distribution**, which is an extreme form of selective distribution. The best example of exclusive distribution is the automobile industry. For example, a city of 100 000 might have a single Toyota dealer or one Cadillac agency. Exclusive distribution arrangements are also found in the marketing of some major appliances and in fashion apparel. Powerful retailers may also negotiate to acquire exclusive distribution.

exclusive distribution
The granting of exclusive rights by manufacturers to a wholesaler or retailer to sell in a geographic region.

Some market coverage may be sacrificed through a policy of exclusive distribution, but this is often offset through the development and maintenance of an image of quality and prestige for the products, with more active attention by the retailer to promote them, and the reduced marketing costs associated with a small number of accounts. Producers and retailers cooperate closely in decisions concerning advertising and promotion, inventory to be carried by the retailers, and prices.

The Legal Problems of Exclusive Distribution The use of exclusive distribution presents a number of potential legal problems. Three problems areas exist: exclusive dealing, tied selling, and market restriction. Each will be examined briefly.

Exclusive dealing prohibits a marketing intermediary (either a wholesaler or, more typically, a retailer) from handling competing products. Through such a contract, the manufacturer is assured of total concentration on the firm's product line by the intermediaries. For example, an oil company may consider requiring all dealers to sign a contract agreeing to purchase all of their accessories from that company.

The legal question is covered in Part IV of the Competition Act, which prohibits exclusive dealing by a major supplier if it is likely to

1. Impede entry into or expansion of a firm in the market.
2. Impede introduction of a product into or expansion of sales of a product in the market.
3. Have any other exclusionary effect in the market, with the result that competition is or is likely to be lessened substantially.[9]

A second problem area is **tied selling**. In this case, a supplier forces a dealer who wishes to handle a product to also carry other products from the supplier or to refrain from using or distributing someone else's product. Tied selling is controlled by the same provision as exclusive dealing.

The third legal issue of exclusive distribution is the use of **market restriction**. In this case, suppliers restrict the geographic territories for each of their distributors. The key issue is whether such restrictions substantially lessen competition. If so, the Restrictive Trade Practices Commission has the power to order the prohibition of such practices. For example, a *horizontal territorial restriction*, where retailers or wholesalers agree to avoid competition in products from the same manufacturer, would likely be declared unlawful.

exclusive dealing
An arrangement whereby a supplier prohibits a marketing intermediary (either a wholesaler or, more typically, a retailer) from handling competing products.

tied selling
An arrangement whereby a supplier forces a dealer who wishes to handle a product to also carry other products from the supplier or to refrain from using or distributing someone else's product.

market restriction
An arrangement whereby suppliers restrict the geographic territories for each of their distributors.

Negotiate with Channels

Having gone through the channel selection process, you may not be able to get the channel that you have so carefully selected for your new line of hair dryers. Consider the situation of the buyer for a large and successful drugstore chain such as London Drugs or Shoppers Drug Mart. Will the buyer automatically stock your new dryer? Not likely, because she or he is faced with a fixed amount of shelf space, of which a certain proportion is already allocated and filled with eleven different dryers. There is never vacant shelf space. To get your product on the shelf, you have to make it so attractive to the buyer that she or he will remove some other product to make space. *If* the buyer does so, it will usually be because you make it profitable to do so.

Normally this is done through offering a good profit margin and promising to affect demand through a strong advertising campaign. It is easier to persuade the buyer that you can do this if you are a well-established supplier such as Black and Decker and have already developed a good relationship with the channel. If you are a new company, your negotiations may well fail, and you will have to turn to other outlets or a different channel arrangement. That is why it is so important to understand the various channel options.

Support the Channel

After a channel of distribution has been set up, the job is not done. Since channels carry many products, they normally do not have time or motivation to pay special attention to your product. Thus it is important to support the channel members' activities through regular calls on channel members, missionary selling, advertising, and other methods. This combination of activities helps to move the product, and as it moves, channels will be happy to carry and support your product, and perhaps other products of yours.

Vertical Marketing Systems

Some channel members, and even entire channels of distribution, act quite independently. They have no formal long-term ties to others in the channel, but build relationships with buyers or sellers in an autonomous fashion.

More commonly, intermediaries have found it desirable to form a **vertical marketing system**. A vertical marketing system (VMS) is a network of channel intermediaries organized and centrally managed to produce the maximum competitive impact. In such a system, the coordination of the various channel members can produce operating efficiencies, deep market penetration, and greater profits. Vertical marketing systems produce economies of scale through their size and the elimination of duplicated services. There are three types of VMS: corporate, administered, and contractual. They are summarized in Table 15.6.

vertical marketing system
A network of channel intermediaries organized and centrally managed to produce the maximum competitive impact.

CORPORATE SYSTEM

When there is single ownership of all stages of the marketing channel, a *corporate vertical marketing system* exists. Holiday Inn owns a furniture manufacturer and a carpet mill. Bata Shoes owns a retail chain of shoe stores. Many McDonald's food outlets are corporate-owned.

ADMINISTERED SYSTEM

Channel coordination is achieved through the exercise of economic and "political" power by a dominant channel member in an *administered vertical marketing system*. Canadian General Electric has a network of major appliance dealers who aggressively display and promote the line because of its strong reputation and brand. Although independently owned and operated, these dealers cooperate with the manufacturer because of the effective working relationships enjoyed over the years and the profits to be realized from selling the widely known, well-designed, broad range of merchandise. Dominance can come from the retail end of the channel too. Wal-Mart and Sears dominate their suppliers, and their demands on suppliers and other intermediaries result in powerful retail operations.

www.ge.com/canada

CONTRACTUAL SYSTEM

The most significant form of vertical marketing is the *contractual vertical marketing system*. It accounts for nearly 40 percent of all retail sales. Instead of the common ownership of channel components that characterizes the corporate

> ▶ **TABLE 15.6 Three Types of Vertical Marketing Systems**

TYPE OF SYSTEM	DESCRIPTION	EXAMPLES
Corporate	Channel owned and operated by a single organization	Bata Shoes Firestone Sherwin-Williams Singer McDonald's (partial)
Administered	Channel dominated by one powerful member that acts as channel captain	Kodak General Electric Corning Glass

Contractual	Channel coordinated through contractual agreements among channel members	Wholesaler-Sponsored Voluntary Chain
		   IGA
		   Canadian Tire
		   Independent Druggists Alliance (IDA)
		   Allied Hardware
		Retail Cooperative
		   Associated Grocers
		Franchise Systems
		   McDonald's (partial)
		   Century 21 Real Estate
		   AAMCO Transmissions
		   Coca-Cola bottlers
		   Ford dealers

VMS or the relative power relationships of an administered system, the contractual VMS is characterized by formal agreements between channel members. In practice, there are three types of agreements: the wholesaler-sponsored voluntary chain, the retail cooperative, and the franchise.

Wholesaler-Sponsored Voluntary Chain The wholesaler-sponsored voluntary chain represents an attempt by the independent wholesaler to preserve a market for the firm's products by strengthening the firm's retailer customers. To enable the independent retailers to compete with the chains, the wholesaler enters into a formal agreement with a group of retailers whereby the retailers agree to use a common name, standardize their facilities, and purchase the wholesaler's products. The wholesaler often develops a line of private brands to be stocked by the members of the voluntary chain. A common store name and similar inventories allow the retailers to achieve cost savings on advertising, since a single newspaper advertisement promotes all retailers in the trading area. IGA, with a membership of approximately 800 food stores, is a good example of a voluntary chain.

www.iga.net/EN

Retail Cooperatives A second type of contractual VMS is the retail cooperative, which is established by a group of retailers who set up a wholesaling operation to compete better with the chains. A group of retailers purchase shares of stock in a wholesaling operation and agree to purchase a minimum percentage of their inventory from the firm. The members may also choose to use a common store name, such as Home Hardware, and develop their own private brands in order to carry out cooperative advertising.

Buying groups like wholesaler-sponsored chains and retail cooperatives are not a new phenomenon in the Canadian distribution industry. They date back at least 50 years, some having evolved from the cooperative movement of the early years of the century. Under the Competition Act, suppliers may charge different prices for different volumes of purchases as long as these prices are available to all competing purchasers of articles of like quantity and quality. And suppliers have done so; it is common practice to offer volume rebates. Thus, buying groups improve the small retailers' bargaining position with their suppliers, thus increasing competition for their large rivals.

In some cases, buying groups have failed because of difficulties with organization and management. In others, the buying group concept has worked very well, with some groups now as large as the chains. The chains themselves have now formed their own buying groups. Recently, five of these large buying groups in the food industry represented some 14 000 stores and accounted for about 85 percent of all retail food sales in Canada.[10] This development leads to the concern that while buying groups may improve the balance of market power in some areas, there is a possibility of abuse of power in others.

Franchises A third type of contractual VMS is the **franchise**. A franchise is an agreement whereby one firm (franchisee) agrees to meet the operating requirements of a successful business (franchisor) in return for the right to carry the name and products of the franchisor. The franchisee pays a predetermined royalty on sales to the franchisor. In addition, the franchisee typically receives a variety of marketing, management, technical, and financial services in exchange for a specified fee. KFC (formerly Kentucky Fried Chicken) started out by franchising its stores, but the company now has the resources to pay for and manage its own stores. Thus it has more control over operations.

Although franchising attracted considerable interest beginning in the late 1960s, the concept actually began 100 years earlier when the Singer Company established franchised sewing-machine outlets. Early impetus for the franchising concept came after 1900 in the automobile industry. The soft-drink industry is another example of franchising, but in this case the contractual arrangement is between the syrup manufacturer and the wholesaler–bottler.

The franchising form that created most of the excitement both in retailing and on Wall Street since the late 1960s was the retailer franchise system sponsored by the service firm. McDonald's Corporation is an excellent example of such a franchise operation. McDonald's brought together suppliers and a chain of hamburger outlets. It provided a proven system of retail operation (the operations manual for each outlet weights over 1 kg) with a standardized product and ingenious promotional campaigns. This enabled lower prices to be offered to customers through the franchisor's purchasing power on meat, buns, potatoes, napkins, and other supplies. In return, the franchisee pays a fee for the use of the name (over $150 000 for McDonald's) and a percentage of gross sales. Other familiar examples include Tim Horton's, Avis, Pizza Hut, and Weight Watchers.

Fast-food franchising has already proven itself in the international market. In Tokyo, London, Rome, Paris, and Moscow, McDonald's hamburgers are con-

franchise
An agreement whereby one firm (franchisee) agrees to meet the operating requirements of a successful business (franchisor) in return for the right to carry the name and products of the franchisor.

www.kfc.com

www.mcdonalds.com

sumed daily. KFC has opened nearly 500 restaurants in Canada and in such locations as Manila, Munich, Nice, Nairobi, Hong Kong, and Japan. In some countries, adjustments to the North American marketing plans have been made to

▶ THE PRACTISING MARKETER

How to Find the Proper Franchise Location

One of the critical success factors in running a successful franchise business is finding a proper location. Prospective investors are advised to scrutinize locations before they take the plunge. Site selection, franchise experts say, is both an art and a science. "There are no hard and fast rules," Marsh & Co. Hospitality Realty Inc. vice-president Ron Scribner says. A thorough site evaluation includes demographic studies, a traffic-flow analysis, an assessment of proximity to public transit and major employment centres, as well as financial projections based on the terms of a lease.

In addition, the potential franchisee should develop a list of questions to gauge whether a site matches the chain's marketing strategy—for example, the age of potential customers, their education, and other important factors.

Computerized census and geographical data may give general information about a neighbourhood, but it won't reveal how people shop, where they will or will not walk, or which side of the street thrives. "You've got to visit sites at different times of the day, on different days of the week, and talk to local retailers," David Black, vice-president of real estate and franchise development for Toronto-based Timothy's World Coffee Inc., says. "I don't think there's any way to choose sites mechanically," Timothy's president Becky McKinnon adds. "The data confirms your intuition." With nonfood chains, such as service franchises, site selection evaluations rely on different criteria entirely. In recent years, Royal LePage Ltd. of Toronto has moved more than 90 percent of its franchise real-estate outlets out of the traditional storefront retail operations and into office space in commercial buildings, while retaining kiosks in major malls for visibility.

Talk to existing franchisees, visit other locations, and take a measure of the dynamics of the local market.

▶ Caveat Emptor

What to steer clear of when selecting a spot for a franchise:

- Sites that lack easy access or don't have adequate parking.
- Locations on the wrong side of the street.
- Outlets where the franchisee is required to pay for substantial renovations, only later to discover that such changes contravene local zoning bylaws.
- Franchises that are located in a given area simply because there are lots of other chain outlets in the immediate vicinity.
- No exit clause. Negotiate a lease that provides an exit clause that will be triggered by major changes in the local market, such as the closing of a nearby office building or government facility that was the source of customers.

Would the above advice hold true in establishing a franchise in another country, such as in France? Why or why not?

Source: Adapted from John Lorinc, "Chains Scout for Top Locations," *The Globe and Mail* (March 23, 1999), p. B12. Reprinted with permission from *The Globe and Mail*.

Many businesses, such as Harvey's, have found franchising to be a successful type of contractual VMS. In this system, the franchisee pays a royalty in exchange for the right to carry the name and products of a well-established business.

match local needs. Although their menu is rigidly standardized in Canada, McDonald's executives approved changes to the menu in outlets in France. KFC replaced french fries with mashed potatoes to satisfy its Japanese customers.

Although many franchises are profitable, the infatuation with the franchising concept and the market performance of franchise stocks have lured dozens of newcomers into the market who have failed. Lacking experience and often with a well-known celebrity's name as their sole asset, many of these firms have disappeared almost as quickly as they entered the market.

The median investment for a franchise varies tremendously from one business area to another. A pet-sitting franchise might sell for as low as $9500, whereas a restaurant franchise will likely average over $250000. In 1999 the average franchise fee was $23 213, and the average investment paid by Canadian franchisees for their franchise (building, supplies, etc.) was $166 603.[11] The great bulk of the nation's franchises are in the "traditional" franchise areas such as car dealers, service stations, and soft-drink bottlers. Figure 15.7 shows a summary of Canadian franchise facts.

Despite the many franchise opportunities available, there are few specific regulations with respect to the proper disclosure of information to prospective franchisees. It is worthwhile to evaluate the opportunity carefully before investing.

The foregoing discussion has shown that vertical marketing systems, whether in the form of corporate, administered, or contractual systems, have become a dominant factor in the consumer goods sector of the Canadian economy. Over 60 percent of the available market is currently in the hands of retail components of VMS.

▶ **FIGURE 15.7 Canadian Franchise Facts, 1999**

Industry Size	
Number of franchisors reported by Francon	1326
Number of corporate owned units	10084
Number of franchised units	65725
Canadian industry total units	**75809**

Did you know that a Canadian franchise opens every two hours, 365 days a year?

Company Size	
Average corporate units per franchisor	7.7
Average franchised units per franchisor	50.7
Average franchisor unit size	58.4

The average number of years in business for a Canadian franchisor is 20.7 years.

The average franchise fee for a Canadian franchisor is $23213.

The average investment paid by Canadian franchisees for their franchise is $166603. This does not include any financing that a franchisee might obtain.

Restaurant categories control over 18000 outlets in Canada.

Burgers, casual dining, chicken, coffee, bakery and donuts, family dining, fast food, ice cream, yogurt and candy, pizza, sandwiches, and Tex Mex.

Miscellaneous products and services	9755 units
Automotive products and services	5695 units

Source: Francon Canada Web site, "Canadian Franchise Fact" page (http://www.francon.com/CDNFACTS.htm), downloaded December 12, 1999.

▶ LEADERSHIP AND COOPERATION IN THE CHANNEL

Leadership and cooperation in the marketing channel are necessary for successfully implementing marketing strategy. Channel leadership is a function of one's power within the distribution channel, and the most powerful often becomes the dominant and controlling member of the channel—the **channel captain**. Historically, the role of channel captain belonged to the manufacturer or wholesaler, since retailers tended to be both small and locally oriented. However, retailers are increasingly taking on the role of channel captain as large retail chains assume traditional wholesaling functions and even dictate product design specifications to the manufacturer. For example, Loblaws Supermarkets in Canada has developed a line of products called President's Choice. Sainsbury's in Britain has its own lines of products as well. Costco has an ever-expanding line of its own Kirkland branded products.

channel captain
The most dominant member of the distribution channel.

Distribution channels must be organized and regarded as a systematic cooperative effort if operating efficiencies are to be achieved. In a sense, the forward-thinking organizations are those that form strategic alliances among channel members in order to take advantage of the competitive attributes each possesses. These alliances include direct channel participants as well as facilitating agencies such as transportation companies, legal organizations, and the like. No longer is it likely that completely independent channel players will dominate the competition in globally oriented industries. Organization and cooperation between independent entities within the channel is a must today.

Cooperation and mutual understanding based on enlightened self-interest are far from the reality of channel relations, according to numerous authors. Instead, many channel relationships are marked by intense rivalry and conflict.

Channel conflict can evolve from a number of sources. For example, a manufacturer of cough lozenges may have planned that its product display would be placed near the cash register to encourage impulse purchases. Many retailers might be unwilling to do this because of many other items taking up the same space. In other situations, a manufacturer might wish certain market information from retailers, but they may not be interested in cooperating. A wholesaler may find that it is being bypassed by a retailer that buys direct from a manufacturer. Manufacturers may wish to dictate the resale prices of their merchandise. These may be lower or higher than the prices that retailers feel are appropriate to their circumstances.

channel conflict
Rivalry and conflict between channel members because of sometimes different objectives and needs.

Channel relationships are dynamic. Just when channel procedures and relationships seem to be sorted out, a competitive action by some channel member upsets the balance, and a whole series of countermoves are triggered to adjust to the changing competitive situation. It is this continuing process that results in the evolution of new and improved channel forms to serve consumer needs.

The study of channels of distribution, and the changes that continually occur, can be fascinating. After this rather extensive overview of channel and distribution strategy, the next two chapters will look more closely at retailing and the process of logistics and supply chain management.

▶ THE PRACTISING MARKETER

www.coca-cola.com

Distribution Is Everything (Almost)

After 112 years of selling mostly sugar water, Coca-Cola Co. is making plans to peddle plain water in plastic bottles.

The soft-drink giant expects to introduce in select markets its own brand of purified bottled water, according to people familiar with the plans. A leading candidate for the brand's name is Dasani. The water will come from the tap or wells, be purified, and then have minerals added, which Coke will sell to its franchised bottlers.

A nationally branded water by Coca-Cola has been the subject of intense speculation in the beverage industry. Many industry executives say that Coke can't wait any longer, given the explosive growth of bottled water in the past few years. Coke officials reason that if consumers are going to drink bottled water, they might as well drink a Coke product.

Furthermore, several Coke bottlers have been urging Coke to market a national brand of water so they don't have to sell a hodgepodge of little-known waters. Currently, Coke bottlers sell a variety of bottled waters, which they make a significant profit on. Several have said they are willing to pay a royalty to Coke if it puts marketing muscle behind a bottled water.

"It's no longer a question of if, but when," said one person familiar with Coke's plans. Others, however, cautioned that several details need to be ironed out and that may have some bearing on a final decision by Coca-Cola chairman M. Douglas Ivester.

Coca-Cola sells a bottled water called BonAqua in several overseas countries. Thanks to health-minded consumers, the bottled water business is now a business worth $4-billion (U.S.) a year, up from $2.65-billion in 1990. Sales of plastic bottles of water, popular because of their convenience, have been the biggest winners, increasing 28 to 30 percent for the past couple of years. PepsiCo Inc. jumped into the water business with its Aquafina brand, first test-marketed in 1994, and the sheer power of Pepsi's vast distribution system has already made Aquafina the top-selling water brand in convenience and gas stores.

For Coke, however, dipping its toe in the water business has been a source of internal debate for years. The biggest obstacle has been financial. Coca-Cola makes it money by selling concentrate to bottlers, independent companies (franchisees) that add water and carbonation to the drinks and distribute them. But with water, Coke can't sell any syrup. Indeed, Mr. Ivester said in June that bottled water is a "tricky subject—we have to be careful that we don't replace high-margin soft drinks with low-margin water."

The mineral packets Coke plans to sell the bottlers would take the place of concentrate and make the venture more financially feasible. The minerals could include small amounts of potassium and magnesium, and would make water taste better, industry executives said. The purification process of reverse osmosis removes all taste from water and gives it a bland flavour, says James Stevens, a veteran bottled water executive and former chief operating officer of Coca-Cola Enterprises Inc., Coca-Cola's largest bottler.

One plus for Coke is that consumers seem far more accepting of purified water over spring water; that makes it easier to create a national brand. Coke has been wary of spring water, because it could mean relying on an outside company to bottle it at the source, according to Mr. Stevens. A bottled-water venture doesn't need to be expensive for Coke. It could vault to the top tier, thanks to its far-flung distribution system. "They'll have a big advantage," said Mr. Stevens.

Explain why franchisees are ready to pay Coke to put out a bottled water when they could easily produce one themselves. What does this article illustrate about the concept of "channel captains"?

Source: Adapted from Nikhil Deogun, "Coke to Peddle Bottled Water," *The Wall Street Journal* in *The Globe and Mail* (November 3, 1998), p. B12. Reprinted by permission.

▶ SUMMARY

The number of actual transactions in an economic system that is comprised of manufacturers and customers can be reduced significantly by inserting one or more intermediaries between the manufacturer and the consumer.

The distribution channel performs several functions in the overall marketing system. These include facilitating the exchange process, sorting, standardizing transactions, holding inventories, assisting in the search process, and transporting.

Channels can be categorized as multistep, two-step, one-step, and direct. In the multistep channel, the product moves from producer to agent/broker to wholesaler to retailer to consumer. An increasingly common phenomenon is the use of more than one marketing channel for similar products.

The term *wholesaler* is applied only to those wholesaling intermediaries that take title to the products they handle. The term *wholesaling intermediary* is a broader term that also includes others who perform important wholesaling activities. These are merchant wholesalers, agents, and brokers.

Trade fairs are periodic shows at which manufacturers in a particular industry display their wares for visiting buyers. International marketers make much use of trade fairs, which work well in certain domestic situations as well.

A manufacturers' agent is essentially an independent salesperson who works on a commission basis for a number of manufacturers of related but noncompeting products. Companies employ manufacturers' agents when they do not have enough sales in an area to warrant having their own sales force, or when they want a special push on certain product lines.

Distribution intensity for various products ranges from intensive to selective to exclusive.

A vertical marketing system (VMS) is a network of channel intermediaries that is organized and centrally managed to produce the maximum competitive impact. The types are corporate, administered, and contractual.

A franchise is an agreement whereby one firm (franchisee) agrees to meet the operating requirements of another successful business (franchisor) in return for the right to carry the name and products of the franchisor.

Channels and channel relationships change. A marketing institution will continue to exist only as long as it fulfills a need by performing a required service. This means that changes in power and function will gradually change over time.

▶ KEY TERMS

agent
auction house
broker
cash-and-carry wholesaler
channel captain
channel conflict
commission merchant
direct-response wholesaler
distribution channels

drop shipper
exclusive dealing
exclusive distribution
facilitating agency
franchise
industrial distributor
intensive distribution
manufacturers' agent
market restriction

marketing intermediary
merchandise mart
merchant wholesaler
public warehouse
rack jobber
reverse channels
retailer
sales branch
sales office
selective distribution

selling agent
sorting
tied selling
trade fairs
truck wholesaler
vertical marketing system
wholesalers
wholesaling
wholesaling intermediaries

▶ INTERACTIVE SUMMARY AND DISCUSSION QUESTIONS

1. The distribution channel performs several functions in the overall marketing system. These include facilitating the exchange process, sorting, standardizing transactions, holding inventories, assisting in the search process, and transporting. Provide an example of each function.

2. In the multistep channel, the product moves from producer to agent/broker to wholesaler to retailer to consumer. Describe how this woks, and the names of intermediary companies, using some product you are familiar with.

3. An increasingly common phenomenon is the use of more than one marketing channel for similar products. In what ways could multiple channels produce channel conflict? Be specific.

4. The term *wholesaler* is applied only to those wholesaling intermediaries that take title to the products they handle. The term *wholesaling intermediary* is a broader term that also includes others that perform important wholesaling activities. Differentiate among merchant wholesalers, agents, and brokers.

5. A marketing institution will continue to exist only as long as it fulfills a need by performing a required service. Does this mean that large retailers will gradually take over from wholesalers and put them out of business? Explain.

6. The number of actual transactions in an economic system comprised of manufacturers and customers can be *reduced* significantly by inserting one or more intermediaries between the manufacturer and the consumer. Explain.

7. Wholesaling intermediaries can be classified based on ownership of the intermediary and on title flows. Assuming that the independent wholesaling intermediary was the first type established in the "ownership" category, discuss the reasons why the other two types in that category might have emerged.

8. Match each of the products in the first column with the most appropriate wholesaling intermediary:

   _____ groceries   a. drop shipper
   _____ potato chips   b. truck wholesaler
   _____ coal   c. auction house
   _____ grain   d. manufacturers' agent
   _____ antiques   e. full-function merchant wholesaler
                                    f. commission merchant

9. Merchant wholesalers take title to products. Agents and brokers may take possession, but do not take title to products. Why is the operating-expense ratio of the merchant wholesaler higher than that of a typical agent or broker?

10. Comment on the following statement: Drop shippers are one type of merchant wholesaler that are good candidates for elimination. All they do is process orders. They don't even handle the goods.

11. The term *broker* also appears in the real-estate and securities fields. Are such brokers identical to the agent wholesaling intermediaries described in this chapter? Explain.

12. Trade fairs are periodic shows at which manufacturers in a particular industry may display their wares for visiting buyers. Explain how an international marketer of agricultural machinery might make use of a trade fair.

13. A manufacturers' agent is essentially an independent salesperson who works on a commission basis for a number of manufacturers of related but non-competing products. Under what circumstances would a company employ manufacturers' agents?

14. Distribution intensity for various products ranges from intensive to selective to exclusive. Which degree of distribution intensity is appropriate for each of the following?
    a. *Maclean's* magazine
    b. Caterpillar bulldozers
    c. Johnson outboard motors
    d. Dove soap
    e. Cuisinart food processors
    f. Kawasaki motorcycles
    g. Waterford crystal

15. Would your answers in question 14 change if your target market was China? If so, how?

16. A vertical marketing system (VMS) is a network of channel intermediaries organized and centrally managed to produce the maximum competitive impact. Distinguish among the following types of VMS: corporate, administered, and contractual.

17. A franchise is an agreement whereby one firm (franchisee) agrees to meet the operating requirements of another successful business (franchisor) in return for the right to carry the name and products of the franchisor. What advantages does franchising offer the small retailer?

18. Why would any manufacturer deliberately choose to limit market coverage through a policy of exclusive coverage?

19. Assume you are planning to set up a retail business (of your choice) on the Internet. Use the Web to locate suitable wholesalers that would supply products. Report on your findings.

To obtain a list of further readings for Chapter 15, please refer to the *Foundations of Marketing* Web site.

Chapter 16
Retailing

On-line retailer eSeeds.com is beginning to sprout some success.

CHAPTER OBJECTIVES
After reading and studying this chapter, you should be able to

1. Explain the role played by retailing in the marketing mix.
2. Outline the decision framework for retailing.
3. Distinguish between limited-line retailers and general-merchandise retailers.
4. Identify and explain each of the six bases for categorizing retailers.
5. Identify the major types of mass merchandisers.
6. Outline the various types of nonstore retailing.
7. Distinguish between chain and independent retailers.
8. Contrast the three types of planned shopping centres.
9. Identify new trends in retailing.

Mala Gunadasa-Rohling is proving that E-retailing can open new doors of opportunity for a small business. Ms. Gunadasa-Rohling, 37, is founder and partner of Tapestry International. The firm designs and maintains Web sites for about 40 garden clubs and societies, and in January 1999, launched eSeeds.com, an on-line retailer of seeds, plants, books, and tools. Ms. Gunadasa-Rohling's base is an office in her Vancouver home, next to the University of British Columbia.

Ms. Gunadasa-Rohling has gardening in her blood: she spent her childhood in England, where her father was a keen gardener and her mother was a whiz with houseplants. She also has a mind for science. She obtained a master of science degree from the University of British Columbia.

Gardening and technology came together in 1995 after the birth of her first child, a daughter. While on maternity leave, she approached the university's botanical garden about putting up a Web site.

Gardening was just beginning to bloom on the Internet. The botanical garden agreed to launch a site, and clubs and societies joined it. They found a home at www.hedgerows.com, designed and maintained by Ms. Gunadasa-Rohling. By the time her six-month leave was over, she had decided to turn the Hedgerows venture into a new career.

Her company, Tapestry, had skimpy revenue at first. Ms. Gunadasa-Rohling originally ran the Hedgerows project largely as a community service, providing Web site installation and maintenance free of charge to gardening groups in Canada and England. But as her virtual garden grew, she attracted some paying clients, including the CBC television's *Canadian Gardener*. She's now working on luring advertisers to the site, and may charge participating clubs in the future.

www.hedgerows.com

Husband Gerald Rohling, a researcher at UBC, works with her as well. The two built the eSeeds business using Net.Commerce, an electronic-commerce package from International Business Machines Corp.

To date, they've invested close to $50 000 in hardware and software to launch the eSeeds data base. Financing for the new business came from their savings and, late last year, through a small-business bank loan.

www.eseeds.com

The University of British Columbia Botanical Garden was the first supplier to sign on with eSeeds. Now the data base includes more than 2000 different products from seven suppliers. Ms. Gunadasa-Rohling hopes to boost that total to 10 000 or more products by year-end. ESeeds earns a commission of about 30 percent of the ticket price of each transaction. This year, eSeeds plans to launch a separate, secure area for wholesalers to sell to retailers.

The couple came close to burning out in the months spent getting eSeeds up and running. "Lots of times, we were working until 2:00 or 3:00 A.M.—our friends and family didn't see us for about 12 months."

Going live with eSeeds in January 1999 was a "huge relief," Ms. Gunadasa-Rohling says. Other high points came when the venture received its first cheque in U.S. funds and its first order from Europe. Tapestry sales were about $40 000 last year and are projected to at least double this year.

The biggest challenge now is surviving in a crowded on-line market. ESeeds is a mere sprout next to players such as Garden.com, an Austin, Texas–based operation that raised more than $20-million (U.S.) in financing last year, carries about 15 000 items, and recently launched a spin-off quarterly magazine.

Ms. Gunadasa-Rohling says her niche will be in selling Canadian goods to Canadian gardeners, many of whom are hungry for information geared to their specific needs—and climate.

"Our focus will be on Canadian suppliers. There are a lot of specialty nurseries in Canada, and we want to give them a chance. The hardest thing was becoming a salesperson. Once I've got a relationship with a client I'm fine—but when it comes to that first call, whenever I pick up the phone, I break out in a cold sweat."

Retailing takes many different forms. It can be a small business, as discussed above, and it also takes the form of huge organizations such as the Hudson's Bay Company.

In Canada, retailing is big business and is a vital part of the national economy. All you have to do is look around you as you travel to and from school. You will probably see several fast-food restaurants, such as Wendy's and Tim Horton's. You will also pass convenience stores such as 7-Eleven, Mac's, and local corner stores. As well, there will be car dealerships, neighbourhood shopping centres, and possibly regional shopping centres with several department stores. You might also pass some retailers that don't sell physical products but instead provide services, such as movie rentals or tax return preparation (e.g., H&R Block).

Retailing is one of this country's largest employers, and the range of occupations is wide. As consumers we mainly see salesclerks, but the industry also includes accountants, merchandise buyers, display specialists, advertising personnel, and distribution and plant specialists. For the marketing student, retail management can be an exciting career.

Source: Adapted from Wendy Stueck, "Founder Sows eSeeds for Online Sales," *The Globe and Mail* (March 22, 1999), p. B5. Reprinted with permission from *The Globe and Mail*.

▶ INTRODUCTION

Because retailers sell the products created by others to the ultimate consumers, retailers are the final link in the marketing channel. In a very real sense, retailers *are* the marketing channel for most consumers, since consumers have little contact with manufacturers and almost none with wholesaling intermediaries. The services provided—location, store hours, quality of salespeople, store layout, Web site, selection, and returns, among others—often figure even more importantly than the physical product in buying decisions.

Retailers are both customers and marketers in the channel. They market goods and services to ultimate consumers and also are the consumers for wholesalers and manufacturers. Because of their critical location in the channel, retailers may perform an important feedback role in obtaining information from customers and transmitting it to manufacturers and other channel members.

Retailing is the "last step of the marketing channel" for the consumer-goods manufacturer. Whether the manufacturer has established a company-owned chain of retail stores or uses several of the thousands of retail stores in Canada, the success of the entire marketing strategy rides on the decisions of consumers in the retail store.

retailing
All the activities involved in selling goods and services to the ultimate consumer.

Retailing may be defined as all the activities involved in selling goods and services to the ultimate consumer. Retailing involves not only sales in retail stores, but also several forms of nonstore retailing. These include telephone and direct-response sales (e.g., Internet selling), automatic merchandising, and direct house-to-house solicitations by salespeople.

▶ EVOLUTION OF RETAILING

www.hbc.com/english.asp

Early retailing in Canada can be traced to the voyageurs, to the establishment of trading posts by the Hudson's Bay Company and others, and to pack peddlers who literally carried their wares to outlying settlements. After the trading post days, the Hudson's Bay and other retailers evolved into the institution known as the *general store*. The general store was stocked with general merchandise to meet the needs of a small community or rural area. Here customers could buy clothing, groceries, feed, seed, farm equipment, drugs, spectacles, and candy. The following account provides a good description of this early retail institution:

> The country store was in many respects a departmental store on a small scale, for a well-equipped store contained a little of everything. On one side were to be seen shelves well filled with groceries, crockery-ware, and a few patent medicines, such as blood purifiers, painkillers, and liniments; on the other side, a well assorted stock of dry goods, including prints, woolens, muslins, calico, cottons, etc. At the back, a lot of hardware, comprising nails, paints, oils, putty, glass, and garden tools, as well as an assortment of boots and shoes—from the tiny copper-toe to the farmer's big cowhide. In the back room, at the rear end of the store, were to be

found barrels of sugar and New Orleans molasses, crates of eggs, and tubs of butter and lard. With this miscellaneous mixture — tea, coffee, dry goods, codfish, and boots and shoes — the odour of the country store was truly a composite one, and trying to the olfactory organs of the visitor. The country merchant was usually a man in good circumstances, for he was obliged in most cases to give a year's credit, the farmers paying their bills in the fall of the year, after the "threshing" or the "killing"; their only source of revenue at any other time being from butter and eggs, which their wives took to the country store, usually once a week, and exchanged for store goods. Perhaps there was no more popular place of meeting than the country store.[1]

The basic needs that caused the general store to develop also doomed this institution to a limited existence. Since the general store owners attempted to satisfy the needs of customers for all types of "store-bought" goods, they carried a small assortment of each good. As the villages grew, the size the market was large enough to support stores specializing in specific product lines, such as groceries, hardware, dry goods, and drugs. Most general stores either converted into more specialized limited-line stores or closed. But the general store did, and in some rural areas still does, fill a need for its customers. General stores are still operated profitably in less developed countries, where income levels cannot support more specialized retailers, and in a few isolated parts of Canada as well.

Innovation and Competition in Retailing

Retailing is an extremely competitive industry. A major determinant of success is to develop a *differential advantage* over competitors. Without a sustainable differential advantage, no retailer will last for long. Therefore, retailing is one of the most dynamic components of the economic system. As consumers, we see these changes occurring almost on a daily basis, yet we often do not think about the retail warfare going on around us.

Retailing operations are remarkable illustrations of the marketing concept in operation. Retail innovations often develop as attempts to better satisfy particular consumer needs, or to make the enterprise more competitive.

As consumers' needs and lifestyles change, institutions emerge to meet this demand. The supermarket appeared in the early 1930s to meet consumer desires for lower prices. Its success was enhanced by the fact that cars and good roads were commonly available. Convenience food stores such as 7-Eleven meet the need today for readily available basic products at all hours. Superstores and membership and warehouse clubs such as Costco serve consumers who want low prices and are willing to travel significant distances, as well as give up services.

www.7-eleven.com

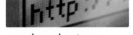
www.homedepot.com

Large-format specialty stores such as Home Depot are a particularly potent competitor, because they provide low prices and breadth and depth of merchandise, as well as services. Department stores provide a wide variety of other products and services to meet other customer needs. The once-powerful Eaton's department store failed to do this and the company (but not its brands) is now history. Vending machines, door-to-door retailers, and mail-order retailing offer buyers convenience. Planned shopping centres provide a balanced array of consumer goods and services and include ample parking for their customers.

The Wheel-of-Retailing Hypothesis

wheel of retailing
Hypothesized process of change in retailing, which suggests that new types of retailers gain a competitive foothold by offering lower prices through the reduction or elimination of services; but once established, they add more services and their prices gradually rise, so that they then become vulnerable to a new low-price retailer with minimum services—and the wheel turns.

M.P. McNair attempted to explain the patterns of change in retailing through what has been termed the **wheel of retailing**. According to this hypothesis, new types of retailers gain a competitive foothold by offering lower prices to their customers through the reduction or elimination of services. Once they are established, however, they evolve by adding more services, and their prices gradually rise. Then they become vulnerable to a new low-price retailer that enters with minimum services—and the wheel turns.

Most of the major developments in retailing appear to fit the wheel pattern. Early department stores, chain stores, supermarkets, and discount stores all emphasized limited service and low prices. In most instances, price levels have gradually increased as services have been added.

There have been some exceptions, however. Suburban shopping centres, convenience food stores, and vending machines were not developed on a foundation of low-price appeals. However, the wheel pattern has been present often enough in the past that it should serve as a general indicator of future developments in retailing.

▶ MARKETING STRATEGY IN RETAILING

The retailer's decision-making process, like the producer's and wholesaler's, centres on the two fundamental steps of (1) analyzing, evaluating, and ultimately selecting a *target market,* and (2) developing a *marketing mix* designed to satisfy the chosen target market profitably. In other words, the retailer must develop a product offering to appeal to the chosen consumer group, set prices, and choose a location and method of distribution. Finally, the retailer has to develop a marketing communications strategy.[2]

Conduct Target Market Research and Analysis

www.canadiantire.com

Target market analysis is essential in retailing. Canada's 119 000 retail establishments are involved in developing specific marketing mixes to satisfy chosen market segments. Like other marketers, retailers must start by selecting the target market to which they wish to appeal. Marketing research is often used in this aspect of retail decision making. For example, retailers entering new countries, or even new markets in the same country, have been surprised that the target market of their home location apparently does not exist in the new location. Canadian Tire expanded to the larger U.S. market with the purchase of White Stores, Inc.,[3] but found U.S. market acceptance of virtual carbon copies of the successful Canadian store so limited that the firm abandoned that market after significant losses. Marks and Spencer, one of Britain's most successful retailers, had similar difficulties when it entered the Canadian market and finally had to abandon this market. Marketing research can help a company adjust to a new environment faster.

▶ THE ETHICAL MARKETER

Ethics on the Internet

"Who said you leave your values at the door when you start doing business on the Web? There are certain fair practices that have to be upheld and respected." In March 1999, the president of Chapters Internet, Rick Segal, sent a letter to chief executive Heather Reisman of Indigo Books saying his company would remove the link to Chaptersglobe.com from Indigo Instruments, an unrelated site that has a Web address (Indigo.com) similar to Indigo Books (Indigo.ca). Indigo Books had threatened to go to court to remove the site, saying Chapters' link on Indigo Instruments, a seller of scientific equipment that does 95 percent of its business in the United States, was a violation of the book retailer's trademark.

Indigo Books was especially irked the original appearance of the link was intentionally designed to make Web users looking for Indigo Books think their search had ended. The original link said, "Looking for Books? Come Here," followed by an exclamation mark that looked similar to Indigo's trademarked logo. Instead, pressing on the link brought Web users to Chaptersglobe.com. Indigo Books was also upset that Chapters had included the word Indigo as a metatag on its Web site. This metatag would give anyone using Indigo in a Web search engine a list of book retailers that would include the Chapters site.

www.indigo.ca

www.chaptersglobe.com

www.chapters.ca

Industry watchers say operators of Web porn sites have used words such as Barbie or Playboy to route Web users to their sites. Chapters initially described these activities as an ingenious use of "guerriila warfare" tactics in the battle for Web customers. Chapters' first response to Indigo Books' protests was to change the look of the site to make it clear it was a link to Chapters' Web site, but maintained it wasn't breaking trademark law. Mr. Segal's letter said "there was never any intent to misuse or infringe on your trademark in any way."

Chapters Inc.'s capitulation in agreeing to remove a link to its Internet address from a site with a name similar to archrival Indigo Books and Music was the only "ethical and legal" solution, said Indigo Books' chief executive Heather Reisman.

What are the implications for Internet retailing if other firms emulate the original Chapters strategy?

The battle of giants.

Source: Adapted from Zena Olijnyk, "The Battle for Web Customers Brings Out Guerrilla Warfare Tactics," *Financial Post* (March 30, 1999), p. C8. Reprinted with permission.

Sometimes a retailer finds it necessary to shift target markets. For example, stores established to serve specialty markets, such as skiers or snowmobilers, have found that lack of snow or changes in consumer recreation habits have forced them to expand or change their offerings to serve more viable target markets. Market selection is as vital an aspect of retailers' marketing strategy as it is for any other marketer.[4]

Develop a Marketing (Retail) Mix That Fits the Target Market

The retail mix is comprised of the following elements: decision about goods and services, prices, location and distribution, and retail image and promotion. The objective is to blend these elements to provide a unique offering to the market.

GOODS AND SERVICES STRATEGY

Retailers must also determine and evaluate their offerings with respect to the following:

- general goods/services categories
- specific lines
- specific products
- inventory depth
- range of assortment

These decisions are determined by the size of the retailer, as well as whether the store tends to concentrate on convenience, shopping, or specialty goods. Other marketing factors can influence goods and/or service offerings. For instance, Toys R Us distinguishes itself by specializing and providing great breadth and depth of assortment at low prices.

Product strategy evolves to meet competition and changing consumer needs. The success of Loblaws' Superstores forced Safeway to develop its large Food for Less establishments. On a more limited scale, a decision by Wal-Mart to provide a special area devoted to youth-oriented CDs would likely have to be matched by Zellers if the new Wal-Mart section proved to be popular.

www.safeway.com

www.walmart.com

RETAIL PRICING STRATEGY

Pricing is another critical element of the retailing mix. The essential decisions concern relative price levels. Does the target market want service and high quality, high-priced merchandise (as offered by Holt Renfrew), or lower-priced items (as offered by Zellers)? Price is such an important variable in the retail marketing mix that it continually drives the establishment of new types of retail operations, such as Costco. These will be discussed in more detail later.

Other pricing decisions concern markups, markdowns, loss leaders, odd pricing, and promotional pricing. The retailer is the channel member with direct responsibility for the prices paid by consumers. As Chapters 13 and 14 pointed out, the prices that are set play a major role in buyer perceptions of the retail market.

LOCATION AND DISTRIBUTION STRATEGY

Real-estate professionals often say that there are three critical factors for establishing a retail establishment: "Location, location, location." A store must be in an appropriate location for the type and price of merchandise carried. Small service outlets such as dry cleaners have discovered that there is a difference between being on the "going to work" side of a busy street and the "going home" side. Other retailers have found success in small strip-type neighbourhood shopping centres that are close to where people live. These centres continue to flourish despite the advent of larger suburban community shopping centres.[5]

retail trade area analysis
Studies that assess the relative drawing power of alternative retail locations.

Retail trade area analysis refers to studies that assess the relative drawing power of alternative retail locations. For example, shoppers might be polled as to where they live, how they get to the stores they shop at, how long it takes, how often they shop, and the like. Similarly, the credit charges of an existing store might be plotted to show what its service area is.

law of retail gravitation
Principle that delineates the retail trade area of a potential site on the basis of distance between alternative locations and relative populations.

Another technique to use is the law of retail gravitation, sometimes called Reilly's law after its originator, William J. Reilly.[6] The **law of retail gravitation**, originally formulated in the 1920s, delineates the retail trade area of a potential site on the basis of distance between alternative locations and relative populations. The formula is

$$\text{Breaking point in km from A} = \frac{\text{km between A and B}}{1 + \sqrt{\dfrac{\text{Population of B}}{\text{Population of A}}}}$$

Assume a retailer is considering locating a new outlet in Town A or Town B, which are located 60 km from each other. The population of A is 80 000 and the population of B is 20 000. One question that concerns the retailer is where people living in a small rural community located on the highway between the two towns 25 km from Town B are likely to shop.

According to the law of retail gravitation, these rural shoppers would most likely shop in Town A even though it is 10 km farther away than Town B. The retail trade area of A extends 40 km toward B, and the rural community is located only 35 km away.

$$\text{Breaking point in km from A} = \frac{60}{1 + \sqrt{\dfrac{20\,000}{80\,000}}} = \frac{60}{1 + \sqrt{.25}} = \frac{60}{1.5} = 40$$

The formula can be applied inversely to find Town B's trade area, yielding a figure of 20 km, which falls 5 km short of the rural community:

$$\text{Breaking point in km from B} = \frac{60}{1 + \sqrt{\dfrac{80\,000}{20\,000}}} = \frac{60}{1 + \sqrt{4}} = \frac{60}{3} = 20 \text{ km}$$

The complete trade area for A or B could be found by similar calculations with other communities.

The application of this technique is limited in an area of urban sprawl, regional shopping centres, and consumers who measure distances in terms of travel time. As a result, a contemporary version of retail trade analysis has been offered by David Huff.

Huff's work is an interurban model that assesses the likelihood that a consumer will patronize a specific shopping centre. Trading areas are expressed in terms of a series of probability contours. The probability that a consumer will patronize a specific shopping centre is viewed as a function of centre size, travel time, and the type of merchandise sought.[7] Such models are more often used for structuring decision making than as a precise, predictive tool.

Other Distribution Decisions Retailers are faced with a variety of other distribution decisions, largely in order to ensure that adequate quantities of stock are available when consumers want to buy. The definition of "adequate" will vary with the service strategy of the retailer. In many traditional retail situations, since the cost of carrying inventory is high, a high-margin, full-service retailer will likely have a greater depth and range of merchandise than a low-margin, limited-time, high-volume outlet. This generalization does not hold in the case of some large-format specialty stores, such as Office Depot.

RETAIL IMAGE AND PROMOTIONAL STRATEGY

Retail image refers to the consumer's perception of a store and of the shopping experience it provides.[8] Promotional strategy is a key element in determining the store's image with the consumer. Another important element is the amenities provided by the retailer — the so-called atmospherics.

Promoting a store with screaming headlines about fantastic once-in-a-lifetime sale prices creates a substantially different image from that using a subdued,

retail image
The consumer's perception of a store and of the shopping experience it provides.

▶ THE CANADIAN MARKETPLACE

A Failure in Global Marketing

Highly successful British retailing institution Marks & Spencer PLC packed up its food and clothing and left Canada in 1999 after years of failing to connect to Canadian tastes. Marks & Spencer Canada Inc. closed all 38 stores in the country and laid off about 900 employees. Parent company Marks & Spencer PLC estimated that leaving Canada cost about $60-million.

"I think the brand ... never really found its niche in the Canadian market," David Stewart, president and chief executive officer in Canada for the company's last two years, said in an interview.

"It was a British concept that was imported and assumed to work in Canada. I put together a North American management team that tried to change it. But [it was] far too late.... There [was] too much to rejig."

Marks & Spencer, known fondly by many for its quality underwear, turned a profit only three times since it set up shop in Canada in 1973: in the 1992–93 year and twice in the 1980s. It had a loyal customer core of mostly expatriate Britons, but never bothered to market itself to others in Canada, observers say.

"They were viewed as being terribly unfashionable," said retail consultant John Williams of J.C. Williams Group Ltd. in Toronto. "[They] had a dowdy image. They were insensitive to the needs of Canadian consumers."

The plans to close [came] amid heated competition among clothing retailers, especially since department store chains Eaton's and The Bay moved more into apparel. The arrival of giant discounter Wal-Mart Canada Inc. in 1994 and other U.S.-based big-box category killers also squeezed virtually all rivals.

You cannot assume that a product or concept that works in your country will work in another.

Source: Adapted from Marina Strauss, "Marks & Spencer to Leave Canada," *The Globe and Mail* (April 29, 1999), p. B1. Reprinted with permission from *The Globe and Mail*.

---

tasteful illustration of obviously stylish, elegant clothing. Similarly, walking into a discount store filled with the smell of caramel popcorn produces an image that is dramatically different from that of entering a beautifully carpeted boutique.

Regardless of how it is accomplished, the objective of retailer promotional strategy should be to align the consumer's perception of the store with other elements of the retailing mix: retail image should match the target market that is selected.

Differentiate Store from Competitors

differentiation triangle
Differentiation of a retail store from competitors in the same strategic group through price, location, and store atmosphere and service.

Differentiation is a key factor in competitive strategy.[9] Retailers can differentiate themselves in many ways. However, three elements — price, location, and store atmosphere and service — are typically used to differentiate stores from the competitors in the same strategic group. The **differentiation triangle** is shown in Figure 16.1.

Changes in these elements do not transform a store from one type to another (e.g., a convenience store to a department store). Yet the way the elements are

▶ THE PRACTISING MARKETER

Loyalty Programs and Relationship Marketing

Loyalty marketing is the process of providing incentives to customers so that they will want to return again and again. Such activities are sometimes called "continuity programs." The development of a loyalty-marketing program is more important for those companies or industries in a commodity-like business, where there is less ability to differentiate by product. Customer loyalty today equals the best sale price.

Airlines started the continuity programs. Their objective was to attract and maintain their principal customer, the business traveller, using frequent-flyer programs. These programs have become so important to the airlines, due to the loyalty factors, repeat business, and marketing value of the frequent-flyer list, that they can't afford to drop them.

One of the most outstanding loyalty programs is the Zellers Club Z program. Zellers developed the first on-line frequent-buyer system (points are given with purchases) in North America. The initial objectives of Club Z included specific financial targets for market penetration, customer shopping frequency, incremental purchase, and new customers. Not only were these targets exceeded, but the program continues to outperform expectations.

Another goal was to increase the frequency of purchase of everyday consumables. Zellers wanted to find a way to drive up sales of such things as shampoo or toothpaste rather than having to "give them away" in order to get customers back into the store.

On an individual customer basis, Zellers wanted to build frequency per customer and spending per customer. The Club Z program enabled the company to delineate a specific day in the week, hour in the day, or department in the store where it could give double points. For example, the fashion department gave double points on Valentine's Day.

Club Z also provides a database so that Zellers knows exactly where Club Z members live and how much they spend. Zellers can thus identify profiles of individuals who are good consumers, and target them. Loyalty programs like this one enable the firm to add an important degree of differentiation to its offerings that truly builds loyalty.

The Hudson's Bay Company is now extending its loyalty programs into Asia. It expects that these will contribute as much as one-third of its overall revenue in five years.[10] **How can the information generated by a loyalty program be used in a relationship marketing program?**

Source: Excerpted from a presentation by Arthur Smith, former executive vice-president of Zellers, in *Marketing* magazine (January 22, 1990), p. 20. Reprinted with permission.

www.zellers.ca

---

used is important, since they give the customer reasons to choose one store over another. For example, location is very important, as we have already discussed.

Price is a powerful tool in the retail mix. It is not always the differentiating factor, but retailers must understand when it does play that role. In such a circumstance, retailers are finding that they cannot "play around" with discounting. Price cuts must be truly significant in order to compete with other retailers who have also chosen price as a means of differentiation.

Stores can also differentiate by improving store atmosphere and customer service. Unfortunately, many retailers have ignored this element's potential and allowed service quality to deteriorate in the pursuit of cost savings. As manufacturers and other service providers are learning to emphasize total quality in their products, retailers also need reevaluate the quality of their service.

▶ **FIGURE 16.1 Differentiation Triangle: Avenues for Differentiation Within Strategic Groups**

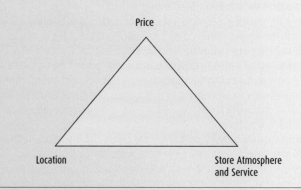

Source: Avijit Ghosh, *Retail Management*, 2nd ed. (Fort Worth, TX: Dryden Press, 1994), pp. 59–60. Copyright © 1994 by The Dryden Press, reprinted by permission of the publisher.

▶ CATEGORIZING RETAILERS

The nation's retailers come in a variety of forms. Since new types of retail operations continue to evolve in response to the changing demands of their markets, no universal classification has been devised. The following characteristics or bases can be used in categorizing them:

- shopping effort expended by customers
- services provided to customers
- product lines
- location of retail transactions
- form of ownership
- margin and turnover

Any retailing operation can be classified using each of these six bases. A 7-Eleven store may be classified as a convenience store (category 1), self-service (category 2), relatively narrow product lines (category 3), in-store retailing (category 4), a member of a corporate chain (category 5), and high margin/high turnover (category 6). Figure 16.2 illustrates the bases for classifying retail operations.

Retailers Classified by Shopping Effort

A classification of consumer goods based on consumer purchase patterns in securing a particular product or service was presented in Chapter 10. Products were classified as convenience, shopping, or specialty goods. This system can be

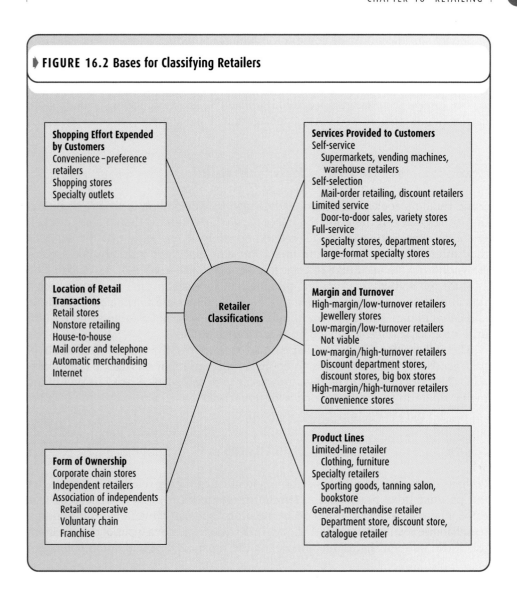

FIGURE 16.2 Bases for Classifying Retailers

Shopping Effort Expended by Customers
Convenience – preference retailers
Shopping stores
Specialty outlets

Services Provided to Customers
Self-service
 Supermarkets, vending machines, warehouse retailers
Self-selection
 Mail-order retailing, discount retailers
Limited service
 Door-to-door sales, variety stores
Full-service
 Specialty stores, department stores, large-format specialty stores

Location of Retail Transactions
Retail stores
Nonstore retailing
House-to-house
Mail order and telephone
Automatic merchandising
Internet

Retailer Classifications

Margin and Turnover
High-margin/low-turnover retailers
 Jewellery stores
Low-margin/low-turnover retailers
 Not viable
Low-margin/high-turnover retailers
 Discount department stores, discount stores, big box stores
High-margin/high-turnover retailers
 Convenience stores

Form of Ownership
Corporate chain stores
Independent retailers
Association of independents
 Retail cooperative
 Voluntary chain
 Franchise

Product Lines
Limited-line retailer
 Clothing, furniture
Specialty retailers
 Sporting goods, tanning salon, bookstore
General-merchandise retailer
 Department store, discount store, catalogue retailer

extended to retailers by considering the reasons consumers shop at a particular retail outlet. The result is a classification scheme in which retail outlets, like consumer goods, are categorized as convenience–preference, shopping, or specialty. The type of retail outlet has a significant influence on the marketing strategies the retailer should select. *Convenience–preference retailers* focus on convenient locations, long store hours, rapid checkout service, and adequate parking facilities. Small food stores, gasoline retailers, and some barber shops are included in this category.

Shopping stores typically include furniture stores, appliance retailers, clothing outlets, and sporting goods stores. Consumers will compare prices, assortments, and quality levels of competing outlets before making a purchase decision. Managers of shopping stores attempt to differentiate their outlets through advertising, window displays, in-store layouts, knowledgeable salespeople, and appropriate merchandise assortments.

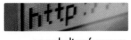

www.holtrenfrew.com

www.birks.com

Specialty retailers provide some combination of product lines, service, and reputation that results in consumers' willingness to expend considerable effort to shop there. Holt Renfrew and Birks have developed a sufficient degree of loyalty among many shoppers to be categorized as specialty retailers.

The foregoing categories are not absolute. The most exclusive specialty store carries handkerchiefs, and many supermarkets have gourmet food departments.

Retailers Classified by Services Provided

Some retailers seek a differential advantage by developing a unique combination of service offerings for the customers who compose their target market. Retailing operations may be classified according to the extent of the services they offer. There is a spectrum of retailer services from virtually no services (self-service) to a full range of customer services (full-service).

Since the self-service retailers provide few services to their customers, location and price are important factors. These retailers tend to specialize in staple and convenience goods that are purchased frequently by customers and require little product service or advice from retail personnel.

The full-service retail establishments focus more on fashion-oriented shopping goods and specialty items and offer a wide variety of services to their clientele. Their prices tend to be higher than those of self-service retailers due to the higher operating costs associated with the services.

Retailers Classified by Product Lines

Perhaps the most commonly used method of categorizing retailers is to consider the product lines they handle. Grouping retailers by product lines produces three major categories: limited-line retailers, specialty retailers, and general-merchandise retailers. Table 16.1 shows retail trade for various types of outlets. From this it can be seen that Canadians spend the most on food and automobiles.

LIMITED-LINE RETAILERS

limited-line store
Retailer that offers a large assortment of a single line of products or a few related lines of products.

A large assortment of a single line of products or a few related lines of products are offered in **limited-line stores**. Their development parallelled the growth of towns when the population grew sufficiently to support them. These operations include such retailers as furniture stores, hardware stores, grocery stores and supermarkets, appliance stores, and sporting goods stores. Examples of limited-line stores include Sherwin-Williams (paint), House of Teak (furniture), Radio Shack (home electronics), Pegabo and Bata (shoes), Calculator World (electronic calculators), Gap (ready-to-wear), and Chapters (books).

These retailers choose to cater to the needs of a specific target market — people who want to select from a complete line in purchasing a particular product. The marketing vice president of a limited-line firm might summarize the limited-line retailer's strategy this way: "Canadian Tire can show customers 5 types of safety boots, but we can show them 25."

Supermarkets The supermarket concentrates mainly on a single line — groceries — but this line contains many different products.

▶ **TABLE 16.1 Total Retail Sales by Trade Group, 1995–1996**

TRADE GROUP	1995	1996	PERCENTAGE CHANGE 1995/1996
	\$000 000		
Supermarkets and grocery stores	49 909.9	49 264.8	-1.3
All other food stores	4 153.6	4 188.3	0.8
Drugs and patent medicine stores	11 943.8	12 405.6	3.9
Shoe stores	1 707.9	1 714.5	0.4
Men's clothing stores	1 645.4	1 544.0	-6.2
Women's clothing stores	4 097.2	4 040.6	-1.4
Other clothing stores	5 464.7	5 378.1	-1.6
Household furniture and appliance stores	8 551.1	8 341.9	-2.4
Household furnishings stores	2 290.2	2 365.0	3.3
Motor vehicle and recreational vehicle dealers	45 591.6	52 285.7	14.7
Gasoline service stations	14 703.6	16 257.0	10.6
Automotive parts, accessories, and services	11 357.8	12 186.2	7.3
General merchandise stores	22 583.6	23 717.8	5.0
Other semidurable goods stores	7 094.0	7 350.8	3.6
Other durable goods stores	5 504.1	5 592.3	1.6
Other retail stores	11 202.2	10 378.9	-7.3
All Stores—Total	211 600.6	217 011.6	2.6

Source: Statistics Canada, *Market Research Handbook, 1998,* Catalogue No. 63-225, p. 122. Reproduced by permission of the Minister of Supply and Services Canada.

A **supermarket** can be defined as a large-scale, departmentalized retail store offering a large variety of food products such as meats, produce, dairy products, canned goods, and frozen foods in addition to various nonfood items. It operates on a *self-service* basis and emphasizes price and adequate parking facilities. Supermarket customer typically shop once or twice a week and make fill-in purchases between each major shopping trip. In 1996, supermarkets and grocery stores accounted for 92.2 percent of food store sales in Canada.[11]

Vigorous competition is a way of life for supermarkets. One Ontario supermarket attempted to increase its share of the market through a well-publicized price-cutting program. The ramifications were quickly felt in other areas of the country where branches of competing chains operate. Retaliation by other supermarkets was swift, and temporary price cuts ensued—as well as reductions in profits. Supermarket profits average only about 1 percent of sales after taxes. However, a high turnover of 20–26 times per year provides attractive returns on investment.

With a razor-thin profit margin, supermarkets compete through careful planning of retail displays in order to sell more merchandise per week and reduce the amount of investment in inventory. Product location is studied carefully in order to expose the consumer to as much merchandise as possible (and increase impulse purchases). In an attempt to respond to the tendency of consumers to

supermarket
Large-scale, departmentalized retail store offering a large variety of food products.

eat many of their meals outside the home, supermarkets have begun to feature their own delicatessens and bakeries and to devote a limited portion of their stores to nonfood items.

Nonfood products such as toiletries, magazines, videos, over-the-counter drugs, prescription pharmaceuticals, and small kitchen utensils are carried for two reasons: (1) consumers have displayed a willingness to buy such items in supermarkets, and (2) supermarket managers like these items because they have a higher profit margin than the food products. Nonfood sales have grown substantially as a percentage of supermarket sales.

The trend in this category is toward larger stores. Many of these, such as Loblaws' Superstores, carry a variety of other merchandise, such as clothing, hardware, and gift items.

SPECIALTY RETAILERS

specialty store
Retailer that handles only part of a single line of products.

A **specialty store** typically handles only part of a single line of products. However, this narrow line is stocked in considerable depth. Such stores include meat markets, shoe stores, bakeries, furriers, and luggage shops. Although some of these stores are operated by chains, most are run as independent small-scale operations. The specialty store is perhaps the greatest stronghold of the independent retailer, who can develop expertise in providing a very narrow line of products for his or her local market.

Specialty stores should not be confused with specialty goods, for the specialty store typically carries convenience and shopping goods. The label "specialty" comes from the practice of handling a specific, narrow line of merchandise.

GENERAL-MERCHANDISE RETAILERS

department store
Large retailer that handles a variety of merchandise.

Department Stores The department store is actually a series of limited-line and specialty stores under one roof. A **department store**, by definition, is a large retailer that handles a variety of merchandise that may include apparel and accessories, home furnishings, cosmetics, housewares, and appliances. It serves the consumer by acting as a one-stop shopping centre for almost all personal and household items.

A distinguishing feature of the department store is indicated by its name. The entire stock is *organized around departments* for the purposes of service, promotion, and control. A general merchandising manager is responsible for the entire store's product planning. Reporting to the merchandising manager are the buyers who manage each department. The buyers typically run the departments almost as independent businesses and are given considerable discretion in merchandising and layout decisions. Acceptance of the retailing axiom that "well-purchased goods are half sold" is indicated in the department manager's title of *buyer*. The buyers, particularly those in charge of high-fashion departments, spend a considerable portion of their time making decisions concerning the inventory to be carried in their departments.

The department store has been the symbol of retailing since the turn of the century. It started in Canada with Timothy Eaton in 1869, when he purchased the 4 m wide dry-goods store and stock of William Jennings for $6500. Eaton established a one-price cash policy (instead of bargaining and paying in produce), and formulated the famous "goods satisfactory or money refunded" guarantee. By 1929, half the retail sales in Canada were made at Eaton's.[12]

▶ INTERNET IMPACT

Web Site Opens Music Store's Doors to the World

The magic of a music amplifier is that it can take the minimal, muted sound of an electric instrument and transform it into a rich, strong, vibrant sound that can be heard across a room or at the other end of a stadium.

Having a Web site does much the same job for his music store, says Glenn Murch, owner of Murch Music in Cambridge, a small city west of Toronto. "Our Web site opens up our store's doors to the entire world," says Mr. Murch, who is sold on the Web as an effective way of building revenue. "We've added a couple of months' worth of sales to our year by going on the Web."

And winning those sales has cost them little in terms of expenditures of either money or time. "We built the Web site ourselves," says Mr. Murch. Maintaining the site at www.murchmusic.com takes only minimal effort, and it allows sales staff to maximize their efforts, responding to on-line inquiries and orders when the store isn't busy, while devoting their complete attention to customers who show up to shop in person.

One big attraction of the Web for Murch Music stems from the store's focus on high-end and vintage instruments. The reality, especially for an outlet in a small community, is that the more specialized the product niche, the fewer the number of potential buyers. Having an on-line presence lets Murch Music overcome that handicap by offering its products to musical enthusiasts around the globe. "I just had an e-mail inquiry from Madrid, Spain, about one of the amplifiers on our site," says Mr. Murch. "I grabbed our digital camera, took three snaps of it, and sent them off in a reply e-mail. Twenty minutes later, I got a phone call with an order request and a credit card number."

In many cases, the Web site isn't so much a promotional medium as simply an easy way for would-be buyers to find out that the store has in stock what they are looking for. Web customers arrive at Murch Music through referrals, via links from manufacturers' sites, or through search engines. "It's a way of reaching out and grabbing that person who really wants to buy that particular item."

The site also acts as a "virtual" store, allowing instrument shoppers to electronically browse through Murch's inventory. If they click on the products link, for instance, they can take a cyber-stroll through the store's aisles, complete with large colour photographs of the instruments, which range from vintage guitars to digital recording machines.

Having a Web site helps Mr. Murch increase customer satisfaction while reducing the time spent on administration and correspondence. In the pre-Web days, if Mr. Murch got an inquiry about an instrument, he had to take some photographs, have the film developed, send the snaps out to the interested party, and then enter into a complicated, slow, and time-consuming series of letters and phone calls to land the sale. With the Web, he can quickly scan in a picture of a new item, answer follow-up queries by e-mail, and complete the sale, all electronically.

In short, says Mr. Murch, "having a Web site is great because it lets us experience terrific growth with very little effort."

Which types of retailers could benefit from using e-commerce as Mr. Murch has done? What are the limitations of this approach?

Source: "Web Site Opens Music Store's Doors to the World," IBM Small Business Advertising Feature, *The Globe and Mail* (June 15, 1999). Reprinted with the expressed permission of IBM Canada Ltd., Copyright © 1999.

Today, almost every urban area in Canada has one or more department stores associated with its downtown area and its major shopping areas. Department stores have had a major impact in many cities. For example, as recently as 1969, Eaton's received 40 percent of every retail dollar (except groceries) in

Winnipeg.[13] Even though Eaton's had to close its doors 30 years later, other department stores remain a significant factor in the market.

The impact of department stores on urban life is not confined to Canada. Such stores are, of course, widespread in the United States. European shoppers associate London with Harrod's and Paris with Au Printemps. Australians associate Melbourne and Sydney with Myers/Cole.

Department stores are known for offering their customers a wide variety of services such as charge accounts, delivery, gift wrapping, and liberal return privileges. In addition, approximately 50 percent of their employees and some 40 percent of their floor space are devoted to nonselling activities. As a result, department stores have relatively high operating costs, averaging between 45 and 60 percent of sales.

Department stores have faced intense competition in the past 30 years. Their relatively high operating costs make them vulnerable to other retailing types such as discount stores and "big box" warehouse stores (discussed later in this section). In addition, department stores are typically located in downtown business districts and experience the problems associated with limited parking, traffic congestion, and urban migration to the suburbs. In 1999, Eaton's declared bankruptcy. Some of its stores were sold to Sears, but many others simply closed.

Successful department stores have displayed a willingness to adapt to competition and changing consumer desires. Reducing prices through lowering service levels has been one notable response by some department stores. Also, department stores have followed the movement of the population to the suburbs by opening major branches in outlying shopping centres. Canadian department stores have led other retailers in maintaining a vital and dynamic downtown through modernizing their stores, extending store hours, emphasizing attracting the trade of tourists and people attending conventions, and focusing on the residents of the central cities.

Variety Stores Retailers that offer an extensive range and assortment of low-priced merchandise are called **variety stores**. Two examples are Fields and Stedmans. Most of the products carried by these stores are quite basic. Consumers seldom have strong preferences for particular brands. Thus stores can carry a limited range in each product line without losing potential customers. The nation's variety stores account for only about 0.64 percent of all retail sales. Variety stores have steadily declined in popularity. Many have evolved into or have been replaced by other retailing categories such as discounting.

Mass Merchandisers Mass merchandisers are direct competitors of department stores. **Mass merchandisers** concentrate on high turnover of items, emphasize lower prices than department stores, and offer reduced services. Typically, they give considerable attention to small appliances, hardware, automotive products, and sporting goods in addition to apparel.

Canadian Tire is an example of a mass merchandiser. Other major types of mass merchandisers are discount houses, hypermarkets, and catalogue retailers.

Discount Houses The birth of the modern **discount house** came at the end of World War II when a New York operation named Masters discovered that a very large number of customers were willing to shop at a store that did not offer such traditional retail services as credit, sales assistance by clerks, and delivery, in exchange for reduced prices. Within a very brief period, retailers throughout the

variety store
Retailer that offers an extensive range and assortment of low-priced merchandise.

mass merchandiser
Retailer that concentrates on high turnover of items, emphasizes lower prices than department stores, and offers reduced services.

discount house
Retailer that, in exchange for reduced prices, does not offer such traditional retail services as credit, sales assistance by clerks, and delivery.

country followed the Masters formula and either changed over from their traditional operations or opened new stores dedicated to discounting. At first the discount stores were primarily involved with selling appliances, but they have spread into furniture, soft goods, drugs, and even food.

The new discounters operated large stores, advertised heavily, and emphasized low prices on well-known brands. And consumers, who had become accustomed to self-service by shopping at supermarkets, responded in great numbers to this retailing innovation. Conventional retailers such as Kresge and Woolworth joined the discounting practice by opening their own Kmart and Woolco stores.

www.kmart.com

As the discount houses move into new product areas, a noticeable increase in the number of services offered as well as a corresponding decrease in the discount margin is evident. Carpeted floors are beginning to appear in discounters' stores, credit is increasingly available, and many discounters are even quietly dropping the term *discount* from their name. Even though they still offer fewer services, their operating costs are increasing as they become similar to the traditional department stores (which have adopted some of the discount stores' practices).

As these trends have continued, and other retailers have adjusted their offerings to compete with them, the original competitive threat of the discount phenomenon has waned. However, the purchase of the aging Woolco operations by American discount chain Wal-Mart has renewed the competitive challenge. Wal-Mart generates differential price advantage through great purchasing power and efficiencies in distribution. In addition to low prices, it competes by offering extra services. Zellers and Canadian Tire are two major retailers that are being especially challenged by Wal-Mart. Kmart, which had a long history, was unable to meet the competition and failed in Canada.

Two new formats have evolved in the discount store category.[14] These are membership and warehouse clubs and large-format specialty stores. An example of a **membership and warehouse club** is Costco. Customers must purchase a membership card (about $35) before they can enter the store. The stores are often located in an industrial subdivision and are constructed like warehouses, with steel walls and roofs and cement floors. They range in size from 9000 to 12 000 m². Customers vie with forklift trucks in the aisles, as all merchandise is stored on tall metal shelving.

membership and warehouse club
Very large, warehouse-type retail store that offers low prices because of its no-frill format and paid membership requirement.

One of each item is displayed, and the price is marked on a card on the shelf. Large-size packaging, in most instances, requires the buyer to purchase a supply that will last several months. There is no service, and prices are low enough that many small businesses are seen buying merchandise for resale. These warehouses are having a sizable impact on the retail market, as well as on the market share of traditional retailers.

The new threat to existing retailers is the development of very large specialty retailers. **Large-format specialty stores** can be of similar size to warehouse clubs. They are known as *category killers*. The characteristics of these stores give some reasons for this name:

large-format specialty store
Large, warehouse-type retail store that specializes in selling a great variety of one category of merchandise at very low prices.

1. They are very large and specialize in one type of merchandise. Each store has a huge variety to choose from.
2. They use low-cost, warehouse-type building structures.
3. They sell a very large volume of merchandise at very low prices. The average gross margin is approximately 8 percent.

4. Their average sales per square metre are $4300 — about twice as much as traditional retailers.

5. These new retailers offer a great deal of service. Consider Home Depot, for example. It looks like a warehouse, has a huge selection of hardware and building items, and even offers "how-to" sessions taught by professionals.

6. These category killers locate in a free-standing suburban location. This gives them 35 to 50 percent lower location costs than in the downtown area. Other costs are often much less than in more congested retail areas.

Another example of a large-format specialty store is Chapters, a bookstore stacked with 100 000 different types of books. Included is live children's entertainment and a cappuccino bar with a reading room. Yet another example is Petsmart, a pet supply store of 1800 m². This is about ten times larger than typical stores. It carries 6500 products to keep animals happy, healthy, and fashionable.

Because of their size and the warehouse-type facility, these two types of retailers are also known as *big box retailers*. The development of these two types of discount operations is a classic example of retailers seeking a differential advantage. In the case of the category killers, they are very strong on at least two aspects of the differential triangle: price and service. Consumers have ready access to virtually anything they want in a particular category without shopping around — and likely at a lower price. Selection plus service at a low price is a hard combination for traditional retailers to beat.

power node
Groupings of two or more large-format retailers that result in large customer drawing power.

In Edmonton, Toronto, and other cities, groupings of two or more large-format retailers in the same areas are forming **power nodes**. These have a large drawing power and are pulling consumers away from traditional shopping areas.

Established retailers are scrambling to compete. Canadian Tire, for example, is increasing the size of its stores and adopting a warehouse format. It has also announced new lower prices.

hypermarket
Mass merchandiser that operates on a low-price, self-service basis and carries lines of soft goods, hard goods, and groceries.

Hypermarkets These giant mass merchandisers operate on a low-price self-service basis and carry lines of soft goods, hard goods, and groceries. **Hypermarkets** are sometimes called superstores, although this latter term has also been used to describe a variety of large retail operations.[15] The *hypermarché*, or hypermarket, began in France and has since spread to a limited degree to Canada and the United States. The Hypermarché Laval outside Montreal was the first to open and had 19 500 m² of selling space (eleven to fifteen times the size of the average supermarket) and 40 checkouts. A typical hypermarket is like a shopping centre in a single store. It sells food, hardware, soft goods, building materials, auto supplies, appliances, and prescription drugs, and has a restaurant, a beauty salon, a barber shop, a bank branch, and a bakery. Many of these superstores are currently in operation throughout the world. It appears that they are more popular in Europe than in North America. This is likely because North America already had many large, well-developed shopping centres before the hypermarket concept arrived.

off-price retailer
Retailer that specializes in selling manufacturers' excess stocks of brand-name merchandise at a discount.

Off-Price Retailers Off-price retailers specialize in selling manufacturers' excess stocks of brand-name merchandise at a discount. **Off-price retailers** stock designer labels or well-known products and sell at prices that approximate wholesale. One of the keys to their success is the ability of buyers to find and take advantage of special price offers from manufacturers that are selling excess merchandise. Winners is an example of such a retailer.

Recycled Merchandise Retailers Interest in recycled merchandise, such as castoff clothes, furniture, and other products, is growing. There are several different types of **recycled merchandise retailers**: pawn shops, thrift shops, and flea markets. Another version is the recycled discount store typified by Value Village. Value Village arranges with the Tuberculosis Society to pick up castoff merchandise from households and purchases this merchandise for resale from the Society. Specialty versions of recycled merchandise retailers have emerged, offering children's clothes, outerwear, and other merchandise.

recycled merchandise retailer
Retailer that sells castoff clothes, furniture, and other products.

Liquidators There are thousands of retailers in the marketplace, and some do not make it. Even successful retailers often have lines of products that they don't want to carry any longer, or they have broken lots of merchandise they want to get rid of. The result is a great deal of products that need to be disposed of. **Liquidators** are specialty retailers who either come into a bankrupt store and handle the closeout, or who buy the entire lot and sell it in their own stores. Liquidation World is a chain of liquidators that is spreading across the country. Buying products for approximately 30 cents on the dollar, the liquidator can offer good value to customers and still be profitable.

liquidator
Specialty retailer that either comes into a bankrupt store and handles the closeout, or buys the entire lot and sells it in its own stores.

Catalogue Retailers These retailers mail catalogues to their customers and operate from a showroom displaying samples of their products. **Catalogue retailers** fill orders from a backroom warehouse. Price is an important factor for catalogue store customers, and low prices are made possible by few services, storage of most of the inventory in the warehouse, reduced shoplifting losses, and handling of products that are unlikely to become obsolete, such as luggage, small appliances, gift items, sports equipment, toys, and jewellery. (Mail-order catalogue retailing is discussed later in this chapter.)

www.liquidationworld.com

catalogue retailer
Retailer that mails catalogues to its customers and operates from a showroom displaying samples of its products.

Retailers Classified by Location of Retail Transactions

A fourth method of categorizing retailers is by determining whether the transaction takes place in a store. While the overwhelming majority of retail sales occur in retail stores, nonstore retailing is important for many products. Nonstore retailing includes direct house-to-house sales, mail-order retailing, and automatic merchandising machines. These kinds of sales account for about 1.7 percent of all retail sales.

HOUSE-TO-HOUSE RETAILING

One of the oldest marketing channels was built around direct contact between the retailer–seller and the customer at the home of the customer—**house-to-house retailing**. It provides convenience for the consumer and allows the manufacturer to control the firm's marketing channel. House-to-house retailing is a minor part of the retailing picture, with less than 1 percent of all retail sales.

House-to-house retailing is conducted by a number of different merchandisers. Manufacturers of such products as bakery and dairy products and newspapers use this channel. Firms whose products require emphasis on personal selling and product demonstrations may also use it. Such products and services include, for example, cosmetics (Avon), vacuum cleaners (Electrolux), household brushes (Fuller Brush Company), encyclopedias (World Book), and insurance.

house-to-house retailer
Retailer that sells products by direct contact between the retailer–seller and the customer at the home of the customer.

Catalogue retailers such as Lands' End, which now offers its catalogue on-line, offer consumers the convenience of shopping without leaving the comfort of their homes.

Some firms — such as Tupperware and Stanley Home Products — use a variation called *party-plan selling,* where a customer gives a party and invites several neighbours and friends. During the party, a company representative makes a presentation of the product, and the host or hostess receives a commission based on the amount of products sold.

The house-to-house method of retailing would appear to be a low-cost method of distribution. No plush retail facilities are required, no investment in inventory is necessary, and most house-to-house salespeople operate on a commission basis. In fact, this method is an extremely high-cost approach to distribution.

Often the distribution cost of a product marketed through retail stores is half that of the same product retailed house-to-house. High travel costs, the problems involved in recruiting and training a huge sales force that generally has a high turnover, nonproductive calls, several layers of commissions, and the limited number of contracts per day result in high operating expenses.

Multilevel Marketing Another version of house-to-house retailing is **multilevel marketing**. This type of marketing depends heavily on the personal influence network of consumers and "positive thinking" techniques. Many different products are sold, from burglar alarms to cosmetics to "wellness" products such as vitamins and meal supplements. Examples of such companies are Amway and Shaklee.

The system depends on a network of people.[16] As many as possible are recruited to sell the products to friends, family, and acquaintances. In return, the salesperson, or "independent distributor," gets a commission. But the real money comes in when the salesperson recruits others who become distributors.

In return for bringing in new people — known in the business as "down-liners" — the recruiter receives a cut of all of their sales. If these new people also recruit, they get a cut of that too. Commissions can travel five or six layers up the network of distributors, depending on the company's policy. A key to making the system work is to keep all the people involved highly motivated. Consequently, a regular series of local and district motivational meetings are a standard requirement.

Critics say multilevel marketers flog a deck of dreams that is stacked against the people who buy it. But supporters see it as an entrepreneurial opportunity that is open to anyone and requires little start-up capital.

Federal regulations require multilevel marketers to disclose realistic earnings forecasts for distributors. For example, Interior Design Nutritional, a spinoff of Nu Skin International, reports that 70 percent of participants earn an annual average of $2000, and according to Amway Canada, the average monthly compensation is $61.[17] This is not much. New candidates are recruited on the basis of the opportunity of earning much more.

About 750 000 Canadians are involved full- or part-time in one or more of the 300 to 400 multilevel marketing companies starting up, progressing, or fizzling out in this country at any given time, according to federal government figures. Although 70 percent of these companies collapse before they are eight months old, it is a multibillion-dollar industry that spans the continent and is rapidly going global. The Better Business Bureau receives between 5000 and 7000 industry-related complaints every year. Most are from people who have stockpiled product they purchased in an effort to keep their sales quotas up, and then could not unload. Others paid substantial fees to become distributors only to find the job was not the paved road to prosperity they were led to expect.

MAIL-ORDER RETAILING

The customers of **mail-order merchandisers** can place merchandise orders by mail, by telephone, or by visiting the mail-order desk of a retail store. Goods are then shipped to the customer's home or to the local retail store.

Many department stores and specialty stores issue catalogues to seek telephone and mail-order sales and to promote in-store purchases of items featured in the catalogues. Among typical department stores, telephone and mail-generated orders account for 15 percent of total volume during the Christmas season.

multilevel marketing
The development of a network among consumers to sell and deliver from one level of consumers to another using social obligation, personal influence, and motivational techniques.

mail-order merchandiser
Retailer that offers its customers the option of placing merchandise orders by mail, by telephone, or by visiting the mail-order desk of a retail store.

▶ THE ETHICAL MARKETER

www.amway.com

Amway's New Method of Recruiting Representatives

Mr. Davies shakes hands as he strides to the front of a curious crowd that has gathered at the Embassy Suites hotel into a well-practised presentation meant to motivate and excite his audience about an amazing business opportunity. The hook comes about a third of the way through his routine. "Internet. E-commerce. Cybermall." He punches out the words, as if each one held the key to a better life. "We know that E-commerce is the way to go," he continues, holding up a copy of *Fortune* magazine emblazoned with the latest trendy E-term. "All you have to do is plug people into the Internet and you'll get paid for it.... Even Martha Stewart is going on-line."

Eventually, the important details begin to surface. After more than an hour of patient listening, the young, fidgety audience of about 150 discovers that Mr. Davies is a senior distributor and recruiter for multilevel marketing company Amway Corp. Clearly disappointed, most of the room clears during a ten-minute break. "Sounds like a pyramid scheme to me," says one twenty-something who decides he's wasted his time. Still, the buzzwords lured him to the meeting, and showing up is the first step to becoming a new recruit in the multilevel marketing operation.

Amway is seeking a new way of recruiting representatives. Ken Wong, associate professor of marketing and business strategy at Queen's University in Kingston, Ontario, says "The fact that you have the Internet out there, there's always going to be people trying to take advantage of it." People are lured by the seeming magic and ease of making money through E-commerce [and] a chance to be on the leading edge of technology."

Multilevel marketing is often equated—mistakenly—with illegal pyramid schemes, in which participants make money solely by signing up new members. Multilevel marketers survive by recruiting a large stable of independent sales representatives who, like most salespeople, earn a commission for the products they sell. Unlike most salespeople, however, these reps also make money from new members. They get a percentage of the revenue that their own recruits generate—and so on, in a top-down structure that resembles a pyramid. Start early enough in the process and have the persistence to stay in the game, and the rewards grow exponentially. Amway is hoping the lure of the Internet will get more people into the game.

Companies such as Amway are not doing anything wrong, says Mr. Wong. Nonetheless, he calls such operations "deceptive" because they feed off the innocent and the naive. "The challenge you face if you're an Amway or someone else is that at some point, you run out of recruits ... you start to exhaust the market," says Mr. Wong, explaining that pyramid-like schemes by nature begin to collapse once a market is saturated.

What do you think of this method of direct marketing and recruiting?

Source: Adapted from Tyler Hamilton, "Sold on the Web," *The Globe and Mail* (March 11, 1999), pp. T1 and T3. Reprinted with permission from *The Globe and Mail*.

Mail-order selling began in Canada in 1894 when Eaton's distributed a slim 32-page booklet to rural visitors at the Canadian National Exhibition in Toronto. That first catalogue contained only a few items, mostly clothing and farm supplies. Simpsons soon followed, and mail-order retailing became an important source of products in isolated Canadian settlements.

Even though mail-order sales represent only a small percentage of all retail sales, this type of retailing is an important channel for many consumers who want convenience and a large selection of colours and sizes.

With the demise of the Eaton's catalogue sales operations in 1976, apparently due to a failure to introduce effective cost and inventory control measures, Sears became the one major mail-order catalogue marketer left in Canada. Sales have been strong. Sears now has nearly 1800 catalogue sales offices across Canada and produces 11 catalogues a year, with a combined distribution of 45 million.[18]

www.sears.ca

Mail-order houses offer a wide range of products — from novelty items (Regal Gifts) to sporting equipment (S.I.R. and L.L. Bean). The growing number of women who work outside the home, increasing time pressures, and a decline in customer service in some department stores seem to be good signs for the success of catalogue sales.

AUTOMATIC MERCHANDISING

Automatic vending machines — the true robot stores — are a good way to purchase a wide range of convenience goods. These machines accounted for over $424.5 million in sales in Canada.[19] Approximately 213 000 vending machines are currently in operation throughout the country.

While automatic merchandising is important in the retailing of some products, it represents less than 1 percent of all retail sales. Its future growth is limited by such factors as the cost of machines and the necessity for regular maintenance and repair. However, with the possibility of credit card readers in these machines, a wide variety of additional, more expensive products can be sold.

Automatically vended products are confined to convenience goods that are standardized in size and weight, with a high rate of turnover. Prices for some products purchased in vending machines are higher than store prices for the same products.

RETAILING THROUGH THE INTERNET

The Internet has become not only an information source and a means of communication, but also an important business tool. Retailing is one area that can be greatly facilitated through its use. For example, Bolen's Books in Victoria set up a home page for the purpose of retailing its line of books. Within a year of starting to retail on the Internet, the company had covered the costs of setting up and running the system. It now receives orders from around the world. Blaney's Travel agency publishes special travel deals on the Internet in order to generate new clients. It offers its travel services to anyone logging onto its home page. These are but two examples of the thousands of firms retailing through the Internet. The applications are limited only by the creativity of the company.

Electronic commerce, or e-commerce, is now a reality. Major initiatives are underway that may revolutionize business transaction processes. On-line business is quickly becoming a mainstream practice in North America and is growing exponentially overseas. Most companies are quickly adapting to the information age, and so should every business.

Benefits of Internet Retailing Internet retailing provides a considerable number of benefits to both consumers and retailers. Consumers enjoy the benefit of convenience — they can shop 24 hours a day from their own homes. Price competition is another benefit. Studies have shown that products in certain retail categories, especially mid- to high-priced commodity-oriented items, sell for lower prices on-line than in traditional stores.[20] Comparison shopping is easy and fast.

How will you shop tSc today?

tSc
The Shopping Channel

Virtually everywhere.

Television shopping channels and on-line shopping sites have gained momentum in recent years, but how widely will they be used?

Selection is another advantage. Consumers can find a much broader and deeper selection of items on the Internet. The vast selection on booksellers' Web sites is a good example. Customization can also be obtained in some Internet purchasing. For example, Dell Computers' Internet site allows customers to custom design the exact computer system that matches their needs and budget.

Information is perhaps the most important benefit to consumers. The Internet provides businesses with a low-cost means of disseminating all types of business information. However, when customers log on to a site, they have very high expectations. Thus great care must be taken by the firm to build a proper site. For example a well-known sports equipment company may produce a great number of camping products; however, if the information provided on its Web site is very limited, the potential buyer will not be able to make an informed choice.

The Internet serves as a communication tool between consumers and retailers. A continuing dialogue can be maintained before and after a product purchase, which can help to create a very high level of customer satisfaction. Similarly, a retailer can undertake on-line surveys and feedback forums that facilitate developing databases on customers' ideas, attitudes, and product preferences.

Retailers can likewise benefit by optimizing their inventory management practices through connections with suppliers and agreements to keep retailers supplied with a steady flow of merchandise rather than a few large lots. In the case of on-line retailing, the Internet can provide a very efficient and profitable means of processing orders. Potential cost savings can be achieved through lower inventory, transaction costs, easier customer service, and lower administration and communication costs.

Internet Retail Spending Trends Retailing on the Internet has turned into big business. As of 2002, business-to-consumer Internet transactions worldwide are expected to reach $450 billion. Some forecasters estimate even higher sales. Compare this with 1996 business-to-consumer transactions of under $1 billion. Business-to-business transactions are expected to reach $150 billion.

Successful Retail Categories Sold on the Internet Products that are best suited for selling on the Internet have the following characteristics:

- They are sold in fragmented markets and involve substantial comparison shopping.
- They have relatively low shipping costs.
- They do not require a physical inspection before a purchase is made.

Figure 16.3 shows the relative potential of various products to be sold on the Internet.

The Importance of Branding Strong brand-name recognition may be even more important in Internet retailing than traditional retailing. Customers are more comfortable ordering products with familiar names and characteristics. This applies to store branding as well as to product branding.

Demographic Characteristics of Internet Users Internet users are, in general, above-average spenders. They also tend to be highly educated people, 18–44 years of age, high-income earners, and white-collar workers. The 12 to 24-year-old segment is also a very attractive target market given its large size, technological sophistication, and willingness to make Internet purchases. Male Internet users have traditionally outnumbered female users. However, this is changing. In 1997 the male/female Internet user ratio had changed to 60 percent/40 percent, and it was expected to gradually change to resemble that of the general public.

Some examples of Canadian companies that do business on the Internet can be found at http://strategis.ic.gc.ca/SSG/ng00079e.html.

The Future of Internet Retailing Computers are found in virtually every business and in a large number of homes. The number of home computers is growing rapidly,

> ▶ **FIGURE 16.3 Potential of Products to Be Sold on the Internet**

Relative Potential	Retail Categories
High	Insurance/financial services Computer hardware/software Travel services Books, magazines, music/videos Flowers, gifts, greeting cards Office supplies
Moderate	Cars Sporting goods Consumer electronics/appliances Food and beverages Collectibles Apparel, shoes, accessories Health and beauty products
Low	Toys and games Tools/home improvement products Home furnishings

and it is expected that within a short time most homes will have one. Bill Gates, CEO of Microsoft, and others in the industry have predicted that as these homes get hooked up to digital information links, it will be only a matter of time before the computer, telephone, television, and on-line information services converge into a single system for handling all home entertainment, education, information, and communication needs.

If you want to watch a movie, play a computer game, buy the latest music recording by your favourite artist, or acquire some new software, you will just dial in to the information highway over the phone line and download whatever product or service you want, charging the cost to a debit or credit card.

The ultimate mix of computer technology, consumerism, and television, however, would come with use of the shopping channel, where consumers could design "virtual shopping malls" in which they were the only customers. These would work by having the consumer designate which shops he or she would like to frequent (from either an on-screen or published catalogue). The system would then respond by displaying a video game–style representation of a mall with shop fronts. The consumer would then use the handheld controller to "walk through" the custom-designed on-screen malls, stopping at the shops whose goods he or she might be interested in buying.

The on-screen shop fronts, when entered, would be replaced with an on-screen catalogue of the goods available in that shop. By pointing at the picture of any item, consumers will be able to get detailed information on it, including price, warranty details, and estimated delivery times.

Will such a system really exist someday? A skeptic would say that predictions of computer retailing have been made for over 30 years. The theme is the same—only the format of the implementation varies. On the other hand, we are much closer to the interactive link described above. It is happening, so a more relevant question is how many people will use such a system?

There are several inhibiting factors. First, many people wish to inspect products personally. The tangible aspects of touch, smell, and sight will remain important for many products. Second, people are concerned about the security of making credit card information available through the Internet. Third, many people prefer the experience of going out to shop. Fourth, personal service will remain important for some products. Finally, people may be unwilling to wait for delivery of products.

Retailers Classified by Form of Ownership

The fifth method of classifying retailers is by ownership. The two major types are corporate chain stores and independent retailers. In addition, independent retailers may join a wholesaler-sponsored voluntary chain, band together to form a retail cooperative, or enter into a franchise arrangement through contractual agreements with a manufacturer, wholesaler, or service organization. Each type has its special characteristics.

Among supermarket chains, Dominion is a well-recognized name. Recent humorous "fresh obsessed" commercials brought the name into Canadians' living rooms.

Our meat manager, on a date.

We're fresh obsessed.

CHAIN STORES

Chain stores are groups of retail stores that are centrally owned and managed and that handle the same lines of products. The concept of chain stores is certainly not new; the Mitsui chain was operating in Japan in the 1600s. The Bay, Zellers, and Reitman's have operated in Canada for many years. Wal-Mart is now a powerful competitor.

The major advantage possessed by chain operations over independent retailers is economies of scale. Volume purchases through a central buying office allow such chains as Provigo and Wal-Mart to obtain lower prices than independents. Since a chain such as Provigo has hundreds of retail stores, specialists in

chain store
Group of retail stores that are centrally owned and managed and that handle the same lines of products.

layout, sales training, and accounting systems may be used to increase efficiency. Advertising can also be effectively used. An advertisement in a national magazine for The Bay promotes every Bay store in Canada.

Chains (excluding food stores) account for approximately one-third of all retail stores, and their dollar volume of sales amounts to 30 percent of all retail sales. At present, chains dominate four fields: department stores, variety stores, shoe stores, and food stores.[21]

Many of the larger chains in Canada have expanded their operations to the rest of the world. Sears now has branch stores in Spain, Mexico, and several countries in South America. Safeway operates supermarkets in Germany, the United Kingdom, and Australia. Bowring's has expanded internationally, as has Wal-Mart.

INDEPENDENT RETAILERS

Independents have attempted to compete with chains in a number of ways. Some independents were unable to do so efficiently and went out of business. Others have joined retail cooperatives (e.g., IGA), wholesaler-sponsored voluntary chains (e.g., IDA), or franchise operations (e.g., Home Hardware). Still others have remained in business by exploiting their advantages of flexibility in operation and knowledge of local market conditions. The independents continue to represent a major part of Canadian retailing.

Retailers Classified by Margin and Turnover

The previous classifications of retailers sometimes tend to overlap one another. Therefore, a very useful method of classification is by gross margin percentage and rate of inventory turnover.[22] Inventory turnover refers to the number of times per year, on average, that a retailer sells its inventory. Jewellery stores have low turnover and therefore must have high margins to survive; grocery stores have high turnover and can make satisfactory net profits on low margins.

Figure 16.4 illustrates this classification system. In reality, the low-margin/low-turnover category is not a viable situation, and there are no good examples. There are, however, many high-margin/low-turnover retailers such as furniture stores, gift shops, and local mom and pop convenience stores.

Low-margin/high-turnover stores are common. Examples are discount department stores such as Zellers, Wal-Mart, and Canadian Tire, and category killers such as Michaels, Office Depot, and Costco.

High-margin/high-turnover stores are also common. Convenience stores such as Mac's, Red Rooster, and 7-Eleven are examples. Having both high margins and high turnover puts the store in a very strong position.

planned shopping centre
Group of retail stores planned, coordinated, and marketed as a unit to shoppers in a particular geographic trade area.

▶ SHOPPING CENTRES

A pronounced shift of retail trade away from the traditional downtown retailing districts and toward suburban shopping centres developed after 1950. A **planned shopping centre** is a group of retail stores planned, coordinated, and marketed

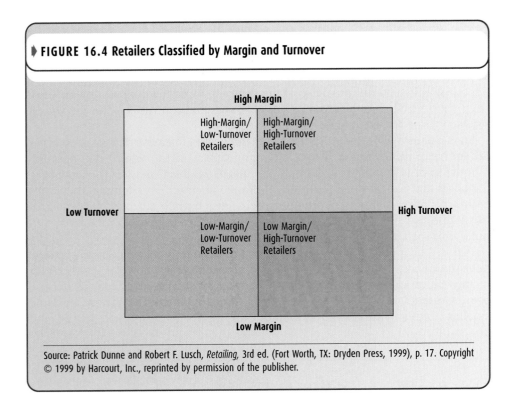

FIGURE 16.4 Retailers Classified by Margin and Turnover

High Margin

High-Margin/ Low-Turnover Retailers	High-Margin/ High-Turnover Retailers
Low-Margin/ Low-Turnover Retailers	Low Margin/ High-Turnover Retailers

Low Turnover — High Turnover

Low Margin

Source: Patrick Dunne and Robert F. Lusch, *Retailing*, 3rd ed. (Fort Worth, TX: Dryden Press, 1999), p. 17. Copyright © 1999 by Harcourt, Inc., reprinted by permission of the publisher.

as a unit to shoppers in a particular geographic trade area. These centres followed population shifts to the suburbs and focused on correcting many of the problems involved in shopping in the downtown business districts. Ample parking and locations away from downtown traffic congestion appeal to the suburban shopper. Additional hours for shopping during the evenings and on weekends facilitate family shopping.

Types of Shopping Centres

There are three types of planned shopping centres. The smallest and most common is the *neighbourhood shopping centre,* which most often comprises a supermarket and a group of smaller stores, such as a drugstore, a laundry and dry cleaner, a small appliance store, and perhaps a beauty shop and barbershop. Such centres provide convenient shopping for perhaps 5000 to 15 000 shoppers who live within a few minutes' commuting time of the centre. These centres typically contain five to fifteen stores whose product mix is usually confined to convenience goods and some shopping goods.

Community shopping centres typically serve 20 000 to 100 000 people in a trade area extending a few kilometres in each direction. These centres are likely to contain 15 to 50 retail stores, with a branch of a local department store or a large variety store as the primary tenant. In addition to the stores found in a neighbourhood centre, the community centre is likely to have additional stores featuring shopping goods, some professional offices, and a bank branch.

The largest planned centre is the *regional shopping centre,* a giant shopping district of at least 30 000 m² of shopping space, usually built around one or more major department stores and containing as many as 300 smaller stores. To be successful, regional centres must be located in areas where at least 150 000 people live within a 30-minute drive of the centre. Characteristically, they are temperature-controlled, enclosed facilities. The regional centres provide the widest product mixes and the greatest depth of each line.

Such a centre is the West Edmonton Mall, located in Jasper Place, a suburb of Edmonton. Said to be the largest shopping centre in the world, the West Edmonton Mall is located in a densely populated area and is easily accessible to both cars and pedestrians. Catering to a range of suburban clientele, the stores at this mall offer a variety of quality merchandise to their customers. Because of its unique features, such as an amusement park, wave pool, skating rink, and hotel, this mall also counts on tourist traffic.

Planned shopping centres account for approximately 40 percent of all retail sales in Canada. Their growth has slowed in recent years, however, as the most lucrative locations are occupied and the market for such centres appears to have been saturated in many regions. Recent trends have moved toward building smaller centres in smaller cities and towns.

▶ SCRAMBLED MERCHANDISING

scrambled merchandising
The retail practice of carrying dissimilar lines to generate added sales volume.

You will not be surprised that a characteristic of retailing is the steady deterioration of clear-cut delineations of retailer types. Anyone who has attempted to fill a prescription recently has been exposed to the concept of **scrambled merchandising**—the retail practice of carrying dissimilar lines to generate added sales volume. The large mass-merchandising drugstore carries not only prescription and proprietary drugs, but also gifts, hardware, housewares, videos, magazines, grocery products, garden supplies, even small appliances. Gasoline retailers sell bread and milk; supermarkets carry antifreeze, televisions, cameras, and stereo equipment.

Scrambled merchandising was born out of retailers' willingness to add dissimilar merchandise lines in order to offer additional high-profit lines, as well as to satisfy consumer demands for one-stop shopping. It complicates manufacturers' channel decisions, because attempts to maintain or increase a firm's market share mean, in most instances, that the firm will have to develop multiple channels to reach the diverse retailers handling its products. On the other hand, customers benefit from increased availability, and retailers benefit from additional sales.

This chapter has described some aspects of the many faces of retailing. As this is the end of the marketing channel that handles millions of products and services, a vast array of retailers can be categorized in several different ways. A basic characteristic of retailing is change. New retail forms are continually emerging. Existing retailers gradually adjust to meet the new competition. If they cannot adjust, they disappear.

▶ SUMMARY

Retailing is big business and a vital part of the national economy. It is comprised of many different types of operations, ranging from fast-food restaurants to convenience stores to department stores to some services to Internet retailers.

The wheel-of-retailing hypothesis postulates that new types of retailers gain a competitive advantage by offering lower prices to their customers through reducing services. Gradually they add services and increase prices, opening the door to new low-cost retailers entering the market.

The retailer's decision process centres on analyzing and selecting a target market and developing a marketing (or retailing) mix designed to satisfy that market.

The law of retail gravitation (Reilly's law) delineates the retail trade area of a potential site on the basis of distance between alternative locations and relative populations.

Differentiation is a key factor in competitive strategy. The differentiation triangle has the following elements: price, location, and store atmosphere and service.

Retailers can be classified in six different ways: (1) shopping effort expended by customers, (2) services provided to customers, (3) product lines, (4) location of retail transactions, (5) form of ownership, and (6) margin and turnover.

▶ KEY TERMS

catalogue retailer
chain store
department store
differentiation triangle
discount house
house-to-house retailer
hypermarket
large-format specialty store
law of retail gravitation
limited-line store
liquidator
mail-order merchandiser
mass merchandiser
membership and warehouse club

multilevel marketing
off-price retailer
planned shopping centre
power node
recycled merchandise retailer
retail image
retail trade area analysis
retailing
scrambled merchandising
specialty store
supermarket
variety store
wheel of retailing

▶ INTERACTIVE SUMMARY AND DISCUSSION QUESTIONS

1. The retailer's decision process centres on analyzing and selecting a target market and developing a marketing (or retailing) mix designed to satisfy that market. Compare and contrast the marketing mix with the retailing mix.

2. The law of retail gravitation (Reilly's law) delineates the retail trade area of a potential site on the basis of distance between alternative locations and relative populations. Assume that a large-format specialty retailer is considering opening an outlet in Town A, population 144 000. The retailing firm wants to know how far its trade area would extend toward Town B (population 16 000), 72 km away. Apply the law of retail gravitation to the retailer's problem. What other factors should be taken into consideration in this location decision?

3. The differentiation triangle has the following elements: price, location, and store atmosphere and service. Explain the importance of this triangle in considering a retailer's competitive options.

4. There are three types of retailers if classified by shopping effort: convenience–preference stores, shopping stores, and specialty retailers. In which of these types would the following products likely fit?
   a. Kodak film
   b. *Foundations of Marketing* textbook
   c. computer paper
   d. fax machine
   e. leather slippers
   f. Cartier watch
   g. picture framing

5. Some examples of general-merchandise retailers include department stores, variety stores, mass merchandisers, and discount houses. If you were marketing a new line of perfume, which of these outlets would you choose to use first? Why?

6. Large-format specialty stores can be of similar size to warehouse clubs. They are known as category killers. Explain why.

7. There are relatively few large warehouse and membership clubs in each community, yet the significance of this type of retail operation to retail competition in general is great. How can this be?

8. Multilevel marketing has several distributor levels, makes use of a personal influence network, and promises great rewards to those who work hard. What is your evaluation of these promised rewards?

9. Chain stores are groups of retail stores that are centrally owned and managed and that handle the same lines of products. Illustrate how the chain store concept results in powerful competition.

10. The wheel-of-retailing hypothesis postulates that new types of retailers gain a competitive advantage by offering lower prices to their customers through reducing services. Gradually they add services and increase prices, opening the door to new low-cost retailers entering the market. List several examples of the wheel of retailing in operation. Can you list examples that do not conform to this hypothesis?

11. What is your assessment of the future of e-commerce or "e-tailing"?

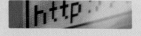

12. Write a brief report comparing, contrasting, and evaluating five different retailing Web sites.

To obtain a list of further readings for Chapter 16, please refer to the *Foundations of Marketing* Web site.

Chapter 17
Logistics and Supply Chain Management

Relocating Hong Kong International Airport involved using a convoy of vehicles and a fleet of barges. The move, with careful planning, was a resounding success.

In the wee hours of the morning on July 5, 1998, Hong Kong made history by carrying out the largest peacetime movement of men and equipment. In just seven hours, Kai Tak, the world's third busiest international passenger airport, was moved to its new home 30 km west to Chek Lap Kok on Lantau Island.

"The relocation operation involved the movement of equipment, vehicles, personnel, and aircraft from Kai Tak to Chek Lap Kok over a 90-day period, culminating in the overnight closure of operations at Kai Tak and the opening of Hong Kong's new international airport seven hours later," says Michael Winarick, a retired British Army colonel who planned the logistics of the airport move.

Equipment to be moved ranged from small tractors, to an entire aero engine.

On move night, there were 1000 vehicle movements, 70 barges transporting heavier loads through Victoria Harbour, and 30 airliners. The heaviest item was an aircraft recovery vehicle big enough to haul a disabled Boeing 747 from the runway.

To help control traffic, 1000 police officers were called in that evening. "The move, without doubt the largest in Hong Kong history, included the separate relocation of 72 business partners and 13 government departments," Winarick says. The airport's business partners involved in the move included government departments, airlines, airport operators, including ramp and cargo handlers, base and line maintenance operators, retail outlets, and airline caterers.

A number of government departments and external agencies helped move-night organizers with things such as traffic control, permits for unlicensed vehicles to travel on public roads, and permits for those vessels entering the marine exclusion zones around both airports.

> **CHAPTER OBJECTIVES**
> After reading and studying this chapter, you should be able to
>
> 1. Relate supply chain management to the other variables of the marketing mix.
> 2. Explain the role of logistics and supply chain management in an effective marketing strategy.
> 3. Describe the objectives of physical distribution.
> 4. Identify and compare the major components of the physical distribution system.
> 5. Discuss some of the basic concepts involved in making transportation decisions.
> 6. Relate the major transportation alternatives to such factors as efficiency, speed, dependability, and cost.
> 7. Discuss the problem of suboptimization in physical distribution.

www.hkairport.com/
welcome/main/index.htm

Because the two airports are so close together, air traffic control concerns dictated that both airports could not be open at the same time, so Kai Tak had to close before Chek Lap Kok could open, leaving Hong Kong without an airport for seven hours. "The need to ensure the cohesion necessary, the tight time schedule on move night, and the discipline so important for ingress and egress at each airport necessitated a military-style operation," says Winarick.

Kai Tak's geographical location in the densely populated Kowloon district of Hong Kong, the fact that the move was scheduled during typhoon season, and part of the route was over one of the world's longest suspension bridges, *Tsing Ma,* were some of the unique problems faced on move night. When implementing the changeover, two movement control centres were set up, one at each airport.

A computer program was designed and developed to monitor the real-time movement details during move night and track the actual move against planned parameters.

The move was a resounding success, Winarick says. All essential equipment was in place to allow operations to begin at 6:30 A.M. at the new airport. During the transfer, there were no major hold-ups. One piece of equipment was delayed 35 minutes, as its blown tire was replaced while on the *Tsing Ma* bridge.

This unusual story illustrates the type of planning that goes on daily in the movement of materials and goods from original source to manufacturer to distributor to customer. People are often amazed when they find out that a courier package sent from Fredericton via FedEx goes first to a massive distribution centre in the southern United States, where it is sorted along with thousands of other packages, and ends up in Edmonton, on schedule, the next morning. It happens because someone has carefully worked out the most efficient way.

Source: Adapted from Sherry Butt, "Hong Kong's Flight Plan," *Calgary Sun,* Resource and Supply Chain Management Supplement (January 1999), p. 8. Reprinted with permission of the *Calgary Sun.*

▶ INTRODUCTION

It is essential to select the right channel of distribution. It is equally important to work out how to distribute products. An example of not-so-efficient distribution occurred when the U.S. armed forces were preparing for the Gulf War in Kuwait (Desert Storm) in 1990. It took over five months to build up the force, and the order-delivery time for spare supplies was 26 days. Half of the 40 000 containers of equipment shipped went unused because soldiers did not know what equipment was in what container. With a better distribution system in 1995, it took only a month to have the Bosnia force in place, and the order-delivery time was seven days.[1]

"Impressive," you say, "but what's that got to do with me?" Distribution affects you every time you go shopping. How many times have you gone to a store and found that the product you wanted was out of stock? For you it was an annoyance. For that retailer, and perhaps the producer, the accumulated out-of-stock situations represent a tremendous loss of business. This loss may be permanent because you and other consumers went somewhere else and never came back.

One of the reasons that The Gap has been so successful is because it has dramatically shortened the delivery time of its clothing. Products that are moving quickly can be replenished at the retail level before current supplies run out, so sales are not missed. Similarly, hot new items can be distributed from central supply depots to catch new fashion waves.

Every item consumed in daily living is affected by logistics. **Logistics** is the process of managing and implementing the physical movement of products from source to place of use. Another way of thinking about logistics is what's involved in having the right materials at the right place at the right time and in the right quantity.

Achieving this goal is no simple matter. Markets can be spread over a region, a province, a country, and even the world. This complex and expensive process has been passed by some companies to **third-party logistics providers**. These are specialist firms that perform virtually all of the logistical tasks that manufacturers or other channel members would normally perform themselves. More and more companies are turning over their logistics decisions to such specialist firms. With third-party logistics, a company can partner with an organization that can fulfill requirements from storage to transportation. This allows the client company to focus on its core business. An example of a third-party logistics provider is Canada Messenger, which has developed a sophisticated distribution and warehouse system that can handle the logistical tasks for its clients.

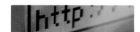

www.gap.com/onlinestore/gap

logistics
The process of managing and implementing the physical movement of products from source to place of use.

third-party logistics provider
Specialist firm that performs virtually all of the logistical tasks that manufacturers or other channel members would normally perform themselves.

The logistics of moving products are complex. Many businesses turn to companies that handle all aspects of logistics, including inventory control and warehousing.

A major part of logistics is **physical distribution (PD)**, which includes the activities involved in getting a product from the end of the production line to the consumer. Physical distribution is more than just transportation. As we will see later, it includes customer service, inventory control, materials handling, protective packaging, order processing, transportation, warehouse site selection, and warehousing.

physical distribution (PD)
Includes the activities involved in getting a product from the end of the production line to the consumer.

As our previous examples illustrated, logistics is a process that can be honed to a high level of efficiency. Logistics has stolen the limelight in business, according to a Logistics in Canada survey conducted by KPMG and *Materials Management* magazine.[2] Companies have proven not only that capabilities in logistics can increase their competitiveness, but that savings in costs go right to the bottom line of the company.

From a cotton grower in India to an assembly line in China to the nearby sporting goods store, many organizations are involved even in producing and delivering a pair of Nikes. They make up the *supply chain.* To obtain efficiencies and gain competitive advantage, it is necessary to consider and manage the entire supply chain. **Supply chain management** is the coordination of the flow of materials and products from the source of raw materials to the production line, and ultimately to the consumer. It includes managing information, cash, and process/work flows.

supply chain management
The coordination of the flow of materials and products from the source of raw materials to the production line, and ultimately to the consumer. It includes managing information, cash, and process/work flows.

The goal of supply chain management is to build flexible and efficient supply chains. To do so, manufacturers need to forge close, long-term ties with their suppliers. They need to work hand in hand to refine products and components, respond to shifts in demand, unclog bottlenecks, and share sensitive information. Research into supply chain management by Chrysler and Ford[3] suggests that the most effective alliances with external suppliers are built on four pillars:

- *Power balancing.* Instead of using their buying leverage to extract concessions from small suppliers, purchasing managers balance their contracts so that neither manufacturer nor supplier is highly dependent on the other.

Companies can rely on J.D. Edwards for supply chain management.

- *Co-specialization.* As they try to balance power, purchasing managers also try to achieve a degree of mutual dependence in their alliances. A supplier might have a factory make parts that work exclusively in one car model, or the car-maker might adapt one of its assembly lines to fit a particular supplier's needs. Often, a manufacturer will decide on "preferred suppliers" for a particular component, which encourages them to move beyond manufacturing and contribute to the design and engineering of components.
- *Target costing.* The cooperative approach extends to pricing as well. Instead of the adversarial system of competitive bidding for contracts, the purchasing managers set target costs based on the manufacturer's goal for the final selling price of the car. Open communication encourages suppliers to engage in joint problem solving, leading to more efficient design and production.
- *Personal ties.* Personal ties among managers are often what keeps alliances productive. One way these can be created is through establishing joint teams to solve problems. This not only improves the flow of information but also encourages each side to feel comfortable with the other. Alliances built along these lines enable manufacturers and suppliers to cooperate closely and share information openly.

From this example of supply chain management in the automotive industry, we can see how the possibilities of developing strong supply chain relationships in other spheres of business are inviting.

▶ THE PRACTISING MARKETER

Patchgear.com Ready to Revolutionize Supply Chain Management

It hasn't happened overnight, but the Internet is revolutionizing the world of retail. In fact, companies like Amazon.com have become darlings of consumers and financial markets alike.

A new Calgary-based company, Patchgear.com, is throwing its hat into the digital ring, with a promise to help companies cut costs from the supply chain.

www.patchgear.com

Patchgear.com builds virtual company stores that are customized and integrated with a company's Intranet or Web site. Companies can stock their digital store from the more than 20 000 products available on the Patchgear.com Web site.

The digital store, or Private On-line Catalogue (POC), functions as the company's distribution facility for safety, footwear, work, and corporate apparel. The technology allows employees to view and order products on-line, and provides administrators with detailed summary information on all transactions and purchases.

The front-end technology is only half of the story. Patchgear.com also handles everything from warehousing and managing inventory to shipping products and negotiating with suppliers.

Patchgear.com feels the low cost, direct environment enabled by its digital information management technology will generate 100 virtual company stores in the first year alone.

In pursuit of its global distribution objectives, Patchgear.com also has a physical presence, with a distribution facility in Edmonton and Houston, Texas.

How does supply chain management make possible the concept being developed by Patchgear.com?

Source: Adapted from "Patchgear.com Ready to Revolutionize Supply Chain Management," *Calgary Sun,* Resource and Supply Chain Management Supplement (January 1999), p. 42. Reprinted by permission of the *Calgary Sun.*

▶ PHYSICAL DISTRIBUTION

The study of physical distribution is one of the classic examples of the systems approach to business problems. The basic notion of a physical distribution system is that it is a set of interrelated parts. The word "system" is derived from the Latin word *systema,* which means an organized relationship among components. In a system, each component must function properly if the system is to be effective and the organizational objectives are to be achieved. A system thus may be defined as an organized group of parts or components linked together according to a plan to achieve specific objectives. The physical distribution system contains the following elements:

- *Customer service.* What level of customer service should be provided?
- *Transportation.* How will the products be shipped?
- *Materials handling and protective packaging.* How do we develop efficient methods of handling products in the factory, warehouse, and transport terminals?
- *Order processing.* How should orders be handled?
- *Inventory control.* How much inventory should be maintained at each location?
- *Warehousing.* Where will the products be located? How many warehouses should be used?

A simple but powerful concept is that these components are interrelated, and *decisions made in one area affect the relative efficiency of other areas.* For example, you might be able to reduce transportation costs by using low-cost, relatively slow water transportation, but this will probably reduce customer service and may increase inventory costs, since the firm may be required to maintain larger inventory levels to compensate for longer delivery times. The logistics manager must balance each component so that no single aspect is stressed to the detriment of the overall distribution system.

The Objective of Physical Distribution

In logistics management, the customer is king. The first question is what level of service is necessary to get and keep the customer's business. The objective of a firm's physical distribution system is to produce a specified level of customer service while minimizing the costs involved in physically moving and storing the product from its production point to the point where it is ultimately purchased.

To achieve this, the logistics manager makes use of three basic concepts that are vital to effective logistics management: (1) the total-cost approach, (2) the avoidance of suboptimization, and (3) the use of cost tradeoffs.

total-cost approach
Holds that all relevant factors in physically moving and storing products should be considered as a whole and not individually.

TOTAL-COST APPROACH

The **total-cost approach** holds that all relevant factors in physically moving and storing products should be considered as a whole and not individually. Thus, each element of the physical distribution system listed above should be included. All of these cost items must be considered as a whole when attempting to meet customer service levels at minimum cost. Management might therefore choose a faster but more expensive transportation mode if the cost of warehousing and materials handling could be reduced beyond the higher cost of transportation.

THE PROBLEM OF SUBOPTIMIZATION

Although the total-cost approach requires that all physical distribution elements must be considered as a whole rather than individually, sometimes this does not happen. **Suboptimization** is a condition in which the manager of each physical distribution function attempts to minimize costs, but due to the impact of one physical distribution task on the others, the results are less than optimal. Consider a football team that is made up of several talented individuals who seldom win games. Team members hold league records in a variety of skills: pass completions, average distance gained per rush, blocked kicks, and average gains on punt returns. Unfortunately, however, the overall ability of the team to accomplish the organizational goal — scoring more points than its opponents — is rarely achieved.

Why does suboptimization occur frequently in physical distribution? The answer lies in the fact that each separate logistics activity is often judged by its ability to achieve certain management objectives, some of which are at cross-purposes with other objectives. Sometimes departments in other functional areas take actions that cause the physical distribution area to operate at less than full efficiency. Psychological factors often come into play here. For example, a product manager might think, "Cartons are bought out of my department's budget, so we'll buy only standard, nonreinforced ones. We don't care if the warehouse staff complain — breakages are their problem, not ours. We'll look good because this department kept costs down." Counteracting this type of attitude is the responsibility of top management, who must convince junior management that they are serious about total cost — which means not complaining about the cost of cartons to one department head and complaining about breakages to the other.

Effective management of the physical distribution function may result in some costs increasing in order to reduce total costs. This means some cost tradeoffs may be required. Of course, reducing any logistics cost assumes that the level of customer service will not be sacrificed.

COST TRADEOFFS

The third fundamental concept of physical distribution is the use of **cost tradeoffs**. This approach assumes that some functional areas of the firm will experience cost increases while others will have cost decreases. The result will be that total physical distribution costs will be minimized, while at no time is the established level of customer service sacrificed. By thinking in terms of a total system and the cost tradeoffs shown in Figure 17.1, management should minimize the total of these costs rather than attempt to minimize the cost of each component.

For example, the Gillette Company, the world's largest producer of safety razors, was faced with an ever-expanding assortment of products due to its expansion into a broad range of toiletry products. To produce good customer service, Gillette shipped by air freight, but this proved to be very expensive.

suboptimization
A condition in which the manager of each physical distribution function attempts to minimize costs, but due to the impact of one physical distribution task on the others, the results are less than optimal.

cost tradeoffs
Approach that assumes that some functional areas of the firm will experience cost increases while others will have cost decreases.

www.gillette.com

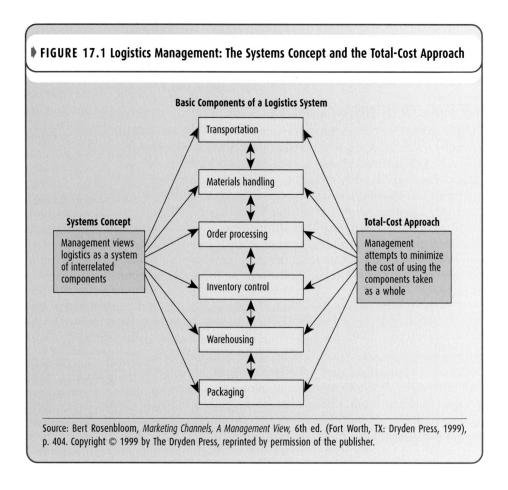

▶ FIGURE 17.1 Logistics Management: The Systems Concept and the Total-Cost Approach

Basic Components of a Logistics System

Transportation

Materials handling

Order processing

Inventory control

Warehousing

Packaging

Systems Concept

Management views logistics as a system of interrelated components

Total-Cost Approach

Management attempts to minimize the cost of using the components taken as a whole

Source: Bert Rosenbloom, *Marketing Channels, A Management View*, 6th ed. (Fort Worth, TX: Dryden Press, 1999), p. 404. Copyright © 1999 by The Dryden Press, reprinted by permission of the publisher.

Through a detailed study of its distribution system, Gillette discovered that its problem was inefficient order processing. By simplifying the paperwork involved, the company was able to reduce the time required to process new orders. Gillette was then able to return to lower-cost surface transportation and still meet previous delivery schedules. The cost tradeoff here was that the order-processing costs increased and transportation costs decreased, and the net result was that total logistics costs decreased.

physical distribution concept
The integration of the total-cost approach, the avoidance of suboptimization, and the use of cost tradeoffs.

The integration of these three basic concepts—the total-cost approach, the avoidance of suboptimization, and the use of cost tradeoffs—forms what is commonly referred to as the **physical distribution concept**. It should be noted that the real uniqueness of the physical distribution concept is not in the individual functions, since each function is performed anyway. Rather, this uniqueness stems from the integration of all of these functions into a unified whole, the objective of which is providing an established level of customer service at the lowest possible distribution costs.

Customer Service

The role physical distribution activities play in providing customer service is critical. Robert Woodruff, former president of The Coca-Cola Company, empha

▶ **THE CANADIAN MARKETPLACE**

"Traiting": Wal-Mart's Method of Managing Inventory

Another reason that Wal-Mart has grown into a leading position in retailing is its inventory management system. Wal-Mart's use of sophisticated inventory technologies has permitted the chain to look beyond the more traditional "merchandising by region to merchandising by individual store." Wal-Mart uses a system called *traiting* to look at both the customers' makeup and their buying preferences at individual stores.

Traiting indexes the product movement at each store with the store's market traits. This is used to determine not only if a given product should be carried in a particular store given the demographic makeup of the trading area, but also where it should be stocked in the store's layout. Traiting permits a store manager to alter total shelf space allotments based on product flow data. That's why in a rural area Wal-Mart may carry more hardware and do-it-yourself merchandise, and in an urban area Wal-Mart will stock more fax paper and other home office supplies. Likewise, a store in one part of a metropolitan area may carry more golf equipment, whereas the Wal-Mart just across town carries more swimming pool supplies.

This doesn't mean that only sales data can be used to support carrying a product. If a store manager finds out that Garth Brooks is going to have a concert in the area, it is reasonable to assume that 1000 Garth Brooks T-shirts will not only be in the manager's store but every other store near where Brooks is touring.

Explain how Wal-Mart makes consumer behaviour analysis and logistics work together to produce a competitive advantage.

Source: Adapted from Patrick Dunne and Robert F. Lusch, *Retailing*, 3rd ed., (Fort Worth, TX: Dryden Press, 1999), p. 16. Copyright © 1999 by Harcourt Inc., reprinted by permission of the publisher.

www.walmart.com

sized the role of physical distribution in his firm's success when he stated that his organization's policy was to "put Coke within arm's length of desire." Having its products available everywhere is one of The Coca-Cola Company's greatest strengths.

Customer service standards are the quality-of-service levels the firm's customers will receive. Companies should set goals and define acceptable performance for the quality of service that they expect to deliver. For example, a customer service standard of one firm might be that 60 percent of all orders will be shipped within 48 hours after they are received, 90 percent in 72 hours, and all orders within 96 hours. Setting the standards for customer service to be provided is an important marketing channel decision. FedEx has a policy of answering the phone after the first ring.

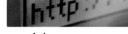

www.fedex.com

Transportation

How will the products be shipped, and by what carrier? The transportation system in Canada is a regulated industry, much like the power industry. The federal and provincial governments perform both promotional and regulatory functions to maintain a viable Canadian transportation system. Transport Canada, a government agency within the federal bureaucracy, supports technological developments associated with the airways, waterways, and highways in Canada.

www.tc.gc.ca/en/menu.htm

The Canadian Transport Commission (CTC), an agency of the federal government, is responsible for the air, rail, pipeline, and inland water components of the transportation industry. Each province has a transportation regulatory agency whose functions are equivalent to those of the CTC. In general, the purpose of government intervention in the transportation sector is to assure the development of a sound, efficient transportation infrastructure while protecting the public against abusive tactics.

CLASSES OF CARRIERS

common carrier
Transportation carrier that provides service to the general public, and is subject to regulatory authority including fee setting.

Three legal forms of transportation carriers exist to provide linkages between the various channel members: common, contract, and private. **Common carriers** must "hold themselves out" to serve the general public for a fee. They must receive appropriate regulatory authority to perform transport service, and must adhere to guidelines and rules as to rate setting, mergers, application of accounting procedures, and financial dealings. Although common carriers provide transportation services between each of the marketing channel intermediaries, they most frequently operate among manufacturers, wholesalers, and retailers moving goods of high value.

contract carrier
Transportation carriers that serves only customers it has contracts with. Contracts include rates to be charged.

Contract carriers do not offer their services to the public at large. Rather, they enter into contractual arrangements with select customers. All rates and charges are included in the contractual instrument, along with additional terms and conditions associated with providing service. Although regulatory requirements for contract carriers are significantly fewer than for common carriers, rules and standards are in effect at both the federal and provincial levels of government to delineate the scope of their authority to provide transportation services. Contract carriers tend to operate between raw material suppliers and manufacturers, and between manufacturers, rather than among wholesalers, retailers, and final customers, since they tend to be commodity and final goods consolidators rather than break-bulk operators.

private carrier
Transportation carrier that provides transportation services for a particular firm and may not solicit other transportation business.

Private carriers are not providers of transportation for a market fee. Instead, they provide transportation services for a particular firm and may not solicit other transportation business. The test to determine whether a carrier is a private or a for-hire carrier is to ask whether the primary business is transportation or not. Legal status depends on the percentage of revenues from transportation activities or the ratio of transportation to nontransportation-related assets. Owing to the exclusive nature of their operations, and the fact that transportation is incidental to the main operations of the firm, private carriers are not subject to economic regulation by either the federal or the provincial governments. They are, however, subject to federal and provincial safety regulations, as are others who use transportation facilities.

There are five major transportation alternatives, referred to as modes, that link the various channel intermediaries. These are *railways, trucking companies, water carriers, air freight,* and *pipelines.* Railways are the largest transporters (as measured by tonne-kilometres of freight) and are considered the most efficient mode in moving bulk commodities over long distances. They are readily available in most locations in North America, although line abandonment has considerably reduced the operating systems of the major rail carriers over the past three decades. Likewise, railways are quite flexible in that many different commodities, raw materials, liquids, grains, and finished goods can be safely and efficiently moved.

Trucking companies compete with railways in several product categories. However, where speed, flexibility, and frequency of service are important, motor carriers often outperform rail carriers. The truck shows its inherent advantage in moving high-valued goods short to intermediate distances. While the rate per tonne-kilometre is often greater for motor than for rail carrier, the service advantages provided by truck often more than compensate for the added expenditures. Furthermore, the variety of available trucking technologies provides the shipper with a broad array of options in transporting goods to market. No other mode rivals trucking in the range of transportation options.

Water carriers are much like rail carriers in that they tend to perform best in moving bulky, low-value commodities long distances. Whether along the inland waterway system, the Great Lakes, or in international commerce, water carriers tend to carry bulk cargoes at rather low speeds. They do have the advantage in international commerce of moving freight of all kinds as no other mode can, given present technologies. Rates per tonne-kilometre tend to be lowest for this mode, reflecting in part the relatively low value per unit of weight of cargoes typically carried by water. The exception to this general case is container service for medium- to high-value goods. Container ships provide manufacturers with the opportunity of extending market channels to locations that are quite distant from sourcing and producing sites. The presence of scale economies in production and distribution permit effective competition with local production.

Air freight is often referred to as "premium transportation" because of the high-cost–high-service nature of the mode. Speed is the single most important factor in selecting air over other freight carriers, and the rate per tonne-kilometre tends to be among the highest of all modes. Cut flowers from southern U.S. growing fields, fresh seafood from Vancouver, and component parts urgently needed for a downed assembly line in Ontario are examples of the types of goods often moved by air freight carriers. In recent years, the demand for expedited small parcel and parcel post service has exploded, and companies like Emery Worldwide and FedEx have developed as a response to this demand.

www.emeryworldwide.com/
eww/emeryweb

Pipeline transportation is the mode least likely to be used within a marketing channel except in specific industries such as oil extraction and refining and coal extraction, and in industries where raw commodities can be pulverized into small pellets or a powder, mixed with water, and transported in suspension.

MULTIMODAL TRANSPORTATION

Since the various modes of transportation have advantages and disadvantages, it is logical that a combination of modes may meet established customer service standards at the lowest cost. Companies such as Canadian Pacific have, for many years, responded to the need for combined modes by providing ocean and rail transportation.

www.cp.ca

Inventory Control

How much inventory should be maintained at each location? Inventory control analysts have developed a number of techniques that aid the physical distribution manager in effectively controlling inventory costs. The most basic is the **economic order quantity (EOQ)** model. This technique emphasizes a cost

economic order quantity (EOQ)
A model that emphasizes a cost tradeoff between inventory holding costs and order costs.

It was a good idea:
Cross the seas with lines of ships.
Cross the land with lines of steel.
Tie the lines, draw them tight,
and make a smaller world.

Forty years ago, a simple idea
changed the world: the box.
The standardized container,
which could be moved at
unheard-of speed, from
trucks to trains to ships.
From land to sea.

Almost overnight,
the world became smaller.
But world trade grew bigger.
Fourteen times bigger, so far.
And as trade grows,
so do railways.

In North America, more freight
volume moves by train than
by any other mode, and rail
container traffic has been
growing at double-digit rates.
Rail is twice as fuel-efficient
as road transport. One train
moves as much as 280 trucks.

Every year Canadian Pacific
moves 150 million tons
of goods across Canada
and the US Midwest and
Northeast, over 15,900 miles
of railway lines.

Which are closely tied
to our shipping lines.

It's a small world.
And a perfect place for trains.

CANADIAN PACIFIC
Energy Transportation Hotels

www.cp.ca

Canadian Pacific has, for more than 100 years, provided Canadians with logistics solutions.

tradeoff between two fundamental costs involved with inventory: inventory holding costs and order costs. As Figure 17.2 indicates, these two cost items are then "traded off" to determine the optimum order quantity of each product.

No aspect of physical distribution strategy has experienced the changes brought about by acceptance of the total quality management (TQM) philosophy as much as inventory practice and policy. Once it is recognized that significant resources are often tied up in inventory, it should come as no surprise that some of the new frontiers in distribution cost savings have accrued from minimizing inventory holding costs. The Japanese capitalized on this simple idea several decades ago with the implementation of **just-in-time (JIT)** inventory systems. The basic idea is to identify stock levels that meet peak efficiency minimums and to trade off higher transportation expenditures for reduced inventory holding expenditures.

The concept can be visualized in the following illustration. Imagine a young couple entering a car dealership in Calgary. They have a vague idea of the features they would like to have in their dream car and have sought out the services of an informed representative to assist them in their purchase decision. The representative activates her computer and asks the young couple for the specific features they would like in their car: exterior and interior colours, fab-

just in time (JIT)
An approach to minimizing inventory costs through identifying minimal inventory levels and arranging with suppliers to replenish stocks just in time to be used in production.

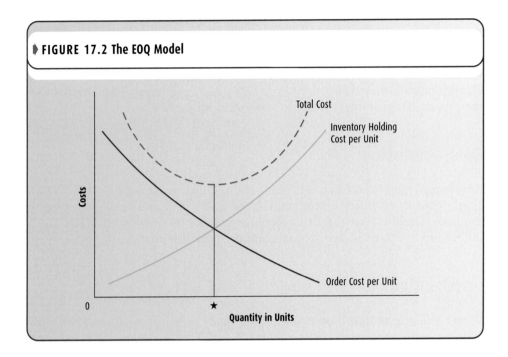

▶ FIGURE 17.2 The EOQ Model

ric type, stereo system, wheel type, suspension, and so forth. As the couple discusses the various options, the representative enters the information into the computer. Once the features have all been selected, she pushes a button and a simulated version of the car with the designated features appears on the monitor.

Assuming the couple agrees on the features and a transaction occurs, the representative activates an order to the manufacturer, which contacts various component suppliers and assembly plants to ship parts for the car. An order is sent to the battery manufacturer, the stereo manufacturer, the engine manufacturer, and to all other component suppliers that contribute to producing the ordered car. From the subassembly plants, the various components are produced and then shipped to the next unit in the manufacturing chain.

The important point is that inventories are not held in large amounts anywhere in the manufacturing or marketing channel. Instead, upon receiving the order, the subassembler produces the component and transports it in minimum efficient lot sizes to the next assembler in the channel. The JIT method results in significant reductions in inventory costs even though transportation costs may increase. Just as important as reducing inventory costs, however, are the gains from reductions in setup and changeover times in procedures and equipment modifications, in more rapid response to changes in market conditions, and in the increased awareness of total quality management by using the most recent technologies in producing component parts.

Protective Packaging and Materials Handling

How do we develop efficient methods of handling products in the factory, warehouse, and transport terminals? All the activities associated with moving products among the manufacturer's plants, warehouses, wholesalers, retailers, and transportation company terminals are called *materials handling*. Two important innovations have developed — combining as many packages as possible into one load (**unitization**) and combining several unitized loads (**containerization**) — which have revolutionized the materials handling field. The materials handling system must be thoroughly coordinated for plants and warehouses that service the various channel intermediaries to perform effectively.

unitization
Combining as many packages as possible into one load.

containerization
Combining several unitized loads.

Order Processing

Businesses today expect not only that orders will be processed quickly and efficiently, but that information regarding the status of the order will be readily available. On-line ordering and computer tracking makes this possible. Such information systems also enable the supplier to be more efficient.

Warehousing

Where will the products be stored? How many warehouses should be used? Warehouses lend themselves exceptionally well to automation, with the com-

www.streamline.com

▶ INTERNET IMPACT

Grocery Shopping on the Internet

For 2000 people near Boston, the Saturday morning assault on the supermarket is only a fleeting and distasteful memory.

They select their groceries and videos over the Internet from Streamline Inc., which delivers their order to their door. Streamline does dry cleaning and photo processing, too.

These on-line shoppers need a garage so the delivery person can access a specially installed refrigerator when they aren't home, and it costs them $30 a month, but after a long week at work, who wants to spend precious time fighting the hordes at the superstore, wailing children in tow?

They are the future, if the cybergurus are right, and they are about to revolutionize business. While it is not clear yet how many companies are actually making money doing business on the Internet, it is certainly changing the way business is being done—creating new winners and losers as the mesh of computers, telecommunications, and the Internet squeezes out the intermediary and brings the customer straight to the warehouse.

Already retailing, financial services, advertising, and information services are beginning to be reshaped in the New Economy. "The last economy was all about quantity and standardization—make it in big, standardize it, and make it as cheap as possible," explained Harry S. Dent, an author and economic forecaster. "But Internet and Intranet technologies will allow companies to totally reorganize—not reengineer—reorganize around the customer. People who can deliver real customization will be the winners."

What will be the role of logistics in facilitating the Internet revolution? Explain.

Source: Excerpted from Jacqueline Thorpe, "Winners and Losers in the New Economy," *Financial Post* (November 19, 1998), p. C16. Reprinted with permission.

puter as the heart of the operation. *Distribution warehouses* are designed to assemble and then redistribute products, whereas **break-bulk warehouses** receive consolidated shipments from a central distribution centre, and then distribute them in smaller shipments to individual customers in more limited areas. Another type of warehouse, the *storage warehouse,* stores products for moderate to long periods of time in an attempt to balance supply and demand for producers and purchasers. Automated warehouse technology that uses bar codes and computerized equipment enables the speedy turnaround of products. This is especially important for products such as computer games, which have high initial demand and short life cycles. These distribution functions are interrelated, and decisions made in one area affect the relative efficiency of other areas.

break-bulk warehouse
Receives consolidated shipments from a central distribution centre, and then distributes them in smaller shipments to individual customers in more limited areas.

▶ INTERNATIONAL PHYSICAL DISTRIBUTION

Canada depends very much on international trade. The continued growth of international commerce has created new responsibilities for many firms' physical distribution departments.

A major problem facing international marketers is the pile of paperwork involved in exporting products. Many specialized international trade documents must be completed for each international shipment. As a result, documentation for the average import or export shipment requires a significant amount of time. Many logistics departments are not large enough to readily deal with these complexities or do not find it worthwhile to do on their own. Therefore, this work is subcontracted to **freight forwarders**—wholesaling intermediaries that specialize in international logistics.

freight forwarder
Wholesaling intermediary that specializes in international logistics.

A significant facilitating factor for the export business has been the advent of containerization and container ships. Shipping companies now use container ships that can make a round trip among Halifax, Bremerhaven, and Rotterdam in fourteen days. Only four days are needed for each crossing of the Atlantic, and another six for the three port calls. This speed allows Canadian exporters to provide competitive delivery schedules to European markets. Similar procedures are followed for other foreign destinations.

The largest volume of Canadian shipments, however, still comprises agricultural products and raw materials (lumber and minerals). The importance of these basic commodities to Canada has resulted in specialized, complex systems at various ports for handling them.

▶ SUMMARY

Every item consumed in daily living is affected by logistics. Logistics is the process of managing and implementing the physical movement of products from source to place of use.

To obtain efficiencies and gain competitive advantage, it is necessary to consider and manage the entire supply chain. Supply chain management is the coordination of the flow of materials and products from the source of raw materials to the production line, and ultimately to the consumer. It includes managing information, cash, and process/work flows.

The study of physical distribution is one of the classic examples of the systems approach to business problems. The goal of a physical distribution system is to produce a specified level of customer service while minimizing the costs involved in physically moving and storing the product from its production point to the point where it is ultimately purchased. The physical distribution system consists of six elements: (1) customer service, (2) transportation, (3) inventory control, (4) protective packaging and materials handling, (5) order processing, and (6) warehousing. These elements are interrelated and must be balanced for a distribution system to run smoothly.

Three basic concepts of the systems approach—the total-cost approach, the avoidance of suboptimization, and cost tradeoffs—combine to form the physical distribution concept.

The logistics manager has available five transportation alternatives: railways, motor carriers, water carriers, air freight, and pipelines. Multimodal transportation systems are available and increasingly used.

Efficient international physical distribution allows a firm to compete more effectively in foreign markets.

▶ KEY TERMS

break-bulk warehouse

common carrier

containerization

contract carrier

cost tradeoffs

economic order quantity (EOQ)

freight forwarder

just in time (JIT)

logistics

physical distribution (PD)

physical distribution concept

private carrier

suboptimization

supply chain management

third-party logistics provider

total-cost approach

unitization

▶ INTERACTIVE SUMMARY AND DISCUSSION QUESTIONS

1. Some say that physical distribution has been one of the last areas in most companies to be carefully studied and improved. How can this be explained?

2. Outline the basic reasons for the increased attention to logistics and supply chain management.

3. The physical distribution system contains the following elements: customer service, transportation, inventory control, protective packaging and materials handling, order processing, and warehousing. Explain how specifying a level of customer service can affect each of the other elements.

4. Customer service standards are an essential element in developing a logistics plan. Who should be ultimately responsible for determining the level of customer service? Why?

5. What are the basic objectives of physical distribution?

6. The five main transportation modes are railway, motor carrier, water carrier, air freight, and pipelines. Outline the basic strengths and weaknesses of each mode of transport.

7. Legal forms of transportation carriers can be categorized as common, contract, and private. In what circumstances would each be used?

8. Under what circumstances are freight forwarders used?

9. Suggest the most appropriate transportation mode for each of the following products, and defend your choices:
   a. iron ore
   b. crude oil
   c. Dash detergent
   d. orchids
   e. heavy earth-moving equipment
   f. lumber

10. The location of distribution warehouses has a significant bearing on costs and customer service. What factors should be considered in locating a new warehouse?

11. Economic order quantity emphasizes a cost tradeoff between two fundamental costs involved with inventory: inventory holding costs and order costs. Explain how EOQ works.

12. Describe how the notion of a cost tradeoff should be applied to the elements of the physical distribution system listed in question 3.

13. Select two companies such as Wal-Mart and FedEx. Using the Internet, research how an emphasis on logistics and supply chain management have contributed to their success.

To obtain a list of further readings for Chapter 17, please refer to the *Foundations of Marketing* Web site.

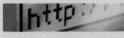

www.walmart.com

www.fedex.com

Part 7
Marketing Communications

Probably the most visible component of marketing is advertising. This is just one component of the mix of variables used by the marketer to communicate with current and potential customers. Marketers are often quick to express opinions about marketing communications, but in reality, marketing communications strategy is quite complex. Part 7 concludes with a chapter dealing with some of the basic concepts of applying marketing communications.

▶ **Chapter 18**
Marketing Communications Strategy

▶ **Chapter 19**
Marketing Communications Applications

This "in-your-face," hard-hitting advertisement from the LCBO is designed to grab viewers' attention and drive the message home.

Chapter 18
Marketing Communications Strategy

▶ **CHAPTER OBJECTIVES**
After reading and studying this chapter, you should be able to

1. Explain the concept of the marketing communications mix.
2. Describe the marketing communications mix as part of the marketing mix.
3. Elaborate on the importance of the integrated marketing communications concept.
4. Outline a theoretical model of the communications process.
5. Show how various marketing communications must conform to this model in order to be effective.
6. Explain and contrast pulling and pushing marketing communications strategies.
7. Discuss the appropriateness of different types of marketing communications objectives.
8. Explain the concept of a marketing communications budget.
9. Discuss the appropriateness of different types of marketing communications budgets.
10. Discuss marketing communications in the light of some public criticisms.

The Liquor Control Board of Ontario (LCBO) has used actual wrecked cars in an outdoor ad campaign to illustrate the dangers of drinking and driving, joining other advertisers who are turning heads with 3-D billboards.

The ambitious campaign, launched in partnership with Mothers Against Drinking and Driving (MADD) Canada, is the first ever for the LCBO. It features more than 200 English and French billboards across Ontario, most with photos of crashed cars, sport-utility vehicles, boats, and snowmobiles. Ten billboards in major cities such as Toronto, London, Ottawa, Hamilton, and Kingston featured actual wrecked automobiles and boats. Many others had lifelike highway signs.

Three-dimensional billboards are becoming increasingly popular with advertisers who want to cut through the billboard clutter. For MADD, the eye-catching ads are the best way to reach males aged 21 to 35, the highest-risk group for drinking and driving, Andrew Murie of MADD says.

"You've got to get in their face with a really hard message," says Mr. Murie, national executive director of Mississauga-based MADD. He says summer is the worst season for drinking-related crashes, and "this advertising campaign graphically shows the tragic consequences that can result." The ads, developed by Communiqué Group of Toronto, carry the tag line "Drinking and Driving is no accident." The campaign has a total budget of $2.4-million. The LCBO, Ontario's liquor retailer, also revived a 90-second cinema ad with the message, "How far will you let drinking take you?" It was scheduled to run on 547 Famous Players and Cineplex Odeon screens to coincide with the holiday season. The hard-hitting cinema ad shows a young man driving home after a night of drinking, only to end up in what appears to be a jail cell. When he passes, ghost-like, through the bars, it becomes apparent he is actually dead.

www.lcbo.com

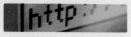

www.madd.ca

An attention-getting device used in a creative way to transmit a message—that is the essence of marketing communications. And the variations that people think up are endless. This is what makes marketing communications one of the most interesting and exciting elements of the marketing mix.

Source: Adapted from John Heinzl, "Wrecked Cars Star in LCBO's 3-D Billboards," *The Globe and Mail* (May 28, 1999), p. M1. Reprinted with permission from *The Globe and Mail.*

▶ INTRODUCTION

You have come up with a wonderful product. You have determined the market segment that it will serve, appraised customer needs, analyzed competitors' offerings, and defined a positioning strategy. How then should your product's advantages be communicated to the target audience?

A vast array of communication alternatives are available. How about direct mail (is it really "junk," as some people claim?) or celebrity advertising? Perhaps the main communication message should be carried by salespeople. But that might cost too much. On the other hand, why waste money by not spending enough on marketing communications? How much *is* "enough"?

These few questions just scratch the surface of the many issues involved in developing and implementing a marketing communications strategy. It is an exhilarating and creative process that requires tough thinking and a very systematic approach. This chapter and the next will introduce the domain of marketing communications.

Marketing communications, the fourth variable in the marketing mix, is defined as all activities and messages that inform, persuade, and influence the consumer in making a purchase decision. Figure 18.1 depicts the relationship between a firm's marketing communications strategy and the other elements of the overall marketing plan.

The marketing manager sets the goals and objectives of the firm's communications approach in accordance with overall organizational objectives and the goals of the marketing plan.

marketing communications All activities and messages that inform, persuade, and influence the consumer in making a purchase decision.

Primed to Score

tse.com

In this advertisement, the Toronto Stock Exchange uses a tangible image to persuade people to invest in the Exchange as it is "primed to score."

Then, based on these goals, the various elements of marketing communications —advertising, personal selling, sales promotion, publicity, and public relations— are formulated in a coordinated plan. This plan, in turn, becomes an integral part of the total marketing strategy for reaching selected consumer segments. Finally, the feedback mechanism, in such forms as marketing research and field reports, closes the system by identifying any deviations from the plan and by suggesting modifications or improvements.

▶ **FIGURE 18.1 Integrating the Marketing Communications Plan into the Total Marketing Mix**

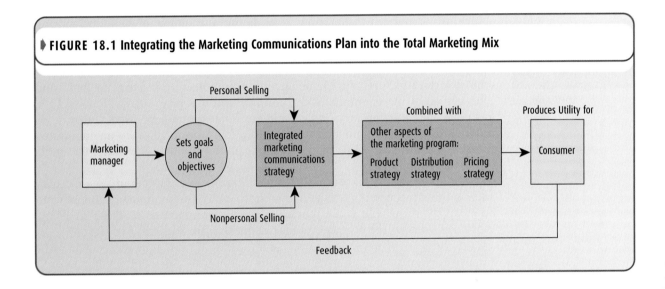

▶ INTEGRATED MARKETING COMMUNICATIONS (IMC)

The foregoing approach is also known as integrated marketing communications (IMC). Formerly, a significant number of firms tended to view the elements of the promotion mix individually, each with its own plans and tactics for influencing the target market. For example, advertising was managed separately from the sales promotion, publicity, and direct marketing functions.

Today it is recognized that the vast array of communication alternatives should be integrated to create the greatest impact. The integrated marketing communications approach looks at company information outputs from the customer's perspective. It recognizes that the customer develops an understanding of the company or the product through a *combination* of many sources: advertising, the Internet, direct mail, billboards, and coupons. In addition, the IMC concept includes all of the other ways that customers learn about the company and product, such as packaging, displays, and sales literature. All communications must be integrated so that the customer receives a unified message. Such communications are coordinated with other elements of the marketing mix to create synergistic effects.

integrated marketing communications (IMC)
A comprehensive marketing communications plan that takes into consideration all the communication disciplines being used and combines them to provide clarity, consistency, and maximum communications impact.

www.toyota.ca

Integrated marketing communications (IMC) has been defined by the American Association of Advertising Agencies as a concept of marketing communications planning that recognizes the added value of a comprehensive plan that evaluates the strategic role of a variety of communication disciplines — for example, general advertising, direct response, sales promotion, and public relations — and combines these disciplines to provide clarity, consistency, and maximum communications impact.[1]

An integrated, comprehensive plan is more difficult to achieve than it sounds. A large number of people within the firm are involved, each with somewhat different responsibilities and perspectives. Furthermore, good information is necessary. An important integrating factor is the availability of high-quality customer databases that contain not only customer names and addresses, but also demographic data, lifestyle information, and brand preferences. Database marketing has been discussed in earlier chapters. Valid information about customers creates a good picture of their needs and wants, making it easier to focus and integrate all of the elements of the communications mix. Toyota, for example, has developed a database of its car buyers. The data can be used not only for product, distribution, and pricing planning, but also to develop an integrated marketing communications plan that supports and enhances the other elements of the marketing mix.

Developing an integrated marketing communications program is a detailed and complex process. As will be shown in this chapter, many decisions have to be made about the role and importance of each promotional element, and how these decisions will fit together to best communicate with target customers.

▶ THE COMMUNICATIONS PROCESS

Figure 18.2 shows a generalized communications process using terminology borrowed from radio and telecommunications.[2] The sender is the *source* of the communications system, since he or she seeks to convey a *message* (a communication of information or advice or a request) to a *receiver* of the communication. The message must accomplish three tasks to be effective:

1. It must *gain the attention* of the receiver.
2. It must *be understood* by both the receiver and the sender.
3. It must *stimulate* the needs of the receiver and *suggest* an appropriate method of satisfying these needs.[3]

The message must be *encoded,* or translated into understandable terms, and transmitted through a communications medium or transfer mechanism. *Decoding* is the receiver's interpretation of the message. The receiver's response, known as *feedback,* completes the system. Throughout the process, *noise* can interfere with the transmission of the message and reduce its effectiveness.

In Figure 18.3, the generalized communications process is applied to marketing communications. The marketing manager is the sender in the system. The message is encoded in the form of sales presentations, advertisements, displays, or publicity releases. The *transfer mechanism* for delivering the message may be a salesperson, print or electronic advertising media, direct mail, the Internet, or a public relations channel.

FIGURE 18.2 A Generalized Communications Process

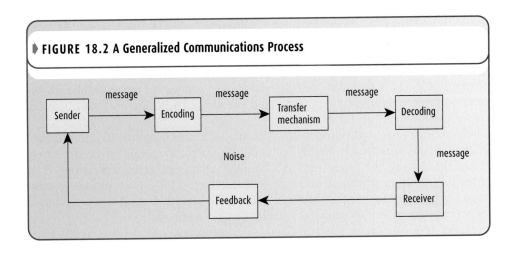

FIGURE 18.3 The Process of Marketing Communications

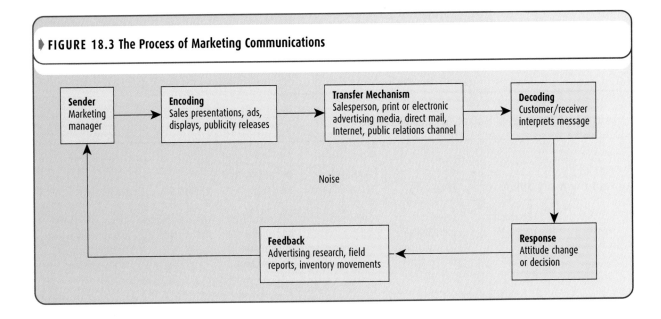

The *decoding* step involves the consumer's interpretation of the sender's message. This is the most troublesome aspect of marketing communications, since consumers often do not interpret a promotional message in the same way as its sender does. Because receivers are likely to decode messages based on their own frames of reference or individual experiences, the sender must be careful to ensure that the message is properly encoded to match the target audience. If the message is decoded properly, there is a greater chance of a positive consumer *response*—an attitude change or decision to purchase.

Feedback is information about the receiver's response to the message. The response may take the form of attitude change, purchase, or nonpurchase. In some instances, a firm may use marketing communications to create a favourable attitude toward its new products or services. Such attitude changes may result in future purchases. In other instances, the objective of the communication is to stimulate consumer purchases. Such purchases indicate positive responses to the firm, its product/service offerings, its distribution channels, its prices, and its promotion. Even nonpurchases can serve as feedback to the sender. They may result from ineffective communication in that the message was not believed, not remembered, or failed to persuade the receiver that the firm's products or services are superior to its competitors. Feedback can be obtained from advertising research, field sales reports, or an analysis of inventory movements.

Noise represents interference at some stage in the communications process. It may result from such factors as competitive promotional messages being transmitted over the same communications channel, misinterpretation of a sales presentation or an advertising message, receipt of the promotional message by the wrong person, or random noise factors, such as people conversing — or leaving the room — during a television commercial.

Table 18.1 illustrates the steps in the communications process with three examples of promotional messages. Although the types of promotion vary from a highly personalized sales presentation to such nonpersonal promotion as a two-for-one coupon and television advertising, each form of promotion goes through each stage in the communications model.

TABLE 18.1 Examples of Marketing Communications

TYPE OF PROMOTION	SENDER	ENCODING	TRANSFER MECHANISM	DECODING BY RECEIVER	RESPONSE	FEEDBACK
Personal selling	Canon Office Equipment	Sales presentation on new model office copier	Canon sales representative	Office manager and employees in local firm discuss Canon sales presentation and those of competing suppliers	Order placed for Canon copier	Information that customers are reacting positively to the message
Two-for-one coupon (sales promotion)	Wendy's Hamburgers	Wendy's marketing department and advertising agency	Coupon inserted in weekend newspaper	Newspaper reader sees coupon for hamburger and saves it	Hamburgers purchased by consumers using the coupon	Information that customers are reacting positively to the message
Television advertising	Movie producer	Advertisement for a new movie is developed by the producer's advertising agency	Network television during programs with high percentage of viewers in target market	Audience sees ad but few decide to go to the movie	Small number of movie tickets purchased	Communication failed to interest and motivate the target market

▶THE MARKETING COMMUNICATIONS MIX

Similar to the marketing mix, in planning marketing communications, numerous variables must be considered and blended together. The **marketing communications mix** is a subset of the marketing mix that blends personal selling and nonpersonal communication (including advertising, sales promotion, public relations, sponsorship marketing, and point-of-purchase communications) by marketers in an attempt to accomplish information and persuasion objectives. Figure 18.4 illustrates this relationship.

Personal selling and advertising are generally the most significant elements of the mix, since they usually account for the bulk of a firm's marketing communications expenditures. However, in any individual company, marketing planners may gain a competitive advantage by emphasizing other elements of the communications mix. A discussion of each of these elements is presented in Chapter 19. Only brief definitions will be given here to set the framework for the overall discussion of marketing communications.

marketing communications mix
The blend of personal selling and nonpersonal communication (including advertising, sales promotion, public relations, sponsorship marketing, and point-of-purchase communications) by marketers in an attempt to accomplish information and persuasion objectives.

Personal Selling

Personal selling may be defined as a seller's promotional presentation conducted on a person-to-person basis with the buyer. It is a direct face-to-face form of promotion. Personal selling was also the original form of promotion. The 1996 census estimated that 554 370 people in Canada work in retail sales.

personal selling
A seller's promotional presentation conducted on a person-to-person basis with the buyer.

Nonpersonal Communication

Nonpersonal communication is divided into advertising, sales promotion, and public relations. Advertising is usually regarded as the most important of these forms.

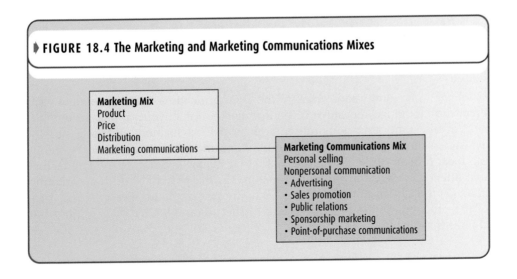

▶ **FIGURE 18.4 The Marketing and Marketing Communications Mixes**

Marketing Mix
Product
Price
Distribution
Marketing communications

Marketing Communications Mix
Personal selling
Nonpersonal communication
• Advertising
• Sales promotion
• Public relations
• Sponsorship marketing
• Point-of-purchase communications

advertising
Paid nonpersonal communication through various media by business firms, nonprofit organizations, and individuals who are in some way identified with the advertising message and who hope to inform or persuade members of a particular audience.

sales promotion
Those marketing activities, other than personal selling, mass media advertising, and publicity, that stimulate consumer purchasing and dealer effectiveness.

sponsorship marketing
The practice of promoting the interests of a company by associating the company or a brand with a specific event.

point-of-purchase communications
Materials designed to influence buying decisions at the point of purchase.

Advertising is paid nonpersonal communication through various media by business firms, nonprofit organizations, and individuals who are in some way identified with the advertising message and who hope to inform or persuade members of a particular audience.[4] It involves the mass media, such as newspapers, television, radio, magazines, and billboards. Business realizes the tremendous potential of this form of communication, and advertising has become increasingly important in marketing. Mass consumption makes advertising particularly appropriate for products that rely on sending the same message to large audiences.

Sales promotion includes "those marketing activities, other than personal selling, mass media advertising, and publicity, that stimulate consumer purchasing and dealer effectiveness, such as displays, shows and expositions, demonstrations, and various nonrecurrent selling efforts not in the ordinary routine."[5] Sales promotion is usually practised together with other forms of advertising to emphasize, assist, supplement, or otherwise support the objectives of the promotional program. It is growing in importance.

Public relations is a component of marketing communications that focuses on creating favourable attention and word of mouth among various publics—including the organization's customers, suppliers, shareholders, and employees; the government; the general public; and the society in which the organization operates. Public relations programs can be either formal or informal. Every organization, whether or not it has a formalized, organized program, must be concerned about its public relations. Publicity generated by such activities can have very positive effects on consumers' product and company knowledge.

Sponsorship marketing is the practice of promoting the interests of a company and its brands by associating the company or a brand with a specific event (such as a hockey tournament or festival) or charitable cause (such as the United Way).

Point-of-purchase communications includes a variety of materials that are designed to influence buying decisions at the point of purchase. Examples are displays, posters, signs, packaging, and even brand names.

▶ FACTORS AFFECTING USE OF MARKETING COMMUNICATIONS MIX ELEMENTS

How can a marketer know which of the communications mix elements to use? Precise quantitative measures to determine the effectiveness of each component of the communications mix in a given market segment are not generally available. Thus, choosing a proper mix of communications elements is one of the most difficult tasks facing the marketing manager. Some of the key factors that affect the choice of mix elements are (1) the objectives of the marketing plan, (2) the actions of competitors, (3) the nature of the market, (4) the nature of the product, (5) the product's stage in the product life cycle, (6) price, and (7) funds available.

▶ THE CANADIAN MARKETPLACE

Sponsorship Marketing Is Big Business

Auto racing is leaving other sports in the dust when it comes to luring corporate sponsors. Companies are expected to pump more than $1-billion (U.S.) into the fast lanes this year. The corporate love-in with auto racing has existed for years, but has recently reached a new plateau in this country as Canadian drivers such as Greg Moore, Paul Tracy, and Jacques Villeneuve make headlines.

In 1998, the Molson Indy in Toronto, a three-day racing and sports marketing extravaganza, attracted twenty major corporate sponsors to put a total of $10-million or more into the event. Industry experts say racing is now more popular with corporate sponsors than traditional favourites such as golf and professional teams and leagues.

North American companies sunk $1.1 billion into racing in 1998. This represents an increase of 30 percent from 1995. In comparison, it was estimated that golf would attract $650-million, while pro sports leagues and teams would receive about $457-million in corporate largesse in 1998.

Still, the million-dollar question for many auto racing neophytes is what benefits do companies really reap from being front and centre at ear-shattering racing events? The answer is simple, said Bill Chipps, editor of International Events Group (IEG) Sponsorship. "It's profile."

Corporate supporters of the Molson Indy—such as Molson Breweries, Federal Express Corp., MCI Communications Corp., Firestone Canada Inc., General Motors Corp., and Player's Ltd.—get their names plastered all over the souped-up cars and the race track walls. The company logo then reaches an estimated five million North American television viewers, and more overseas.

www.iam.ca/touts/
indy.html

Popular and high-profile events, like the Molson Indy, are important promotional venues for marketers. Large corporations, such as Shell Oil, sponsor these events and get wide exposure.

"In short, they get a lot of bang for the buck," said Mr. Chipps, adding that studies of NASCAR and CART events have shown 80 percent of attendees are likely to purchase the product or service of a race sponsor over that of a nonsponsor.

The target demographics of the sport are also appealing to sponsors. Although more than two-thirds of spectators at the Molson Indy site are male, the female participation rate is slowly growing. Of the men, about 51 percent are in the 26-to-44 age group, old enough to make a decent living and young enough to want to spend it. The lion's share of attendees are also university or college graduates, and more than 35 percent make over $75 000 a year.

All this spells major purchasing power, which has brought a new breed of sponsor besides the traditional auto parts and services firms. For instance, the lineup for the 1998 Molson Indy

included Montclair water, Pizza Pizza Ltd., Snapple drinks, Burger King Corp., and Bell Mobility. "The Molson Indy attracts a mixed bag of sponsors who are international businesses," said Jeff Carefoote, president of Molstar Sports & Entertainment. "It's a great way for them to differentiate their brands."

Are some products more suitable for sponsorship marketing than others?

Source: Adapted from Gayle MacDonald, "Auto Racing Attracts Heavy Sponsor Traffic," *The Globe and Mail* (July 17, 1998), pp. B1 and B5. Reprinted with permission from *The Globe and Mail*.

Objectives of the Marketing Plan

The first consideration in developing a communications mix is the objectives of the marketing plan. As outlined in Chapter 6, the marketing plan makes specific decisions about each element of the marketing mix. The role that marketing communications should play in that plan has to be clearly defined. Is its role to provide supplemental support to an aggressive pricing strategy, for example, or will marketing communications be used to promote product features? If promoting product features, what are the best ways to communicate the message?

Actions of Competitors

Considering competitors' actions is important in developing marketing strategy, and it is of critical importance to understand the communications program of competitors. The marketer must decide whether to match competitors' communications mix or to develop a different mix that counters the competition's strategy more effectively.

Nature of the Market

The marketer's target audience has a major impact on what type of communications mix elements will work best. In cases where there is a limited number of buyers (as, for example, with a manufacturer of printing presses), personal selling may prove highly effective. However, markets that are characterized by a large number of potential customers scattered over a large geographic area may make the cost of contact by personal salespeople prohibitive; in such instances, marketers may make extensive use of advertising (as, for example, is done for Kodak film).

The type of consumer also affects the marketing communications mix. A target market that is made up of business purchasers or retail and wholesale buyers is more likely to require personal selling than one consisting of ultimate consumers. Also, because the value of their purchases is significant, it is economically feasible to use personal selling.

Nature of the Product

Another important factor in determining an effective marketing communications mix is the product itself. Highly standardized products with minimal servicing requirements are less likely to depend on personal selling than are higher-priced custom products that are technically complex and require servicing. Consumer goods are more likely to rely heavily on advertising than are business goods.

Within each product category, marketing communications mixes vary. For instance, in business marketing, installations typically involve a heavy reliance on personal selling compared with the marketing of operating supplies. Convenience goods rely heavily on manufacturer advertising, and personal selling plays a role only in getting the product distributed.

On the other hand, personal selling is often more important in marketing shopping goods, and both personal selling and nonpersonal selling are important in marketing specialty goods. Finally, personal selling is likely to be more important in marketing products that are characterized by trade-ins.

Stage in the Product Life Cycle

The marketing communications mix must also be tailored to the stage in the product life cycle. In the introductory stage, heavy emphasis is placed on personal selling to inform the marketplace of the merits of the new product and to gain distribution. Salespeople contact marketing intermediaries to secure interest and commitment to handle the new product. Trade shows and exhibitions are frequently used to inform and educate prospective dealers and ultimate consumers. Any advertising at this stage is largely informative, and sales promotional techniques, such as samples and cents-off coupons, are designed to influence consumer attitudes and stimulate initial purchases.

As the product moves into the growth and maturity stages, advertising becomes more important in attempting to persuade consumers to make purchases. Personal-selling efforts continue to be directed at intermediaries in an attempt to expand distribution. As more competitors enter the marketplace, advertising stresses product differences in an attempt to persuade consumers to purchase the firm's brand. Reminder advertisements begin to appear in the maturity and early decline stages. Sponsorship marketing may be used at this time.

Price

The price of the product is a sixth factor in the choice of marketing communications mix elements. Advertising is a dominant mix component for low-unit-value products due to the high costs per contact involved in personal selling. The cost of a sales call by an intermediate level sales representative, for example, has been estimated at nearly $93, excluding overhead costs.[6] As a result, it has become unprofitable to promote lower-value products through personal selling. Advertising, by contrast, permits a low promotional expenditure per sales unit since it reaches mass audiences. For low-value consumer products, such as chewing gum, soft drinks, and snack foods, advertising is the only feasible means of promotion.

Funds Available

A very real barrier to implementing any marketing communications strategy is the size of the budget. If a 30-second television commercial costs a packaged-goods company $100 000 to shoot, and one 30-second showing nationally during a special even costs $6000 or more, television advertising is costly. Even though the message is received by millions of viewers and the cost per contact is relatively low, such an expenditure for just one showing would exceed the entire promotional budget of thousands of firms.

For many new or smaller firms, the cost of national mass advertising is prohibitive, so they are forced to seek less expensive, and possible less efficient, methods. One common approach involves using smaller, local media. Neighbourhood retailers may not be able to advertise in metropolitan newspapers or on local radio and television stations; apart form personal selling, therefore, their limited promotional budgets may be allocated to an eye-catching sign, one of the most valuable promotional devices available to small retailers, or local circulation of handbills. A well-designed Web site is another reasonably priced option.

Table 18.2 summarizes the factors that influence the determination of marketing communications mix elements for a marketing program.

▶ **TABLE 18.2 Factors That Influence the Marketing Communications Mix**

	EMPHASIS ON	
FACTOR	**Personal Selling**	**Advertising**
Objectives of the Marketing Plan	Affects all decisions in the mix	
Actions of Competitors	Decide whether to match competitors and/or to develop a different mix	
Nature of the Market		
Number of buyers	Limited number	Large number
Geographic concentration	Concentrated	Dispersed
Type of customer	Business purchaser	Ultimate consumer
Nature of the Product		
Complexity	Custom-made, complex	Standardized
Service requirements	Considerable	Minimal
Type of good	Business	Consumer
Use of trade-ins	Trade-ins common	Trade-ins uncommon
Stage in the Product Life Cycle	Introductory and early growth stages	Latter part of growth stage and maturity and early decline stages
Price	High unit value	Low unit value
Funds Available	Affects all decisions in the mix	

▶ MARKETING COMMUNICATIONS STRATEGY— PULL OR PUSH?

Broadly speaking, there are two marketing communications policies that may be employed: a pulling strategy and a pushing strategy. A **pulling strategy** is a promotional effort by the seller to stimulate final-user demand, which then exerts pressure on the distribution channel. The plan is to build consumer demand for the product by means of advertising so that channel members will have to stock the product to meet that demand. If a manufacturer's advertising efforts result in shoppers' requesting the retailer to stock an item, they will usually succeed in getting that item on the retailer's shelves, since most retailers want to stimulate repeat purchases by satisfied customers. For example, grocery retailers are unwilling to stock a new product unless the manufacturer mounts a significant advertising and promotional program. They realize that it is necessary to pull the product through the channel.

A pulling strategy may be required to motivate marketing intermediaries to handle a product when they already stock a large number of competing products. When a manufacturer decides to use a pulling strategy, personal selling is often largely limited to contacting intermediaries, providing requested information about the product, and taking orders. Advertising and sales promotion are the most commonly used marketing communications elements in a pulling strategy.

By contrast, a **pushing strategy** relies more heavily on personal selling. Here, the objective is the promotion of the product first to the members of the marketing channel, who then participate in its promotion to the final user. This can be done through personal-selling efforts by the firm's sales force, cooperative advertising allowances, trade discounts, and other dealer supports. Such a strategy is designed to produce marketing success for the firm's products by motivating representatives of wholesalers or retailers to spend a disproportionate amount of time and effort in promoting these products to customers. For example, a lawn mower manufacturer may decide to provide high margins plus other incentives to dealers to encourage them to push their brand rather than competitors' brands. Thus money is spent in this way rather than on extensive advertising.

While pulling and pushing are presented here as alternative policies, it is unlikely that many companies will depend entirely on either strategy. In most cases, marketers employ a mixture of the two.

Timing

In situations where both advertising and personal selling are used, timing is another factor to consider in developing a marketing communications strategy. Figure 18.5 shows the relative importance of advertising and selling in different periods of the purchase process. During the pre-transactional period (before the actual sale), advertising has been found to be more important than personal selling. It is often argued that one of the primary advantages of a successful adver-

pulling strategy
A promotional effort by the seller to stimulate final-user demand, which then exerts pressure on the distribution channel.

pushing strategy
The promotion of the product first to the members of the marketing channel, who then participate in its promotion to the final user.

▶ THE PRACTISING MARKETER

www.naya.com

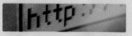

www.coca-cola.com

When Distribution Is in Trouble, Turn to Advertising

Canadian bottled water company Naya Inc. watched its sales surge for five years, but found itself paddling hard in 1999.

Naya was a success story. The Mirabel, Que.-based company had a trendy product—bottled water in small containers, which is the fastest-growing beverage in North America—a snappy advertising slogan ("hungry for life, thirsty for Naya"), and about 65 percent of its volume distributed by Coca-Cola Enterprises Inc., one of the most powerful networks in the world.

Sales were growing yearly by at least 30 percent, said Steven Wasik, Naya's vice-president of marketing. Things were going so well that in 1997, the bottler bid to acquire privately held Naya, though a deal was never reached. Then, a key part of the picture changed. Coca-Cola Co., which owns 39 percent of Coca-Cola Enterprises, its largest bottler, decided to introduce a bottled water brand of its own called Dasani, and Naya executives were told that they would have to start looking for a new distributor.

"This came as a great surprise," Mr. Wasik said. "We had fully expected to be able to coexist with Dasani." The Dasani brand is purified tap water with added minerals. Naya is bottled from a pair of Canadian springs and is priced higher than Dasani, Mr. Wasik said, though not as high as Danone SA's Evian, a French spring water that Coca-Cola Enterprises has also distributed.

A spokeswoman for the bottler said: "We believe a purified water such as Dasani provides Coca-Cola Enterprises with a high-growth, high-profit product that will capture a significant share of the bottled water category. For consumers who are only interested in a natural spring water, we will continue to offer Evian."

Notice of the change came to Naya in November 1998 and went into effect in May 1999. Mr. Wasik said the company has switched to a distribution method that uses brokers to provide its products to stores. Other beverage companies, including Triarc Cos., the owner of Snapple and RC Cola, rely on the method. But it has its drawbacks. "Obviously, the convenience store, the gas stations, and other smaller accounts are a greater challenge for us," Mr. Wasik said.

Others were blunter. "This is going to be a substantial body blow for Naya," said John Sicher, publisher of *Beverage Digest,* a U.S.-based industry newsletter. "They are probably going to lose somewhere in the range of 30 percent of their volume. The reason is, when a product is distributed in the Coke bottling system, it's in every vending machine, nook, and cranny in the United States."

To counteract the loss of Coca-Cola Enterprises, Naya has been working the public relations machines overtime. A large ad in the April 1999 issue of *Beverage World,* a U.S. trade publication, thanked the bottler for the memories. "It's been a great relationship," the ad read in part. "While you supplied the distribution strength, we supplied the finest-quality product and a commitment to invest in marketing through advertising, promotions, and sponsorships. Together, we took an already successful brand and made it better."

The point, Mr. Wasik said, was to let retailers know that Naya—and not Coca-Cola—had been the promotional force behind the brand. "It was our way, and we hope a classy way, of saying here's the real deal," he said.

Then it issued a release titled "How Naya Kicked the Coke Habit." In it, Naya all but lambasted the Coca-Cola system dropping it and even took a shot at Dasani. "In our opinion, by replacing Naya natural spring water with a purified bottled water, Coke is emphasizing cost savings over quality," Naya president, Stu Levitan, said in the release.

Can this marketing communications strategy make the difference for Naya? Is this a pushing strategy? Why or why not?

Source: Adapted from Constance L. Hays, "Naya Set Adrift after Coke Sinks Distribution Deal," *The New York Times* in *The Globe and Mail* (May 28, 1999), p. B6. Reprinted with permission from *The New York Times.*

tising program is that it sensitizes prospects to the product, and it assists the salesperson in approaching the prospect. Personal selling becomes more important than advertising during the transactional phase of the process. In most situations, personal selling is the actual mechanism for closing the sale. In the post-transactional stage, advertising regains primacy in the communication effort. It serves as an affirmation of the customer's decision to buy a particular good or service, as well as a reminder of the product's favourable qualities, characteristics, and performance.

▶ FIGURE 18.5 Relative Importance of Advertising and Selling

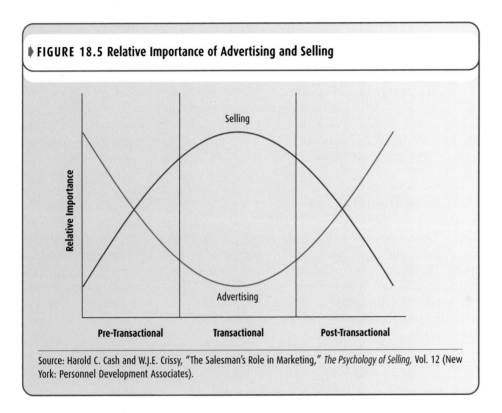

Source: Harold C. Cash and W.J.E. Crissy, "The Salesman's Role in Marketing," *The Psychology of Selling,* Vol. 12 (New York: Personnel Development Associates).

▶ MARKETING COMMUNICATIONS OBJECTIVES

"Set clear objectives" is an axiom of good business. However, management has always found that determining exactly what it expects marketing communications to achieve is a perplexing problem. In most cases, it is too simplistic to expect a direct correlation between advertising and sales results. Generally, strategy for this mix element should be oriented toward achieving clearly stated, measurable communications objectives.

The specific objective must vary with the situation. However, the following can be considered objectives of marketing communications: (1) to provide information, (2) to increase demand, (3) to differentiate the product, (4) to accentuate the value of the product, (5) to stabilize sales, and (6) in a limited number of situations, to produce sales.

Providing Information

The traditional function of marketing communications was to inform the market about the availability of a particular product. Indeed, a large part of modern marketing communications efforts is still directed at providing product information to potential customers. An example of this is the typical university or college extension course program advertisement appearing in the newspaper. Its content emphasizes informative features, such as the availability of different courses. Southam Business Information has employed an interesting idea in advertising to potential business advertisers. The ad shows the back of a station wagon covered with bumper stickers, and then makes the point "To communicate effectively, deal with one idea at a time." The ad educates potential advertisers and shows how Southam can help.

The informative function often requires repeated customer exposures. For instance, "in a ... study concerning customer acceptance of a new durable good, it was found that ... at least several months were required after introduction (and accompanying promotion) before consumers became generally aware of the item and somewhat familiar with its characteristics."[7]

Increasing Demand

www.pg.com

The primary objective of most marketing communications efforts is to increase the demand for a specific brand of product or service. This can be shown by using the familiar demand curves of basic economics (see Figure 18.6). Successful promotion can shift demand from schedule 1 to schedule 2, which means that greater quantities can be sold at each possible price level. Procter & Gamble has done this successfully with its Tide detergent.

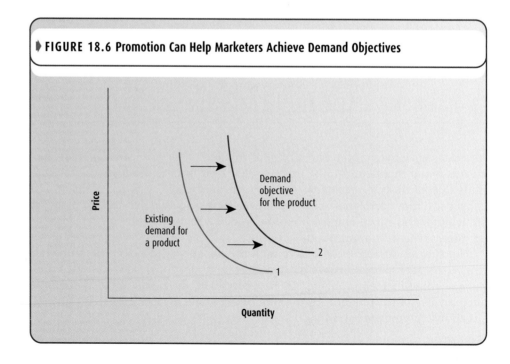

▶ **FIGURE 18.6 Promotion Can Help Marketers Achieve Demand Objectives**

Differentiating the Product

Product differentiation is often an objective of the firm's marketing communications efforts. Homogeneous demand, represented by the horizontal line in Figure 18.7, means that consumers regard the firm's product as no different from that of its competitors. In such cases, the individual firm has no control over such marketing variables as price. A differentiated demand schedule, in contrast, permits more flexibility in marketing strategy, such as price changes.

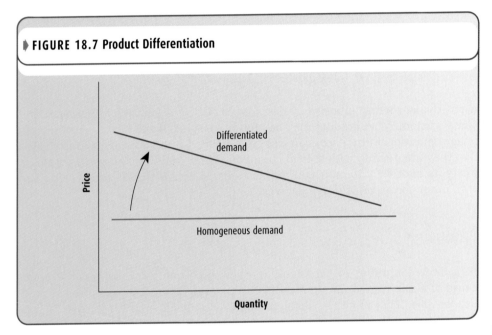

▶ **FIGURE 18.7 Product Differentiation**

For example, McCain, a producer of frozen vegetables, advertises the dependable high quality and good taste of its products. This differentiates these products from others. Consequently, some consumers who want these attributes are willing to pay a higher price for McCain than they would for other brands. Similarly, the high quality and distinctiveness of Cross pens are advertised, resulting in Cross's ability to ask for and obtain a price that is 100 times that of some disposable pens.

With the exception of commodities, most products have some degree of differentiation, resulting in a downward-sloping demand curve. The angle of the slope varies somewhat according to the degree of product differentiation.

Accentuating the Value of the Product

Marketing communications can point out important features of a product to buyers, thereby accentuating the value of the product. The good or service might then be able to command a higher price in the marketplace. For example, status-oriented advertising may allow some retail clothing stores to command higher prices than others. The demand curve that faces a prestige store may be less responsive to price differences than that of a competitor without a quality reputation. The responsiveness to price differences is shown in Figure 18.8.

Stabilizing Sales

A company's sales are not uniform throughout the year. Fluctuations can occur for cyclical, seasonal, or other reasons. Reducing these variations is often an objective of the firm's marketing communications strategy.

Other objectives of stabilizing sales are to create brand loyalty and to increase repeat purchases. These advertising objectives are two of the most important purposes of promotional activity.

Building Positive Corporate Image

A positive corporate image provides a great deal of assurance to potential and actual customers. A product may be chosen because of the perceived company image, and repeat purchases can also be enhanced when customers are satisfied that they are dealing with a good company. Thus, building a positive corporate image is another common communications objective that is often combined with other communication objectives.

Producing Sales

In a limited number of situations, marketing communications are the direct cause of a sale. One example is a direct marketing campaign that offers a product for sale. This might be done through direct mail or the Internet. If consumers respond with orders, the cause-and-effect relationship between the mes-

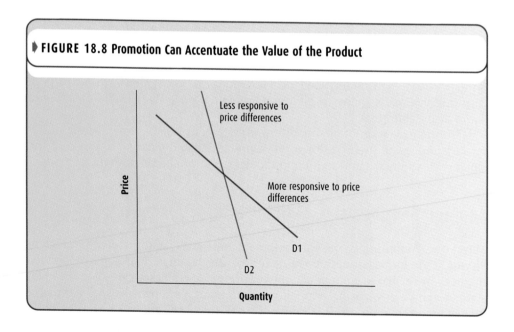

▶ **FIGURE 18.8 Promotion Can Accentuate the Value of the Product**

sage and the response is clear. TV, radio, and newspaper advertising that offers various items on sale can also bring a flow of purchasers. Note that producing sales is only one of the legitimate expectations for marketing communications, and is not considered the predominant one.

▶ ADVERTISING PLANNING

Advertising plans provide the framework for properly implementing marketing communications strategy. Advertising planning begins with effective research. Information from research allows management to make strategic decisions, which are then translated into tactical execution, budgeting, copywriting, scheduling, and the like. Finally, there must be some feedback mechanism for measuring the effectiveness of the advertising. The elements of advertising planning are shown in Figure 18.9.

▶ FIGURE 18.9 Elements of Advertising Planning

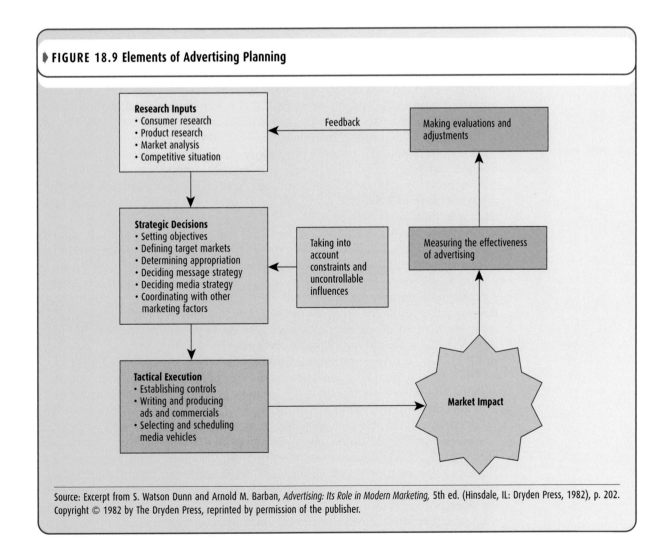

Source: Excerpt from S. Watson Dunn and Arnold M. Barban, *Advertising: Its Role in Modern Marketing,* 5th ed. (Hinsdale, IL: Dryden Press, 1982), p. 202. Copyright © 1982 by The Dryden Press, reprinted by permission of the publisher.

There is a real need to follow a sequential process in making advertising decisions. Novice advertisers are often guilty of being overly concerned with the technical aspects of designing advertisements while ignoring the more basic steps, such as market analysis. The type of advertisement that is employed in any particular situation is largely related to the planning phase of this process.

▶ BUDGETING FOR MARKETING COMMUNICATIONS EFFORTS

Marketing communications budgets can differ not only in amount but also in composition. Business-to-business marketers generally invest a larger proportion of their budgets in personal selling than in advertising, while the reverse is usually true of most consumer-products producers.

How Much Should Be Spent on Marketing Communications?

Theoretically, the optimal method of determining how much to spend on marketing communications (known as a marketing communications budget) is to expand it until the cost of each additional increment equals the additional incremental revenue received. In other words, the most effective allocation procedure is to increase expenditures until each dollar of expense is matched by an additional dollar of profit. This procedure — called *marginal analysis* — results in the maximization of the input's productivity. The difficulty arises in identifying this optimal point. In practice, doing so is virtually impossible.

The common methods of determining a marketing communications budget are percentage of sales, fixed sum per unit, meeting competition, and the task-objective method.

Percentage of sales is a very common (but dangerous) way of allocating budgets. The percentage can be based on either past (for example, previous-year) or forecasted (current-year) sales. While the simplicity of this plan is appealing, it is not an effective way of achieving the basic communications objectives. Arbitrary percentage allocations (whether applied to historical or future sales figures) fail to allow the required flexibility. Furthermore, such reasoning is circular, because the advertising allocation is made to depend on sales, rather than vice versa, as it should be. Consider, for example, the implications of a decline in sales — advertising investment would fall just when it was needed most.

The *fixed sum per unit* approach differs from percentage of sales in only one respect: it applies a predetermined allocation to each sales or production unit. This also can be set on either a historical or a forecasted basis. Producers of high-value consumer durable goods, such as cars, often use this budgeting method.

Another traditional approach is simply to match competitors' outlays — in other words, *meet competition* — on either an absolute or a relative basis. However, this kind of approach usually lead to a status quo situation at best, with each company retaining its market share. Meeting the competition's budget does not necessarily relate to the objectives of promotion and, therefore, seems inappropriate for most contemporary marketing programs.

▸ THE CANADIAN MARKETPLACE

A Unique Marketing Communications Method

If you're the corporate equivalent of a gnat, how do you compete against titans such as IBM and Hewlett-Packard? That's the problem facing systems integrator KTI Kanatek Technologies Inc., which makes its living helping large corporations and government organizations manage data and conduct e-business.

Rather than bowing to the superior marketing budgets of its multinational rivals, however, Kanatek has come up with a uniquely Canadian solution: hockey. As in the Kanatek Silicon Valley Challenge, an annual event pairing corporate executives with NHL legends.

Two teams of high-tech players square off in the game, with former pros sprinkled in. This year, Lanny MacDonald, Laurie Boschman, and Mike Gartner joined in the fun.

Started three years ago by Kanatek president Terry Kell and chief executive Peter Karneef as a means of generating publicity for the company, the event has become an Ottawa mainstay, with more than 900 people showing up at the Corel Centre this year just to watch. Clients come from the U.S. and as far away as Europe to play. In keeping with techie form, the game is broadcast live on the Internet.

This year, in addition to the hockey, Kanatek added a one-day conference called Cybertrends. "It's a thank you to our customers, and it's also an opportunity for our clients to meet one another and to facilitate relationships," Mr. Kell said. "Delegates come to hear about real-life situations."

These are exciting times for Kanatek. The small, Kanata-based company expects to ink sales of $50-million to $60-million in 1999, and is looking to aggressively expand its client base. For the third year running, it was named one of the 50 best-managed private companies in Canada by the *Financial Post.*

Since its inception, the company's average rate of annual growth has been 25 percent. Now, however, the plan is to grow bigger, faster—a plan that includes an aggressive marketing campaign, a focus on product development, and a concerted effort to penetrate existing accounts more deeply. "All our development in the marketplace has been in terms of word of mouth," Mr. Kell said. "We're going to raise our profile in the marketplace, and we're going to get the company ready to go to the next level of business."

Marketing communications can be accomplished in many ways. What do you think of Kanatek's approach to competing with the large advertisers mentioned in the article?

Source: Excerpted from Jennifer Campbell, "Kanatek Shines on the Ice and the Net," *Financial Post* (April 26, 1999). Reprinted with permission.

|http://|
www.kanatek.com

The **task-objective method** of developing a marketing communications budget is based on a sound evaluation of the firm's communications objectives, and is thus better attuned to modern marketing practices. It involves two sequential steps:

1. The organization must define the realistic communication goals the firm wants the marketing communications mix to accomplish—for example, a 25 percent increase in brand awareness, or a 10 percent rise in consumers who realize that the product has certain specific differentiating features. The key is to specify quantitatively the objectives to be accomplished. They then become an integral part of the marketing communications plan.

2. The organization, on the basis of experience and expert advice, must determine the amount and type of marketing communications activity required to accomplish each of these objectives. The communications activities thus identified, and costed out, determine the firm's budget.

task-objective method
A sequential approach to allocating marketing communications budgets that involves two steps: (1) defining the realistic communication goals the firm wants the marketing communications mix to accomplish, and (2) determining the amount and type of marketing communications activity required to accomplish each of these objectives.

THE GLOBE AND MAIL
CANADA'S NATIONAL NEWSPAPER • WWW.GLOBEANDMAIL.COM
To subscribe, call 1-800-387-5400.

Think where it will take you.

With new competition from the *National Post,* existing newspapers, such as *The Globe and Mail,* stepped up their marketing communications. What objectives and goals would the papers need to define for such a campaign?

A crucial assumption underlies the task-objective approach: that the productivity of marketing communications expenditures is measurable. That is why the objectives must be carefully chosen, quantified, and coordinated with the rest of the marketing mix. Generally, an objective like "We wish to achieve a 5 percent increase in sales" is an ill-conceived marketing objective, because a sale is the culmination of the effects of *all* elements of the marketing mix. A more appropriate advertising objective might be "To make 30 percent of the target market aware of the facilities available at our health spa."

▶ MEASURING THE EFFECTIVENESS OF MARKETING COMMUNICATIONS

It is widely recognized that part of a firm's marketing communications effort is ineffective. John Wanamaker, a successful nineteenth-century retailer, once observed, "I know half the money I spend on advertising is wasted; but I can never find out which half."

Measuring the effectiveness of marketing communications is an extremely important research question, particularly among advertisers. Studies aimed at this measurement objective face several major obstacles, among them the difficulty of isolating the effect of the marketing communications variable.

Most marketers would prefer to use a **direct-sales results test** to measure the effectiveness of marketing communications. Such a test attempts to ascertain for each dollar of promotional outlay the corresponding increase in revenue. The primary difficulty involves controlling the other variables that operate in the marketplace. A $1.5 million advertising campaign may be followed by an increase in sales of $20 million. However, this shift may have more to do with a sudden price hike by the firm's leading competitor than with the advertising expenditure. Therefore, advertisers are turning to establishing and assessing achievable, measurable objectives.

direct-sales results test
A test that attempts to ascertain for each dollar of promotional outlay the corresponding increase in revenue.

With the increasing sophistication of marketing analysts, analytical techniques, and computer-based marketing information systems, banks of historical data on marketing communications expenditures and their effects are being subjected to ever more scrutiny. More and more is being learned about measuring and evaluating the effects of marketing communications activity. While the technical literature in marketing reveals much of what is happening in this critical area, firms are reluctant to release much of this information. Not only do they wish to keep their proprietary information about how the market works to themselves for competitive reasons, but they do not want competitors to know the methods and decision routines used in planning marketing communications activity.

Other methods of assessing marketing communications effectiveness include inquiries about the product, about changes in attitudes toward the product, and about improvements in public knowledge and awareness. One indicator of probable advertising effectiveness is the elasticity or sensitivity of sales to marketing communications based on historical data concerning price, sales volume, and advertising expenditures.

It is difficult for the marketer to conduct research in a controlled environment like other disciplines can set up. The difficulty of isolating the effects of marketing communications causes many to abandon all attempts at measurement. Others, however, turn to indirect evaluation. These researchers concentrate on quantifiable factors, such as recall (how much is remembered about specific products or advertisements) and readership (the size and composition of the audience). But it remains difficult to relate these variables to sales. Does extensive ad readership actually lead to increased sales? Another problem is the high cost of research. To assess the effectiveness of marketing communications expenditures correctly may require a significant investment.

▶ THE VALUE OF MARKETING COMMUNICATIONS

Various aspects of marketing communications have often been the target of criticism. A selection of these includes the following:

- "Advertising contributes nothing to society."
- "Most advertisements and sales presentations insult my intelligence."

- "Promotion 'forces' consumers to buy products they cannot afford and do not need."
- "Advertising and selling are economic wastes."
- "Salespeople and advertisers are usually unethical."

Consumers, public officials, and marketers agree that all too often many of these complaints are true. Some salespeople do use unethical sales tactics. Some product advertising is directed at consumer groups that can least afford to purchase the particular item. Many television commercials are banal and annoying.

A marketing strategy or an ethical issue?

"I know what you're thinking, but just for a minute, think of the media exposure."

While such components of the marketing communications mix as advertising can certainly be criticized on many counts, it is important to remember that marketing communications play a crucial role in modern society. This point is best explained by looking at the importance of marketing communications on the business, economic, and social levels.

Business and Nonprofit Enterprise Importance

Marketing communications is essential for both profit and nonprofit organizations, both large and small. The long-term rise in outlays for advertising and other communications elements is well documented and certainly attests to management's faith in this element of the marketing communications mix. It is difficult to conceive of an enterprise that does not attempt to promote its goods or services in some way or another. Most modern institutions simply cannot survive in the long run without communicating with their market.

Nonbusiness enterprises also recognize the importance of this variable. The Canadian government is consistently one of the largest advertisers in Canada, promoting many programs and concepts. Religious organizations have also acknowledged the importance of promoting what they do. Even labour organizations have used marketing communications channels to make their viewpoints known to the public at large. In fact, advertising now plays a larger role in nonprofit organizations than ever before.

Economic Importance

Advertising has assumed a degree of economic importance, if for no other reason than that it is an activity that employs thousands of people. More importantly, however, effective advertising has allowed society to derive the benefits of learning about new products and new ways of doing things. This can set many economic activities into motion. Advertising creates awareness around the world and stimulates global trade.

Marketing communications strategies that increase the number of units sold permit economies in the production process, thereby lowering the production costs assigned to each unit of output. Lower consumer prices then allow these products to be available to more people. Similarly, advertising subsidizes the informational content of newspapers and the broadcast media. In short, advertising pays for many of the enjoyable entertainment and educational aspects of contemporary life, as well as lowers product costs.

Social Importance

Criticism such as "Most advertising messages are tasteless" and "Advertising contributes nothing to society" disregard the foregoing economic facts. Furthermore, they ignore the fact that no commonly accepted set of standards or priorities exists within our social framework. We live in a varied economy that is characterized by consumer segments with differing needs, wants, and aspirations. What is tasteless to one group may be quite informative to another. Advertising is faced with an "averaging" problem that escapes many of its critics. The one generally accepted standard in a market society is freedom of choice for the consumer. Consumer buying decisions eventually determine what is acceptable practice in the marketplace.

Advertising has become an important factor in the campaigns to achieve such socially oriented objectives as stopping smoking, promoting family planning, encouraging physical fitness, eliminating drug abuse, and supporting countless benevolent causes. Advertising performs an informative and educational task that makes it extremely important in modern society. As with everything else in life, it is how one uses advertising, not advertising itself, that can be criticized.

▶ THE ETHICAL MARKETER

Messages Invade Calls

The telephone, last sanctuary of private communications in the Information Age, is about to be invaded by advertising. Former MCI Communications Inc. executive Perry Kamel, who has an eye for unusual promotional opportunities, is launching a long-distance service called FreeWay that offers callers free minutes for every commercial message they hear.

Meanwhile, a number of small calling card firms, including one called Free for All Systems Inc. in Ft. Lauderdale, Fla., are offering free long-distance calls to consumers willing to listen to 20-second commercials during long-distance conversations.

Most major long-distance carriers vow they will never permit advertising on their phone lines. But the activity has caught the eye of a few carriers, including long-distance giant AT&T Corp., which already has a recorded voice telling customers the time in the region they are calling to.

FreeWay allows customers to make a free call by dialing an 800 number. Customers then enter a special identification code and the number they want to reach. They are then required to listen to a brief commercial message, earning two free minutes of talk time for each message heard.

"Our members are volunteering to hear messages for something of tangible value. We've gotten a very positive response so far," Mr. Kamel says. Phone users, of course, have long been assaulted by ads and promotions while waiting on hold on business customer-service lines. But for more than half a century, phone calls have largely been a sanctuary from the onslaught of ads and promotional messages that television viewers, radio listeners, e-mail users, and Web surfers endure.

"We haven't seen the real onslaught yet; people are just now beginning to think how to market in these spaces," Washington communications lawyer Leonard Kennedy says. Experts say it will be an uphill battle.

"I wouldn't be a bit surprised that if phone companies increase 'hang time' to deliver these advertising messages during calls, they may very well be left with a lot of customers choosing to hang up instead of waiting for a call to complete," says John Kamp, senior vice-president at the American Association of Advertising Agencies in Washington.

Is there an ethical dimension to this issue, or is it a purely commercial proposition?

Source: Excerpted from Jube Shiver, Jr., "Pauses while Phones Connect Provide Space for Advertisements," *National Post* (February 1, 1999), p. C9. Reprinted with permission.

▶ SUMMARY

Today it is recognized that the vast array of communications alternatives should be integrated to create the greatest impact. Integrated marketing communications is a comprehensive marketing communications plan that takes into consideration all the communication disciplines being used and combines them to provide clarity, consistency, and maximum communications impact.

A generalized model of the communications process includes the following elements: sender, encoding, transfer mechanism, decoding, and receiver. The marketing communications mix comprises the following elements: personal selling and nonpersonal communication (which comprises advertising, sales promotion, public relations, sponsorship marketing, and point-of-purchase communications).

The factors that influence the use of marketing communications mix elements are the nature of the market, nature of the product, product's stage in the product life cycle, price, and funds available.

A pulling strategy is a promotional effort by the seller to stimulate final-user demand, which then exerts pressure on the distribution channel. A pushing strategy is the promotion of the product first to the members of the marketing channel, who then participate in its promotion to the final user.

Six different types of objectives are the focus of different marketing communications strategies: (1) to provide information, (2) to increase demand, (3) to differentiate the product, (4) to accentuate the value of the product, (5) to stabilize sales, and (6) to produce sales. The last objective is significant, but is not the most important one for most companies.

The common methods of determining the amount of money to be spent on marketing communications are percentage of sales, fixed sum per unit, meeting competition, and the task-objective method.

Marketing communications is sometimes maligned. However, three categories of contributions are made by this part of the marketing mix: business importance, economic importance, and social importance.

▶ KEY TERMS

advertising
direct-sales results test
integrated marketing
  communications (IMC)
marketing communications
marketing communications mix
personal selling

point-of-purchase communications
public relations
pulling strategy
pushing strategy
sales promotion
sponsorship marketing
task-objective method

▶ INTERACTIVE SUMMARY AND DISCUSSION QUESTIONS

1. A generalized model of the communications process includes the following elements: sender, encoding, transfer mechanism, decoding, and receiver. Using this model, explain how a sales presentation could be structured to make it work better. Using this model, show how a sales presentation could become ineffective.

2. The marketing communications mix comprises the following elements: personal selling and nonpersonal communication (which comprises advertising, sales promotion, public relations, sponsorship marketing, and point-of-purchase communications). Using Xerox copiers as an example, propose a realistic communications mix, and explain how it should blend with the rest of the marketing mix.

3. The factors that influence the use of marketing communications mix elements are the nature of the market, nature of the product, product's stage in the product life cycle, price, and funds available. If CD players are in the late growth stage of the product life cycle, what would be an appropriate type of advertising message for a CD player manufacturer?

4. A pulling strategy is a promotional effort by the seller to stimulate final-user demand, which then exerts pressure on the distribution channel. A pushing strategy is the promotion of the product first to the members of the marketing channel, who then participate in its promotion to the final user. Would you use a pushing strategy for introducing a new line of drinks that would compete with products such as Clearly Canadian? Explain.

5. Six different types of objectives are the focus of different marketing communications strategies: (1) to provide information, (2) to increase demand, (3) to differentiate the product, (4) to accentuate the value of the product, (5) to stabilize sales, and (6) to produce sales. Give examples of situations in which each type of objective would be appropriate.

6. Explain the effects of advertising being used to shift the demand curve to the right.

7. The common methods of determining the amount of money to be spent on marketing communications are percentage of sales, fixed sum per unit, meeting competition, and the task-objective method. Discuss the pros and cons of the percentage-of-sales method.

8. A new store that features specialty music geared to the 35–45 age group is about to open. Describe exactly how the store could establish a communications budget using the task-objective method.

9. Marketing communications is sometimes maligned. However, three categories of contributions are made by this part of the marketing mix: business importance, economic importance, and social importance. Defend the proposition that marketing communications offers a significant social contribution.

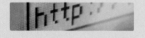

10. Select two products that are widely advertised. Find advertisements for these products in the traditional media and on the Web. What conclusions can you make about Web advertising?

To obtain a list of further readings for Chapter 18, please refer to the *Foundations of Marketing* Web site.

Chapter 19
Marketing Communications Applications

DoubleClick is riding on the wave of a new type of marketing communication—Internet advertising.

▶ **CHAPTER OBJECTIVES**
After reading and studying this chapter, you should be able to

1. Identify the categories of advertisements.
2. Identify and discuss the main advertising media.
3. Describe the process of creating an advertisement.
4. Explain public relations and its functions.
5. Discuss sales promotion and its various elements.
6. Classify the three basic types of selling.
7. Outline the seven steps in the sales process.
8. Specify the functions of sales management.

Tony Nethercutt points to a big white swatch of emptiness as his computer pulls up a page on the World Wide Web. Then he coyly tells his audience: "All that space is still available. It can still be yours. But there's a great land rush going on for advertising space on the Internet. Eventually, there will be a bidding war for sites like this."

Across the table, two executives listen eagerly to the ad salesman's presentation. They are looking for new ways to promote their Armor All line of car cleansers.

On-line advertising is new territory for them, but Mr. Nethercutt beckons with a $50 000 (U.S.) opportunity to reach a targeted audience. His proposal: Put their message on the Web pages of Kelley Blue Book Inc., the Bible of used-car data.

After a moment's pause, marketing manager Cary Rosenzweig nods his head. "I'm very supportive," he says. "This is the right thing to do."

Mr. Nethercutt's triumph is part of a wider coming of age for cyberspace advertising. Not long ago, much of his pitch would have been laughable. Few companies outside the technology field wanted to advertise on the Internet, and those that tried were hardly dazzled by the results. By some estimates, more than 80 percent of the Internet's available ad slots in 1997 went unsold. Now, on-line advertising is booming. On-line ad spending isn't just keeping pace with increased use of the Internet—it is rising appreciably faster.

Whether on-line advertising can live up to its champions' hopes is unclear. Rates are steep enough that some marketers wonder whether the response justifies the cost. Most advertisers pay at least as much to reach an Internet audience—typically $10 to $40 per 1000 viewers—as they would for TV or magazine ads.

www.doubleclick.net

Mr. Nethercutt represents DoubleClick Inc., a new kind of company. It is an ad-sales network that represents more than 70 sites on the Internet. In practically every call, Mr. Nethercutt woos advertisers with the notion that he can deliver just those parts of the vast Internet audience most valuable to them. If they want to reach women, he plays up DoubleClick clients such as foodtv.com, an offshoot of cable television's Food Network.

If customers want even more precise targeting, Mr. Nethercutt can often oblige. One advertising manager wants to reach people in one city, but not the nearby suburbs of a neighbouring city, where his cellular-phone company can't deliver service. "No problem," Mr. Nethercutt says. In the brief moment when Internet users wait for a Web page to be delivered to their screen, DoubleClick's computers can identify the area code being serviced. People in the selected area code would get the company ad; those elsewhere wouldn't. "Nice," the advertising manager says. "The customer has been targeted before he knows it."

Increasingly, on-line advertisers aren't just moving money to the sites they like; they are stepping forward with ideas about how to change the sites into better vehicles for their messages. And the people who run Web sites aren't taking offence, the way their cousins in print and television might. Instead, they are braiding advertisers' stories into the central message of their sites.

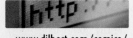

www.dilbert.com/comics/
dilbert/financial/index.html

DoubleClick, for example, persuaded Scott Adams, the cartoonist who draws Dilbert, to include a "financial section" on his Web site, with stock portfolios for his favourite characters. This new section appears in the centre of dilbert.com's home page, surrounded by cartoon strips and background facts about Dilbert. But it is paid advertising, packed with plugs for on-line trader Datek Securities Inc.

Source: Adapted from George Anders, "Internet Ad Targeting Gets More Precise," *The Wall Street Journal* in *The Globe and Mail* (December 3, 1998), p. C8. Reprinted by permission.

▶ INTRODUCTION

Time is money. Consider the advertising industry: major advertisers routinely spend thousands of dollars for 30 or 60 seconds of air time. Advertisers want to convince you that their car will make your driving easier, their clothes will make you more attractive, and they offer many other ways to improve your whole life. They buy over $9 billion worth of advertising each year in this process. This includes spending on television (the number one medium by sales), radio, newspapers, magazines, billboards, telephone directories, direct mail, Web advertising, and many other media.

Marketing communications efforts constantly change and evolve. With the advent of the Internet, a new and important advertising medium has emerged. The opening story illustrates how advertising can be used on the Internet. Advertising is becoming an integral part of Internet activity, just as it is of television, newspapers, radio, and so on. The range of marketing communications options is vast.

The previous chapter introduced the topic of marketing communications strategy, communication theory and the communications process, the marketing communications mix, and the process of advertising planning. You now know that the objectives of marketing communications are to provide information, stimulate demand, differentiate the product, accentuate the value of the product, stabilize sales, or, in some cases, actually produce sales. This chapter will discuss the major advertising media and illustrate the main marketing communications applications: advertising, publicity, sales promotion, and personal selling.

▶ ADVERTISING

If you wanted to be the next prime minister of Canada, you would need to communicate with every possible voting Canadian. If you invented a new computer game and went into business to sell it, your chances of success would be slim without informing and persuading children and young people of its uniqueness. In both these situations you would discover, as have countless others, that you would need to use advertising to communicate with buyers or voters. In the previous chapter, advertising was defined as paid nonpersonal communication through various media by business firms, nonprofit organizations, and individuals who are in some way identified with the advertising message and who hope to inform or persuade members of a particular audience.

Today's widespread markets make advertising an important part of business. Since the end of World War II, advertising and related expenditures have risen faster than gross domestic product and most other economic indicators. Furthermore, about 45 500 people were employed in advertising in 1998, according to the Statistics Canada Web site.

Three advertisers — General Motors of Canada, BCE Inc., and the government of Canada — spent more than $89 million each for advertising in 1998.[1] It is par-

www.statcan.ca/english/
Pgdb/Economy/Finance/
fin11.htm

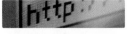

www.gmcanada.com

ticularly noteworthy that federal and provincial governments are such a major force in Canadian advertising. The federal government more than doubled its total spending since 1993. Total 1996 advertising media expenditures were about $9.4 billion. This means that about $313 is spent on advertising each year for every person in Canada.

When considered on a sector basis, retail, automotive, and business equipment and services are the three biggest advertising spenders. Table 19.1 ranks the top ten industry sector advertisers in Canada. When the two categories of automotive advertising are combined, the automotive industry becomes the largest advertiser.

▶ TABLE 19.1 The Top Ten Advertising Sectors in Canada, 1998

RANK	SECTOR	EXPENDITURES ($)
1	Retail	953 472 600
2	Automotive	753 841 800
3	Business Equipment and Services	521 617 900
4	Food	395 613 400
5	Financial Services and Insurance	388 013 200
6	Entertainment	314 755 700
7	Local Automotive Dealer Advertising	266 628 700
8	Travel and Transportation	249 321 600
9	Restaurants and Catering Services	199 322 900
10	Media	165 477 300

Source: A.C. Nielsen. Reprinted by permission.

▶ THE ROOTS OF MARKETING

Some Early Advertising Methods

Some form of advertising aimed at boosting product sales has probably existed since the development of the exchange process.[2] Most early advertising was vocal. Criers and hawkers sold various products, made public announcements, and chanted advertising slogans like this one (now familiar to many as a nursery rhyme):

One-a-penny, two-a-penny, hot-cross buns
One-a-penny, two for tuppence, hot-cross buns

Signs were also used in early advertising. Most were symbolic and identified products and services. In Rome, a goat signified a dairy; a mule driving a mill, a bakery; a boy being whipped, a school.

Later, the development of the printing press greatly expanded advertising's capability. A 1710 advertisement in the *Spectator* billed one tooth powder as "the Incomparable Powder for cleaning of Teeth, which has given great satisfaction to most of the Nobility and Gentry in England."

Advertising expenditures as a proportion of sales vary among industries and companies. Wide differences exist among industries. Advertising spending can range from 0.2 percent (as is the case with iron and steel foundries) to more than 7 percent of sales (as in the soap and detergent industry). Cosmetics companies are often cited as an example of firms that spend a high percentage of their funds on advertising and promotion.

Until 1990, professionals such as doctors and dentists were restricted in the amount of advertising they could do. In June 1990, the Supreme Court of Canada struck down prohibitions on advertising by the Royal College of Dental Surgeons of Ontario as a violation of freedom of expression. This means that not only dentists but other professionals, such as lawyers, accountants, and architects, are free to advertise their services. Thus, consumers should be more fully informed about available services, as they are for products.

One identifying feature of advertising in the last half of the twentieth century was its concern for researching the markets that it attempts to reach. Originally, advertising research dealt primarily with media selection and the product. Then, advertisers became increasingly concerned with aiming their messages more specifically through determining the appropriate demographics (such characteristics as the age, gender, and income level of potential buyers). Now, understanding consumer behaviour has become an important aspect of advertising strategy. As discussed in Chapter 3, psychographics can be useful in describing potential markets for advertising appeals. Increased knowledge of such factors as lifestyle and personal attitudes has led to improved advertising decisions.

▶ THE CANADIAN MARKETPLACE

Advertising Industry Jargon

Above-the-Line Advertising that uses catchy, creative techniques and often appeals to the subconscious.

AIDA Attention, interest, desire, and action: the classic model of how advertising works.

AM Drive, PM Drive Radio time slots.

Below-the-Line Less creative advertising, such as sales promotions and direct marketing.

Bounce Back Any ad campaign that asks you to fill in a personal information card and send it back.

Cost per Thousand (CPM) The cost, per 1000 people reached, of buying advertising space in a given medium.

Full-Service Agency An advertising agency that handles all aspects of the advertising process, from planning to placement. May handle other aspects of marketing communication and public relations as well.

HH Share The percentage of total households that own a TV or radio and are tuned in to a program.

In-Home Advertising on broadcast and cable television and the Internet.

Market Blitz A short but broad campaign that uses a lot of repetition over different advertising media.

Narrowcasting Using a broadcast medium to appeal to audiences with special interests.

Out-of-Home Radio and outdoor advertising.

Premium An item offered free or at a low price as an incentive to purchase the advertised product or service.

Tombstone Ad An ad without pictures.

Vertical Publications Publications whose editorial content deals with the interests of a specific industry, such as *Infectious Wastes News.*

The emergence of the marketing concept, with its emphasis on a company-wide consumer orientation, saw advertising take on an expanded role as marketing communications assumed greater importance in business. Advertising provides an efficient, inexpensive, and fast method of reaching consumers. Its extensive use now rivals that of personal selling. Advertising has become a key ingredient in effectively implementing the marketing concept.

Categories of Advertisements

There are two basic types of advertisements: product and institutional. Product advertising can be subdivided into informative, persuasive, and reminder-oriented categories.

Product advertising deals with the nonpersonal selling of a particular good or service. It is the type we normally think of when the subject of advertising comes up. **Institutional advertising**, by contrast, is concerned with promoting a concept, idea, or philosophy, or the goodwill of an industry, company, or organization. It is often closely related to the public relations function of the enterprise.

INFORMATIVE PRODUCT ADVERTISING

All advertising seeks to influence the audience, as does any type of communication. **Informative product advertising** seeks to develop demand through presenting factual information on the attributes of the product or service. For example, an advertisement for a new hydrogen fuel cell car would attempt to persuade through citing the various unique product or service features of that car, as well as providing assurances of satisfaction. Informative product advertising tends to be used in promoting new products, to announce their availability and characteristics that will satisfy needs. Thus it is often seen in the introductory stages of the product life cycle.

PERSUASIVE PRODUCT ADVERTISING

In **persuasive product advertising**, the emphasis is on using words or images to try to create an image for a product and to influence attitudes about it. In contrast to informative product advertising, this type of advertising contains little objective information. Coca-Cola and Pepsi use persuasive techniques in their lifestyle advertisements featuring a group of happy people enjoying the product. Persuasive advertising is generally used more in the growth and maturity stages of the product life cycle.

REMINDER-ORIENTED PRODUCT ADVERTISING

The goal of **reminder-oriented product advertising** is to reinforce previous promotional activity by keeping the product or service name in front of the public. It is used in the maturity period as well as throughout the decline phase of the product life cycle. An example of a reminder-oriented advertising campaign is Maytag's lonely service repairman series. The signs on the boards of hockey arenas are other examples of reminder-oriented advertising. Figure 19.1 illustrates the general relationship between the type of advertising and the stage of the life cycle.

product advertising
Nonpersonal selling of a particular good or service.

institutional advertising
Promoting a concept, idea, or philosophy, or the goodwill of an industry, company, or organization.

informative product advertising
Advertising that seeks to develop demand through presenting factual information on the attributes of a product or service.

persuasive product advertising
Advertising that emphasizes using words or images to try to create an image for a product and to influence attitudes about it.

www.coca-cola.com

www.pepsiworld.com

reminder-oriented product advertising
Advertising whose goal is to reinforce previous promotional activity by keeping the product or service name in front of the public.

Kool-Aid's mascot is so well-recognized that even its company name is not required on this billboard advertisement. Motorists passing by are instantly reminded of the product.

INSTITUTIONAL ADVERTISING

As mentioned earlier, institutional advertising seeks to increase public knowledge of a concept, idea, philosophy, industry, or company. For example, egg marketers have run a series of advertisements on the desirability of eating eggs. Similarly, the dairy industry has extolled the value of butter through a long-running series of advertisements. When the oil industry was experiencing some unfavourable publicity, it decided that it had a positive story to tell. It increased its advertising budget to educate the public about the industry's contributions to society. Other firms, such as Volvo, have continuously advertised their innovativeness and reliability.

Media Selection

One of the interesting phenomena in the world of high-tech recorded music is the small but significant group of consumers who prefer vinyl records to CDs. They argue that the music on vinyl is "warmer" and not as "antiseptic" as on CDs. Suppose you want to advertise to these people. A mass television campaign might reach them, but you would waste your message on most of the audience. The proper approach would be to find an advertising medium that is more focused on that group. Perhaps you could reach them through an audiophile magazine, or through the Internet.

One of the most important decisions in developing an advertising strategy is media selection. A mistake at this point can cost a company literally millions of dollars in ineffectual advertising. Media strategy must achieve the communications goals mentioned earlier.

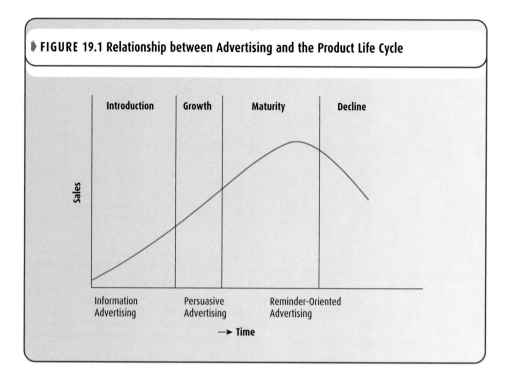

▶ FIGURE 19.1 Relationship between Advertising and the Product Life Cycle

Research should identify the target market, determine its size and characteristics, and then match the target with the audience and effectiveness of the available media. The objective is to achieve adequate media coverage without advertising beyond the identifiable limits of the potential market. Finally, alternative costs are compared to determine the best possible media purchase.

There are many types of advertising media, and the characteristics of some of the more important ones will be considered here. The advantages and disadvantages of each are shown in Table 19.2 and discussed briefly below. Net advertising revenues by medium are shown in Figure 19.2.

TELEVISION

www.cbc.ca

Television is the largest advertising medium. It now accounts for about 21 percent of total advertising volume. Since 1991, it has grown by 22 percent. Television advertising can be divided into three categories: network, national spot, and local spot. The Canadian Broadcasting Corporation, the Canadian Television Network, and Global Television are the three national networks. Network advertising usually accounts for over two-thirds of the total television advertising expenditures. A national "spot" refers to non-network broadcasting used by a general advertiser. For example, Black & Decker might choose to place an advertisement in several cities across the country without buying time from a television network. Local spots, primarily used by retailers, consist of locally developed and sponsored commercials. Television advertising offers the following advantages: impact, mass coverage, repetition, flexibility, and prestige. Its disadvantages include the temporary nature of the message, high costs, high mortality rates for commercials, some evidence of public distrust, and lack of selectivity.

> **TABLE 19.2 Advantages and Disadvantages of Various Advertising Media**

MEDIUM	ADVANTAGES	DISADVANTAGES
Television Advertising	• Demonstration ability • Intrusion value • Ability to generate excitement • One-on-one reach • Ability to use humour • Effective with salesforce and trade • Ability to achieve impact	• Rapidly escalating cost • Erosion of viewing audiences • Audience fractionalization • Zipping and zapping • Clutter
Newspaper Advertising	• Audience in appropriate mental frame to process messages • Mass audience coverage • Flexibility • Ability to use detailed copy • Timeliness	• Clutter • Not a highly selective medium • Higher rates for occasional advertisers • Mediocre reproduction quality • Complicated buying for national advertiser • Changing composition of readers
Radio Advertising	• Ability to reach segmented audiences • Intimacy • Economy • Short lead times • Transfer of imagery from TV • Use of local personalities	• Clutter • No visuals • Audience fractionalization • Buying difficulties
Magazine Advertising	• Some magazines reach large audiences • Selectivity • Long life • High reproduction quality • Ability to present detailed information • Authoritative conveying of information • High involvement potential	• Not intrusive • Long lead times • Clutter • Somewhat limited geographic options • Variability of circulation patterns by market
Direct Mail	• Selectivity • Intense coverage • Speed • Flexibility of format • Complete information • Personalization	• High cost per person • Dependence on quality of mailing list • Consumer resistance
Internet Advertising	• Ability to reach segmented audiences • Ability to change message quickly • High user interest in medium • Use of colour and limited motion graphics • Ability to bridge to extensive message and to advertiser's Web site • Can close a sale and take order	• Limited initial message length • Clutter • Uncertain effectiveness of new medium • Consumer resistance • Concern about security of information

(continued)

▶ **TABLE 19.2** *(continued)*

MEDIUM	ADVANTAGES	DISADVANTAGES
Outdoor Advertising	• Broad reach and high frequency levels • Geographic flexibility • Low cost per thousand • Prominent brand identification • Opportune purchase reminder	• Nonselectivity • Short exposure time • Difficult to measure audience size • Environmental problems

Source: Adapted from Terrance A. Shimp, *Advertising, Promotion, and Supplemental Aspects of Integrated Marketing Communications* (Fort Worth, TX: Dryden Press, 1997), pp. 324ff.

▶ **FIGURE 19.2 Net Advertising Revenues by Medium**

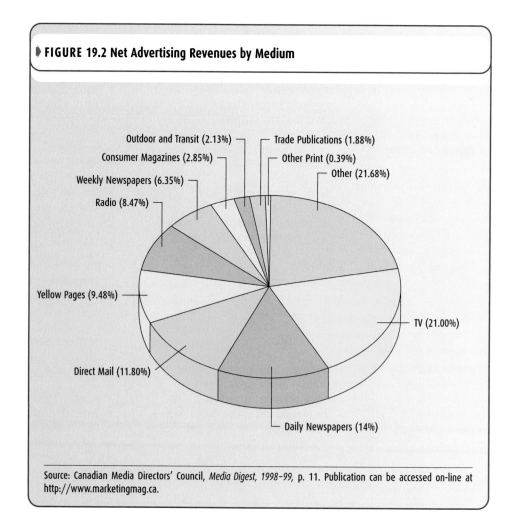

Source: Canadian Media Directors' Council, *Media Digest, 1998–99*, p. 11. Publication can be accessed on-line at http://www.marketingmag.ca.

▶ THE CANADIAN MARKETPLACE

The Mathematics of Sponsoring Television Sports

Recently a $600-million ABC/ESPN television deal was signed with the National Hockey League. Experts have done the math on the deal, and the numbers still don't make any sense. ESPN and ESPN2 are paying $70-million a season for a total of 130 games. The revenue required for ESPN to break even is difficult to determine, because subscription rates contribute to its revenue, and rates can be hiked.

ABC's financial commitment is more straightforward. It ponied up $50-million a year for the rights to 16 to 20 games (four to seven in the regular season; one a week in the playoffs, the entire final).

Generally, a hockey game produces about 56 commercial spots 30 seconds in length. Over 20 games, that adds up to 1120 spots. ABC, to make back its $50-million investment, will need to charge more than $45 000 a spot over 20 games (assuming the Cup final goes a full seven games).

But the most money that Fox Sports ever received for a 30-second spot in a Cup final was $45 000. Regular season ads sell for only $25 000. So how can ABC even come close to breaking even?

Said one television insider, "The ABC offer was based less on business than emotion. Disney wanted to knock off Fox and I think Michael Eisner's love for hockey had a lot to do with the price that was paid." Eisner is the chairman/CEO of the Disney Co., which owns ABC/ESPN and the NHL's Anaheim Mighty Ducks.

Consider how this insight into the mathematics of commercial television might apply to the advertising rights for other programs.

Source: Adapted from "William Houston's World of Television and Radio Sports," *The Globe and Mail* (August 29, 1998), p. A24. Reprinted with permission from *The Globe and Mail*.

espn.go.com

abc.go.com

NEWSPAPERS

Newspapers are the second-largest advertising medium. About 20.5 percent of Canada's total advertising revenues are spent on newspaper advertising.[3] The primary advantages of newspapers are flexibility (advertising can vary from one locality to the next), community prestige (newspapers have a deep impact on the community), intense coverage (in most places, about nine out of ten homes can be reached by a single newspaper), and reader control of exposure to the advertising message (unlike audiences of electronic media, readers can refer back to newspapers). The disadvantages are a short lifespan, hasty reading (the typical reader spends only 20 to 30 minutes on the newspaper), and poor reproduction. Advertising in daily newspapers has decreased by 9 percent since 1991, while advertising in weeklies and community papers has grown by 22 percent.

RADIO

Radio continues to hold its share of advertising revenue. Advertisers using the medium of radio can also be classified as network or local advertisers. Radio accounts for about 8.5 percent of total advertising volume. The advantages of radio advertising are immediacy (studies show that most people regard radio as the best source for up-to-date news); low cost; flexibility; practical, low-cost audience selection; and mobility (radio is an extremely mobile broadcast medium). Radio's disadvantages include fragmentation (for instance, Montreal has fifteen

AM and FM stations), the unavailability of the advertising message for future reference, and less available research information than for television.

MAGAZINES

Magazines are divided into such diverse categories as consumer magazines, farm and business publications, and directories. They account for about 5 percent of all advertising. The primary advantages of magazine advertising are selectivity of target markets, quality reproduction, long life, the prestige associated with some magazines, and the extra services offered by many publications. Canadian consumer magazines have pioneered many controlled distribution techniques. Our postal code system, with its six-digit forward sortation area (FSA) and local delivery unit (LDU), can be linked with census data at the enumeration area (EA) level to produce well-defined circulation clusters based on demographics, life cycles, or other interest–activity profiles. The primary disadvantage is that magazines lack the short-term flexibility of newspapers, radio, and television.

DIRECT MAIL

Growing by 23 percent since 1991, direct mail is a very significant advertising medium. It now accounts for 11.8 percent of advertising revenues. Sales letters, postcards, leaflets, folders, broadsides (which are larger than folders), booklets, catalogues, and house organs (periodicals issued by an organization) are all forms of direct-mail advertising. The advantages of direct mail include selectivity, intensive coverage, speed, format flexibility, complete information, and the personalization of each mailing piece. Direct-mail purchasers also tend to be consistent buyers by mail. A disadvantage of direct mail is its high cost per reader. Direct-mail advertising also depends on the quality of the mailing list. Often those unfamiliar with the effectiveness of direct mail condemn it all as "junk mail." They are very surprised to find that many people respond positively to such advertising. In fact, marketing research surveys consistently show a majority who say they prefer to receive it. Effectively used, direct mail is a successful and lucrative marketing tool. Direct mail can be used for many purposes, including informative, persuasive, and reminder-oriented advertising. However, a major function is to generate direct orders. Direct response marketing is further discussed on pages 554–56.

INTERNET ADVERTISING

Internet advertising is growing rapidly. Financial services lead all major industry sectors in Internet advertising, which is in line with growth in the areas of PC banking and electronic commerce. Internet advertising can be used for informative, persuasive, and reminder-oriented advertising. It is also a powerful means of direct marketing.

The types of advertising available on the Web are also rapidly changing. Currently, "banner advertising," an electronic strip that usually appears at the top or bottom of a Web page, accounts for more than 59 percent of total industry revenues.[4] New forms of Web advertising are emerging that go beyond the static company logo and message in a banner ad. Advertisers are developing Web ads that incorporate interactivity, electronic commerce, sound, and animation. An example is a banner ad from John Hancock Mutual Life Insurance Co.

www.jhancock.com

that lets users enter their children's ages to find out how much money must be invested each month for a college education. These types of functional, entertaining, and compelling ads are helping to drive direct response, often without the user having to click through an advertiser's Web site.[5]

As discussed more fully in Chapters 2 and 16, e-commerce has become a powerful marketing force. As more and more well-known companies such as IBM, AT&T, and Microsoft advertise on the Web, other firms follow their lead. Consumers are responding with more on-line shopping. An important contributing factor is the establishment of new security technology that allays consumer fears that key personal information is unprotected.

www.ibm.com

www.attcanada.ca

Key to marketers' evaluation of Web ad buying is the ability to measure Web site traffic and verify how many ad impressions are delivered. While the industry still lacks standards, progress has been made toward providing more measurement and independent auditing services.

www.microsoft.com

As the Web moves into living rooms and hotel rooms, advertiser interest in Web advertising will grow with the expanded target audience. Internet advertising has become an important advertising medium that can provide unique opportunities for the advertiser.

OUTDOOR ADVERTISING

Posters (commonly called billboards), painted bulletins or displays (such as those that appear on building walls), and electric spectaculars (large, illuminated, and sometimes animated signs and displays) make up outdoor advertising. Accounting for 2.1 percent of advertising volume, this form of advertising has the advantages of quick communication of simple ideas, repetition, and the ability to promote products that are available for sale nearby. Outdoor advertising is particularly effective in metropolitan and other high-traffic areas. Disadvantages of the medium are the brevity of its message and public concern over aesthetics; however, a simple message can be extremely powerful.

Selecting outdoor advertising media presents many opportunities and challenges. Aside from the main media categories listed above, many others can serve an important role in communicating with selected target markets. Table 19.3 lists the main categories. Within each category there are often several companies that provide media opportunities. For example, eight firms provide supermarket advertising services, and two handle washroom advertising. Details on these and other media can be found in the Canadian Media Directors' Council, *Media Digest* at http://www.marketingmag.ca.

Organizing the Advertising Function

While the ultimate responsibility for advertising decisions often rests with top marketing management, how the advertising function is organized varies among companies. A producer of a technical industrial product may be served by a one-person operation primarily concerned with writing copy for trade publications. A consumer-goods company, on the other hand, may have a large department staffed with advertising specialists.

The advertising function is usually organized as a staff department reporting to the vice president (or director) of marketing. The director of advertising is an executive position that heads the functional activity of advertising. The individ-

---

▶ **TABLE 19.3 Other Advertising Media**

Aerial advertising	Programs (for theatres, concerts, trade shows, etc.)
Airport display advertising	
Bar, restaurant, and hotel advertising	Receptacle advertising
Brochure advertising	Religious publications
Cable advertising	Scholarly publications
Campus advertising	Shopping centre advertising
Closed-circuit advertising	Sports advertising (e.g., rinkboard panels)
Coupon advertising	Stadium advertising
Directories, annuals, and almanacs	Supermarket advertising
Elevator advertising	Tabletop advertising (e.g., tent cards)
Exhibition centre advertising	Theatre screen advertising
Farm publications	Truck advertising
Medical advertising	University and school advertising
Mobile signage	Video screen advertising
Mural signage	Washroom advertising
Parking lot advertising	Yellow pages/telephone directory advertising
Product postcard service	

---

ual filling this slot should not only be a skilled and experienced advertiser, but also be able to communicate effectively within the organization. The success of a firm's promotional strategy depends on the advertising director's willingness and ability to communicate both vertically and horizontally. The major tasks typically organized under advertising include advertising research, art, copywriting, media analysis, and, in some cases, sales promotion.

ADVERTISING AGENCIES

advertising agency
A marketing specialist firm that assists the advertiser in planning and preparing its advertisements.

Many advertisers also use an independent advertising agency. The **advertising agency** is a marketing specialist firm that assists the advertiser in planning and preparing its advertisements.

The first advertising agents were simply newspaper space salespeople. They went from company to company selling the idea of advertising products in the paper. Since many of their potential clients knew little about advertising, some salespeople began to offer additional services, such as artwork and copywriting. The need for these services grew, and advertising agencies evolved as a result.

Within such organizations exists a cross-section of talents. There are creative people who dream up an advertisement or advertising campaign. They or others may write the copy for the advertisement, and still others are involved in producing artwork or commercials. Media specialists in the agency know the many media types and select and schedule ads to reach the right target market. Another group of people who call on clients and liaise between clients, the creative group, and the production people in the agency are known as account executives.

There are several reasons why advertisers use an agency for at least a portion of their advertising. Agencies are typically staffed with highly qualified

▶ THE PRACTISING MARKETER

New Advertising Media

Traditional ad space is getting cluttered and expensive. What's an aggressive company to do? The answer may be in your produce bin.

Take a close look at your banana. It has a couple of things to tell you about television. Or, rather, a television network is using your banana to tell you a thing or two—not just about television, but about the ever-changing world of advertising. Across North America, 22 million bananas, 4.4 million of them in Canada, have been affixed with little yellow labels bearing the ABC network logo, sporting such clever slogans as "TV. Zero Calories" and "Another Fine Use of Yellow" (referring to ABC's official corporate colour, in case you didn't know).

These tiny billboards, about one centimetre by two centimetres, may have passed a new threshold for brevity in advertising.

"It is increasingly more difficult to impact consumers, and the banana labels are a very novel medium to cut through the clutter," Brian Fox, president of the Fruit Label Company, told reporters in August. His boss, CEO Irv Weinhaus, was even more enthusiastic: "The response we have received to date from potential users of this fun new medium is amazing," he told the Business Wire news service. "Our phones have not stopped ringing."

▶ Comparing the Price of Fruit with Other Media

Advertising messages are popping up on apples, bananas, and limes for another good reason: They're a cheap way to reach lots of people.

- Advertising sticker on 12 million apples: $120000 (U.S.).
- 30-second ad on a TV series watched by 1 million Canadians: $20000.
- 30-second ad on a hockey game watched by 2 million Canadians: $50000.
- 15-second ad on the same game: $32500.
- 10-second ad on the same game: $25000.
- 30-second ad on the final episode of *Seinfeld,* watched by 76.3 million people: $1.7 million (U.S.).
- 30-second ad on the 1998 Super Bowl, watched by 138.4 million people: $1.3 million (U.S.).
- Full-page ad in a newsmagazine reaching 500000 Canadians: $30000.
- Full-page ad in a newspaper with 350000 subscribers: $43000.

Would you spend your advertising budget on this medium?

Source: Adapted from Doug Saunders, "The Incredible Shrinking Advertising Message," *The Globe and Mail* (September 2, 1998), p. A14. Reprinted with permission from *The Globe and Mail.*

---

specialists who provide a degree of creativity and objectivity that is difficult to maintain in a corporate advertising department. In some cases using an agency reduces the cost of advertising, since the agency does not require many of the fixed expenses associated with internal advertising departments. Effective use of an advertising agency requires a close relationship between advertiser and agency.

▶ INTERNET IMPACT

www.sportsline.com

Internet advertising has become a reality for marketers. However, most advertisements get lost in the sea of information on the Internet. Few get the recognition or have the impact of these ads from Auction Universe, which won a Bronze 1999 Marketing Award for Web Banners.

The Trouble with Web Advertising

With a glut of space to sell, media outfits on the Net are fighting for viewers and advertisers. Only the most ingenious sites will survive.

By most standards SportsLine USA is a new-media success story. It's the second most popular sports site on the Internet, behind ESPN. It benefits from a valuable alliance with CBS Sports. Its ad revenues keep climbing. However, with a glut of space to sell, media outfits on the Internet are fighting for viewers and advertisers.

Consequently, even SportsLine is paying people to visit its site. It doesn't call it that, exactly, but SportsLine has created a "rewards" program that gives users points, similar to airline frequent-flier miles, for viewing pages and buying things. An avid sports fan (or anyone with nothing better to do) who visits frequently and clicks on enough pages can exchange points for T-shirts, movie passes, $5 and $10 restaurant certificates, hockey pucks, and baseballs, along with automatic entries in a $1 million sweepstakes. As you surf through all the freebies, it's easy to forget why you came in the first place—to check the scores.

SportsLine isn't alone. To generate traffic, Internet publishers are spending more money than ever on marketing and promotion. But advertisers have countless choices on-line, so the rates that publishers can charge for ads are coming down. In essence, many new-media companies are buying eyeballs at high prices and selling them at low prices—not a good thing, even in the Through the Looking Glass world of Internet economics.

Advertising rates are declining. CPMs—the cost to advertisers of showing an ad 1000 times—dropped by some 5 percent during 1998, to about $35, according to Adknowledge, a company that helps clients buy ads. Ad buyers who are just seeking mass impressions can buy them for $5 per 1000 or less from aggregators like Flycast, a firm that gathers unsold inventory on Web sites and sells it to sponsors at bargain prices.

No one should be terribly surprised by this. Since the beginnings of the World Wide Web, publishers have celebrated their ability to deliver more information than any other medium because they have unlimited space. The trouble is, the same goes for ad space, creating an oversupply. Fuelling the glut is the fact that barriers to entry on the Internet are low, particularly when compared with other media businesses like radio and TV, which operate with finite spectrum and airtime.

"There's an unlimited supply of banner real estate out there, and that can only drive the prices down," says Chase Franklin, CEO of Qpass. His company helps publishers that can't survive on advertising alone charge small fees for digital content. "We're firing a shot across the bow at the absurd notion that all information on the Internet ought to be free," he says.

The big will only get bigger. Big portals like Yahoo! and Excite have the scale to invest tens of millions of dollars in technology that will enable them to target ads: they can measure an advertiser's return on investment with a sophistication that old media can't match. "We can direct an ad to a West Coast audience that is predominantly male and between the ages of 18 and 25," says Yahoo's Jerry Yang. Says Excite founder Joe Kraus: "The ultimate promise of the Internet is the ability to generate TV-sized audiences and to target a single individual."

As for the rest—the hundreds, if not thousands, of news, sports, women's, health, entertainment, and community sites—only the best will become real businesses.

(continued)

> **▶ INTERNET IMPACT** *(continued)*
>
> Those allied with TV and cable networks have an edge; they get promotion and access to video, which will become important with the spread of broadband.
>
> But even the strongest companies face perils. Fewer users are clicking on banners. New technology enables consumers to block ads. And there's the "Where's the beef?" factor—no Internet banner ever coined a catch phrase or caused a user to laugh out loud or hum a jingle. And no one has ever argued about who had the best commercials on SuperBowl.com.
>
> **On the basis of this information, what advice would you give to an Internet advertising company? To a potential Internet advertiser?**
>
> Source: Adapted from Marc Gunther, "The Trouble with Web Advertising," *Fortune* 139 (April 12, 1999), pp. 147–48.

Creating an Advertisement

A major step in the advertising process is developing and preparing an advertisement, which should flow logically from the promotional theme selected. This step should thus be a complementary part of the marketing mix, with its role in total marketing strategy carefully determined. For example, a reminder-oriented advertising campaign would not be the best way to introduce a new product. In addition, major factors to consider when preparing an advertisement are its creativity, its continuity with past advertisements, and possibly its association with other company products.

What should an advertisement accomplish? Regardless of the exact appeal that is chosen, an ad should (1) gain attention and interest, (2) inform or persuade, and (3) eventually lead to buying action.

Gaining attention should be productive. That is, the reason for gaining consumers' attention should be to instill some recall of the product. Consider the case of The Gillette Company, which had a chimpanzee shave a man's face in a commercial. After tests in two cities, one Gillette man observed, "Lots of people remembered the chimp, but hardly anyone remembered our product. There was fantastic interest in the monkey, but no payoff for Gillette."[6] The advertisement gained the audience's attention, but it failed to lead to buying action. An ad that fails to gain and hold the receiver's attention is ineffective.

Together, information and persuasion are the second factor to consider when creating an advertisement. For example, insurance ads typically specify the features of the policy and may use testimonials to persuade prospects.

Stimulating buying action is often difficult, however, since an advertisement cannot actually close a sale. Nevertheless, if the first steps have been accomplished, the advertising has likely been worthwhile. Too many advertisers fail to suggest how receivers of the message can buy the product if they so desire.

RETAIL ADVERTISING

Retail advertising is the advertising done by stores that sell goods or services directly to consumers. Retail advertising accounts for a sizable portion of total advertising expenditures. Supermarkets advertise weekly specials, restaurants and fast-food chains promote the quality of their products, and lawyers advertise such services as handling accident claims.

The quality of retail advertising varies greatly. Some, like that of McDonald's, is created by professionals and generally follows the procedures described previously. Other retail advertising, like much local automobile dealer advertising, appears to be slapped together by rank amateurs. Because retail advertising is frequently prepared without the benefit of professional advertising experience or adequate research, there is considerable scope for improving the effectiveness of such advertising.

One aspect of advertising that involves a retailer–manufacturer relationship is **cooperative advertising**. This involves the sharing of advertising costs between the retailer and the manufacturer. For example, Maple Leaf Foods may pay 50 percent of the cost of a 50 cm^2 area of a supermarket chain's weekly newspaper ad that features one or more of Maple Leaf's products.

Cooperative advertising benefits both retailer and manufacturer. It permits the retailer to secure additional advertising that it would not otherwise have. The manufacturer benefits from having retailers share in advertising costs. In addition, retailers that have invested in the advertisement will not only carry the manufacturer's product but also try to be sure of having enough in stock to satisfy demand.

cooperative advertising
The sharing of advertising costs between the retailer and the manufacturer.

The Advertising Campaign: Integrated Marketing Communications

A company that develops a marketing communications strategy often does not restrict its plan to advertising alone. Just as a military campaign combines many elements in a strategic effort to meet objectives, the elements of the communications mix are blended to provide maximum consumer impact. As an example of a complete advertising campaign, suppose that we are planning an advertising campaign for the opening of a new women's fashion store in downtown Calgary.

To announce the opening of the new store, we could use a variety of advertising media, including local magazines, public transit posters, billboards, radio, newspapers, direct mail, and public relations. We might arrange for Calgary issues of *Flare* and *Maclean's* to include special sections with a mix of ads and "advertorials" (advertisements that look like editorials). Radio stations could be used first for "teaser" ads, which are designed to stimulate interest but not reveal the sponsor, and then for "launch" or opening ads.

In addition, we could send a direct mailing to 20 000 households that have demographic characteristics approximating our target market. Moreover, we could establish a Web site that contains up-to-the minute reports on fashion trends, and has links to selected fashion magazines and other sites of interest to the fashion-conscious woman. This Web site would be promoted in our advertisements.

Next, we could design a distinctive and eye-catching shopping bag that customers will be proud to carry their purchases in. Finally, in order to get some free media publicity, we could invite the mayor, a group of dignitaries, and the media to a ribbon-cutting ceremony followed by a reception.

Message Themes

Advertising messages are delivered using many classic techniques. The structure of the message; the use of various appeals, such as humour, sex, and fear; and the use of comparative advertising are examples.

STRUCTURE

Since readers tend to skim advertising, a number of subheadings that summarize the entire message are usually an advantage. Because of many competing stimuli, it is necessary to attract the audience's attention. Bold headlines, colour, sound effects, louder sound during a television commercial, and unusual images are only a few of the methods used by advertisers.

USE OF HUMOUR, SEX, AND FEAR

Most people say they love humour in advertising, and many think that all advertisements should use this technique. Unfortunately, with advertising, it is not that simple. Even advertising humour classics, such as those developed by Alka Seltzer a few years ago, failed. Humour must not detract from the central message the advertiser wishes to deliver. Also, many attempts at humour in advertising are not that funny. The bottom line in advertising is to communicate the advertiser's message.

In order to gain attention, some advertisers use sexual images. It is now believed that unless such images are used in a setting that is natural to the product, this approach does not help. Furthermore, society has become resistant to advertisers who seem to be exploiting people in their advertising. For example, women's groups have objected to the brewing industry about their thinly disguised sex/lifestyle ads. A classic longitudinal study of the effects of erotic content on brand recall showed that as erotic content increases, the probability of people correctly recalling the associated brand decreases.[7]

Fear is another technique used in advertising. Advertisers sometimes appeal to people's fear of social stigma in their ads for deodorants, breath sweeteners, and dandruff treatments. Antidrinking advertisements showing powerful images of fatal car crashes have been created to limit drinking by young people. Life insurance companies sometimes use the fear of dying or of leaving loved ones uncared for in their advertising appeals. Research has shown that fear appeals can be effective unless the appeal is so strong that individuals psychologically repress the message because it disturbs them too much.

COMPARATIVE ADVERTISING

Comparative advertising makes direct promotional comparisons with competitive brands. The strategy is best employed by firms that do not lead the market.

Companies used to be afraid to mention the name of their competitor's product because that was thought to be a "free" reminder about that product, sometimes going to ridiculous lengths. For example, a salesperson would refer only to "that other product" or use some other euphemism. Everyone listening immediately substituted the competing brand for the euphemism.

This is seen both in personal selling and in advertising. Many advertisers are now choosing to compare their products directly with those of competitors. The comparison can sometimes take the form of an attack on the competition.

comparative advertising
Advertising that makes direct promotional comparisons with competitive brands.

"Sometimes when my boss is out, I yahoo in his chair."

www.yahoo.ca

Do You YAHOO!?

Marketing communications that use humour often fail, as they distract the audience from the real message. In this advertisement, Yahoo! Canada uses humour while ensuring that it does not detract from the key message—selling the company itself.

© 1999 by Yahoo! Inc.

Comparative advertising can be challenged in the courts, as was the case when Robin Hood Multifoods compared a pie crust made with its shortening to one made with Maple Leaf Foods Inc. Tenderflake and Gainsborough lard. The court ordered Robin Hood to pull its ads because they would "have the effect of diminishing Maple Leaf's reputation and lead to a loss of goodwill as well. They tend to create the impression that ... [Maple Leaf's] product will be a misshapen pie and not a normal pie."[8]

Advertisers sometimes get carried away using the comparative approach. During the 1993 federal election campaign, the Conservatives used an adver-

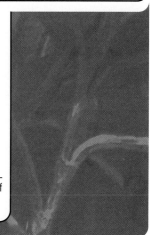

▶ THE ROOTS OF MARKETING

Your Message Must Crash through the Wall

Many years ago, the famous advertiser William Bernbach put it well when he said,

You must crash through the wall!

What brand of vanity or indifference leads us to believe that we can ... sit alongside world-shaking events and even be noticed? Our reader is confronted daily with history-making news. The papers are filled with sensationalism ... With this deafening roar of frightening conflict beating about his ears, how do we expect him to hear our advertising story? How are we going to pierce this wall around him? ... And if we pierce this wall, how are we going to get through that second wall, an almost impenetrable wall of competition crying its wares?

Only a message with a tremendous vitality carried in a dramatic graphic treatment will ever reach your consumer. What's the use of saying all the right things in the world if nobody's going to read them? And believe me, nobody's going to read them if they are not done with freshness, originality, and imagination.

Source: Excerpted from William Bernbach, address to Western Region Annual Meeting, American Association of Advertising Agencies, Pebble Beach, CA, November 13, 1965.

tisement emphasizing Jean Chrétien's partially paralyzed mouth. The outcry among all Canadians caused the ad to be pulled after only one day.

Marketers who contemplate using comparative advertising should ensure that they can prove their claims, because such advertising has the potential of producing lawsuits. From a long-run perspective, advertisers need to decide whether a more solid product and company image can be created with a message devoted to communicating about and positioning a product in its own right, or by comparing the product with others.

These are a few examples of the many technical issues in creating advertising messages. Creating messages is serious business—thousands of messages are wasted every day because advertisers use worn-out phrases and unimaginative messages.

Table 19.4 provides a summary of important points made by William Bernbach concerning advertising messages.

Assessing the Effectiveness of an Advertisement

For many firms, advertising represents a major expenditure, so it is imperative to determine whether a campaign is accomplishing its promotional objectives. Determining advertising's effectiveness, however, is one of the most difficult undertakings in marketing. In consists of two primary elements—pretesting and post-testing.

PRETESTING

Pretesting is the assessment of an advertisement's effectiveness before it is actually used. It includes a variety of evaluative methods. For example, to test magazine advertisements, the ad agency Batten, Barton, Durstine & Osborn cuts ads out of advance copies of magazines and then "strips in" the ads it wants to test. Interviewers later check the impact of the advertisements on the readers who

pretesting
The assessment of an advertisement's effectiveness before it is actually used.

> **TABLE 19.4 Important Points about Advertising Messages**

1. Crash through the wall! Not to be different is virtually suicide.
2. Impressions outweigh numbers.
   - Nobody counts the number of ads you show, they just remember the impressions you make.
   - Make your ad so provocative, so artful, that it is many times more effective than your competitors'.
3. Create personality.
   - Differentiate your ad from the competition's, and produce individuality.
4. Don't waste the reader's time.
   - Don't just get attention with an easy, irrelevant gimmick. Make sure the attention-getting element stems from your product.
5. Make your ads memorable.

Source: Adapted from William Bernbach, address to Western Region Annual Meeting, American Association of Advertising Agencies, Pebble Beach, CA, November 13, 1965.

receive free copies of the revised magazine. Television advertisements can be pretested before airing by measuring the responses of a representative sample of prospective customers. Many other techniques are used for pretesting advertising.

POST-TESTING

post-testing
The assessment of advertising copy after it has been used.

Post-testing is the assessment of advertising copy after it has been used. Pretesting is generally a more desirable testing method than post-testing because of its potential cost savings. But post-testing can be helpful in planning future advertisements and in making adjustments to current advertising programs.

In one of the most popular post-tests, the *Starch Readership Studies,* interviewers ask people who have read selected magazines whether they have read various ads in them. A copy of one of the magazines is used as an interviewing aid, and each interviewer starts at a different point in the magazine. For larger ads, respondents are also asked about specifics such as headlines and copy. All readership or recognition tests assume that future sales are related to advertising readership.

Regardless of the exact method used, marketers must realize that pretesting and post-testing are expensive and must, therefore, be used as effectively as possible.

Direct Response Marketing

direct response marketing
An interactive system of marketing that uses one or more advertising media to effect a measurable response directly to the advertiser.

Marketers have increasingly used various advertising media to make a selling offer directly to the target market. The results of these direct marketing efforts have been so impressive that this practice has grown steadily. **Direct response marketing** is an interactive system of marketing that uses one or more advertising media to effect a measurable response directly to the advertiser, not to an intermediary as in the case of general product advertising.

Two distinguishing words are measurable and response. Direct response marketing uses various media such as the Internet, catalogues, direct mail, magazines, television, radio, and newspapers to make a specific offer. The purpose of this offer is to elicit a direct positive response (usually, an order). This contrasts with general advertising for the purpose of creating an image, or communicating for some other purpose.

Direct response marketing anticipates a relatively immediate response (sale) that can be measured against the marketing effort. For example, a television offer of a special CD set might encourage buyers to phone an 800 number or write in to order it and charge it to their credit card. If the campaign costs $70 000 and orders amount to $200 000, the marketer can take other costs into consideration and readily calculate whether or not the direct marketing effort was profitable. As another example, Tilley Endurables elicits direct orders for its Tilley hat and other casual clothing in *The Globe and Mail* and other print media along with a number of other direct marketers. As mentioned earlier, Dell Computers, a manufacturer, has enjoyed phenomenal success through direct response marketing. America OnLine (AOL) and other Internet providers are other examples. Direct response marketing and general advertising are compared in Table 19.5.

Much direct marketing is done through direct mail. Computerization has made this medium extremely versatile, and direct mail can be very focused. For

TABLE 19.5 Comparison of Direct Response Marketing and General Advertising

DIRECT RESPONSE MARKETING	GENERAL ADVERTISING
Selling to individuals. Customers are often identifiable by name, address, and purchase behaviour.	Mass selling. Buyers are identified as broad groups sharing common demographic and psychographic characteristics.
Products may have added value or service.	
Distribution is an important product benefit.	Product benefits do not always include convenient distribution channels.
The medium is the marketplace.	The retail outlet is the marketplace.
Marketer controls product until delivery.	Marketer may lose control as product enters distribution channel.
Advertising is used to motivate an immediate order or inquiry.	Advertising is used for cumulative effect over time to build image, awareness, loyalty, or benefit recall. Purchase action is deferred.
Repetition is used in ad.	Repetition is used over time.
Consumers feel a high perceived risk— product is bought unseen. Recourse is distant.	Consumers feel less risk—have direct contact with the product and direct recourse.

Source: Reprinted from Bob Stone, *Successful Direct Marketing Methods*, 5th ed. (Lincolnwood, IL: NTC Publishing Group, 1994). Used with permission of NTC/Contemporary Publishing Group, Inc.

example, you receive a personalized letter inviting you to a mutual funds seminar. Another arrives announcing a special concert featuring the music you like. These letters were aimed directly at you because you subscribe to a financial magazine or order CDs regularly from a club by mail.

Information about potential mail recipients is so important that an industry has evolved to collect and rent databases. These not only provide names and addresses, but also past purchase behaviour.[9] List houses, or list brokers, specialize in collecting lists and keeping them up to date. A direct marketer must find the right combination of lists to use. This may be done by going directly to the list rental division of major publications or organizations, or to a broker that specializes in selecting lists. About 2000 lists are for rent in Canada.

Lists from many sources are combined, and duplicate names are removed. Renting lists generally costs 5 or 6 cents a name. Those who rent their lists usually insist on approving samples of the material that will be mailed. The renter agrees to one use per rental.

Mailing lists never enter the possession of the renter. Rather, the provider sends a computer tape or disks via the broker to one of several businesses that specialize in combining computer lists and generating labels, envelopes, and customized letters. It is at this stage that duplicates and those on various "do-not-mail" lists are removed. Labels and materials then move on to a mailing house, which stuffs the envelopes and puts them in the mail. List specialists also exist for Internet addresses. Currently, such lists are generally quite cheap. However, costs will rise as the target audience is refined and made more specific.

The range of products offered by direct marketing is large, ranging from computers (sold by Dell) to tax preparation to pest control and many other services. But not everyone prefers to buy directly from manufacturers — many consumers enjoy shopping and browsing in person.

A problem with direct response marketing is that because consumers have difficulty avoiding and ignoring it, there is a fair amount of animosity toward its continuous flow. In addition, privacy sometimes becomes an issue. This writer recently received a letter that said, "You have more than 15 000 frequent-flyer air mile points. You can increase them by accepting our offer." How did the direct marketer know how many points I had? Why did the airline company release this information? Direct marketers may learn about consumer purchase behaviour from the list categories they purchase, but they should be careful not to make consumers feel that their privacy has been compromised.

Direct response marketing is used successfully in a growing number of applications and is an important part of marketing. The main threat to its viability is negative public reaction to the intrusiveness of this medium (especially direct mail). Despite a rather small and vocal consumer group that opposes direct response marketing, it continues to thrive.

Using Celebrities to Promote the Company and Its Products

Even though Wayne Gretzky has retired, his name continues to be associated with several different products. Some of the corporate names that have sought his endorsement are the Hudson's Bay Co., Post Cereals, McDonald's, Canadian Imperial Bank of Commerce, Zurich Financial Services Group, Tylenol, and

The general populace isn't merely lacking culture, it's lacking calcium. In fact, 60% of men and 90% of women don't get enough. The enlightened among us, however, drink 3 glasses of milk a day. A practice that can prevent a Freudian condition known as "calcium envy."

got milk?

FRASIER ©1999 NATIONAL FLUID MILK PROCESSOR PROMOTION BOARD

The Milk Board has often used celebrities to promote milk. This advertisement features the cast from the popular television sitcom *Frasier.*

Campbell Soup. Many companies believe that **celebrity marketing**—having celebrities lend their name and influence to the promotion of a product—is worth the cost of paying the celebrity for his or her endorsement of the product. These marketers feel that there will be a positive association between the public acceptance of the celebrity and the acceptance of their product. Advertisers hope that the characteristics celebrities represent—beauty, courage, talent, ath-

celebrity marketing
Having celebrities lend their name and influence to the promotion of a product.

letic ability, and sex appeal — will create a positive image for their brand. If consumers like the celebrity, they may like the brand. Well-liked Bill Cosby is perfect for endorsing Jell-O.

While the risk is perhaps not too great, if the celebrity falls out of favour, the company has to try to quickly dissociate itself from that person. This happened to Hertz when O.J. Simpson was accused of murdering his ex-wife.

Celebrity marketing can be expensive. Nora beverages of Mirabel, Quebec, uses role model marketing instead. **Role model marketing** associates a product with the positive perception of a type of individual or a role. Nora sells its Naya brand bottled water in almost 3000 vending machines across North America. In one campaign, it placed 40 machines along Los Angeles County beaches — an unusual locale for the units. The company also donated $185 000 to help operate these beaches. In exchange, the company was allowed to advertise on lifeguard stands ("Naya — made when the world was still pure") and put its logo on the time and temperature blackboards. The role model association here was with 150 healthy-looking lifeguards. Lifeguards are held in high esteem—they take care of their bodies, and it is assumed that they are concerned about nutrition.[10] As the cost of celebrity marketing increases and the availability of suitable celebrities decreases, role model marketing is a useful alternative.

role model marketing
Marketing technique that associates a product with the positive perception of a type of individual or a role.

▶ SALES PROMOTION

In addition to advertising, sales promotion is another type of nonpersonal selling. It does not have as high a profile as some other marketing communications activities, but is extremely important. As advertising media become more cluttered with competing messages, marketers are turning to an increased use of sales promotion. A study of marketing communications expenses of Canadian packaged goods companies showed that sales promotion accounted for about half as much as advertising expenditures.[11] As we learned in Chapter 18, sales promotion may be defined as the use of incentives to stimulate consumers to purchase a product or deal with a supplier. It includes such activities as point-of-purchase advertising; specialty advertising; samples, coupons, and premiums; loyalty points; deals; rebates; and contests. More than one of these options may be used in a single promotional strategy, but probably no promotional strategy has ever used all the options in a single program. While they are not mutually exclusive, sales promotion methods are generally employed on a selective basis.

Sales promotion techniques may be used by all members of a marketing channel — manufacturers, wholesalers, and retailers — and are typically targeted at specific markets. For example, a manufacturer such as Texize Corporation might combine trial sample mailings of a new spot remover to consumers with a sales contest for wholesalers and retailers who handle the new product. In both instances, the sales promotion techniques are designed to supplement and extend the other elements of the firm's promotional mix.

Point-of-Purchase Advertising

Displays and demonstrations that seek to promote the product at a time and place closely associated with the actual decision to buy are called **point-of-purchase advertising**. The in-store promotion of consumer goods is a common example. Such advertising can be extremely useful in carrying forward a theme developed in another element of promotional strategy. A life-sized display of a celebrity used in television advertising, for instance, can become a realistic in-store display. Displays also serve as an effective attention-getter and reminder.

point-of-purchase advertising
Displays and demonstrations that seek to promote the product at a time and place closely associated with the actual decision to buy.

Specialty Advertising

Specialty advertising is a sales promotion medium that uses useful articles to carry the advertiser's name, address, and advertising message to reach target customers. The Roots of Marketing box illustrates that this is one of the oldest marketing practices.

Examples of contemporary advertising specialties carrying a firm's name include calendars, pencils, pens, paperweights, matchbooks, mugs, coasters, pocket diaries, shopping bags, memo pads, balloons, measuring sticks, key rings, glasses, and hundreds of other items.

specialty advertising
Sales promotion medium that uses useful articles to carry the advertiser's name, address, and advertising message.

▶ THE ROOTS OF MARKETING

Specialty Advertising Traced to the Middle Ages
Specialty advertising has been traced to the Middle Ages, when wooden pegs bearing the names of artisans "were given to prospects to be driven into their walls and to serve as a convenient place upon which to hang armour."[12] Undoubtedly, many earlier marketers followed similar practices.

Samples, Coupons, Premiums, Deals, Rebates, and Loyalty Programs

The distribution of samples, coupons, and premiums is one of the best-known sales promotion techniques. Sampling involves giving away a free item in an attempt to obtain consumer acceptance. This may be done door to door, by mail, through demonstrations, or as an insertion into packages containing other products. Sampling is especially useful in promoting new products.

Coupons offer a discount, usually some specified price reduction, on the next purchase of a product. Coupons are readily redeemable with retailers, who also receive a handling fee. Mail, magazines, newspapers, package insertions, and in-store displays are standard methods of distributing coupons.

Premiums, bonus items given free with the purchase of another product, have proven effective in getting consumers to try a new product or a different brand. Service stations, for example, use glassware, ice scrapers, and beach balls to convince noncustomers to patronize their station. Premiums are also used to encourage response to direct-marketing offers. The value of premium giveaways runs into millions of dollars each year.

Deals to consumers are price reductions designed to encourage trial use of a product or to counteract a competitor's promotion. Deals are also commonly used to encourage retailers to stock enough merchandise. For example, Old Dutch might offer retailers one free case of potato chips with every dozen purchased. The retailers then benefit from selling this "100 percent profit" case of chips. The manufacturer also gains because the deal encourages retailers to stock lots of product. Deals are short-term in nature.

Rebates have several uses. In some cases, they are used to encourage consumers to purchase. For example, Kodak offered a $4 rebate to consumers who purchased a package of five films. The consumer had to mail in a form and proof of purchase. Rebates are also used to induce channel member loyalty to a manufacturer. A carpet manufacturer keeps track of the number of metres of carpeting sold by a retailer during the year, and provides a rebate of 25, 35, or 40 cents per metre depending on whether the retailer sells up to one of three preset targets.

loyalty program
A program that gives rewards, such as points or free air miles, with each purchase in order to stimulate repeat business.

www.zellers.ca

Loyalty programs stimulate repeat purchases. Similar in concept to rebates, some businesses assign points, based on value, to every purchase. The points are automatically posted by computer after each purchase. After a customer has accumulated a certain number of points, they may be used to purchase products. Zellers Club Z points are an outstanding example. Club Z now has over 10 million members and an incredible reach of 65 percent of all Canadian households.[13] The introduction of Club Z points was a major factor in making Zellers one of the leading retailers in the country and Club Z one of the most successful reward clubs in North America. Strategic alliances have been established with AT&T Canada and CIBC. Now certain purchases from these organizations translate into Club Z points.[14] Airline companies such as Air Canada have also created a great deal of loyalty with their frequent-flyer air-mile programs. Grocery retailers almost force customers to join their loyalty group because they offer deep price cuts on selected items to members.

Contests

Firms may sponsor contests to attract additional customers, offering substantial cash or merchandise prizes to call attention to their products. The number of such contests is almost infinite. A company might consider employing a specialist in developing this type of sales promotion because of the variety and complexity of schemes available.

Trade Shows

A small machinist company in central Manitoba invented a machine to hold, dispense, and measure heavy rolls of carpeting. This was an excellent product with worldwide potential. How could this firm with little marketing experience, no sales force, and no international experience distribute its product? A series of trade shows was the answer that resulted in sales and interested dealerships in several different countries.

A **trade show** is an organized exhibition of products based on a central theme. The theme might be Canadian manufactured products, agricultural products, or toys, for example. The trade show is held in a centre that is accessible to buyers and runs for a specified number of days. Each exhibitor rents display space and has personnel available to answer questions. Trade shows are organized by trade associations, businesses, and governments (to promote products in another country). For example, the Canadian government organizes an annual trade show of Canadian agricultural machinery in Dubbo, Australia. It also organizes the rental of enough space for several Canadian companies that might be interested in joining to form a Canadian presence at other trade shows.

trade show
An organized exhibition of products based on a central theme.

▶ PUBLIC RELATIONS AND PUBLICITY

Public relations, or PR, is the component of marketing communications that focuses on fostering goodwill between a company and its various publics. PR efforts are aimed primarily at consumers, employees, suppliers, stockholders, governments, the general public, labour groups, and citizen action groups.[15]

Public relations can be integrated with advertising and other elements of the promotion mix to accomplish objectives other than goodwill. It can also increase brand awareness, build favourable attitudes toward a company and its products, and encourage purchases.

Public relations involves a number of functions and activities. One is providing advice to executives on the impact of their actions on the public. Another is producing publications, such as brochures for stockholders and newsletters for employees. **Publicity** is a third important aspect of PR. Publicity involves disseminating positive information about company activities and products, or overcoming negative attention. Publicity is not paid advertising—it is accomplished through contact with the news media, through news releases, and through press conferences.

Publicity depends on some characteristic, activity, or event to make it "newsworthy" and to stimulate media attention. In North America, over 100 000 media editors are constantly searching for news and public interest stories, including stories about interesting new products, product uses, and services.

The publicity campaign for the Furby toy is a classic example of the power of publicity. Planned almost a year before, the campaign was orchestrated with the advertising and promotion campaign to peak in December 1998. The ultimate sales response was overwhelming.

Publicity is also generated with attention-getting activities. Kellogg's uses a larger-than-life mascot of Tony the Tiger for appearances at public venues. "Kids go nuts—they love the characters," says Carol Reader, product manager for children's cereals at Kellogg Company. "This is a very inoffensive way to remind people about a product."[16]

Publicity has a number of advantages and disadvantages. One advantage is its greater credibility because the information is perceived to be offered by an unbiased source (the media). Another advantage is that coverage often occurs with

public relations
The component of marketing communications that focuses on fostering goodwill between a company and its various publics.

publicity
Normally unpaid communication that disseminates positive information about company activities and products.

www.kelloggs.com

▶THE ETHICAL MARKETER

Trading on Another's Brand Equity

Pfizer, the pharmaceutical company, has alleged that a firm specializing in knockoffs of famous fragrances is unfairly trying to capitalize on the sweet smell of Viagra's success. Pfizer, the maker of the blockbuster anti-impotence drug, has filed a trademark lawsuit against Park Plaza Fragrances, a New York company that Pfizer says is marketing "Viagra" brand fragrances without its authorization.

Park Plaza's selection of the name "reeks" of an attempt to exploit Viagra's famous name for its own benefit, Pfizer alleges in the suit. The drug maker is seeking an injunction to stop Park Plaza from using the Viagra name. "Without the explosive fame of Pfizer's Viagra trademark, the premise of [Park Plaza's] name selection would be meaningless," it said.

Park Plaza officials could not be reached for comment. It sells "smell-alike" versions of famous fragrances like Chanel No. 5 and CK One at cut-rate prices. The "Viagra" men's and women's fragrances it sells are coloured blue, like Viagra pills, and sell for about $1.50 (U.S.) per one-ounce bottle, according to the suit—about one-seventh the cost of a single Viagra pill.

What do you think of Park Plaza's actions? Does Pfizer really have a concern?

Source: Adapted from "Pfizer Sues Over 'Viagra' Fragrance," *Dow Jones* in the *Financial Post* (December 23, 1998), p. D7. Reprinted with permission.

---

great speed, which is further enhanced by word of mouth. The public interest generated can often be considerably greater than could be created with an advertising campaign. If an editor thinks your message is newsworthy and runs it, others are likely to pick it up, and terrific momentum can occur.

The disadvantage of publicity is that it is out of the control of the marketer in terms of execution or timing. Thus, it is not possible to count on the fact that there will be any publicity at all, what actually will be said about the product, or when this might happen. Even if the story is run, the marketer cannot be sure what will be said. Furthermore, each medium is likely to try covering the topic from a different angle. Photos and videotapes provide some control because they cannot be so readily edited.

The process of gaining publicity is a delicate one that requires good relationships with the media. The marketing company's publicist prepares a kit with a write-up, or press release, on the product and any other relevant materials such as pictures, videotapes, and other background information. The objective is to present the message as conveniently as possible without removing the possibility for the media to create their own angle on the story. Some media will publish the press release as it is, while others never do so because they view it as advertising. Many times, marketers will provide a spokesperson that the media can build the story around.

Publicity can also be generated through publicity stunts or giving the product away to celebrities. Tilley advertises that its sports clothing is worn by Sir Edmund Hillary, the first man to climb Mt. Everest. Products are often given away to charities or to be won as contest prizes. In the case of some products, such as cars and computer software, the product is lent to media specialists on the topic so that they can try it and write about it.

The media are very aware of the publicity objectives of marketers, and they are sensitive to being manipulated. Therefore, they are usually very careful about promoting performance superiority claims. Thus, marketers should supply them with independent test performance results if available.

▶ PERSONAL SELLING

Personal selling was defined in Chapter 18 as a seller's promotional presentation conducted on a person-to-person basis with the buyer. Selling is an inherent function of any business enterprise. Accounting, engineering, personnel management, and other organizational activities are useless unless the firm's product can be sold to someone. Thousands of sales employees bear witness to the importance of selling in the Canadian economy. While advertising expenses in the average firm may represent from 1 to 3 percent of total sales, selling expenses are likely to equal 10 to 15 percent of sales. In many firms, personal selling is the single largest marketing expense.

As Chapter 18 pointed out, personal selling is likely to be the primary component of a firm's marketing communications mix when customers are concentrated geographically; when orders are large; when the products or services are expensive, technically complex, and require special handling; when trade-ins are involved; when channels are short; and when the number of potential customers is relatively small.

In instances where personal selling is the primary component of a firm's marketing mix, advertising may be used in a support role to assist the salespeople. Much of Avon's advertising is aimed at assisting the neighbourhood salesperson by strengthening the image of Avon, its products, and its salespeople. Table 19.6 summarizes the factors that affect personal selling's importance in the overall marketing communications mix.

avon.avon.com

Categories of Selling

The sales job has evolved into a professional occupation. Today's salesperson is more concerned with helping customers select the correct product to meet their needs than with simply selling whatever is available. Modern professional salespeople advise and assist customers in their purchase decisions. Where repeat purchases are common, the salesperson must be certain that the buyer's purchases are in his or her best interest, or else no future sales will be made. The interests of the seller are tied to those of the buyer. This is another example of the importance of relationship marketing discussed in earlier chapters.

Not all sales activities are alike. While all sales activities assist the customer in some way, the exact tasks that are performed vary from one position to another. Three basic types of selling can be identified: (1) order processing, (2) creative selling, and (3) missionary selling.

Most sales jobs do not fall into any single category. Instead, we often find salespeople performing all three types of selling to a certain extent. A sales engi-

> **TABLE 19.6 Factors Affecting the Importance of Personal Selling in the Promotional Mix**

	PERSONAL SELLING IS LIKELY TO BE MORE IMPORTANT WHEN	ADVERTISING IS LIKELY TO BE MORE IMPORTANT WHEN
Consumer is	geographically concentrated, relatively small in number	geographically dispersed, relatively large in number
Product is	expensive, technically complex, custom-made, requires special handling, frequently involves trade-ins	inexpensive, simple to understand, standardized, requires no special handling, requires no trade-ins
Price is	relatively high	relatively low
Channels are	relatively short	relatively long

neer for a computer firm may be doing 50 percent missionary selling, 45 percent creative selling, and 5 percent order processing. In other words, most sales jobs require staff to engage in a variety of sales activities. However, most selling jobs are classified on the basis of the primary selling task that is performed. We will examine each of these categories.

ORDER PROCESSING

order processing
Selling at the wholesale and retail levels; involves identifying customer needs, pointing out these needs to the customer, and completing the order.

Order processing is most often typified by selling at the wholesale and retail levels. Salespeople who handle this task must do the following:

1. *Identify customer needs.* For instance, a soft-drink route salesperson determines that a store that normally carries inventory of 40 cases has only 7 cases left in stock.
2. *Point out the needs to the customer.* The route salesperson informs the store manager of the inventory situation.
3. *Complete or write up the order.* The store manager acknowledges the situation, the driver unloads 33 cases, and the manager signs the delivery slip.

Order processing is part of most selling jobs, but becomes the primary task in a routine or repeat buying situation when needs can be readily identified and then acknowledged by the customer. Getting business is more a matter of trading on the reputation of the company, which the customer has already decided to deal with.

CREATIVE SELLING

creative selling
Selling that involves making the buyer see the worth of the item.

Creative selling is much more demanding. Often, customers first have to be found, then helped to make a purchase decision. When a considerable degree of analytical decision making on the part of the consumer is involved in purchasing a product, the salesperson must skillfully solicit an order from a prospect. To do so, creative selling techniques must be used. New products often require a high degree of creative selling. The seller must make the buyer see the worth of the item. Creative selling may be the most demanding of the three selling tasks.

An example of how a sales job evolves into creative selling is found in one chemical company. Originally, selling chemicals was a relatively straightforward job. The salesperson was assigned a territory and dispatched to tap every possible customer. She or he was told little about the division's goals or about the profitability of the list of products. Salespeople's marching orders were uncomplicated: sell all you can, as fast as you can.

But the salesperson's job has become much more complex. Now the company tells salespeople: "Don't just sell — we need information. What do our customers need? What is the competition doing? What sort of financial package do we need to win the order?" Salespeople also are expected to mediate disputes between the credit department and slow-paying customers and to sort out customer complaints concerning the company's products. They must keep informed of fast changes in both government regulations and world chemical markets. In short, the salesperson's job requires applying informed management skills to solving customers' problems.

MISSIONARY SELLING

Missionary selling is an indirect type of selling; people sell the goodwill of a firm and provide customers with technical or operational assistance. For example, a toiletries company salesperson may call on retailers to look after special promotions and overall stock movement, although a wholesaler is used to take orders and deliver merchandise. In more recent times, technical and operational assistance, such as that provided by a systems specialist, have also become a critical part of missionary selling.

missionary selling
Selling that emphasizes selling the firm's goodwill and providing customers with technical or operational assistance.

Characteristics of Successful Salespeople

The saying "Salespeople are born, not made" is untrue. Most people have some degree of sales ability. Each of us is called upon to sell others our ideas, philosophy, or personality at some time. However, some individuals adapt to selling more easily than others. Selling is not an easy job; it involves a great deal of hard work. Many college and university graduates find it an extremely rewarding and challenging career.

Effective salespeople are self-motivated individuals who are well-prepared to meet the demands of the competitive marketplace. The continuing pressure to solve buyers' problems requires that salespeople develop good work habits and exhibit considerable initiative.

Successful salespeople are not only self-starters, they are also knowledgeable businesspeople. Salespeople are also in the peculiar position of having their knowledge tested almost continually, so sales success is often a function of how well a salesperson can handle questions. Salespeople must know their company, their products, their competition, their customers, and themselves. They must also be able to analyze customer needs and fit them with products and services that satisfy those needs.

The Sales Process

The sales process involves seven steps. While the terminology may vary, most authorities agree on the following sequence:

1. prospecting and qualifying
2. approach
3. presentation
4. demonstration
5. handling objections
6. closing
7. follow-up

PROSPECTING AND QUALIFYING

prospecting
Identifying potential customers.

Prospecting—identifying potential customers—is difficult work that often involves many hours of diligent effort. Prospects may come from many sources: previous customers, friends and neighbours, other vendors, nonsales employees in the firm, suppliers, and social and professional contacts. New sales personnel often find prospecting frustrating, since there is usually no immediate payoff. But without prospecting, there are no future sales. Prospecting is a continuous process because there will always be a loss of some customers over time, a loss that must be compensated for with new customers or the discovery of potential customers who have never been contacted. Many sales management experts consider prospecting to be the very essence of the sales process.

qualifying
Determining that the prospect is really a potential customer.

Qualifying—determining that the prospect is really a potential customer—is another important sales task. Not all prospects are qualified to become customers. Qualified customers are people with both the money and the authority to make purchase decisions. A person with an annual income of $25 000 may wish to own a $70 000 car, but this person's ability to actually become a customer must be questioned.

APPROACH

approach
The initial contact between the salesperson and the prospective customer.

Once the salesperson has identified a qualified prospect, he or she collects all available information relative to the potential buyer and plans an **approach**—the initial contact between the salesperson and the prospective customer. All approaches should be based on comprehensive research. The salesperson should find out as much as possible about the prospect and the environment in which the prospect operates.

PRESENTATION

presentation
The act of giving the sales message to a prospective customer.

When the salesperson gives the sales message to a prospective customer, she or he makes a **presentation**. The seller describes the product's major features, points out its strengths, and concludes by citing illustrative successes. The seller's objective is to talk about the product or service in terms that are meaningful to the buyer—that is, to discuss benefits rather than technical specifications. Thus, the presentation is the stage where the salesperson relates product features to customer needs. The presentation should be clear and concise, and should emphasize the positive.

DEMONSTRATION

demonstration
Actions that supplement, support, and reinforce what the salesperson has already told the prospect.

Demonstration can play a critical role in a sales presentation. A demonstration ride in a new car allows the prospect to become involved in the presentation. It awakens customer interest in a way no amount of verbal presentation can. Demonstrations supplement, support, and reinforce what the salesperson has already told the prospect.

"Best salesman we ever had!"

Demonstration awakens
customer interest.

The key to a good demonstration is planning. A unique demonstration is more likely to gain a customer's attention than a "usual" sales presentation. But such a demonstration must be well planned and executed if a favourable impression is to be made. The need for the salesperson to check and recheck all aspects of the demonstration before delivering it cannot be overemphasized.

HANDLING OBJECTIONS

A vital part of selling involves handling objections. It is reasonable to expect a customer to say, "Well, I really should check with my family," "Perhaps I'll stop back next week," or "I like everything except the colour." A good salesperson, however, should use each **objection** as a cue to provide additional information. In most cases, an objection such as "I don't like the bucket seats" is really the customer's way of asking what other choices or product features are available. A customer's question reveals an interest in the product. It allows the seller an opportunity to expand a presentation by providing additional information.

objection
Reveals a customer's interest in a product and can be used as a cue to provide additional information.

CLOSING

closing
The act of asking the prospect for an order.

The moment of truth in selling is the **closing**, for this is when the salesperson asks the prospect for an order. A salesperson should not hesitate during the closing. If he or she has made an effective presentation based on applying the product to the customer's needs, the closing should be the natural conclusion.

A surprising number of salespeople have a hard time actually asking for an order. But to be effective, they must overcome this difficulty.

FOLLOW-UP

follow-up
The post-sales activities that often determine whether a person will become a repeat customer.

The post-sales activities that often determine whether a person will become a repeat customer constitute the sales **follow-up**. To the maximum extent possible, sales representatives should contact their customers to find out if they are satisfied with their purchases. This step allows the salesperson to psychologically reinforce the buyer's original decision to buy. It gives the seller an opportunity, in addition to correcting any sources of discontent with the purchase, to secure important market information and to make additional sales. Car dealers often keep elaborate records on their previous customers. This allows them to remind individuals when they might be due for a new car. One successful travel agency never fails to telephone customers on their return from a trip. Proper follow-up is a logical part of the selling sequence.

Managing the Sales Effort

sales management
Securing, maintaining, motivating, supervising, evaluating, and controlling the field sales force.

The selling function is made effective through **sales management**, which involves securing, maintaining, motivating, supervising, evaluating, and controlling the field sales force. The sales manager is the link between the firm and the marketplace through the sales force. The sales manager has a challenging task that involves interpreting and implementing company strategy through a diverse group of sales representatives. Similarly, since the sales force also represents the customers, the sales manager must represent customers' and sales representatives' needs and concerns to senior management.

The sales manager performs seven basic managerial functions: (1) recruitment and selection, (2) training, (3) organization, (4) supervision, (5) motivation, (6) compensation, and (7) evaluation and control. Each of these is an elaborate and demanding task; unfortunately, describing them in detail is beyond the scope of this book. An interested reader can refer to many books on sales management.

▶ SUMMARY

This chapter has discussed the major advertising media and has illustrated the main marketing communications applications: advertising, public relations and publicity, sales promotion, and personal selling.

Today's widespread markets make advertising an important part of business. Advertising expenditures as a proportion of sales vary among different industries and companies because of the different role that advertising plays in the different marketing mixes.

There are four basic types of advertising: informative product advertising, persuasive product advertising, reminder-oriented product advertising, and institutional advertising.

Advertisements have to be created with both the consumer and the advertising medium in mind. Selecting advertising media is an important task that enables the marketer to precisely direct the message. Television and newspapers are the most important advertising media, followed by direct mail.

Cooperative advertising involves the retailer and the manufacturer sharing advertising costs. Comparative advertising makes direct promotional comparisons with competitive brands.

Direct response marketing is an interactive system of marketing that uses one or more advertising media to effect a measurable response or transaction at any location.

Public relations is the component of marketing communications that focuses on fostering goodwill for the company. One aspect of PR is publicity, which is normally unpaid communication that disseminates positive information about company activities and products.

adage.com

Celebrity marketing is the process of engaging celebrities to lend their names and influence in promoting a product. Role model marketing associates a product with the positive perception of a type of individual or role.

www.adcouncil.org

Sales promotion includes such activities as point-of-purchase advertising; specialty advertising; samples, coupons, premiums, deals, rebates, loyalty programs; contests; and trade shows.

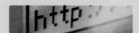

www.adweek.com

The three basic types of selling are order processing, creative selling, and missionary selling. The sales process involves seven steps: prospecting and qualifying, approach, presentation, demonstration, handling objections, closing, and follow-up.

There are a growing number of useful Web sites that can provide further insight on the topics discussed in this chapter. Web sites such as those for the Ad Age Group, the Ad Council, *Adweek* magazine, and the University of Texas at Austin Department of Advertising are good places to start.

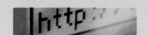

advertising.utexas.edu/world/index.html

▶ KEY TERMS

advertising agency	informative product advertising
approach	institutional advertising
celebrity marketing	loyalty program
closing	missionary selling
comparative advertising	objection
cooperative advertising	order processing
creative selling	persuasive product advertising
demonstration	point-of-purchase advertising
direct response marketing	post-testing
follow-up	presentation

pretesting
product advertising
prospecting
public relations
publicity
qualifying

reminder-oriented product advertising
role model marketing
sales management
specialty advertising
trade show

▶ INTERACTIVE SUMMARY AND DISCUSSION QUESTIONS

1. Advertising expenditures as a proportion of sales vary among different industries and companies because of the different role that advertising plays in the different marketing mixes. Rank the following industries in terms of proportionate advertising expenditures (1 = lowest proportion), and then explain your reasoning.
   ___ Soap/detergent   ___ Chemicals   ___ Restaurant

2. Advertising is the most important component in the marketing mix for positioning a product. A product can be positioned by attributes, price/quality, competitor, application, product user, and product class. Give an example of each.

3. There are four basic types of advertising: informative product advertising, persuasive product advertising, reminder-oriented product advertising, and institutional advertising. What type of advertising would you recommend for Ford Motor Company? For Compaq computers? For Mohawk gas? Explain your reasoning.

4. Television is the second-largest advertising medium. Television advertising can be divided into three categories: network, national spot, and local spot. When would each be used, and who would be the likely users?

5. "The final step in the advertising process is the development and preparation of an advertisement." Outline the earlier steps.

6. Cooperative advertising involves the sharing of advertising costs between the retailer and the manufacturer. Develop an argument favouring or opposing the use of cooperative advertising by a marketer who is currently preparing an advertising plan. Make any assumptions that are necessary.

7. Comparative advertising makes direct promotional comparisons with competitive brands. Suggest a list of conditions under which a company should consider using comparative advertising.

8. The famous advertiser and head of DDB Advertising Agency William Bernbach said about advertising, "You must crash through the wall." Explain and elaborate on the meaning of this statement.

9. Direct marketing is an interactive system of marketing that uses one or more advertising media to effect a measurable response or transaction at any location. Compare and contrast this with general advertising.

10. Publicity is generating awareness about a product beyond regular advertising methods. Discuss the advantages and limitations of using publicity.

11. Develop a plan for a publicity campaign for a newly opened dry cleaner in a strip mall near a residential neighbourhood.

12. Celebrity marketing is the process of engaging celebrities to lend their names and influence in promoting a product. Role model marketing associates a product with the positive perception of a type of individual or role. Give an example of a role model marketing campaign.

13. Sales promotion includes such activities as point-of-purchase advertising; specialty advertising; samples, coupons, premiums, deals, rebates, and loyalty programs; contests; and trade shows. Sales promotion seems to be growing at the expense of advertising. How can this be?

14. The three basic types of selling are order processing, creative selling, and missionary selling. Give an example of each.

15. The expression "Salespeople are born, not made" is untrue. Explain why.

16. The sales process involves seven steps: prospecting and qualifying, approach, presentation, demonstration, handling objections, closing, and follow-up. Distinguish between the sales process and a sales call.

17. Select three products of interest. Find a Web advertisement, a TV advertisement, and a print advertisement for each. Compare them and write an evaluation of their estimated role and value in marketing the products.

To obtain a list of further readings for Chapter 19, please refer to the *Foundations of Marketing* Web site.

Part 8
Additional Marketing Management Considerations

This book has thus far dealt with the fundamental components of marketing; however, by no means is this the whole story of marketing. These concepts will be examined in much more depth in senior-level courses.

There are two other important topics that should be considered here. The first is the application of marketing in the international environment, or global marketing. The second is the application of marketing to not-for-profit organizations such as charities, religious groups, associations, and government organizations. These topics have been mentioned throughout the book but are discussed in greater detail in Chapters 20 and 21.

▶ **Chapter 20**
Global Marketing

▶ **Chapter 21**
Not-for-Profit Marketing

Coffee bars such as Starbucks are attempting to make inroads with their products in China. However, these cafes face a formidable challenge—converting 1.24 billion tea drinkers, with a 5000-year-old tea-drinking history, to coffee lovers.

Chapter 20
Global Marketing

▶ CHAPTER OBJECTIVES

After reading and studying this chapter, you should be able to

1. Discuss some of the fundamental concepts that underlie international business.
2. Identify aspects of marketing strategy that are important in the global marketplace.
3. Outline the environment for international business.
4. Explain how the marketing mix may be affected by competition in a global environment.
5. Outline various approaches to global marketing that are taken by companies.
6. Discuss the various modes of entry into international markets.

Tranquillity still reigns supreme inside the Lao She Tea House. Patrons sip their chrysanthemum tea under red lanterns. A young girl in a red silk *qipao* delicately plucks a Chinese harp on the tea house's stage.

A book publisher from out of town tilts back his cup, considers China's 5000 years of tea-drinking history, and scoffs at the new invader from the West bearing bags of beans.

"Starbucks?" Chen Dapeng asks, leaning back on his antique stool inside the tea house, named after one of China's famous writers. Never heard of them."

The West Coast's formidable pusher of caffeine opened its first coffee bar in Beijing last week, part of a plan by Starbucks to try to convert this country of 1.24 billion tea drinkers into coffee lovers.

On hearing that the West Coast juggernaut was on its way, one Beijing magazine for foreigners declared: "Resistance is futile ... you will be assimilated."

Well, maybe not. Turning the Chinese into coffee junkies has been tried by the West before.

Consider this bullish piece on coffee in the Oct. 19, 1946, edition of the *China Weekly Review:* "China's masses in this year of grace in 1946 have discovered coffee. Once sipped only by the well-to-do, coffee today delivers its exhilarating 'lift' to the labouring classes; the rickshaw coolie, pedicab man, domestic servant, and even occasionally the lowly beggar out to celebrate a bumper crop of alms."

But more than 50 years later, the coffee culture has yet to catch on in a big way.

For reasons of both habit and national pride, China's drink of choice remains tea, served either in dainty porcelain cups or the thick mason jars that Chinese workers plant on their desk, to sip endless cups of *cha* throughout the day.

"Coffee is a Western thing," Mr. Chen said. "In China, ordinary Chinese will always prefer tea over coffee."

www.starbucks.com

However, Starbuck's first coffee bar on the Mainland, ensconced in the China World Hotel, Beijing's swankiest, is undeniably doing a brisk business. Lines are long and many of the clients are young Chinese, most of whom are impressed with the caffe lattes that sell for about $4 a cup and up.

"This is the best cup of coffee I've ever had," one 30-something Beijinger said, trying her first cafe latte loaded with hazelnut syrup. "It's smooth."

Starbucks, which plans to open more bars this year in Beijing, has taken great pains to replicate the atmosphere and taste of its coffee bars in North America. It flew some of its Chinese staff to Seattle, where the first Starbucks started in 1971, to teach them how to create that Starbucks experience and the proper West Coast attitude.

And China's Starbucks barristas—as they insist on being called—wear the same uniforms and use the same coffee lingo as their West Coast peers. Indeed, the Chinese employees are learning English fast to handle such terms as frappacino.

The thing about coffee houses in China, however, is that you won't exactly see a real slice of Chinese life. The Starbucks clientele is the Chinese MTV set, with hip clothes, expensive haircuts, and the latest in cellular phone equipment. As one of Starbucks' own Chinese staff said, it's going to take a while for the masses to catch on.

"Chinese who have lived in the West come here," she said as she piled up some bags of coffee beans. "But ordinary Chinese like tea. They don't come here much."

Even some of Starbucks hip, young patrons think the sip-and-go culture isn't Chinese. "It cannot replace tea in China," said Chen Yan, 25.

Chinese hungering for a taste of the West will drink coffee. But most regard Starbucks, which boasts that it is trying to create "an enduring global brand," with the same wariness they reserve for other Western imports such as McDonald's and Pizza Hut: a rich interloper that shouldn't be allowed to diminish the greater Chinese culture or make too much profit off the Chinese people.

Inside the Lao She Tea House, not far from Tiananmen Square, it is evident that tea is viewed as something steeped in the essence of being Chinese.

"Yes, boys and girls like to go to disco bars and cool places such as coffee bars," said Lan Ping, the owner of a bookstore who was visiting in the tea house recently.

"But we scholars like to go to a tea house like this, where things are quiet. This is what ordinary Chinese do: Drink tea, not coffee."

And that won't change for a long time. In Beijing's Starbucks, they will serve you tea.

But at the Lao She Tea House, ask for a cup of coffee and the waitress's smile evaporates and she lifts her nose in a huff. "This is a Chinese tea house," she said haughtily. "We have no coffee."

The potential market in China is almost mind-boggling. With the world's largest population, many businesses have targeted this country as a potential market for their products. However, the challenges of breaking into the market are also enormous. Two of these challenges are cultural norms and nationalism, which are faced in many global ventures. Starbucks and many other companies have seen the possibilities and accepted the challenge of becoming involved in the global marketplace, where many companies have found great success.

International marketing is growing rapidly. It not only is good for business, but also provides tremendous career opportunities for marketing graduates who are willing to become involved in doing business in an unfamiliar culture.

Source: Adapted from Miro Cernetig, "Starbucks' Tempest in China's Teapot," *The Globe and Mail* (January 22, 1999), pp. A1 and A11. Reprinted with permission from *The Globe and Mail*.

▶ INTRODUCTION

International trade is vital to a nation and its business for several reasons. International business expands the market for a country's or firm's products and thus makes possible further production and distribution economies. An added benefit to an exporting firm that has global trade experience is that it can compete more effectively with foreign competitors who enter this market at a later date. Furthermore, international involvement is the only way many firms can survive in the competitive world marketplace. Global marketing can also mean more jobs at home. It is estimated that some 11 000 new jobs are supported by every billion export dollars.

Some Canadian companies depend heavily on their ability to sell their products abroad. For companies like General Motors, MacMillan Bloedel, Alberta and Southern Gas, Nortel Networks, and others, the majority of sales dollars come from customers in other countries. Many smaller companies have also discovered the value of selling into international markets. Indeed, some companies, like high-tech Seastar Optics of Sidney, B.C., would find it difficult to survive without international sales. For such companies, the Canadian market may not even be large enough for their specialized products.

Business is now international. Whether you are a farmer, a small local retailer, a wholesaler, or one of the established Canadian telecommunications companies, you will be affected by global competition. International goods, services, and competitors are found in virtually every aspect of the Canadian (and every other country's) economy. In developing business strategy, this international dimension must be as carefully considered as the domestic environment.

Some 2 million Canadians—1 in 5 of the labour market—work in areas that are directly or indirectly related to export trade. Thus, there is a good chance that every single Canadian has a close connection with export trade through family or friends. Thirty cents of every dollar of our gross national product (GNP) comes from our exports.

www.gm.com

www.mbltd.com

www.sga-aso.com

www.nortelnetworks.com/index.html

Our exports pay for the things we import to meet our high standard of living expectations—our morning orange juice, fresh vegetables in winter, wool and cotton clothes, TV sets, some cars, and some computers. On another level, exports also pay for the interest and dividends on foreign investment, for the deficit on tourism, for access to foreign technologies, and for the borrowing that different levels of government use to finance our economic development.

Globalization is vital to a nation.

In other words, foreign trade is important to Canada from both the *exporting* and the *importing* viewpoints. International trade is more important to the economy of some countries than others. Countries such as the United Kingdom, Belgium, the Scandinavian countries, and New Zealand also heavily depend on international trade. On the other hand, although the United States is both the largest exporter and the largest importer in the world, its exports account for only about 7.7 percent of its gross national product. Compare this with the percentages for Belgium (46 percent) and the former West Germany (23 percent). Canadian exports account for about 30 percent of our GNP. Canada's leading trading partners are shown in Table 20.1. The United States is clearly our chief trading partner, supplying about 77.0 percent of our imports and buying about 83.7 percent of our exports.

There are both similarities and differences between international and domestic marketing. This chapter examines characteristics of the global marketplace,

> **TABLE 20.1 Canadian Imports and Exports of Goods on a Balance-of-Payments Basis**

	1993	1994	1995	1996	1997	1998
	\$ Millions					
Exports From:	**190 213.1**	**228 167.1**	**265 333.9**	**279 891.8**	**301 381.4**	**322 262.4**
United States	149 099.7	181 049.3	205 690.6	222 341.6	242 481.6	269 496.6
Japan	9 184.5	10 788.5	13 286.1	12 417.1	12 269.3	9 513.1
European Union	12 009.5	13 039.8	18 256.3	17 356.7	17 033.7	17 798.1
Other OECD[a]	3 361.7	4 536.0	4 563.4	5 086.5	8 091.6	7 511.5
Other countries[b]	16 557.6	18 753.5	23 537.6	22 690.0	21 505.1	17 943.2
Imports To:	**177 123.2**	**207 872.5**	**229 936.5**	**237 917.2**	**277 707.8**	**303 399.7**
United States	130 244.3	155 661.3	172 516.5	180 217.4	211 424.9	233 634.8
Japan	8 477.4	8 315.4	8 427.6	7 229.9	8 712.3	9 651.3
European Union	14 026.4	16 404.3	20 289.1	20 589.8	24 246.8	25 447.8
Other OECD[a]	4 683.9	7 364.7	7 942.3	9 041.5	11 378.1	11 368.3
Other countries[b]	19 691.1	20 126.9	20 761.0	20 838.6	21 945.6	23 297.6
Balance	**13 089.9**	**20 294.6**	**35 397.4**	**41 974.6**	**23 673.6**	**18 862.7**
United States	18 855.4	25 388.0	33 174.1	42 124.2	31 056.7	35 861.8
Japan	707.1	2 473.1	4 858.5	5 187.2	3 557.0	-138.2
European Union	-2 016.9	-3 364.5	-2 032.8	-3 233.1	-7 213.1	-7 649.7
Other OECD[a]	-1 322.2	-2 828.7	-3 378.9	-3 955.0	-3 286.5	-3 856.8
Other countries[b]	-3 133.5	-1 373.4	2 776.6	1 851.4	-440.5	-5 354.4

[a] Organisation for Economic Co-operation and Development excluding the United States, Japan, and EU countries.

[b] Countries not included in the European Union or the OECD.

Source: "Imports and Exports on a Balance-of-Payments Basis," http://www.statcan.ca/english/Pgdb/Economy/International/gblec02a.htm, downloaded November 28, 1999. Reproduced by permission of the Minister of Supply and Services Canada.

environmental influences on marketing, and the development of an international marketing mix. Most of this chapter considers global marketing from the perspective of a company. However, we will first introduce the basic concepts of international trade from a nation's point of view.

▶ MEASURING A COUNTRY'S INTERNATIONAL TRADE ACTIVITY

Since imports and exports are important contributors to a country's economic welfare, governments and other organizations are concerned about the status of various components of international marketing. The concepts of balance of trade and balance of payments are a good starting point for understanding international business.

Balance of Trade

balance of trade
The relationship between a country's exports and its imports.

A nation's **balance of trade** is determined by the relationship between a country's exports and its imports. A favourable balance of trade (trade surplus) occurs when the value of a nation's exports exceeds its imports. This means that, other things being equal, new money would come into the country's economic system via the sales abroad of the country's products. An unfavourable balance of trade (trade deficit), by contrast, results when imports exceed exports. The net money flow would then be outward, other things being equal.

On the whole, Canada has maintained a favourable balance of trade. However, as Table 20.1 shows, Canada has a large balance with the United States that masks negative balances with a number of other trading partners.

Balance of Payments

balance of payments
The flow of money into or out of a country.

A country's balance of trade plays a vital role in determining its **balance of payments**, the flow of money into or out of a country. However, other factors are also important. A favourable balance of payments (or "current account") indicates that there is a net money inflow; an unfavourable balance of payments means that there is a net money outflow from the country.

The balance of payments is also affected by such factors as tourism, interest on foreign borrowings, military expenditures abroad, investment abroad, and foreign aid. A money outflow caused by these factors may exceed the money inflow from a favourable balance of trade and leave a nation with an unfavourable balance of payments.

Figure 20.1 shows that Canada has had a positive merchandise trade balance. However, because of a negative nonmerchandise balance, the overall balance of payments has been negative since 1987, except for 1996. Thus, Canadian residents spent more than they earned abroad. Figure 20.2 provides additional details. Despite a strong trade surplus, the balance on services is negative, and the deficit on investment income (primarily Canada's debt) is huge.

Exchange Rate Adjustments

exchange rate
The rate at which a nation's currency can be exchanged for other currencies or gold.

When the real value of a currency is out of line with international currencies in terms of relative buying power, the **exchange rate**, the rate at which a nation's currency can be exchanged for other currencies or gold, may change. (See the Practising Marketer box for an unusual but practical example.) Some countries try to fix the exchange rate. In Canada we have a floating rate. Fluctuations in the exchange rate have a significant impact on both the balance of trade and the balance of payments. Because of this, government policy may lead to efforts to stem significant fluctuations by buying or selling foreign—for example, U.S.—currency.

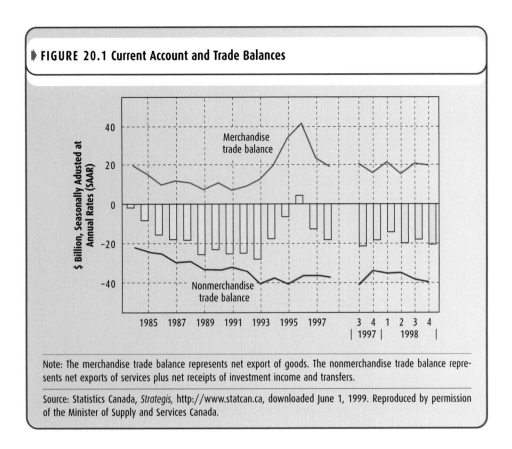

▶ FIGURE 20.1 Current Account and Trade Balances

Note: The merchandise trade balance represents net export of goods. The nonmerchandise trade balance represents net exports of services plus net receipts of investment income and transfers.

Source: Statistics Canada, *Strategis*, http://www.statcan.ca, downloaded June 1, 1999. Reproduced by permission of the Minister of Supply and Services Canada.

Devaluation occurs when a nation reduces the value of its currency in relation to gold or some other currency. Devaluation of the dollar has the effect of making Canadian products less expensive abroad and trips to Canada cheaper for foreign visitors, thus enhancing export trade. On the other hand, imports are more expensive. As a result, cross-border shopping becomes much less attractive. **Revaluation**, a less typical case, occurs when a country adjusts the value of its currency upward. This makes imports cheaper and exports more expensive. Either of these actions may force firms to modify their world marketing strategies.

devaluation
Situation in which a nation reduces the value of its currency in relation to gold or some other currency.

revaluation
Situation in which a country adjusts the value of its currency upward.

The Case for Open Trade[1]

It is better for a country to be open to, and to facilitate trade with, other countries. Open trade between countries benefits those countries, including consumers and business in general. There is a strong case for an open trading system. One piece of evidence is the experience of world trade and economic growth since World War II. Since that time, tariffs have fallen steeply and now average less than 4 percent in industrialized countries. During the first decades after the war, world economic growth averaged about 5 percent per year, a high rate that was partly the result of lower trade barriers. World trade grew even faster, averaging about 8 percent during the period. There is a definite statistical link between freer trade and economic growth.

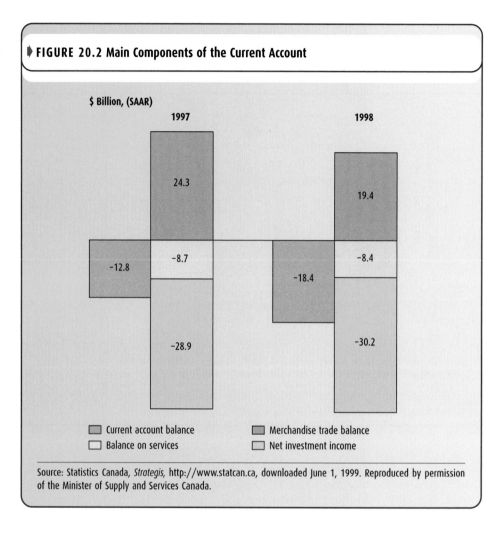

▶ **FIGURE 20.2 Main Components of the Current Account**

Source: Statistics Canada, *Strategis*, http://www.statcan.ca, downloaded June 1, 1999. Reproduced by permission of the Minister of Supply and Services Canada.

▶ **THE PRACTISING MARKETER**

www.mcdonalds.com

Big MacCurrencies

Some readers find our Big Mac index hard to swallow. This year, however, has been one to relish for burgernomics. When the euro was launched at the start of the year, most forecasters expected it to rise. The Big Mac index, however, suggested the euro was overvalued against the dollar—and it has indeed fallen.

The Big Mac index was devised thirteen years ago as a light-hearted guide to whether currencies are at their "correct" level. It is based upon one of the oldest concepts in international economics: purchasing power parity (PPP)—the notion that a dollar, say, should buy the same amount in all countries. In the long run, argue PPP fans, currencies should move toward the rate that equalizes the prices of an identical basket of goods and services in each country.

Our "basket" is a McDonalds' Big Mac, which is produced in more than 100 countries. The Big Mac PPP is the exchange rate that would leave hamburgers costing the same in America as abroad. Comparing actual exchange rates with PPPs signals whether a currency is under- or overvalued.

(continued)

▶ THE PRACTISING MARKETER *(continued)*

Our correspondents have once again been munching their way around the globe. The first column of the table shows local-currency prices of a Big Mac; the second converts them into dollars. The American price (the average in four cities, including tax) has dropped by 5 percent over the past year, to $2.43. Elsewhere, the cheapest Big Mac is in Malaysia ($1.19), whereas in Switzerland it costs a beefy $3.97. Hence the Swiss franc is the most overvalued currency (by 64 percent), the ringgit the most undervalued (by 51 percent).

The third column calculates Big Mac PPPs. For example, dividing the Japanese price by the American price gives a dollar PPP of ¥121, implying that the yen is spot on McParity. The price of a Big Mac varies widely within the euro area, but the average price (weighted by GDP) in the eleven countries is 2.52 eurodollars, or $2.71 at current exchange rates. This implies that despite its fall, the euro is still 11 percent overvalued. The table also shows prices in the euro's biggest member countries—ranging from the equivalent of $2.87 in France to $2.43 in Spain. Since their currencies are now irrevocably fixed, this gap can only be narrowed by prices falling in France or rising in Spain.

The currencies of the European economies that have decided to stay outside the euro are all noticeably overvalued. For example, according to the Big Mac index, sterling is overvalued by 26 percent against the dollar and by 13 percent against the euro.

In contrast, most of the emerging-market currencies, notably those in East Asia, Russia, and Brazil, are significantly undervalued against the dollar, following large devaluations. There is one big exception: the Israeli shekel is 42 percent overvalued.

We admit that the Big Mac is an imperfect measure of PPP, because prices may be distorted by trade barriers, sales taxes, and differences in the cost of nontraded inputs such as rents. But experience suggests that investors ignore burgernomics at their peril.

It is now time to lay down our chips: according to the Big Mac index, sterling and the non-euro currencies will fall over the next year or so; the shekel is likely to suffer a sharp fall; but China, where Big Macs are almost as cheap as in Malaysia, does not need to devalue the yuan.

▶ The Hamburger Standard

	BIG MAC PRICES		IMPLIED PPP[a] OF THE DOLLAR	ACTUAL $ EXCHANGE RATE (30/03/99)	UNDER(-)/ OVER (+) VALUATION AGAINST THE DOLLAR (%)
	In Local Currency	In Dollars			
United States[b]	$2.43	2.43	—	—	—
Argentina	Peso2.50	2.50	1.03	1.00	+3
Australia	A$2.65	1.66	1.09	1.59	−32
Brazil	Real2.95	1.71	1.21	1.73	−30
Britain	£1.90	3.07	1.28[c]	1.61[c]	+26
Canada	C$2.99	1.98	1.23	1.51	−19
Chile	Peso1,25	2.60	518	484.00	+7
China	Yuan9.90	1.20	4.07	8.28	−51
Denmark	Dkr24.75	3.58	10.19	6.91	+47

(continued)

▶ THE PRACTISING MARKETER (continued)

▶ **The Hamburger Standard** (continued)

	BIG MAC PRICES		IMPLIED PPP[a] OF THE DOLLAR	ACTUAL $ EXCHANGE RATE (30/03/99)	UNDER(-)/ OVER (+) VALUATION AGAINST THE DOLLAR (%)
	In Local Currency	In Dollars			
Euro area	Euro2.52	2.71	0.97[d]	1.08[d]	+11
France	FFr8.50	2.87	7.20	6.10	+18
Germany	DM4.95	2.72	2.04	1.82	+12
Italy	Lire4,500	2.50	1852.00	1799.00	+3
Netherlands	Fl5.45	2.66	2.24	2.05	+10
Spain	Pta375	2.43	154.00	155.00	0
Hong Kong	HK$10.2	1.32	4.20	7.75	-46
Hungary	Forint299	1.26	123.00	237.00	-48
Indonesia	Rupiah14,500	1.66	5967.00	8725.00	-32
Israel	Shekel13.9	3.44	5.72	4.04	+42
Japan	¥294	2.44	121.00	120.00	0
Malaysia	M$4.52	1.19	1.86	3.80	-51
Mexico	Peso19.9	2.09	8.19	9.54	-14
New Zealand	NZ$3.40	1.82	1.40	1.87	-25
Poland	Zloty5.50	1.38	2.26	3.98	-43
Russia	Rouble33.5	1.35	13.79	24.7	-44
Singapore	S$3.20	1.85	1.32	1.73	-24
South Africa	Rand8.60	1.38	3.54	6.22	-43
South Korea	Won3,000	2.46	1235.00	1218.00	+1
Sweden	SKr24.0	2.88	9.88	8.32	+19
Switzerland	SFr5.90	3.97	2.43	1.48	+64
Taiwan	NT$70.0	2.11	28.8	33.2	-13
Thailand	Baht52.0	1.38	21.4	37.6	-43

[a] Purchasing-power parity: local price dived by price in United States
[b] Average of New York, Chicago, San Francisco, and Atlanta
[c] Dollars per pound
[d] Dollars per euro

Source: "Big MacCurrencies," *The Economist* (April 3, 1999), p. 66. Reprinted with permission. Table: McDonald's and *The Economist*.

There are strong reasons for the link. All countries, including the poorest, have assets — human, industrial, natural, financial — that they can employ to produce goods and services for their domestic markets or to compete overseas.

We can benefit when these goods and services are traded. Simply put, the principle of *comparative advantage* (discussed in more detail in a later section) says that countries prosper most by taking advantage of their assets in order to concentrate on what they can produce best, and then by trading these products for products that other countries produce best.

Firms do exactly that quite naturally on the domestic market. But what about the international market? Most firms recognize that the bigger the market, the greater their potential—they can expand until they are at their most efficient size, and they can have access to large numbers of customers.

Will Trade Take Away from a Nation's Self-Sufficiency?

The Pacific island republic of Nauru has only a few thousand people but one of the richest deposits of phosphate in the world. New Zealand has a very productive sheep and cattle industry. Singapore has about 3 million people crowded into a small area. However, it has become one of the largest ports in the world, and has specialized in being a financial and information centre for the entire region. Kuwait has rich oil fields but few other industries or resources. Should these countries try to diversify their product base in order to increase their self-sufficiency?

The economic argument is that nations are usually better off specializing in certain products or marketing activities. By doing what they do best, nations are able to exchange products for foreign-made goods they need. Nauru could attempt to develop a tourist trade, but it has opted to specialize in phosphate mining. This allows the country a higher standard of living than would be possible through diversified business enterprises.

Nevertheless, a nation should not necessarily remain fixated on producing certain products or services. Just as the ability to compete well in certain products can shift from company to company, the same can happen between countries. Over time, countries (and their businesses) need to evolve from a pure commodity approach in order to become more efficient in world trade, and thus create more economic opportunity for their people.

For example, if "specialization" means selling nonrenewable resources, a country could find itself without a specialty and have a devastating balance of trade when these resources diminish. Canada faces this problem to some degree. For example, it has quite a high volume of trade with Japan and has generally maintained a positive balance of trade with that country. The problem for Canada is that it sells Japan mostly raw materials (coal, wood, pulp, softwood lumber, precious metals, fish, and wheat) while importing manufactured goods from Japan (cars, computers, telecommunications equipment, and photographic products). Canada is not likely to run out of its resources because most are renewable. The problem is that this trade does not create as many jobs as secondary manufacturing. The challenge is to expand exports of finished goods that create more jobs at home.

Specialization by countries sometimes produces odd situations. A classic example is the many Canadian tourist souvenirs and flags for sale in Canada that are made in China or some other country. Similarly, a number of "Buy Canadian" stickers can be found on the rear bumpers of Subarus and Toyotas.

Comparative Advantage: Trade Is Beneficial

Understanding the concepts of absolute and comparative advantage is important to the study of global trade. These concepts explain why all countries can benefit from trade.

ABSOLUTE ADVANTAGE

absolute advantage
A nation has an absolute advantage in the marketing of a product if it is the sole producer or can produce a product for less than anyone else.

A nation has an **absolute advantage** in the marketing of a product if it is the sole producer or can produce a product for less than anyone else. Since few nations are sole producers and economic conditions rapidly alter production costs, examples of absolute advantage are rare. However, suppose country A is better at making tractors, and country B is better at making computers. Clearly, both would benefit if A specialized in tractors and B specialized in computers, and then they traded. This is a case of absolute advantage.

COMPARATIVE ADVANTAGE

comparative advantage
A nation has a comparative advantage if it can produce a given product more efficiently per unit of output than it can produce other products.

What if a country is bad at making everything? Will trade drive all producers out of business? The answer is no. The reason is the principle of comparative advantage, one of the most powerful concepts in international trade. A nation has a **comparative advantage** if it can produce a given product more efficiently per unit of output than it can produce other products.

According to the principle of comparative advantage, countries A and B still stand to benefit from trading with each other even if A is better than B at making everything. The concept of comparative advantage, although a bit complicated, explains why it is beneficial for all nations to trade with one another. Comparative advantage is a *relative* concept. In comparison with country B, what goods should country A trade?

If A is far better at making tractors and only slightly better at making computers, then A should still invest resources in what it does best — making tractors — and export the product to B. B should still invest in what it does best — making computers — and export that product to A, even if it is not as efficient as A. Both would still benefit from the trade. A country does not have to be best at anything to gain from trade. That is comparative advantage.

Country A should produce and trade those products that it can. Thus, if country A produces tractors more efficiently per unit of output than it can produce other products, it should concentrate on producing tractors.

Country A should also buy products that it might produce, but less efficiently, from country B. A should do this even if it could produce these products more efficiently than country B. In total, A's outputs will be maximized by concentrating on its most efficiently produced product. This is because A's total productive capacity is fixed, and thus should be devoted to products that it makes most efficiently.

Country B has a comparative advantage in the product that it trades to country A because it is the one that B is most efficient at producing. Trade can be beneficial to both countries regardless of absolute costs. Nations will usually produce and export those goods in which they have the greatest comparative advantage and import those items in which they have the least comparative advantage (or the greatest comparative disadvantage).

Figure 20.3 suggests how the comparative advantage concept works for Canada. The export commodities tend to be those in which there is a comparative advantage. Being an industrialized nation with ample natural resources, Canada tends to export manufactured items, such as cars and machinery, and natural resources, such as grain, wood, and ores. By contrast, countries with lower-cost labour tend to specialize in products that require a significant labour content, such as textiles, shoes, and clothing.

▶ FIGURE 20.3 Leading Commodities in Canadian Foreign Trade

Merchandise Exports

	$ Billion	% Change, 1997–98
Total	323.4	7.4
Agricultural and fishing products	25.2	2.0
Energy products	23.4	−12.8
Forestry products	35.5	1.7
Industrial goods and materials	57.4	3.2
Machinery and equipment	78.8	15.9
Automotive products	79.2	13.1
Other consumer goods	12.5	17.2

Merchandise Imports

	$ Billion	% Change, 1997–98
Total	304.0	9.8
Agricultural and fishing products	17.3	10.8
Energy products	8.7	−17.8
Forestry products	2.5	5.2
Industrial goods and materials	60.3	10.9
Machinery and equipment	101.6	11.4
Automotive products	66.8	10.1
Other consumer goods	34.6	16.8

Source: Statistics Canada *Strategis,* http://www.statcan.ca, downloaded June 1, 1999. Reproduced by permission of the Minister of Supply and Services Canada.

Despite the principle of comparative advantage, there are noneconomic reasons for not specializing in certain items. Some countries refuse to specialize their productive efforts because they want to be self-sufficient. The Communist nations typically followed this pattern, to their disadvantage and downfall. It gradually became clear that it is impossible for a country to be fully self-sufficient. Self-sufficiency is in turn motivated by security concerns and the desire for high national status. Still other nations adopt the self-sufficiency viewpoint only for certain commodities that they regard as important to their long-run development. For instance, a country might choose to maintain self-sufficiency in weapons production for defence reasons.

▶ COMPETING IN THE INTERNATIONAL MARKET

While some Canadian firms have never ventured outside their own domestic market, others have discovered the challenges as well as the payoffs of marketing abroad. In some ways, marketing in Malaysia is very similar to marketing in Canada. That is, the marketing principles discussed in this book apply everywhere. However, the economic environment and culture often result in significant differences in the implementation of a marketing plan.

Market size, for example, means different things in different countries. Thailand has a population twice as large as Canada's. However, it potential market for many products is quite small, since the per capita income is only about $3800, compared with Canada's $30 000. On the other hand, there could well be a very profitable market niche of well-to-do customers in Thailand.

▶ INTERNET IMPACT

www.yahoo.ca

Yahoo Winning with Global, Local Mix

Yahoo Inc. has become the Internet's most popular destination, with more than 60 million users in 18 countries, by thinking globally and acting locally.

Yahoo's efforts to dominate Canada gained momentum in May of 1999 when the Web portal launched several new features tailored for the local market—enhancing its competitive edge against Canadian rivals such as Canoe, Sympatico.ca, and Canada.com.

In an ideal demonstration of how Yahoo endears itself to foreign markets, Jeff Mallett, Yahoo's president and chief operating officer, flew to Toronto for a day from the company's headquarters in Santa Clara, Calif., to launch the new features on the Canadian Web site, www.yahoo.ca, and meet with media that were happy to promote a local-boy-makes-good story.

Yahoo's successful penetration of foreign markets is based on its ability to leverage its extensive content, technological expertise, and financial muscle to create one-stop destinations—otherwise called "portals"—in a market with an overabundance of options.

By adding information relevant to each market, Yahoo has replicated the marketing savvy used by global companies such as Nike Inc. and Coca-Cola Ltd. Without a doubt, Yahoo has become one of the world's best-known brand names on the Internet. The company's Web sites attract more than 7 billion page views a month worldwide.

Would the "global/local" strategy work as well for other businesses?

Source: Excerpted from Mark Evans, "Yahoo Winning with Global, Local Mix," *The Globe and Mail* (May 24, 1999), p. B5. Reprinted with permission from *The Globe and Mail*.

Buyer Behaviour

There are many influences on buyer behaviour. Some of these, as discussed in Chapters 2 and 8, represent components of the external environment, as well as cultural and individual elements. In international marketing, the culture of the country is a key factor. For example, business gifts are commonly given, but the process and circumstances are very different from country to country. In Latin America, it is customary to present business gifts only after negotiations have been completed. Also, gifts that bear logos are considered cheap. On the other hand, business transactions can suffer if gifts are deemed too personal. Business visitors to the Arab world should understand that Arabs believe their public image to be greatly enhanced by lavish gift giving. The giver who pays tribute to an Arab's honour and enhances that person's self-esteem presents the most successful gift.

The cultural nuances cannot be underestimated. In Japan, for instance, it is wise not to say "no" when asked a question. When a Japanese client asks if it is possible to modify a particular product, it may be better to say, "I'll think about it" or "Let me get back to you in a few days." Marketers must be careful that their marketing strategies comply with local customs, tastes, and buying practices.

In some cultures, long-term relationships are very important. When, for example, Nortel Networks became the first non-Japanese telecommunications company to make a major sale to Nippon Telegraph and Telephone with a $250-million seven-year deal, it was the culmination of a four-year marketing effort. Much of this effort was "trust-building" work. The company president alone made eleven trips to Japan within a space of six months.

Economic and Societal Factors

International marketing is also affected and influenced by economic and societal factors. The economic status of some countries makes them less (or more) likely candidates for international business expansion. Nations with lower per capita income may still represent a market but packaging may have to change (for example, sizes may have to be much smaller). Wealthier countries can prove to be prime markets for the products of many Canadian industries, particularly those involved with consumer goods and advanced business products, but there are frequently wealthy market segments to be found in less well-off countries.

Many products have failed abroad simply because the producing firm tried to use the same marketing strategy that was successful at home. Consider an advertising strategy based primarily on using print media that features testimonials. Such a campaign would have dim prospects in a less developed nation with a high degree of illiteracy. Other marketing practices can be transferred successfully. It all depends — and that is why a systematic market assessment is even more important in marketing to anther country than in your own market, where you have knowledge and experience.

North American products do not always meet the needs of foreign consumers. Products that are strongly culture-bound are usually the most difficult to market globally. Foods, for example, have widely different acceptance levels in different countries. White Canadians find many Asian foods too "adventurous." Asians, on the other hand, find some Canadian foods very boring. Similarly, products that are used in the course of daily living are often difficult to transfer to another country because ways of doing things are different. Until recently, washing machines in Europe operated differently from those in North America. Therefore, for a company from either continent to just export its prod-

▶ THE PRACTISING MARKETER

Do Your Homework Before You Leave Canada

About five years ago, Barbara Barde waltzed into the offices of a Japanese television company armed with a program already in production, but in need of investment to complete. She met with the boss, who was a model of Japanese civility.

Her pitch was a flop.

"I really thought it was a good idea and they should put money into it," she says. "I think … they thought I hadn't paid my dues in their marketplace. They didn't know me."

In retrospect, Ms. Barde, 51, founder of Toronto-based Up Front Entertainment Inc., says her idea could have been a winner if she had done more research, spent more time with her prospective Japanese partner, and learned a little more about the person she would be meeting.

But the experience also taught her something about exporting. "You could see he was fairly uncomfortable about doing business with me. I have no doubt it was based on gender."

A federally commissioned survey of female business owners engaged in exporting suggests her experience is not isolated. *Beyond Borders: Canadian Businesswomen in International Trade* reports there is a host of gender issues that affect the way women do business at home and internationally.

However, the study revealed that among the 254 business operators surveyed, international marketing is generally considered to be the biggest obstacle to breaking into foreign markets. The women said the cost of developing new markets, obtaining information, setting up distribution channels, coping with government regulations, and finding partners were their biggest challenges.

Cultural issues and not being taken seriously were most often cited as problems, the report says.

"Cultural challenges were most often cited in the context of business transactions in Asia, the Middle East, South Africa, India and South America," according to the report.

▶ How to Go Global

Female business owners offer tips for clearing the gender hurdle:

- Build owner credibility first.
- Work with Canadian trade commissioners to be introduced to potential clients.
- Avoid personal or phone contact in certain countries.
- Use e-mail only with certain customers.
- Have a male employee handle certain client companies.
- Avoid some social events.
- Change business cards to indicate clearly the owner's position.
- In some cases, lay down the law that customers must deal with the female business owner.

Source: *Beyond Borders.*

Why do you think that aspects other than gender showed up as the most important obstacles when breaking into new markets?

Source: Adapted from Dawn Walton, "Female Exporters Face Gender Factor," *The Globe and Mail* (March 10, 1999), p. B9. Reprinted with permission from *The Globe and Mail.*

uct to the other would have not been very successful, because consumers would not be familiar with the washing process. Likewise, a North American laundry detergent (which does not contain perborate) may not satisfy Europeans who are used to washing their laundry at near-boiling temperatures.

Political and Legal Factors

The international marketer may find that the political environment of another country requires some modifications in the ways of doing business. For example, China is a socialist, centrally planned economy. Companies wishing to do business there must obtain permission from several layers of government. Doing business in another country means that a company is a guest in that country. Success requires recognizing the political priorities of the host.

International relations can also affect business activities. For example, during the Bosnian crisis, the Canadian government, as well as others, would not allow its country's firms to do business with Serbia. Similarly, the United States has a long-standing trade embargo against Cuba. It has even tried to prosecute firms from Canada and other countries that trade with Cuba.

Each country has evolved a legal system that reflects the values of its culture. As in Canada, most countries have many laws that control the way business is done. For example, Malaysia has laws against cigarette advertising, but the cigarette companies have found a way around these laws by adding other products, such as clothing, to their line. Then they prominently advertise brand names such as Marlborough, ostensibly to promote the other products. A different set of rules can be found in Canada, where a third of a cigarette package must be in black and white, with the words "Smoking can kill you" printed on it.

Canadians marketing food products in the United States find that the requirements for stating the contents are different and more strict than in Canada. All commercials in the United Kingdom and Australia must be cleared in advance. In The Netherlands, ads for candy must also show a toothbrush. Some nations have **local content laws** that specify the portion of a product that must come from domestic sources. This may force a manufacturer to ship a product unassembled and to have the assembly done in the host country. These examples suggest that managers involved in international marketing must be well-versed in legislation that affects their specific industry.

local content laws
Laws specifying the portion of a product that must come from domestic sources.

The legal environment for Canadian firms operating abroad can be divided into three dimensions:

- Canadian law
- international law
- laws of host nations

CANADIAN LAW

International business is subject to various trade regulations, tax laws, and import/export requirements. One significant provision in the Competition Act exempts from anticombines laws groups of Canadian firms that act together to develop foreign markets. An example is the cartel of Canadian uranium producers, which is designed to increase prices received in international markets.

cartel
The monopolistic organization of a group of firms.

The intent of allowing this is to give Canadian industry economic power equal to that possessed by foreign cartels. A **cartel** is the monopolistic organization of a group of firms. Companies operating under this provision must not reduce competition within Canada and must not use "unfair methods of competition." It is hard to say whether companies can cooperate internationally and remain competitive without collusion in the domestic market. Canadian law also restricts the export of certain strategic goods, such as sophisticated computer technology, atomic components, and military hardware, to certain countries.

INTERNATIONAL LAW

friendship, commerce, and navigation (FCN) treaties
Treaties that address many aspects of commercial relations with other countries; such treaties constitute international law.

International law can be found in the treaties, conventions, and agreements that exist among nations. Canada has many **friendship, commerce, and navigation (FCN) treaties**. These treaties address many aspects of commercial relations with other countries, such as the right to conduct business in the treaty partner's domestic market, and constitute international law.

Other international agreements concern international standards for various products, patents, trademarks, reciprocal tax treaties, export control, international air travel, and international communications. For example, the leading nations of the world established the International Monetary Fund, which facilitates foreign exchange transactions among nations to conduct international trade.

LAWS OF HOST NATIONS

www.cadburyschweppes.
com

The legal requirements of host nations affect foreign marketers. For example, some nations limit foreign ownership in their business sectors. Global marketers obey the laws and regulations of the countries within which they operate. The amount and type of advertising allowed are also prescribed by law in many countries. A host of other trade regulations must be understood and met by the foreign marketer. Australia's competition watchdog (The Australian Competition and Consumer Commission) blocked a plan by The Coca-Cola Company to buy soft drink brands from Cadbury Schweppes PLC. It ruled that the merger would result in a market structure where the leading carbonated drinks in almost every category would be controlled by The Coca-Cola Company.

▶ CANADIAN GOVERNMENT ASSISTANCE TO EXPORTERS

Exporting is of great importance to a country. It creates jobs and helps bring about a positive balance of trade, thus making the entire economy more prosperous. Consequently, governments have active programs to help companies become more active in the global marketplace. Provincial governments provide information and guidance to businesses and have even set up foreign trade offices in major markets such as Japan, Hong Kong, and Britain.

The Canadian government has trade officers in every embassy and consulate around the world. These people seek out opportunities for Canadian goods and services and send this information back to Canada. They also help Canadian businesspeople make the right contacts when travelling abroad. Furthermore, trade officers may arrange trade shows that demonstrate Canadian products. For example, in Australia, a large Canadian agricultural equipment show is held in Dubbo, a big agricultural town.

In Canada, Foreign Affairs and International Trade Canada has trade officers in many major cities; these individuals facilitate export planning by Canadian firms and connect them with the overseas consulates. Their offices are also good sources of secondary data concerning exporting and various countries. The Internet is also proving to be a useful source of data on global marketing planning.

Through Foreign Affairs and International Trade Canada offices, the Canadian government administers various travel support programs in the form of loans to firms that need to go to a foreign market to initiate trade. If the venture is successful, the loan must be paid back.

www.dfait-maeci.gc.ca/
menu-e.asp

Whatever you make, we'll help it travel.

Madawaska makes doors. And we're helping them open more, around the world. We're Ontario Exports Inc., the lead trade agency of the Government of Ontario. Whatever your business, we can provide you with market intelligence, introduce your goods or services to foreign buyers, and more. Contact us and see the world. Because exports mean jobs. For everyone. Ph. (416) 314-8200 or Toll Free: 1 877-468-7233 (outside Toronto) web: www.ontario-canada.com/export

ONTARIO EXPORTS INC.
OPENING DOORS WORLDWIDE

Because exports mean jobs for Ontario, the provincial government has established agencies, such as Ontario Exports Inc., to provide guidance and information to export businesses.

The Export Development Corporation (EDC) is a Canadian Crown corporation that provides financial services to Canadian exporters and foreign buyers in order to facilitate and develop export trade. It does this through a wide range of insurance, guarantee, and loan services not normally provided by the private sector. Through its export financing programs, EDC extends to the Canadian exporter's foreign buyer the medium- or long-term financing required to purchase Canadian goods or services.

With EDC's accounts receivable insurance, Canadian firms can protect their export sales against nonpayment by foreign buyers for up to 90 percent of the value of their sales. EDC's insurance essentially transfers the foreign buyer's risk to EDC, enabling the exporter to make more sales in more countries. Up to 85 percent of the Canadian portion of an export deal can generally be financed.

www.edc.ca

Export Development Corporation (EDC) helps Canadian exporters open doors to global markets by providing insurance and financial solutions.

Once the Canadian exporter has fulfilled the terms of the commercial contract and has provided the appropriate documentation, EDC pays the exporter on behalf of the foreign buyer/borrower. Exporters in other countries have access to similar support facilities from their governments through Export Credit Agencies.

EDC thus assumes all subsequent payment risk and collects payments from the borrower over the life of the loan. EDC's export financing services include direct loans; lines of credit and protocols, which are streamlined financing facilities set up between EDC and a foreign bank; note purchase agreements, under which the EDC buys promissory notes issued by foreign banks to Canadian exporters for the purchase of Canadian goods or services; and specialized credits. EDC facilitates this by (normally) assuming the commercial and political risks, including insolvency or default by the buyer and blockage of funds in a foreign country.

EDC will also make long-term loans to foreign buyers of Canadian capital goods and services. Funds are disbursed directly to Canadian suppliers on behalf of the borrower, in effect providing the exporters with cash sales. EDC policy is to achieve maximum private-sector involvement in export financing; it therefore provides 100 percent guarantees to banks and financial institutions to facilitate the exporters' banking arrangements.

▶ THE MARKETING MIX IN THE GLOBAL SETTING

A fundamental marketing principle is that the marketing mix must be designed to meet the needs of the target market. This holds whether the marketing is done in Canada or a foreign market. Thus, depending on the international situation, some marketing elements may be relatively unchanged, whereas others require significant modification.

Some products seem to be "global" products, and virtually the same marketing mix can be used everywhere. Examples are Levi jeans, Coca-Cola, Rolex watches, and most business products. In these cases, a universal comprehension of the product exists or has been developed through international media, or there are common behaviour patterns between countries. A computer is not "culture-bound," whereas a food item, or the place and method of serving it, could be very much an acquired preference that is moulded by culture. For example, many Germans accustomed to heavy, dark bread might find Canadian mass-produced bread unappetizing. It seems that "culture-boundness" is a function of time — products that have been around the longest, like food and articles of clothing, are the most culture-bound. New products, like computers and cell phones, are less culture-bound.

www.us.levi.com

Adaptation is required for many products — and for managerial styles. Let us consider a few examples of adaptations to the marketing mix.

Product Decisions

Cutomer expectations define quality and value, and those expectations are not always the same as they are in Canada. Nortel Networks learned that lesson after it sold its SL-1 telephone answering and switching system to a large Japanese department store. Among the features of the product is one called "music on hold." Both Japanese and North American customers are familiar with this. However, familiarity and expectations are two different things. The Japanese *expect* to hear music under all circumstances while waiting to be connected. The SL-1 gave them music while they waited to be connected to a particular department, but if that call was transferred to somebody else, no music would play. As a result, the Japanese callers assumed they had been disconnected and they hung up. Rather than trying to reshape the listening habits of 130 million Japanese, the company redesigned its system to meet Japanese expectations.

▶ THE PRACTISING MARKETER

A McDonald's That Doesn't Serve a Big Mac

McDonald's has arrived in India. It set up shop in a fairly low-key manner and *abandoned* the Big Mac! In fact, it serves a chicken burger, potato cutlets, and some other items unheard of at any other McDonald's outlet in the world.

To understand the brilliance behind McDonald's strategy, one has to understand more about the environment and culture of India. There is a common myth in the West that India is a vegetarian country. Actually, the majority of Indians are nonvegetarian, including Hindus. But, as with certain lobby groups in the West, the vegetarian segment in India is a very vocal and powerful minority. Such groups have also lashed out against foreign companies with claims of the damage these companies are doing to the livestock population and to the health of the people by serving meat. So, there was a potential danger that McDonald's new outlets would be picketed as "disseminators of dangerous foreign culture" and "vendors of holy cows."

Initially, the outlets were picketed, but the whole movement fizzled out when it was discovered that there was nothing to protest about. Indians consume millions of chickens every day, in every way, including hundreds of thousands of chicken burgers. So that was not an argument that would win sympathy.

Think about it. A McDonald's that doesn't serve a Big Mac or a small Mac, but is quietly widening its outlet base in posh localities and will be a major player in a few years. The question to ask ourselves: Is the burger really McDonald's core value, or is it something much stronger, that allows such changes in strategy without hurting the brand?

A point to remember is that McDonald's was already very well known to a number of the customers in whose localities it has set up shop. They are the "holiday and study abroad" segment, and McDonald's is standard fare because of price and standardization. (Yes, the members of this segment enjoy the beef Big Mac when abroad, because they don't ask what's inside.) Isn't marketing the most fun you can have with your clothes on?

How would you react if you went into one of these outlets? Does this adaptation mean that you can't count on McDonald's for its famous standardization and reliability anymore? Why or why not?

Source: Adapted from a communication from Larry Grant, http://www.larrygrant.net, to GINLIST@LIST.MSU.EDU. Reprinted with permission.

Government-established product standards often differ among countries. Host-country standards obviously must be met. For example, a Canadian marketer of packaged food products must meet specific nutritional label information requirements. Similarly, electrical products must meet varying codes from country to country. Germany, for example, has very rigid requirements for products such as fax machines that are connected to the telephone system. Thus, well-known brands accepted in Canada may not be allowed in Germany.

Pricing Decisions

When exporting, a cost-plus approach to pricing can quickly destroy potential opportunities. This is because more intermediaries are often required. If all these intermediaries take a standard markup based on a percentage of the cost they pay, the resulting price increase can be so large that the product is priced out of the foreign market. Table 20.2 shows an example of how a product that retails for $10.01 in Canada could end up being priced at $18.30 in a foreign market if a simple cost-plus pricing approach is used. This could well make the product uncompetitive in the foreign market. This problem can be avoided by reconsidering the internal costing system, as well as whether the standard markups are necessary in this situation.

▶ **TABLE 20.2 How Prices Can Mount When Exporting to a Foreign Market**

	DOMESTIC EXAMPLE	FOREIGN EXAMPLE (IMPORTER AND WHOLESALER IMPORTING DIRECTLY)
Manufacturing net	$5.00	$5.00
Transport, c.i.f.[a]	n.a.	1.10
Tariff (20 percent c.i.f. value)	n.a.	1.22
Importer pays	n.a.	7.32
Importer margin when sold to wholesaler (25% on cost)	n.a.	1.83
Wholesaler pays landed cost	5.00	9.15
Wholesaler margin (33⅓% on cost)	1.67	3.05
Retailer pays	6.67	12.20
Retail margin (50% on cost)	3.34	6.10
Retailer price	10.01	18.30

[a] c.i.f. = cost, insurance, and freight

Because exchange rates fluctuate, marketers must be careful to consider whether the price that they are asking for will be enough at the time of delivery. The currency of the deal might devaluate, thus possibly wiping out all profits. Because of this, a stable, commonly traded currency such as U.S. dollars may be chosen as the currency of payment.

If a country has limited foreign exchange reserve, it may not be able to afford to pay for a product in foreign currency. It is sometimes necessary to think about payment in different terms. For example, Nortel Networks sometimes agrees to accept payment in kind from customers. "Deals often hinge on how willing companies are to set aside more cherished commercial practices and accept payment in the form of copper, sugar cane, bamboo, rice, or even a boatload of figs," says Alan Lytle, Nortel's vice-president of marketing.

Marketing Communications

In Canada, sales representatives sometimes try to develop rapport with a client by asking about his or her family. In Saudi Arabia, this could be taken as an insult. Advertising messages also vary from country to country. In France, sexually explicit advertising is more common than in Canada, and the British tend to use more humour.

The newly promoted global advertising manager for a brand of toothpaste for children was puzzled. The company's highly successful ad campaign, which had boosted sales in Canada, the United States, Europe, and Australia, was not well received by the folks in the Bangkok office. "Too American" they kept repeating. So, the manager showed them the French and British versions of the campaign. Still, the Bangkok staff was uneasy, and, as politely as their Thai upbringing allowed, told the manager that the campaign would not work in their country. It had to do with the "pat on the head" that appeared in a scene that closed all commercials in the campaign. This gesture was meant to express the parents' appreciation of their child's good brushing with the toothpaste. But one does not touch the head of another person in many Asian countries. Thus, to make the communication successful, a different way of showing approval had to be found.

Because communication is so entwined with culture, the subtle nuances that make messages acceptable or unacceptable should be, at least, monitored by a local communicator before use. Preferably, local communicators should develop the message so that it accords with pre-established company strategy.

> The logistics of moving products globally are often complicated and costly. Canadian exporting firms, however, can turn to The Logistics Institute for help in making sound logistic decisions.

Thanks to logistics, lobsters can fly.

To places like Paris, Munich and Tokyo. And hundreds of cities in between. But rather than wings, they're powered by the magic of logistics. A science so capable, it can send 5.5 million live lobsters airborne every year.

Just ask the world's largest exporter of live lobster, Clearwater Fine Foods in Bedford, Nova Scotia. "Lobsters are like eggs—an accident waiting to happen," sighs Clearwater distribution director Ron Carter, a Professional Logistician (P. Log.). Preventing mishaps is why Clearwater's lobsters spend several days in an Olympic-sized pool to relax after they're caught, and before being stored for up to a year in vast arrays of capsule hotel rooms called "dry land pounds" flushed with sea water straight from the Atlantic.

When they're ready to be air freighted, the lobsters are packed in 30-pound styrofoam trays and wrapped in sea-soaked newspaper, a process which provides them with enough oxygen to survive the journey—usually to a linen-clad table in an elegant setting.

Having a ready supply of premium, hard-shell lobster in and out of season calls for the kinds of organizational skills only professional logisticians can provide. Which is why Clearwater relies so heavily on people like Ron Carter.

Professional logistics is helping a growing number of Canadian companies, some of which (Canadian Tire, IBM, Nabisco and Xerox Canada, to name a few) have enrolled as corporate members of the Canadian Professional Logistics Institute, the national governing body dedicated to teaching, developing and promoting logistics.

To find out how your business can also benefit from corporate membership in the Logistics Institute, perhaps you should call us today. We could be just the lift you need.

The Logistics Institute ™ CANADIAN PROFESSIONAL LOGISTICS INSTITUTE
10 King Street East, 4th Floor, Toronto, Ontario M5C 1C3
Tel: (416) 363-3005   Fax: (416) 363-5598
e-mail: loginfo@istar.ca   website: www.loginstitute.ca

Logistics. The driving force of human achievement.

local communicator before use. Preferably, local communicators should develop the message so that it accords with pre-established company strategy.

Distribution Decisions

Distribution is one of the major problems in developing a marketing plan for a foreign market. This is especially true of exporting—the logistics of moving products are often very complicated. Fortunately, service firms called freight forwarders specialize in distribution and can be counted on to help solve the physical distribution problem. Obviously, both the service provided and the transportation add to the cost structure and must be reflected in the price or compensated for by reducing other costs.

Another problem is deciding which channels of distribution to use. The system may be quite different from what the Canadian marketer is accustomed to. In some countries, it may be difficult to find the necessary wholesaling intermediaries. In Japan, the opposite is

▶ **THE PRACTISING MARKETER**

Product Image Varies by Country

The image of Mercedes varies significantly between North America and its home in Germany. The image in North America is that of a very prestigious, well-made car—the car young as well as old can aspire to. In contrast, Cadillac has become the car for the aging executive near retirement. It's boring. Mercedes is exciting.

In Germany, the Mercedes has the image of a car for the "butter and egg" man—an aging, potbellied executive. It is a boring brand, similar to Cadillac in North America. In Germany, BMW and Porsche are exciting.

The Mercedes is the same product, but its history and evolution in each market is quite different. The marketing that works in one country may not work in the other.

It seems that people's needs are similar. Human nature is the same all over, but the role, position, and perception of a brand in one culture can differ wildly from those in another culture. Standardization may save money in manufacturing, but it can reduce the edge that a marketer has if practised too dogmatically.

What are the lessons for an international marketer?

Source: Adapted from a communication from Joel Baumwoll, joelb@THORN.NET, to GINLIST@LIST.MSU.EDU. Reprinted with permission.

www.mercedes-benz.ca

true: channels of distribution normally consist of many layers of wholesalers that sell the product to others of their kind, that finally sell it to the retailer. As in the domestic market, the marketer has to solve the problem of how to persuade the channels to carry and promote the product.

From the foregoing discussion, it is clear that the marketing mix is likely to require some adaptation before success in the foreign market can be achieved. An attitude of openness and flexibility is essential.

Companies who want international success must be willing to adapt their products and marketing strategies to the needs of the customer and the attitudes and business practices of the country they are operating in, no matter how demanding these may be.

If that means having to make major and costly product modifications to meet the technical requirements and customer expectations, so be it.

If it means investing years of time and money in order to build trust and establish a presence to win that first contract, then that too has to be done.

If it means applying a sensitive understanding of cultural behaviour, such as learning the language, then that must be done as well.

And if it means fashioning an appealing financed cooperative marketing package that maximizes the benefits of the products you sell, that must be done.

Only by embracing these kinds of value-charged initiatives can you hope to surmount the complex barriers and challenges of international marketing. Companies that do will find themselves well on the way to global competitive success. Companies that don't will sadly discover their respective customers don't care about their work.[2]

▶ COMPANY APPROACHES TO GLOBAL MARKETING

A variety of approaches to global marketing can be seen. Some firms do not get involved at all. Others export occasionally when an order happens to arrive from overseas or possibly when they have some excess product. Both of these could be classified as "not-committed approaches."

Among firms committed to international business, Warren Keegan has identified four different approaches: ethnocentric, polycentric, regiocentric, and geocentric.[3]

ethnocentric company
Firm that assumes that its way of doing business in its home market is the proper way to operate, and tries to replicate this in foreign markets.

A company that is **ethnocentric** assumes that its way of doing business in its home market is the proper way to operate, and tries to replicate this in foreign markets. As the previous discussion has shown, such an inflexible approach is likely to severely inhibit the effectiveness of a firm's efforts in another country.

polycentric company
Firm that assumes that every country is different and that a specific marketing approach should be developed for each separate country.

The opposite of the ethnocentric approach is the **polycentric** approach. Companies that are polycentric assume that every country is different and that a specific marketing approach should be developed for each separate country. This attitude certainly overcomes the inflexibility of ethnocentricity. For many firms, being insightful enough to see the pitfalls of the ethnocentric approach and being willing to adapt have become the foundation of success and are cause for some pride. Such an approach can be more cost, however, because the marketing must be custom-tailored to each individual country.

regiocentric company
Firm that recognizes that countries with similar cultures and economic conditions can be served with a similar marketing mix.

As business has become more global in its orientation, managers have found that it is not always necessary to develop a separate plan for each country. A **regiocentric** approach recognizes that countries with similar cultures and economic conditions can be served with a similar marketing mix. As has been mentioned earlier, in the case of some products it is possible to take a **geocentric** approach. This means developing a marketing mix that meets the needs of target consumers in all markets. Note that this is different from an ethnocentric approach. Depending on the circumstances, polycentric, regiocentric, and geocentric strategies can each be appropriate.

geocentric company
Firm that develops a marketing mix that meets the needs of target consumers in all markets.

▶ MODES OF INTERNATIONAL ACTIVITY

Firms can participate in the international market in a number of ways and to a lesser or greater extent. The lowest level of participation is indirect exporting and importing; the highest levels are joint ventures and foreign production and marketing.

indirect international trade
Exporting and/or importing only through other domestic companies that trade internationally.

Indirect Exporting and Importing

A company that is involved in **indirect international trade** does not attempt to buy or sell in other countries. However, some of the companies it does business with will be involved in exporting or importing. For example, a supplier produces and sells parts to Monarch Pumps, which markets its products in many countries. Similarly, the supplier buys from a Canadian distributor some components that are made in Germany to include in its product. Although the supplier has no direct contact with foreign firms, it is a vital part of the international market.

Direct Exporting and Importing

Some companies are more committed to **direct international trade**. They may produce in Canada and then seek to export a portion of their output to foreign markets. For example, the developer of a software program for managing trucking distribution companies markets the product in both Canada and the United States, and considers which other countries would have similar needs. Conversely, an oil company imports crude oil from Venezuela or the Middle East to refineries in Montreal in order to sell the finished product in eastern Canada.

Triple E, a Canadian recreational vehicle manufacturer, is involved in both importing and exporting. The firm directly imports certain components from the United States and other countries. It also exports its RVs directly to Europe, as well as selling them in Canada.

direct international trade
Exporting directly to markets and/or importing directly from suppliers in other countries.

Licensing

Licensing allows a firm in another country to produce and sell a product for a fee paid to the licensing company. For example, the Canadian inventor of a commercial trash compactor displays her product at a trade show. Among the visitors to her booth is a Taiwanese businessman. Impressed with the product, he offers to produce and sell it in Taiwan under licence. The licence agreement gives him the know-how and legal right to produce the compactor in Taiwan at a set fee per unit. This saves the Canadian inventor a great deal of trouble. However, normally the return on licences is quite low, and it may be difficult to monitor patent control.

licensing
Granting authority to produce and sell a product developed in one country in another.

Joint Venture

In an international **joint venture**, a company sets up a business in a foreign market by going into partnership with a local enterprise. Such an arrangement allows for financial risk to be shared and reduces the problems inherent in doing business in a foreign country, because the partner can supply knowledge of local marketing and production practices. More specifically, the partner can supply knowledge of the market itself (local tastes and preferences) and established relationships with local organizations (wholesalers, retailers, government agencies, banks) and customers. A joint venture requires a much greater commitment of resources than importing, exporting, or licensing. General Motors and Suzuki, in Ingersoll, Ontario, is an example of an international joint venture. In China, a country of great potential but high risk, nearly 50 000 joint ventures were established in the first fifteen years after China started allowing them.[4]

joint venture
A partnership of firms from different countries, often to set up a local business in a country that is foreign to one of the partners.

Foreign Production and Marketing

direct investment
The ownership and management of production and/or marketing facilities in a foreign country.

Direct investment in another country requires the greatest commitment to global enterprise. In such an enterprise, a firm invests in facilities, staff, and marketing programs in a foreign market without a local partner. If the enterprise is successful, the rewards do not have to be shared, and the business can operate freely without the need to make decisions jointly with a foreign partner. Canadian auto-parts manufacturer Magna International has such an operation in Mexico.

Multinational Enterprise

multinational corporation (MNC)
A corporation that produces and markets goods and services in several countries.

A company that handles its own foreign production and marketing may be, or could become, a **multinational corporation (MNC)**. An MNC produces and markets in several countries; it has a world orientation rather than loyalty to any one country. Thus, it chooses to produce in whichever country happens to be the best for the job. An MNC's marketing strategies in various countries are often similar or interrelated, and may follow a common theme.

Alcan Aluminum is a multinational corporation headquartered in Canada, but its products can be found around the world. The company has branches in many world markets. With approximately 80 percent of its sales originating outside Canada, the company must think in global rather than domestic terms.

▶ STARTING INTERNATIONAL OPERATIONS[5]

Before deciding to "go international," a company needs to ensure that it has the following elements: a strong senior management commitment, adequate resources, a viable product, and strategic planning.

Management Commitment

Developing and implementing a strategic plan for an international venture requires a substantial investment of financial and human resources for a considerable period before any profits are seen. Therefore, it is crucial that senior management be committed to an international venture before embarking on it.

Adequate Resources

Before making any decision to export, a company needs to thoroughly review its domestic performance and capabilities. For example, sales profit margins and prices should be compared with those of the industry. If competitors are already exporting, this is a positive sign that there may be a good opportunity in the international market.

@boogie

www.cdwarehouse.com is an **IBM** e-business

IBM, a multinational firm, assumes a polycentric approach in its global marketing. Does its new e-commerce technology imply any change in its approach?

The company's own resources should be thoroughly assessed. Does it have the financial and human resources to research foreign markets? Does it have the production capacity to ensure prompt deliveries when orders come in? Reliability is one of the most essential requirements for success in selling internationally.

Viable Product

The exportability of the product should be determined by considering the following factors:

- Who will use the product?
- Who will make the purchasing decisions in the foreign country?
- Will the product be purchased throughout the year or on a seasonal basis?
- From whom is the product being purchased now?
- Will the product have to be modified to adapt to specific market nuances or regulations? If so, what will this cost?
- Is the product easy to ship? Are there any special handling costs?
- Is the product competitive on the basis of price, quality, and delivery?

Strategic Export Planning

Export strategy should be part of overall corporate strategy. The company must be clear about its expectations of an international venture as well as fully aware of its own limitations. For example, if the company is not prepared to spend the time and money to research the market and to adapt and produce the proper type and quantity of products, then it should not be considering the export market.

Once management decides to examine the feasibility of an international venture, it should begin by scanning possible markets. Countries first considered would normally be those that are geographically close, similar in language and culture, or familiar to company officials. The preliminary scanning should include factors such as market size, political and economic stability, competition, distribution, and profit potential. This initial survey provides management with the information to select the four or five most likely markets for further analysis. Such an analysis considers the market, product (already discussed), price, distribution, and marketing communications. A few examples of the relevant issues for each factor follow.

THE MARKET

- What are the tariff barriers, import quotas, and internal taxes for the product?
- What is the size and the sector of the market that will purchase the product?
- What is the long-term potential, based on future growth, for each sector?
- Who are the major competitors, and what is their market share? Is the market politically and economically stable?

THE PRICE

- What is the profitability at various pricing levels?
- Can the pricing match or better the competition and still have a healthy profit margin?
- If pricing cannot match the competition, can the product still sell because of product superiority, ability to deliver, and after-sales servicing?

DISTRIBUTION

- What methods of distribution are available in the country, and which is the most reliable and cost-efficient?

- What markups are normally sought by intermediaries in the industry?
- Who are the main importers; what are their reputations, capabilities, and financial strengths?
- What types of carriers are needed? What are the transportation costs? How frequent and reliable are the various modes of transportation?
- Is there an agent capable of providing satisfactory technical services?

MARKETING COMMUNICATIONS

- What are the types and costs of advertising in the individual markets, and which are best suited to the needs of the product?
- What are the advertising practices of competitors? What percentage of their gross profit goes into advertising, and what media do they advertise in?
- Where and when do trade fairs and exhibitions take place, and what opportunities exist for participating in them?

Some of this information is available from provincial business and trade departments as well as Foreign Affairs and International Trade Canada. After gleaning as much information as possible in Canada, it is very important for the marketer to make a trip to the target country to size up the situation.

After an analysis that takes the foregoing factors into consideration, the business will be in a better position to decide whether it should proceed with an international venture. Such an appraisal also provides the groundwork for developing the company strategy that is necessary to enter the foreign market. It is a challenging task. However, those who proceed in a systematic fashion generally find that going international is worthwhile.

▶ INTEGRATION OF WORLD MARKETS

One country would find it difficult to produce all the goods and services it needed, so international trade occurs. Nevertheless, every country tends to jealously protect its own producers and markets. This results in a maze of laws, tariffs, and restrictions that need to be overcome by trading firms.

Over the years, all nations have recognized that there is a need for an open trading system based on multilaterally agreed-upon rules. Protectionism leads to bloated and inefficient companies and can, in the end, lead to factory closures and job losses. Consequently, in 1948 many countries negotiated a General Agreement on Tariffs and Trade (GATT), which was revised periodically. However, in 1995, after a massive set of negotiations (known as the Uruguay Round because that country was the host), the World Trade Organization was established to do much more than the GATT. A major objective of the WTO is to reduce protectionism.

The **World Trade Organization (WTO)** is an international organization that deals with the rules of trade between nations. The WTO agreements are the legal rules for international commerce and trade policy. The agreements have three main objectives: to encourage free trade, to further open international trade through negotiation, and to provide a way to settle disputes between countries.[6]

World Trade Organization (WTO) The international body that deals with the rules of trade between nations.

www.wto.org

Principles of the Trading System

Five fundamental principles run throughout all WTO agreements and form the foundation of the multilateral trading system. Trade should be

1. *Without discrimination* — a country should not discriminate between its trading partners (they are all, equally, granted "most-favoured-nation" or MFN status); and it should not discriminate between its own and foreign products, services, or nationals (they are given "national treatment").
2. *Freer* — with barriers coming down through negotiation.
3. *Predictable* — foreign companies, investors, and governments should be confident that trade barriers (including tariffs, nontariff barriers, and other measures) should not be raised arbitrarily; more and more tariff rates and market-opening commitments are "bound" in the WTO.
4. *More competitive* — by discouraging "unfair" practices such as export subsidies and dumping products at below cost to gain market share.
5. *More beneficial for less developed countries* — by giving them more time to adjust, greater flexibility, and special privileges.[7]

Trade Agreements

free trade area
Area established by agreement among two or more nations within which participants agree to free trade of goods and services among themselves.

Some countries decide to go further and make agreements to open their borders for trading with one another. The North American Free Trade Agreement (NAFTA) among Canada, the United States, and Mexico is an example of this. Even though inter-country trade was very large, each country agreed that it would be to the advantage of all to further simplify the process.

Different types of arrangements are used to achieve greater economic integration. The simplest approach is a **free trade area**, within which participants agree to free trade of goods and services among themselves. Normally such agreements are phased in over a period of time to allow companies in both countries to adjust. NAFTA is an example.

customs union
Agreement among two or more nations that establishes a free trade area, plus a uniform tariff for trade with nonmember nations.

A **customs union** establishes a free trade area, plus a uniform tariff for trade with nonmember nations. The former European Community (EC), comprising Belgium, Britain, Denmark, France, Germany, Greece, Ireland, Italy, Luxembourg, Portugal, The Netherlands, and Spain, is the best example of a customs union.

common market
A customs union that also allows factors of production such as labour, capital, and technology to flow freely among members.

As these nations gained experience, they went further and formed a **common market**. The common market is a customs union that also allows factors of production such as labour, capital, and technology to flow freely among members. Thus there are no restrictions on immigration and cross-border investment. Under a common market, this mobility of production factors allows them to be employed most productively.

economic union
A common market that also requires members to harmonize monetary policies, taxation, and government spending. In addition, a common currency is used by members.

In 1993, these nations went beyond a common market to form an **economic union**. The European Union (EU) officially came into being January 1, 1994. It goes beyond a common market and also requires members to harmonize monetary policies, taxation, and government spending. In addition, member countries use a common currency. The euro has been established and is being phased into use by EU members. The individual countries give up control of the value of their currency and social programs to some degree. A final step in this evolution would be a political union.

The European Union (EU) has results in a trading bloc that is unparallelled in history. It now constitutes a giant single market of nearly 400 million consumers. The rest of the world watches it with fascination and some nervousness. Some nations worry that the EU could turn into Fortress Europe, slamming the door on trade with its members.

The **North American Free Trade Agreement (NAFTA)** started with the Canada–U.S. **Free Trade Agreement (FTA)**. It reinforced the long-term trading relationship between Canada and the United States. Each country has traditionally been the other's biggest customer. NAFTA includes Mexico and builds on the trading and other relationships among the three countries.

In the world marketplace, the United States has been the target of many trading countries. This has resulted in serious negative trade balances for the United States. Gradually that country began to put significant restrictions on trade, restrictions that threatened Canadian business as well. In addition, the United States arbitrarily made judgements about whether Canadian firms were trading "fairly." The potential of further restrictions and arbitrary decisions encouraged Canada to negotiate the Free Trade Agreement, which had been under discussion.

All tariffs were scheduled to be gradually eliminated according to a timetable over a ten-year period. Companies can now bid on government procurement projects worth $25 000 (U.S.) or more in other countries. This now gives companies in each country access to government business through NAFTA. A Trade Commission was created to supervise the agreement. As well, a dispute settlement mechanism and panels of individuals to settle disputes were established.

NAFTA has created hardships for some industries as companies settle their operations in one country or another. On the other hand, it presents great opportunities for others who seek them out. The concept is now well enough accepted by the three member nations that further expansion is being undertaken. Canada has established a similar relationship with Chile, which is expected to become the fourth member of NAFTA, and other South American countries will be added as they develop economically and politically.

The evolution of the European Union and NAFTA has made other nations, such as Japan and other Asian countries, somewhat concerned about the possible negative effects of trading blocs on those on the outside. Asia Pacific countries have formed a working group called the Asia Pacific Economic Council (APEC) to consider economic matters. Canada and the United States are members of this group. It is too soon to tell whether APEC will develop into a trading bloc as well. There are a number of other regional trade agreements among the nations of the world.

The global marketplace is dynamic and exciting. It is clear that the growth of most firms will depend on some involvement in foreign marketing. The movement toward globalization of business is accelerating, and this will create many opportunities for the student of marketing who wants to be part of the world marketplace.

Trade Restrictions

Assorted trade restrictions can greatly affect world trade. These restrictions are most commonly expressed through tariffs. A **tariff** is a tax levied against prod-

North American Free Trade Agreement (NAFTA)
The agreement establishing a free trade area among Canada, the United States, and Mexico that followed the FTA.

Free Trade Agreement (FTA)
The agreement establishing a free trade area between Canada and the United States that preceded NAFTA.

tariff
A tax levied against products imported from abroad.

ucts imported from abroad. Some tariffs are based on a set tax per unit. Others are figured on the value of the imported product. Tariffs may be classified as either revenue or protective tariffs. *Revenue tariffs* are designed to raise funds for the government. Most of the Canadian government's revenue in the early years of Confederation came from this source. *Protective tariffs* are designed to raise the price of imported goods to that of similar domestic products or higher. In the past, it was believed that a country should protect its infant industries by using tariffs to keep out foreign-made products. Some foreign goods would still enter, but the addition of a high tariff payment would make the domestic products competitive. Protective tariffs are usually higher than revenue tariffs. Different interest groups argue about whether or not tariffs should be raised to protect employment and profits in domestic Canadian industry. It is debatable whether, in the long run, such a goal is obtainable through tariff protection.

import quota
A limit set on the amount of products that may be imported in a certain category.

There are other forms of trade restrictions. An **import quota** sets a limit on the amount of products that may be imported in a certain category. One country may use unofficial quotas to limit imports. When Canadian hog farmers began to take over the U.S. Midwest market, U.S. officials "discovered" that Canadian meat might have certain additives that might be "harmful" and, therefore, restricted imports. The objective of import quotas is to protect local industry and employment and preserve foreign exchange. The ultimate form of a quota is an **embargo**, a complete ban on importing a particular product. When British cattle began to suffer from mad cow disease, the whole world shuddered at the thought of humans contracting the disease. Therefore, most countries placed an embargo on British beef until they could be sure that it was safe.

embargo
A complete ban on importing a particular product.

Foreign trade can also be regulated by exchange control through a central bank or government agency. **Exchange control** means that firms gaining foreign exchange by exporting must sell their foreign exchange to the central bank or agency, and importers must buy foreign exchange from the same organization. The exchange control authority can then allocate, expand, or restrict foreign exchange according to existing national policy.

exchange control
Requirement that firms gaining foreign exchange by exporting must sell their foreign exchange to the central bank or agency, and importers must buy foreign exchange from the same organization.

Dumping—A Marketing Problem

In a battle between shoe manufacturers and retailers, Revenue Canada sided with Canadian manufacturers and imposed dumping charges on imported women's footwear from low-cost overseas producers. It was expected that between $22 million and $41 million in dumping charges would be imposed. Importers, including retailers, contended that most of the new charges will be passed on to consumers through price increases of up to 30 percent. Canadian show manufacturers argued that this estimate was much exaggerated.

dumping
Practice of selling products at significantly lower prices in a foreign market than in a nation's own domestic market.

The term **dumping** is applied to situations in which products are sold at significantly lower prices in a foreign market than in a nation's own domestic market. If foreign goods sell in Canada for substantially lower prices than Canadian products, the likely consequence is a loss of jobs here. Revenue Canada Customs and Excise Branch investigates alleged cases of dumping. If there is a preliminary determination of dumping, the Deputy Minister submits the finding to the Anti-Dumping Tribunal. The tribunal must make an inquiry within 90 days and issue a finding as to whether dumping is causing or likely to cause national injury to the production in Canada of like goods. This may lead to the imposition of anti-dumping duties by Customs and Excise. The tariff charge is designed

▶ THE CANADIAN MARKETPLACE

Battling for Trade

The powerful U.S. lumber industry says Canadian rivals are literally poking holes in boards to do an end-run around the Canada–U.S. lumber accord and it wants the loophole plugged.

The Washington-based Coalition for Fair Lumber Imports has mounted a fierce lobbying campaign to reverse an obscure U.S. Customs ruling that it says has spawned a booming cross-border trade in predrilled boards.

The fight has become so political that some now predict it could re-ignite one of the fiercest trade wars in Canada–U.S. history. Montana Senator Max Baucus warned recently that the board issue could strain relations and undo a landmark accord that ended years of sparring between the two countries.

"[In 1997 U.S. Customs] decided that a board with a small hole drilled in one end is not a board anymore," Mr. Baucus complained. "So Canadian mills are drilling lots of holes."

The Canadian government also intervened, arguing that U.S. Customs officials had put the studs in the right category in the first place.

At issue is whether a 2x4-inch or 2x6-inch board is considered lumber, and therefore subject to strict quotas and prohibitive export fees (from Canada), or "joinery and carpentry," which enters the United States virtually duty-free. The holes are used by electricians when they thread wiring through the wood frame of newly built homes.

Canfor Corp. of Vancouver won the right to export studs with predrilled holes to the United States under the more advantageous category.... A Canfor official denied that the company is deliberately trying to circumvent the lumber accord. "I wouldn't say there's a loophole," said Ralph Eastman. "There's a demand for our product and we are filling a need."

But John Ragosta, a Washington lawyer who leads the Coalition for Fair Lumber Imports, said lumber producers are abusing the system by shipping countless boards that are never used for their intended purpose by electricians. The coalition argues that boards with holes are priced the same as those without and are used for the same purpose. "The argument that 'we need these holes to put wires through' is just hokum," he said.

"It is a U.S. issue," said Jake Kerr, chairman and chief executive of Lignum Ltd., a sawmilling company, who speaks for the lumber industry. "We support the lumber agreement. We don't look on this as a loophole issue. This is a product that the U.S. Customs says is not part of the deal. I don't know what could be expected of us."

He added that the U.S. industry has no right to call the Canadian industry "a bad guy in the deal."

Who do you think is right? Is anyone "right"?

Source: Adapted from Barrie McKenna, "Lumber Battle Looms over Predrilled Studs," *The Globe and Mail* (March 5, 1998), pp. B1 and B6. Reprinted with permission from *The Globe and Mail*.

to protect Canadian business and employment by raising the product's price up to what it sells for in its home market.

Some critics have argued that fear of the dumping procedure and its tariff causes many foreign markets to keep their export prices higher than would normally be the case. The result, it is argued, is higher prices for the Canadian consumer. It is likely that dumping will remain a controversial topic in international trade for some time. Periodically, it is expected that countries will invoke dumping claims to protect industries that are suffering from international competition. International trade-regulating bodies, such as the World Trade Organization, will then have to resolve the issue.

▶ SUMMARY

Global business is one of the most important economic activities for Canada. It expands the market for a country's or firm's products. Some 11 000 new jobs are supported by every billion export dollars.

A nation's balance of trade is determined by the relationship between its exports and its imports. If a nation exports more than it imports, it has a favourable balance of trade. However, because of foreign travel and interest payments, the overall balance of payments may be negative.

The marketing mix in the global context could be similar to that at home, but is likely to be different because of the need to adjust to the environment in a foreign market.

Devaluation occurs when a nation reduces the value of its currency in relation to gold or some other currency. If a currency is devalued, it makes exports cheaper to other nations and imports more expensive to the importing country.

The concept of comparative advantage explains why it is beneficial for all nations to trade with one another. The concept says that countries prosper most by taking advantage of their assets in order to concentrate on what they can produce best, and then by trading these products for products that other countries produce best.

GATT was an international trade agreement to gradually lower tariffs among countries. It has been replaced with the World Trade Organization (WTO), the international body that deals with the rules of trade between nations. The WTO agreements have three main objectives: to encourage free trade, to further open international trade through negotiation, and to provide an impartial means of settling trade disputes between countries.

Dumping is a situation in which products are sold at significantly lower prices in a foreign market than in the producing nation's own domestic market. Countries try to penalize dumping because it creates unfair competition for their businesses.

The legal environment for Canadian firms operating abroad can be divided into three dimensions: Canadian law, international law, and the laws of host nations. All three are significant and must be understood and followed by the international marketer.

Four different approaches to involvement in international business are ethnocentric, polycentric, regiocentric, and geocentric. An ethnocentric approach is likely to be the least effective.

Firms can participate in the international market in a number of ways and to a lesser or greater extent. The lowest level of participation is indirect exporting and importing; the highest levels are joint ventures and foreign production and marketing.

World markets are being drawn together through various treaties among nations. Four significant types of trading arrangements have emerged: free trade area, customs union, common market, and economic union. The European Union is an economic union, making it one of the most powerful trade arrangements in the world.

For most countries, and especially Canada, international trade is essential to long-term prosperity and jobs. Canada's national policy promotes international trade wherever possible.

▶ KEY TERMS

absolute advantage
balance of payments
balance of trade
cartel
common market
comparative advantage
customs union
devaluation
direct international trade
direct investment
dumping
economic union
embargo
ethnocentric company
exchange control
exchange rate
Free Trade Agreement (FTA)

free trade area
friendship, commerce, and
   navigation (FCN) treaties
geocentric company
import quota
indirect international trade
joint venture
licensing
local content laws
multinational corporation (MNC)
North American Free Trade
   Agreement (NAFTA)
polycentric company
regiocentric company
revaluation
tariff
World Trade Organization (WTO)

▶ INTERACTIVE SUMMARY AND DISCUSSION QUESTIONS

1. Global business is one of the most important economic activities for Canada. Why is it important to Canadian firms? To the Canadian economy?

2. A nation's balance of trade is determined by the relationship between its exports and its imports. If a nation exports more than it imports, how can it have a negative balance of *payments?*

3. Is the marketing mix in the global context likely to be different from that in the domestic context?

4. Devaluation occurs when a nation reduces the value of its currency in relation to gold or some other currency. Explain how devaluation is likely to affect trade.

5. The concept of comparative advantage explains why it is beneficial for all nations to trade with one another. Comparative advantage is a *relative* concept. In *comparison with* nation B, what goods should nation A trade?

6. GATT was an international trade agreement to gradually lower tariffs among countries. The World Trade Organization is a much broader international trade-facilitating body. Why is international trade so important?

7. Dumping is a situation in which products are sold at significantly lower prices in a foreign market than in the producing nation's own domestic market. If countries are seeking to lower tariffs, and therefore prices, isn't dumping a good thing? Why or why not?

8. The legal environment for Canadian firms operating abroad can be divided into three dimensions: Canadian law, international law, and the laws of host

nations. What do Canadian law and international law have to do with business a Canadian company conducts in another country?

9. The concept of the marketing mix applies in international marketing just as it does in domestic marketing. However, marketing in a foreign country may not be the same as in Canada, even for the same product. Explain.

10. Four different approaches to involvement in international business are ethnocentric, polycentric, regiocentric, and geocentric. Explain each of these approaches.

11. World markets are being drawn together through various treaties among nations. Four significant types of trading arrangements have emerged: free trade area, customs union, common market, and economic union. Differentiate among the four.

12. Trade restrictions such as import quotas and embargoes may be employed to restrict or to stimulate international marketing activities. Why might a country do each of these, and what would be the effect?

13. Comment on the following statement: "It is sometimes dangerous for a firm to attempt to export its marketing strategy."

14. Give an example — hypothetical or actual — of a firm for each of the following approaches to international marketing. How would the marketing mix compare with that used in the home market?
    a. exporting in response to external demand
    b. ethnocentric approach
    c. polycentric approach
    d. regiocentric approach
    e. geocentric approach

15. The following business opportunity was listed in *CandExport:*

    > Singapore — a services and supplies company wishes to import *water treatment products for the pharmaceutical, food and beverages industries.* Contact Randy Yang, Marketing Manager Jelen Supplies and Services, Singapore. Tel_____; Fax _____; Telex _____.

    Assume that you work for a company that supplies such products. Outline the possible opportunities that such a venture might bring to your firm, and then list the possible problems. What steps should be taken to fully follow up on this advertisement?

16. Assume that you market a product in Canada on which there is a 20 percent U.S. tariff for such products coming from Canada and a 25 percent Canadian tariff for products coming from the United States. In two years the product will be tariff-free under the terms of NAFTA. What are the challenges and opportunities of such a change? What should your company do in anticipation of the change?

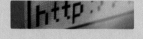

17. Assume that your company makes high-quality tennis, badminton, and squash racquets. It is considering the possibility of marketing them in Malaysia. Using the Internet, determine whether there would be a market for your products. Also, find out whether any restrictions or conditions have to be met to enter the Malaysian market.

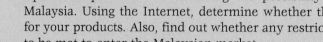

To obtain a list of further readings for Chapter 20, please refer to the *Foundations of Marketing* Web site.

COFFEE BREAK™

LA PAUSE-CAFÉ™

September 23 is Alzheimer
Coffee Break™ Day.

Brendan Shanahan, Star NHL hockey player with the Detroit Red
Wings and National Coffee Break™ spokesperson, would like your
help in raising money to fight Alzheimer Disease.
How can you help? Host a coffee break yourself. It's easy!
Call us at 1-800-616-8816 to receive your host kit.

Alzheimer *Society*

www.alzheimer.ca

Pfizer

National Patron

The Alzheimer Society recognizes that marketing is also essential for not-for-profit organizations. With its Coffee Break™ campaign, the Society turns an ordinary ritual of coffee drinking into a significant gesture of gift giving.

Sylvia Mitchell is expecting a few friends to drop in to Middleton Baptist Church for coffee. Actually, if things work out, about 150 local residents will come by, and each one will leave a few dollars in the collection box and pick up some pamphlets about Alzheimer's disease.

Mrs. Mitchell, whose 47-year-old husband, Steve, is suffering from the grave neurological disease, is hosting one of 12 000 Alzheimer's Coffee Breaks being held in Canada.

▶ **CHAPTER OBJECTIVES**
After reading and studying this chapter, you should be able to

1. Outline the primary characteristics of nonprofit organizations that distinguish them from profit-seeking organizations.
2. Show that marketing applies to nonprofit organizations in the same way it does to businesses.
3. Identify the main categories of marketing in nonprofit settings.
4. Apply the marketing mix to nonprofit settings.

The fundraiser is a prototype for successful charitable events, striking proof that it is still possible to carve out a niche in the highly competitive $10-billion-a-year fundraising field.

The idea underlying Coffee Break is devilishly simple: Sponsors, either individuals or corporations, invite people for coffee and ask for a small donation in return.

www.alzheimer.ca

"The secret of our success, I think, is that we have been able to transform an ordinary ritual into a significant gesture," said Andrea Olson, director of marketing, development and communications at the Alzheimer Society of Canada.

A simple habit, such as buying a cup of coffee, becomes a charitable act. And because most Coffee Breaks have an educational component, the event raises awareness not only of the Alzheimer Society but of a disease whose prevalence is increasing at an alarming rate.

For Terry Smethurst, whose mother-in-law is one of 250 000 Canadians with Alzheimer's, there is also powerful symbolism in drinking coffee, because people affected by the disease first lose their rituals and then their ability to communicate, things that most people take for granted.

"To me, it's a super idea because when you sit down for coffee, everybody talks about their problems," said Ms. Smethurst, who is hosting a Coffee Break at the Royal Canadian Legion Hall in Watrous, Sask.

"When you get talking, you realize how many people are affected, and maybe you can help them. That's probably more important than the money."

Last year, that Coffee Break raised $770, part of the $630 000 collected across the country. But, more important, it was one of 32 such events in the pharmacies, hair salons, fire halls, and churches of the small town, making Watrous the biggest per-capita fundraiser in the country.

At a time when many charities are abandoning long-time special events because they are being crowded out or their revenues are failing, Coffee Break has not only growth potential but the likelihood of a long life span. If every coffee drinker got into the habit of giving a loonie, to Coffee Break, for example, it would raise millions of dollars annually.

Like many fundraising events, it also has a corporate component. For example, National Public Relations Inc.—because one of the company's executives has a mother with Alzheimer's—provides hundreds of hours of high-priced marketing help gratis. All the printing and publicity also comes in the form of in-kind donations.

The Alzheimer Society has two corporate sponsors who make big cash donations and host king-size Coffee Breaks. Pfizer Canada Inc. of Kirkland, Que., makes the only drug available to treat the symptoms of Alzheimer's, and Imperial Life Financial (Desjardins-Laurentian Life Assurance in Quebec), as a big insurance company, knows the financial impact of a disease that is a $4-billion-a-year economic drain.

At Imperial Life, for example, most representatives will host a Coffee Break, and the celebration at corporate headquarters in Toronto will raise several thousand dollars.

Restaurants, big and small, are also coming on board quickly. This year, McDonald's restaurants in Quebec will add their marketing muscle to the cause. In Manitoba, the provincial restaurant association has enticed restaurants into giving a fixed percentage of their day's receipts to the charity.

Another staple of modern fundraising events is a celebrity spokesperson, and the Alzheimer Society has a powerful one in hockey star Brendan Shanahan.

The Detroit Red Wings player was 21 when he lost his father, Donal, to Alzheimer's, and he has lent his time and name to the cause in his honour because "I'm dedicated to continuing his fight." Mr. Shanahan is a big giver himself and will probably be passing the hat at the team's training camp.

For Mrs. Mitchell, who had never been involved in a fundraising event before hosting her Coffee Break, it is also about doing her part against a disease that devastates individuals and their families.

"Three years ago, I didn't know what I was getting into. I just said: 'I'm going to do it. I'm going to do it for Steve,'" she said.

The first year, she raised $700, the next $1100. In 1998, Mrs. Mitchell was joined by about 25 volunteers and her 6 children. (Her husband's illness is so advanced that he is in a nursing home.) She is also participating in a handful of other Coffee Breaks in the Annapolis Valley.

"The way I look at it, if we raise $100 or $1000, it will be more than we had the day before. That money will go to research and it will go to helping families. All those cups of coffee, it adds up."

The Coffee Break is part of a successful marketing program by the Alzheimer's Society that simultaneously raises funds, distributes educational material, and raises the profile of both Alzheimer's disease and the Society in the community.

Source: Adapted from André Picard, "Charity Made Easy," *The Globe and Mail* (September 24, 1998), pp. A1 and A4. Reprinted with permission from *The Globe and Mail*.

▶ INTRODUCTION

Too often, people look at the *advertising* that is done by nonprofit organizations (NPOs)[1] and equate it with marketing. By now, the reader will realize that marketing is much more than just advertising or selling. Marketing involves applying the entire marketing mix in accordance with a well-planned marketing strategy.

For example, the Alzheimer Society's products are Alzheimer's disease education and research. There are two target markets for this organization: potential donors and those who need to be educated. Because of this, the Society has two highly interrelated marketing strategies. Both education and research are in accord with people's needs for health information and medical care, but if support for the Society's efforts is to continue, the public must perceive the Society's products to be valuable.

Potential donor segments must be identified in order to appeal to the various motivations in the population. For those who have family members or friends with Alzheimer's, fear of the disease might be a motivation. Others may simply recognize that this is a worthy cause. Corporate donors may have less obvious motivations to which the Society should appeal. Marketing research may be necessary to develop a complete picture of the factors that would create a favourable response to an appeal for funds. The two major corporate donors mentioned in the opening vignette appear to have a direct stake in controlling Alzheimer's disease.

Marketing research may also be needed in order to learn how best to communicate current findings and advice concerning Alzheimer's disease and to distribute appeal literature.

Other tasks for the Society are to find, manage, and motivate the thousands of volunteers who collect funds for its work. This process has some similarities to sales management in a profit organization but is broader in scope, especially since motivating volunteers is different from motivating paid employees.

Above all, proper marketing planning will greatly improve the direction and effectiveness of this nonprofit organization. Not only has the Alzheimer Society discovered the benefits of this approach, but many other nonprofit organizations have also successfully applied marketing thinking to their efforts.

In Chapter 1, marketing was defined as the process of planning and executing the conception, pricing, promotion, and distribution of ideas, goods, and services to create exchanges that satisfy individual and organizational objectives. Although much of the text up to now has concentrated on organizations that operate for profit, the activities of the Alzheimer Society are as representative of modern marketing activities as are the marketing programs of IBM, Wendy's, and Maple Leaf Foods. Our definition of marketing is sufficiently comprehensive to encompass nonprofit as well as profit-seeking organizations.

A substantial portion of our economy is composed of **nonprofit organizations (NPOs)**—those whose primary objective is something other than returning a profit to their owners. An estimated one of every ten service workers and one of six professionals are employed in the nonprofit sector. The nonprofit sector includes thousands of religious organizations, social service organizations, museums, libraries, colleges and universities, symphony orchestras and other music organizations, and organizations such as government agencies, political parties, and labour unions.

Nonprofit organizations can be found in both public and private sectors of society. In the public sector, federal, provincial, and local governmental units and agencies whose revenues are derived from tax collection have service objectives that are not keyed to profitability targets. One part of Foreign Affairs

nonprofit organization (NPO)
Organization whose primary objective is something other than returning a profit to its owners.

The primary objective of nonprofit organizations is something other than profit.

Reprinted with special permission of King Features Syndicate.

"We're a nonprofit organization—we don't intend to be, but we are!"

and International Trade Canada, for instance, provides services that facilitate exports of Canadian products. A provincial department of natural resources regulates conservation and environmental programs. The local animal control officer enforces ordinances that protect both people and animals.

Some public-sector agencies may be given revenue or behaviour goals. An urban-transit system might be expected to pay a great deal of its costs out of revenues, for example. But society does not expect these units to routinely produce a surplus that is returned to taxpayers.

▸ THE PRACTISING MARKETER

Improving Transit Service
Seattle-area commuters no longer have to stare at the horizon and wonder how long it will be before the next bus pulls up. In selected stations around the city, they can simply check an airport-style ARRIVALS screen and go back to their papers.

The new Transit Watch kiosks use an existing system for tracking the fleet via radio transmissions. Buses send back signals that tell how far they've travelled on their routes. Transit Watch takes the data and uses the history of the route to estimate arrival times, refreshing the information every 30 seconds.

Two kiosks were installed at busy stops in June and November 1998. Two more are being added at a plant of corporate partner Boeing. And Seattle isn't the only city trying to keep the commuters happy. Atlanta, Blacksburg, Va., and Ann Arbor, Mich., also have real-time bus-information systems.

"People come away from these kiosks with the idea that the system is running better," says state transit official Pete Briglia, "even though you haven't really given them anything other than information."

Mr. Briglia implies that the arrivals screens are not actually helping the system run better but merely give the appearance of running better. From a marketing perspective, do you agree? Is there a difference? Can you relate these issues to the gap model of service quality discussed in Chapter 12?

Source: "Magical Bus Stops," *Time Digital* (May 24, 1999), p. 7. Reprinted with permission.

The private sector offers an even more diverse array of nonprofit settings. Art institutes, churches, labour unions, private schools, the United Way, the Rotary Club, and the local country club all serve as examples of private-sector, nonprofit organizations. The diversity of these settings suggests how pervasive organizational objectives other than profitability really are in a modern economy.

The market offering of the nonprofit organization is frequently more nebulous than the tangible goods or service provisions of profit-seeking firms. Table 21.1 lists social issues and ideas, ranging from family planning to using motorcycle helmets, that represent the offerings made by some nonprofit organizations to their publics.

The diversity of these issues suggests the size of the nonprofit sector and the marketing activities involved in accomplishing the objectives of these organizations. They are different from their profit-seeking counterparts in a number of ways.

> **TABLE 21.1 Social Issues Marketed by Nonprofit Organizations**

Abortion rights	Fire prevention	911 (emergency number)
Affirmative action	Fluoridation	Nonsmokers' rights
Alcoholism control	Forest fire prevention	Nuclear energy
Birth defects	Foster parenthood	Physical fitness
Blood	Fraternal organizations	Police, support of
Blue laws	Free enterprise	Pollution control
Buy Canadian goods	Freedom of the press	Population control
Cancer research	French immersion	Prison reform
Capital punishment	Gay rights	Religion
CARE packages	Housing cooperatives	Right to life
Carpooling	Legalized gambling	Save the whales
Child abuse	Literacy	Seatbelt use
Child adoption	Littering prevention	Solar energy
Consumer cooperatives	Mass transportation	STD hotline
Crime prevention	Mental health	Suicide hotline
Drunk driving	Metric system	Tax reform
Energy conservation	Military recruiting	UNICEF
Euthanasia	Motorcycle helmets	United Way
Family planning	Museums	

Source: Most of these issues are listed in Seymour H. Fine, *The Marketing of Ideas and Social Issues* (New York: Praeger, 1981), pp. 13–14. Copyright © 1981 by Praeger Publishers, New York. Reprinted by permission of Greenwood Publishing Group, Inc., Westport, CT.

▶ CHARACTERISTICS OF NONPROFIT ORGANIZATIONS

Nonprofit organizations have a special set of characteristics that affect their marketing activities. Like the profit-oriented service offerings discussed in Chapter 12, *the product offered by a nonprofit organization is often intangible*. A hospital's diagnostic services exhibit marketing problems similar to those inherent in marketing a life insurance policy.

A second feature of nonprofit organizations is that *they must deal with multiple publics*. As Professor Philip Kotler points out,

Nonprofit organizations normally have at least two major publics to work with from a marketing point of view: their clients and their funders. The former pose the problem of *resource allocation* and the latter, the problem of *resource attraction*. Besides these two publics, many other publics surround the nonprofit organization and call for marketing programs. Thus a college can direct marketing programs toward prospective students, current students, parents of students, alumni, faculty, staff, local business firms, and local government agencies. It turns out the business organizations also deal with a multitude of publics but their tendency is to think about marketing only in connection with one of the publics, namely their customers.[2]

A customer or service user *may have less influence than a customer of a profit-seeking (or for-profit) firm.* A government employee may be far more concerned with the opinion of a member of the Cabinet than with that of a service user. Furthermore, nonprofit organizations often possess some degree of monopoly power in a given geographical area. As an individual, a person might object to the local United Way's inclusion of a crisis centre among its supported agencies, but as a contributor who accepts the merits of the United Way appeal, this same person recognizes that a portion of total contributions will go to the agency in question.

▸ THE PRACTISING MARKETER

The United Way's Statement of Principles for Donors' Rights
The donor participates in the very essence of our mission and purpose, exercises rights, prerogatives, and fundamental privileges that must be recognized at all times and without reservation.

This document was approved by the membership of United Way of Canada–Centraide Canada at its March 1998 Annual General Meeting. Member United Ways–Centraides are expected to comply with these guidelines. These guidelines were developed for United Ways–Centraides in Canada.

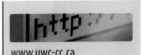

www.uwc-cc.ca

- The right to be informed of the organization's mission and purpose and to become a member of the organization if the donor so wishes;
- The right to know the identity of the organization's officers and members of the Board of Directors and to expect that they act with the greatest transparency, integrity, and discernment in implementing the organization's mission and purpose for the best interests of the community;
- The right to have access to the organization's annual financial statements and to easily obtain a copy;
- The right to know how donations, directly or indirectly contributed to the organization, are distributed, and to be assured that donated funds are used as intended by the donor;
- The right to be treated with consideration and respect by the organization and to receive appropriate acknowledgment and recognition;
- The right to confidentiality regarding personal information about donors and facts about their donations;
- The right to expect that all relationships between the organization's representatives and the donor will be professional in nature;
- The right to be informed of the exact nature of the relationship that exists between fundraisers and the organization;
- The right to expect that the organization will not share or sell a mailing list that includes the donor's name, without providing the donor with a meaningful opportunity to decline;
- The right to ask questions of the organization and to expect prompt, truthful, and complete answers in an easy-to-understand manner.

Why might the United Way have decided that a statement of principles of donors' rights was necessary?

Source: United Way, "Statement of Principles for Donors' Rights," http://www.unitedway.ca/english/docs/principles_of_donors_rights.html, downloaded June 15, 1999. Reprinted with permission.

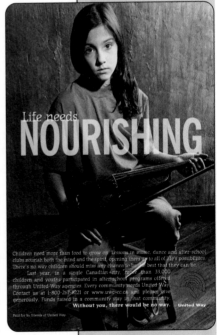

The United Way, like other nonprofit organizations, is responsible not only to its service users (clients) but also to its funders (those whom the organization must attract for donations).

Another problem involves *the resource contributor, such as a legislator or a financial backer, who interferes with the marketing program.* It is easy to imagine a political candidate harassed by financial supporters who want to replace an unpopular campaign manager (the primary marketing position in a political campaign).

Perhaps the most commonly noted feature of the nonprofit organization is its lack of a **bottom line**, which refers to the overall-profitability measure of performance. That is, *nonprofit organizations have goals other than profit.* While a nonprofit organization may attempt to maximize its return from a specific service, less measurable goals such as service level standards are the usual substitute for an overall evaluation. The net result is that it is often difficult to set marketing objectives that are in line with overall organizational goals.

Another characteristic is the *lack of a single clear organizational structure.* Nonprofit organizations refer to constituencies that they serve, but these are often considerably less exact than the shareholders of a profit-oriented corporation. Nonprofit organizations often have multiple organizational structures. A hospital might have an administrative structure, a professional organization consisting of medical personnel, and a volunteer organization that dominates the board of trustees. These people may sometimes work at cross-purposes and not be totally in line with the marketing strategy that has been devised.[3]

A final characteristic of the nonprofit sector is that it is sometimes inefficient. Often two or more NPOs work toward the same "cause." For example, there may be several affirmative-action groups. Religious organizations, many with very similar objectives, abound and overlap. This could be seen as a duplication or multiplication of efforts. Clearly, however, there is competition in many cases, and the competition is not only to win a larger portion of the client target market. In fundraising, the same types of NPOs sometimes compete for donor support. In addition, competition for personnel, such as fundraisers, occurs.

While the above factors may also characterize some profit-oriented organizations, they are certainly prevalent in nonprofit settings. These characteristics affect the implementation of marketing efforts in such organizations and must be considered in the development of an overall strategy.

▶ TYPES OF NONPROFIT MARKETING

Although nonprofit organizations are at least as varied as profit-seeking organizations, it is possible to categorize them based on the type of marketing each requires. The three major types of marketing among NPOs are person marketing, social marketing, and organization marketing.

Person Marketing

Person marketing refers to efforts designed to cultivate the attention, interest, and preference of a target market toward a person.[4] This type of marketing is typically employed by political candidates and celebrities.

bottom line
The overall-profitability measure of performance.

person marketing
Efforts designed to cultivate the attention, interest, and preference of a target market toward a person.

▶ THE ROOTS OF MARKETING

The History of the United Way

The United Way–Centraide (UW-C) movement had its roots in Canada in the early part of the twentieth century. At that time, Catholic, Protestant, and Jewish charities began to raise funds to strengthen their communities. Over the years, the UW-C was known as the Red Feather, the Community Chest, and the United Appeal. In the 1970s, these organizations adopted the name of United Way and Centraide. Since the mid-70s, the UW-C movement in Canada has grown and adapted quickly to embrace the diversity of evolving communities.

- 1887 first United Community campaign organized in Denver, Colorado
- 1917 federated campaigns began in Montreal and Toronto
- 1922 federation for community service began in Winnipeg
- 1935 Red Feather started in Quebec City and the Community Chest in Regina
- 1939 a national organization began
- 1945 there were 36 federations raising $7 182 787
- 1950 there were 65 federations
- 1957 adoption of the national association title "Community Funds and Councils of Canada"
- 1972 Community Funds and Councils of Canada became incorporated on April 1st and became a separate body from the Canadian Council on Social Development
- 1973 adoption of the name United Way
- 1974 in November, the national association name was changed to United Way of Canada
- 1975 adoption of the name Centraide
- 1978 United Way of Canada and the Canadian Council on Social Development had completely separated
- 1978 United Way of Canada–Centraide Canada signed a formal agreement with United Way of America through United Way International
- 1979 there were over 70 UWs-Cs raising $84 872 760
- 1996 the UW-C hand symbol was registered in Canada
- 1998 there are 126 UWs-Cs across Canada who raised in 1997 $266 212 479 (5 percent increase over previous year) to fund more than 4300 agencies/programs and directed gifts to more than 10 000 organizations

What is distinctive about the United Way that has allowed it to be so successful in attracting donations over the years? Why are other charities not able to duplicate this success?

Source: United Way, "History," http://www.unitedway.ca/english/index.cfm?area=6, downloaded June 18, 1999. Reprinted with permission.

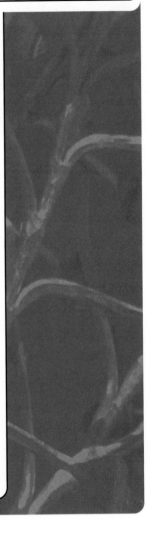

Leadership campaigns for political parties are good examples of person marketing. Serious contenders conduct research into the various voter segments and develop strategies to reach them. Similarly, in a profit-seeking setting, various musicians are carefully marketed to subsegments of the total market. The marketing mix for marketing Shania Twain is different from that for Céline Dion.

Social Marketing

The second type of nonprofit marketing deals with causes and social issues rather than an individual. **Social marketing** refers to "the analysis, planning,

social marketing
The analysis, planning, execution, and evaluation of programs designed to influence the voluntary behaviour of target audiences in order to improve their personal welfare and that of society.

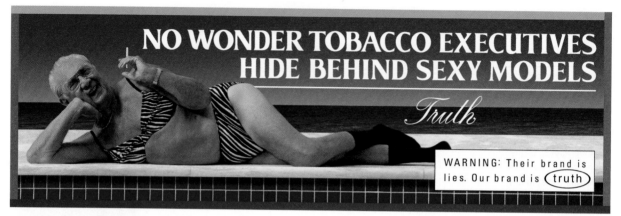

Antismoking campaigns like this one are examples of social marketing that have, in recent years, used hardhitting, controversial messages to get people to give up the health-hazardous habit.

execution, and evaluation of programs designed to influence the voluntary behaviour of target audiences in order to improve their personal welfare and that of society."[5]

Social marketing is distinct from other forms of marketing, including other forms of nonprofit marketing, in that its goal is explicitly and singularly to work to the benefit of the target audience by influencing the target audience's behaviour.

The importance of wearing sunscreen is an idea currently being marketed in several countries. Antismoking marketing programs have been so successful that many people have quit smoking, and legislation has been passed that forbids smoking in public places.

Organization Marketing

organization marketing Attempts to influence others to accept the goals of, receive the services of, or contribute in some way to an organization.

The third type of nonprofit marketing, **organization marketing**, attempts to influence others to accept the goals of, receive the services of, or contribute in some way to an organization. Included in this category are *mutual benefit* organizations, such as churches, labour unions, and political parties; *service* organizations, such as colleges, universities, hospitals, and museums; and *government* organizations, such as military services, police and fire departments, the post office, and local communities.[6]

> ## ▶ UNDERSTANDING OF MARKETING BY NONPROFIT ORGANIZATIONS

Nonprofit organizations often have too limited an understanding of marketing. In many cases, marketing is taken to mean simply marketing communications. Developing well-thought-out marketing strategy, as well as considering other components of the marketing mix — product development, distribution, and pricing strategies — have too often been largely ignored. Marketing, considered and practised merely as aggressive promotion, is a short-lived, surface-level solution to a variety of organizational problems and objectives. For instance, one university decided to "adopt marketing" and thought it was doing so by planning to release balloons containing scholarship offers. And a "marketing planning" conference for a private school consisted mainly of developing new slogans for advertisements.

Professor Seymour H. Fine conducted a survey of nonprofit organizations to assess the degree of marketing sophistication present. His findings, illustrated in Table 21.2, revealed that many respondents were unaware of, or at least reluctant to admit, the presence of marketing efforts in their organization. Although this study was done some time ago, it is fair to say that nonprofit appreciation of the benefits of marketing still lacks that of profit-oriented firms.

> ▶ **TABLE 21.2 Responses of Selected Nonprofit Organization Representatives**

NONPROFIT ORGANIZATION	RESPONSE TO THE QUESTION "DO YOU HAVE A MARKETING DEPARTMENT OR EQUIVALENT?"
Public health service official	"Marketing fluoridation is not a function of government—promotion and public awareness is."
Administrator of regional women's rights group	"We have never thought of ourselves as marketing a product. We have people who are assigned equal pay for work of equal value as their 'item.'"
Group crusading for the rights of the left-handed	"Don't understand the term [marketing]; we do lobbying, letter writing to appropriate government and commercial concerns."
A national centre for the prevention of child abuse	"We disseminate information without the marketing connotation. Besides, demand is too great to justify marketing."
Recruiting officer	"Not applicable."

Source: Adapted from Seymour H. Fine, *The Marketing of Ideas and Social Issues* (New York: Praeger, 1981), p. 53. Copyright © 1981 by Praeger Publishers, New York. Used by permission of Greenwood Publishing Group, Inc., Westport, CT.

Nonprofit organizations need to take the time to develop a comprehensive marketing approach. One university, for example, conducted a comprehensive marketing audit that designated strong and weak areas in its product mix (program offerings). It was then possible to develop strategies after the basic parameters of market, resources, and mission had been identified and analyzed.

▶ IMPORTANCE OF MARKETING TO NONPROFIT ORGANIZATIONS

Marketing as a recognized function is a late arrival to managing nonprofit organizations. The practices of improved accounting, financial control, personnel selection, and strategic planning were all implemented before formal marketing planning. Nevertheless, nonprofit organizations have begun to accept marketing enthusiastically. For example, university administrators attend seminars and conferences to learn how to better market their institutions.

Marketing's rise in the nonprofit sector could not be continued without a successful track record. While it is often more difficult to measure results in nonprofit settings, marketing can already point to examples of success. The Church of the Nazarene in Canada, for instance, has used a telemarketing campaign called "Phones for You" to develop a target clientele interested in supporting the start of new churches. And one art gallery's marketing analysis resulted in defining two distinct market segments it should serve. Marketing is increasingly an accepted part of the operational environment of successful nonprofit organizations. Table 21.3 presents a hypothetical job description for a marketing director at a university.

▶ DEVELOPING A MARKETING STRATEGY

The need for comprehensive marketing planning and control rather than a mere increase in marketing communications expenditures has already been noted. Substantial opportunities exist for effective, innovative strategies, since there has been little previous marketing effort in most nonprofit settings.

Marketing Research

Many decisions in nonprofit settings (as well as in business) are based on little, if any, research. For example, numerous Canadian art galleries arbitrarily establish programs and schedules with little or no reference to audience marketing research. In contrast, the Victoria Symphony (see the Practising Marketer box) was motivated and informed by market research.

Adequate marketing research can be extremely important in a variety of nonprofit settings. Resident opinion surveys in some cities have proven valuable to public officials.[7] Analyzing projected population trends has led school boards to build new schools and to phase out others.

Product Strategy

www.redcross.ca

Nonprofit organizations face the same product decisions as profit-seeking firms. They must choose a product, service, person, idea, or social issue to be offered to their target market. They must decide whether to offer a single product or a mix of related products. They must make product identification decisions. The fact that the United Way symbol and the Red Cross trademark are as familiar as the golden arches of McDonald's or the Shell logo illustrates the similarity in the use of product identification methods.

TABLE 21.3 Job Description: Director of Marketing for a University

Position Title: Director of Marketing

Reports to: A vice-president designated by the president

Scope: University-wide

Position Concept: The director of marketing is responsible for providing marketing guidance and services to university officers, school deans, department chairpersons, and other agents of the university

Functions: The director of marketing will
1. Contribute a marketing perspective to the deliberations of the top administration in its planning of the university's future
2. Prepare data that might be needed by any officer of the university on a particular market's size, segments, trends, and behavioural dynamics
3. Conduct studies of the needs, perceptions, preferences, and satisfaction of particular markets
4. Assist in the planning, promotion, and launching of new programs
5. Assist in the development of communication and promotion campaigns and materials
6. Analyze and advise on pricing questions
7. Appraise the workability of new academic proposals from a marketing point of view
8. Advise on new student recruitment
9. Advise on current student satisfaction
10. Advise on university fundraising

Responsibilities: The director of marketing will
1. Contact individual officers and small groups at the university to explain services and to solicit problems
2. Rank the various requests for services according to their long-run impact, cost-saving potential, time requirements, ease of accomplishment, cost, and urgency
3. Select projects of high priority and set accomplishment goals for the year
4. Prepare a budget request to support the anticipated work
5. Prepare an annual report on the main accomplishments of the office

Major Liaisons: The director of marketing will
1. Relate most closely with the president's office, admissions office, development office, planning office, and public relations department
2. Relate secondarily with the deans of various schools and chairpersons of various departments

Source: Philip Kotler, "Strategies for Introducing Marketing into Nonprofit Organizations," *Journal of Marketing* (January 1979), p. 42. Reprinted by permission of the American Marketing Association.

Recognizing that classical music can be intimidating or considered just plain boring, the Victoria Symphony adjusted its program mix to appeal to wider audiences while staying in harmony with its mission. A common failure among nonprofit organizations is assuming that heavy promotional efforts can overcome a poor product strategy or marketing mix. For example, some liberal arts colleges tried to use promotion to overcome their product mix deficiencies when students became increasingly career-oriented. Successful institutions adjust their product offerings to reflect customer demand.

▶ THE PRACTISING MARKETER

kafka.uvic.ca/~fa225/
STUDENT/HELEN/
Symphony.html

To attract a young audience and guarantee future audiences, the Victoria Symphony revamped its sedate message and created this advertisement.

Check out the awesome power of classical music! a highly energetic, learn as much as you can, totally non-conventional concert to preview our season.

All for just $9.99

If you like what you hear and purchase season tickets in September, we'll give you the Test Drive price back!

Friday
August 27 at 8pm
Farquhar Aditorium,
UVic Centre

Saturday
August 28 at 8pm
Royal Theatre

Call 385-6515
or 386-6121

Media Partner

VICTORIA SYMPHONY

The Victoria Symphony's Marketing Approach

Bums in the seats. That's the objective of every performing arts publicist. And in these days of declining disposable income and increasing competition for entertainment dollars, publicists are, by necessity, becoming conspicuously creative in their quest to fill houses.

Discounts, theme shows, singles nights—you name it, they're doing it.

For the Victoria Symphony, a 1997 marketing study, which looked at audience stats, served as a wake-up call, says marketing and public relations coordinator Adrienne Holierhoek.

"There were some striking findings," she says. For example, "we have a serious portion of our subscribers over 80, so 10 years from now, it's realistic to think our audience could drop significantly."

At the same time, she notes, symphonies across the country have been jolted into economic reality by the demise of a number of significant orchestras.

"Watching them drop like flies is scary.... I think it's a wakeup call right across the country."

While the local orchestra is still on top of its game, Holierhoek and symphony management have realized they'd better start taking some preventative measures before it's too late.

"We need to catch the eye—or ear—of younger people now, to guarantee future audiences," she says.

With that in mind, the symphony completely revamped its programming for the 1998–99 season. Instead of the sedate-sounding Grand Masters, Classics, Great Romantics, and Pops series of previous years, the program featured titles like Passion for Classics and Enchanted by the Masters—concerts designed for the serious classical music lover.

The bestselling Pops series remained unchanged. And the symphony has a whole new series for sale—Rendezvous with Friends, which features "snippets that people will know, put together in a thematic way," says Holierhoek. "We try not to water down what we do but, rather, to take the essence of what we do and put it in a context for people who may not be as familiar with the classics."

The five-part concert series features theme nights like an all-Mozart program, storm scenes, comic symphonies, and an evening of grand finales.

"It's a real risk for us, but we needed to do something to bring new audiences in." To further that purpose, the symphony came up with another new hook in 1998—the Test Drive the Symphony concert, Friday at UVic.

"That's a way of taking all these new things and saying, 'Look what we've done,'" says Holierhoek. "If you look through the brochure and it looks like a whole bunch of mumbo jumbo to you, then come to this concert."

Under the baton of Brian Jackson, the orchestra will play samples of each of the upcoming concert series, with commentary in between.

"It's not going to be a two-hour sales pitch," says Holierhoek. "But we're expecting a lot if people there to be newcomers to the symphony, so they'll probably pick up a few things that they didn't know—about instruments, about acoustics, about UVic, about music."

And if audience members like what they hear well enough to subscribe to the symphony, they'll get their $9.99 back.

Is there a symphony orchestra or other performing arts group in your area? What strategies are those organizations using to attract new audiences? What suggestions could you offer them?

Source: Adapted from Diane Dakers, "Marketing 101," *Times Colonist* (August 27, 1998), p. D1. Reprinted with permission.

Pricing Strategy

Pricing is typically a very important element of the marketing mix for nonprofit organizations. For its "Test Drive" concert, the Victoria Symphony set a price at about one-half to one-third the regular ticket price to encourage participation — plus that ticket price could count toward a future subscription.

Pricing strategy can be used to accomplish a variety of organizational goals in nonprofit settings. These include

- *Profit maximization.* While nonprofit organizations by definition do not cite profitability as a primary goal, there are numerous instances in which they do try to maximize their return on a single event or a series of events. The $1000-a-plate political fundraiser is an example.
- *Cost recovery.* Some nonprofit organizations attempt to recover only their actual cost of operating. Mass transit, colleges, and airports are common examples. The amount of recovered cost is often dictated by tradition, competition, or public opinion.
- *Providing market incentives.* Other nonprofit groups follow a penetration pricing policy or offer a free service to encourage increased usage of the product or service. Winnipeg's bus system policy of free fares on special "Dash" buses in the downtown area reduces traffic congestion, encourages retail sales, and minimizes the effort required to use downtown public services.
- *Market suppression (demand deterrance).* Price is sometimes used to discourage consumption. In other words, high prices are used to accomplish social objectives and are not directly related to the costs of providing the product or service. Illustrations of suppression include tobacco and alcohol taxes, parking fines, tolls, and gasoline excise taxes.[8]

▸ THE PRACTISING MARKETER

It Seemed Like a Good Idea ...

Call it a failed experiment in charity. You'll see plenty of people dropping donations into the collection boxes scattered around Almudena Cathedral in Madrid. But hardly anyone stops at the credit-card machine by the doorway—people prefer handing over money the old-fashioned way.

The cathedral, which sits next to the Royal Palace, opened in 1993 after 110 years of construction, but its interior is still unfinished. Hoping to increase donations, the church had the credit-card machine installed last year, but fewer than a dozen people a month have used it.

Well, it *sounded* like a good idea: the machine was proposed by a credit-card company, which figured that since credit cards were so popular in Spain—outpacing even personal cheques as the preferred method of payment—people would take to the cash-free charity box.

It's scheduled to be removed shortly. Just hope church officials resist the remote-videocam-confessional-booth idea.

Why might visitors to a cathedral be reluctant to use credit cards to make contributions? How might market research have prevented this mistake from happening?

Source: "Church Disses Credit," *Time Digital* (May 24, 1999), p. 7. Reprinted with permission.

Distribution Strategy

Distribution channels for nonprofit organizations tend to be short, simple, and direct. If intermediaries are present in the channel, they are usually agents, such as an independent ticket agency or a specialist in fundraising. Even so, there are opportunities for creativity. For its "Test Drive the Symphony" concert, the Victoria Symphony performed in a different venue. Also, every summer the orchestra rents a barge and performs from Victoria's harbour, while the audience sits on lawnchairs or blankets on the banks.

Nonprofit organizations often fail to exercise caution in planning and executing the distribution strategy. For example, organizers of recycling centres sometimes complain about lack of public interest when their real problem is an inconvenient location or lack of adequate drop-off points. In a number of cities, this problem has been solved by dropping blue boxes off at people's homes. By contrast, some public agencies, like health and social welfare departments, have set up branches in neighbourhood shopping centres to be more accessible to their clientele. Nonprofit marketers must carefully evaluate the available distribution options if they are to be successful in delivering their products or in serving their intended consumers.

Marketing Communications Strategy

It is common to see or hear advertisements from nonprofit organizations such as educational institutions, churches, and public service organizations.

Marketing communications are affected by a variety of factors, including relative involvement in the nonprofit setting, pricing, and perceived benefits.[9] But overall, marketing communications are seen by many nonprofit managers as the primary solution to their marketing problems. As noted earlier, this view is often naive, but it does not diminish the importance of this mix element in a nonprofit setting.

www.recruiting.dnd.ca

All types of marketing communications elements have been used. The Canadian Armed Forces has used television advertising to attract recruits. Fundraising for some support groups for the handicapped is done through personal selling over the telephone. Volunteers are an essential part of the marketing program for many nonprofit organizations. They are used to "sell" (canvass) by phone or in person. Such individuals pose a significant "sales management" problem. With a paid sales force, it is easy to demand certain behaviour on the part of personnel or to provide various financial incentives to affect their behaviour. Similar methods are not as readily available with volunteers. Other stimulation and incentives, such as public recognition or receptions, are used as substitutes. Even so, it is unlikely that the same effects can be achieved.

Advertising is a desirable marketing communications option. However, because the cost of media is high, fundraising drives often rely on publicity and public relations efforts, such as appearances on TV talk shows, to promote their product. In the Victoria Symphony's case, in addition to print ads, the orchestra benefited from the publicity of the in-depth newspaper article reproduced in the Practising Marketer box.

▶ THE FUTURE OF NONPROFIT MARKETING

While marketing has gained increasing acceptance in the nonprofit sector of society, it is still viewed with suspicion by some of the people involved. The heavy emphasis on marketing communications is one reason. Marketing efforts in nonprofit organizations often lack the sophistication and integration found in the marketing of profit-oriented industries. Marketing is too often seen as the "quick-fix" solution to a more basic problem. To combat this, nonprofit marketers must market their own discipline in a realistic and socially responsible manner. The client must be helped to understand the opportunities, benefits, behaviour modifications, and commitment involved in adopting the marketing concept in a nonprofit setting.

▶ SUMMARY

A nonprofit organization is one whose primary objective is something other than returning a profit to its owners. The marketing mix is just as applicable to not-for-profit marketing as it is to for-profit marketing.

The special characteristics of nonprofit organizations are as follows:

- often intangible product
- often dealing with multiple publics
- customer may have less influence than a customer of a profit-seeking organization
- lack of a bottom line
- lack of a single clear organizational structure
- inefficient operation

Three types of marketing among NPOs are person marketing, social marketing, and organization marketing. Market suppression, or demand deterrence, is sometimes practised in nonprofit marketing.

▶ KEY TERMS

bottom line
nonprofit organization (NPO)
organization marketing

person marketing
social marketing

▶ INTERACTIVE SUMMARY AND DISCUSSION QUESTIONS

1. A nonprofit organization is one whose primary objective is something other than returning a profit to its owners. Give an example of other core objectives that such organizations could have.

2. Explain how each of the following special characteristics of nonprofit organizations might affect the way nonprofit organizations practise marketing.
   a. often intangible product
   b. often dealing with multiple publics
   c. customer may have less influence than a customer of a profit-seeking organization
   d. lack of a bottom line
   e. lack of a single clear organizational structure
   f. inefficient operation

3. Three types of marketing among NPOs are person marketing, idea marketing, and organization marketing. For which of these would the application of marketing principles be the most difficult? Explain.

4. The marketing mix is just as applicable to not-for-profit marketing as it is to for-profit marketing. Would there be any differences in applying the marketing mix in the case of not-for-profit marketing? Use examples to explain your answer.

5. Market suppression, or demand deterrence, is sometimes practised in non-profit marketing. Give examples of this. Which of the elements of the marketing mix would most likely be applicable in accomplishing market suppression?

6. Cite several examples of circumstances in which penetration pricing might be practised by public utilities.

7. How would you assess the marketing performance of the following?
   a. your college or university
   b. Canadian Postal Workers Union
   c. Planned Parenthood
   d. the re-election committee of a local politician

8. Outline the marketing program of your college or university. Make any reasonable assumptions necessary. Where are the major strengths and weaknesses of the current program? What recommendations would you make for improvement?

9. Why might there be a greater tendency for a nonprofit organization to define marketing inaccurately?

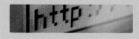

10. Visit the Web sites of two nonprofit organizations and two for-profit organizations. How are they similar? How are they different? What do you think accounts for the differences?

To obtain a list of further readings for Chapter 21, please refer to the *Foundations of Marketing* Web site.

Notes

Chapter 1

1. Peter F. Drucker, *The Practice of Management* (New York: Harper and Row, 1954), p. 37.
2. Richard P. Bagozzi, "Marketing as an Organized Behavioral System of Exchange," *Journal of Marketing* (October 1974), p. 77. Further work by Bagozzi on this subject appears in "Marketing as Exchange," *Journal of Marketing* (October 1975), pp. 32–39, and in "Marketing as Exchange: A Theory of Transactions in the Marketplace," *American Behavioral Scientist* (March–April 1978), pp. 535–36.
3. Richard P. Bagozzi, "Marketing as an Organized Behavioral System of Exchange," p. 77.
4. Wroe Alderson, *Marketing Behavior and Executive Action* (Homewood, IL: Irwin, 1957), p. 292.
5. "AMA Board Approves New Marketing Definition," *Marketing News* (March 1, 1985), p. 1.
6. Many discussions of this topic have suggested that marketing passed through a series of "eras": product, sales, and market orientations. However, Ronald A. Fullerton shows that there is little historical support for the concept of progression through various eras in his article "How Modern Is Modern Marketing? Marketing's Evolution and the Myth of the 'Production Era,'" *Journal of Marketing* (January 1988), pp. 108–25.
7. Henceforth, the term "product" will apply to both goods and services, except as otherwise noted. The marketing princi-ples that apply to products nor-mally apply to services as well.
8. Theodore Levitt, *Innovations in Marketing* (New York: McGraw-Hill, 1962), p. 7.
9. Ajay K. Kohli and Bernard J. Jaworski, "Market Orientation: The Construct, Research Propositions, and Managerial Implications," *Journal of Marketing* (April 1990), pp. 1–18; Bernard J. Jaworski and Ajay K. Kohli, "Market Orienta-tion: Antecedents and Conse-quences," *Journal of Marketing* (July 1993), pp. 53–70.
10. Mansour Javidan and John Rigby, *Marketing,* Proceedings of the Annual Conference of the Administrative Sciences Association of Canada, Vol. 11, Part 3, pp. 147–56.
11. Edna Buchanan, "Lucky Luciano," *Time* 152:23 (December 7, 1998), p. 130.
12. "AMA Board Approves New Marketing Definition," p. 1.

Chapter 2

1. For a detailed discussion of how to create an effective envi-ronmental scanning system, see Peter R. Dickson, *Marketing Management,* 2nd ed. (Fort Worth, TX: Dryden Press, 1997), pp. 93–109.
2. Simon Tuck, "Toys in the Hood," *The Globe and Mail* (February 18, 1999), p. T1.
3. "Play Money," *Maclean's* (May 31, 1999), p. 51.
4. Erika Rasmusson, "Wanted: Profitable Customers," *Sales and Marketing Management* (May 1999), pp. 28–34.
5. Andrew Van Velzen, "Secular Society Gave Couple Their Niche: The Wedding Business," *The Globe and Mail* (August 14, 1989), p. C1.
6. Many economists argue that society is capable of preventing future depressions through the intelligent use of various eco-nomic policies. Thus, a reces-sion is followed by a period of recovery.
7. The concept of environmental forecasting is examined in T.F. Mastri, "Environmental Forecasting," *Fairleigh Dickinson University Business Review* (Winter 1973), pp. 3–10.
8. Interesting articles related to this topic include Philip Kotler and Sidney J. Levy, "Demar-keting, Yes, Demarketing," *Harvard Business Review* (November–December 1971), pp. 74–80; David W. Cravens, "Marketing Management in an Era of Shortages," *Business Horizons* (February 1974), pp. 79–85; A.B. Blankenship and John H. Holmes, "Will Shortages Bankrupt the Marketing Concept?" *MSU Business Topics* (Spring 1974), pp. 13–18; Philip Kotler, "Marketing during Periods of Shortages," *Journal of Marketing* (July 1974), pp. 20–29; Zohrab S. Demirdjian, "The Role of Marketing in an Economy of Affluence and Shortages," *Business and Society* (Spring 1975), pp. 15–21; Nessim Hanna, A.H. Kizilbash, and Albert Smart, "Marketing Strategy under Conditions of Economic Scarcity," *Journal of Marketing* (January 1975), pp. 63–67; Sunier C. Aggarwal, "Prepare for Continual Materials Shortages," *Harvard Business Review* (May–June

1982), pp. 6–10; Joseph Deutsch, "Effects of a Public Advertising Campaign on Consumer Behavior in a Demarketing Situation," *International Journal of Research in Marketing* 2:4 (1985), pp. 287–90; and Guprit S. Kindra, "Demarketing Inappropriate Health Care Consumption," *Journal of Health Care Marketing* 15:2 (Summer 1995), pp. 10–14.

9. John Kohut, "Competition Body Charges NutraSweet with Monopolizing Canadian Market," *The Globe and Mail* (June 2, 1989).

10. Adapted from Drew Fagan, "Tribunal Sours NutraSweet's Success," *The Globe and Mail* (October 5, 1990).

11. Consumer and Corporate Affairs, personal communication.

12. Consumer and Corporate Affairs, *Misleading Advertising Bulletin* (July–September 1986), p. 11.

13. Alan Toulin, "Pulling Cuban Pajamas Leaves Wal-Mart Exposed," *Financial Post* (March 4, 1997), p. 3.

Chapter 3

1. See Scott M. Smith and Leland L. Beik, "Market Segmentation for Fund Raisers," *Journal of the Academy of Marketing Science* (Summer 1982), pp. 208–16.

2. Statistics Canada, *Quarterly Demographic Statistics,* Catalogue No. 91-002, 13:1, p. 16.

3. This section relies heavily on Harry H. Hiller, *Canadian Society: A Sociological Analysis* (Scarborough, ON: Prentice-Hall, 1976), pp. 13–37.

4. Statistics Canada, *Canada Year Book 1999,* p. 51.

5. Statistics Canada, *Annual Demographic Statistics, 1998,* Catalogue No. 91-213-XPB, p. 3.

6. Statistics Canada, Population by Mother Tongue, 1996 Census, http://www.statcan.ca.

7. T.R. Weir, "Population Changes in Canada, 1867–1967," *Canadian Geographer* 2:4 (1967), p. 198.

8. Statistics Canada, *A National Overview, Population and Dwelling Counts,* Catalogue No. 93-357-XPB, p. 183.

9. *Annual Demographic Statistics, 1998,* p. 27.

10. Larry H. Long, "On Measuring Geographic Mobility," *Journal of the American Statistical Association* (September 1970).

11. Kenneth Runyon, *Consumer Behavior* (Columbus, OH: Merrill, 1980), p. 35.

12. *Annual Demographic Statistics, 1998,* p. 14.

13. Statistics Canada, *Canada at a Glance, 1999,* Catalogue No. 12-581-XPE, p. 6.

14. These examples are from an earlier life-cycle study—see William D. Wells and George Gubar, "Life Cycle Concept in Marketing Research," *Journal of Marketing Research* (November 1966), p. 362; see also Frederick W. Derrick and Alane K. Lehfeld, "The Family Life Cycle: An Alternative Approach," *Journal of Consumer Research* (September 1980), pp. 214–17; Robin A. Douthitt, "Family Composition, Parental Time, and Market Goods: Life Cycle Trade-Offs," *Journal of Consumer Affairs* 24:1 (Summer 1990), pp. 110–33; Rob Lawson, "Patterns of Tourist Expenditure and Types of Vacation Across the Family Life Cycle," *Journal of Travel Research* 29:4 (Spring 1991), pp. 12–18; and Fabian Linden, "Welcome to the Middle Ages," *Across the Board* 28:7 (July–August 1991), pp. 9–10.

15. Statistics Canada, *Market Research Handbook, 1999,* Catalogue No. 63-224-XPD, p. 36.

16. The 1985 data have been obtained from Statistics Canada, *Income Distributions by Size in Canada, 1985,* Catalogue 13-207, p. 71. The 1996 data have been obtained from Statistics Canada, *Income Distributions by Size in Canada, 1996,* Catalogue No. 13-207-XPB, p. 96.

17. Statistics Canada, *Changes in Income in Canada, 1970–1980,* Catalogue No. 99-941.

18. John Chaplin, "Pigeonholes for Consumers," *Marketing Magazine* (October 16, 1989), p. 1.

19. For a complete discussion of the Environics segments see Michael Adams, *Sex in the Snow: Canadian Social Values at the End of the Millennium* (Toronto: Viking, 1997).

20. John J. Burnett, "Psychographic and Demographic Characteristics of Blood Donors," *Journal of Consumer Research* (June 1981), pp. 62–86; Mary Ann Lederhaus and Ronald J. Adams, "A Psychographic Profile of the Cosmopolitan Consumers," in *Proceedings of the Southwestern Marketing Association,* eds. Robert H. Ross, Frederic B. Kraft, and Charles H. David (Wichita, KS: Southwestern Marketing Assoc., 1981), pp. 142–45; J. Paul Merenski, "Psychographics: Valid by Definition and Reliable by Technique," *Developments in Marketing Science,* ed. Venkatakrishna V. Bellur (Miami Beach: Academy of Marketing Science, 1981), pp. 161–66; Jack A Lesser, "The Generalizability of Psychographic Market Segments across Geographic Locations," *Journal of Marketing* 50:1 (January 1986), pp. 18–27;

"Psychographics Help Marketers Find and Serve New Market Segments: Scenario for Setting Psychographics to Work," *Marketing News* 21:9 (April 24, 1987), pp. 4–5; and Rebecca Piirto, "Clothes with Attitude," *American Demographics* 12:10 (October 1990), pp. 10, 52, 54.

21. Daniel Yankelovich, "New Criteria for Market Segmentation," *Harvard Business Review* (March–April 1964), pp. 83–90.

22. See Russell I. Haley, "Benefit Segmentation: A Decision-Oriented Research Tool," *Journal of Marketing* (July 1968), pp. 30–35.

23. Peter R. Dickson, *Marketing Management,* 2nd ed. (Fort Worth, TX: Dryden Press, 1997), p. 190.

24. Peter R. Dickson, *Marketing Management,* p. 187.

25. Statistics Canada, Population by Mother Tongue, 1996 Census, http://www.statcan.ca.

Chapter 4

1. This section is based on materials written by J.D. Forbes, University of British Columbia.

2. "Small Clothes Are Selling Big," *Business Week* (November 16, 1981), pp. 152, 156.

3. Joseph P. Guiltinan, Gordon W. Paul, and Thomas Madden, *Marketing Management, Strategies, and Programs,* 6th ed. (New York: McGraw-Hill, 1997).

4. A similar analysis is suggested in Robert M. Fulmer, *The New Marketing* (New York: Macmillan, 1976), pp. 34–37; Philip Kotler, *Marketing Management: Analysis, Planning, Implementation, and Control,* 7th ed. (Englewood Cliffs, NJ: Prentice-Hall, 1991), pp. 263–86; E. Jerome McCarthy and

William D. Perreault, *Basic Marketing: A Global Managerial Approach,* 11th ed. (Homewood, IL: Irwin, 1993), pp. 81–104; and Roger Brooksbank, "The Anatomy of Marketing Positioning Strategy," *Marketing Intelligence and Planning* 12:4 (1994), pp. 10–14.

5. "Properly Applied Psychographics Add Marketing Luster," *Marketing News* (November 12, 1982), p. 10.

6. Victoria Burrus, "A Burning Ambition," *The Globe and Mail* (August 8, 1994), p. B4.

Chapter 5

1. Official definition of the American Marketing Association.

2. John A. Gardner, "Marketing Research in Canada," in *Cases and Readings in Marketing,* ed. R.H. Rotenberg (Toronto: Holt, Rinehart and Winston, 1974), p. 221.

3. Bertram Schoner and Kenneth P. Uhl, *Marketing Research: Information Systems and Decision Making* (New York: Wiley, 1975), p. 199.

4. Wide Area Telephone Service is a telephone company service that allows a business firm to make unlimited long-distance calls for a fixed rate per region.

5. "Marketing Intelligence Systems: A DEW Line for Marketing Men," *Business Management* (January 1966), p. 32.

6. "Marketing Management and the Computer," *Sales Management* (August 20, 1965), pp. 49–60; see also Leon Winer, "Putting the Computer to Work in Marketing," *Pittsburgh Business Review* (November–December 1972), pp. 1–5ff; and "Computer-Assisted Marketing," *Small Business Reports* 14:5 (May 1989), pp. 76–78.

Chapter 6

1. For a more detailed discussion, see Yoram Wind and Thomas S. Robertson, "Marketing Strategy: New Directions for Theory and Research," *Journal of Marketing* (Spring 1983), pp. 12–15.

2. George S. Day and Robin Wensley, "Assessing Advantage: A Framework for Diagnosing Competitive Superiority," *Journal of Marketing* (Summer 1983), p. 82.

3. This story was related by Mr. Birney during a visit to an MBA class at the University of Manitoba.

4. This list of questions is adapted from O.C. Ferrel, Michael D. Hartline, George H. Lucas, Jr., and David Luck, *Marketing Strategy,* Dryden Press, (Fort Worth, TX: 1999), p. 43.

5. Peter Chandler, "Strategic Thinking," *Business Victoria* (May 1994), p. 7.

6. Alfred R. Oxenfeld and William L. Moore, "Customer or Competitor: Which Guideline for Marketing?" *Management Review* (August 1978), pp. 43–48.

7. Benson P. Shapiro, "Getting Things Done," *Harvard Business Review* (September–October, 1985), p. 28.

Chapter 7

1. Adapted from William A. Brand, "Use the Right Measures to Track Marketing Performance," *Sales and Marketing Management in Canada* (February 1988), p. 33.

2. Robert C. Blattberg, *Chain Store Age* 74 (January 1998), pp. 46–49.

3. P.M. Dawkins and F.F. Reichheld, "Customer Retention as a Competitive Weapon," *Directors and Boards* (Summer 1990), pp. 42–47.

4. Francis Buttle and Rizal Ahmad, "Loving, Retaining and Losing Customers — How National First Bank Retains Its Corporate Direct Customers," in *Market Relationships,* Track 1, ed. Per Andersson (Stockholm: European Marketing Academy, 1998), p. 241.

5. Blattberg, *Chain Store Age,* pp. 46–49.

6. This section is based on Jac Fitz-enz, *Benchmarking Staff Performance* (San Francisco: Jossey-Bass Publishers, 1993), pp. 8–17.

7. Rahul Jacob, "TQM, More than a Dying Fad?" *Fortune* (October 18, 1993), p. 67.

8. George Day, "CSC Index" presentation at ASAC Conference, Lake Louise, May 1993.

9. Based on Robert C. Camp, *Benchmarking: The Search for Industry Best Practices that Lead to Superior Performance* (Milwaukee: ASQC Quality Press, 1989), p. 4.

10. Adapted from Howard Schlossberg, "Customer Satisfaction Serves and Preserves," *Marketing News* (May 28, 1990), p. 8.

11. This section is based on Charlotte Klopp and John Sterlicchi, "Customer Satisfaction Just Catching on in Europe," *Marketing News* (May 28, 1990), p. 5.

12. Katherine Doherty, "Pillsbury Measures Customer Service," *U.S. Distribution Journal* 223:12 (December 15, 1996), p. 10.

13. C. Gronroos, "Relationship Marketing: The Strategy Continuum," *Journal of the Academy of Marketing Science* 23:4 (April 1995), pp. 252–54.

14. Ivan Snehota and Magnus Soderlund, "Relationship Marketing — What Does It Promise and What Does It Deliver?" in *Market Relationships,* Track 1, ed. Per Andersson (Stockholm: European Marketing Academy, 1998), p. 313.

15. "Relationship Marketing," *Chain Store Age Executive with Shopping Centre Age* 74:7 (July 1998), p. 4B.

16. This section is based on Thomas Stewart, "Brace for Japan's New Strategy," *Fortune* (September 21, 1992), pp. 63–68.

17. James T. Rothe, Michael G. Harvey, and Candice E. Jackson, "The Marketing Audit: Five Decades Later," *Journal of Marketing Theory and Practice* (Summer 1997), pp. 1–16.

Chapter 8

1. This definition is adapted from James F. Engel, Roger D. Blackwell, and Paul W. Miniard, *Consumer Behavior,* 7th ed. (Hinsdale, IL: Dryden Press, 1993), p. 4.

2. See Kurt Lewin, *Field Theory in Social Science* (New York: Harper and Row, 1964), p. 25; see also C. Glenn Walters, "Consumer Behavior: An Appraisal," *Journal of the Academy of Marketing Science* (Fall 1979), pp. 237–84.

3. "Learning How to Please the Baffling Japanese," *Fortune* (October 5, 1981), p. 122.

4. Adapted from Engel, Blackwell, and Miniard, *Consumer Behavior,* 7th ed., p. 63.

5. Statistics Canada, *Canada Year Book 1999,* Catalogue No. 11-402-XPE, p. 99.

6. Statistics Canada, *Market Research Handbook, 1999,* Catalogue No. 63-224-XPB, p. 104.

7. Royal Commission on Bilingualism and Biculturalism.

8. Del I. Hawkins, Kenneth A. Coney, and Roger J. Best, *Consumer Behavior: Implications for Marketing Strategy,* 5th ed. (Homewood, IL: Irwin, 1992), pp. 137–38. The quotation is adapted from S.E. Asch, "Effects of Group Pressure upon the Modification and Distortion of Judgments," in E.E. MacCoby et al., eds., *Readings in Social Psychology* (New York: Holt, Rinehart and Winston, 1958), pp. 174–83.

9. Bruce Carroll, Compusearch Web site (www.polk.ca), August 8, 1999.

10. Carroll, Compusearch Web site, August 8, 1999.

11. Gillian Rice, "Lifestages," *Academy of Marketing Science News* 2 (October 1990), p. 4.

12. Engel, Blackwell, and Miniard, *Consumer Behavior,* 7th ed., pp. 176–82; see also Wilson Brown, "The Family and Consumer Decision Making," *Journal of the Academy of Marketing Science* (Fall 1979), pp. 335–43; Gary L. Sullivan, "The Family Purchase Decision Process: A Cross-Cultural Review and Framework for Research," *Southwest Journal of Business and Economics* 6:1 (Fall 1988), pp. 43–63; Erich Kirchler, "Spouses' Joint Purchase Decisions: Determinants of Influence Tactics for Muddling through the Process," *Journal of Economic Psychology* 14:2 (June 1993), pp. 405–38; and John B. Ford, "Perception of Marital Roles in Purchase Decision Processes: A Cross-Cultural Study," *Journal of the Academy of Marketing Science* 23:2 (Spring 1995), pp. 120–31.

13. A.H. Maslow, *Motivation and Personality* (New York: Harper and Row, 1954), pp. 370–96.

14. A.H. Maslow, *Motivation and*

Personality, p. 382; see also George Brooker, "The Self-Actualizing Socially Conscious Consumer," *Journal of Consumer Research* (September 1976), pp. 107–12; and James Rada, Jr., "What Makes Buyers Buy?" *American Salesman* 40:2 (February 1995), pp. 16–19.

15. E.E. Lawlor and J.L. Suttle, "A Causal Correlational Test of the Need Hierarchy Concept," *Organizational Behaviour and Human Performance* 3 (1968), pp. 12–35; see also Jerry L. Gray and Frederick A. Starke, *Organizational Behavior: Concepts and Applications,* 3rd ed. (Columbus, OH: Merrill, 1988), pp. 25–29; and James L. Gibson, John M. Ivancevich, and James H. Donnelly, Jr., *Organizations: Behavior, Structure, Processes,* 7th ed. (Homewood, IL: Irwin, 1991), pp. 102–105.

16. George Katona, *The Powerful Consumer* (New York: McGraw-Hill, 1960), p. 132; see also Engel, Blackwell, and Miniard, *Consumer Behavior,* 7th ed., pp. 490–91.

17. John Brooks, "The Little Ad That Isn't There," *Consumer Reports* (January 1958), pp. 7–10; see also Del Hawkins, "The Effects of Subliminal Stimulation on Drive Level and Brand Preference," *Journal of Marketing Research* (August 1970), pp. 322–26; and Kathryn T. Theus, "Subliminal Advertising and the Psychology of Processing Unconscious Stimuli: A Review of Research," *Psychology and Marketing* 11:3 (May–June 1994), pp. 271–90.

18. See James H. Myers and William H. Reynolds, *Consumer Behaviour and Marketing Management* (Boston: Houghton Mifflin, 1967), p. 14.

19. Richard P. Barthol and Michael J. Goldstein, "Psychology and the Invisible Sell," *California Management Review* (Winter 1959), p. 34.

20. One researcher reports that some overt behaviour in pathologically prone individuals can be influenced if they appeal to the appropriate unconscious wish: see Jack Saegert, "Another Look at Subliminal Perception," *Journal of Advertising Research* (February 1979), pp. 55–57.

21. Stuart Henderson Britt, "How Weber's Law Can Be Applied to Marketing," *Business Horizons* (February 1975), pp. 21–29.

22. Learning is perhaps the most thoroughly researched field in psychology, and several learning theories have been developed. For a discussion of these theories, see Engel, Blackwell, and Miniard, *Consumer Behavior,* 7th ed., pp. 425–55.

23. This section is based on Michael L. Rothschild and William C. Gaidis, "Behavioral Learning Theory: Its Relevance to Marketing and Promotion," *Journal of Marketing* (Spring 1981), pp. 70–78.

24. See J.P. Liefeld, "Problem Recognition," in *Consumer Decision-Making: An Annotated Bibliography* (Ottawa: Consumer and Corporate Affairs, 1979).

25. B.M. Campbell, "The Existence of Evoked Set and Determinants of Its Magnitude in Brand Choice Behavior," in John A. Howard and Lonnie Ostrom, eds., *Buyer Behavior: Theoretical and Empirical Foundations* (New York: Knopf, 1973), pp. 243–44.

26. For a thorough discussion of purchase location, see David L. Loudon and Albert J. Della Bitta, *Consumer Behavior: Concepts and Applications,* 3rd ed. (New York: McGraw-Hill, 1988), pp. 631–51.

27. These categories were originally suggested in John A. Howard, *Marketing Management Analysis and Planning* (Homewood, IL: Irwin, 1963); the discussion here is based on Donald R. Lehmann, William L. Moore, and Terry Elrod, "The Development of Distinct Choice Process Segments over Time: A Stochastic Modelling Approach," *Journal of Marketing* (Spring 1982), pp. 48–50.

Chapter 9

1. Dartnell Corporation, "Dartnell's 30th Sales Force Compensation Survey" (Palm Beach Gardens, FL, 1999).

2. Dartnell Corporation, "Dartnell's 30th Sales Force Compensation Survey" (Palm Beach Gardens, FL, 1999).

3. The development of the new type of pole and the problems involved in its adoption are described in Arch G. Woodside, "Marketing Anatomy of Buying Process Can Help Improve Industrial Strategy," *Marketing News* (May 1, 1981), Section 2, p. 11.

4. Statistics Canada, "Consolidated Federal, Provincial, Territorial and Local Government Expenditures, Fiscal Years 1990/1991 to 1994/1995," from *Public Sector Finance, 1995–1996,* Catalogue No. 68-212.

5. Statistics Canada, "Consolidated Federal, Provincial, Territorial and Local Government Expenditures, Fiscal Years 1990/1991 to 1994/1995," from *Public Sector Finance, 1995–1996,* Catalogue No. 68-212.

6. Oracle Web site (www.oracle.com), March 22, 2000.

7. Government of Canada (Team Canada Inc.), "Beyond the Website." Catalogue No. C2-446/1999E, p. 5.

Chapter 10

1. A good summary of the product life cycle is contained in George S. Day, "The Product Life Cycle: Analysis and Application Issues," *Journal of Marketing* (Fall 1981), pp. 60–67; see also Gerald J. Tellis and C. Merle Crawford, "An Evolutionary Approach to Product Growth Theory," *Journal of Marketing* (Fall 1981), pp. 125–32.
2. This section relies on George S. Day, "The Product Life Cycle," pp. 60–65.
3. Ben M. Enis, Raymond LaGrace, and Arthur E. Prell, "Extending the Product Life Cycle," *Business Horizons* (June 1977), pp. 45–56.
4. William Qualls, Richard W. Olshavsky, and Ronald E. Michaels, "Shortening the PLC: An Empirical Test," *Journal of Marketing* (Fall 1981), pp. 76–80.
5. For a further discussion of fashions and fashion life cycles, see Avijit Ghosh, *Retail Management,* 2nd. ed. (Fort Worth TX: Dryden Press, 1994), pp. 340–42, or Patrick Dunne and Robert F. Lusch, *Retailing,* 3rd. ed. (Fort Worth TX: Dryden Press, 1999), pp. 339–47.
6. Enis, LaGrace, and Prell, "Extending the Product Life Cycle."
7. Gail Bronson, "Baby Food It Is, but Gerber Wants Teen-Agers to Think of It as Dessert," *Wall Street Journal* (July 17, 1981).
8. Everett M. Rogers, *Diffusion of Innovations,* 4th ed. (New York: Free Press, 1995), pp. 243–51.

9. For a discussion of the characteristics of early adopters, see Jagish N. Sheth, Banwari Mittal, and Bruce I. Newman, *Customer Behaviour* (Orlando, FL: Harcourt Brace, 1999), pp. 320–22, and Frank Alpert, "Innovator Buying Behaviour Over Time: The Innovator Buying Cycle and the Cumulative Effects of Innovations," *Journal of Product and Brand Management* 3:2 (1994), pp. 50–62.
10. Ronald Marks and Eugene Hughes, "Profiling the Consumer Innovator," in *Evolving Marketing Thought for 1980,* eds. John H. Summey and Ronald D. Taylor (New Orleans: Southern Marketing Association, 1980), pp. 115–18; Elizabeth Hirschman, "Innovativeness, Novelty Seeking and Consumer Creativity," *Journal of Consumer Research* (December 1980), pp. 283–95; and Richard W. Olshavsky, "Time and the Rate of Adoption of Innovations," *Journal of Consumer Research* (March 1980), pp. 425–28.
11. For a more thorough discussion of the speed of the adoption process, see Everett M. Rogers, *Diffusion of Innovations,* 4th ed.
12. This discussion relies on Patrick E. Murphy and Ben M. Enis, "Classifying Products Strategically," *Journal of Marketing* (July 1986), pp. 24–42. Note that these authors argue that their classification system can be applied equally well to business products.

Chapter 11

1. http://www.bombardier.com.
2. Bill Abrams, "Despite Mixed Record, Firms Still Pushing for New Products," *Wall Street Journal* (November 12, 1981).

3. http://www.wto.org/wto/statis/stat.htm.
4. "The Money-Guzzling Genius of Biotechnology," *The Economist* (May 13, 1989), p. 69.
5. David S. Hopkins, *New Product Winners and Losers* (New York: Conference Board, 1980); see also "Booz Allen Looks at New Products' Role," *Wall Street Journal* (March 26, 1981).
6. Abrams, "Despite Mixed Record," p. 25.
7. Robert Cooper, "The New Prod System: The Industry Experience," *Journal of Product Innovation Management* (June 1992), pp. 113–27.
8. Roger Calantone and Robert G. Cooper, "New Product Scenarios: Prospects for Success," *Journal of Marketing* (Spring 1981), p. 49.
9. Robert G. Cooper, "The Myth of the Better Mousetrap: What Makes a New Product a Success?" *Business Quarterly* (Spring 1981), pp. 71, 72.
10. Reported in Ann M. Morrison, "The General Mills Brand of Manager," *Fortune* (January 12, 1981), pp. 99–107; another interesting discussion appears in "Brand Management System Is Best, but Refinements Needed," *Marketing News* (July 9, 1982), p. 12.
11. Jacob M. Duker and Michael V. Laric, "The Product Manager: No Longer on Trial," in *The Changing Marketing Environment: New Theories and Applications,* eds. Kenneth Bernhardt et al. (Chicago: American Marketing Association, 1981), pp. 93–96; and Peter S. Howsam and G. David Hughes, "Product Management System Suffers from Insufficient Experience, Poor Communication," *Marketing News* (June 26, 1981), p. 8.

12. Adapted from John R. Rockwell and Marc C. Particelli, "New Product Strategy: How the Pros Do It," *Industrial Marketing* (May 1982), p. 50.

13. Rockwell and Particelli, "New Product Strategy," p. 50.

14. Quoted in Mary McCabe English, "Marketers: Better than a Coin Flip," *Advertising Age* (February 9, 1981), p. S-15. Copyright 1981 by Crain Communications, Inc.

15. Dylan Landis, "Durable Goods for a Test?" *Advertising Age* (February 9, 1981), pp. S-18, S-19.

16. Committee on Definitions, *Marketing Definitions: A Glossary of Marketing Terms* (Chicago: American Marketing Association, 1960), pp. 9–10.

17. "A Worldwide Brand for Nissan," *Business Week* (August 24, 1981), p. 104.

18. Meir Statman and Tyzoon T. Tyebjee, "Trademarks, Patents, and Innovation in the Ethical Drug Industry," *Journal of Marketing* (Summer 1981), pp. 71–81.

19. Bill Abrams, "Brand Loyalty Rises Slightly, but Increase Could Be Fluke," *Wall Street Journal* (February 7, 1982).

20. Frances Phillips, "Private Label Appliances Vie with National Brands," *Financial Post* (August 13, 1983).

21. *Market Research Facts and Trends* (November–December 1989), p. 1.

22. "Packaging Linked to Ad's Effect," *Advertising Age* (May 3, 1982), p. 63.

23. Bill Abrams and David P. Garino, "Package Design Gains Stature as Visual Competition Grows," *Wall Street Journal* (August 6, 1981).

24. Robert Ball, "Warm Milk Wakes Up the Packaging Industry," *Fortune* (August 7, 1982), pp. 78–82.

25. Patricia Lush, "Tide's In, Plastic's Out in Environmentally Safer Pouches," *The Globe and Mail* (September 6, 1989).

Chapter 12

1. Statistics Canada, *Market Research Handbook 1999,* Catalogue No. 63-224-XPB, p. 64.

2. World Trade Organization (http://www.wto.org/wto/intltrad/internat.htm), March 30, 2000.

3. L. Berry, "Services Marketing Is Different," in *Marketing Management and Strategy: A Reader,* eds. P. Kotler and K.K. Cox (Englewood Cliffs, NJ: Prentice-Hall, 1988), p. 278.

4. A. Rushton and D. Carson, "The Marketing of Services: Managing the Intangibles," *European Journal of Marketing* (1989), p. 31.

5. J. Bateson, "Do We Need Services Marketing?" in *Marketing Management and Strategy,* eds. Kotler and Cox, pp. 278–86.

6. Valarie A. Zeithaml, A. Parsuraman, and Leonard L. Berry, "Problems and Strategies in Services Marketing," *Journal of Marketing* (Spring 1985), p. 33.

7. Theodore Levitt, "The Industrialization of Service," *Harvard Business Review* (September–October 1976), pp. 63–74.

8. L. Berry, "Services Marketing Is Different," p. 281.

9. L. Berry, "Services Marketing Is Different," p. 281.

10. G.L. Shostack, "Breaking Free from Product Marketing," *Journal of Marketing* (April 1977), pp. 73–80.

11. L. Berry, "Services Marketing Is Different," p. 281; and A. Rushton and D. Carson, "The Marketing of Services," p. 31.

12. A. Parasuraman, Valarie Zeithaml, and Leonard Berry, "A Conceptual Model of Service Quality and Its Implications for Future Research," *Journal of Marketing* 49 (Fall 1985), pp. 41–50.

Chapter 13

1. Adapted from David J. Schwartz, *Marketing Today,* copyright © 1981 by Harcourt Brace Jovanovich, Inc.

2. See William J. Baumol, "On the Theory of Oligopoly," *Economica* (August 1958), pp. 187–98; see also William J. Baumol, *Business Behavior, Value, and Growth* (New York: Harcourt Brace and World, 1967).

3. An interesting discussion appears in Carl R. Frear and John E. Swan, "Marketing Managers' Motivation to Revise Their Market Share Goals: An Expectancy Theory Analysis," in *Southwestern Marketing Proceedings,* eds. Robert H. Ross, Frederic B. Kraft, and Charles H. Davis (Wichita, KS: 1981), pp. 13–16; see also William Brand, "Pricing Strategies for Profit," *Sales and Marketing Management in Canada* 27:11 (December 1986), p. 30–31.

4. This section is adapted from Edwin G. Dolan, *Basic Economics* (Toronto: Holt, Rinehart, and Winston, 1984), pp. 57–58; and Ross D. Eckert and Richard H. Leftwich, *Price System and Resource Allocation,* 10th ed. (Chicago: Dryden Press, 1988), pp. 55–58.

5. For a discussion of the application of price elasticity to a consumer service, see Steven J.

Skinner, Terry L. Childers, and Wesley H. Jones, "Consumer Responsiveness to Price Differentials: A Case for Insurance Industry Deregulation," *Journal of Business Research* (December 1981), pp. 381–96.

6. Some problems of using economic models in practice are discussed in Kent B. Monroe and Albert J. Della Bitta, "Models of Pricing Decisions," *Journal of Marketing Research* (August 1978), pp. 413–28; see also Robert J. Dolan and Abel P. Jeuland, "Experience Curves and Dynamic Models: Implications for Optional Pricing Strategies," *Journal of Marketing* (Winter 1981), pp. 52–62.

Chapter 14

1. Walter J. Primeaux, Jr., "The Effect of Consumer Knowledge and Bargaining Strength on Final Selling Price: A Case Study," *Journal of Business* (October 1970), pp. 419–26; another excellent article is James R. Krum, "Variable Pricing as a Promotional Tool," *Atlanta Economic Review* (November–December 1977), pp. 47–50.

2. Bernie Faust et al., "Effective Retail Pricing Policy," *Purdue Retailer* (Lafayette, IN: Agricultural Economics, 1963), p. 2.

3. Karl A. Shilliff, "Determinants of Consumer Price Sensitivity for Selected Supermarket Products: An Empirical Investigation," *Akron Business and Economic Review* (Spring 1975), pp. 26–32.

4. John F. Willenborg and Robert E. Pitts, "Perceived Situational Effects on Price Sensitivity," *Journal of Business Research* (March 1977), pp. 27–38.

5. Jack C. Horn, "The High-Class Nickel Discount," *Psychology Today* (September 1982).

6. See David M. Georgoff, "Price Illusion and the Effect of Odd–Even Retail Pricing," *Southern Journal of Business* (April 1969), pp. 95–103; see also Dik W. Twedt, "Does the '9 Fixation in Retailing Really Promote Sales?" *Journal of Marketing* (October 1965), pp. 54–55; Benson P. Shapiro, "The Psychology of Pricing," *Harvard Business Review* (July–August 1968), pp. 14–16; David M. Georgoff, *Odd–Even Retail Price Endings: Their Effects on Value Determination, Product Perception, and Buying Propensities* (East Lansing, MI: Michigan State University, 1972); and JoAnn Carmin, "Pricing Strategies for Menus: Magic or Myth?" *Cornell Hotel and Restaurant Administration Quarterly* 31:3 (November 1990), pp. 44–50.

7. See, for instance, I. Robert Andrews and Enzo R. Valenzi, "The Relationship between Price and Blind-Rated Quality for Margarines and Butter," *Journal of Marketing Research* (August 1970), pp. 393–95; Robert A. Peterson, "The Price–Perceived Quality Relationship: Experimental Evidence," *Journal of Marketing Research* (November 1970), pp. 525–28; David M. Gardner, "An Experimental Investigation of the Price/Quality Relationship," *Journal of Retailing* (Fall 1970), pp. 25–41; Arthur G. Bedelan, "Consumer Perception as an Indicator of Product Quality," *MSU Business Topics* (Summer 1971), pp. 59–65; and R.S. Mason, "Price and Product Quality Assessment," *European Journal of Marketing* (Spring 1974), pp. 29–41.

8. J. Douglass McConnell, "An Experimental Examination of the Price–Quality Relation-

ship," *Journal of Business* (October 1968), pp. 439–44; see also J. Douglass McDonnell, "The Alphabet and Price as Independent Variables: A Note on the Price–Quality Question," *Journal of Business* (October 1970), pp. 448–51; Jerry B. Gotlieb, "Effects of Price Advertisements on Perceived Quality and Purchase Intentions," *Journal of Business Research* 22:3 (May 1991), pp. 195–210; and William B. Dodds, "Effects of Price, Brand, and Store Information on Buyers' Product Evaluations," *Journal of Marketing Research* 28:3 (August 1991), pp. 307–19.

9. James H. Myers and William H. Reynolds, *Consumer Behavior and Marketing Management* (Boston: Houghton-Mifflin, 1967), p. 47.

10. See Kent B. Monroe and M. Venkatesan, "The Concepts of Price Limits and Psychophysical Measurement: A Laboratory Experiment," in *Marketing Involvement in Society and the Economy,* ed. Philip R. McDonald (Cincinnati: American Marketing Association, 1969), pp. 345–51.

11. *Market Spotlight* (Edmonton: Alberta Consumer and Corporate Affairs, March 1979).

12. J. Edward Russo, "The Value of Unit Price Information," *Journal of Marketing Research* (May 1977), pp. 193–201.

13. This is one of many important terms outlined in a publication called *INCOTERMS,* published in Paris in September 1999 by the International Chamber of Commerce.

14. See Mary Louise Hatten, "Don't Get Caught with Your Prices Down: Pricing in Inflationary Times," *Business Horizons* (March–April 1982), pp. 23–28.

Chapter 15

1. Committee on Definitions, *Marketing Definitions: A Glossary of Marketing Terms* (Chicago: American Marketing Association, 1960), p. 10; some authors limit the definition to the route taken by the *title* to the goods, but this definition also includes agent wholesaling intermediaries who do not take title but who do serve as an important component of many channels.

2. This section is adapted from Louis W. Stern and Adel I. El-Ansary, *Marketing Channels,* 3rd ed. (Englewood Cliffs, NJ: Prentice-Hall, 1989), pp. 7–12.

3. The first five functions were developed in Wroe Alderson, "Factors Governing the Development of Marketing Channels," in *Marketing Channels for Manufactured Products,* ed. Richard M. Clewitt (Homewood, IL: Irwin, 1954), pp. 5–22.

4. Donald A. Fuller, "Aluminum Beverage Container Recycling in Florida: A Commentary," *Atlanta Economic Review* (January–February 1977), p. 41.

5. Industry, Science and Technology Canada, *Wholesale Trade Industry Profile* (Ottawa, 1988), p. 7.

6. An interesting discussion of types of wholesaling appears in J. Howard Westing, "Wholesale Indifference," *The Courier* (Spring 1982), pp. 3, 8.

7. James R. Moore and Kendell A. Adams, "Functional Wholesaler Sales Trends and Analysis," in *Combined Proceedings,* ed. Edward M. Mazze (Chicago: American Marketing Association, 1976), pp. 402–405.

8. For a profile of the typical manufacturers' agent, see Stanley D. Sibley and Roy K. Teas, "Agent Marketing Channel Intermediaries' Perceptions of Marketing Channel Performance," in *Proceedings of the Southern Marketing Association,* eds. Robert S. Franz et al. (New Orleans: 1978), pp. 336–39.

9. Combines Investigation Act, Part IV.1, 31.4, 1976.

10. Lawson A.W. Hunter, "Buying Groups," *Agriculture Canada: Food Market Commentary* 5:4, p. 15.

11. Downloaded from Francon Canada Web site at http://www.francon.com/CDNFACTS.htm.

Chapter 16

1. "Canuck," *Pen Pictures of Early Pioneer Life in Upper Canada* (Toronto: Coles, 1972), pp. 80–82.

2. Interesting discussions include Sak Onkvisit and John J. Shaw, "Modifying the Retail Classification System for More Timely Marketing Strategies," *Journal of the Academy of Marketing Science* (Fall 1981), pp. 436–53; and Bobby C. Vaught, L. Lyn Judd, and Jack M. Starling, "The Perceived Importance of Retailing Strategies and Their Relationships to Four Indexes of Retailing Success," in *Progress in Marketing: Theory and Practice,* eds. Ronald D. Taylor, John J. Bennen, and John H. Summey (Carbondale, IL: Southern Marketing Association, 1981), pp. 25–28.

3. Frances Phillips, "Canadian Tire Finds Texas Trail a Bit Bumpy," *Financial Post* (March 26, 1983).

4. A good discussion appears in Mary Carolyn Harrison and Alvin C. Burns, "A Case for Departmentalizing Target Market Strategy in Department Stores," in *Progress in Marketing: Theory and Practice,* eds. Taylor, Bennen, and Summey, pp. 21–24.

5. Clayton Sinclair, "The New Priorities for Shopping Centres," *The Financial Times of Canada* (March 21, 1983).

6. The following discussion of Reilly and Huff's work is adapted from Joseph Barry Mason and Morris Lehman Mayer, *Modern Retailing: Theory and Practice,* 5th ed. (Homewood, IL: BPI/Irwin, 1990), pp. 679–81.

7. Huff's work is described in David Hugg, "A Probabilistic Analysis of Consumer Spatial Behavior," in *Emerging Concepts in Marketing,* ed. William S. Decker (Chicago: American Marketing Association, 1972), pp. 443–61; shopping centre trade areas are also discussed in Edward Blair, "Sampling Issues in Trade Area Maps Drawn from Shopper Surveys," *Journal of Marketing* (Winter 1983), pp. 98–106.

8. Retail images are discussed in a variety of articles, for example, Pradeep K. Korgaonbar and Kamal M. El Sheshai, "Assessing Retail Competition with Multidimensional Scaling," *Business* (April–June 1982), pp. 30–33; Jack K. Kasulis and Robert F. Lush, "Validating the Retail Store Image Concept," *Journal of the Academy of Marketing Science* (Fall 1981), pp. 419–35; and Julie Baker, "The Influence of Store Environment on Quality Inferences and Store Image," *Journal of the Academy of Marketing Science* 22:4 (Fall 1994), pp. 328–39.

9. This section is based on Avijit Ghosh, *Retail Management,* 2nd

ed. (Fort Worth, TX: Dryden Press, 1994), pp. 59–60.

10. Susan Bourette, "Hudson's Bay Expands Loyalty Programs in Asia," *The Globe and Mail* (September 30, 1998), p. B5.

11. Calculated from Table 16.1, Total Retail Sales by Trade Group, 1995–1996. Statistics Canada, *Market Research Handbook, 1998,* Catalogue No. 63-225, p. 122.

12. See Ian Brown, "The Empire That Timothy Built," *Financial Post Magazine* (May 1978), pp. 16–47.

13. Ian Brown, "The Empire That Timothy Built," p. 20.

14. Some of this section is based on Ken Jones, Wendy Evans, and Christine Smith, "New Formats in the Canadian Retail Economy," paper presented at the Retailing and Services Conference, Lake Louise, Alberta (May 7–10, 1994).

15. Superstores are discussed in Myron Gable and Ronald D. Michman, "Superstores— Revolutionizing Distribution," *Business* (March–April 1981), pp. 14–18.

16. This section is based on Tamsen Tilson, "Multilevel Marketing Sells Costly Dreams," *The Globe and Mail* (October 6, 1994).

17. Tyler Hamilton, "Sold on the Web," *The Globe and Mail* (March 11, 1999), p. T1.

18. Quoted by Mr. Knox, a Sears executive in Toronto.

19. Statistics Canada, *Vending Machine Operators,* 1988, Catalogue No. 63-213.

20. This section is based on Industry Canada, "Canadian Internet Retailing Report," http://strategis.ic.gc.ca/SSG/ir01582e.html, September 27, 1999.

21. Statistics Canada, *Market Research Handbook, 1990,* Catalogue No. 63-224.

22. This section is based on Patrick Dunne and Robert F. Lusch, *Retailing,* 3rd ed. (Fort Worth, TX: Dryden Press, 1999), p. 17.

Chapter 17

1. Peter R. Dickson, *Marketing Management* (Fort Worth, TX: Dryden Press, 1997), p. 457.

2. Sherry Butt, "Planning for Success," *Calgary Sun,* Resource and Supply Chain Management Supplement (January 1999), p. 2.

3. The four pillars and their descriptions are based on John T. Landry, "Supply Chain Management: The Case for Alliances," *Harvard Business Review* 76 (November– December 1998), pp. 24–25.

Chapter 18

1. Don E. Schultz, "Integrated Marketing Communications: Maybe Definition Is in the Point of View," *Marketing News* (January 18, 1993), p. 17.

2. Similar communications processes are suggested in David K. Berlo, *The Process of Communications* (New York: Holt, Rinehart and Winston, 1960), pp. 23–38; and Thomas S. Robertson, *Innovative Behavior and Communication* (New York: Holt, Rinehart and Winston, 1971), p. 122; see also Claude Shannon and Warren Weaver, *The Mathematical Theory of Communication* (Urbana, IL: University of Illinois Press, 1978), p. 7; and Wilbur Schramm, "The Nature of Communication between Humans," in *The Process and Effects of Mass Communication,* rev. ed. (Urbana, IL: University of Illinois Press, 1971), pp. 3–53.

3. Wilbur Schramm, "The Nature of Communication between Humans," pp. 3–53.

4. S. Watson Dunn and Arnold M. Barban, *Advertising: Its Role in Modern Marketing,* 7th ed. (Chicago: Dryden Press, 1990), p. 9.

5. Committee on Definitions, *Marketing Definitions: A Glossary of Marketing Terms* (Chicago: American Marketing Association, 1960), p. 20.

6. Extrapolation based on "Dartnell's 30th Sales Force Compensation Survey" (Palm Beach Gardens, FL, 1999), p. 20.

7. Terrence V. O'Brien, "Psychologists Take a New Look at Today's Consumer," *Arizona Review* (August–September 1970), p. 2.

Chapter 19

1. Canadian Media Directors' Council, *Media Digest, 1998–99,* p. 11. Publication can be accessed on-line at http://www.marketingmag.ca.

2. This section follows in part the discussion in S. Watson Dunn and Arnold M. Barban, *Advertising: Its Role in Modern Marketing,* 7th ed. (Chicago: Dryden Press, 1990), pp. 16–19.

3. Canadian Media Directors' Council, *Media Digest, 1998–99,* p. 11. Publication can be accessed on-line at http://www.marketingmag.ca.

4. "Web Ads Top $10m; Marketing Research Firm Ernst and Young, LLP and The Internet Advertising Bureau of Canada Predicts Revenues from Internet Advertising to Increase," *Computer Dealer News* 23:14 (June 15, 1998), p. 18.

5. "Web Ads Top $10m," p. 18.

6. William M. Carley, "Gillette Co. Struggles as Its Rivals Slice at

Fat Profit Margin," *Wall Street Journal* (February 2, 1972), p. 1.

7. Ralph B. Weller, C. Richard Roberts, and Colin Neuhaus, "A Longitudinal Study of the Effect of Erotic Content upon Advertising Brand Recall," *Current Issues and Research in Advertising* (1979), pp. 145–61.

8. Marina Strauss, "Ontario Judge Rules Pie Crust Ads Are Half-Baked," *The Globe and Mail* (October 14, 1994), p. B1.

9. This section draws from Jim Steinhart, "Their Aim Is True," *The Globe and Mail* (February 15, 1994).

10. Marina Strauss, "Vending Machines Get the Picture," *The Globe and Mail* (August 18, 1994), p. B6.

11. Ken Riddel, "New Study Shows Sales Promotion Spending May Be Inflated," *Marketing Magazine* (April 23, 1990), pp. 1, 3.

12. Walter A. Gaw, *Specialty Advertising* (Chicago: Specialty Advertising Association, 1970), p. 7.

13. Maurice Simms, "Retailers Pin Hope on Marketing Skill," *The Globe and Mail* (February 15, 1994), p. B28.

14. http://www.hbc.com/zellers

15. Terrance A. Shimp, *Advertising, Promotion, and Supplemental Aspects of Integrated Marketing Communications* (Fort Worth, TX: Dryden Press, 1997), p. 554.

16. Johanna Powell, "Mascot Maker Finds Success Is Little More than Child's Play," *Financial Post* (September 11, 1989).

Chapter 20

1. This section is adapted from "About the WTO: The Case for Open Trade," World Trade Organization, http://www.wto.org/wto/about/facts3.htm,

June 21, 1999.

2. "Northern Telecom: Mastering the International Market," *Business to Business Marketing* 94:13 (March 27, 1989), p. B12.

3. Warren Keegan, *Global Marketing Management* (New York: McGraw-Hill, 1989), pp. 31–33.

4. Philip R. Cateara and John L. Graham, *International Marketing* (Boston: Irwin/McGraw-Hill, 1999), p. 331.

5. This section is adapted from Geoff Nimmo and Michael Macdonald, *Export Guide: A Practical Approach,* 6th ed. (Ottawa: External Affairs and International Trade Canada), Spring 1993, pp. 3–4.

6. This paragraph is adapted from "About the WTO: Summary," World Trade Organization, http://www.wto.org/wto/about/facts0.htm, June 21, 1999.

7. These five principles are excerpted from "About the WTO: Principles of the Trading System," World Trade Organization, http://www.wto.org/about/facts2.htm, June 21, 1999.

Chapter 21

1. Also referred to as "not-for-profit" organizations; we will use the two terms interchangeably in this chapter.

2. Philip Kotler, *Marketing for Nonprofit Organizations* (Englewood Cliffs, NJ: Prentice-Hall, 1982), p. 9.

3. These differences and others are outlined in Harvey W. Wallender, III, "Managing Not-for-Profit Enterprises," *Academy of Management Review* (January 1978), p. 26; Cecily Cannon Selby, "Better Performance for 'Nonprofits,'" *Harvard Business Review* (September–October 1978), pp. 93–95; see also John

M. Gwin, "Constituent Analysis: A Paradigm for Marketing Effectiveness in the Not-for-Profit Organization," *European Journal of Marketing* 24:7 (1990), pp. 43–48; and Katherine Gallagher, "Coping with Success: New Challenges for Nonprofit Marketing," *Sloan Management Review* 33:1 (Fall 1991), pp. 27–42.

4. Kotler, *Marketing for Nonprofit Organizations,* p. 482.

5. Alan R. Andreason, *Marketing Social Change: Changing Behaviour to Promote Health, Social Development and the Environment* (San Francisco: Jossey-Bass, 1995), p. 7.

6. David J. Rachman and Elaine Romano, *Modern Marketing* (Hinsdale, IL: Dryden Press, 1980), p. 576; the delineation of person, social, and organization marketing is proposed by Professors Rachman and Romano.

7. James M. Stearns, John R. Kerr, and Robert R. McGrath, "Advances of Marketing for Functional Public Policy Administration," in *Proceedings of the Southern Marketing Association,* eds. Robert S. Franz, Robert M. Hopkins, and Alfred G. Toma (Atlanta, GA: November 1979), pp. 140–43.

8. This section is based on Philip Kotler, *Marketing for Nonprofit Organizations,* pp. 306–309; see also Chris T. Allen, "Self-Perception Based Strategies for Stimulating Energy Conservation," *Journal of Consumer Research* (March 1982), pp. 381–90.

9. Michael L. Rothschild, "Marketing Communications in Nonbusiness Situations or Why It's So Hard to Sell Brotherhood Like Soap," *Journal of Marketing* (Spring 1979), pp. 11–20.

Credits

Glossary

absolute advantage A nation has an absolute advantage in the marketing of a product if it is the sole producer or can produce a product for less than anyone else.

accelerator principle The disproportionate impact that changes in consumer demand have on business market demand.

accessory equipment Second-level capital items that are used in the production of products and services but are usually less expensive and shorter-lived than installations.

adoption process A series of stages consumers go through, from learning of a new product to trying it and deciding to purchase it regularly or to reject it.

advertising Paid nonpersonal communication through various media by business firms, nonprofit organizations, and individuals who are in some way identified with the advertising message and who hope to inform or persuade members of a particular audience.

advertising agency A marketing specialist firm that assists the advertiser in planning and preparing its advertisements.

affective component One's feelings or emotional reactions.

agent A wholesaling intermediary that differs from the typical wholesaler in that the agent does not take title to the goods.

AIO statements Statements about activities, interests, and opinions that are used in developing psychographic profiles.

approach The initial contact between the salesperson and the prospective customer.

Asch phenomenon The impact that groups and group norms can exhibit on individual behaviour.

aspirational group A type of reference group with which individuals wish to associate.

attitudes A person's enduring favourable or unfavourable evaluations of some object or idea.

auction house An agent wholesaling intermediary that brings buyers and sellers together in one location and allows potential buyers to inspect the merchandise before purchasing through a public bidding process.

average cost Obtained by dividing total cost by the quantity associated with this cost.

average variable cost The total variable cost divided by the related quantity.

balance of payments The flow of money into or out of a country.

balance of trade The relationship between a country's exports and its imports.

BCG growth-share matrix Plots market share relative to the market share of the largest competitor, against market growth rate.

benchmarking The comparison of performance with industry best practices.

benefit segmentation Depends on advanced marketing research techniques that focus on benefits the consumer expects to derive from a product.

bids Price quotations from potential suppliers.

bottom line The overall-profitability measure of performance.

brand A name, term, sign, symbol, or design (or some combination of these) used to identify the products of one firm and to differentiate them from competitive offerings.

brand equity Represents the value customers (and the stock markets) place on the sum of the history the customer has had with a brand.

brand extension The decision to use a popular brand name for a new product entry in an unrelated product category.

brand insistence The ultimate stage of brand loyalty, when consumers will accept no alternatives and will search extensively for the product.

brand name Words, letters, or symbols that make up a name used to identify and distinguish the firm's offerings from those of its competitors.

brand preference The second stage of brand loyalty, when, based on previous experience, consumers will choose a product rather than one of its competitors — if it is available.

brand recognition The first stage of brand loyalty, when a firm has developed enough publicity for a brand that its name is familiar to consumers.

break-bulk warehouse Receives consolidated shipments from a central distribution centre, and then distributes them in smaller shipments to individual customers in more limited areas.

break-even analysis A means of determining the number of goods or services that must be sold at a given price in order to generate sufficient revenue to cover total costs.

broker An agent wholesaling intermediary that brings buyers and sellers together; operates in industries with a large number of small suppliers and purchasers.

business-to-business market Firms that produce or acquire goods and services to be used, directly or indirectly, in the production of other goods and services or to be resold.

buying centre The key individuals who participate in a buying decision.

cannibalizing Situation involving one product taking sales from another offering in a product line.

capital items Long-lived business assets that must be depreciated over time.

cartel The monopolistic organization of a group of firms.

cash-and-carry wholesaler Limited-function merchant wholesaler that performs most wholesaling functions except financing and delivery.

cash discount Reduction in price that is given for prompt payment of a bill.

catalogue retailer Retailer that mails catalogues to its customers and operates from a showroom displaying samples of its products.

celebrity marketing Having celebrities lend their name and influence to the promotion of a product.

census A collection of marketing data from all possible sources.

chain store Group of retail stores that are centrally owned and managed and that handle the same lines of products.

channel captain The most dominant member of the distribution channel.

channel conflict Rivalry and conflict between channel members because of sometimes different objectives and needs.

closing The act of asking the prospect for an order.

cluster sample A probability sample that is generated by randomly choosing one or more areas or population clusters and then surveying all members in the chosen cluster(s).

cognitive component The knowledge and beliefs one has about an object or concept.

cognitive dissonance The postpurchase anxiety that occurs when there is a discrepancy between a person's knowledge and beliefs (cognitions).

commission merchant An agent wholesaling intermediary that takes possession when the producer ships goods to a central market for sale.

common carrier Transportation carrier that provides service to the general public, and is subject to regulatory authority including fee setting.

common market A customs union that also allows factors of production such as labour, capital, and technology to flow freely among members.

communication Personal selling, advertising, sales promotion, and publicity.

company elasticity Refers to the sensitivity to changes in price that a particular company or brand faces.

comparative advantage A nation has a comparative advantage if it can produce a given product more efficiently per unit of output than it can produce other products.

comparative advertising Advertising that makes direct promotional comparisons with competitive brands.

competitive bidding A process by which buyers request potential suppliers to make price quotations on a proposed purchase or contract.

competitive environment The interactive process that occurs in the marketplace in which different organizations seek to satisfy similar markets.

component parts and materials Finished business-to-business goods that actually become part of the final product.

conative component The way one tends to act or behave.

concept testing A marketing research project that attempts to measure consumer attitudes and perceptions relevant to a new-product idea.

consumer behaviour The activities of individuals in obtaining, using, and disposing of goods and services, including the decision processes that precede and follow these actions.

consumer goods Those products and services purchased by the ultimate consumer for personal use.

consumer innovators The first purchasers — those who buy a product at the beginning of its life cycle.

containerization Combining several unitized loads.

contract carrier Transportation carrier that serves only customers it has contracts with. Contracts include rates to be charged.

convenience products Products that are lowest in terms of both effort and risk.

convenience sample A nonprobability sample based on the selection of readily available respondents.

cooperative advertising The sharing of advertising costs between the retailer and the manufacturer.

corporate strategy The overall purpose and direction of the organization that is established in the light of the challenges and opportunities found in the environment, as well as available organizational resources.

cost-plus pricing Pricing technique using base cost figure per unit to which is added a markup to cover unassigned costs and to provide a profit.

cost tradeoffs Approach that assumes that some functional areas of the firm will experience cost increases while others will have cost decreases.

creative selling Selling that involves making the buyer see the worth of the item.

credence qualities Qualities for which, even after purchasing, the buyer must simply trust that the supplier has performed the correct service.

cue Any object existing in the environment that determines the nature of the response to a drive.

culture The complex of values, ideas, attitudes, institutions, and other meaningful symbols created by people that shape human behaviour, and the artifacts of that behaviour, transmitted from one generation to the next.

customs union Agreement among two or more nations that establishes a free trade area, plus a uniform tariff for trade with nonmember nations.

demand variability In the business market, the impact of derived demand on the demand for interrelated products used in producing consumer goods.

demarketing The process of cutting consumer demand for a product, because the demand exceeds the level that can reasonably be supplied by the firm or because doing so will create a more favourable corporate image.

demographic segmentation Dividing an overall market on the basis of characteristics such as age, gender, and income level.

demonstration Actions that supplement, support, and reinforce what the salesperson has already told the prospect.

department store Large retailer that handles a variety of merchandise.

depreciation The accounting concept of charging a portion of the cost of a capital item as a deduction against the company's annual revenue for purposes of determining its net income.

derived demand Demand for a product used by business derived from (or linked to) demand for a consumer good.

devaluation Situation in which a nation reduces the value of its currency in relation to gold or some other currency.

differentiation triangle Differentiation of a retail store from competitors in the same strategic group through price, location, and store atmosphere and service.

diffusion process The filtering and acceptance of new products and services by the members of a community or social system.

direct international trade Exporting directly to markets and/or importing directly from suppliers in other countries.

direct investment The ownership and management of production and/or marketing facilities in a foreign country.

direct response marketing An interactive system of marketing that uses one or more advertising media to effect a measurable response directly to the advertiser.

direct-response wholesaler Limited-function merchant wholesaler that relies on catalogues rather than on a sales force to contact retail, industrial, and institutional customers.

direct-sales results test A test that attempts to ascertain for each dollar of promotional outlay the corresponding increase in revenue.

disassociative group A type of reference group with which an individual does not want to be identified.

discount house Retailer that, in exchange for reduced prices, does not offer such traditional retail services as credit, sales assistance by clerks, and delivery.

distribution The selection and management of marketing channels and the physical distribution of goods.

distribution channels The paths that goods — and title to these goods — follow from producer to consumer.

drive Any strong stimulus that impels action.

drop shipper Limited-function merchant wholesaler that takes orders from customers and places them with producers, which then ship directly to the customers.

dumping Practice of selling products at significantly lower prices in a foreign market than in a nation's own domestic market.

dynamic break-even analysis Combines the traditional break-even analysis model with an evaluation of consumer demand.

economic environment The factors in a region or country that affect the production, distribution, and consumption of its wealth. Key elements are monetary resources, inflation, employment, and productive capacity.

economic order quantity (EOQ) A model that emphasizes a cost tradeoff between inventory holding costs and order costs.

economic union A common market that also requires members to harmonize monetary policies, taxation, and government spending. In addition, a common currency is used by members.

elasticity A measure of the responsiveness of purchasers and suppliers to changes in price.

electronic exchange An organized group of buyers and sellers from a specific industry linked together electronically.

embargo A complete ban on importing a particular product.

Engel's Laws As family income increases, (1) a smaller percentage goes for food, (2) the percentage spent on housing and household operations and clothing will remain constant, and (3) the percentage spent on other items will increase. Engel's Laws As family income increases, (1) a smaller percentage goes for food, (2) the percentage spent on housing and household operations and clothing will remain constant, and (3) the percentage spent on other items will increase.

environmental scanning The process by which the marketing manager gathers and sorts information about the marketing environment.

escalator clause Allows the seller to adjust the final price based on changes in the costs of the product's ingredients between the placement of the order and the completion of construction or delivery of the product.

ethnocentric company Firm that assumes that its way of doing business in its home market is the proper way to operate, and tries to replicate this in foreign markets.

evaluative criteria Features the consumer considers in making a choice among alternatives.

evoked set The number of brands that a consumer actually considers in making a purchase decision.

exchange control Requirement that firms gaining foreign exchange by exporting must sell their foreign exchange to the central bank or agency, and importers must buy foreign exchange from the same organization.

exchange process The means by which two or more parties give something of value to one another to satisfy felt needs.

exchange rate The rate at which a nation's currency can be exchanged for other currencies or gold.

exchange risk The risk of negotiating a price in another nation's currency and finding upon delivery of the product that the currency's value has dropped in relation to your country's currency.

exclusive dealing An arrangement whereby a supplier prohibits a marketing intermediary (either a wholesaler or, more typically, a retailer) from handling competing products.

exclusive distribution The granting of exclusive rights by manufacturers to a wholesaler or retailer to sell in a geographic region.

expense items Products and services that are used within a short period of time.

experience qualities Characteristics of products that can be assessed mainly through using them.

exploratory research Learning about the problem area and beginning to focus on specific areas of study by discussing the problem with informed sources within the firm (a process often called situation analysis) and with knowledgeable others outside the firm (the informal investigation).

facilitating agency An agency that provides specialized assistance for regular channel members (such as producers, wholesalers, and retailers) in moving products from producer to consumer.

fads Fashions with abbreviated life cycles.

family brand Brand name used for several related products.

family life cycle The process of family formation, development, and dissolution.

fashions Currently popular products that tend to follow recurring life cycles.

fiscal policy The receipts and expenditures of government.

flexible pricing A variable price policy.

FOB plant The buyer must pay all the freight charges.

follow-up The post-sales activities that often determine whether a person will become a repeat customer.

franchise An agreement whereby one firm (franchisee) agrees to meet the operating requirements of a successful business (franchisor) in return for the right to carry the name and products of the franchisor.

Free Trade Agreement (FTA) The agreement establishing a free trade area between Canada and the United States that preceded NAFTA.

free trade area Area established by agreement among two or more nations within which participants

agree to free trade of goods and services among themselves.

freight absorption The seller permits the buyer to subtract transportation expenses from the bill.

freight forwarder Wholesaling intermediary that specializes in international logistics.

friendship, commerce, and navigation (FCN) treaties Treaties that address many aspects of commercial relations with other countries; such treaties constitute international law.

generic name A brand name over which the original owner has lost exclusive claim because all offerings in the associated class of products have become generally known by the brand name (usually that of first or leading brand in that product class).

generic products Food and household staples characterized by plain labels, little or no advertising, and no brand names.

geocentric company Firm that develops a marketing mix that meets the needs of target consumers in all markets.

geographic segmentation Dividing an overall market into homogeneous groups based on population location.

Hazardous Products Act A major piece of legislation that consolidated previous legislation and set significant new standards for product safety; defines a hazardous product as any product that is included in a list (called a schedule) compiled by Consumer and Corporate Affairs Canada or Health and Welfare Canada.

high-involvement products Products for which the purchaser is highly involved in making the purchase decision.

house-to-house retailer Retailer that sells products by direct contact between the retailer–seller and the customer at the home of the customer.

hypermarket Mass merchandiser that operates on a low-price, self-service basis and carries lines of soft goods, hard goods, and groceries.

hypothesis A tentative explanation about the relationship between variables as a starting point for further testing.

implementation and control Consist of putting the marketing plan into action as well as doing ongoing monitoring and gathering feedback on how well the plan is accomplishing the stated marketing objectives.

import quota A limit set on the amount of products that may be imported in a certain category.

indirect international trade Exporting and/or importing only through other domestic companies that trade internationally.

individual brand Brand that is known by its own brand name rather than by the name of the company producing it or an umbrella name covering similar items.

individual offering Single product within a product line.

industrial distributor A wholesaler that operates in the business-to-business goods market and typically handles small accessory equipment and operating supplies.

industrial goods Those products purchased to be used, either directly or indirectly, in the production of other goods or for resale.

industry or market elasticity Refers to changes in total demand resulting from general changes in price across the industry.

inflation A rising price level that results in reduced purchasing power for the consumer.

informative product advertising Advertising that seeks to develop demand through presenting factual information on the attributes of a product or service.

inseparability A characteristic of services in which the product is produced and consumed simultaneously.

installations Major capital assets that are used to produce products and services.

institutional advertising Promoting a concept, idea, or philosophy, or the goodwill of an industry, company, or organization.

intangible attributes Those attributes that cannot be experienced by the physical senses.

integrated marketing communications (IMC) A comprehensive marketing communications plan that takes into consideration all the communication disciplines being used and combines them to provide clarity, consistency, and maximum communications impact.

intensive distribution A form of distribution that attempts to provide saturation coverage of the potential market.

interactive marketing Term used to describe the interrelationship between the employee and the customer.

internal marketing A marketing effort aimed at those who provide the service so that they will feel better about their task and therefore produce a better product.

international pricing Setting prices to be charged to buyers in other countries taking into consideration exchange risk, price escalation through multiplication of channels, and transportation.

inventory adjustments Changes in the amounts of materials a manufacturer keeps on hand.

joint demand Demand for an industrial product that is related to the demand for other industrial goods.

joint venture A partnership of firms from different countries, often to set up a local business in a country that is foreign to one of the partners.

judgement sample A nonprobability sample of people with a specific attribute.

just in time (JIT) An approach to minimizing inventory costs through identifying minimal inventory levels and arranging with suppliers to replenish stocks just in time to be used in production.

label The part of a package that contains (1) the brand name or symbol, (2) the name and address of the manufacturer or distributor, (3) information about product composition and size, and (4) information about recommended uses of the product.

large-format specialty store Large, warehouse-type retail store that specializes in selling a great variety of one category of merchandise at very low prices.

law of retail gravitation Principle that delineates the retail trade area of a potential site on the basis of distance between alternative locations and relative populations.

learning Changes in knowledge, attitudes, and behaviour, as a result of experience.

licensing Granting authority to produce and sell a product developed in one country in another.

lifestyle The mode of living.

lifetime-customer value (LCV) The sum of all future-customer revenue streams minus product and servicing costs, acquisition costs, and remarketing costs.

limited-line store Retailer that offers a large assortment of a single line of products or a few related lines of products.

line extension The development of individual offerings that appeal to different market segments but are closely related to the existing product line.

liquidator Specialty retailer that either comes into a bankrupt store and handles the closeout, or buys the entire lot and sells it in its own stores.

list price The rate normally quoted to potential buyers.

local content laws Laws specifying the portion of a product that must come from domestic sources.

logistics The process of managing and implementing the physical movement of products from source to place of use.

loss leader Goods priced below cost to attract customers.

low-involvement products Products with little significance, either materially or emotionally, that a consumer may purchase first and evaluate later (while using them).

loyalty program A program that gives rewards, such as points or free air miles, with each purchase in order to stimulate repeat business.

mail-order merchandiser Retailer that offers its customers the option of placing merchandise orders by mail, by telephone, or by visiting the mail-order desk of a retail store.

manufacturers' agent An independent salesperson who works for a number of manufacturers of related but noncompeting products.

marginal cost The change in total cost that results from producing an additional unit of output.

markdown A reduction in the price of an item.

market People with the willingness, purchasing power, and authority to buy.

market development strategy Finding new markets for existing products.

market orientation A focus on understanding customer needs and objectives, then making the business serve the interests of the customer rather than trying to make the customer buy what the business wants

to produce.

market price The amount that a consumer pays.

market restriction An arrangement whereby suppliers restrict the geographic territories for each of their distributors.

market segmentation Grouping people according to their similarity in one or more dimensions related to a particular product category.

market share objective To control a specific portion of the market for the firm's product.

marketing The process of planning and executing the conception, pricing, promotion, and distribution of ideas, goods, and services to create exchanges that satisfy individual and organizational objectives.

marketing audit A comprehensive appraisal of the organization's marketing activities. It involves a systematic assessment of marketing plans, objectives, strategies, programs, activities, organizational structure, and personnel.

marketing channels The steps or handling organizations that a good or service goes through from producer to final consumer.

marketing communications All activities and messages that inform, persuade, and influence the consumer in making a purchase decision.

marketing communications mix The blend of personal selling and non-personal communication (including advertising, sales promotion, public relations, sponsorship marketing, and point-of-purchase communications) by marketers in an attempt to accomplish information and persuasion objectives.

marketing concept An organization-wide philosophy that holds that the best route to organizational success is to find an unserved or under-served need in society and meet that need better than anyone else, while still meeting long-term organizational objectives.

marketing functions Buying, selling, transporting, storing, grading, financing, risk taking, and information collecting and disseminating.

marketing information system A set of routine procedures to continuously collect, monitor, and present internal and external information on company performance and opportunities in the marketplace.

marketing intermediary A business firm operating between the producer and the consumer or business purchaser.

marketing mix The blending of the four elements of marketing to satisfy chosen consumer segments.

marketing objectives and strategy Flow from the situation analysis. They are a statement of what the organization intends to accomplish with its marketing program and the general strategic approach it will take.

marketing plan A specific detailed statement of how the marketing mix will be used to realize the marketing strategy.

marketing research The systematic gathering, recording, and analyzing of data about problems relating to the marketing of goods and services.

marketing strategy A strategy that focuses on developing a unique long-run competitive position in the market by assessing consumer needs and the firm's potential for gaining competitive advantage.

markup The amount a producer or channel members adds to cost in order to determine the selling price.

mass merchandiser Retailer that concentrates on high turnover of items, emphasizes lower prices than department stores, and offers reduced services.

membership and warehouse club Very large, warehouse-type retail store that offers low prices because of its no-frill format and paid membership requirement.

membership group A type of reference group to which individuals actually belong.

merchandise mart Permanent exhibition at which manufacturers rent showcases for their product offerings.

merchant wholesaler A wholesaler who takes title to the products carried.

microculture A subgroup with its own distinguishing modes of behaviour.

missionary selling Selling that emphasizes selling the firm's goodwill and providing customers with technical or operational assistance.

modified rebuy A situation in which purchasers are willing to reevaluate their available options.

monetary policy The manipulation of the money supply and market rates of interest.

monopolistic competition A market structure with a large number of buyers and sellers where heterogeneity in good and/or service and usually geographical differentiation allow the marketer some control over price.

monopoly A market structure with only one seller of a product with no close substitutes.

motive An inner state that directs us toward the goal of satisfying a felt need.

MRO items Business-to-business supplies, so called because they can be categorized as maintenance items, repair items, and operating supplies.

multilevel marketing The development of a network among consumers to sell and deliver from one level of consumers to another using social obligation, personal influence, and motivational techniques.

multinational corporation (MNC) A corporation that produces and markets goods and services in several countries.

multi-offer strategy The attempt to satisfy several segments of the market very well with specialized products and unique marketing programs aimed at each segment.

national brand (manufacturer's brand) A brand promoted and distributed by a manufacturer.

need The perceived difference between the current state and a desired state.

negotiated contract The terms of the contract are set through talks between the buyer and the seller.

new task buying First-time or unique purchase situations that require considerable effort on the part of the decision makers.

nonprobability sample A sample chosen in an arbitrary fashion so that each member of the population does not have a representative chance of being selected.

nonprofit organization (NPO) Organization whose primary objective is something other than returning a profit to its owners.

North American Free Trade Agreement (NAFTA) The agreement establishing a free trade area among Canada, the United States, and Mexico that followed the FTA.

North American Industrial Classification System (NAICS) A coding system used to categorize different types of businesses and products (formerly the Standard Industrial Classification, or SIC).

objection Reveals a customer's interest in a product and can be used as a cue to provide additional information.

odd pricing Prices are set ending in some amount just below the next rounded number.

off-price retailer Retailer that specializes in selling manufacturers' excess stocks of brand-name merchandise at a discount.

oligopoly A market structure in which there are relatively few sellers.

oligopsony A market in which there are only a few buyers.

opinion leaders Trendsetters — individuals who are more likely to purchase new products early and to serve as information sources for others in a given group.

order processing Selling at the wholesale and retail levels; involves identifying customer needs, pointing out these needs to the customer, and completing the order.

organization marketing Attempts to influence others to accept the goals of, receive the services of, or contribute in some way to an organization.

penetration pricing An entry price for a product that is lower than what is estimated to be the long-term price.

perception The meaning that each person attributes to incoming stimuli received through the five senses.

perceptual screen The filter through which messages must pass.

performance gap The difference between the company's performance and that of the best of the best.

person marketing Efforts designed to cultivate the attention, interest, and preference of a target market toward a person.

personal selling A seller's promotional presentation conducted on a person-to-person basis with the buyer.

persuasive product advertising Advertising that emphasizes using words or images to try to create an image for a product and to influence attitudes about it.

physical distribution (PD) Includes the activities involved in getting a product from the end of the production line to the consumer.

physical distribution concept The integration of the total-cost approach, the avoidance of suboptimization, and the use of cost tradeoffs.

planned shopping centre Group of retail stores planned, coordinated, and marketed as a unit to shoppers in a particular geographic trade area.

point-of-purchase advertising Displays and demonstrations that seek to promote the product at a time and place closely associated with the actual decision to buy.

point-of-purchase communications Materials designed to influence buying decisions at the point of purchase.

political–legal environment The laws and interpretation of laws that require firms to operate under competitive conditions and to protect consumer rights.

polycentric company Firm that assumes that every country is different and that a specific marketing approach should be developed for each separate country.

population or **universe** The total group that the researcher wants to study.

positioning Shaping the product and developing a marketing program in such a way that the product is perceived to be (and actually is) different from competitors' products.

post-testing The assessment of advertising copy after it has been used.

power node Groupings of two or more large-format retailers that result in large customer drawing power.

preference products Products that are slightly higher on the effort dimension and much higher on risk than convenience products.

presentation The act of giving the sales message to a prospective customer.

prestige objectives Establishing relatively high prices in order to develop and maintain an image of quality and exclusiveness.

pretesting The assessment of an advertisement's effectiveness before it is actually used.

price The value that a buyer exchanges for a good or service.

price escalation The increase in final price in a foreign market over a domestic price because of having to pay for the services of additional channel members to get the product to that market.

price limits Limits within which product quality perception varies directly with price.

price lining The practice of marketing merchandise at a limited number of prices.

price structure An outline of the selling price and the various discounts offered to intermediaries.

pricing The methods of setting competitive, profitable, and justified prices.

pricing policy A general guideline based on pricing objectives that is intended for use in specific pricing decisions.

primary data Data being collected for the first time.

private brand A brand promoted and distributed by a wholesaler or retailer.

private carrier Transportation carrier that provides transportation services for a particular firm and may not solicit other transportation business.

probability sample A sample in which every member of the population has a known chance of being selected.

producers Those who transform goods and services through production into other goods and services.

product A total bundle of physical, service, and symbolic characteristics designed to produce consumer want satisfaction.

product advertising Nonpersonal selling of a particular good or service.

product development strategy Introducing new products into identifiable or established markets.

product diversification strategy The development of new products for new markets.

product improvement strategy A modification in existing products.

product life cycle A product's progress through introduction, growth, maturity, and decline stages.

product line A series of related products.

product management Decisions about what kind of product is needed, its uses, package design, branding, trademarks, warranties, guarantees, product life cycles, and new product development.

product managers (brand managers) Individuals assigned one product or product line and given responsibility for determining its objectives and marketing strategies.

product mix The assortment of product lines and individual offerings available from a company.

product orientation A focus on the product itself rather than on the consumer's needs.

product portfolio The complete collection of products or services that a company produces.

profit centre Any part of the organization to which revenue and controllable costs can be assigned, such as a department.

profit maximization The point where the addition to total revenue is just balanced by an increase in total cost.

promotional allowance Extra discount offered to retailers so that they will advertise the manufacturer along with the retailer.

promotional price A lower-than-normal price used as an ingredient in a firm's selling strategy.

prospecting Identifying potential customers.

psychographic segmentation Uses behavioural profiles developed from analyses of the activities, opinions, interests, and lifestyles of consumers in identifying market segments.

psychographics The use of psychological attributes, lifestyles, and attitudes in determining the behavioural profiles of different consumers.

psychological pricing The use of prices to suggest values of a product or attributes of a product/price offering.

public relations The component of marketing communications that focuses on fostering goodwill between a company and its various publics.

public warehouse Independently owned storage facility.

publicity Normally unpaid communication that disseminates positive information about company activities and products.

pulling strategy A promotional effort by the seller to stimulate final-user demand, which then exerts pressure on the distribution channel.

pure competition A market structure in which there is such a large number of buyers and sellers that no one of them has a significant influence on price.

pushing strategy The promotion of the product first to the members of the marketing channel, who then participate in its promotion to the final user.

qualifying Determining that the prospect is really a potential customer.

quantity discount Price reduction granted for large purchases.

quota sample A nonprobability sample that is divided so that different segments or groups are represented in the total sample.

rack jobber Wholesaler that provides the racks, stocks the merchandise, prices the goods, and makes regular visits to refill the shelves.

raw materials Farm products (such as cattle, wool, eggs, milk, pigs, and canola) and natural products (such as coal, copper, iron ore, and lumber).

rebate Refund by the seller of a portion of the purchase price.

reciprocity Extending purchasing preference to suppliers who are also customers.

recycled merchandise retailer Retailer that sells castoff clothes, furniture, and other products.

reference group A group whose value structures and standards influence a person's behaviour.

regiocentric company Firm that recognizes that countries with similar cultures and economic conditions can be served with a similar marketing mix.

reinforcement The reduction in drive that results from a proper response.

relationship marketing Identifying and establishing, maintaining and enhancing, and, when necessary, also terminating relationships with customers and other stakeholders, at a profit, so that the objectives of all parties involved are met, through a mutual exchange and fulfillment of promises.

reminder-oriented product advertising Advertising whose goal is to reinforce previous promotional activity by keeping the product or service name in front of the public.

research design A series of advance decisions that, taken together, make up a master plan or model for conducting the investigation.

response The individual's reaction to the cues and drives.

retail image The consumer's perception of a store and of the shopping experience it provides.

retail trade area analysis Studies that assess the relative drawing power of alternative retail locations.

retailer A store that sells products purchased by individuals for their own use and not for resale.

retailing All the activities involved in selling goods and services to the ultimate consumer.

revaluation Situation in which a country adjusts the value of its currency upward.

reverse channels The paths goods follow from consumer to manufacturer or to marketing intermediaries.

role The rights and duties expected of an individual in a group by other members of the group.

role model marketing Marketing technique that associates a product with the positive perception of a type of individual or a role.

sales branch Manufacturer-owned facility that carries inventory and processes orders to customers from available stock.

sales management Securing, maintaining, motivating, supervising, evaluating, and controlling the field sales force.

sales maximization The pricing philosophy analyzed by economist William J. Baumol. Baumol believes that many firms attempt to maximize sales within a profit constraint.

sales office Manufacturer-owned facility that does not carry stock but serves as a regional office for the firm's sales personnel.

sales orientation A focus on developing a strong sales force to convince consumers to buy whatever the firm produces.

sales promotion Those marketing activities, other than personal selling, mass media advertising, and publicity, that stimulate consumer purchasing and dealer effectiveness.

scrambled merchandising The retail practice of carrying dissimilar lines to generate added sales volume.

search qualities Physical qualities that enable products to be examined and compared. This eases the task of choosing among them.

secondary data Previously published matter.

segment elasticity Refers to the sensitivity to changes in price that a particular segment exhibits.

selective distribution The selection of a small number of retailers to handle the firm's product line.

selling agent An agent wholesaling intermediary that is responsible for the total marketing program for a firm's product line.

service A product without physical characteristics — a bundle of performance and symbolic attributes designed to produce consumer want satisfaction.

shaping The process of applying a series of rewards and reinforcement so that more complex behaviour can evolve over time.

shopping products Products that are usually purchased only after the consumer has compared competing products.

simple random sample A probability sample in which every item in the relevant universe has an equal opportunity of being selected.

single-offer strategy The attempt to satisfy a large or a small market with one product and a single marketing program.

situation analysis Considers the internal circumstances of the organization or product, the external environment, competitive activity, and characteristics of the customer that may be relevant to the marketing plan.

skimming pricing Choosing a high entry price; to sell first to consumers who are willing to pay the highest price, and then reduce the price.

social class The relatively permanent divisions in a society into which individuals or families are categorized based on prestige and community status.

social marketing The analysis, planning, execution, and evaluation of programs designed to influence the voluntary behaviour of target audiences in order to improve their personal welfare and that of society.

societal marketing concept An organization-wide philosophy that holds that the best route to organizational success is to find an unserved or underserved need in society and meet that need better than anyone else, while still meeting long-term organizational objectives and also considering the long-term impact on society.

sociocultural environment The mosaic of societal and cultural components that are relevant to the organization's business decisions.

sorting The process that alleviates discrepancies in assortment by reallocating the outputs of various producers into assortments desired by individual purchasers.

specialty advertising Sales promotion medium that uses useful articles to carry the advertiser's name, address, and advertising message.

specialty products Products that are highest in both effort and risk, due to some unique characteristics that cause the buyer to prize that particular brand.

specialty store Retailer that handles only part of a single line of products.

specifications A specific description of a needed item or job that the buyer wishes to acquire.

sponsorship marketing The practice of promoting the interests of a company by associating the company or a brand with a specific event.

SSWDs Single, separated, widowed, or divorced people.

stagflation High unemployment and a rising price level at the same time.

status Relative position in a group.

status quo objectives Objectives based on maintaining stable prices.

stock turnover The number of times the average inventory is sold annually.

straight rebuy A recurring purchase decision involving an item that has performed satisfactorily and is therefore purchased again by a customer.

subliminal perception A subconscious level of awareness.

suboptimization A condition in which the manager of each physical distribution function attempts to minimize costs, but due to the impact of one physical distribution task on the others, the results are less than optimal.

supermarket Large-scale, departmentalized retail store offering a large variety of food products.

supplies Regular expense items necessary in the daily operation of a firm, but not part of its final product.

supply chain management The coordination of the flow of materials and products from the source of raw materials to the production line, and ultimately to the consumer. It includes managing information, cash, and process/work flows.

supply curve The marginal cost curve above its intersection with average variable cost.

SWOT analysis The combined summary of the internal analysis and the environmental analysis. Stands for *strengths, weaknesses, opportunities,* and *threats.*

systematic sample A probability sample that takes every nth item on a list, after a random start.

tangible attributes Those attributes that can be experienced by the physical senses, such as sight, touch, and smell.

target market A market segment that a company chooses to serve.

target market decision analysis The evaluation of potential market segments.

target return objectives Either short-run or long-run goals, usually stated as a percentage of sales or investment.

tariff A tax levied against products imported from abroad.

task-objective method A sequential approach to allocating marketing communications budgets that involves two steps: (1) defining the realistic communication goals the firm wants the marketing communications mix to accomplish, and (2) determining the amount and type of marketing communications activity required to accomplish each of these objectives.

technological environment The applications of knowledge based on scientific discoveries, inventions, and innovations.

test marketing Selecting areas considered reasonably typical of the total market, and introducing a new product to these areas with a total marketing campaign to determine consumer response before marketing the product nationally.

third-party logistics provider Specialist firm that performs virtually all of the logistical tasks that manufacturers or other channel members would normally perform themselves.

tied selling An arrangement whereby a supplier forces a dealer who wishes to handle a product to also carry other products from the supplier or to refrain from using or distributing someone else's product.

total-cost approach Holds that all relevant factors in physically moving and storing products should be considered as a whole and not individually.

total customer satisfaction Providing a good or service that fully and without reservation conforms to the customer's requirements.

trade discount Payment to channel members or buyers for performing some marketing function normally required of the manufacturer.

trade fairs Periodic shows at which manufacturers in a particular industry display their wares for visiting retail and wholesale buyers.

trade industries Organizations, such as retailers and wholesalers, that purchase for resale to others.

trade show An organized exhibition of products based on a central theme.

trade-in Deduction from an item's price of an amount for the customer's old item that is being replaced.

trademark A brand that has been given legal protection and has been granted solely to its owner.

transfer price The price for sending goods from one company profit centre to another.

truck wholesaler Limited-function merchant wholesaler that markets products that require frequent replenishment.

uniform delivered price The same price (including transportation expenses) is quoted to all buyers.

unit pricing Stating prices in terms of some recognized unit of measurement (such as grams or litres) or a standard numerical count.

unitization Combining as many packages as possible into one load.

Universal Product Code A code readable by optical scanners that can print the name of the item and the price on the cash register receipt.

usage rate Divides the market by the amount of product consumed, and/or the degree of brand loyalty.

utility The want-satisfying power of a product or service.

value A subjective term that is defined by the customer; part of customer expectations, which are a combination of cost, time, quantity, quality, and human factors.

value added The increase in value of input material when transformed into semifinished or finished goods.

variety store Retailer that offers an extensive range and assortment of low-priced merchandise.

venture-team concept An organizational strategy for developing new products through combining the management resources of marketing, technology, capital, and management expertise in a team.

vertical marketing system A network of channel intermediaries organized and centrally managed to produce the maximum competitive impact.

vertical Web community A site that acts as a comprehensive source of information and dialogue for a particular vertical market.

warranty A guarantee to the buyer that the supplier will replace a defective product (or part of a product) or refund its purchase price during a specified period of time.

Weber's Law The higher the initial intensity of a stimulus, the greater the amount of the change in intensity that is necessary in order for a difference to be noticed.

wheel of retailing Hypothesized process of change in retailing, which suggests that new types of retailers gain a competitive foothold by offering lower prices through the reduction or elimination of services; but once established, they add more services and their prices gradually rise, so that they then become vulnerable to a new low-price retailer with minimum services — and the wheel turns.

wholesalers Wholesaling intermediaries who take title to the products they handle.

wholesaling The activities of intermediaries who sell to retailers, other wholesalers, and business users but not in significant amounts to ultimate consumers.

wholesaling intermediaries Intermediaries who assume title, as well as agents and brokers who perform important wholesaling activities without taking title to the products.

World Trade Organization (WTO) The international body that deals with the rules of trade between nations.

zone pricing The market is divided into different zones and a price is established within each.

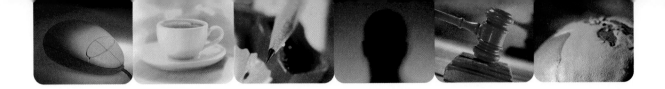

Index

READER REPLY CARD

We are interested in your reaction to *Foundations of Marketing*, Seventh Canadian Edition by M. Dale Beckman and John M. Rigby. You can help us to improve this book in future editions by completing this questionnaire.

1. What was your reason for using this book?

   ☐ university course ☐ college course ☐ continuing education course
   ☐ professional   ☐ personal   ☐ other _____
      development   interest   _____

2. If you are a student, please identify your school and the course in which you used this book.

3. Which chapters or parts of this book did you use? Which did you omit?

4. What did you like best about this book? What did you like least?

5. Please identify any topics you think should be added to future editions.

6. Please add any comments or suggestions.

7. May we contact you for further information?

   Name: _____

   Address: _____

   Phone: _____

   E-mail: _____

(fold here and tape shut)

0116870399-M8Z4X6-BR01

Larry Gillevet
Director of Product Development
HARCOURT CANADA
55 HORNER AVENUE
TORONTO, ONTARIO
M8Z 9Z9